Applied ASP .NET 4 in Context

Adam Freeman

Applied ASP.NET 4 in Context

ISBN-13 (pbk): 978-1-4302-3467-8

ISBN-13 (electronic): 978-1-4302-3468-5

Trademarked names, logos, and images may appear in this book. Rather than use a trademark symbol with every occurrence of a trademarked name, logo, or image we use the names, logos, and images only in an editorial fashion and to the benefit of the trademark owner, with no intention of infringement of the trademark.

The use in this publication of trade names, trademarks, service marks, and similar terms, even if they are not identified as such, is not to be taken as an expression of opinion as to whether or not they are subject to proprietary rights.

President and Publisher: Paul Manning
Lead Editor: Ewan Buckingham
Technical Reviewer: Fabio Claudio Ferracchiati
Editorial Board: Steve Anglin, Mark Beckner, Ewan Buckingham, Gary Cornell, Jonathan Gennick, Jonathan Hassell, Michelle Lowman, James Markham, Matthew Moodie, Jeff Olson, Jeffrey Pepper, Frank Pohlmann, Douglas Pundick, Ben Renow-Clarke, Dominic Shakeshaft, Matt Wade, Tom Welsh
Coordinating Editors: Jennifer Blackwell and Mary Tobin
Copy Editors: Marilyn Smith and Kim Wimpsett
Production Support: Patrick Cunningham
Indexer: Broccoli Indexing & Proofreading Services
Artist: SPi Global
Cover Designer: Anna Ishchenko

Distributed to the book trade worldwide by Springer Science+Business Media, LLC., 233 Spring Street, 6th Floor, New York, NY 10013. Phone 1-800-SPRINGER, fax (201) 348-4505, e-mail orders-ny@springer-sbm.com, or visit www.springeronline.com.

For information on translations, please e-mail rights@apress.com, or visit www.apress.com.

Apress and friends of ED books may be purchased in bulk for academic, corporate, or promotional use. eBook versions and licenses are also available for most titles. For more information, reference our Special Bulk Sales–eBook Licensing web page at www.apress.com/bulk-sales.

The information in this book is distributed on an "as is" basis, without warranty. Although every precaution has been taken in the preparation of this work, neither the author(s) nor Apress shall have any liability to any person or entity with respect to any loss or damage caused or alleged to be caused directly or indirectly by the information contained in this work.

The source code for this book is available to readers at www.apress.com.

Dedicated to my lovely wife, Jacqui Griffyth.

Contents at a Glance

Contents

About the Author

Adam Freeman is an experienced IT professional who has held senior positions in a range of companies, most serving recently as chief technology officer and chief operating officer of a global bank. Now retired, he spends his time writing and training for his first competitive triathlon. This is his twelfth book on programming and his tenth on .NET.

About the Technical Reviewer

Fabio Claudio Ferracchiati is a senior consultant and a senior analyst/developer using Microsoft technologies. He works for Brain Force (`www.brainforce.com`) in its Italian branch (`www.brainforce.it`). He is a Microsoft Certified Solution Developer for .NET, a Microsoft Certified Application Developer for .NET, a Microsoft Certified Professional, and a prolific author and technical reviewer. Over the past ten years, he's written articles for Italian and international magazines and coauthored more than ten books on a variety of computer topics.

Acknowledgments

I would like to thank everyone at Apress for working so hard to bring this book to print. In particular, I would like to thank Jennifer Blackwell for keeping me on track and Ewan Buckingham for commissioning and editing this revision. I would also like to thank my technical reviewer, Fabio, whose efforts made this book far better than it would have been otherwise.

PART I

■ ■ ■

Getting Started

Before you can begin to explore the ASP.NET framework, we have some preparation to do. In the next three chapters, I'll describe the structure of the book, show you how to set up your workstation and server for ASP.NET development, and provide a high-level overview of how the various parts of the ASP.NET framework fit together.

CHAPTER 1

Introduction

My first experience with ASP.NET wasn't very positive. It was back in 2003, and I had agreed to write a book for Microsoft Press about using ASP.NET to create XML web services.

This was when ASP.NET 1.0 was released. In those days, .NET was interesting but nothing special. It was widely regarded as Microsoft's attempt to compete with Java, and the whole platform had a "me too" feel about it. ASP.NET itself was a very rigid and limited platform. It hadn't been thought through and had a lot of rough edges. It was difficult to use, the tools support was lacking, and programmers had to work hard to get even the most basic functionality working.

Most Microsoft products follow a standard pattern of evolution. Version 1 shows promise but is rushed out the door and has major flaws. It is more a statement of intent rather than something to bet on. Version 2 fixes the worst flaws and delivers more of the original promise. Version 3 starts to look polished, but there are breaking changes. Version 4 is a solid performer, which adds innovative features and has the capability to lead the market segment.

This is the story of ASP.NET (and, of course, .NET as a whole). We are at the point where Microsoft excels: building on a solid and widely adopted product set to produce tools and features that shine. ASP.NET 4 is a very solid web application platform. It is packed with features, contains a choice of development frameworks, and has excellent tool support in Visual Studio. ASP.NET has reached maturity and *is* a platform to bet on.

In this book, I'll take you on a tour through ASP.NET, starting with the core platform features, moving on to the Web Forms and MVC framework development frameworks, and finishing with the information you need to know to successfully deploy an ASP.NET web application.

As we go from chapter to chapter, you'll learn everything you need to write effective ASP.NET web applications and understand how to solve the most commonly encountered web application challenges.

Who Should Read This Book?

This book was written for programmers who have some experience with C# and the .NET Framework and have a basic knowledge of web technologies such as HTML and HTTP. No prior knowledge of ASP.NET, Web Forms, or the MVC framework is required. You should have a basic familiarity with Visual Studio.

What Is Covered in This Book?

This book covers the major features of ASP.NET version 4, including core platform features, Web Forms, and the MVC framework. The emphasis of this book is about *applying* ASP.NET. To that end, I cover the core features in depth and leave the more academic and theoretical coverage to other authors. This book is about getting things done with ASP.NET.

What Is the Structure of This Book?

There are five parts to this book. The first helps you get ready to use ASP.NET and to understand the building blocks of the ASP.NET platform. By the end of these chapters, you will have all the software you require installed and ready to go.

Part II introduces the core features of the ASP.NET platform. You will learn how ASP.NET handles browser requests, how to create ASP.NET web pages, how to apply JavaScript to those pages, and how to create and consume web services.

Part III covers Web Forms, a set of features designed to make developing web applications similar to developing traditional Windows programs. Web Forms has fallen out of favor lately, but it is a powerful and flexible system, and it is worth taking the time to read these chapters.

Part IV covers the MVC framework, which is a relatively new addition to ASP.NET and which has stolen the limelight from Web Forms in the ASP.NET world. The MVC framework takes an approach to web application development that has a lot in common with platforms such as Ruby on Rails.

Part V covers some advanced topics, including web application security and deployment.

What Do You Need to Read This Book?

To get the most benefit from this book, you should have a modern Windows PC, set up for .NET development. Chapter 3 gives you complete details of the software you will need. With the exception of Windows itself, Microsoft makes free-of-charge versions of every software component that this book requires. These free versions are suitable for following all the examples in this book, with the exception of some unit testing examples in Part IV (for which a paid-for edition of Visual Studio is required).

Part V of this book includes examples of deploying an ASP.NET web application to a server. These tasks require a machine running Windows Server 2008 R2. These examples are optional. Many ASP.NET developers don't need to deploy the application they create themselves since these tasks are handled by operations teams.

Getting the Example Code

The code for all the examples in this book is freely available for download from Apress.com. Most of the more substantial examples relate to triathlons. As I write this book, I am training for my first competitive triathlon, and I felt that these were better examples than the stock or employee tracking examples that programming books usually contain.

Finding More Information

I have tried to cover everything important in ASP.NET, but there are bound to be aspects that interest you that I have left out. If that should be the case, then I recommend the resources described next.

The MSDN Library

The MSDN library contains a lot of useful information about ASP.NET, although the quality and depth can be patchy. The starting point for ASP.NET 4 is at `http://msdn.microsoft.com/en-us/library/ee532866.aspx`.

Online Forums

Numerous web sites discuss ASP.NET. The one that seems to have the most knowledgeable participants and the lowest amount of useless noise is Stackoverflow.com. This site is not specific to ASP.NET, but there is a very active .NET and ASP.NET community, and when you get stuck, chances are someone has had the same problem and has already asked for help.

Other Books

I have written a couple of other books you might like to consider as complements to this one. I wrote a more traditional ASP.NET 4 reference with Matt MacDonald called *Pro ASP.NET 4 in C# 2010*. This is focused more on the Web Forms side of things but provides broad coverage. I also wrote *Pro ASP.NET MVC 3 Framework* with Steve Sanderson. Steve is a member of the Web Platform and Tools team at Microsoft, the group responsible for the MVC framework. Both of these books are published by Apress.

Summary

ASP.NET 4 is a fantastic platform for web development. The depth of functionality and the breadth of options are excellent, especially if you are moving to web application development from another area of .NET. As we go through this book, you'll see just how rich the ecosystem is and how rapidly and easily we can create functional and robust web applications.

CHAPTER 2

Getting Ready

We must do some preparation before we can start working with ASP.NET. In the following sections, I'll tell you what you need.

I have split the preparation into two sections. You'll need to install a couple of additional components when you reach the part of the book that deals with the part of ASP.NET called the MVC framework. The rest of ASP.NET is installed as part of Visual Studio and .NET 4, but you need an update and an additional third-party library to get the best from the MVC framework.

Installing Visual Studio 2010

The first step in preparing a workstation for development with ASP.NET is to install Visual Studio 2010. Visual Studio is Microsoft's integrated development environment (IDE), a tool that you will most likely have used if you have done any prior development for a Microsoft platform.

Microsoft produces a range of different Visual Studio 2010 editions, each of which has a different set of functions and attracts a different price. For this book, you will require one of the following editions:

- Visual Studio 2010 Professional

- Visual Studio 2010 Premium

- Visual Studio 2010 Ultimate

The features that we require are available in all three editions, and all three editions are equally suited to our purposes. Install Visual Studio as you would any Windows application and make sure that you have the latest updates and service packs installed.

USING VISUAL WEB DEVELOPER EXPRESS

Microsoft produces a set of light-weight versions of Visual Studio known as the *Express editions*. The Express edition for web application development is called *Visual Web Developer 2010 Express*. Microsoft differentiates the Express editions by removing some features, but you can still use Visual Web Developer to create ASP.NET applications.

You should be able to follow most of the examples in this book using Visual Web Developer, but there are some features I rely on in later chapters that are not present. In short, you *can* use Visual Web Developer as your IDE when reading this book, but you'll find certain examples more challenging to follow, and you'll be on your own if you have problems.

The complete installation for Visual Studio 2010 Ultimate edition is 7.8GB and includes programming languages and features that you won't require. If you don't want to give up that much space, you can select just the components we need for this book, as shown in Figure 2-1.

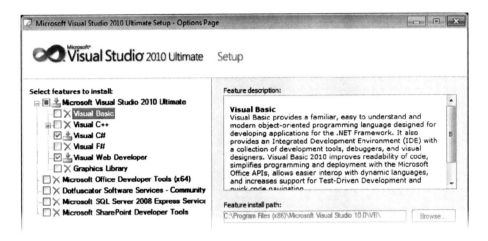

Figure 2-1. *Installing the required Visual Studio features*

We require only the Visual C# and Visual Web Developer features. By default, the Visual Studio setup process includes SQL Server 2008 Express, but I recommend you uncheck this option and follow the instructions later in the chapter to install the database to get the latest version.

The exact set of features available to be installed will vary based on the Visual Studio edition and the operating system you are using, but as long as you check at least those options shown in Figure 2-1, you will have the key components required for ASP.NET framework development: Visual Studio, version 4 of the .NET Framework, and some of the behind-the-scenes features that we will use such as the built-in development application server.

■ **Note** The Visual Web Developer feature will cause Visual Studio 2010 installer to set up version 2 of the MVC framework on your computer. Don't worry about this. I'll show you how to upgrade to MVC 3 later in this chapter.

Installing the Essential Software

Microsoft releases some of the components we need on different schedules. The easiest way to update the components is to use the *Web Platform Installer* (WebPI). The WebPI is a free tool provided by

Microsoft that downloads and installs components and products for the overall Microsoft web platform. There is a wide range of software available, including popular third-party add-ons.

To get the WebPI, go to http://microsoft.com/web/downloads and click the download link, as shown in Figure 2-2. Microsoft changes the layout of this page from time to time, so you might see something different when you visit.

Figure 2-2. *Downloading the Web Platform Installer*

Download and run the installer. The name is a little confusing: this is the installer for the Web Platform Installer. The download is a regular Windows installer, which installs the WebPI tool and you can then use to download and install web application components. The WebPI will start automatically, and you will see the selection window, as shown in Figure 2-3.

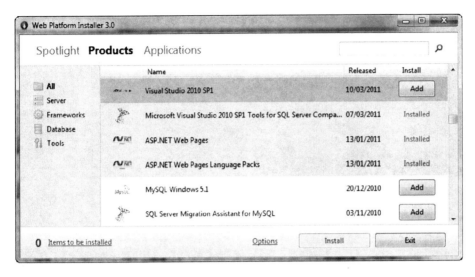

Figure 2-3. The Web Platform Installer

There are three categories across the top of the screen. The components we are interested in are available in the Products category. Locate the following components either by scrolling through the list (selecting the subcategories on the left side of the screen) or by using the search box:

- Visual Studio 2010 SP1

- SQL Server Express 2008 R2

For each component, click the Add button. When you have make your selections, click Install to being the download and installation process.

■ **Tip** Using the WebPI to install SQL Server Express on the workstation assumes that you want your development environment and your database running on the same computer. If you prefer them to be on different machines, as I do, simply run the WebPI on your database machine as well.

Installing Optional Components

There are a couple of additional components that you might like to consider using. They are not required for this book, but I find them useful on a day-to-day basis.

IIS Express

Visual Studio includes a web server that you can use to run and debug your MVC framework applications. For the most part, it does everything that we require, and we'll be using it throughout this book.

As useful as it is, the built-in server, known as the ASP.NET Development Server, doesn't support the full range of options that are available in IIS. As a simple example, the built-in server doesn't support SSL. It is possible to use the full, non-Express edition of IIS as you develop an application, but you will lose the tight integration with Visual Studio that is available with the ASP.NET Development Server.

An alternative is to use IIS Express, which includes the tight integration from the built-in server and the full feature set of IIS. IIS Express is still a development server, meaning you should not try to use it to deliver your application to real users, but it makes the development process much more consistent with how the application will operate once it has been deployed. IIS Express is installed as part of Visual Studio 2010 Service Pack 1.

SQL Server 2008 R2 Management Studio Express

All the database operations that I perform in this book can be done through Visual Studio, but for broader database administration, I like to use the SQL Server Management Tools. You can get the SQL Server Management Studio through the WebPI tool.

■ **Note** Visual Web Developer has limited support for managing databases. You will need Management Studio Express if you are using this edition of Visual Studio.

Getting Ready for the MVC Framework

In Part IV of this book, I introduce the part of ASP.NET called the MVC framework. This is a relatively new addition to ASP.NET and follows a different release cycle. The easiest way to install the latest version of the MVC framework (version 3 with the Tools Update release) is to use the WebPI tool again. In the Products section, you will find an item called ASP.NET MVC 3. Click the Add button and then the Install button to perform the installation (see Figure 2-4).

Figure 2-4. Installing MVC 3 using the Web PI tool

■ **Note**   You can install the MVC framework before reaching Part IV of this book. The only problem you will encounter is that the versions of some of the JavaScript libraries that I use in Chapter 9 are different. This is because the latest version of the MVC installer includes more recent jQuery versions.

Ninject

In Chapter 23, I introduce a concept called *dependency injection*. This requires what a *dependency injection container*. I have selected the open source and freely available Ninject. I have included the required Ninject libraries in the source code download for this book (available at Apress.com), but you can download the latest version from Ninject.org.

MVC Framework Source Code

Microsoft publishes the source code to the MVC framework so that it can be downloaded and inspected. You don't need the source code to use the MVC framework, and I won't refer to the source code in this book, but when you hit a problem that you just can't figure out, being able to refer to the source code can be invaluable. You can get the MVC framework source code from `http://aspnet.codeplex.com`.

Summary

You are now ready to begin developing ASP.NET applications. In the next chapter, I'll give you an overview of how ASP.NET fits together, and then we can begin digging into the details.

CHAPTER 3

Putting ASP.NET in Context

ASP.NET is a *framework*, or tool kit, for creating *web applications*. These are applications that operate over a network, largely (but not exclusively) where a user employs a web browser to communicate with a server over an intranet or the Internet. In this chapter, I will give you a high-level overview of ASP.NET and explain how I have mapped the key elements into the different parts of this book.

An Overview of ASP.NET

Web applications have special demands. The way that browsers work, the nature of HTTP (the protocol over which most web application operate), and the separation of the server from the client all affect the nature of web applications and web application programming. ASP.NET provides the features we need to meet those special demands and create an application that we can deliver using web technology.

ASP.NET is not a new technology. ASP.NET 1.0 was released as part of the wider .NET framework more than a decade ago. At the time that ASP.NET 1.0 was introduced, Visual Basic was a dominant force in the programming world, and Microsoft created ASP.NET to bring the Visual Basic programming model to the web development world, including concepts such as drag-and-drop controls, events, and design surfaces. These features are wrapped up in a feature set called Web Forms (which I cover in Part III of this book), predicated on the idea that the developer doesn't need to have direct knowledge of or control over the underlying HTML and HTTP.

This may seem like an odd concept today, when almost every developer has at least a basic knowledge of HTTP and HTML, but it made perfect sense at the time. There was a huge population of Visual Basic developers, and Microsoft wanted to protect this market segment by giving them web development tools that built on their existing experience.

Note When I refer to the Visual Basic model, I don't mean the language itself; rather, I mean the approach, tools, and environment that Visual Basic programmers use. The Visual Basic language has struggled since the introduction of .NET. Many programmers have moved to C#, leaving the market segment for Visual Basic .NET much reduced.

ASP.NET 1 introduced some core themes that have underpinned all versions of ASP.NET, including the most recent version, ASP.NET 4:

- *It has close integration with the .NET Framework:* ASP.NET is very tightly bound to the .NET Framework, such that ASP.NET applications are hosted in the .NET runtime and all the features of the .NET Framework (LINQ, the Entity Framework, automatic garbage collection, and so on) are available to ASP.NET programmers.

- *ASP.NET applications are compiled:* We build ASP.NET applications using a mix of annotated HTML and C# classes. But everything, including the marked-up HTML, is compiled into .NET classes to improve performance.

- *Visual Studio provides comprehensive support for ASP.NET:* We create ASP.NET applications just as we would any other kind of Visual Studio project. There is support for IntelliSense, debugging, and packaging and deployment, just as there is for other application types. You could choose to build an ASP.NET application outside of Visual Studio, but it would be much harder to do.

- *ASP.NET supports all .NET Framework languages:* Even though C# has emerged as the dominant .NET language, we can write ASP.NET applications using any of the languages supported by .NET. This includes Visual Basic .NET and F#. Microsoft had a brief foray into supporting other languages on .NET, including Ruby and Python, but that seems to have died recently.

- *ASP.NET is tightly integrated into IIS:* To deploy and run an ASP.NET application, you really need to use IIS, which is Microsoft's web application server. IIS is available only for Windows and works best on Windows Server. In embracing ASP.NET, you are adopting an entire stack of tools from Microsoft. They are pretty good tools, but there isn't any diversity available.

If you have done any other kind of .NET development, these themes will make it easier for you to learn ASP.NET programming. The tools are very similar, the approach to creating and managing projects is the same, and, of course, C# is a familiar language when it comes to writing the code segments of a web application.

The Structure of ASP.NET

ASP.NET has evolved since it was first released, and the importance of the Web Forms programming model has lessened. We can tease ASP.NET into two sections: Web Forms and the core platform, as illustrated in Figure 3-1.

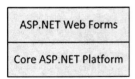

Figure 3-1. Separating ASP.NET into the core platform and Web Forms

Although I have made the distinction clear in the figure, the separation between the core platform and Web Forms is actually pretty porous. The core platform was originally designed solely to support Web Forms, and so even when we are using just core platform features, we are adopting some Web Forms characteristics.

The reason that this separation is useful—however poorly defined it might be—is because of a recent addition to ASP.NET: the *MVC framework*. The MVC framework (MVC stands for Model-View-Controller) follows a development style that is very different from Web Forms, such that we are closely involved in the HTML and HTTP that our application produces and consumes. This means we have to reshape the ASP.NET diagram, as shown in Figure 3-2.

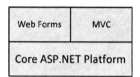

Figure 3-2. *Adding MVC to ASP.NET*

With the addition of the MVC framework, we can choose between two radically different approaches to web application development. Both approaches can take advantage of the underlying core platform features.

The Core ASP.NET Platform

As part of its evolution, ASP.NET has broadened the set of core features that underpin ASP.NET applications. These are features such as standardized error handling, a page metaphor for servicing browser requests, state management features so that we can build continuity across a series of stateless HTTP requests, support for creating XML and JSON web services, and features for managing the URLs that our web application presents to the world.

Since ASP.NET version 4, Visual Studio creates ASP.NET projects with built-in support for jQuery, a popular JavaScript library. I have included jQuery as one of the core platform features, since it can be used by Web Forms and MVC framework applications.

You'll need to master the core ASP.NET features to get the most out of both Web Forms and the MVC framework. The set of features that the core platform supports is extensive, and as I'll show you in Part II of the book, they can be used to create web applications in their own right.

Web Forms

Web Forms is a set of user interface controls that are built on top of the core ASP.NET platform to create the classic Visual Basic style of application development. Even though the idea behind this style of development has gone out of fashion, there is still a lot to be gained by using Web Forms and the associated Visual Studio support to create applications.

Since the introduction of the MVC framework, Web Forms has fallen out of the limelight. This is a shame and doesn't reflect the reality of ASP.NET development, which is that the vast majority of ASP.NET applications are created using Web Forms.

Aside from the issue of the hide-the-details Web Forms design philosophy, there are some additional limitations. The first is that Web Forms creates a stateful application by embedding hidden data into the HTML forms that are sent to the browser. The amount of data can grow quite significantly, which can make complex Web Forms applications unsuitable for Internet-facing applications (although this is rarely a problem within intranets, where bandwidth is much more plentiful and a lot cheaper).

The second drawback is that it is virtually impossible to perform unit testing on a Web Forms application. Unit testing is a concept that emerged into the mainstream after ASP.NET was released, and there is little support for anything other than integration testing available.

The third drawback, and the most serious to my mind, is that Web Forms applications are difficult to maintain over the long term. The application model that Web Forms pushes the developer toward means that markup, application state, and data models are blurred together, which in turn means that most large Web Forms applications gradually become a morass of spaghetti code, and changes often have unexpected (and unwanted) effects. That's not to say it can't be done, but if long-term maintenance is important to you (and it should be in most situations), then you are probably better off using the MVC framework.

But it is not all bad in the world of Web Forms. They are widely used around the world because they are simple to learn, allow rapid development, and contain functionality for every common scenario that arises in mainstream web development. To my mind, the sweet spot for Web Forms development is rapid prototyping and short-lived (but urgently required) web applications. If unit testing and maintenance are not priorities, for whatever reason, then Web Forms can be incredibly powerful. I suggest you read the chapters that cover Web Forms, even if you purchased this book for the coverage of the MVC framework. Web Forms can be useful for experimenting with different user experience approaches and general proof-of-concept work.

The MVC Framework

The MVC framework is a very modern approach, driven by the widespread adoption of frameworks such as Ruby on Rails. The MVC framework is well-suited to building large-scale applications that have to be maintained over time, but it contains a lot of concepts that will be new to .NET developers and so has a relatively large up-front investment.

The key difference from Web Forms is that MVC framework developers are expected to have a comprehensive knowledge of HTML and HTTP. There is no hiding of the details here. This is more demanding of the developer, but it leads to applications that are more suited to the nature of HTTP and allows total flexibility over the HTML that is generated and sent to the browser.

The MVC framework is built around a design pattern called MVC, which stands for Model-View-Controller. You break our applications into these three areas, called *concerns*, and through this separation, you create applications that are easier to test and easier to maintain. I'll explain more about the MVC pattern and how it is reflected in the MVC framework in Chapter 22. You don't need comprehensive knowledge of the MVC pattern to write MVC framework applications, but it does help to understand why things operate the way they do in an MVC framework web application.

Aside from requiring the developer to learn new concepts, the main drawback of the MVC framework is that it is a while before a web application takes shape. There is a greater up-front investment. This is a sensible investment for applications that will be around a while, because this investment pays dividends over the long term by making the application easier to maintain. But if you are looking to put together a quick-and-dirty demo, then Web Forms offers a better prospect.

I really like the MVC framework, but I also like Web Forms. The key to success is to know the strengths and weaknesses of each and to have a good enough knowledge of both to be able to switch between them at will. This is the purpose of this book.

Understanding Related Technologies

I have described the major components of ASP.NET, but there are a lot of affiliated technologies that you will encounter as you begin web application development. In the following sections, I describe some of the most widely known and explain how they relate to ASP.NET and to this book.

Dynamic Data

Many web applications simply exist to provide access to a database. There is no application logic as such, just a reasonably direct mapping between a set of grid-based and form-based web pages and a set of database tables.

Dynamic Data is a set of features that were added to ASP.NET version 4, specifically to allow rapid development of this kind of application, but it hasn't really caught on. I think this is because it falls in a gap between Web Forms and the MVC framework. If you are going to learn a new approach to web application development, you might as learn the MVC framework. It is because of this lack of widespread adoption that I have omitted Dynamic Data applications from this book, giving me more space to focus on the rest of ASP.NET.

Silverlight

Silverlight is Microsoft's answer to Adobe Flash, designed for rich browser experiences and integrated with other .NET technologies and languages. Recently, Microsoft announced that it would be focusing on HTML5 as its preferred approach to rich web pages, leaving Silverlight as the development platform for Windows Phone products. I don't cover Silverlight in this book, not least because it is in danger of becoming a niche platform. If you are interested in Silverlight development, I recommend *Pro Silverlight 4 in C#*, written by Matthew MacDonald and published by Apress.

HTML5

HTML5 is an emerging standard for web pages, tidying up some of the duplication and redundancy in HTML version 4 and incorporating some new interactivity features. Microsoft has started adding basic support for HTML5 elements in ASP.NET, but it is in its early days, and it will be a while before HTML5 matures—and longer still before Microsoft delivers credible tooling in this space. I don't cover HTML5 in this book, but if you are interested in further details, I suggest another of my books, *The Definitive Guide to HTML5*, also published by Apress.

jQuery and ASP.NET Ajax

jQuery is a popular JavaScript library that simplifies using JavaScript, hides a lot of the inconsistencies between browsers, and has a rich ecosystem of plug-in functionality. As of ASP.NET 4, Microsoft has embraced the open source jQuery, which is included in all ASP.NET 4 projects. I discuss and demonstrate jQuery in Chapters 10 and 11. Version 3 of the MVC framework relies on jQuery to deliver unobtrusive client validation and Ajax, which I explain in Chapters 29 and 30, respectively.

jQuery replaces the ASP.NET Ajax library. This was developed by Microsoft but was tricky to use correctly and generated some very messy web pages. You can still elect to use ASP.NET AJAX, but jQuery is easier to use, is more flexible, and produces cleaner web pages.

IIS and Windows Server

ASP.NET applications are deployed to Internet Information Services (IIS). IIS is included in a number of different Windows editions, including some of the workstation products, although IIS will process a limited number of concurrent requests on a workstation.

For serious applications, you will need to use Windows Server. In Chapter 32, I show you how to prepare Windows Server 2008 R2 (the current version as I write this), and in Chapter 33, I show you how to use Visual Studio to deploy an ASP.NET application to IIS.

Summary

In this chapter, I set out some context for the different parts of ASP.NET and how they fit together. I explained how Web Forms was designed to apply the classic Visual Basic development methodology to web applications and how the MVC framework does away with this to follow an entirely different approach. I also touched on some of the technologies that are commonly associated with ASP.NET and explained where you can find further details, either in this book or further afield.

With the preamble addressed, we can begin development in earnest. In the next chapter, I'll introduce you to *pages*, one of the core ASP.NET platform concepts.

PART II

■ ■ ■

Getting to Know ASP .NET

We are ready to start digging into the ASP.NET framework. Over the next eight chapters, I'll introduce you to the core features that you can use to create web applications. As you'll learn, the ASP.NET framework provides a comprehensive set of capabilities, covering every aspect of web development. We'll use these features to build a stand-alone web application and set the scene for the other parts of this book, which explore the that are built on top of ASP.NET (such as Web Forms and the MVC framework).

CHAPTER 4

Working with Pages

The main objective of most ASP.NET web applications is to generate HTML content that will be displayed in a web browser (although you can use ASP.NET to produce other kinds of data, as you'll learn in later chapters).

In this chapter, we are going to look at the core mechanism that ASP.NET provides for generating HTML: *the ASP.NET web page*. Getting a good grip on this topic is a big step toward understanding ASP.NET as a whole, and you will be surprised at how simply and elegantly this all works.

We are going to start with a simple HTML file and explore different ways of combining C# and HTML to generate the same result in the browser. Using dynamic content features to reproduce static HTML may seem odd, but it provides a nice foundation for gradually introducing C# to generate content programmatically. In later chapters, we'll build on these techniques to produce content that is genuinely dynamic. Here, we will start with the basics.

Getting Started with Pages

In this chapter, we are going to start with an empty project and add items to it manually. To create the project, follow these steps:

1. In Visual Studio, select File ➤ New ➤ Project. This will bring up the New Project dialog.

2. Click the Visual C# templates in the Installed Templates section, select the Web category, and then click the ASP.NET Empty Web Application template.

▨ **Caution** The set of templates displayed in the New Project dialog will differ based on the Visual Studio edition you have installed and the options you selected during installation. Take care to select the right template. There are some with similar names, and it is easy to pick the wrong one. Also make sure that you have selected the template from the Visual C# category. You will see templates with the same name available for each .NET language you have installed. We'll use most of the other C# ASP.NET templates as we work our way through the following chapters, but you can ignore them for now.

---

3.   Set the name of the project as `SimplePages`, as shown in Figure 4-1.

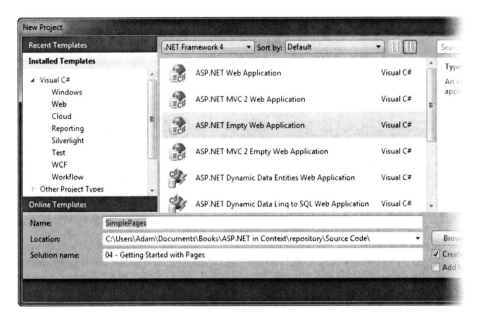

Figure 4-1. Creating an empty ASP.NET project

4.   Click the OK button to create the project.

5.   Select View ➤ Solution Explorer. In the Solution Explorer, you can see the items that have been added to the project, as shown in Figure 4-2. As this is an empty project, Visual Studio creates only the bare essentials.

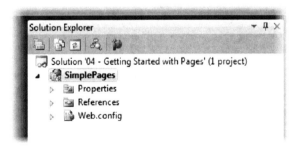

Figure 4-2. The contents of the empty project

You will be familiar with these items if you have used Visual Studio to create other kinds of .NET projects. The `Properties` item contains the settings for your project—build options, deployment configuration, and so on. The `Web.config` file contains the configuration information for our ASP.NET application. This is similar to `App.config`, which you will have seen if you have used Visual Studio to create other types of .NET applications. The `References` item contains the references to the .NET assemblies that our project needs to run.

Adding a Web Page

One of the fundamental concepts in ASP.NET is *programmatically generated web pages*, more commonly known as *dynamic web pages*, or simply *dynamic pages*. A dynamic page mixes program logic (in our case, C# code) with HTML to create content that will be displayed in a client browser. Such a page is dynamic because the code portions of the web page are evaluated for each browser request, allowing you to produce different content. This is in contrast to *static* content, such as a regular HTML files or an image file, where the same content is always sent to the users' browsers.

ASP.NET supports two different, but related, models for combining program logic and HTML: using code blocks or using code-behind files. We'll explore both of these techniques in this chapter.

The best place to start with a dynamic web page is, oddly enough, with a regular HTML file. There are two reasons for this:

- We are going to explore one feature at a time, and the templates that Visual Studio has for dynamic pages make some assumptions about which features are to be used.

- Introducing dynamic elements to a static page lets you see the close relationship between static and dynamic content, and, as you'll discover, emphasizes the important role that static content plays in dynamic pages.

Creating an HTML File

To add an HTML file to the Visual Studio project, follow these steps:

1. Select Project ➤ Add New Item.

2. Select the HTML Page template from the Web category of the Add New Item dialog.

3. Set the name of the page to `Default.html`, as shown in Figure 4-3. As you will see throughout this book, ASP.NET has a number of naming conventions that most web application projects follow. These are optional, but following them can have some benefits. Not only will other developers recognize the purpose of files or directories with certain names, but Visual Studio will as well. Also, some convenience features work based on these conventions. The first such convention is that the starting point for your web application is a page called `Default`, which is why our HTML page is called `Default.html`.

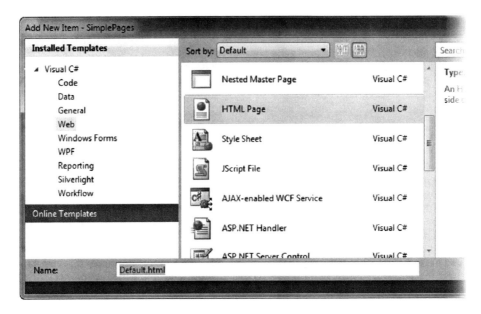

Figure 4-3. *Adding an HTML page to the project*

■ **Tip**   You may have noticed that the default file name extension for the Visual Studio HTML file template is `.htm`. This is a historical holdover from the days when Windows could deal with only three-letter file name extensions. I use the more conventional four-letter extension `.html`, which is not only more descriptive, but is consistent with the extensions used for other ASP.NET file types, such as `.aspx`. If you are having any kind of problem involving HTML pages, the first thing to check is the file name extension. More often than not, you'll find that you are referring to a page using the `.html` extension, but you created the file with the `.htm` extension.

---

4. Click OK to dismiss the Add New Item dialog and create the HTML file.

5. Edit the contents of the file so that they match the HTML shown in Listing 4-1.

Listing 4-1. *A simple HTML file*

```
<!DOCTYPE html PUBLIC "-//W3C//DTD XHTML 1.0 Transitional//EN"
 "http://www.w3.org/TR/xhtml1/DTD/xhtml1-transitional.dtd">
<html xmlns="http://www.w3.org/1999/xhtml">
<head>
    <title>My Web Page</title>
</head>
<body>
    <div>
```

```
        Here are some numbers I like:
        <ul>
            <li>0</li>
            <li>1</li>
            <li>2</li>
            <li>3</li>
        </ul>
    </div>
    <div>
        Here are some things I like to do:
        <ol>
            <li>Swim</li>
            <li>Cycle</li>
            <li>Run</li>
        </ol>
    </div>
    <div>
        Here is an image:
        <img src="Images/triathlon.png" alt="Triathlon Symbols" />
    </div>
    <div>
        <a href="SecondPage.html">This is a link to another page</a>
    </div>
</body>
</html>
```

This HTML page contains a list of numbers, a list of activities, an image, and a link to another page. Before we view this page, we need to add the image and the second HTML page to our project.

▪ **Tip**   I am not going to cover HTML in any depth in this book. You will be able to follow the examples in this book just fine if you have a basic knowledge of HTML. If you are new to HTML or want to build on your knowledge, I suggest reading *Beginning HTML with CSS and XHTML*, by David Schultz and Craig Cook (Apress, 2007). I also recommend looking at the HTML source for web sites that catch your eye. All of the mainstream web browsers will let you inspect the HTML on a web page, and this can be a good way to see how sites are constructed.

Adding the Second HTML Page

To add a new HTML file to the project, follow these steps:

1. Select Project ➤ Add New Item.

2. In the Add New Item dialog, choose the HTML Page template from the Web section.

3. Give the new page the name SecondPage.html.

4. Click Add to create the file.

5. Edit the contents of the new file to match Listing 4-2.

Listing 4-2. *Adding a second HTML file*

```
<!DOCTYPE html PUBLIC "-//W3C//DTD XHTML 1.0 Transitional//EN"
 "http://www.w3.org/TR/xhtml1/DTD/xhtml1-transitional.dtd">
<html xmlns="http://www.w3.org/1999/xhtml">
<head>
    <title>My Second HTML File</title>
</head>
<body>
    <div>
        Here are some colors I like:
        <ul>
            <li>Green</li>
            <li>Red</li>
            <li>Yellow</li>
            <li>Blue</li>
        </ul>
    </div>
</body>
</html>
```

This is a simple file that contains a list of colors.

Adding the Image

By convention, images are stored in a separate directory, typically called **Images**. You could create this folder in your project directory and refer to the images it contains without adding them to the Visual Studio project. However, I prefer to have all of the files of my web applications (including static content) as part of my project. One reason is that it allows me to use the Visual Studio version control support for all files.

Visual Studio is a bit finicky when it comes to adding external content to a project. If you select Project ➤ Add Existing Item, you can select your images files, but they will be added to your project at the same level as your HTML files. I find this confusing, because the location of the image files on the disk has not changed, so the layout of the project on the disk and the layout shown in the Solution Explorer window do not match up.

Instead, I prefer to create a directory first by selecting Project ➤ New Folder and giving it the name **Images**. This creates the directory on the disk where I can copy my image files. I then select the **Images** folder in the Solution Explorer, select Project ➤ Add Existing Item, and select my images. This provides a project view that matches the way that the files are arranged on disk, as shown in Figure 4-4.

Figure 4-4. *Adding an image to the project*

UNDERSTANDING PAGE REFERENCES

I advise you not to use absolute paths when referencing content in your project. For example, the absolute path for my image file is C:\Users\Adam\Documents\Books\ASP.NET in Context\repository\Source Code\04 - Working with Pages\SimplePages\Images\triathlon.png. I could have used this path in the HTML file to reference the image, but if I did, I would have problems when I deployed the project to a server, unless I used the exact same path. Many projects are deployed to servers that belong to third-party hosting companies, and you usually won't be able to control the paths to which your project is deployed.

To avoid this problem, use references that are project-relative or file-relative, as follows:

- A *project-relative reference* begins with the / character, such as /Images/triathlon.png. If you use this style of reference, ASP.NET will start at the root folder for your project and look for a file called triathlon.png in a folder called Images.

- A *file-relative reference* omits the / character, as in Images/triathlon.png. If you use this kind of reference, ASP.NET will look in the folder that contains your page file for a folder called Images and the triathlon.png file inside it. You can use file-relative paths to navigate the directory structure of your project. For example, ../../Images/triathlon.png407.90 will look for the Images folder up two levels from the page file.

Viewing the HTML File

To view the HTML file, right-click `Default.html` in the Solution Explorer and select View in Browser from the pop-up menu. This will display the HTML page in a browser window—which browser depends on your system configuration. My preferred browser is Google Chrome, and because this is set as my Windows default browser, this is where Visual Studio displays the content. You might recognize the window header shown in Figure 4-5.

Here are some numbers I like:

- 0
- 1
- 2
- 3

Here are some things I like to do:

1. Swim
2. Cycle
3. Run

Here is an image:
This is a link to another page

Figure 4-5. *Displaying the HTML file*

You can change the browser that Visual Studio uses by right-clicking a page and selecting the Browse With menu item. You will be presented with a dialog that lists all of the available browsers on your computer, as shown in Figure 4-6.

Figure 4-6. Selecting the browser to use in Visual Studio

You can use this window to set the default Visual Studio browser by selecting it and clicking the Set as Default button. In Figure 4-6, I have selected the built-in browser that is part of Visual Studio. This is based on Internet Explorer, and it is the browser I have tended to use for the figures in this book. You can also select a different browser to view a single page just once, which is handy when you want to compare the way that different browsers display the same pages.

When you selected View in Browser, an ASP.NET Development Server icon appears on your Windows taskbar with a balloon, as shown in Figure 4-7.

Figure 4-7. The ASP.NET Development Server

Visual Studio includes a full-featured ASP.NET server, which is started when you view pages in your project. By *full-featured*, I mean that the development server implements all of the ASP.NET features. However, it doesn't implement all the features that a production web application server needs. You need Internet Information Services (IIS) for that (which is discussed in Chapters 32 and 33). Still, it is very useful to be able to test a web application on your development machine directly from your Visual Studio project.

You can see from the balloon in Figure 4-7 that the development server is monitoring port 1939 on my machine. The port is selected randomly, so you will see different port numbers used. If you look at the browser window in Figure 4-5, you can see that the URL for loading our HTML page uses that port. The name localhost refers to the local machine, so the URL for testing our HTML page is http://localhost:1939/Default.html. If you click the link at the bottom of the page, the second static

HTML file will be requested from the ASP.NET development server and displayed in the browser, as shown in Figure 4-8.

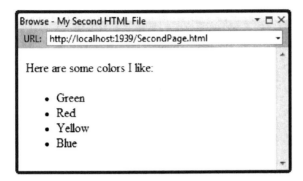

Figure 4-8. *Displaying the second HTML file*

If you have a lot of pages and other items in your Visual Studio ASP.NET project, it can be annoying to search for the page you want to view in the Solution Explorer, right-click it, and select the appropriate menu item. An alternative approach is to select the page, right-click, and pick Set as Start Page. This may not seem like an improvement, but once you have set your start page, you can select Debug ➤ Start Debugging or Start Without Debugging, and your selected page will be rendered and displayed. See Chapter 7 for details on using the Debug menu to debug the rendering process for an ASP.NET web page.

Making a Page Dynamic with Code Blocks

The pages we created in the previous section are *static*, meaning that the content is fixed. It doesn't matter how many times you request the URLs associated with those files, the content returned to the browser will always be the same. The ASP.NET server treats static content as *opaque*, meaning that it doesn't look inside the files or process them, except to return their contents to the client browser.

The counterpart to a static web page is a *dynamic web page*, which mixes HTML content with program logic that the ASP.NET server executes to generate content. The HTML that results from a request to a dynamic page can vary based on the output of the program logic. In this section, we will convert our HTML file to a dynamic page and look at one of the two approaches that ASP.NET supports for mixing the program logic with the HTML: using code blocks. Later, we'll demonstrate the other approach, which is using code-behind files.

The ASP.NET server differentiates between static and dynamic files using the file name extensions. There are a set of extensions, such as `.aspx` and `.cshtml`, that are treated as dynamic. You'll see the different extensions for dynamic files as we progress through the book.

To begin the process of converting our HTML file to a dynamic page, we must rename the file— ASP.NET page files have the `.aspx` file extension. The `.aspx` file extension is one of the most important In ASP.NET. It tells the server that this is a dynamic web page file.

To rename the file, select the `Default.html` file in the Solution Explorer, right-click, select Rename, and change the name to `Default.aspx`. You will see a dialog warning you about changing the file name extension, as shown in Figure 4-9. Click the Yes button to dismiss the dialog and change the file name.

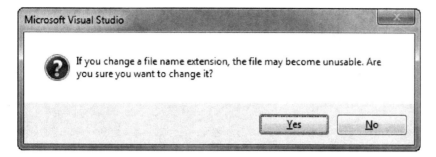

Figure 4-9. *Changing the extension of a file name*

Adding the Page Directive

The .aspx file extension tells ASP.NET that a file should be processed as a dynamic web page, but it doesn't tell the server *how* it should be processed. To do that, we need to add a Page directive.

A *directive* is an ASP.NET instruction that starts with the character sequence <%@ and ends with the sequence %>. In between those sequences, it contains a series of attribute values, each of which tells the ASP.NET framework something about the file. The most commonly found directive is the Page directive, which tells the ASP.NET framework how to process the file. We are going to start with a basic Page directive:

```
<%@ Page Language="C#" %>
```

This is a simple Page directive that tells ASP.NET we are using the C# language. If we don't add this directive, ASP.NET assumes that we are using Visual Basic. The Page directive goes at the top of our .aspx file, like this:

```
<%@ Page Language="C#" %>

<html xmlns="http://www.w3.org/1999/xhtml">
<head>
    <title>My Web Page</title>
</head>
<body>
...
```

Adding a Code Block

We needed to use the Page directive to specify C# because our real goal in this section is to add *code blocks* to our web page. A code block, sometimes known as a *code fragment*, is a set of C# statements that the ASP.NET server will execute when the page is requested by a browser. In our static HTML file, we have the following:

```
...
<div>
    Here are some numbers I like:
    <ul>
        <li>0</li>
        <li>1</li>
        <li>2</li>
        <li>3</li>
    </ul>
</div>
<div>
...
```

We can use a code block to create the list of numbers with C# statements, as shown in Listing 4-3, where the code block is highlighted in bold.

Listing 4-3. *A simple code block*

```
...
<div>
    Here are some numbers I like:
    <ul>
        <%
            for (int i = 0; i < 4; i++) {
                Response.Write(string.Format("<li>{0}</li>", i));
            }
        %>
    </ul>
</div>
<div>
...
```

How do code blocks work? To explain this, we'll take a closer look at what we have added to the page.

Defining a Code Block

A code block starts with <% and ends with %>. Any code statements that the ASP.NET server finds between those delimiters will be compiled and executed. The formatting of a code block is relatively flexible. I like to have just one set of delimiters, but you can mix and match where you place them, like this:

```
<ul>
    <% for (int i = 0; i < 4; i++) { %>
    <%    Response.Write(String.Format("<li>{0}</li>\n", i)); %>
    } %>
</ul>
```

You can delimit individual statements or groups of statements. The preceding example shows both techniques. The first part of the **for** loop is delimited on its own, and the next two code lines are grouped together. The ASP.NET server is clever enough to figure out that these delimited statements are related and treats them as a single code block.

Breaking down the Code Block Statements

There are three parts to our example code block:

- The first part is a standard C# `for` loop. The loop initializer creates an `int` variable called `i` with an initial value of `0`. The loop iterator increments the variable, and the loop condition terminates the loop when four iterations have been performed.

- The second part of the code block is the call to the static `String.Format` method:

  ```
  String.Format("<li>{0}</li>\n", i)
  ```

  This statement allows us to use the .NET composite string-formatting feature to generate the HTML for each list item. Notice that we are responsible for generating well-formed HTML list items, not just the numeric values for our list. Also notice that we append the `\n` character sequence to the end of each string we create. This is ignored by the web browser, but it makes the HTML that is generated easier to read by separating the list item onto separate lines (albeit at the cost of transferring additional characters to the web browser).

- The final part of the code block is the call to the `Response.Write` method, which inserts the result of the `String.Format` call into the HTML that will be returned to the browser. When you use the `Response.Write` method, the string that you pass as a parameter is placed in the HTML at the location where the ASP.NET server encountered the code block. This means that our calls to this method result in the individual list items being placed in between the `ul` tags.

■ **Note**   ASP.NET provides a series of classes that simplify writing code blocks, the most useful of which is `Response.Write`. You can find more information about these classes, including the use of `Response.Write`, in Chapter 5.

Adding and Calling Methods

The code block in Listing 4-3 is self-contained, but if we want to perform the same task in several different code blocks, we can define a common method and refer to it from different code blocks. Listing 4-4 demonstrates defining two methods.

Listing 4-4. Defining methods in a dynamic web page

```
<%@ Page Language="C#"%>
<script runat="server">
    protected string GetImageName() {
        return "Images/triathlon.png";
    }
```

```
        protected string GetImageAlt() {
            return "Triathlon Symbols";
        }
</script>
<html xmlns="http://www.w3.org/1999/xhtml">
<head>
...
```

You define one or more methods inside a `script` tag. The convention is to define all of your methods near the top of your dynamic page, but they can be placed anywhere you like, as long as they are defined before you refer to them. You must define your `script` tag with the `runat` attribute set to `server`. If you don't do this, ASP.NET won't recognize your `script` tag as one that contains C# code.

Listing 4-4 defines two simple methods:

- `GetImageName` returns the name of the only image in the project.

- `GetImageAlt` returns a string to be used as the value for the `alt` attribute of the `img` tag.

We can use these methods in a couple of ways. The first is to use an equal sign (=) inside the delimiters and call the method name, like this:

```
<div>
<img src="<% =GetImageName() %>" alt="<% =GetImageAlt() %>" />
</div>
```

This is shorthand that inserts the result from the method we called into the HTML for the response, without needing to use the `Response.Write` method. This approach is ideally suited to setting attribute values in HTML elements, as shown in the example.

We can also call the methods inside a regular code block, This is more commonly used to create entire HTML elements, like this:

```
<%
    Response.Write(string.Format("<img src=\"{0}\" alt=\"{1}\"/>",
        GetImageName(), GetImageAlt()));
%>
```

Viewing a Dynamic Web Page

A dynamic page can contain multiple directives, `script` tags, and code blocks. Listing 4-5 shows the contents of the `Default.aspx` file, updated to include the `Page` directive, the methods, and the code blocks from the previous sections.

Listing 4-5. A complete dynamic web page

```
<%@ Page Language="C#" %>
<script runat="server">
    protected string GetImageName() {
        return "Images/triathlon.png";
    }
```

```
    protected string GetImageAlt() {
        return "Triathlon Symbols";
    }
</script>
<html xmlns="http://www.w3.org/1999/xhtml">
<head>
    <title>My Web Page</title>
</head>
<body>
    <div>
        Here are some numbers I like:
        <ul>
            <%
                for (int i = 0; i < 4; i++) {
                    Response.Write(string.Format("<li>{0}</li>", i));
                }
            %>
        </ul>
    </div>
    <div>
        Here are some things I like to do:
        <ol>
            <li>Swim</li>
            <li>Cycle</li>
            <li>Run</li>
        </ol>
    </div>
    <div>
        Here is an image:
        <img src="<% =GetImageName() %>" alt="<% =GetImageAlt() %>"
    </div>
    <div>
        <a href="SecondPage.html">This is a link to another page</a>
    </div>
</body>
</html>
```

To view this page, right-click the `Default.aspx` item in the Solution Explorer window and select View in Browser from the pop-up menu.

At this point, something very cool happens: ASP.NET extracts the statements from the code blocks and `script` regions and uses them to create a temporary C# class. The methods defined in the `script` regions are added as methods to the class. The HTML and the statements in the code block are combined in another method to generate the output. Listing 4-6 shows the temporary class generated for our page.

Listing 4-6. The automatically generated temporary C# class for a dynamic web page

```csharp
namespace ASP {

    public class default_aspx : System.Web.UI.Page,
        System.Web.SessionState.IRequiresSessionState, System.Web.IHttpHandler {

        protected string GetImageName() {
            return "Images/triathlon.png";
        }

        protected string GetImageAlt() {
            return "Triathlon Symbols";
        }

        private void @__Render__control1(System.Web.UI.HtmlTextWriter @__w,
            System.Web.UI.Control parameterContainer) {

            @__w.Write("\r\n<html xmlns=\"http://www.w3.org/1999/xhtml\">\r\n<head>\r\n" +
                "<title>My Web Page</title>\r\n</head>\r\n<body>\r\n<div>\r\n" +
                "Here are some numbers I like:\r\n<ul>\r\n");

            for (int i = 0; i < 4; i++) {
                Response.Write(string.Format("<li>{0}</li>", i));
            }

            @__w.Write("</ul>\r\n</div>\r\n<div>\r\nHere are some things I like to " +
                "do:\r\n<ol>\r\n<li>Swim</li>\r\n<li>Cycle</li>\r\n<li>Run</li>" +
                "\r\n</ol>\r\n</div>\r\n<div>\r\nHere is an image:\r\n<img src=");

            @__w.Write(GetImageName() );

            @__w.Write("\" alt=\"");

            @__w.Write(GetImageAlt(); );

            @__w.Write("\"\r\n</div>\r\n<div>\r\n<a href=\"SecondPage.html\">This is" +
                "a link to another page</a>\r\n    </div>\r\n\r\n    ");

            @__w.Write("\r\n</body>\r\n</html>\r\n");
        }
    }
}
```

This class is responsible for *rendering* the web page that it represents. This means that it transforms the contents of the .aspx web page file (including the code blocks) and produces an HTML result to be displayed in a browser.

I have removed some additional methods and cleaned up the formatting of this class to fit it on the page, but you can clearly see the approach that ASP.NET has taken to cope with the mix of code and HTML, and you can also see that it is pretty simple. The methods from our `script` region have been moved as is to be methods in the class. In the method that writes the content, you can see that a series of `Write` statements push the HTML sections and the output from the code blocks to the output to the browser.

LOCATING TEMPORARY CLASS FILES

You don't need to inspect the temporary classes to use ASP.NET, but it can be interesting to see how features are translated into C# code. Finding the temporary classes can be a bit tricky and requires some patience.

You can find the directory where the classes are created and compiled by reading the static `System.Web.HttpRuntime.CodegenDir` property in your page. For me, all temporary ASP.NET files are in the `C:\Adam\AppData\Local\Temp\Temporary ASP.NET Files` directory, but if you are using a different operating system or ASP.NET configuration, your files may be stored elsewhere.

On my system, the files for this project are in the `root\1f7bc190\d0a76116` subdirectory. The name of your subdirectory will differ and a bit of rooting around is required. You'll find a C# code file and some dynamic-link library (DLL) files. The trick is to look for a file that resembles your dynamic page file name— something like `default.aspx.cdcab7d2.compiled`. You can't read this file, but it tells you that you are in the right place. Open some of the `.cs` files, and you'll find those temporary classes.

When the ASP.NET server receives a request for our dynamic page, it creates the temporary class, compiles it, and then calls the method in the compiled code to create the HTML page that will be sent back to the browser. This output will combine the static HTML regions and the results created by the code blocks in our `.aspx` file. All of this is done at the ASP.NET server, and only HTML is returned to the browser. The browser is unaware of the dynamic nature of our web page and never sees the C# statements. Figure 4-10 shows our dynamic page as it appears in the browser.

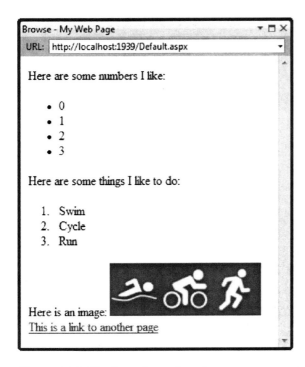

Figure 4-10. *Viewing a dynamic web page*

Notice that we didn't need to compile anything in the project explicitly. ASP.NET takes care of creating, compiling, and executing the temporary class for us. If we make any changes to the .aspx file, the ASP.NET server will re-create and recompile the temporary class for us. For example, change the code block that generates the numeric sequence as follows and save the file:

```
<ul>
    <% for (int i = 0; i < 5; i++) {
        Response.Write(String.Format("<li>{0}</li>\n", i));
    }
    %>
</ul>
```

Now select Reload or Refresh in your browser, and you'll see the page displayed with fewer numeric values, as shown in Figure 4-11. We didn't need to do anything explicit to tell Visual Studio or ASP.NET to re-create and compile the temporary class. The ASP.NET server detected the change in the .aspx file and regenerated and recompiled the temporary class automatically when the browser request was processed.

Figure 4-11. Changes in a dynamic web page

The temporary class for a dynamic web page is created and compiled only when there is a change in the `.aspx` file. Otherwise, once a class has been created and compiled, it will be reused for subsequent requests for the same page.

Using a Code-Behind File

Code blocks are great for simple tasks and are especially well-suited to setting values for HTML element attributes, as we did for the `img` element in the previous section. Their main drawback is that they are harder to read and maintain than regular C# files, because the code statements are dispersed throughout the page and mingled in with the HTML.

A common use for code blocks is to insert values into JavaScript files, so that we can refer to elements in an ASP.NET web page. You will see how this is done, and understand why it is required, in Chapter 9. For more complex pages, a more useful (and commonly used) approach is to separate the HTML and directives into one file and the C# code into another. When you do this, the C# file is called the *code-behind file*, and the class that is contains is called the *code-behind class*.

Preparing the Page File

We need to make a couple of changes to our web page file so that we can use a code-behind file:

- Update our `Page` directive so that ASP.NET knows we want to use a code-behind file and knows how to find it.

- Add attributes to the HTML elements that we want to work with.

The following sections demonstrate both of these changes.

Setting the Page Directive

The first step toward using a code-behind file is to prepare our page file. We begin by updating the `Page` directive, like this:

```
<%@ Page CodeFile="Default.aspx.cs" Inherits="SimplePages.Default" %>
<html xmlns="http://www.w3.org/1999/xhtml">
<head>
...
```

The first new attribute in the directive is `CodeFile`. This tells the ASP.NET server the name of the C# file that contains the program logic for this web page. The naming convention for code-behind files is to use the name of the web file (`Default.aspx`) and append the normal file name extension for that kind of code file. For C#, that is `.cs`, giving us a code-behind file name of `Default.aspx.cs`.

A single C# code file can contain multiple classes. The second new attribute is `Inherits`. This tells the ASP.NET server which class in the code file should be used; that is, which class is the code-behind class in the code-behind file. If you are using the `Namespace` directive to group your classes together, then you must include the namespace in the value for the `Inherits` attribute. We will follow the convention of using the project name as the namespace and the page name as the class name. This gives us an `Inherits` value of `SimplePages.Default`.

▓ **Tip**   You don't need to include the `Language` attribute in the `Page` directive when you are using code-behind files, only when working with code blocks. But if you do include it, you can mix code blocks and code-behind techniques to create dynamic content.

Assigning Element IDs

The second change we need to make is to add some attributes to the HMTL elements that we want to work with in our code. When we used code blocks, the placement of the code statements determined where in the rendered HTML the effect of the code blocks would be applied. Our `for` loop created list items inside the list where the code block was placed—all very nice and direct.

Things are more complicated when the code statements are in a separate file, and we resolve this by giving identifiers to the parts of the HTML that we know we want to work on. Here is an example applied to the one of the HTML list elements:

```
...
<ul id="numberList" runat="server"/>
...
```

Assigning an ID gives an HTML element a name that we can refer to in our code later. This example assigns the `id` a value of `numberList`.

▓ **Note**   The convention for `id` attribute values is to use *camel case*. This means that the first letter is lowercase, and the first letter of any subsequent concatenated word is uppercase—for example, `numberList` or `secondPageLink`. This is because the names that you assign though the `id` attributes will be transformed into C# class fields, and camel case is the standard form for field names.

Each HTML element that we want to modify in our C# code must also have the **runat** attribute with a value of **server**. This tells the ASP.NET server that an element is in scope for a code-behind file. If you omit the **runat** attribute, or use a value other than **server**, the ASP.NET server will ignore your HTML element, and you won't be able to refer to it in your code-behind class.

■ **Tip** You'll see the **runat** attribute used throughout ASP.NET. If you want to bring something into sight of ASP.NET, you will generally need to apply **runat="server"** somewhere in your page file. It is easy to forget to do this. If you are having problems where ASP.NET doesn't recognize some element or component in your page file, the first thing to check is the presence of **runat**.

Listing 4-7 shows the updated contents of the **Default.aspx** file. The code blocks and **script** section from the previous examples are removed, and we update the **Page** directive to reference a code-behind file and class, and add **id** and **runat** attributes to the HTML elements that we are going to be working with.

Listing 4-7. *Preparing for a code-behind file*

```
<%@ Page CodeFile="Default.aspx.cs" Inherits="SimplePages.Default" %>
<html xmlns="http://www.w3.org/1999/xhtml">
<head>
    <title>My Web Page</title>
</head>
<body>
    <div>
        Here are some numbers I like:
        <ul id="numberList" runat="server" />
    </div>
    <div id="thingsListDiv" runat="server"/>
    <div>
        Here is an image:
        <img id="image" runat="server" />
    </div>
    <div>
        <a id="secondPageLink" runat="server" />
    </div>
</body>
</html>
```

The file shown by Listing 4-7 contains HTML elements in four different conditions:

- The first is where the element exists, but has no content. This is the case for the ul element. We have a list, but there is nothing in the list.

- The second condition is an element that is missing attributes. This is the case for the img element, which lacks the src and alt attributes.

- The third condition is represented by the a element, which is missing an href element and the content to describe the link.

- The final condition is where the element doesn't exist (yet). I have removed the ordered list (ol) element and its contents and the text that preceded the list in earlier examples. We'll use this element as a demonstration of how to add new content to a page.

We will use the code file to add list items, the missing attributes, and the link description.

Creating the Code-Behind Class

To create the code-behind file, follow these steps:

1. In Visual Studio, select Project ➤ Add Class. This will open the familiar Add New Item dialog.

2. Select the Class template, as shown in Figure 4-12.

3. Set the name of the class to be Default.aspx.cs (this is the name we specified in the Page directive in the previous section).

4. Click the OK button to create the new file.

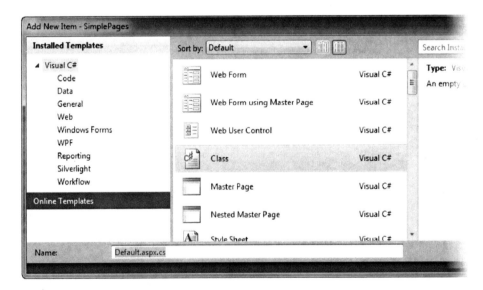

Figure 4-12. Adding a code-behind class file

The new code file is created as a subitem of Default.aspx, as shown in Figure 4-13. This is done based on the name of the code file, rather than the values in the Page directive. This is one reason why following the naming convention for code-behind files is so common: it helps keep web application projects tidy by grouping dynamic page files and their associated code-behind files together.

Figure 4-13. *A code file associated with a web page file*

Editing the Code-Behind File

You can open the code file for editing in several ways:

- Expand the `Default.aspx` item in the Solution Explorer window, and then double-click the `Default.aspx.cs` file.

- Right-click `Default.aspx` and select the View Code menu item.

- You can edit the `.aspx` file itself by right-clicking `Default.aspx` and selecting the View Markup menu item. (You'll use the third option in the pop-up menu, View Designer, when we look at web forms in Chapter 14.)

Open the code file however you prefer, and edit it so that it matches Listing 4-8.

Listing 4-8. *A code-behind file*

```
using System;
using System.Text;
using System.Web.UI;

namespace SimplePages {

    public partial class Default : Page {

        protected void Page_Load(object sender, EventArgs e) {

            // create a string builder so we can efficiently compose HTML
            StringBuilder builder = new StringBuilder();
```

```
/////////////////////////////////
// deal with the numbers list //
/////////////////////////////////

// create the HTML list items for the numeric list
for (int i = 0; i < 4; i++) {
    builder.AppendFormat("<li>{0}</li>\n", i);
}

// set the content of the number list
numberList.InnerHtml = builder.ToString();

/////////////////////////////////
// deal with the things list //
/////////////////////////////////

// clear the StringBuilder so we can use it again
builder.Clear();
// append the string
builder.AppendLine("Here are some things I like to do:");
// append the list and the list items
builder.AppendLine("<ol>");
foreach (string str in new string[] {"Swim", "Cycle", "Run"}) {
    builder.AppendFormat("<li>{0}</li>\n", str);
}
builder.AppendLine("</ol>");
// set the contents of the div element
thingsListDiv.InnerHtml = builder.ToString();

/////////////////////////////
// deal with the image //
/////////////////////////////
image.Src = "/Images/triathlon.png";
image.Alt = "Triathlon Symbols";

/////////////////////////////
// deal with the link //
/////////////////////////////
secondPageLink.HRef = "SecondPage.html";
secondPageLink.InnerHtml = "This is a link to another page";


            }
        }
    }
}
```

Understanding the Code-Behind Class

This class shown in Listing 4-8 is a simple one, but there is a lot going on, not all of which is obvious from the statements. Let's start with the namespace and class definition statements:

```
namespace SimplePages {
    public partial class Default : Page {
    ...
```

The namespace and the name of the class must match the values we set in the Page directive of the .aspx file. In our example, this means that the namespace is called SimplePages and the class is called Default.

Our Default class is derived from the Page class, which is contained in the System.Web.UI namespace. If you are observant, you will have noticed that this is the same base as for the temporary class that ASP.NET generated to make the code blocks work . As you will see, the support for code-behind files and the support for code blocks have a lot in common.

The Default class is defined with the **partial** modifier, making this a *partial class*. A partial class is one that is defined in one or more code files. The individual pieces are combined to produce a single class during compilation. The partial class is the secret glue that ASP.NET uses to join together the .aspx web page file and the .cs code-behind file. When the ASP.NET server receives a request for our dynamic page, it creates another part of the same partial class and uses it to define a protected field for each HTML element to which we have added an id attribute (and for which we have set the runat attribute to be server).

Working with HTML Controls

Listing 4-8 shows the *other* partial class for Default. This class is generated automatically by ASP.NET and is not produced with legibility in mind, so I had to tidy it up to make it readable. The results are in Listing 4-9.

Listing 4-9. *The partial class containing fields*

```
using System.Web.UI.HtmlControls;
namespace SimplePages {

    public partial class Default : System.Web.SessionState.IRequiresSessionState {

        protected HtmlGenericControl numberList;
        protected HtmlGenericControl thingsListDiv;
        protected HtmlImage image;
        protected HtmlAnchor secondPageLink;

    }
}
```

You can see that there is a field for each id value we added to the .aspx file. ASP.NET includes a set of classes that are used to represent HTML elements. For example, the anchor (<a>) element is represented by the HtmlAnchor class, and the image (<img>) element is represented by the HtmlImage class. These classes are known as *HTML controls*, and can be found in the System.Web.UI.HtmlControls namespace.

■ **Note** If you follow these examples in Visual Studio, you'll see that references to the HTML controls in the code-behind file are flagged as errors. This is because Visual Studio doesn't know about and can't access the other partial class that ASP.NET will create. You can ignore these errors, because the compilation will be handled by ASP.NET, rather than by the standard Visual Studio C# compiler. Alternatively, selecting an `.aspx` code file, right-clicking, and selecting View in Browser will generate a request for your dynamic web page, and trigger the compilation process if it is required.

The `System.Web.UI.HtmlControls` namespace contains 34 classes. Table 4-1 lists the most commonly used HTML control classes, along with their corresponding HTML elements.

Table 4-1. *Commonly Used HTML Control Classes*

HTML Element	HTML Control Class
`<a>`	`HtmlAnchor`
`<button>`	`HtmlButton`
`<img>`	`HtmlImage`
`<link>`	`HtmlLink`
`<table>`	`HtmlTable`
`<tr>`	`HtmlTableRow`
`<td>` and `<th>`	`HtmlTableCell`
`<textarea>`	`HtmlTextArea`

■ **Tip** There are also HTML control classes for HTML form and input elements. You'll see these in Chapter 6, when we look at the ASP.NET support for creating and handling forms.

Working with Generic HTML Controls

When there isn't an HTML control for a given HTML element, the `HtmlGenericControl` class is used instead, and this is the case for the two list elements in the web page file.

The HTML controls defined in the generated partial class are available for use in the code-behind file, so the `numberList` field can be used to work with the HTML element that has the `id` attribute of that name, like this:

```
StringBuilder builder = new StringBuilder();

for (int i = 0; i < 4; i++) {
    builder.AppendFormat("<li>{0}</li>\n", i);
}

numberList.InnerHtml = builder.ToString();
```

This example creates a `System.Text.StringBuilder` object and uses it in conjunction with a `for` loop to compose the HTML that should be displayed inside the HTML `ul` element.

All HTML controls have a pair of properties that you can use to set the contents of an HTML element: `InnerHtml` and `InnerText`. You can see that I have assigned the `InnerHtml` property in the code fragment to the contents of the `StringBuilder`. Using the `InnerText` property parses the string to map the < and > characters to the HTML escape sequences < and >. The `InnerHtml` property doesn't perform this conversion.

The `InnerText` and `InnerHtml` properties are used when you want to define the contents of an HTML element. This is one of the conditions we have set out to address in our code file. Here is part of the HTML sent to the browser that shows the effect of the code statements operating on the `numberList` element:

```
<ul id="numberList">
<li>0</li>
<li>1</li>
<li>2</li>
<li>3</li>
</ul>
```

You can see that the HTML composed using the `StringBuilder` and assigned to the element using the `InnerHtml` property has formed the contents of the list.

Here is the same approach applied to the ordered list:

```
builder.AppendLine("Here are some things I like to do:");
// append the list and the list items
builder.AppendLine("<ol>");
foreach (string str in new string[] {"Swim", "Cycle", "Run"}) {
    builder.AppendFormat("<li>{0}</li>\n", str);
}
builder.AppendLine("</ol>");
// set the contents of the div element
thingsListDiv.InnerHtml = builder.ToString();
```

The HTML element in this case is a `div`, and we want to insert some text, a list, and the list items inside the element. We build up the content, including the text and the HTML elements (such as `ol` and `li`), and then use the `InnerHtml` property to set the content of the `div` element that we want to enclose the list. This produces the following HTML:

```
<div id="thingsListDiv">Here are some things I like to do:
<ol>
<li>Swim</li>
<li>Cycle</li>
<li>Run</li>
</ol>
</div>
```

Working with Element-Specific HTML Controls

Each of the element-specific HTML controls defines properties that are specific to the supported element. For example, the `HtmlImage` class defines the `Src` property to set the value of the `src` attribute and the `Alt` property to set the value of the `alt` attribute, like this:

```
image.Src = "Images/triathlon.png";
image.Alt = "Triathlon Symbols";
```

These code statements create the following HTML in the response to the browser:

```
<img src="/Images/triathlon.png" id="image" alt="Triathlon Symbols" />
```

■ **Note** Each element can potentially have a lot of properties. You can easily look up properties in the .NET Framework class library.

The properties in an HTML control class tend to relate to element attributes, but you can still use the `InnerHtml` and `InnerText` properties as well. Here are the statements that configure the a element in our code file:

```
secondPageLink.HRef = "SecondPage.html";
secondPageLink.InnerHtml = "This is a link to another page";
```

The first statement uses the `HRef` property to set an element attribute, and the second statement uses the `InnerHtml` property to set the contents that the element will enclose. These statements result in the following HTML when our page file is requested:

```
<a href="SecondPage.html" id="secondPageLink">This is a link to another page</a>
```

Using the Event Handler Method

The last aspect of Listing 4-8 we need to explore is the location of the code statements that use the HTML control classes, This is in the `Page_Load` method, which has the following definition:

```
protected void Page_Load(object sender, EventArgs e) {
```

The ASP.NET system has a set of events that are invoked to signal that different parts of the web application life cycle are occurring. You'll learn more about these events in Chapter 5, but we'll take a quick look at one particular event now, because it is central to the way that ASP.NET web pages are rendered. This is the `Page.Load` event.

The `Page` class has a number of events, one of which is called `Load`, so we have the `Page.Load` event. This is one of the events called when the page is requested by a browser and is represented by the `Page_Load` method in the `Page` class.

We don't need to explicitly register our method as a handler for the `Load` method. This is done for us by ASP.NET automatically through a feature known as *auto event wire-up*. As a result of this, any code statements that we place in the `Page_Load` method will be executed each time the page is requested.

USING MANUAL EVENT WIRE-UP

Auto event wire-up looks for methods whose names match the pattern *Page_EventName* and registers those methods as handlers for the appropriate event. Auto event wire-up is general useful and enabled by default, but you are not required to take advantage of this feature. You can disable this feature through the Page directive, like this:

```
<%@ Page CodeFile="Dynamic2.aspx.cs" Inherits="SimplePages.Dynamic2"
AutoEventWireup="false" %>
```

When auto event wire-up is disabled, the Page_Load method won't be called unless you wire the method to the Load event. The simplest way to do this is in a constructor for the Dynamic2 class, like this:

```
public Dynamic2() {
    Load += Page_Load;
}
```

If you disable auto event wire-up, then you are responsible for registering methods delegated for all of the ASP.NET events that you are interested in. If you disable auto event wire-up and your web application behaves unexpectedly, then missing event registrations are a good place to start looking.

Viewing a Page with a Code-Behind Class

All that remains is to view the page, which we do as before—by selecting View in Browser from the pop-up menu that appears when we right-click the page in the Solution Explorer window. You can see the result in Figure 4-14.

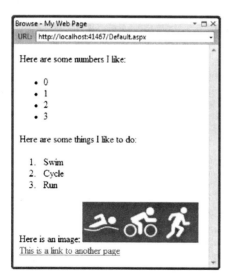

Figure 4-14. *Viewing a page with a code-behind file*

Of course, this page looks the same as the one we built with code blocks. This is a signature of ASP.NET: you can achieve the same result in many different ways. At first, this can be maddening. Trying to work out the best approach for a given problem can be frustrating. In general, the best approach is the one that you prefer using, because ASP.NET ends up rendering the pages in much the same way. The different techniques exist only so that you can express the needs of your web application as elegantly and appropriately as possible.

If we consider the choice of using code blocks or code-behind files, we can see how this works out. Using code-behind files, as part of the on-demand compilation process, ASP.NET parses our `.aspx` file and looks for HTML elements that have an `id` attribute and a `runat` attribute with a value of `server`. The ASP.NET compiler then generates a partial class that corresponds to our code-behind class and creates protected HTML control fields for each of the HTML elements we have tagged. These fields are typed as either an element-specific HTML control, such as `HtmlImage`, or as `HtmlGenericControl` if there isn't a specific control available for the element. The code statements in the code-behind file refer to these HTML controls and use them to set HTML element attributes and content in the `Page_Load` method, which ASP.NET automatically binds to the `Load` event in the `Page` class. And all of this happens when a browser requests our `.aspx` page, although once all of the processing and compilation has been done, subsequent requests are handled using the classes compiled for the initial one.

This is the same approach that is used when dealing with code blocks. The choice of which approach to take is based on which you prefer. Often, especially with regard to code blocks and code-behind classes, you will mix and match multiple techniques in a single web page. We'll do exactly that when we come to use JavaScript in Chapter 9.

Summary

Rendering dynamic HTML content is right at the heart of ASP.NET, and in this chapter, we have explored how this is implemented. You will see the combination of web page files and code-behind files used throughout ASP.NET. Now that you have seen how ASP.NET achieves this, you'll find that peeking behind the curtain of higher-level features such as web forms and the Model-View-Controller (MVC) pattern to be easier and more informative.

When we used the `Page_Load` method in our code-behind files, we touched on the ASP.NET event system, which we will look at in more depth in Chapter 5. ASP.NET implements events that are invoked at key stages in the web application life cycle. We used one of them to hook our C# code into our HTML output. There are other uses for these events, as you will see in later chapters. For now, it is enough to be aware of the existence of these events.

In the next chapter, we'll turn our attention to the different kinds of events that ASP.NET applications emit, and look at how we can get information about the requests received from the browser and take control of the response that is sent in return.

CHAPTER 5

Working with Context and Events

The ASP.NET processing model depends on some behind-the-scenes features to render pages. These are the ASP.NET *event model* and a set of *contexts*. The event model is used to indicate the progress of the rendering process as it passes through different stages. You caught a glimpse of this when we used the `Page_Load` method in the code-behind classes in the previous chapter. The context objects give us information about the request from the client browser and let us configure the response that will be returned. We took advantage of one of the context features when we used the `Response.Write` method in code blocks in the previous chapter.

In this chapter, we'll look at the event model and the context features in more depth. Mostly, these are features that you won't use on a daily basis. You'll put your page-processing statements in the `Page_Load` method of your code-behind class or use the `Response.Write` method in your code blocks, and won't need to go any deeper. That said, there are two reasons for reading this chapter. First, a knowledge of how ASP.NET presents events and context information will help you understand the topics in the chapters that follow. Second, there will come a day when you need to do something different in your ASP.NET web application, and odds are that you will need to respond to a different event or use a different context feature. When that day comes—and it will—you can refer back to this chapter to find the information you need.

Working with ASP.NET Events

ASP.NET implements a set of events that indicate different stages in the life cycle of a web application. We touched on one such event in the previous chapter, when we added C# statements to the `Page_Load` method of our code-behind class and relied on the auto event wire-up feature to associate this method with the `Page.Load` event. In this section, we'll dig deeper into these events to understand what they represent and how they can be used.

Page Events

The first kind of ASP.NET events we will look at are *page events*. These events are invoked as the ASP.NET server processes a request for page. You can register a handler for page events in your code-behind class to respond to the different parts of the life cycle.

The page events are defined within the System.Web.UI.Page class, which is the base class for the .aspx web page code-behind classes that you saw in the previous chapter. Most of the time, we care about only the Load event. By the time that this event is called, the ASP.NET server has processed the details of the request from the web browser and initialized the HTML controls to represent the elements in the web page, so it's ready to start the process of rendering the response.

That said, the other page events can be useful to perform specific actions either before or after the ASP.NET server has reached the sweet spot that is the Load event. Here, we'll look at some potentially useful page events. (Some events are best used for features that we will discuss in later chapters, and I'll point you toward those chapters in the upcoming discussions of the events.)

Let's start by creating another Visual Studio project and adding a web page, as follows:

1. Select File ➤ New ➤ Project.

2. Click the Visual C# templates in the Installed Templates section, select the Web category, and then click the ASP.NET Empty Web Application template.

3. Set the name of the project to ContextAndEvents, as shown in Figure 5-1.

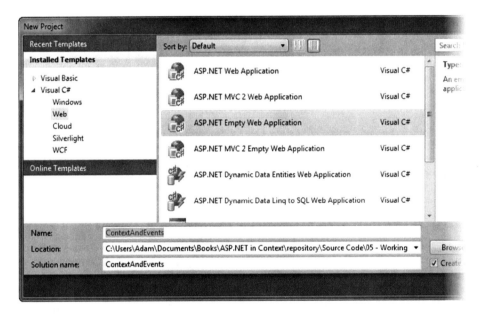

Figure 5-1. *Creating the ContextAndEvents project in Visual Studio*

4. Select Project ➤ Add New Item.

5. Select the Web Form template.

6. Give the new file the name Default.aspx.

7. Edit the file so that its contents match Listing 5-1.

Listing 5-1. *Adding a web page to the project*

```
<%@ Page Language="C#" AutoEventWireup="true"
CodeBehind="Default.aspx.cs" Inherits="ContextAndEvents.Default" %>

<!DOCTYPE html PUBLIC "-//W3C//DTD XHTML 1.0 Transitional//EN"
  "http://www.w3.org/TR/xhtml1/DTD/xhtml1-transitional.dtd">

<html xmlns="http://www.w3.org/1999/xhtml">
<head runat="server">
    <title></title>
</head>
<body>
    <h3 id="placeHolderH3" runat="server">This is a place holder</h3>
</body>
</html>
```

This is a very simple page. The body contains an H3 element with the id of placeHolderH2 and a runat value of server, so that we can refer to and work with the element in the code-behind file.

Understanding the Page Event Sequence

There are a lot of events in the Page class, but most of them are of interest only when you are developing controls, such as the HTML controls you saw in the previous chapter. Some events that are helpful to the ASP.NET application developer are described in Table 5-1 in the order in which they occur in the page life cycle.

Table 5-1. *Useful Page Events*

Event Name	Description
PreInit Init InitComplete	These three events are invoked as the ASP.NET server processes the request from the client browser and populates the context for the request.
Load	This is the most important event for ASP.NET web application developers. The code to configure the page controls is typically placed in a handler for this event.
PreRender	This event is called before the page is rendered, and it can be used to make any final changes to the response.
Unload	This event is called after the response has been sent back the browser. It is often used to release resources such as database connections.

The Initialization Events

The PreInit, Init and InitComplete methods are invoked early in the page-processing life cycle—too early to be helpful to most developers. That said, there are a couple of useful actions you can perform.

The `PreInit` method can be used to specify a master page programmatically, rather than in a `Page` directive. ASP.NET master pages provide consistent visual styling across the pages of a web application, as discussed in Chapter 9.

The `Init` event is a good place to create resources that you will need for your page, such as database connections. The counterpart to this event is `Unload`, which is described a little later in the chapter. ASP.NET doesn't restore view state data until just before the `InitComplete` method is invoked. View state is a persistence feature, as described in Chapter 6. If you need to read or modify view state data, you must wait until at least this method in the event sequence.

The Load Event

The `Page.Load` event is the most important of the page events. It is where we work with the HTML controls to populate the content of the web page. Many programmers use only this event when they create ASP.NET web applications. We employed this method when we worked with code-behind classes in Chapter 4, and you'll see it throughout the rest of the book, because it occurs in almost every example.

Listing 5-2 contains a very simple demonstration of responding to the `Load` event in a code-behind class.

Listing 5-2. *Responding to the Load page event*

```
using System;

namespace ContextAndEvents {

    public partial class Default : System.Web.UI.Page {

        protected void Page_Load(object sender, EventArgs e) {
            placeHolderH3.InnerText = "This message was changed in the Page_Load method";
        }
    }
}
```

This example uses the `InnerText` property of the `HtmlGenericControl` object that ASP.NET has created to represent the `H3` element in the web page. These same techniques were used in the previous chapter. The result of viewing the `Default.aspx` web page with this code-behind class is shown in Figure 5-2.

Figure 5-2. *The effect of responding to the Load event*

Putting your code statements in the `Page_Load` method, which is called when the `Load` event is invoked, is the right thing to do 99 times out of a 100.

The PreRender Event

The PreRender event is invoked just before ASP.NET renders the HTML for the page. To render the page, the server combines the output from the code blocks or code-behind class with the static HTML elements to produce a result that the browser can consume and display. The dynamically generated class in the previous chapter (Listing 4-6) demonstrates how to do this in detail.

The most common action performed in response to the PreRender method is to make last-minute changes that rely on the final state of all of the controls on the page. Usually, you don't need to do this, and you can rely on the Load event, but situations do arise when you want to derive part of the display from one or more controls. Listing 5-3 extends the code-behind class for the Default.aspx web page to respond to the PreRender event.

Listing 5-3. *Responding to the PreRender event*

```
using System;

namespace ContextAndEvents {

    public partial class Default : System.Web.UI.Page {

        protected void Page_Load(object sender, EventArgs e) {
            placeHolderH3.InnerText = "This message was changed in the Page_Load method";
        }

        protected void Page_PreRender(object sender, EventArgs e) {
            placeHolderH3.InnerText
                = "This message was changed in the Page_PreRender method";
            Response.Write("<h4>This message comes from the Page_PreRender method</h4>");
        }
    }
}
```

The Page_PreRender method is automatically registered as a handler for the Page.PreRender event by the auto event wire-up system. In this method, we have changed the value of the InnerText property of the H3 element in the web page and called the Response.Write method. You saw the Response.Write method when we used code blocks in Chapter 4, and it forms part of the ASP.NET context features that we will explore in the "Working with Context" section later in this chapter. Figure 5-3 shows the Default.aspx page when viewed after the additions shown in Listing 5-3 are applied to the code-behind class.

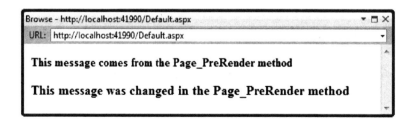

Figure 5-3. *The effect of responding to the PreRender event*

You can see that the change made to the H3 element in the Page_PreRender method overrides the change made in the Page_Load method. This is because the PreRender event is called after the Load event. The text written using Response.Write appears before the H3 text because the contents of the controls are not written to the response until after the PreRender event has been invoked. So, our call to Response.Write has put our text ahead of the contents of the controls. This behavior is something to be aware of if you use this method.

Listing 5-4 shows the HTML that is sent to the browser. You can see that the text we wrote using Response.Write appears outside the HTML element.

Listing 5-4. *The HTML source for the Default.aspx page*

```
<h4>This message comes from the Page_PreRender method</h4>

<!DOCTYPE html PUBLIC "-//W3C//DTD XHTML 1.0 Transitional//EN"↵
  "http://www.w3.org/TR/xhtml1/DTD/xhtml1-transitional.dtd">

<html xmlns="http://www.w3.org/1999/xhtml">
<head><title>

</title></head>
<body>

    <h3 id="placeHolderH3">This message was changed in the Page_PreRender method</h3>

</body>
</html>
```

Most browsers will display text that appears outside a valid HTML element, but you shouldn't rely on this always being the case. If you want to insert content into the page, you should do so using an HTML control.

The Unload Event

The Unload event is invoked when the page has been rendered. This event offers an opportunity to release any external resources that your page might still be holding on to, such as database connections, open files, and so on.

We explore the use of data in ASP.NET web applications in Chapter 8, but we do so using the Entity Framework, which helpfully manages the connections to the database on our behalf.

Application Events

Application events are those that represent change of note for the entire web application. This is in contrast to page events, which are specific to a particular page request.

Application events are handled using a *global application class*. To create such a class, follow these steps:

1. In Visual Studio, select Project ➤ Add New Item.

2. Select the Global Application Class template from the Add New Item dialog, as shown in Figure 5-4.

Figure 5-4. *Adding a global application class*

3. Application event handlers are represented in ASP.NET by files that have the suffix `.asax`. The convention is to use the name `Global.asax`, and you can see that Visual Studio suggests this name when you select the Global Application Class template. Click the Add button to create the new item.

You will see that two items have been added to the project in the Solution Explorer: `Global.asax` and its code-behind file, `Global.asax.cs`. As you can see in Listing 5-5, there isn't much content to `Global.asax` by default.

Listing 5-5. *The Global.asax file*

```
<%@ Application Codebehind="Global.asax.cs" Inherits="ContextAndEvents.Global"
Language="C#" %>
```

The `Global.asax` file contains an `Application` directive, which is like the `Page` directive you saw in the previous chapter, but is used exclusively by `.asax` files. It tells the ASP.NET system to treat the specified code-behind class as a handler for application events. The code-behind class is created with handlers for some of the available events, as shown in Listing 5-6.

Listing 5-6. *The Global.asax.cs file*

```
using System;
using System.Collections.Generic;
using System.Linq;
using System.Web;
using System.Web.Security;
using System.Web.SessionState;
```

```
namespace ContextAndEvents {

    public class Global : System.Web.HttpApplication {

        protected void Application_Start(object sender, EventArgs e) {

        }

        protected void Application_End(object sender, EventArgs e) {

        }

        protected void Session_Start(object sender, EventArgs e) {

        }

        protected void Session_End(object sender, EventArgs e) {

        }

        protected void Application_AuthenticateRequest(object sender, EventArgs e) {

        }

        protected void Application_Error(object sender, EventArgs e) {

        }

        protected void Application_BeginRequest(object sender, EventArgs e) {

        }
    }
}
```

Understanding the Application Event Sequence

The sequence for application events is not as simple as for page events. Some of the events are invoked only when your application starts, some each time a request is received, and others somewhere in between.

Applications events are defined as part of the System.Web.HttpApplication class, which is the base class used for the Global.asax code-behind class. Automatic event wiring ensures that methods are associated with an event, so that the Application_Start and Application_End methods are registered as handlers for the Start and End events. respectively. The most useful application events are described in Table 5-2.

Table 5-2. *Useful Application Events*

Event Name	Description
Start End	The Start event is invoked when the web application starts. The End event is invoked just before the application is destroyed.
Session.Start Session.End	These events are called when a new session is started or an existing session finishes. See Chapter 6 for details on the ASP.NET session feature.
AuthenticateRequest	This event is invoked when ASP.NET has established the identity of a user. See Chapter 34 for details on ASP.NET authentication.
Error	This event is invoked when a page encounters an error that cannot be handled elsewhere. See Chapter 7 for details on ASP.NET error handling.
BeginRequest EndRequest	The BeginRequest event is invoked as one of the first actions when the ASP.NET server receives a request from a client. The EndRequest is invoked as one of the last actions when the ASP.NET server has processed a request.

The Start and End Events

The Start event is invoked when ASP.NET creates the application to service your requests. This involves setting up the application and session state features (which we explore in Chapter 6), and generally getting ready to process the first client request.

The End event is invoked when ASP.NET is shutting down your application and releasing the resources it holds. This could be because you have restarted the server, deployed an update of your application, or the ASP.NET server has not received requests for your pages for some time.

The Start event is a good place to create resources that will be used throughout your application, and the End event is a good place to ensure that they are released. You must not assume that your application will be started and then run forever, which means taking care to balance the actions in the Start and End events to free up things like data connections and streams to files.

The Session Events

The ASP.NET session feature provides support for associating page requests (using cookies or URL rewriting) to form a session for a user. The Session.Start and Session.End events are invoked when sessions are created and destroyed. We'll discuss the session feature in detail in Chapter 6.

The Authentication and Error Events

The AuthenticateRequest event is invoked when ASP.NET has established the identity of the user who has made a request. We will investigate the ASP.NET authentication features in Chapter 34.

The Error event is invoked when there is an exception processing a page request and that exception cannot be handled by the page itself. ASP.NET has a very rich approach to dealing with errors, which is the topic of Chapter 7.

The Application Request Events

The BeginRequest and EndRequest events are invoked when the ASP.NET server starts to process and finishes processing a request for a page in a web application, respectively. Listing 5-7 shows a Global.asax code-behind class that has handlers for these events.

Listing 5-7. Handling the BeginRequest and EndRequest events

```
using System;

namespace ContextAndEvents {
    public class Global : System.Web.HttpApplication {

        protected void Application_BeginRequest(object sender, EventArgs e) {
            Response.Write(
                string.Format("<p>Request processing started at: {0}<p>",
                    GetTimeString()));
        }

        protected void Application_EndRequest(object sender, EventArgs e) {
            Response.Write(
                string.Format("<p>Request processing finished at: {0}<p>",
                    GetTimeString()));
        }

        private string GetTimeString() {
            return DateTime.Now.ToString("hh:mm:ss:ff");
        }
    }
}
```

The event handler methods in Listing 5-7 use the Response.Write method to insert strings into the response sent to the browser. You can see the effect of these statements in Figure 5-5.

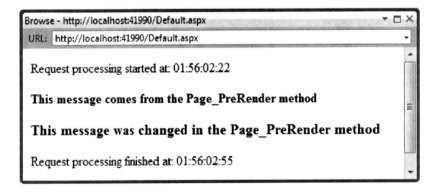

Figure 5-5. Handling the application request events

The event handler methods in Listing 5-7 insert messages into the HTML response to indicate the times that the processing of the page starts and finishes. These messages appear outside the HTML element in the response.

■ **Tip**   While Listing 5-7 demonstrates the way in which the `BeginRequest` and `EndRequest` events are invoked, adding messages to the HTML content isn't a great way to measure the page-processing performance of ASP.NET. Instead, use the tracing features described in Chapter 7.

Working with Context

The complement to the application and page events is the *context,* which is provided by ASP.NET. The available contexts allow you to do the following:

- Get information about the request received from the client.

- Configure aspects of the response that will be returned.

- Issue instructions to the ASP.NET server as the request is processed.

The ASP.NET contexts are request, response, and server. Let's see how they can be put to use.

The Request Context

You can get details of the request made by the client through the **Page.Request** property, which returns an instance of the **System.Web.HttpRequest** class. To demonstrate this class, let's make some changes to the **Default.aspx** web page in the example project, as shown in Listing 5-8.

Listing 5-8. The revised Default.aspx web page

```
<%@ Page Language="C#" AutoEventWireup="true" CodeBehind="Default.aspx.cs"
Inherits="ContextAndEvents.Default" %>

<!DOCTYPE html PUBLIC "-//W3C//DTD XHTML 1.0 Transitional//EN"
"http://www.w3.org/TR/xhtml1/DTD/xhtml1-transitional.dtd">

<html xmlns="http://www.w3.org/1999/xhtml">
<head runat="server">
    <title></title>
</head>
<body>

    <div id="contextDiv" runat="server"/>

</body>
</html>
```

This page contains a `div` element, which has `ID` and `runat` attributes so that we can refer to it using the ASP.NET HTML control feature described in Chapter 4. The `HttpRequest` class defines a range of properties that give information about the request, two of which are read by the code-behind class shown in Listing 5-9.

Listing 5-9. *A code-behind class that reads HttpRequest properties*

```
using System;

namespace ContextAndEvents {

    public partial class Default : System.Web.UI.Page {

        protected void Page_Load(object sender, EventArgs e) {

            WriteContextValue("Path", Request.Path);
            WriteContextValue("HttpMethod", Request.HttpMethod);
        }

        private void WriteContextValue(string nameParam, string valParam) {
            contextDiv.InnerHtml += string.Format("<b>{0}:</b> {1}</p>",
                nameParam, valParam);
        }

    }
}
```

You can obtain the `HttpRequest` object simply by calling `Request`. This is because the `Page` class is the base for code-behind classes, meaning that the `Request` property is inherited. Listing 5-9 reads two properties from the `HttpRequest` object and inserts HTML into the page to list their properties. You can see the effect of this in Figure 5-6. (I have removed the code we added to `Global.asax` earlier, to simplify the output.)

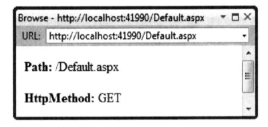

Figure 5-6. *Reading properties from the HttpRequest object*

HttpRequest Properties

Table 5-3 describes some of the more widely used properties of the `HttpRequest` class. Bear in mind that these properties give details of the request made by the client. You use the response context to set values that will be returned as a result of the page being processed, as you'll see later in this chapter.

Table 5-3. *Useful HttpRequest Properties*

Name	Description
AcceptTypes	Returns a `string[]` containing the MIME types that the browser can accept
Browser	Returns information about the capabilities of the client browser (used in the next example)
Cookies	Returns the set of cookies that the browser has included in the request
Form	Used to access form variables when the browser submits a form to the ASP.NET server (ASP.NET has a more sophisticated way of dealing with forms, as described in Chapter 6)
Headers	Returns a collection of the request headers
HttpMethod	Returns the HTTP method of the request, such as `GET`, `POST`, and so on
IsAuthenticated	Returns `true` if the request has been authenticated by the ASP.NET server (see Chapter 34 for details of authentication)
IsLocal	Returns `true` if the request has originated on the local machine—that is, the browser and ASP.NET server are running on the same computer
Params	Returns a combined collection of key/value pairs from the request query string, form variables, and cookies
Path	Returns the path of the requested web page
QueryString	Returns the query string part of the requested URL as a collection of key/value pairs
Url	Returns the URL that the browser has requested, including the hostname and port
UserAgent	Returns the user-agent string that the browser identifies itself with

Varying Content Based on the Browser

For most web applications, there is little need to get too deeply involved in the details of the request, but there are times when this information can be invaluable. For example, Internet Explorer doesn't fully implement a particular Cascading Style Sheets (CSS) feature, as we will discuss in Chapter 10. We might choose to deal with this omission by varying the content of our response based on the type of browser that has been used to make the request. Listing 5-10 demonstrates how we can do this using the Browser property, which provides information about the client browser.

Listing 5-10. *Varying content based on the client browser*

```
using System;

namespace ContextAndEvents {

    public partial class Default : System.Web.UI.Page {

        protected void Page_Load(object sender, EventArgs e) {

            switch (Request.Browser.Browser) {
                case "Chrome":
                    contextDiv.InnerText = "Request made using Google Chrome";
                    break;
                case "IE":
                    contextDiv.InnerText = "Request made using Internet Explorer";
                    break;
                default:
                    contextDiv.InnerText
                        = string.Format("Request made using other browser: {0}",
                            Request.Browser.Browser);
                    break;
            }
        }
    }
}
```

The `Browser` property returns a `System.Web.HttpBrowserCapabilities` object, and we can get the name of the browser family by reading the oddly named `Browser.Browser` property. This returns a name such as `Chrome` or `IE`, without additional version or platform information. You can see the effect of requesting the `Default.aspx` page with the code-behind class in Listing 5-10 in Figure 5-7. If the browser family name isn't detailed enough for your needs, you can get the browser version by reading the `Browser.Version` property.

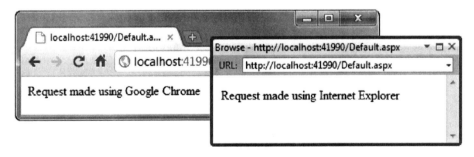

Figure 5-7. *Varying the content of a page based on the browser*

■ **Note** The HttpBrowserCapabilities class contains properties that reveal a lot of very specific information about what a browser is capable of supporting, although some of the information is derived from a database of such capabilities, rather than directly from the client. In your code, you should not assume that the HttpBrowserCapabilities class is able to identify all browsers or their capabilities.

The Response Context

The Page.Response property is the complement of the Request property. It returns a System.Web.HttpResponse object that can be used to configure aspects of the response that will be sent back to the browser.

HttpResponse Properties and Methods

Some of the most commonly used properties of the HttpResponse class are described in Table 5-4. You will note that many of the property names are the same as for the HttpRequest class. The difference is that the request details represent the information that the browser sent, and the response details influence what the browser will receive.

Table 5-4. *Useful HttpResponse Properties*

Name	Description
ContentType	Sets the MIME type of the response to the browser
Cookies	Returns the set of cookies that will be sent to the browser
Headers	Returns the collection of headers that will be sent to the browser
IsClientConnected	Returns true if the browser has maintained a network connection to the ASP.NET server
RedirectLocation	Sets the value of the HTTP Location header
Status	Sets the description of the response status
StatusCode	Sets the HTTP status code

In addition to the properties show in Table 5-4, the HttpResponse class defines a number of convenience methods that set combinations of response properties to achieve a specific result. The most useful of these methods are described in Table 5-5.

Table 5-5. *Useful HttpResponse Methods*

Name	Description
AppendCookie(HttpCookie)	Adds a new cookie to the response. The cookie is represented by a System.Web.HttpCookie object.
AppendHeader(string, string)	Adds a new header to the response. The first string parameter is the name of the value, and the second is the value.
Clear()	Removes all of the headers and content from the response.
ClearContent()	Removes all of the content from the response, but leaves the headers intact.
ClearHeaders()	Removes all of the headers from the response, but leaves the content intact.
End()	Sends the headers and content to the browser and stops further execution of the page.
Redirect(string) Redirect(string, bool)	Redirects the client to a new URL. If the bool argument is true, the execution of the current page is terminated.
Write(string)	Writes the contents of the string parameter to the response.

As you saw in Chapter 4, the Write method is commonly used in code blocks. The other methods are not used anywhere near as much, with the exception of the Redirect method, which is described next.

Redirecting the Client

The Redirect method can be useful, especially when combined with the request content. For example, we might choose to redirect users to a different page based on the type of browser they use, as Listing 5-11 shows.

Listing 5-11. *Redirecting to another page based on browser type*

```
using System;

namespace ContextAndEvents {

    public partial class Default : System.Web.UI.Page {

        protected void Page_Load(object sender, EventArgs e) {
```

```
            switch (Request.Browser.Browser) {
                case "Chrome":
                    Response.Redirect("ChromePage.aspx", true);
                    break;
                case "IE":
                    Response.Redirect("IEPage.aspx", true);
                    break;
                default:
                    Response.Redirect("UnsupportedPage.aspx", true);
                    break;
            }
        }
    }
}
```

Viewing the Default.aspx page will cause the browser to be redirected to one of three pages: ChromePage.aspx, IEPage.aspx, or UnsupportedPage.aspx. You can see the effect of the redirections in Figure 5-8.

Figure 5-8. *Redirecting to pages based on browser type*

The Server Context

The server context isn't really a context at all. It is a collection of useful methods that can be helpful in processing requests. It is known as the *server context* because some of the methods depend on the other context objects.

HttpServerUtility Methods

You access the server context through the Page.Server property, which returns a System.Web.HttpServerUtility object. The most useful methods available in the HttpServerUtility class are described in Table 5-6.

Table 5-6. Useful HttpServerUtility Methods

Name	Description
ClearError()	Marks the last error encountered processing the current page as being handled (see Chapter 7 for details of ASP.NET error handling).
GetLastError()	Retrieves the last error encountered processing the current page.
HtmlEncode(string) HtmlDecode(string)	Encodes and decodes a **string** to remove or restore illegal HTML characters.
Transfer(string) Transfer(string, bool)	Ends the execution of the current page and starts execution of the page specified by the **string** parameter. If the **bool** parameter is true, the query string and form data will be removed.
UrlEncode(string) UrlDecode(string)	Encodes and decodes a **string** to remove or restore characters that are illegal in a URL.

The **ClearError** and **GetLastError** methods are the most important ones in the **HttpServerUtility** class. They are essential in implementing an error-handling policy in an ASP.NET application. You can find full details of ASP.NET error handling and the use of these two methods in Chapter 7.

Transferring a Request

The **Transfer** method can be used to transfer execution from one page to another. This is not the same as redirecting the browser to another page.

When you *redirect*, a message is sent to the browser asking it to request the other page. The browser may choose not to follow the redirection instruction, but if it does, there will have been two requests from the browser: one for the original page and one for the page to which the browser has been redirected. In essence, the browser is aware of the redirection. In Figure 5-8, a request for **Default.aspx** has resulted in a redirect to **IEPage.aspx**, and you can see this second URL in the browser display.

When you *transfer* control, the process takes place entirely within the ASP.NET server, and the browser is not aware that the page that is rendered to create the response is not the same as the page that was requested. Listing 5-12 provides a demonstration of using the **Transfer** method.

Listing 5-12. Using the Server.Transfer method

```
using System;

namespace ContextAndEvents {

    public partial class Default : System.Web.UI.Page {

        protected void Page_Load(object sender, EventArgs e) {
```

```
        switch (Request.Browser.Browser) {
            case "Chrome":
                Response.Redirect("ChromePage.aspx", true);
                break;
            case "IE":
                Server.Transfer("IEPage.aspx", true);
                break;
            default:
                Response.Redirect("UnsupportedPage.aspx", true);
                break;
        }
    }
  }
}
```

This is very similar to the redirect example (Listing 5-11), except that the calls to Response.Redirect are replaced with calls to **Server.Transfer**. You can see the effect of this change in Figure 5-9.

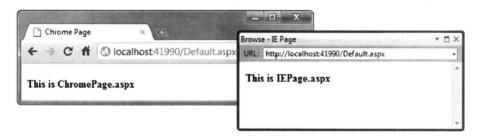

Figure 5-9. *Using the Server.Transfer method*

If you look closely at Figure 5-9, you will see that both browser windows are displaying the URL for the Default.aspx page, but the content is from ChromePage.aspx or IEPage.aspx. The transition from one page to the other happens without the browser's knowledge.

Passing Information Between Pages

If you are redirecting or transferring a request to another page, it can be useful to pass some information from the first to second pages. You don't need to worry about setting the various context objects, because ASP.NET will take care of that automatically, but it can be helpful to provide guidance to the second page as to what you want it to do.

As a simple example, suppose we want to select between two messages that the second page can display. There are several ways to do this. One is to use the session state feature that is described in Chapter 6. Another is to add the information to the query string part of the URL, so that the URL we redirect or transfer to looks like this:

SecondPage.aspx?messageToDisplay=first

This URL contains a key messageToDisplay with a value of first. This can be read by the page that we transfer to and used to determine its behavior. Listing 5-13 contains a page, called SecondPage.aspx, which will be used to display one of two messages.

Listing 5-13. *The SecondPage.aspx markup*

```
<%@ Page Language="C#" AutoEventWireup="true" CodeBehind="SecondPage.aspx.cs"
Inherits="ContextAndEvents.SecondPage" %>

<!DOCTYPE html PUBLIC "-//W3C//DTD XHTML 1.0 Transitional//EN"
"http://www.w3.org/TR/xhtml1/DTD/xhtml1-transitional.dtd">

<html xmlns="http://www.w3.org/1999/xhtml">
<head runat="server">
    <title>Second Page</title>
</head>
<body>
    <h4 id="placeholderH4" runat="server"/>
</body>
</html>
```

Listing 5-14 shows the code-behind class for the `SecondPage.aspx` web page. This class retrieves the value of the `messageToDisplay` key using the `QueryString` property of the request context object.

Listing 5-14. *The Second.aspx.cs code-behind class*

```
using System;

namespace ContextAndEvents {

    public partial class SecondPage : System.Web.UI.Page {

        protected void Page_Load(object sender, EventArgs e) {

            // get the instruction as to which message to display
            // from the query string
            string messageToDisplay = Request.QueryString["messageToDisplay"];
            if (messageToDisplay != null) {
                if (messageToDisplay == "first") {
                    placeholderH4.InnerText = "This is the first message";
                } else {
                    placeholderH4.InnerText = "This is the second message";
                }
            } else {
                // there was no message instruction
                placeholderH4.InnerText = "No message instruction specified";
            }
        }
    }
}
```

The last piece of this example is shown in Listing 5-15. This is the code-behind class of the `Default.aspx` web page. The markup for this page doesn't matter, because it transfers to `SecondPage.aspx`.

Listing 5-15. The Default.aspx.cs code-behind class

```
using System;

namespace ContextAndEvents {

    public partial class Default : System.Web.UI.Page {

        protected void Page_Load(object sender, EventArgs e) {

            switch (Request.Browser.Browser) {
                case "Chrome":
                    Server.Transfer("SecondPage.aspx?messageToDisplay=first", true);
                    break;
                case "IE":
                    Server.Transfer("SecondPage.aspx?messageToDisplay=second", true);
                    break;
                default:
                    Server.Transfer("SecondPage.aspx", true);
                    break;
            }
        }
    }
}
```

You can see how we encode the instruction about which message to display into the URL that we transfer to, and the same approach can be taken when redirecting. If you view **Default.aspx** using Google Chrome, you will see the first message. If you are using Internet Explorer, you will see the second message. You can see the result from both browsers in Figure 5-10.

Figure 5-10. Passing information during a page transfer

Passing Context Using the HttpContext Class

The final context feature we will look at is the **HttpContext** class. This class has two main features:

- It allows you to access all of the other context objects from anywhere in your code.

- It provides an alternative means of passing information between pages.

Now let's see how these features can prove useful to ASP.NET developers.

Accessing Context from Outside the Page Class

Having access to the various context objects through properties of the Page class is perfect when you are deriving from that class and annoying when you are not. If you want to access context information from another class, you have two choices:

- Take care to pass the required information as parameters through each subsequent method call.

- Access the static Current property of the HttpContext class and access all of the context objects that relate to the current page's request through the HttpContext object that is returned.

Listing 5-16 provides a demonstration of accessing context information from outside the Page class.

Listing 5-16. Accessing context information from outside the Page class

```
using System;
using System.Web;

namespace ContextAndEvents {

    public partial class Default : System.Web.UI.Page {

        protected void Page_Load(object sender, EventArgs e) {

            // create an instance of the other class
            MyOtherClass myObject = new MyOtherClass();

            // call a method that relies on context
            myObject.TransferBasedOnBrowser();
        }
    }

    class MyOtherClass {

        public void TransferBasedOnBrowser() {
            // get the HttpContext object
            HttpContext myContext = HttpContext.Current;

            // switch on the browser type
            switch (myContext.Request.Browser.Browser) {
                case "Chrome":
                    myContext.Server
                        .Transfer("SecondPage.aspx?messageToDisplay=first", true);
                    break;
                case "IE":
                    myContext.Server
                        .Transfer("SecondPage.aspx?messageToDisplay=second", true);
                    break;
```

```
            default:
                myContext.Server
                    .Transfer("SecondPage.aspx", true);
                break;
        }
    }
}
}
```

The code-behind class in Listing 5-16 creates an instance of `MyOtherClass` and calls the `TransferBasedOnBrowser` method. This method relies on the request and server context objects. To get these, we call the static `HttpContext.Current` property and read the `Request` and `Server` properties. These return the `HttpRequest` and `HttpServerUtility` classes that relate to the current page request. We can then detect the browser type and perform transfers without needing to pass the context objects and method parameters.

The `HttpContext` class contains properties for each of the context objects, and each has the same name as the equivalent property in the `Page` class. So, you can access the `HttpRequest` object via the `Request` property, the `HttpResponse` object via the `Response` property, and so on.

You must not store and reuse the `HttpContext` objects. A new one is created for each page request, and trying to use an old one will cause an exception.

Passing Information Using the Items Collection

An additional feature of the `HttpContext` class is the `Items` property, which can be used to pass name/value pairs around during the processing of a page. The most common use for this is as an alternative means of passing instructional information to a page during a transfer or redirection. Listing 5-17 demonstrates using the `Items` collection in the code-behind class of `Default.aspx`.

Listing 5-17. Using the HttpContext Items feature

```
using System;
using System.Web;

namespace ContextAndEvents {

    public partial class Default : System.Web.UI.Page {

        protected void Page_Load(object sender, EventArgs e) {

            switch (Request.Browser.Browser) {
                case "Chrome":
                    Context.Items.Add("messageToDisplay", 1);
                    break;
                case "IE":
                    Context.Items.Add("messageToDisplay", 2);
                    break;
            }
```

```
            Server.Transfer("SecondPage.aspx");

        }
    }
}
```

Note that when you are working in a class derived from **Page**, you can access the **HttpContext** object using the **Context** property. This is equivalent to calling the static **Current** property.

The **Items** property returns a standard C# collection. You add values by passing the name and value as parameters to the **Add** method. An advantage of this approach is that you can pass data between pages using C# types, rather than being restricted to using **string** values. Listing 5-18 shows the corresponding code-behind class for **SecondPage.aspx**.

Listing 5-18. Reading values from the HttpContext Items collection

```
using System;

namespace ContextAndEvents {

    public partial class SecondPage : System.Web.UI.Page {

        protected void Page_Load(object sender, EventArgs e) {

            // get the instruction as to which message to display
            // from the HttpContext Items collection
            int messageToDisplay = Context.Items.Contains("messageToDisplay")
                ? (int)Context.Items["messageToDisplay"] : 0;

            if (messageToDisplay == 1) {
                    placeholderH4.InnerText = "This is the first message";
            } else if (messageToDisplay == 2) {
                placeholderH4.InnerText = "This is the second message";
            } else {
                // there was no message instruction
                placeholderH4.InnerText = "No message instruction specified";
            }
        }
    }
}
```

We access the data within the **Items** collection by using an indexer, passing in the name we specified in the other class as the index value. The collection class returns the stored values as **object** instances, so we need to cast them to the desired type; in this case, we cast to an **int** value.

Summary

In this chapter, you have seen two of the features that help form a foundation for ASP.NET. The event model allows you to hook into the ASP.NET page-rendering process at different states in the life cycle, and the various context objects let you gain information about what the browser has asked for and configure the response that will be sent back in return.

This chapter contained a number of references to other chapters. This is an indication of just how deep-rooted the event and context features are in ASP.NET. We have touched on everything from error handling, to forms processing, to authentication and session management. You'll find full details of each of these features in the chapters that follow, and you'll see how ASP.NET builds up a rich and complex set of features that simplify building web applications.

Working with Forms and State

Two key features in a web application are user input and state. We need user input to create useful applications. The user selects some function or enters some data, and our application responds accordingly. In a traditional deployed application, this interaction model is intrinsic to the software. In a web application, we rely on HTML forms.

We rely on state in order to store data on behalf of the user and access it in response to web requests. Web application state can be complex, because the underlying technology is broadly stateless. Fortunately, ASP.NET provides a range of different state mechanisms, and you just need to pick the one that best suits your application's needs. In this chapter, we will look at the features of the four most important and widely used states: form, view, session, and application.

To explore these features, we will walk through producing a simple calculator that solves one of my triathlon training issues. I'm a number-oriented guy. and I record all of my training sessions. When I run and cycle, I use a training computer wristwatch with various sensors that give me a lot of detailed information, including distance, pace, heart rate, and so on. All of this data is uploaded into my training diary.

The sensors communicate with the watch wirelessly, but at a frequency that doesn't pass very far through water. When I train in the swimming pool, I need to manually record the number of laps I swam and how long it took to swim them. From this, I can estimate the calories I have burned and the distance I swam. Along the way, I need to convert the distance from meters (which is how pool lengths are expressed where I live) to miles (which is how I record my other training). The examples in this chapter are based on a simple conversion calculator that uses my time and distance in meters to calculate the distance in miles, the calories I have burned (an estimate), and the pace at which I swam.

Working with Forms

In this section, we'll build a web application that is based on a form. HTML forms (which rely on the HTML `<form>` element) are the foundation for web applications. As with our previous examples, we'll start with the HTML and then add the C# code as a code-behind file. As we create this project, you'll learn how you can build on the HTML control model that you saw in Chapter 4 to define an HTML form and process the form when it is submitted to the ASP.NET server.

Creating a Form

As with the previous chapters, we need to create an ASP.NET project before we can begin to explore the features that are the focus of this chapter. To create the project, follow these steps:

1. In Visual Studio, select File ➤ New ➤ Project.

2. Click the Visual C# templates in the Installed Templates section, select the Web category, and then click the ASP.NET Empty Web Application template, as shown in Figure 6-1.

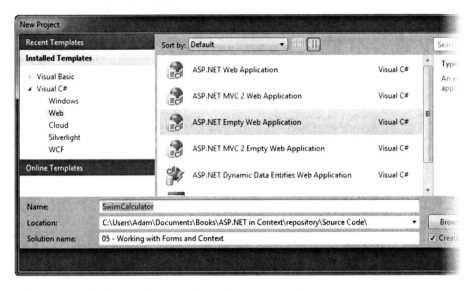

Figure 6-1. Selecting the Empty Web Application template

3. Enter `SwimCalculator` as the name for the new project, and then click OK to create the project.

4. We want to add a dynamic web page, so select Select Project ➤ Add New Item and choose the Web Form item from the list of templates, as shown in Figure 6-2.

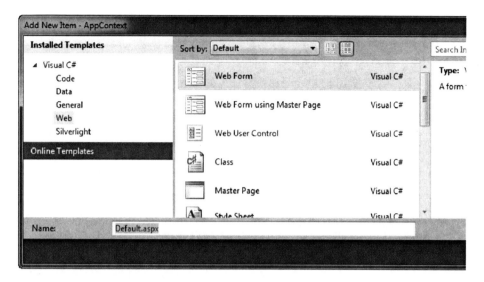

Figure 6-2. Adding a dynamic web page

5. Set the name of the new page to be **Default.aspx**, and then click OK to create the new file.

Don't be confused by the name of the template. Visual Studio assumes that you want to use the dynamic web page with the Web Forms framework, and the basic building block for this is a Web Form, which we'll discuss in Chapter 6 If you expand the **Default.aspx** item in the Solution Explorer window, you'll see two items: **Default.aspx.cs** and **Default.aspx.designer.cs**, as shown in Figure 6-3. The first is the code-behind file, and the second is the corresponding partial class that will contain the fields representing the HTML controls. These are added to the project when you create a web page using the Web Form template, so that Visual Studio doesn't report errors in the code-behind file.

Figure 6-3. The code files associated with a dynamic web page

The first is the code-behind file and the second is the corresponding partial class that will contain the fields representing the HTML controls (these are added to the project when you create a web page using the Web Forms template so that Visual Studio doesn't report errors in the code-behind file).

If you have used almost any web application, you'll be familiar with the HTML **form** element, which is how users can provide input to your application. Open the web file (**Default.aspx**), and you'll see that the template we used to create the project gives us a **form** element, as shown in Listing 6-1.

Listing 6-1. A web page containing a form

```
<%@ Page Language="C#" AutoEventWireup="true" CodeBehind="Default.aspx.cs"↵
 Inherits="SwimCalculator.Default" %>

<!DOCTYPE html PUBLIC "-//W3C//DTD XHTML 1.0 Transitional//EN"↵
 "http://www.w3.org/TR/xhtml1/DTD/xhtml1-transitional.dtd">

<html xmlns="http://www.w3.org/1999/xhtml">
<head runat="server">
    <title></title>
</head>
<body>
    <form id="form1" runat="server">
    <div>

    </div>
    </form>
</body>
</html>
```

ASP.NET does something interesting with forms—something that is quite cool, but requires the use of at least one piece of context to make sense. ASP.NET uses the same **Page** class to generate *and* process the form. That is to say, the **Default.aspx** web file and its associated **Default.aspx.cs** code-behind file are responsible for generating the HTML page, processing the form when it is submitted, and generating whatever page is required to display the result of processing the form.

Let's work through an example to help put this in context, starting with the **form** element:

```
<form id="form1" runat="server">
...
</form>
```

When the ASP.NET server is processing a web browser's request for a dynamic web page that contains a **form** element with a **runat** attribute with a value of **server**, it sets the **action** attribute to refer back to the current page. This is the attribute that specifies where the **form** will be posted back. In the following sections, we'll build on this feature to demonstrate using context to handle a form.

Completing the Form

To complete the form, we need to add the following:

- Some **input** elements that will allow the user to enter data and submit the form

- Some CSS styles to lay out the display elements

- An element to hold the result of our calculation

Listing 6-2 shows the completed **Default.aspx** file.

Listing 6-2. The completed web form

```
<%@ Page Language="C#" CodeBehind="Default.aspx.cs" Inherits="SwimCalculator.Default" %>

<!DOCTYPE html PUBLIC "-//W3C//DTD XHTML 1.0 Transitional//EN"↵
 "http://www.w3.org/TR/xhtml1/DTD/xhtml1-transitional.dtd">

<html xmlns="http://www.w3.org/1999/xhtml">
<head id="Head1" runat="server">
    <title>Swimming Calculator</title>
    <style type="text/css">
        div.label { margin:5px; height:20px}
        input.textinput { margin:2px;width:75px; height:16px }
    </style>
</head>
<body>
    <form id="form1" runat="server">

    <div style="width:200px;">

        <div style="width:auto; min-width:50%; float:left; text-align:right">
            <div class="label">Laps:</div>
            <div class="label">Pool Length:</div>
            <div class="label">Minutes:</div>
            <div class="label">Calories/Hour:</div>
        </div>

        <div id="inputs" style="width:auto; float:left">
          <div><input class="textinput" id="lapsInput" type="text" runat="server" /></div>
          <div><input class="textinput" id="lengthInput" type="text" runat="server" /></div>
          <div><input class="textinput" id="minsInput" type="text" runat="server" /></div>
          <div><input class="textinput" id="calsInput" type="text" runat="server" /></div>
        </div>

        <div style="text-align:center; clear:both;">
            <input id="button" value="Calculate" type="submit" />
        </div>

        <div id="results" runat="server"/>
```

```
        </div>
        </form>
</body>
</html>
```

We have included some of the CSS styles by defining a **style** within the **head** element, and added others directly by defining **style** attributes to individual elements. This is going to be a very simple application, so we are not going to use master pages.

We have not changed the **form** element. We are going to rely on the ASP.NET server to add attributes to this element when the page is rendered.

There are three groups of content in this file: **input** elements, a submit button, and an element for adding our results.

We first have a set of **input** elements, like this one:

```
<div><input class="textinput" id="lapsInput" type="text" runat="server" /></div>
```

These have a value of **text** for the **type** attribute, which means that they will be displayed as single-line text-input boxes. Notice that we have set the **runat** attribute to **server**, so that we can work with each **input** element by its name, as we did in the previous chapter. These four inputs will be used to capture data from the user. The labels that precede them in Listing 6-2 indicate to the user the purpose of each **input** element:

```
<div class="label">Laps:</div>
```

The submit button provides the user a means of posting the form back to our web application. We add a submit button as follows:

```
<input id="button" value="Calculate" type="submit" />
```

This element creates a button labeled Calculate. When the button is clicked, the user's browser will submit the form back to the ASP.NET server.

The final element of interest is one that we will use as a hook to add the results of the calculation:

```
<div id="results" runat="server"/>
```

This element won't affect the appearance of the web page when it is displayed in the browser, but the **runat** element will let us add content to the element using the code-behind file, which is how we will display the results.

Creating the Calculation Code

A widely used convention is to separate code that is not directly related to rendering a page into individual classes. This approach is part of a larger design philosophy, which is often referred to as ensuring a *separation of concerns,* The basic premise is that classes should focus on one function or feature and overlap as little as possible. This is a key idea in the design of the MVC framework, which we explore in Chapter 22.

Another reason to separate code into distinct classes is to reduce duplication of a function or feature that is shared between multiple pages. This is generally a good thing, because you don't need to maintain and test the same code in many different places.

In accordance with the first part of this convention, we'll create a class that contains the logic for performing our swimming calculation, as follows:

1. I think it's a good idea to keep the application logic classes in a separate namespace from the main web application, so to start, select the project in the Solution Explorer and select Project ➤ New Folder.

2. As with other C# projects, the name of the directory corresponds to the namespace, so change the name of the folder to **Calculations**.

3. Select the new folder in the Solution Explorer and select Project ➤ Add Class.

4. Pick the Class template and set the name to **SwimCalculator.cs**.

5. Open the new class file and edit the contents to match Listing 6-3.

Listing 6-3. *The calculation logic class for the swim calculator*

```
using System;

namespace SwimCalculator.Calculations {

    public struct SwimCalcResult {
        public float Distance;
        public float Calories;
        public float Pace;
    }

    public class SwimCalc {
        private const float metersToMiles = 0.00062137119223733f;
        private const float minsPerHour = 60f;

        public static SwimCalcResult PerformCalculation(int lapsParam, int lengthParam,
            int minsParam, int calsPerHourParam) {

            // validate the parameter values - we need all values to be greater than zero
            foreach (int paramValue in new[] {lapsParam, lengthParam,
                minsParam, calsPerHourParam}) {

                if (paramValue < 1) {
                    // this is not a value we can work with
                    throw new ArgumentOutOfRangeException();
                }
            }

            // create the result
            SwimCalcResult result = new SwimCalcResult();

            result.Distance = (lapsParam * lengthParam) * metersToMiles;
            result.Calories = (minsParam / minsPerHour) * calsPerHourParam;
            result.Pace = (minsParam * minsPerHour) / lapsParam;
```

```
        // return the result
        return result;
    }
  }
}
```

When following the separation of concerns principle, you end up with two kinds of classes: self-contained classes and bridge classes.

The *self-contained* class provides a function or feature in isolation. The class shown in Listing 6-3 is an example of this kind of class. Even though we are building a web application, there is no relationship between the **SwimCalculator** class and ASP.NET.

COMPILING APPLICATION LOGIC CLASSES

ASP.NET doesn't automatically recompile your application logic classes when they are modified. This means that you must be sure to recompile your project in Visual Studio by selecting Build ➤ Build *<ProjectName>* when you have made a change. Alternatively, if you right-click a page file and select View in Browser, Visual Studio will recompile any changed classes before showing the preview.

The **SwimCalc** class contains a static method called **PerformCalculation**, which takes a set of **int** parameters to use as the basis for our calculations. The results from this method are returned using the **SwimCalcResult** structure. There are no references to the page file or the HTML **form** element, even though the parameters for the **PerformCalculation** method correspond to the **input** elements in the **Default.aspx** page file.

The *bridge* class connects one area of concern with another. In the case of our example web application, this bridging role is fulfilled by the code-behind class, which connects the functionality of ASP.NET with the calculation functionality provided by the **SwimCalc** class.

Creating the Code-Behind Class

For this example, we need to rely on a useful piece of context that ASP.NET provides through the **Page.IsPostBack** property. This property returns **false** when the page is first requested, and **true** when the user has clicked the button on the page to submit the form. This is how ASP.NET can rely on a single page file and code-behind file to both generate and process HTML forms. Listing 6-4 shows the code-behind file for the swim calculator example.

Listing 6-4. The code-behind file for the swim calculator

```
using System;
using System.Text;
using SwimCalculator.Calculations;

namespace SwimCalculator {

    public partial class Default : System.Web.UI.Page {

        protected void Page_Load(object sender, EventArgs e) {
```

```csharp
        if (!IsPostBack) {

            // this is the initial request to view the page
            // - we want to use this opportunity to set some default values
            // for the input fields
            lapsInput.Value = "1";
            lengthInput.Value = "20";
            minsInput.Value = "60";
            calsInput.Value = "1070";

        } else {
            // define the int values that will hold the values from the input elements
            int laps, length, mins, cals;

            // try to get the values from the form elements as ints
            if (int.TryParse(lapsInput.Value, out laps)
                && int.TryParse(lengthInput.Value, out length)
                && int.TryParse(minsInput.Value, out mins)
                && int.TryParse(calsInput.Value, out cals)) {

                // all of the input values were successfully converted to int values
                try {

                    // perform the calculation
                    SwimCalcResult calcResult
                        = SwimCalc.PerformCalculation(laps, length, mins, cals);

                    // compose the results
                    StringBuilder stringBuilder = new StringBuilder();
                    stringBuilder.AppendFormat("<p>Distance: {0:F2} miles</p>",
                        calcResult.Distance);
                    stringBuilder.AppendFormat("<p>Calories Burned: {0:F0}</p>",
                        calcResult.Calories);
                    stringBuilder.AppendFormat("<p>Pace : {0:F0} sec/lap</p>",
                        calcResult.Pace);

                    // set the results text
                    results.InnerHtml = stringBuilder.ToString();

                } catch (ArgumentOutOfRangeException) {
                    results.InnerText = "Error: parameter out of range";
                }

            } else {
                // at least one of the input values could not be converted to an int
                results.InnerText = "Error: could not process input values";
            }
        }
    }
  }
 }
}
```

There are two branches to the code in Listing 6-4. The branch is selected based on the value of the **IsPostBack** property of the **Page** class, which is, of course, the base for our code-behind class. When the **IsPostBack** property is **false**, the page is being rendered for initial viewing; that is, the user wants to see the page that contains the **form** element. In this situation, we use the **Value** property of the **HtmlInputText** class to set the initial values for the **input** elements (the **HtmlInputText** class is the HTML control that ASP.NET uses to represent **input** elements with a **type** attribute value of **text**):

```
if (!IsPostBack) {
    lapsInput.Value = "1";
    lengthInput.Value = "20";
    minsInput.Value = "60";
    calsInput.Value = "1070";
...
```

We could have done this using HTML in the page file, but we needed something to demonstrate the two request modes for a page that contains a **form**. When the user clicks the Calculate button on the form, the browser submits the data to the ASP.NET server, which renders our page again, this time with the **IsPostBack** property set to **true**, indicating that the **form** has been used.

In this situation, we use the HTML controls that represent the **input** elements to get the data that the user has input (by reading the **Value** property) and try to parse whatever the user has entered to **int** values. ASP.NET defines HTML controls for **form** elements, as described in Table 6-1.

Table 6-1. *ASP.NET HTML Controls for Forms*

HTML Element	HTML Control Class
`<input type="button">`	HtmlImputButton
`<input type="checkbox">`	HtmlInputCheckBox
`<input type="file">`	HtmlInputFile
`<input type="hidden">`	HtmlInputHidden
`<input type="password">`	HtmlInputPassword
`<input type="radio">`	HtmlInputRadioButton
`<input type="reset">`	HtmlInputReset
`<input type="submit">`	HtmlInputSubmit
`<input type="text">`	HtmlInputText

The **input** elements in the example form are all of the type **text** and are represented using the **HtmlInputText** class in the code-behind class.

If we can parse all four values in the **input** elements, then we move on to perform the calculation and display the results by setting the contents of the **result** element that we left as a hook in the **Default.aspx** file. If we can't parse the user input, or if there is an error when performing the calculation, we use the results hook to display an error to the user.

You can see the way that the code-behind class bridges between ASP.NET and the **SwimCalc** class. The values are extracted from the form data, parsed. and then passed on to the **SwimCalc. PerformCalculation** method. The results from the calculation are then mapped back to ASP.NET so that they can be displayed to the user. This is a very common pattern for code-behind files, and you'll see it repeated in other examples and when we look at web application frameworks later in the book.

Using the Form

All that remains is to view the web page and use the form. Right-click **Default.aspx** in the Solution Explorer and select View in Browser. You'll see a web page like the one shown in Figure 6-4.

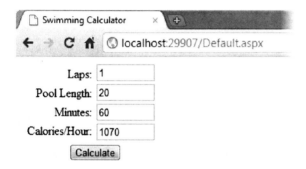

Figure 6-4. *A web page containing a form*

You can see how the **input** elements have been displayed as text boxes and buttons by the browser. If you enter some values in the text boxes and click the Calculate button, you will see the results, as shown in Figure 6-5.

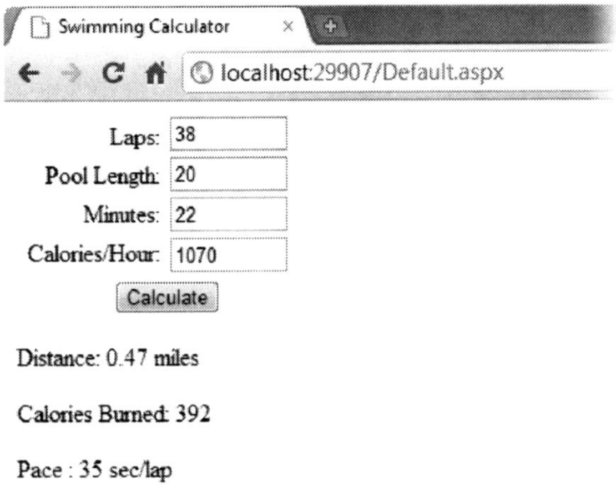

Figure 6-5. *Displaying the results of processing a form*

If you enter values that are not integers or values that are integers but are less than one, you will see an error message, instead of the results.

■ **Note**   You may have noticed something unexpected in the form display. The values that you entered before you clicked the Calculate button are displayed in the page that shows the result, but there are no statements in the code-behind file that set these values. How does this happen? The answer is that ASP.NET automatically sets the contents of the **input** elements based on the values submitted with the form. We'll talk more about this, and how to change the default values, in the "Using Form Input State" section later in this chapter.

Putting Forms in Context

The swimming calculator is a very simple web application, but it demonstrates some important features and behaviors of ASP.NET:

- How the HTML **form** element is automatically completed to refer back to the page that contains it (the **Default.aspx** page file in this case). This example demonstrates one of the main ways that the user can interact with an ASP.NET web application: via the HTML **form** mechanism. There are other approaches (which we'll look at in Chapter 11, when we discuss Ajax), but forms are used very widely.

- How ASP.NET uses context information to tell us that this is happening, through the **Page.IsPostBack** property. This allows us to differentiate between actions we need to perform to set up the page in the first place and actions we need to perform to process a form submission from the user.

- How to generate truly dynamic pages based on data that the user has provided. Our code-behind file connects the features of the ASP.NET page we created with the calculation classes that provide our application logic.

Although this is a simple application, you can see the pattern that emerges when you separate code based on concerns. This is an important pattern that you'll see repeated often in ASP.NET.

Using a form brings us to the point where we are generating truly dynamic content. The page that is generated in response to a form being submitted depends on the data that the user enters into the input fields.

Working with State

Our calculator example is dynamic, but *stateless*, meaning that no information is carried over from one request to the next. This is the default condition for a web application. For simple processing, statelessness isn't a problem. In our example, a user provides some swimming data, and the results of the calculations are returned. There isn't any need to carry data from one request to another, because each request is entirely self-contained.

For more complex applications, you generally need access to data that spans multiple requests. This data is called *state*, and a web application that relies on it is called *stateful*. ASP.NET provides four forms of state:

- *Form input state*: In this state, the input fields show the values that users entered before they clicked the submit button.

- *View state*: This feature allows you to store data in a hidden input field of a **form** element in a web page.

- *Session state*: This is similar to the view state, except that only the session identifier is included in the response sent to the client, and any data you store using the session state is kept on the server.

- *Application state*: This state lets you store data that is available when processing all requests, regardless of session status.

WHY DO WE NEED STATE FEATURES?

You might wonder why we need state features. After all, in regular applications, C# objects are used to maintain and represent state. Why can't we just add fields to our code-behind classes?

The answer is that a new instance of a code-behind class is created to process each and every request and then destroyed afterward. At any moment, there might be several objects created from our code-behind class simultaneously processing requests from different users, or one user, or no users. You just can't tell. And since we can't rely on code-behind objects being kept around, we need to take alternative measures to persist data across the life of multiple page requests.

Using Form Input State

The most basic form of state is one that you have already seen, but it might not have been obvious. If you look back at Figure 6-5, you might notice something odd. The input fields show the values entered before the user clicked the submit button, but the only code we wrote that set these values provided the defaults the first time that the page was requested.

When a form is submitted, the ASP.NET server uses the form data to set the **Value** properties of the HTML control objects before calling the **Page_Load** method. If you don't change the values in the code, these values are included in the result. This behavior is generally desirable. In our swim calculator application, for example, it means that the results and the values that led to them are displayed simultaneously.

But sometimes you will want to have the default values appear instead of the input values. To override the default form input state behavior, you need to set values for the inputs when the form is requested and submitted. Listing 6-5 shows these changes to the swim calculator code-behind file in bold.

Listing 6-5. *Overriding form input state*

```
using System;
using System.Text;
using SwimCalculator.Calculations;

namespace SwimCalculator {

    public partial class Default : System.Web.UI.Page {

        protected void Page_Load(object sender, EventArgs e) {

            if (IsPostBack) {
                // define the int values that will hold the values from the input elements
                int laps, length, mins, cals;
                ...
            }

            // set the values for the input fields
            lapsInput.Value = "1";
            lengthInput.Value = "20";
            minsInput.Value = "60";
            calsInput.Value = "1070";
        }
    }
}
```

The values of the HTML controls are explicitly set to the default values every time that the page is processed, instead of only when the page is initially requested (when value of the **IsPostBack** property is **true**). I have omitted the statements that process the form submission, because these are unchanged from the earlier listing. If you apply these changes, view the web page, and submit the form, you will see that the results page shows the default values, as illustrated by Figure 6-6.

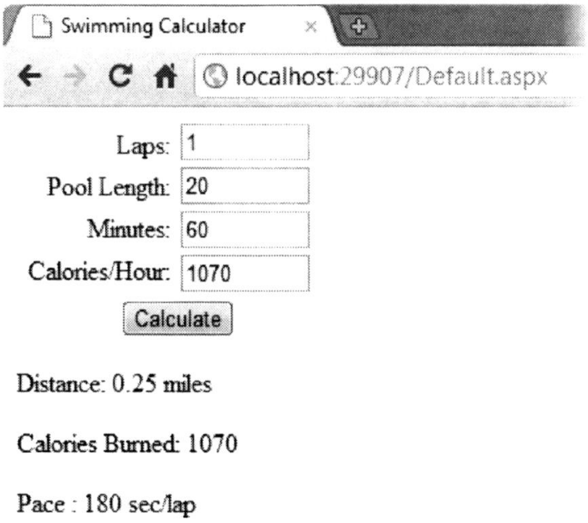

Figure 6-6. *Overriding form input state*

Using View State

Using the view state feature, you can store data in a hidden input field of a **form** element, and then when the **form** is submitted, you can read the data back and use it in whatever way makes sense for your web application. The view state feature can be used only in web pages that contain a **form** element.

View state is used extensively by the Web Forms framework, which is covered in Chapter 13 but can be used more broadly. You will see this in action as we extend our swimming calculator example to use the view state feature.

Setting and Getting View State Data

The view state feature is accessed through the **ViewState** property of the **Page** class, which is inherited by the code-behind class. You set values using a **string** indexer that specifies a key for the data, like this:

```
ViewState["myString"] = "Hello World";
```

This statement assigns **Hello World** to the key **myString** in the view data. To read the data back, you use the same key in the indexer and assign the result to a variable, like this:

```
string myString = (string)ViewState["myString"];
```

The getter of the **ViewState** indexer returns an **object**, which must be cast to the correct data type. This means that in order to retrieve data from the view state, you must know the key and the data type.

You can store any serializable data type. This includes the built-in C# types, arrays, and collection classes. If you want to store custom data types, you must apply the **Serializable** attribute to the type. Here's how the **Serializable** attribute is applied to the **SwimCalcResult** structure:

```
[Serializable]
public struct SwimCalcResult {
    public float Distance;
    public float Calories;
    public float Pace;
}
```

Once the **Serializable** attribute has been applied, we can store the instance of **SwimCalcResult** in the view state, like this:

```
ViewState["lastResults"] = calcResult;
```

We can read back the results as follows:

```
SwimCalcResult oldResults = (SwimCalcResult)ViewState["lastResults"];
```

Listing 6-6 shows the **Default.aspx.cs** code-behind class updated to use view state (the changes are shown in bold).

Listing 6-6. Using view state

```
...
try {

    // perform the calculation
    SwimCalcResult calcResult
        = SwimCalc.PerformCalculation(laps, length, mins, cals);

    // compose the results
    StringBuilder stringBuilder = new StringBuilder();
    stringBuilder.Append("<b>Results</b>");
    stringBuilder.AppendFormat("<p>Distance: {0:F2} miles</p>",
        calcResult.Distance);
    stringBuilder.AppendFormat("<p>Calories Burned: {0:F0}</p>",
        calcResult.Calories);
    stringBuilder.AppendFormat("<p>Pace : {0:F0} sec/lap</p>",
        calcResult.Pace);

    // set the results text
    results.InnerHtml = stringBuilder.ToString();

    // clear the stringbuilder so we can reuse it
    stringBuilder.Clear();
    stringBuilder.Append("<b>Previous results</b>");

    // get the previous results if they are in the view data
    if (ViewState["lastResults"] != null) {
        float[] oldDataArray = (float[])ViewState["lastResults"];
```

```
        // we have some old results to work with
        stringBuilder.AppendFormat("<p>Distance: {0:F2} miles</p>",
            oldDataArray[0]);
        stringBuilder.AppendFormat("<p>Calories Burned: {0:F0}</p>",
            oldDataArray[1]);
        stringBuilder.AppendFormat("<p>Pace : {0:F0} sec/lap</p>",
            oldDataArray[2]);
    } else {
        stringBuilder.Append("<p>No previous results are available</p>");
    }

    // set the view state data
    ViewState["lastResults"] = new float[] { calcResult.Distance,
        calcResult.Calories, calcResult.Pace };

    oldresults.InnerHtml = stringBuilder.ToString();

} catch (ArgumentOutOfRangeException) {
    results.InnerText = "Error: parameter out of range";
}
...
```

Notice that we store the view data using an array of **float** values. This is because we are going to decode the view state data in the next section, and that's easier when using built-in C# types. In a real project, applying the **Serializable** attribute to your custom types is a more convenient technique.

After setting the contents of the **results** control, we check to see if there is any view data available using the key **lastResults**. If there is, we retrieve the data as follows:

```
float[] oldDataArray = (float[])ViewState["lastResults"];
```

We use the data to build the contents of the **StringBuilder**, which we first cleared so we could reuse it. If there is no view data, we set the content of the **StringBuilder** to be a message to that effect. After we have finished with the old data, we assign the new results to the view data using the same key:

```
ViewState["lastResults"] = new float[] { calcResult.Distance, calcResult.Calories,
calcResult.Pace };
```

Finally, we use the contents of the **StringBuilder** to set the **InnerHtml** property of an HTML element called **oldresults**, which we add to the **Default.aspx** file, as follows:

```
...
<div>
    <div id="results" runat="server" style="float:left; width:123px;"/>
    <div id="oldresults" runat="server" style="float:left; width:123px; padding-left:2px"/>
</div>
...
```

We also add a style to the **results** element so that the current results and the new results will be displayed side by side. And now, when we submit the form more than once (that is, load the page, submit the form once to get some initial results, and then submit it again), we can see the previous results alongside the current results, as demonstrated by Figure 6-7.

Figure 6-7. *Using view state*

Decoding View State

If you look at the HTML source for the swim calculator web application in your browser, you will see an **input** element like this one:

```
<input type="hidden" name="__VIEWSTATE" id="__VIEWSTATE"
value="/wEPDwUJNTcyMjA2OTI4DxYCHgtsYXNOUmVzdWx0cxQpWlN5c3RlbS5STaW5nbGUsIG1zY29ybGliLCBWZXJzaW9
uPTQuMC4wLjAsIEN1bHR1cmU9bmV1dHJhbCwgUHVibGljS2V5VG9rZW49Yjc3YTVjNTYxOTM0ZTA4OQMIop4FPwgAwAVEC
LdtKoIWAgIDD2QWBAIJDxYCHglpbm5lcmhObWwFXDxiPlJlc3VsdHM8L2I+PHA+RGlzdGFuY2U6IDAuNTIgbWlsZXM8L3A
+PHA+Q2Fsb3JpZXMgQnVybmVkOiA1MzU8L3A+PHA+UGFjZSA6IDQzIHNlYy9sYXA8L3A+ZAILDxYCHwEFZTxiPlByZXZpb
3VzIHJlc3VsdHM8L2I+PHA+RGlzdGFuY2U6IDAuNDcgbWlsZXM8L3A+PHA+Q2Fsb3JpZXMgQnVybmVkOiA1MzU8L3A+PHA
+UGFjZSA6IDQ3IHNlYy9sYXA8L3A+ZGRKAgJ3DtyzoMWTNtevE26AtDRGW/+i43QiVYa4h/M8nw==" />
```

This is how the view state data is included in the web page that is sent back to the web browser—as an **input** element called **__VIEWSTATE** that contains a Base 64-encoded string. The type of the **input** is hidden, which means that it is not displayed to the user. When the ASP.NET server receives a form post that contains this input, it decodes the content and uses it to populate the data behind the **Page.ViewState** property.

■ **Caution** Although the view data field is not displayed in a web page, it is part of the source HTML and can be seen and decoded by the user. The user may also remove or tamper with the data. You should not rely on the view data for any critical application data, including anything to do with security.

Listing 6-7 shows the decoded view data, which ends up as an XML document. (If you want to experiment with decoding, which is a complicated task, a number of helpful tools available online make the process somewhat easier.)

Listing 6-7. Decoding view state data

```
<?xml version="1.0" encoding="utf-16"?>
<viewstate>
  <Pair>
    <Pair>
      <String>572206928</String>
      <Pair>
        <ArrayList>
          <IndexedString>lastResults</IndexedString>
          <Array>
            <Single>0.5219518</Single>
            <Single>535</Single>
            <Single>42.85714</Single>
          </Array>
        </ArrayList>
        <ArrayList>
          <Int32>3</Int32>
          <Pair>
            <ArrayList>
              <Int32>9</Int32>
              <Pair>
                <ArrayList>
                  <IndexedString>innerhtml</IndexedString>
                  <String>&lt;b&gt;Results&lt;/b&gt;&lt;p&gt;Distance: 0.52↵
 miles&lt;/p&gt;&lt;p&gt;Calories Burned: 535&lt;/p&gt;&lt;p&gt;Pace : 43↵
sec/lap&lt;/p&gt;</String>
                </ArrayList>
              </Pair>
              <Int32>11</Int32>
              <Pair>
                <ArrayList>
                  <IndexedString>innerhtml</IndexedString>
                  <String>&lt;b&gt;Previous results&lt;/b&gt;&lt;p&gt;Distance: 0.47↵
 miles&lt;/p&gt;&lt;p&gt;Calories Burned: 535&lt;/p&gt;&lt;p&gt;Pace : 47↵
sec/lap&lt;/p&gt;</String>
                </ArrayList>
              </Pair>
            </ArrayList>
          </Pair>
        </ArrayList>
      </Pair>
    </Pair>
  </Pair>
</viewstate>
```

You can see the previous results data added to the view state in bold. The individual values are **Single** elements. **Single** is the underlying .NET type that is mapped to a C# **float**.

Disabling View State

Most of the data in Listing 6-7 has nothing to do with the results data assigned to the view data. If you look closely, you can see that part of the data is the values that were assigned to the **InnerHTML** property of the two **div** controls at the bottom of the web page.

ASP.NET uses view state to store information about controls. If you assign a value to a property that cannot be expressed using standard HTML, the value of the property may be added to the view state. Sometimes, this just adds to the amount of data that is sent to and from the client browser, without adding any value to the web application. For example, we don't rely on being able to read the **InnerHTML** property of the **div** controls in the swimming calculator web application.

To disable view state entirely for a page, we can set the **EnableViewState** attribute of the **Page** directive to **false**, like this:

```
<%@ Page Language="C#" CodeBehind="Default.aspx.cs" Inherits="SwimCalculator.Default"
EnableViewState="false" %>
```

This disables view state entirely for the page, meaning that any use of the **ViewData** property in the code-behind class will be ignored. You can get and set data as normal in your code, but the data will be quietly discarded.

■ **Note** The __VIEWSTATE input is still included in the HTML, even when the view data feature has been disabled. However, the XML form contains no data and is relatively small.

If you want to be more selective, you can apply the **enableviewstate** attribute for individual controls, as follows:

```
<div id="results" runat="server" enableviewstate="false"/>
<div id="oldresults" runat="server" enableviewstate="false"/>
```

This leaves the view state feature enabled on the page so that you can store your data, but prevents ASP.NET from storing the value of the **InnerHTML** property for the two **div** controls. You can disable individual controls in this way. If you apply the **enableviewstate** attribute to a control that contains other controls, the setting also applies to those children.

```
<div runat="server" enableviewstate="false">
    <div id="results" runat="server"/>
    <div id="oldresults" runat="server"/>
</div>
```

The view state feature is disabled for all three **div** elements, even though it's applied only once. This allows you to disable view state for regions of your page if required, although you must ensure that the control to which you apply the **enableviewstate** attribute also has the **runat** attribute with a value of **server**. If that is not the case, view state won't be disabled.

Using Session State

If you have done any kind of web programming, you will almost certainly be familiar with the idea of session state. When the server receives an initial request from a web browser, a new session is created, and an identifier representing the session is included in the response to the client. Subsequent requests include the identifier, which the server uses to associate a set of requests together. A session has a fixed lifetime, which is extended each time the server receives a request that includes the identifier.

The key difference between session state and view state is that only the session identifier is included in the response that is sent to the client, while the data stored remains on the server. This helps reduce the amount of data sent between the browser and the server, and prevents the user from being able to view and modify the state data. You must remain cautious, however. The session identifier can be seen by the user, and anyone with malicious intent can try to steal someone else's session by editing the identifier.

Setting and Getting Session State Data

Using the session state feature is similar to using the view state feature. The **Page.Session** property provides access to the feature through your code-behind class, and you associate data with a key, as follows:

```
Session["lastResults"] = calcResult;
```

You retrieve data using the same key value. Data is returned as an object, and it must be cast to the correct data type, like this:

```
SwimCalcResult oldData = (SwimCalcResult)Session["lastResults"];
```

You can use any C# type as session data. You don't need to worry about serialization, because the data is not included in the response to the client. And you don't need to worry about the size of the data for the same reason.

Listing 6-8 shows the code-behind file **Default.aspx.cs** updated from the previous example to use session state instead of view state.

Listing 6-8. Using session state

```
...
// set the results text
results.InnerHtml = stringBuilder.ToString();

// clear the stringbuilder so we can reuse it
stringBuilder.Clear();
stringBuilder.Append("<b>Previous results</b>");

// get the previous results if they are in the view data
if (Session["lastResults"] != null) {
    SwimCalcResult oldData = (SwimCalcResult)Session["lastResults"];
```

```
        // we have some old results to work with
        stringBuilder.AppendFormat("<p>Distance: {0:F2} miles</p>",
            oldData.Distance);
        stringBuilder.AppendFormat("<p>Calories Burned: {0:F0}</p>",
            oldData.Calories);
        stringBuilder.AppendFormat("<p>Pace : {0:F0} sec/lap</p>",
            oldData.Pace);
    } else {
        stringBuilder.Append("<p>No previous results are available</p>");
    }

    // set the view state data
    Session["lastResults"] = calcResult;

    oldresults.InnerHtml = stringBuilder.ToString();
    ...
```

Listing 6-8 stores the **SimCalcResult** as the data item, rather than using individual **float** values, but in all other respects, the only code difference is that we access the state using the **Session** property. The effect of those changes is more significant because of the way that the data is stored, but in code terms, moving from view state to session state data is pretty straightforward.

■ **Note** ASP.NET automatically manages concurrency for session data, so that only one request with a given session identifier is processed at a time. Other simultaneous requests that share the session identifier are queued up and processed in sequence.

ASP.NET takes responsibility for associating the correct session data for the page request that your code-behind class has been instantiated to service. You don't need to use session state keys that include the session identifier, for example. In Listing 6-8, different users can be performing swimming calculations simultaneously, and ASP.NET will ensure that the data associated with the **lastResults** key is the correct data for that user.

Configuring Session State

Session state is enabled by default, but can be explicitly controlled using the **EnableSessionState** attribute in the **Page** directive, as follows:

```
<%@ Page Language="C#" CodeBehind="Default.aspx.cs" Inherits="SwimCalculator.Default"↵
EnableSessionState="True" %>
```

For more advanced configuration, you must edit the **Web.config** file and make changes that affect all of the pages in your application that use session state. To do this, you must add a **sessionState** section to the **system.web** part of the **Web.config** file. Listing 6-9 shows the **Web.config** updated to disable the session state feature (with the addition in bold).

Listing 6-9. Using the Web.config file to disable session state

```
<?xml version="1.0"?>
<configuration>
  <system.web>
    <compilation debug="true" targetFramework="4.0" />
    <sessionState mode="Off"/>
  </system.web>
</configuration>
```

There are many configuration options for session state, most of which are not of interest to us in this chapter—options for storing session information in a database, for example. However, three options are worth noting, and each requires modifications to the **Web.config** file.

Using Cookieless Session Identifiers

By default, the session identifier is passed to the client as a cookie. Some users prefer not to use cookies and with this in mind, you can elect to use "cookieless" session state. In this case, the ASP.NET server rewrites the URLs for your web application so that they include the session identifier. Listing 6-10 shows how to enable cookieless session state in the **Web.config** file.

Listing 6-10. Using cookieless session identifiers

```
<?xml version="1.0"?>
<configuration>
  <system.web>
    <compilation debug="true" targetFramework="4.0" />
    <sessionState cookieless="true"/>
  </system.web>
</configuration>
```

When you view the **Default.aspx** web page, you will see that your browser is redirected to a URL that contains a session identifier, like this one:

```
http://localhost:29907/(S(zieasch53qws15e4rzdan100))/Default.aspx
```

By rewriting the URL, ASP.NET can keep track of sessions without needing to rely on cookies. A nice compromise is the auto-detect feature, which tries to set a cookie, but falls back to URL rewriting if the cookie isn't accepted. To use this feature, set the value of the **cookieless** attribute to **AutoDetect** in the **Web.Config** file, like this:

```
<?xml version="1.0"?>
<configuration>
  <system.web>
    <compilation debug="true" targetFramework="4.0" />
    <sessionState cookieless="AutoDetect"/>
  </system.web>
</configuration>
```

Managing Session Expiry

As you have seen, there are two parts to a session: the data that is stored on the server and the identifier that is used by the client. The ASP.NET server uses the identifier to recognize that a request is part of one user's set of interactions with a web application, retrieves the stored data associated with that session, and makes that data available to your application code. At some point, the user will stop making requests, and if the user hasn't performed an action that indicates the end of a session to your application, you are left with data on the server associated with a session identifier that will not be used again.

You don't want to keep this data around forever. Eventually, it would exhaust your ability to store and manage it. So you set a grace period that defines the session lifetime. If the server doesn't receive a request with a given session identifier during this grace period, then the session is considered to have *expired*, and the data associated with the session is destroyed. Conversely, if the server *does* receive a request during the grace period, then the countdown resets, and the wait begins again.

If the server receives a request that contains an expired session identifier, it creates a new session automatically, but of course, the data from the old session has been deleted. For this reason, some caution is required in deciding what should be stored in session state, and what the user will see and need to do when a session has expired.

■ **Caution** Data stored using the session state feature will be lost if the web application is stopped or restarted, even though the session has not expired.

Determining the appropriate grace period for the sessions in your web application is important, especially if you are dealing with a high volume of requests from a wide community of users. If you set the period to be too short, the session will expire while the user is still using the application. If you set the period to be too long, you will be overwhelmed by the need to store session data that will never be needed again.

You set the grace period in the **Web.config** file using the **timeout** attribute on the **sessionState** element, as shown in Listing 6-11.

Listing 6-11. Setting the session timeout value

```xml
<?xml version="1.0"?>
<configuration>
  <system.web>
    <compilation debug="true" targetFramework="4.0" />
    <sessionState timeout="60"/>
  </system.web>
</configuration>
```

The value assigned to the **timeout** attribute specifies the number of minutes that the ASP.NET server will wait without receiving a request for a given session before considering that session expired and deleting the associated data. In Listing 6-11, the session will expire if a request has not been received in 60 minutes.

■ **Tip** Details of active sessions and the data associated with them are stored in the ASP.NET server process by default. ASP.NET includes support for storing this information and data in a SQL Server database, and you can even implement your own session management system if you have unusual project requirements. See the MSDN documentation for details.

Using Application State

With application state, you can store data and have it is available when processing all requests, irrespective of session status. Unlike session data, application data doesn't expire, which means that you don't need to worry about timeouts. However, you are responsible for managing the overall set of data, including removing data that is no longer required, to ensure that you don't exhaust the server resources.

■ **Caution** Data stored using the application state feature will be available for as long as the web application is running. If the application is stopped or restarted, the application state data is lost. Be careful when modifying the files of a running web application. The dynamic recompilation process causes the application to be restarted.

Setting and Getting Application State Data

Application state is accessed through the **Application** property of the **Page** class, and the form for setting and getting application state data is consistent with the other types of state. Listing 6-12 shows the code-behind class for the swim calculator web application updated to use application state, instead of session state (the changes are marked in bold).

Listing 6-12. Using application state

```
...
// clear the stringbuilder so we can reuse it
stringBuilder.Clear();
stringBuilder.Append("<b>Previous results</b>");

// get the previous results if they are in the view data
if (Application["lastResults"] != null) {
    SwimCalcResult oldData = (SwimCalcResult)Application["lastResults"];

    // we have some old results to work with
    stringBuilder.AppendFormat("<p>Distance: {0:F2} miles</p>",
        oldData.Distance);
    stringBuilder.AppendFormat("<p>Calories Burned: {0:F0}</p>",
        oldData.Calories);
```

```
        stringBuilder.AppendFormat("<p>Pace : {0:F0} sec/lap</p>",
            oldData.Pace);
} else {
    stringBuilder.Append("<p>No previous results are available</p>");
}

// set the view state data
Application["lastResults"] = calcResult;
oldresults.InnerHtml = stringBuilder.ToString();
...
```

As you can see, we simply replace references to the **Session** property with references to the **Application** property. So, setting and getting values uses the same key/indexer approach you saw with the other types of state.

The effect of these changes is that our web application now displays the previous results using the last calculation performed by any request, not just the one from the current session. To try this out, perform a calculation using one browser and then another. You will see the results from the first request displayed in the Previous Results section of the response to the second request.

Removing Data from the Application State

The ASP.NET server doesn't automatically remove data from the application state. This is something you must do yourself. The problem is that your interactions with application state arise when you are processing page requests, and taking the time to manage the state data will slow down your response to the client. For this reason, application state is better suited for storing data items that don't change and that will be used throughout the life of the web application. Database connections are a prime example.

If you do need to remove something from the application state, you can do so by calling the **Remove** method on the **HttpApplicationState** object that is returned when you read the **Application** property in the **Page** class, like this:

```
Application.Remove("lastResults");
```

This statement removes the data associated with the key **lastResults**.ey **lastResults**.

Putting State in Context

The ASP.NET state features are essential to building a web application of any complexity. You can't rely on the usual C# object state, because new objects are created to process each page. If you want data to persist across requests, you need to use one of the state features. which are summarized in Table 6-2.

Table 6-2. *Summary of ASP.NET State Features*

Type	Data Life	Data Location
Form input state	One request	Individual HTML **input** elements
View state	One request	Hidden field in the web browser response
Session state	Multiple requests, plus grace period	Session identifier stored in a cookie or request URL; state data stored on the server
Application state	Life of web application	Server

The choice of state feature depends on the following:

- Size and scale of your web application
- Security implications of the data being stored
- Longevity and frequency that the data changes
- Whether the data is used by some, all, or just one user

The view, session, and application state features are accessed through properties in the **Page** class. These properties return a specialized collection object that lets you perform more complex operations than simply getting and setting data, as we did in the examples. Table 6-3 summarizes the relationship between each of these state features, their associated **Page** properties, and the implementation classes.

Table 6-3. *ASP.NET State Features*

State	Page Property	Implementation Class
View state	`ViewState`	`System.Web.UI.StateBag`
Session state	`Session`	`System.Web.SessionState.HttpSessionState`
Application state	`Application`	`System.Web.HttpApplicationState`

▨ **Tip**   The ASP.NET state data is stored in the memory of the ASP.NET server by default. You can select different storage approaches, which is useful if you expect a lot of state data or you need to share the same data among multiple servers that are delivering the same application. A popular approach for large-scale applications is to store the data in a relational database, such as SQL Server. You can find details for setting up the database and configuring the ASP.NET framework on MSDN site.

On one hand, I encourage you to look at these classes and explore other actions you can perform on state data. On the other, I advise caution if you find yourself needing to do anything other than getting and setting state data. The state management features are best suited to storing small amounts of relatively simple data, which is then used to provide context and continuity between web page requests. As a general guide, anything more complex is likely better stored in a database (see Chapter 8).

Summary

This chapter presented the key features that move you to being able to build web applications that generate content that is driven by input provided by users or by state information—or, as is often the case, by a combination of both.

Understanding how ASP.NET works with HTML forms is important. It forms the underpinnings of both MVC and Web Forms, which are the two dominant ASP.NET web application frameworks. HTML forms are the main way in which users can change the state of an application, but not the only way. You'll see another example when we look at Ajax in Chapter 11.

The ASP.NET state features simplify the process of creating a coherent web application out of a series of otherwise disconnected web page requests. The trick with state of any kind is to use it sparingly. There are two dangers. The first is that you consume too many resources, either in the network traffic required to transmit a lot of view state data or in the memory required to store server-side data. The second danger is mixing the code that manages state data with the code that renders page responses, which goes against the separation of concerns approach we touched on in the previous chapter.

You'll see other approaches for data management when we look at working with databases (Chapter 8).

CHAPTER 7

Handling Errors

Your web application won't always behave as you want it to behave. It doesn't matter how carefully you plan and code your application, there will come a time when you are faced with a bug, an error, or some other kind of unexpected behavior.

There are two facets to dealing with errors:

- How errors are represented to users. As you'll see, the default approach is far from ideal. Fortunately, some helpful features are available to improve the situation, and each will be demonstrated in this chapter.

- Tracking down the cause of an error. The main technique is to use the ASP.NET tracing feature, which lets you instrument your code so that you can understand its execution. In this chapter, you'll learn how to enable tracing and customize it to give additional insight into your code. We'll also touch on using the debugging features of Visual Studio, which let you follow a request as it is being processed.

Handling Errors

To demonstrate the different techniques for handling errors, we need a web application that will generate them on demand. To that end, we'll create an ASP.NET application that will let us select one of three different C# exceptions to throw when we submit a form.

Creating the Handling Errors Example

To create the sample project, follow these steps:

1. Create a new Visual Studio project using the ASP.NET Empty Web Application template.

2. Given the project the name Handling Errors, as shown in Figure 7-1.

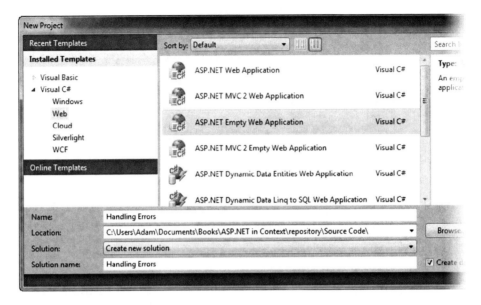

Figure 7-1. *Creating the Handling Errors project*

3.   To add a web page, select Project ➤ Add New Item.

4.   Select the Web Form template, set the name to Default.aspx, and click the Add button.

5.   Open the Default.aspx file and edit the contents so that they match Listing 7-1.

Listing 7-1. *The error-generating web page*

```
<%@ Page Language="C#" AutoEventWireup="true" CodeBehind="Default.aspx.cs"↵
 Inherits="Handling_Errors.Default" %>

<!DOCTYPE html PUBLIC "-//W3C//DTD XHTML 1.0 Transitional//EN"↵
 "http://www.w3.org/TR/xhtml1/DTD/xhtml1-transitional.dtd">

<html xmlns="http://www.w3.org/1999/xhtml">
<head runat="server">
    <title></title>
    <style type="text/css">
        label {display:block}
    </style>
</head>
<body>
    <form id="form1" runat="server">
    <div style="width:250px">
        <b>Select Exception Type:</b>
```

```
        <label for="ArgumentOutOfRangeException">
            <input type="radio" name="exceptionType" id="ArgumentOutOfRangeExceptionControl"
                value="ArgumentOutOfRangeException" runat="server" checked="true"/>
            ArgumentOutOfRangeException
        </label>

        <label for="InvalidOperationException">
            <input type="radio" name="exceptionType" id="InvalidOperationExceptionControl"
                value="InvalidOperationException" runat="server" />
            InvalidOperationException
        </label>

        <label for="NotImplementedException">
            <input type="radio" name="exceptionType" id="NotImplementedExceptionControl"
                value="NotImplementedException" runat="server" />
            NotImplementedException
        </label>

        <input type="submit" id="button" value="Submit" />
    </div>
    </form>
</body>
</html>
```

This web page creates a form that contains three radio buttons and a regular button to submit the form. Select File ➤ View in Browser to see how the page is rendered. There are slight differences in how radio buttons are displayed in browsers, but you should see something similar to Figure 7-2.

Figure 7-2. *Displaying the error-generating HTML*

The page offers a radio button for each of three C# exception types. We will select the exception we want to see by checking the appropriate button and clicking Submit. The code-behind file that handles this, Default.aspx.cs, is shown in Listing 7-2.

Listing 7-2. The code-behind class for the Handling Exceptions example

```csharp
using System;

namespace Handling_Errors {

    public partial class Default : System.Web.UI.Page {

        protected void Page_Load(object sender, EventArgs e) {

            if (IsPostBack) {
                if (this.ArgumentOutOfRangeExceptionControl.Checked) {
                    throw new ArgumentOutOfRangeException();
                } else if (this.InvalidOperationExceptionControl.Checked) {
                    throw new InvalidOperationException();
                } else if (this.NotImplementedExceptionControl.Checked) {
                    throw new NotImplementedException();
                }
            }
        }
    }
}
```

The class shown in Listing 7-2 is very simple. The HTML input elements are represented by the HtmlInputRadioButton control class, whose property Checked returns true if the button is checked. We test each HTML control in turn and throw the appropriate exception.

Testing the Handling Errors Example

Once you have created the project and edited the page and class files, select File ➤ View in Browser. Make sure that the topmost radio button is selected (the one for ArgumentOutOfRangeException) and click the Submit button. The form will be submitted to the ASP.NET server, the code-behind class will be invoked, and an ArgumentOutOfRangeException will be thrown. In the browser, you'll see something similar to Figure 7-3.

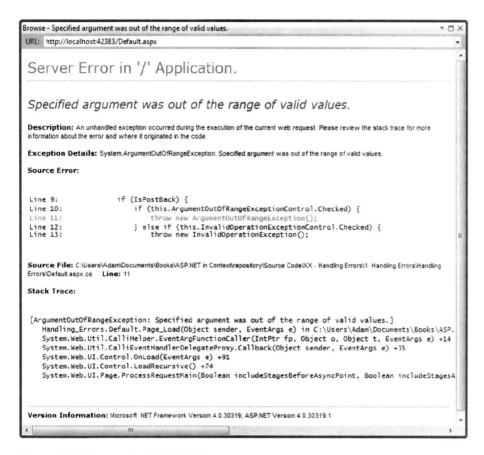

Figure 7-3. The standard ASP.NET error page

Figure 7-3 shows the standard ASP.NET response when an exception is encountered, widely known as the Yellow Screen of Death. When you are developing an ASP.NET, the yellow screen can be very informative. You can clearly see the code where the exception was thrown, details of the stack trace, and information about the exception itself.

As useful as the yellow screen can be to the developer, it is pretty much useless to the end user:

- It doesn't tell the user what has gone wrong.

- It doesn't offer any instructions as to what to do next.

- It exposes the details of your web application.

To show the yellow screen to users is considered unprofessional and unhelpful—so much so that a lot of this chapter is about how to replace it with something more helpful.

The exceptions thrown by the example result in *unhandled errors*, which just means that the exceptions have not been dealt with using a try/catch block in the code-behind class.

So, ASP.NET must do something with the exception, and the default behavior is to display the yellow screen. Fortunately, ASP.NET supports a range of error-handling features that let you show the user something more useful (and less revealing and dangerous) than a stack trace.

Handling Errors in Pages

The first approach to handling errors is to do so in the code-behind class. ASP.NET provides a mechanism for doing this through the Error event defined in the Page class, which is usually the base for code-behind classes. The Error event is invoked when ASP.NET encounters an exception while rendering a page. Listing 7-3 shows how to handle an exception using the Event method.

Listing 7-3. *Handling an exception through the Page.Error event*

```
using System;

namespace Handling_Errors {

    public partial class Default : System.Web.UI.Page {

        protected void Page_Load(object sender, EventArgs e) {

            if (IsPostBack) {
                if (this.ArgumentOutOfRangeExceptionControl.Checked) {
                    throw new ArgumentOutOfRangeException();
                } else if (this.InvalidOperationExceptionControl.Checked) {
                    throw new InvalidOperationException();
                } else if (this.NotImplementedExceptionControl.Checked) {
                    throw new NotImplementedException();
                }
            }
        }

        protected void Page_Error(object sender, EventArgs e) {

            // get the exception that has caused the Error event to be invoked
            Exception ex = Server.GetLastError();

            // check the type of the exception - we only want to deal with
            // the ArgumentOutOfRangeException in this class
            if (ex is ArgumentOutOfRangeException) {
                // write a message
                Response.Write("<h3>Error Page: ArgumentOutOfRangeException</h3>");
                Response.Write("<p>A useful description for the user</p>");
                Response.Write("<a href=\"/Default.aspx\">Click here to start over<a>");
                // clear the error
                Server.ClearError();
            }
        }
    }
}
```

The Page_Error method is called when an error occurs processing the page request. The auto event wiring introduced in Chapter 4 ensures that this method is called when the Page.Error method is invoked.

We get the exception that has been thrown by calling the Server.GetLastError method. You saw this method in Chapter 5 when we looked at the server state object:

```
Exception ex = Server.GetLastError();
```

We want to handle only the ArgumentOutOfRangeException in this class, so we test the type of the exception using the is keyword. If this is the right kind of exception, we use the Response.Write method to compose HTML that will be displayed to the user:

```
Response.Write("<h3>Error Page: ArgumentOutOfRangeException</h3>");
Response.Write("<p>A useful description for the user</p>");
Response.Write("<a href=\"/Default.aspx\">Click here to start over<a>");
```

The error message in this example is just a placeholder. In a real web application, the error message to the user should describe *what* went wrong, give some indication as to *why* it happened, and present some next steps.

The last step in handling the error is to call the Server.ClearError method, like this:

```
Server.ClearError();
```

The ClearError method tells the ASP.NET server that you have handled the exception, and no further action is required. If you don't call this method, the exception is escalated, and the Yellow Screen of Death will be displayed. This can be useful if you want to process the exception without handling it; for example, you may want to create a log entry.

Run the web application, make sure that the ArgumentOutOfRangeException option is checked, and click the Submit button. You will see the results of handling the exception, as shown in Figure 7-4.

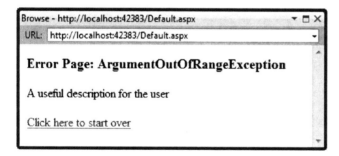

Figure 7-4. *Handling an exception*

We have handled only one of the exception types in the code-behind class, meaning that if you select either of the other options, you will still see the yellow screen.

Using a Custom Error Page

In the previous example, we generated the HTML for the error page programmatically. This approach is fine for simple applications, but it doesn't scale very well. This is not ideal, since you want to consistently handle the same kinds of exceptions in a lot of different pages. Instead, it is good practice to separate the error-handling code from the error page. We can do this by creating a web page specifically for displaying an error. Listing 7-4 shows the changes to the Page_Error method in the Default.aspx.cs file.

Listing 7-4. *Referring to a custom error page*

```
protected void Page_Error(object sender, EventArgs e) {

    // get the exception that has caused the Error event to be invoked
    Exception ex = Server.GetLastError();

    // check the type of the exception - we only want to deal with
    // the ArgumentOutOfRangeException in this class
    if (ex is ArgumentOutOfRangeException) {
        // show the custom error page
        Server.Transfer("/CustomError.aspx");
    }
}
```

We still want to handle only the ArgumentOutOfRangeException in the code-behind class, but instead of writing the HTML directly to the response, we use the Server.Transfer method to render a page called CustomError.aspx, which is shown in Listing 7-5.

Listing 7-5. *A custom error web page*

```
<%@ Page Language="C#" AutoEventWireup="true" CodeBehind="CustomError.aspx.cs"↵
 Inherits="Handling_Errors.CustomError" %>

<!DOCTYPE html PUBLIC "-//W3C//DTD XHTML 1.0 Transitional//EN"↵
 "http://www.w3.org/TR/xhtml1/DTD/xhtml1-transitional.dtd">

<html xmlns="http://www.w3.org/1999/xhtml">
<head runat="server">
    <title>Web Application Error</title>
</head>
<body>

    <div id="exceptionType" runat="server"/>

    <div id="message" runat="server"/>

    <a href="/Default.aspx" runat="server">Click here to start over</a>

</body>
</html>
```

The web page in Listing 7-5 contains three elements that will be used to display the type of the exception, the message to the user, and a link to the main application page. Listing 7-6 shows the CustomErrorPage.aspx.cs code-behind file that sets the content.

Listing 7-6. *The code-behind class for the error page*

```
using System;

namespace Handling_Errors {
    public partial class CustomError : System.Web.UI.Page {

        protected void Page_Load(object sender, EventArgs e) {

            // get the exception that we are dealing with
            Exception ex = Server.GetLastError();

            // check that we have an exception - if we don't
            // then transfer the user to the main page
            if (ex != null) {

                // set the content of the HTML controls based on the exception
                exceptionType.InnerHtml = string.Format("<h3>Error page: {0}</h3>",
                    ex.GetType().ToString());
                message.InnerHtml = "<p>A useful description for the user</p>";

                // clear the error
                Server.ClearError();

            } else {
                Server.Transfer("/Default.aspx");
            }
        }
    }
}
```

When you call another page using the Server.Transfer method, the state of the request is kept intact, allowing you to call the Server.GetLastError method to get the same exception that caused the original problem. In the CustomError class in Listing 7-6, we use the details of the exception to set some of the content.

Note that we check to see if there is a an exception to process. This is a useful check in the event that a user requests the CustomErrorPage.aspx file directly from the browser. In this case, we use Server.Transfer to display the main page instead.

Now when you run the application and select the first exception type, you see the custom page, as shown in Figure 7-5.

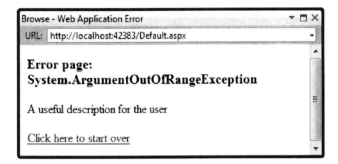

Figure 7-5. *Displaying an error through a custom page*

Using a Page Controller

By using a custom error page, we separated the code that handles the exception from the page that displays the error. However, we still end up with some code duplication, because we need to put error-handling code in every page in our project. That's OK if every page has different error-handling needs, but most projects have groups of pages that should be treated in the same way. A nice solution to this is to create a common class that derives from Page. You can then use that as the base for two or more of your code-behind classes. This is sometimes called a *page controller* class.

To add a page controller, select Project ➤ Add Class and change the name to be PageController.cs. This will be a base class for our code-behind classes, so we need to create only a C# class, and not an ASP.NET web page. Edit the contents of the PageController.cs file to match Listing 7-7.

Listing 7-7. *Handling errors in a common base class*

```
using System;
using System.Web.UI;

namespace Handling_Errors {

    public class PageController : Page {

        protected virtual void Page_Error(object sender, EventArgs e) {
            // get the exception that has caused the Error event to be invoked
            Exception ex = Server.GetLastError();

            // check the type of the exception - we only want to deal with
            // the ArgumentOutOfRangeException in this class
            if (ex is ArgumentOutOfRangeException) {
                // show the custom error page
                Server.Transfer("/CustomError.aspx");
            }
        }
    }
}
```

Page controllers can contain any code that you want to share among your Page classes. In this example, we added a Page_Error method that will be inherited by derived classes. We annotated the class with the virtual keyword, so the method can be overridden by derived classes as required.

Page_Error handles errors in the same way as the previous example: the CustomError.aspx page is shown if the exception that caused the error is an ArgumentOutOfRangeException.

To take advantage of the page controller, we need to modify our code-behind class so that is derived from PageController, as follows:

```
using System;

namespace Handling_Errors {

    public partial class Default : PageController {

        protected void Page_Load(object sender, EventArgs e) {

            if (IsPostBack) {
                if (this.ArgumentOutOfRangeExceptionControl.Checked) {
                    throw new ArgumentOutOfRangeException();
                } else if (this.InvalidOperationExceptionControl.Checked) {
                    throw new InvalidOperationException();
                } else if (this.NotImplementedExceptionControl.Checked) {
                    throw new NotImplementedException();
                }
            }
        }
    }
}
```

We changed the base class from Page to PageController and removed the Page_Error method, so that the version in the PageController class isn't overridden or hidden.

Our simple example contains only one web page, but in a real project, you would apply these changes to all of the pages, so that the common-error handling code is used.

Handling Errors with the Application

Any errors that are not handled by a page become *application errors*. These types of errors can be handled by adding a method to a global application class, as you saw when we looked at the ASP.NET event model in Chapter 5. To create a global application class, follow these steps:

1. In Visual Studio, select Project ➤ Add New Item.

2. Select the Global Application Class item from the list of templates, as shown in Figure 7-6.

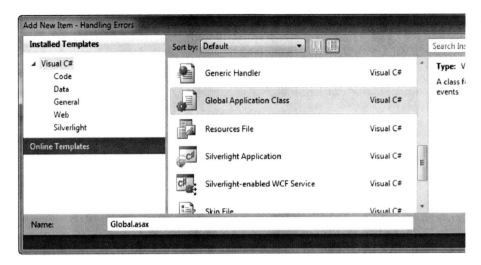

Figure 7-6. *Adding a global application class*

3. The name of the new class is set to `Global.asax` by default. Click the Add button to add the class to the project.

4. We can now add our error-handling code to the `Application_Error` method. We'll use the `Global.asax` class to handle instances of the second of our three exception types, `InvalidOperationException`, as shown in Listing 7-8.

Listing 7-8. Handling an exception in the global application class

```csharp
using System;
using System.Web;

namespace Handling_Errors {
    public class Global : System.Web.HttpApplication {

        protected void Application_Error(object sender, EventArgs e) {
            // get the exception that has caused the Error event to be invoked
            Exception ex = Server.GetLastError();

            // convert the exception so that we have an HttpUnhandledException
            HttpUnhandledException unhandledEx = ex as HttpUnhandledException;

            // check the type of the inner exception - we only want to deal with one type
            if (unhandledEx != null
                && unhandledEx.InnerException is InvalidOperationException) {
```

```
        // show the custom error page
        Server.Transfer("/CustomError.aspx");
    }
}
}
}
```

The `Application_Error` method in the `Global` class will be called only if there is an error that is not handled in a `Page` class; that is, there is no `Page_Error` method, or the `Page_Error` method that exists doesn't result in the `Server.ClearError` method being called.

The exception that caused the error is packaged up inside an instance of the `System.Web.HttpUnhandledException` class, and this is what will be returned if you call the `Server.GetLastError` method from inside the `Application_Error` method. You can get the original exception through the `InnerException` property.

In Listing 7-8, we unpack the inner exception and check to see if it is an instance of `InvalidOperationException`. If it is, we call `ServerTransfer` to display our custom error page. For this example, we used the same error page as for page-level errors, but you could easily use different pages to handle application-level errors.

Update the `CustomError.aspx.cs` file to deal with the `HttpUnhandledException` class, as shown in Listing 7-9.

Listing 7-9. *Working with the HttpUnhandledException class*

```
using System;
using System.Web;

namespace Handling_Errors {
    public partial class CustomError : System.Web.UI.Page {

        protected void Page_Load(object sender, EventArgs e) {

            // get the exception that we are dealing with
            Exception ex = Server.GetLastError();

            // we need to unpack HttpUnhandledException instances so that
            // we get the inner exception to work with
            if (ex is HttpUnhandledException) {
                ex = ((HttpUnhandledException)ex).InnerException;
            }

            // check that we have an exception - if we don't
            // then transfer the user to the main page
            if (ex != null) {

                // set the content of the HTML controls based on the exception
                exceptionType.InnerHtml = string.Format("<h3>Error page: {0}</h3>",
                    ex.GetType().ToString());
                message.InnerHtml = "<p>A useful description for the user</p>";
```

```
            // clear the error
            Server.ClearError();

        } else {
            Server.Transfer("/Default.aspx");
        }
      }
    }
  }
}
```

The changes (shown in bold) have the effect of getting the value of the InnerException property if the Exception returned by the Server.GetLastError method is an instance of HttpUnhandledException.

Configuring Custom Errors

The third and final approach to handling errors is to use the Web.config file. Any error that is not handled by the page of the application will be handled by the policy defined in the configuration file. Listing 7-10 shows such a policy.

Listing 7-10. *Configuring an error-handling policy*

```
<?xml version="1.0"?>

<configuration>
  <system.web>
    <compilation debug="true" targetFramework="4.0" />

    <customErrors mode="On" defaultRedirect="/StaticError.html">
      <error statusCode="404" redirect="/Default.aspx"/>
    </customErrors>

  </system.web>
</configuration>
```

As its name suggests, the customErrors element defines the policy for handling errors using custom pages. The first attribute is mode, which can be set to one of the following values:

- The Off value disables custom pages for unhandled errors. This means that the Yellow Screen of Death will be displayed for errors that are not handled in either the page or the Global class.

- The On value enables custom error pages so that the page specified by the defaultRedirect attribute will be displayed when an error isn't handled by either the page or the Global class.

■ **Note** The customErrors setting does not affect the error handling performed by the Page or Global classes. It controls only what happens if an error is not handled elsewhere.

- The RemoteOnly value displays the yellow screen when an error occurs while showing a page to a browser running on the same computer as the web application. It uses the custom error page for any other computer.

BE WARY OF REMOTEONLY CUSTOM ERRORS

The RemoteOnly option for displaying custom errors might seem like a handy feature, but I don't think it has any place in the tool kit of a professional programmer.

There are two broad situations when you can use the RemoteOnly feature:

- In development, when you want to see the details of an error

- In production, when you want to try to re-create a problem reported by a user

In development, you can disable custom errors in the Web.config file explicitly. And this is good practice, because mostly you will want to develop your web application by seeing exactly what the user will see.

In production, you shouldn't be trying to re-create errors at all. The very fact that you are trying to get information about an error will suggest that you don't know what causes it or what the impact will be. At the very least, you risk interrupting service to other users. Keep your testing to your development/test systems, and leave the production systems to service users.

The page referred to by the value of the defaultRedirect attribute must be a static HTML page. This is to avoid the issue where an error arises processing the page that was intended to display an error. There must be a final "it-has-all-gone-wrong" error page, and this is it. So, we are limited to HTML.

The static page referred to in Listing 7-10 is called StaticError.html and its contents are shown in Listing 7-11. Add StaticError.html to the Visual Studio project using the HTML Page template.

Listing 7-11. A static error page

```
<!DOCTYPE html PUBLIC "-//W3C//DTD XHTML 1.0 Transitional//EN"
"http://www.w3.org/TR/xhtml1/DTD/xhtml1-transitional.dtd">
<html xmlns="http://www.w3.org/1999/xhtml">
<head>
    <title>Web Application Error</title>
</head>
<body>
    <h3>A serious error has occurred</h3>
    <p>A useful message to the user</p>
    <a href="Default.aspx">Click here to start over</a
</body>
</html>
```

The third type of exception that our web application throws will trigger the custom error handling defined in the Web.config file. (The first and second kind were handled by the Page and Global classes, respectively.) Run the web application, check the NotImplementedException option, and click the Submit button. You'll see the static error page, as shown in Figure 7-7.

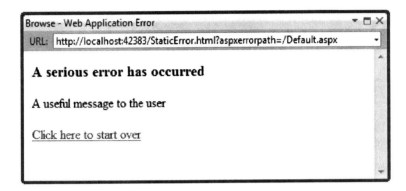

Figure 7-7. The static custom error page

In Listing 7-10, we added the following line:

```
<error statusCode="404" redirect="/Default.aspx"/>
```

The `customErrors` element in the `Web.config` file supports custom actions for HTTP error codes. The code 404 occurs when a request is received for a file that can't be found. The configuration element shown in this line tells the ASP.NET server to redirect the user to the `Default.aspx` file when this error occurs. You can use multiple error elements to set your policy for different error codes. If there is no policy set for a given code, the page specified by the `defaultRedirect` attribute will be used.

Putting Error Handling in Context

You don't need to handle errors in your ASP.NET application, but if you don't handle them, you'll end up displaying the Yellow Screen of Death to your users. Not only does this annoy and confuse users, but it provides detailed information about your application that you probably won't want disseminated.

ASP.NET provides a flexible model for handling exceptions, and you can use it in whatever way makes sense for your application. The basic flow for unhandled errors is illustrated in Figure 7-8. You can opt into some or all of these stages.

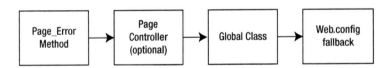

Figure 7-8. The error-handling sequence

You have seen how the `Page_Error` method is automatically wired to the `Page.Error` event and called if exceptions arise that are not handled by a standard `try/catch` code block. A variation on this technique is the page controller pattern. That pattern consolidates common error-handling code in a base class, which is then derived by individual code-behind classes. These derived classes can elect to selectively override the page controller error logic or to rely on the base implementation entirely.

Errors that are not handled by the page code-behind class can be handled in the Global class, using the Application_Error method, which is wired to the Application.Error event. Exceptions are passed indirectly to this method using the HttpUnhandledException class, and they must be unpacked before they can be used.

The fallback for errors that have not been handled elsewhere is the policy set in the Web.config file. Otherwise unhandled errors can be represented to the user by a static HTML page as a last resort. You should set a Web.config error policy as a minimum for your ASP.NET web applications to ensure that you don't display the yellow screen.

Using ASP.NET Tracing

The combination of C# exceptions and ASP.NET error handling deal with one kind of web application programming problem: a *hard failure*, where something specific goes wrong and is expressed using an exception. A hard failure results in an ASP.NET error, and the process of debugging becomes finding out what caused the exception and remedying the situation. It can be more difficult to diagnose a *soft failure*, where there is no exception but the web application doesn't behave as it should.

One tool to help track down the cause of soft failures is ASP.NET *tracing*, which provides detailed information about how a request was processed. As you'll see, this information can be used to get details of state and session data (see Chapter 6 for details on using the state features), performance details for each state in the request handling, and any additional information that you add to help figure out the problem.

For this part of the chapter, we need a simple web application that suffers from a soft failure.

Creating the TraceDemo Example

To focus on the ASP.NET tracing feature, rather than building a complex example, we'll create a simple summing calculator.

Create a new Visual Studio project called TraceDemo using the ASP.NET Empty Web Application template and add a web page called Default.aspx using the Web Form template. The contents of this file are shown in Listing 7-12.

Listing 7-12. The Default.aspx file for the TraceDemo example

```
<%@ Page Language="C#" AutoEventWireup="true" CodeBehind="Default.aspx.cs"
Inherits="TraceDemo.Default"%>

<!DOCTYPE html PUBLIC "-//W3C//DTD XHTML 1.0 Transitional//EN"
"http://www.w3.org/TR/xhtml1/DTD/xhtml1-transitional.dtd">

<html xmlns="http://www.w3.org/1999/xhtml">
<head runat="server">
    <title>Trace Demo</title>
</head>
<body>
    <form id="form1" runat="server">
```

```
    <div>
        Number: <input type="text" id="numericValue" runat="server" />
        <input type="submit" value="Add" />

        <div style="clear:both;margin:2px">
            Running total: <span id="runningTotal" runat="server" />
        </div>
    </div>
    </form>
</body>
</html>
```

This page has a simple layout that lets the user enter a value and an Add button, which will add the entered value to a running total when clicked. Figure 7-9 shows how this HTML page appears in the browser.

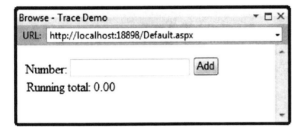

Figure 7-9. *The TraceDemo application*

The code-behind file contains the class shown n Listing 7-13.

Listing 7-13. *The Default.aspx.cs file for the TraceDemo example*

```
using System;

namespace TraceDemo {

    public partial class Default : System.Web.UI.Page {

        protected void Page_Load(object sender, EventArgs e) {

            // define a variable for the running total
            float total = 0;

            // get the running total from the session if possible
            if (Session["runningTotal"] != null) {
                total = (float)Session["runningTotal"];
            }
```

```
        if (IsPostBack) {
            // this is a form post - get the value from the HTML control
            string data = numericValue.Value;
            // try to parse the data to a numeric value
            if (data != null) {
                float incrementalValue = 0;
                if (float.TryParse(data, out incrementalValue)) {
                    total += incrementalValue;
                }
            }
        }

        // update the running total on the HTML control
        runningTotal.InnerText = string.Format("{0:F2}", total);

        // update the value stored in the session
        Session["runningTotals"] = total;
        }
    }
}
```

This class retrieves the running total from the session state data and, if this is a form post, parses and adds the value entered by the user to that total. The bug (shown in bold) is a simple typo. Its result is that different keys are used to set and get the session state data. Because of this, the running total will not increment properly, and will instead show only the previously entered value.

Enabling Tracing

You can enable tracing on individual ASP.NET pages by adding the Trace attribute to the Page directive, like this:

```
<%@ Page Language="C#" AutoEventWireup="true" CodeBehind="Default.aspx.cs"↵
 Inherits="TraceDemo.Default" Trace="true" %>
```

If the Trace value is true, then tracing will be performed each time that the page is requested.

To enable tracing for all pages in a web application, you can add a trace element to the Web.config file, like this:

```
<?xml version="1.0"?>

<configuration>
    <system.web>
        <compilation debug="true" targetFramework="4.0" />
        <trace enabled="true" pageOutput="true" requestLimit="50" localOnly="false"/>
    </system.web>
</configuration>
```

The requestLimit parameter specifies how many page requests should be traced. The default is 10, after which the application returns to normal behavior and tracing will not be performed. The value in the example specifies that the first 50 requests should be traced.

Usually, trace information is displayed only on requests from the same machine on which the ASP.NET server is running. To change this, set the localOnly attribute to false, as in this example.

We'll look at the effect of the pageOutput attribute later in this chapter, in the "Enabling the Trace Viewer" section.

Performing a Trace

Once you have enabled tracing, you simply request the page of interest. For our simple example, there is only one page: Default.aspx. Select this file in the Solution Explorer window, and then select File ➤ View in Browser.

The page will be processed as normal, but details about how it was processed will be appended to the bottom of the response to the browser, as shown in Figure 7-10.

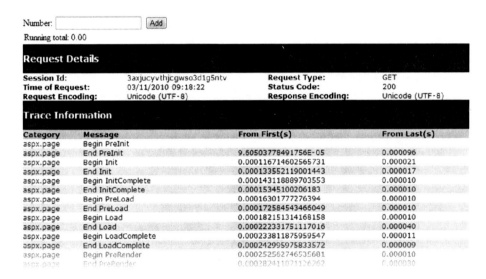

Figure 7-10. *Viewing tracing information*

A single page trace contains a lot of information. Here, we'll look at the most useful sections in detail:

- Request Details

- Trace Information

- Control Tree

- Session State

- Application State

- Request Cookies Collection

- Response Cookies Collection

The remaining trace sections provide details of the values in form input fields, a complete list of headers, query string values, and so on. All of these sections can be useful, but you'll find that most soft problems can be diagnosed using one of the sections in this list.

■ **Note** The way that the information is structured on the web page doesn't suit the printed page. Consider downloading the example or re-creating it and following along with your own trace information.

The first thing to note is that the response includes the web application. At the top of the page are the HTML elements that make up our simple display. The application remains fully functional while tracing is being performed.

The Request Details Section

The first trace section is called Request Details and contains summary information about the request, as you can see in Figure 7-11.

Request Details			
Session Id:	3axjucyvthjcgwso3d1g5ntv	Request Type:	GET
Time of Request:	03/11/2010 09:18:22	Status Code:	200
Request Encoding:	Unicode (UTF-8)	Response Encoding:	Unicode (UTF-8)

Figure 7-11. The Request Details section

The most useful information is the session ID, the request type (a GET in this case), and the HTTP status code for the response to the client (200 for this example, which means OK).

The Trace Information Section

The Trace Information section shows each of the events that occur in the processing of an ASP.NET page and the amount of time that each event took, as shown in Figure 7-12.

Trace Information			
Category	Message	From First(s)	From Last(s)
aspx.page	Begin PreInit		
aspx.page	End PreInit	9.60503778491756E-05	0.000096
aspx.page	Begin Init	0.0001167114602565731	0.000021
aspx.page	End Init	0.000133552119001443	0.000017
aspx.page	Begin InitComplete	0.00014311888897035533	0.000010
aspx.page	End InitComplete	0.00015345100206183	0.000010
aspx.page	Begin PreLoad	0.00016301777276394	0.000010
aspx.page	End PreLoad	0.000172584543466049	0.000010
aspx.page	Begin Load	0.000182151314168158	0.000010
aspx.page	End Load	0.000222331751117016	0.000040
aspx.page	Begin LoadComplete	0.000233811875959547	0.000011
aspx.page	End LoadComplete	0.000242995975833572	0.000009

Figure 7-12. The Trace Information section

These events represent small amounts of time, but they can be very useful in helping to track down performance problems. Times are shown relative to the first event (the start of the PreInit event) and to the previous event. From this example, we see that the amount of time taken to process code in the code-behind class was 0.000040 second (this is shown as the time from the Begin Load and End Load entries).

We will come back to this section of the trace output again when we look at using custom trace messages a little later in this chapter.

The Control Tree Section

The Control Tree section displays information about the size of each of the HTML elements in the page, as shown in Figure 7-13. This information is useful when the size of the response to the browser is causing problems. In Chapter 5, you saw how the view state feature can unexpectedly increase the amount of data sent between the server and the client. Part of the trace information lets you see if this is the case.

Control Tree				
Control UniqueID Type		Render Size Bytes (including children)	ViewState Size Bytes (excluding children)	ControlState Size Bytes (excluding children)
__Page	ASP.default_aspx	1012	0	0
ctl02	System.Web.UI.LiteralControl	174	0	0
ctl00	System.Web.UI.HtmlControls.HtmlHead	43	0	0
ctl01	System.Web.UI.HtmlControls.HtmlTitle	30	0	0
ctl03	System.Web.UI.LiteralControl	14	0	0
form1	System.Web.UI.HtmlControls.HtmlForm	761	0	0
ctl04	System.Web.UI.LiteralControl	39	0	0
numericValue	System.Web.UI.HtmlControls.HtmlInputText	59	0	0
ctl05	System.Web.UI.LiteralControl	129	0	0
runningTotal	System.Web.UI.HtmlControls.HtmlGenericControl	35	28	0
ctl06	System.Web.UI.LiteralControl	4	0	0
ctl07	System.Web.UI.LiteralControl	34	0	0
ctl08	System.Web.UI.LiteralControl	20	0	0

Figure 7-13. *The Control Tree section*

This is an ASP.NET-centric view of the HTML, so all of the HTML elements are represented using HTML control classes. An element will be represented using the LiteralControl class if the element was not made visible to ASP.NET with the runat attribute. For each element, you can see the number of bytes it occupies in the response to the client, the number of associated view state bytes, and details of the control state. Control state is similar to view state, and it is used extensively by the Web Forms framework, which we will come to in Chapter 13

In Figure 7-13, you can see that the runningTotal element has been assigned 28 bytes of view state data. This is a small amount of data, but it isn't being used by the application and could be significant in a more complex page in a high-volume web application. See Chapter 6 for details on how to disable unwanted view state.

The State Sections

The next four sections show information about different kinds of state, as shown in Figure 7-14. The first two are session and application state, which you saw in Chapter 6.

In Figure 7-14, there is only one piece of session state for our application. This is the cause of our bug, and you can see that the key is runningTotals. You can also see the type of the data (in this case, System.Single, which is the .NET counterpart for the C# float type) and the value of the data (0 in this example). We might spot our bug using this data, but it requires a good eye for detail. We'll cover an easier way of diagnosing the problem using custom trace messages, as described in the next section.

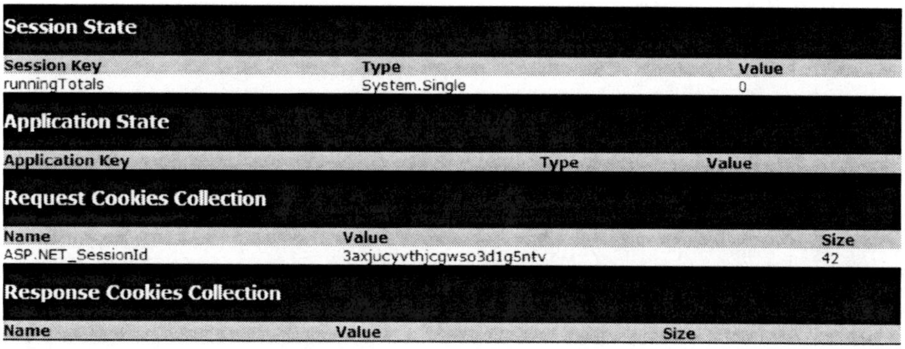

Session State		
Session Key	**Type**	**Value**
runningTotals	System.Single	0

Application State		
Application Key	**Type**	**Value**

Request Cookies Collection		
Name	**Value**	**Size**
ASP.NET_SessionId	3axjucyvthjcgwso3d1g5ntv	42

Response Cookies Collection		
Name	**Value**	**Size**

Figure 7-14. The session, application, and cookie sections

The other two sections show the cookies associated with the request and response. There is only one cookie in this trace, and it contains the session identifier. See Chapter 6 for details on how to use sessions with or without cookies.

Adding Custom Trace Messages

The most useful part of the trace feature is the ability to add you own messages to be included in the tracing process when a page is requested.

The Page.Trace property returns a System.Web.TraceContext object, which you can use to add statements to your code. The output from these statements will be included in the trace information for the page associated with the code. The two key methods from the TraceContext class are Write and Warn, as demonstrated in Listing 7-14.

Listing 7-14. Adding custom trace statements to a code-behind class

```
using System;

namespace TraceDemo {

    public partial class Default : System.Web.UI.Page {

        protected void Page_Load(object sender, EventArgs e) {
            Trace.Write("---Started");
```

```
        // define a variable for the running total
        Trace.Write("Initializing local variable");
        float total = 0;

        // get the running total from the session if possible
        if (Session["runningTotal"] != null) {
            Trace.Write("Session state data obtained");
            total = (float)Session["runningTotal"];
        } else if (IsPostBack) {
            Trace.Warn("No session state data found");
        } else {
            Trace.Write("No session data for initial request");
        }

        if (IsPostBack) {
            // this is a form post - get the value from the HTML control
            string data = numericValue.Value;
            Trace.Write(string.Format("User has entered data: {0}", data));
            // try to parse the data to a numeric value
            if (data != null) {
                float incrementalValue = 0;
                if (float.TryParse(data, out incrementalValue)) {
                    total += incrementalValue;
                    Trace.Write(string.Format("Numeric value: {0}, new total: {1}",
                        incrementalValue, total));
                } else {
                    Trace.Warn("Cannot parse data to float value");
                }
            } else {
                Trace.Warn("No data has been provided by user");
            }
        }

        // update the running total on the HTML control
        Trace.Write("Setting display for total");
        runningTotal.InnerText = string.Format("{0:F2}", total);

        // update the value stored in the session
        Trace.Write("Setting new state data value");
        Session["runningTotals"] = total;
        Trace.Write("---Finished");
    }
  }
}
```

The statements shown in bold are additions that call either Trace.Write or Trace.Warn. The Write method is used to instrument an expected operation in your page—something that will indicate normal progress. The Warn method is used to flag a potential problem. Here is an example of both statements in use:

```
if (Session["runningTotal"] != null) {
    Trace.Write("Session state data obtained");
    total = (float)Session["runningTotal"];
} else if (IsPostBack) {
    Trace.Warn("No session state data found");
} else {
    Trace.Write("No session data for initial request");
}
```

The expectation in the code is that there will be session state data available for all but the initial request, when the session itself will be created. The call to Trace.Write prints a message to the trace log when the session data is successfully retrieved.

We might have a problem if there is no session data, so the example uses the Trace.Warn method to print a warning message to the trace log if this is the case. If you view the page, the messages written using the Trace.Write and Trace.Warn methods are included in the Trace Information section, as shown in Figure 7-15.

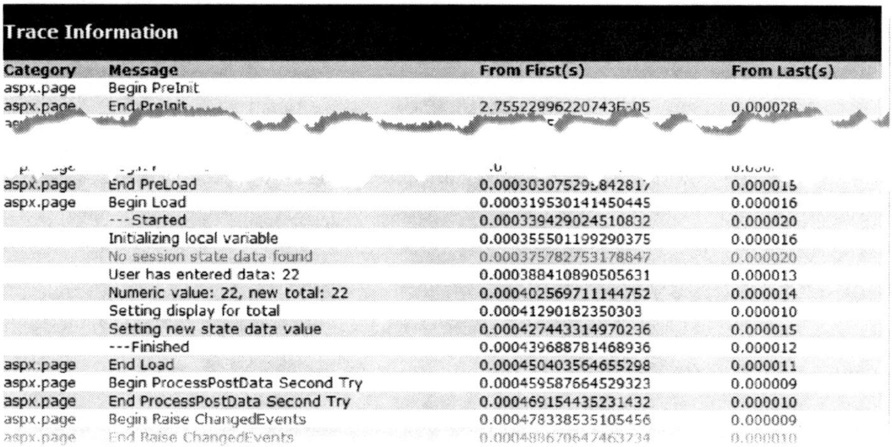

Category	Message	From First(s)	From Last(s)
aspx.page	Begin PreInit		
aspx.page	End PreInit	2.75522996220743E-05	0.000028
...			
p...ge	...g...	.0	0.000.
aspx.page	End PreLoad	0.00030307529:84281?	0.000015
aspx.page	Begin Load	0.000319530141450445	0.000016
	---Started	0.000339429024510832	0.000020
	Initializing local variable	0.000355501199290375	0.000016
	No session state data found	0.000375782753178847	0.000020
	User has entered data: 22	0.000388410890505631	0.000013
	Numeric value: 22, new total: 22	0.000402569711144752	0.000014
	Setting display for total	0.00041290182350303	0.000010
	Setting new state data value	0.000427443314970236	0.000015
	---Finished	0.000439688781468936	0.000012
aspx.page	End Load	0.000450403564655298	0.000011
aspx.page	Begin ProcessPostData Second Try	0.000459587664529323	0.000009
aspx.page	End ProcessPostData Second Try	0.000469154435231432	0.000010
aspx.page	Begin Raise ChangedEvents	0.000478338535105456	0.000009
aspx.page	End Raise ChangedEvents	0.000488670647463234	0.000010

Figure 7-15. *Displaying the custom trace messages*

The ASP.NET server adds the output from any statements that call the Trace.Write or Trace.Warn methods it encounters while processing the page to the trace data. Using this output, you can follow the flow of your page code as it is performed. The Trace.Warn method produces red output to attract attention. In our example, one statement is marked in red, and it tells us that no session state data has been found. The trace in Figure 7-15 is the result of entering the value 22 in the input element and clicking the Add button several times.

This is the clue that helps you find your bug. You can see from the trace messages that the state data is being updated. This tells you that something is going wrong when you get or set the data. You could add more trace messages to help pin down the problem further. In this simple example, a visual inspection of the code shows that there is a mismatch in the keys used to get and set the session state data.

Using the Trace Viewer

Appending the trace information to the page isn't always convenient. The trace viewer feature displays the set of traced requests on a single page and lets you choose which ones are of interest. This is especially useful when you are trying to understand a problem that spans multiple requests or even multiple pages.

Enabling the Trace Viewer

To switch to the trace viewer, set the value of the pageOutput attribute to false, as shown in Listing 7-15.

***Listing 7-15.** Enabling trace viewing*

```
<?xml version="1.0"?>

<configuration>
   <system.web>
      <compilation debug="true" targetFramework="4.0" />
      <trace enabled="true" pageOutput="false" requestLimit="50"/>
   </system.web>
</configuration>
```

This change causes the trace data to be stored rather than displayed at the end of the page. The requestLimit attribute is especially important when tracing in this way. You must ensure that the limit is high enough to store the number of traces that you need to re-create your soft failure.

Viewing a Trace in the Trace Viewer

The first step is to re-create the problem. Select the page you want to start with and select File ➤ View in Browser. Use your web application as your users would. For example, try to add the values 20, 30, and 40.

When you have finished using the web application, navigate to the page Trace.axd. If your application was available at http://localhost:1234/Default.aspx, then navigate to http://localhost:1234/Trace.axd. This is the URL of the trace viewer, which is shown in Figure 7-16.

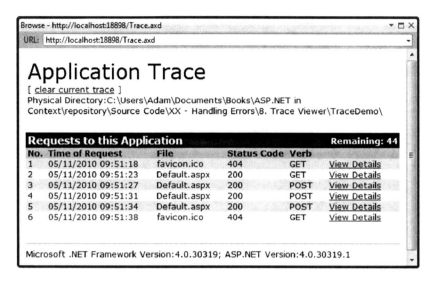

Figure 7-16. *The ASP.NET trace viewer*

All of the requests to the ASP.NET server are shown. Not all of these are useful, even in this simple example.

You can see that there are two requests for favicon.ico, which represent the browser asking for the icon to display alongside the URL. We don't have a favicon.ico file in our web application project, and so the status code for these requests is 404, meaning that the file requested was not found.

The remaining requests are all for Default.aspx, and they all completed successfully (status code 200). The first request was a GET, but all of the rest were POSTs. This is what you would expect for a form-based ASP.NET web application.

Notice the Remaining label at the right side of the black box in Figure 7-16. This indicates how many more requests will be traced before the application reverts to normal behavior. You can restart the trace (and reset this counter) by clicking the clear current trace link at the top of the page.

You can see the details of any individual request by clicking the appropriate View Details link. This takes you to a summary page that contains the same trace information you saw earlier.

The trace viewer makes it easier to find some kinds of bugs. The problem in our example web application is a good case in point. If you view the details or each request in turn, you will quickly notice the message (marked clearly in red to catch the eye) that warns there is no session state data.

The downside of the trace viewer is that it captures *every* request to the ASP.NET server, and that can make it hard to figure out what is going on, as Figure 7-17 demonstrates.

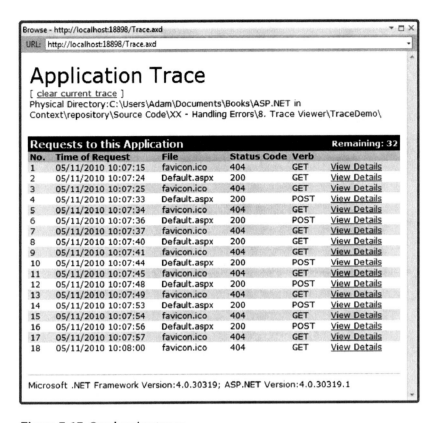

Figure 7-17. Overlapping traces

The weakness of the trace viewer is that you can't filter the data. To create the set of traces shown in Figure 7-17, I interleaved requests from two browser windows. This is still a simple sequence of requests, but the result is a lot more meaningless requests (the favicon.ico file is especially popular). and you will need to view the details of every request to work out which ones are associated with the two sessions.

The trace viewer is at its most useful when you can minimize the number of requests that are not directly related to your bug hunt.

■ **Tip**   Some commercial tracing packages for ASP.NET feature detailed filtering and analytics. My experience with such packages has been mixed. The analysis tools can be useful, but you must use custom trace classes to instrument your web application. Few projects are organized enough to have negotiated licenses for advanced diagnostics and to have performed the instrumentation before a serious problem emerges. By the time you realize you could benefit from the tools, you don't have the time or opportunity to obtain them and put them in place.

Putting ASP.NET Tracing in Context

The ASP.NET tracing feature can be exceptionally useful when you're trying to track down behavioral bugs in a web application. These are bugs that don't cause an error, but that mean the application doesn't perform as expected.

The simplest way to start tracing is to view the information appended to the end of a page response. Detailed information is provided for each of the events that occurs in the page life cycle and the request/response overall.

The real power comes with custom trace messages, which let you instrument the flow of your page code, as well as flag potential error conditions. Trace messages won't identify a bug, but they can give you a solid understanding of the region of your code that is responsible for the problem.

I am a big fan of the trace feature. It gives me insight to where the processing effort for a page is being spent and provides a foundation for detailed instrumentation. By habit, I turn to this feature early in my debugging process.

Using the Visual Studio Debugger

Visual Studio includes a powerful and flexible debugger. You can use it as an alternative to tracing to discover the root cause for all kinds of errors and bugs. The advantage of using the debugger is that you can follow the execution of the code as it happens, rather than relying on a trace summary that is available after the request has been processed.

Debugging an ASP.NET page request is just like debugging a regular C# program. You set breakpoints, run the program, and wait for the debugger to break. Once this happens, you can step through the code to follow its execution. In this section, I'll show you how to selectively break the debugger to get fine-grained control over the debug process.

Setting a Breakpoint

The first step in using the debugger is to set a breakpoint. This is where the debugger will interrupt normal execution of your code and pass control to you.

The problem with breakpoints is that, by default, they are quite crude. A statement that has a breakpoint is reached, and execution is stopped. That can be a problem when it comes to debugging ASP.NET, because the same code can be used for different tasks, such as to process a GET and a POST. Two techniques can be used to make a breakpoint more specific: set a conditional breakpoint or use a programmatic breakpoint.

Listing 7-16 shows the code-behind class that we will use in this section (I have removed the trace statements that were added in the previous section).

Listing 7-16. The code-behind class for the debugger example

```csharp
using System;

namespace TraceDemo {

    public partial class Default : System.Web.UI.Page {

        protected void Page_Load(object sender, EventArgs e) {
```

```
        // define a variable for the running total
        float total = 0;

        // get the running total from the session if possible
        if (Session["runningTotal"] != null) {
            total = (float)Session["runningTotal"];
        }

        if (IsPostBack) {
            // this is a form post - get the value from the HTML control
            string data = numericValue.Value;
            // try to parse the data to a numeric value
            if (data != null) {
                float incrementalValue = 0;
                if (float.TryParse(data, out incrementalValue)) {
                    total += incrementalValue;
                }
            }
        }

        // update the running total on the HTML control
        runningTotal.InnerText = string.Format("{0:F2}", total);

        // update the value stored in the session
        Session["runningTotals"] = total;
    }
  }
}
```

Setting a Conditional Breakpoint

If you are using either the Professional or Ultimate editions of Visual Studio 2010, you can set conditional breakpoints. This feature is not available in Visual Web Developer 2010 Express (advanced debugging features are one of the ways that Microsoft differentiates the premium versions from the Express editions of Visual Studio). See the next section for an alternative approach that works on all editions.

We are going to set a breakpoint that will be triggered only when we are dealing with a POST request and there is no session state data available. The first step is to right-click the following statement in the Visual Studio code editor:

```
if (IsPostBack) {
```

Select Debug ➤ Toggle Breakpoint to add a breakpoint to the selected statement. Visual Studio indicates a breakpoint by coloring the text red and adding a red circle in the margin alongside the statement, as shown in Figure 7- 18.

```
            total = (float)Session["runningTotal"];
    }

    if (IsPostBack) {
            // this is a form post - get the value from the HTML control
            string data = numericValue.Value;
            // try to parse the data toa numeric value
            if (data != null) {
                    float incrementalValue = 0;
```

Figure 7-18. *Adding a breakpoint*

This breakpoint will stop execution every time that it is encountered. To make the breakpoint more specific, right-click the red circle in the margin and select Condition from the pop-up menu. This will open the Breakpoint Condition window, as shown in Figure 7-19.

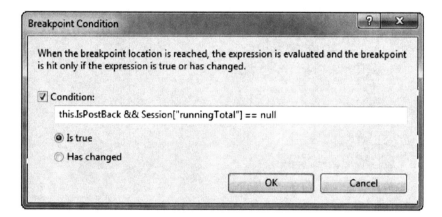

Figure 7-19. *Setting the condition for a breakpoint*

Conditions are stated as C# expressions. The condition is evaluated each time that the breakpoint is encountered, and execution will break if the condition evaluates to true.

It is up to the programmer to make sure that the expression will evaluate as intended. To help reduce the chances of a typo, Visual Studio will provide autocomplete assistance as you type.

There is a lot of flexibility in the range of conditions that can be handled. In our example, we want our breakpoint to work when we are processing a POST request and there is no session state data, so the condition is as follows:

```
this.IsPostBack && Session["runningTotal"] == null
```

The condition that you enter will vary based on the location of the breakpoint. For example, if we added a breakpoint inside the code block that follows the if statement we selected, we would need to test for the availability of the session state data, because the breakpoint would be reached only if the IsPostBack property returned true.

Setting a Programmatic Breakpoint

The .NET Framework class library includes support for creating breakpoints programmatically. Unlike the technique shown in the previous section, this approach works for all editions of Visual Studio.

I like the advanced debugging features that come with the premium editions of Visual Studio, but I tend to use programmatic breakpoints when working with ASP.NET. In part, this is because I like to switch between the lighter Express editions and the heavier (and sometimes slower) Ultimate edition, and programmatic breakpoints are handled consistently across both versions.

The ability to break the debugger comes with the System.Diagnostics.Debugger class, which includes the Break method. Wrap the call to the Break method in an if clause to make the break selective, as demonstrated by Listing 7-17 (with additions shown in bold).

Listing 7-17. A programmatic breakpoint

```
using System;
using System.Diagnostics;

namespace TraceDemo {

    public partial class Default : System.Web.UI.Page {

        protected void Page_Load(object sender, EventArgs e) {

            // define a variable for the running total
            float total = 0;

            // get the running total from the session if possible
            if (Session["runningTotal"] != null) {
                total = (float)Session["runningTotal"];
            }

            if (IsPostBack && Session["runningTotal"] == null) {
                Debugger.Break();
            }

            if (IsPostBack) {
                // this is a form post - get the value from the HTML control
                string data = numericValue.Value;
                // try to parse the data to a numeric value
                if (data != null) {
                    float incrementalValue = 0;
                    if (float.TryParse(data, out incrementalValue)) {
                        total += incrementalValue;
                    }
                }
            }

            // update the running total on the HTML control
            runningTotal.InnerText = string.Format("{0:F2}", total);
```

```
            // update the value stored in the session
            Session["runningTotals"] = total;
        }
    }
}
```

This is not as elegant as using a Visual Studio conditional breakpoint, because the code and the breakpoint are mixed together, but it gets the job done, and you can readily see the conditions under which the breakpoint will halt execution of the code.

Selecting the Start Page

Before we start debugging, we need to ensure that the correct page will be displayed when the debugger starts. You don't need to do this for projects where there is only one page, such as our example, but few web applications have only one page.

Select Project ➤ <ProjectName> Properties (where <ProjectName> is the name of your Visual Studio project). Click the Web tab in order to see the Start Action options available for your project, as shown in Figure 7-20.

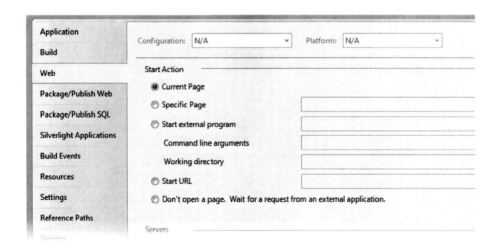

Figure 7-20. *The Start Action options for an ASP.NET project*

The default option is Current Page, which means that the page selected in the Solution Explorer window will be the one that is loaded initially. You can also select a specific page, or elect not to open a page—in which case, nothing will happen until you request a page using a web browser.

Running the Debugger

Once you have set your breakpoints and selected your start page, you can run the debugger. Select Debug ➤ Start Debugging. The simple application will be loaded into a browser. The breakpoint won't execute until we make a form post, so enter a value in the text box, and then click the Add button.

When the breakpoint is reached (and the condition satisfied if you are using the Visual Studio breakpoints), Visual Studio will open the code file for the page and display the breakpoint. Execution of the web application has been stopped and passed to your control. You can use the items in the Debug menu to step through the code, and use the Locals window to see how the state of your Page class changes as processing is performed.

Summary

Bugs will emerge in any application, and web applications are no exception. Fortunately, ASP.NET contains some mature and useful features that let you handle problems as they appear in production and track them down during testing.

In this chapter, we have explored the ASP.NET features for handling errors in web applications. These provide a flexible and multistage system with a good range of choices as to how different types of errors can be handled. ASP.NET errors are equated with C# exceptions, which are classified as hard failures, meaning that a readily detectable failure is apparent when the problem arises, and ASP.NET is unable to process a page request without using one of the error-handling features.

By contrast, a soft failure doesn't cause a C# exception. The page request is handled without error, but the web application doesn't behave in the desired way. You saw how to use the ASP.NET trace feature to instrument your code and gain insight into how it operates. We also briefly touched on using the Visual Studio debugger as an alternative to tracing.

Working with Data

Most web applications rely on a database of some sort. The .NET Framework has a range of different data-access technologies, many of which are part of ADO.NET—the family of .NET technologies that provide unified and consistent access to relational databases.

All of the data technologies can be used with ASP.NET. This chapter demonstrates the use of two of the most important and widely used: the Entity Framework and the Language Integrated Query (LINQ) feature. This combination allows you to work with data using regular C# classes and objects, freeing you from needing to include SQL statements in your code. But don't worry if you prefer some other combination of technologies. Although some of this chapter is specific to LINQ and the Entity Framework, the broader design and best practice principles apply to any data store.

In this chapter, we will create a data model from the sample database included with the download for this book and use it to create a web application that will let us list, create, update, and delete triathlon events. This is considered a CRUD (create, read, update, delete) application.

Creating the Data Model

The Entity Framework is an *object-relational mapping* (ORM) system that allows us to work with relational data using C# objects. What makes this possible is a *data model*, which uses C# classes to represent the tables and columns in the database.

Visual Studio contains a wizard that simplifies creating the data model and adding it to a project. We are going to build a model using the sample database included in the download that accompanies this book. This database is called TrainingData, and it is intended to track triathlon training data.

Follow these steps to create the data model:

1. Create a new Visual Studio project using the ASP.NET Empty Web Application template, as shown in Figure 8-1. Name this project DataApp.

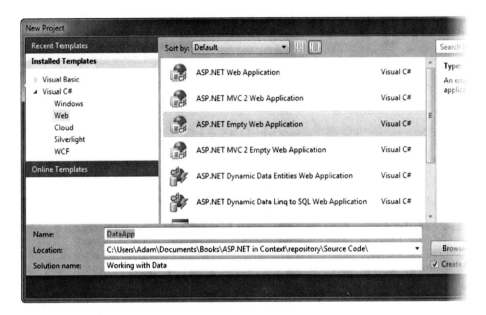

Figure 8-1. *Creating the DataApp project*

2. Select Project ➤ Add New Item from the menu, and then select the ADO.NET Entity Data Model template from the Data template category.

3. The convention is to give the entity data model a name that corresponds with the database we are modeling. Set the name to TrainingModel.edmx, as shown in Figure 8-2, and then click the Add button.

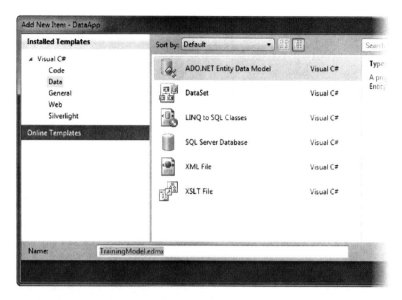

Figure 8-2. Adding the ADO.NET entity data model item

4.   The Entity Data Model Wizard starts. We are going to create a data model from an existing database, so select the Generate from database option, as shown in Figure 8-3. (The alternative is to create the model first and then use it to create the database.) Click Next to continue.

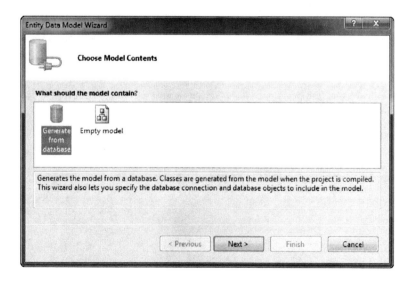

Figure 8-3. Selecting the source of the entity data model

5. On the next screen, we define the connection to the data, as shown by Figure 8-4. Click the New Connection button.

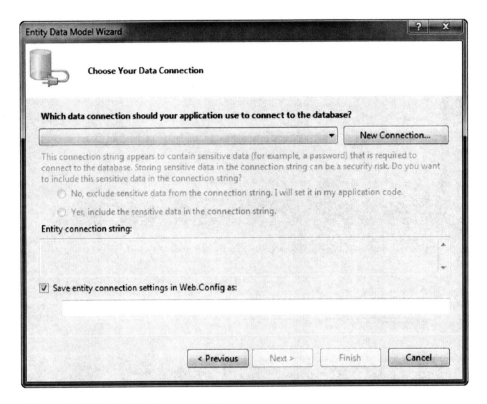

Figure 8-4. *Selecting the data connection*

6. The Connection Properties dialog appears. Visual Studio can make different kinds of database connections, including to existing databases running on database servers. We are going to use an approach that lets us specify a file containing the database, which Visual Studio will attach to the SQL Server instance we installed in Chapter 2. Click the Change button, and select the Microsoft SQL Server Database File option from the set data source options, as shown in Figure 8-5. Then click the OK button.

Figure 8-5. *The Connection Properties dialog*

7. Click the Browse button to select the database file. We want to use the
TrainingData.mdf file included in the download that accompanies this book.
Many of the projects in the chapters that follow require a data model, so you
will want the file to be somewhere easy to find. I created a directory called
C:\TrainingData and copied the TrainingData.mdf and TrainingData_log.mdf
files there. Click OK after selecting the file.

8. Now the wizard's Choose Your Data Connection window has been populated
with the details of our selected database connection, as shown in Figure 8-6.
The populated window includes the connection string that contains the
information that ADO.NET needs to connect to the database. We don't want to
need to include this string in our code when we use the entity data model, so
ensure that the checkbox is checked so that the connection string is stored in
the Web.config file, and then click the Next button.

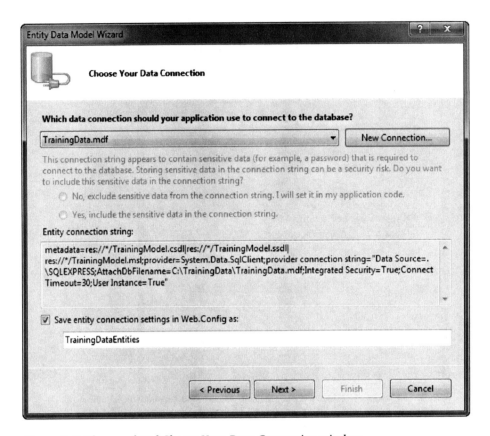

Figure 8-6. The populated Choose Your Data Connection window

9. You will see the dialog shown in Figure 8-7. At this point, you can choose to copy the database file into the project, so that the connection string will be updated automatically. I recommend leaving the database file outside the project, because this will make it easier to create the projects in the later chapters that rely on the same file. Click either the Yes or No button to dismiss the dialog.

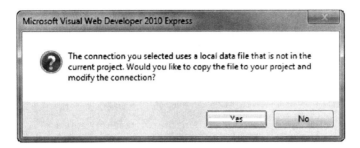

Figure 8-7. Choosing whether to copy the data file to the project

10. You are prompted to specify which parts of the database to include in the data model, as shown in Figure 8-8. The database we are using is pretty simple, but it contains additional tables and stored procedures that were created when I modeled the schema using the SQL Server Management Studio tool. These additions are harmless, but we don't need them included in the entity data model. Expand the Tables item and check the Athletes, Events, EventTypes, and ReferenceTimes tables. Then expand the Stored Procedures item and select the GetPersonalRanking and GetReferenceRanking stored procedures.

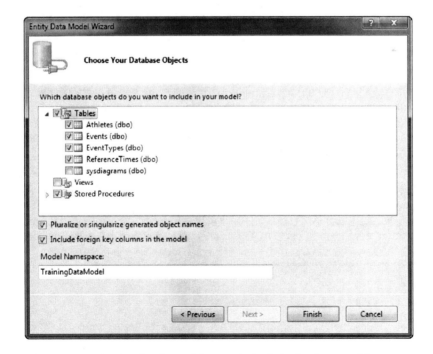

Figure 8-8. Selecting database objects to include in the data model

11. Ensure that the two checkboxes are checked. Checking the first item means that the classes that are created to model rows in tables are pluralized or singularized. For example, the class created to represent a row in the table `Athletes` will be called `Athlete`. This is a convenience feature that makes working with the objects in the entity data model feel more natural. The second checkbox enforces foreign key relationships between tables. There are several foreign key relationships in the `TrainingData` database.

12. The name of the namespace that is used to contain the classes that comprise the entity data model is generated automatically. You can change it if required, but in this chapter, we'll stick with the default value of `TrainingDataModel`. Once you have selected the tables and procedures, and checked the boxes, click the Finish button to create the data model.

It can take a while to create the model, but you'll see some changes to your project once the process has completed. There are some new references, which are required to support the Entity Framework, as well as two new project files:

- `TrainingModel.edmx`, which is the data model

- `TrainingModel.Designer.cs`, which contains the classes that have been created to model the tables and rows of the database

---

SELECTING A DATABASE SERVER FOR YOUR WEB APPLICATION

The most suitable database server for your ASP.NET web application is the one that you already understand.

The potential advantages offered by one database server over another are slim at best. And any advantages are usually outweighed by the series of complex and subtle performance issues and unexpected behaviors that emerge as your DBAs come up to speed on the inner workings of an entirely new product. Learning to build and tune a database takes time, so if you (or your team) have experience using one product family, you should stick with it, irrespective of whether it is SQL Server, Oracle, MySQL, or even something nonrelational.

If you are truly starting from scratch and have no prior experience to build on, I recommend that you consider how your web application will be hosted. Most hosting providers assume that ASP.NET web applications will require SQL Server, and offer attractive combined pricing. SQL Server isn't the most dynamic of products, but it is a good all-round database server. And, of course, it is thoroughly tested for interoperability with .NET.

Viewing the Entity Data Model

The `TrainingModel.edmx` file is opened automatically when the data model is created. It shows a visual representation of each of the classes that has been created. These are known as *entity classes*. Figure 8-9 shows the model for my project. Yours might look slightly different, depending on how Visual Studio has laid out the display.

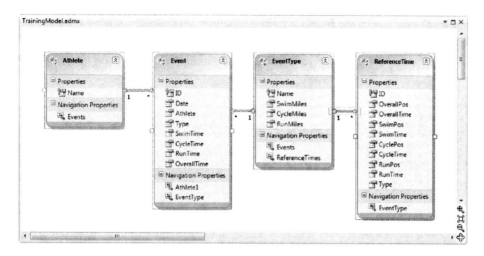

Figure 8-9. *A visual representation of the entity data model*

Each of the four items in Figure 8-9 represents an entity class, and objects created from these classes will be used to represent rows from their associated tables. The `TrainingData` database includes four tables (excluding the ones added by the modeling process):

- The `Athletes` table contains a list of names.

- The `EventTypes` table contains details of different kinds of triathlons.

- The `Events` table contains details of triathlons run by people named in the `Athletes` table.

- The `ReferenceTimes` table contains the results of races local to me for comparison purposes. It has one for each type of event listed in the `EventTypes` table.

You can see from Figure 8-9 that these tables have led to the entity classes `Athlete`, `Event`, `EventType`, and `ReferenceTime`.

Each of these classes has a set of properties that correspond to the columns of the table it represents. These properties are C# types. The mapping to and from SQL types is taken care of for us automatically. As an example, Table 8-1 shows the columns and types of the `Event` class, which represents a row in the `Events` table.

Table 8-1. *C# and SQL Types for the Event Class/Events Table*

Property/Column	C# Type	SQL Type
ID	int (System.Int32)	int
Date	System.DateTime	date
Athlete	string (System.String)	varchar(50)
Type	string (System.String)	varchar(50)
SwimTime	System.TimeSpan	time(0)
CycleTime	System.TimeSpan	time(0)
RunTime	System.TimeSpan	time(0)
OverallTime	System.TimeSpan	time(0)

When you create a new Event object or modify an existing one (which we'll do later in this chapter), you work with the C# types, such as string and TimeSpan, without needing to worry about the translation to and from the SQL types.

Importing the Stored Procedures

Even though we imported the stored procedures from the database into the entity model, we must take an extra step before they are available for use in our web application. We need to take this step so that the Entity Framework knows how to represent the result from the stored procedure. The purpose of the GetPersonalRanking procedure is to compare triathlon times with previous personal performance. The result is a two-column table that contains the range of triathlon activities (swim, run, cycle) and the ranking of each. We are going to create a new entity type that will represent the result of calling this stored procedure. We'll also create a new entity type for the GetReferenceRanking procedure.

Follow these steps to import the stored procedures:

1. Open the TrainingModel.edmx file so that the entity model diagram shown in
    Figure 8-9 is displayed. Open the Model Browser window using the View menu
    (this item may be under the Other Windows submenu, depending on the
    Visual Studio edition you are using). Expand the tree of items so that you can
    see that Stored Procedures list, as shown in Figure 8-10.

Figure 8-10. *The Model Browser window*

2. Right-click the procedure called GetPersonalRanking and select Add Function
    Import from the pop-up menu.

3. The Add Function Import dialog opens. Click Get Column Information. This
    will get the details of the stored procedure result and display them in the table
    at the bottom of the dialog box, as shown in Figure 8-11.

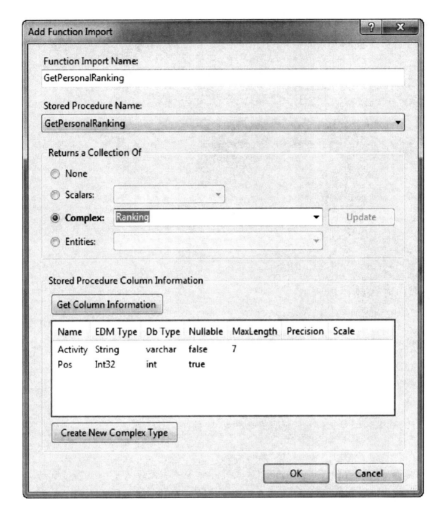

Figure 8-11. The Add Function Import dialog

4. Click the Create New Complex Type button. This will create a new entity type that will have properties for the Activity and Pos columns of the result.

5. Change the default name of the type in the Complex text box to Ranking. Then click OK to import the stored procedure and create the new entity type.

6. Right-click the GetReferenceRanking procedure in the Model Browser window and repeat steps 2 through 5, except this time, instead of clicking the Create New Complex Type button, select the Complex radio button and select Ranking from the drop-down list. In this way, we use the same entity type to represent the results from both stored procedures.

Now that we have created the data model, we can begin to use it in our web application.

Using the Data Model

The basic approach to using the entity data model is to create an instance of the *entity context* class and then use its properties to access the contents of the tables. In the tables, each row is represented by *entity objects,* which are instantiations of the *entity classes* that you saw modeled in Figure 8-9. We can use these objects and properties to query and manipulate the data in the database, as the following sections demonstrate.

Querying the Data Model

Listing 8-1 shows the contents of a web page to add to our project using the name ListEvents.aspx.

Listing 8-1. A simple web page

```
<%@ Page Language="C#" AutoEventWireup="true" CodeBehind="ListEvents.aspx.cs"↵
 Inherits="DataApp.ListEvents" %>

<!DOCTYPE html PUBLIC "-//W3C//DTD XHTML 1.0 Transitional//EN"↵
 "http://www.w3.org/TR/xhtml1/DTD/xhtml1-transitional.dtd">

<html xmlns="http://www.w3.org/1999/xhtml">
<head runat="server">
    <title>Event List</title>
</head>
<body>
    <form id="form1" runat="server">

        <table id="resultsTable" runat="server" rules="cols">
            <tr>
                <th>Date</th>
                <th>Athlete</th>
                <th>Event Type</th>
                <th>Swim</th>
                <th>Cycle</th>
                <th>Run</th>
                <th>Overall</th>
            </tr>
        </table>

    </form>
</body>
</html>
```

This page contains a simple table with columns to match each of the properties in the Event entity class. The associated code-behind file, ListEvents.aspx.cs, is shown in Listing 8-2.

Listing 8-2. *The ListEvents.aspx.cs file*

```csharp
using System;
using System.Web.UI.HtmlControls;

namespace DataApp {

    public partial class ListEvents : System.Web.UI.Page {

        protected void Page_Load(object sender, EventArgs e) {

            // create the entity data model context object
            using (TrainingDataEntities context = new TrainingDataEntities()) {

                // enumerate the objects in the context.Events property - these
                // correspond to the rows in the Events table in the database
                foreach (Event ev in context.Events) {
                    // process the entity object
                    ProcessEvent(ev);
                }
            }
        }

        private void ProcessEvent(Event eventParam) {

            // create a new table row
            HtmlTableRow row = new HtmlTableRow();

            row.Cells.Add(CreateTableCell(eventParam.Date.ToString("MM/dd")));
            row.Cells.Add(CreateTableCell(eventParam.Athlete));
            row.Cells.Add(CreateTableCell(eventParam.Type));
            row.Cells.Add(CreateTableCell(eventParam.SwimTime.ToString()));
            row.Cells.Add(CreateTableCell(eventParam.CycleTime.ToString()));
            row.Cells.Add(CreateTableCell(eventParam.RunTime.ToString()));
            row.Cells.Add(CreateTableCell(eventParam.OverallTime.ToString()));

            // add the row to the table
            resultsTable.Rows.Add(row);
        }

        private HtmlTableCell CreateTableCell(string textParam) {
            return new HtmlTableCell() { InnerText = textParam };
        }
    }
}
```

In the Page_Load method, we create a new instance of the entity context class. The name of the class is set to be the name of the database with Entities appended. For our example, since the database is called TrainingData, the context class is called TrainingDataEntities. We create this instance using the default constructor, like this:

```csharp
TrainingDataEntities context = new TrainingDataEntities();
```

This object is our entry point into the entity data model and the database that it represents. Almost everything is taken care of automatically. We don't need to manage connections to the database server, convert data types, or even issue queries to load data.

THE LIFE CYCLE OF THE ENTITY CONTEXT OBJECT

In Listing 8-2, we create the context object inside a `using` code block. This means that the object will be disposed of as soon as it is out of scope. A context object ties up resources in memory and in the database server. To ensure that your web application can scale properly, it is important to explicitly dispose of the context object when you have finished with it. A `using` block is the simplest and most reliable way:

```
using (TrainingDataEntities context = new TrainingDataEntities()) {
    ... use data model
}
```

However, don't be tempted to create a single context object and share it between requests. This causes problems when modifications to the database cause errors.

An entity context has properties that represent each table in the database. In the case of the `TrainingDataEntities`, these properties are called `Athletes`, `EventTypes`, `Events`, and `ReferenceTimes`. Each of these properties returns a collection of entity objects that represent the rows in the appropriate table. For example, the `Events` property returns a collection of `Event` objects, each of which represents one row from the `Events` table. You don't need to explicitly load the data to access the rows; you just use the collection as you would any other collection. In Listing 8-2, we enumerated all of the `Event` objects using a foreach loop, as follows:

```
foreach (Event ev in context.Events) {
    ProcessEvent(ev);
}
```

I have split out the code that processes each `Event` object to emphasize the way that these objects are accessed through the context object. Each entity class defines properties that correspond to the columns of the table to which it belongs. We read these properties in the `ProcessEvent` method in order to add a row to the HTML table defined in the `ListingEvents.aspx` page:

```
private void ProcessEvent(Event eventParam) {

    // create a new table row
    HtmlTableRow row = new HtmlTableRow();

    row.Cells.Add(CreateTableCell(eventParam.Date.ToString("MM/dd")));
    row.Cells.Add(CreateTableCell(eventParam.Athlete));
    row.Cells.Add(CreateTableCell(eventParam.Type));
    row.Cells.Add(CreateTableCell(eventParam.SwimTime.ToString()));
    row.Cells.Add(CreateTableCell(eventParam.CycleTime.ToString()));
    row.Cells.Add(CreateTableCell(eventParam.RunTime.ToString()));
    row.Cells.Add(CreateTableCell(eventParam.OverallTime.ToString()));
```

```
    // add the row to the table
    resultsTable.Rows.Add(row);
}
```

These properties return C# types, as described in Table 8-1. We read the value of each property and use these values to create `HtmlTableCell` objects; `HtmlTableCell` is the ASP.NET HTML control that represents the HTML `td` element. These are then added to an `HtmlTableRow`, which is the control that represents the `tr` element. Viewing the `ListEvents.aspx` page produces a simple table containing all of the data in the `Events` table, as shown in Figure 8-12.

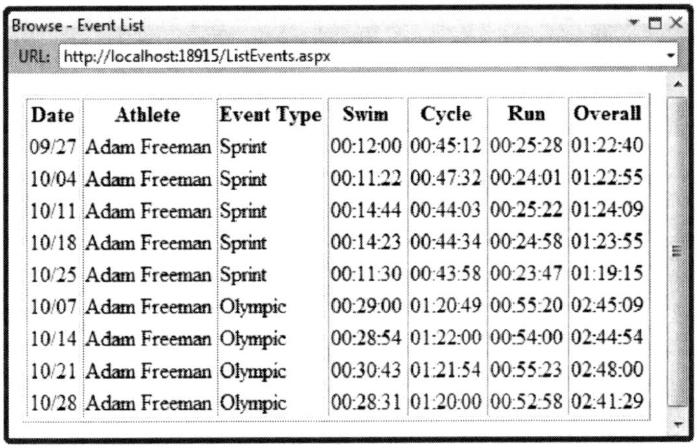

Date	Athlete	Event Type	Swim	Cycle	Run	Overall
09/27	Adam Freeman	Sprint	00:12:00	00:45:12	00:25:28	01:22:40
10/04	Adam Freeman	Sprint	00:11:22	00:47:32	00:24:01	01:22:55
10/11	Adam Freeman	Sprint	00:14:44	00:44:03	00:25:22	01:24:09
10/18	Adam Freeman	Sprint	00:14:23	00:44:34	00:24:58	01:23:55
10/25	Adam Freeman	Sprint	00:11:30	00:43:58	00:23:47	01:19:15
10/07	Adam Freeman	Olympic	00:29:00	01:20:49	00:55:20	02:45:09
10/14	Adam Freeman	Olympic	00:28:54	01:22:00	00:54:00	02:44:54
10/21	Adam Freeman	Olympic	00:30:43	01:21:54	00:55:23	02:48:00
10/28	Adam Freeman	Olympic	00:28:31	01:20:00	00:52:58	02:41:29

Figure 8-12. Displaying entity data in a page

Using LINQ to Query the Data Model

In the previous example, we displayed all of the data contained in the `Events` table by enumerating all of the `Event` objects available through the `Events` property of the context object. To filter data, we could inspect each of the `Event` objects and discard the ones that don't meet our criteria. But a more elegant solution is to use LINQ. To be more specific, we should use LINQ to Entities, which is the dialect of LINQ that operates on entity data models. A LINQ to Entities query is translated into a SQL query that retrieves only the data that matches the `where` clause you specify. This avoids the situation where you retrieve data only to discard it in your application, something that becomes particularly troublesome when you work with tables that contain a lot of rows.

Listing 8-3 demonstrates some additions to the `ListEvents.aspx` page file (shown in bold) that provide the user input we will use to filter data.

Listing 8-3. Adding a select control to the page

```
<%@ Page Language="C#" AutoEventWireup="true" CodeBehind="ListEvents.aspx.cs"↵
 Inherits="DataApp.ListEvents" %>
```

```
<!DOCTYPE html PUBLIC "-//W3C//DTD XHTML 1.0 Transitional//EN"↩
 "http://www.w3.org/TR/xhtml1/DTD/xhtml1-transitional.dtd">

<html xmlns="http://www.w3.org/1999/xhtml">
<head runat="server">
    <title>Event List</title>
    <style type="text/css">
        *.standardDiv {float:left; padding:10px}
        select {width:120px}
        label {vertical-align:top}
    </style>
</head>
<body>
    <form id="form1" runat="server">

        <table id="resultsTable" runat="server" rules="cols">
            <tr>
                <th>Date</th>
                <th>Athlete</th>
                <th>Event Type</th>
                <th>Swim</th>
                <th>Cycle</th>
                <th>Run</th>
                <th>Overall</th>
            </tr>
        </table>

        <div class="standardDiv">
            <label>Event Type:</label>
            <select id="eventSelector" runat="server">
                <option>All</option>
            </select>
        </div>

        <div class="standardDiv">
            <input type="submit" value="Submit" />
        </div>
    </form>
</body>
</html>
```

We add a `select` control (with an option of `All`), a form button labeled Submit, and some structure elements and CSS to create a simple layout. The corresponding code changes, applied to the `ListEvents.aspx.cs` file, are shown in Listing 8-4.

155

Listing 8-4. *Filtering entity data using LINQ*

```
using System;
using System.Collections.Generic;
using System.Linq;
using System.Web.UI.HtmlControls;

namespace DataApp {

    public partial class ListEvents : System.Web.UI.Page {

        protected void Page_Load(object sender, EventArgs e) {

            // create the entity data model context object
            using (TrainingDataEntities context = new TrainingDataEntities()) {

                // populate the select control if needed
                if (ViewState["setupComplete"] == null) {
                    foreach (string name in context.EventTypes.Select(item => item.Name)) {
                        eventSelector.Items.Add(name);
                    }
                    ViewState["setupComplete"] = true;
                }

                // define the collection of events that we will process
                IEnumerable<Event> eventsToProcess;

                if (IsPostBack && eventSelector.Value != "All") {

                    // perform a LINQ query to filter the data
                    eventsToProcess = from item in context.Events
                                      where item.Type == eventSelector.Value
                                      select item;
                } else {
                    // this is either the initial get request or the user has performed
                    // a POST with the ALL filter set - either way, we want to list all
                    // of the data items, with no filtering
                    eventsToProcess = context.Events;
                }

                // process the selected events
                foreach (Event ev in eventsToProcess) {
                    // process the entity object
                    ProcessEvent(ev);
                }
            }
        }
    }
}
```

```
        private void ProcessEvent(Event eventParam) {

            // create a new table row
            HtmlTableRow row = new HtmlTableRow();

            row.Cells.Add(CreateTableCell(eventParam.Date.ToString("MM/dd")));
            row.Cells.Add(CreateTableCell(eventParam.Athlete));
            row.Cells.Add(CreateTableCell(eventParam.Type));
            row.Cells.Add(CreateTableCell(eventParam.SwimTime.ToString()));
            row.Cells.Add(CreateTableCell(eventParam.CycleTime.ToString()));
            row.Cells.Add(CreateTableCell(eventParam.RunTime.ToString()));
            row.Cells.Add(CreateTableCell(eventParam.OverallTime.ToString()));

            // add the row to the table
            resultsTable.Rows.Add(row);
        }

        private HtmlTableCell CreateTableCell(string textParam) {
            return new HtmlTableCell() { InnerText = textParam };
        }
    }
}
```

There are two LINQ queries in this modified code-behind class. Here's the first one (shown in bold):

```
if (ViewState["setupComplete"] == null) {
    foreach (string name in context.EventTypes.Select(item => item.Name)) {
        eventSelector.Items.Add(name);
    }
    ViewState["setupComplete"] = true;
}
```

This query simply selects the value of the Name property of each object returned by the EventTypes property of the context object. We use the results of the LINQ query to populate the contents of the HTML select element in the page the first time that the page is loaded, and use the view state feature to ensure that this happens only when needed (see Chapter 6 for details on the view state). This LINQ query is expressed using *method syntax*, where the LINQ extension methods are called directly.

The second LINQ query filters the Event objects when the user has selected a value other than All in the drop-down list, as follows:

```
eventsToProcess = from item in context.Events
    where item.Type == eventSelector.Value
    select item;
```

This second query uses *query syntax*, meaning that it relies on the C# keyword that supports LINQ queries, such as from, in, where, or select.

Both method and query syntax queries are fully supported in LINQ to Entities, and you can use the technique that is most comfortable for you. In real projects, I tend to use query syntax for simple queries and switch to method syntax when things are more complicated. But there is really no advantage in using one syntax over the other.

Now view the page, select either Sprint or Olympic from the drop-down list, and then click the Submit button. You can see the effect of filtering the data, as shown in Figure 8-13.

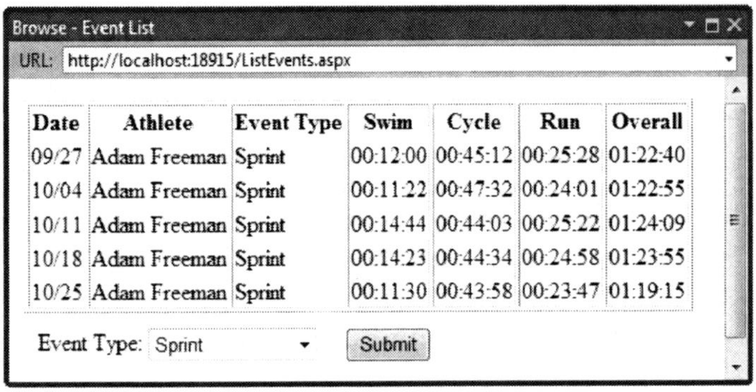

Figure 8-13. *Filtering entity data using LINQ*

Calling Stored Procedures

The stored procedures that we added to the model and then explicitly imported are presented as methods of the context object. The parameters of the method correspond to the parameters of the stored procedure. As an example, Listing 8-5 shows the SQL definition of the GetPersonalRanking stored procedure.

Listing 8-5. *The GetPersonalRanking stored procedure*

```
CREATE PROCEDURE [dbo].[GetPersonalRanking]
        @AthleteName varchar(50),
        @EventType varchar(50),
        @SwimTime time(0),
        @CycleTime time(0),
        @RunTime time(0),
        @OverallTime time(0)
AS
BEGIN

select 'Swim' as Activity, COUNT(*) as Pos from Events where type= @EventType AND athlete=↵
  @AthleteName AND SwimTime <= @SwimTime
UNION
select 'Cycle' as Activity, COUNT(*) as Pos from Events where type= @EventType AND athlete=↵
  @AthleteName AND CycleTime <= @CycleTime
UNION
select 'Run' as Activity, COUNT(*) as Pos from Events where type= @EventType AND athlete=↵
  @AthleteName AND RunTime <= @RunTime
UNION
```

```
SELECT 'Overall' as Activity, COUNT(*) as Pos from Events where type = @EventType AND↵
 athlete = @AthleteName AND OverallTime <= @OverallTime
UNION
select 'Count' as Activity, COUNT(*) as Pos from Events where type= @EventType AND athlete=↵
 @AthleteName

END
```

This procedure has six parameters, which represent a single event performed by a single athlete. The parameters specify the name of the athlete, the type of event, the time taken to perform each stage of the triathlon, and the overall time. These parameters are used as the basis for a series of SELECT statements, which determine how the event performance compares to previous recorded events.

The results are combined using UNION statements to produce a table containing rows that rank stage and overall times, as well as report the number of recorded events, as shown in Table 8-2.

Table 8-2. *Stored Procedure Results*

Activity	Pos
Swim	2
Cycle	7
Run	4
Overall	3
Count	18

The stored procedure is represented in the entity data model as a method called GetPersonalRanking. The types of the parameters are translated from the SQL types into C# types. Invoking the procedure is just like calling any other method:

```
IEnumerable<Ranking> ranks = context.GetPersonalRanking("Adam Freeman", "Sprint", SwimTime,
    CycleTime, RunTime, OverallTime);
```

The result type for the GetPersonalRanking method is IEnumerable<Ranking>. Remember that Ranking is the complex type we defined when we imported the stored procedure earlier. The IEnumerable<Ranking> result contains one Ranking for each row of the result table. Since there are five SELECT queries in the stored procedure, we can expect five Ranking instances in the IEnumerable. Like the other entity classes you have seen, Ranking has properties that represent the columns of the table, so there are Activity and Pos properties.

The results of this stored procedure are a little awkward to deal with, as shown in Table 8-2. If you are working on a new project, you can design the database so that it is closely tailored to your application needs. You can make sure that every result is perfectly suited to something you need to know, and presented in a way that's easy to deal with. However, as your project matures and new versions are released, you reach a point where the database isn't such a good fit, but the cost and risk of changing the database are prohibitive. If you have a database that is shared between projects, the risk and complexity presented by schema changes are much higher. And if you are working with databases that are core corporate functions, such as billing or human resource department records, then the obstacles to making changes are often insurmountable.

So, there will come a point in your web application project where you don't have such a good fit between the queries that you want to make and the stored procedures that are available. You must deal with results that are not quite what you want—much like the results shown in Table 8-2. In the next section, we will extend our example web application to include ranking information, but we are going to use only the Overall result. You'll learn two simple techniques to get that data out of the results returned by the stored procedures in the TrainingData database.

Using LINQ to Filter Stored Procedure Results

The first technique is to use LINQ to find the row that has an Activity value of Overall, which we can do like this:

```
int personalRank = context.GetPersonalRanking(ev.Athlete, ev.Type, ev.SwimTime,
                        ev.CycleTime, ev.RunTime, ev.OverallTime)
        .Where(item => item.Activity == "Overall")
        .Select(item => item).First().Pos ?? -1;
```

In this query, we are doing the following:

- Using an Event entity object to set the parameters for calling the stored procedure

- Filtering the set of Ranking objects to find the Overall ranking

- Calling the First extension method (because we know that there will be only one matching result)

- Reading the Pos parameter to get the ranking we want.

The Pos column is expressed as nullable int values, which means that the value will be null if there is no match for the SELECT statements in the stored procedure. So, the last step is to use the null coalescing operator to get a default value of -1 if the Pos parameter is null.

The second approach is to transform the result objects into a new data type that has fields for each of the different elements in the stored procedure result. Listing 8-6 provides an example of such a type, called RankingSet, which enumerates through the Ranking entity objects returned from the stored procedures and sets the values of public fields.

Listing 8-6. *The RankingSet class*

```
using System.Collections.Generic;

namespace DataApp {

    public class RankingSet {
        public int SwimRank = -1;
        public int CycleRank = -1;
        public int RunRank= -1;
        public int OverallRank = -1;
        public int RankCount = -1;

        public RankingSet(IEnumerable<Ranking> sourceParam) {
```

```
        foreach (Ranking rank in sourceParam) {
            switch (rank.Activity) {
                case "Swim":
                    SwimRank = rank.Pos ?? -1;
                    break;
                case "Cycle":
                    CycleRank = rank.Pos ?? -1;
                    break;
                case "Run":
                    RunRank = rank.Pos ?? -1;
                    break;
                case "Overall":
                    OverallRank = rank.Pos ?? -1;
                    break;
                case "Count":
                    RankCount = rank.Pos ?? -1;
                    break;
            }
        }
    }
}
}
```

I tend to prefer this approach, mainly because I find it creates a more easily understood set of code statements.

Using Stored Procedures in a Project

To demonstrate the use of stored procedures, we will add two columns to the table in the page in the example application, and use them to display the Overall personal and reference rankings. Listing 8-7 shows the additions to the ListEvents.aspx file.

Listing 8-7. Adding columns to the ListEvents page

```
...
<table id="resultsTable" runat="server" rules="cols">
    <tr>
        <th>Date</th>
        <th>Athlete</th>
        <th>Event Type</th>
        <th>Swim</th>
        <th>Cycle</th>
        <th>Run</th>
        <th>Overall</th>
        <th>Rank</th>
        <th>Ref Rank</th>
    </tr>
</table>
...
```

Listing 8-8 shows the changes to the code-behind class to support these two new columns, using the RankingSet class shown in Listing 8-6 (with the key changes in bold).

Listing 8-8. Modifying the ListEvents.aspx.cs file

```
using System;
using System.Collections.Generic;
using System.Linq;
using System.Web.UI.HtmlControls;

namespace DataApp {

    public partial class ListEvents : System.Web.UI.Page {

        protected void Page_Load(object sender, EventArgs e) {

            // create the entity data model context object
            using (TrainingDataEntities context = new TrainingDataEntities()) {

                // populate the select control if needed
                if (ViewState["setupComplete"] == null) {
                    foreach (string name in context.EventTypes.Select(item => item.Name)) {
                        eventSelector.Items.Add(name);
                    }
                    ViewState["setupComplete"] = true;
                }

                // define the collection of events that we will process
                IEnumerable<Event> eventsToProcess;

                if (IsPostBack && eventSelector.Value != "All") {

                    // perform a LINQ query to filter the data
                    eventsToProcess = from item in context.Events
                                      where item.Type == eventSelector.Value
                                      select item;
                } else {
                    // this is either the initial get request or the user has performed
                    // a POST with the ALL filter set - either way, we want to list all
                    // of the data items, with no filtering
                    eventsToProcess = context.Events;
                }

                // process the selected events
                foreach (Event ev in eventsToProcess) {
```

```
                    // get the personal ranking information
                    int personalRank = new RankingSet(
                        context.GetPersonalRanking(ev.Athlete,
                        ev.Type, ev.SwimTime, ev.CycleTime,
                        ev.RunTime, ev.OverallTime)).OverallRank;

                    // get the reference rank information
                    int referenceRank = new RankingSet(
                        context.GetReferenceRanking(ev.Type,
                        ev.SwimTime, ev.CycleTime, ev.RunTime,
                        ev.OverallTime)).OverallRank;

                    // process the entity object
                    ProcessEvent(ev, personalRank, referenceRank);
                }
            }
        }

        private void ProcessEvent(Event eventParam, int personalRankParam,
            int referenceRankParam) {

            // create a new table row
            HtmlTableRow row = new HtmlTableRow();

            row.Cells.Add(CreateTableCell(eventParam.Date.ToString("MM/dd")));
            row.Cells.Add(CreateTableCell(eventParam.Athlete));
            row.Cells.Add(CreateTableCell(eventParam.Type));
            row.Cells.Add(CreateTableCell(eventParam.SwimTime.ToString()));
            row.Cells.Add(CreateTableCell(eventParam.CycleTime.ToString()));
            row.Cells.Add(CreateTableCell(eventParam.RunTime.ToString()));
            row.Cells.Add(CreateTableCell(eventParam.OverallTime.ToString()));

            // add the ranking information
            row.Cells.Add(CreateTableCell(personalRankParam.ToString()));
            row.Cells.Add(CreateTableCell(referenceRankParam.ToString()));

            // add the row to the table
            resultsTable.Rows.Add(row);
        }

        private HtmlTableCell CreateTableCell(string textParam) {
            return new HtmlTableCell() { InnerText = textParam };
        }
    }
}
```

We call the stored procedures, just as we would any other C# method, and the results to create additional table cells to display the ranking information. You can see the effects when you display the ListEvent.aspx page, as shown in Figure 8-14.

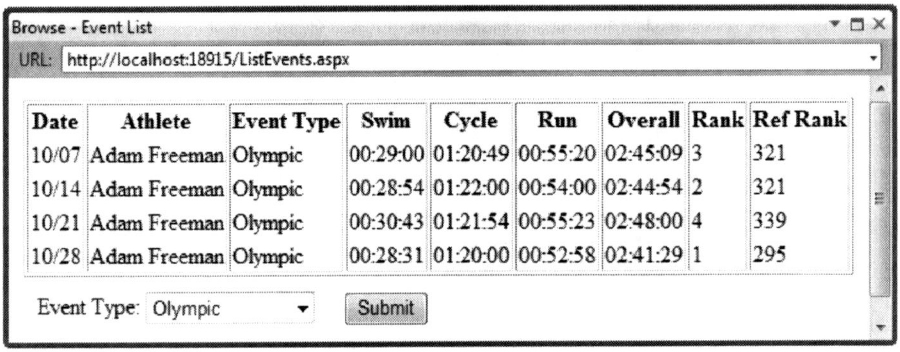

Figure 8-14. *Using stored procedures to add ranking information*

Consolidating the Data-Access Code

Most ASP.NET projects have more than one page that needs to use the data model. A common approach to avoiding duplicating the same code is to consolidate the code that deals with the data model into one or more common classes, which are then used by all of the page classes. We will follow this approach before extending the example web application to create, modify, and delete data. Listing 8-9 shows this class, called DataAccess, which contains methods that perform the functionality from the examples so far.

Listing 8-9. *The DataAccess class*

```
using System.Collections.Generic;
using System.Linq;
using System;

namespace DataApp {

    public static class DataAccess {

        ///////////////////////////////////
        // EventType related methods //
        ///////////////////////////////////

        public static string[] GetEventTypeNames(TrainingDataEntities contextParam) {
            return contextParam.EventTypes.Select(e => e.Name).ToArray();
        }

        ///////////////////////////////////
        // Athlete related methods //
        ///////////////////////////////////
```

```csharp
        public static string[] GetAthleteNames(TrainingDataEntities contextParam) {
            return contextParam.Athletes.Select(e => e.Name).ToArray();
        }

        //////////////////////////////
        // Ranking related methods //
        //////////////////////////////

        public static RankingSet GetReferenceRanking(TrainingDataEntities contextParam,
            Event eventParam) {

            return new RankingSet(contextParam.GetReferenceRanking(eventParam.Type,
                eventParam.SwimTime, eventParam.CycleTime,
                eventParam.RunTime, eventParam.OverallTime));
        }

        public static RankingSet GetPersonalRanking(TrainingDataEntities contextParam,
            Event eventParam) {

            return new RankingSet(contextParam.GetPersonalRanking(eventParam.Athlete,
                eventParam.Type, eventParam.SwimTime, eventParam.CycleTime,
                eventParam.RunTime, eventParam.OverallTime));
        }

        //////////////////////////////
        // Event related methods //
        //////////////////////////////

        public static IEnumerable<Event> GetAllEvents(TrainingDataEntities contextParam) {
            return contextParam.Events;
        }

        public static IEnumerable<Event> GetEventsByType(TrainingDataEntities contextParam,
            string typeParam) {

            return contextParam.Events.Where(e => e.Type == typeParam).Select(e => e);
        }
    }
}
```

The most important aspect of the DataAccess class is that the first parameter of each method is a context object—an instance of the TrainingDataEntities class. When consolidating access to the entity data model, it can be tempting to try to create a single instance of the context object and share it between requests.

The context object has been designed to be instantiated and disposed of often, so that features such as connection pooling are used, even though you do not explicitly control connections when you create the context. Therefore, the best way to consolidate data-access code is rely on a context object that is created by the page code-behind class and ensure that this object is disposed of before the page method exits. Listing 8-10 shows the Page_Load method from the ListEvents.aspx.cs file after it has been updated to use the methods in the DataAccess class.

Listing 8-10. *Updating the ListEvents.aspx.cs code-behind class*

```
...
protected void Page_Load(object sender, EventArgs e) {

    // create the entity data model context object
    using (TrainingDataEntities context = new TrainingDataEntities()) {

        // populate the select control if needed
        if (ViewState["setupComplete"] == null) {
            foreach (string name in DataAccess.GetEventTypeNames(context)) {
                eventSelector.Items.Add(name);
            }
            ViewState["setupComplete"] = true;
        }

        // define the collection of events that we will process
        IEnumerable<Event> eventsToProcess;

        if (IsPostBack && eventSelector.Value != "All") {

            // get the events filtered by event type
            eventsToProcess = DataAccess.GetEventsByType(context, eventSelector.Value);

        } else {
            // get all of the events
            eventsToProcess = DataAccess.GetAllEvents(context);
        }

        // process the selected events
        foreach (Event ev in eventsToProcess) {

            // get the personal ranking information
            int personalRank  = DataAccess.GetPersonalRanking(context, ev).OverallRank;

            // get the reference rank information
            int referenceRank = DataAccess.GetReferenceRanking(context, ev).OverallRank;

            // process the entity object
            ProcessEvent(ev, personalRank, referenceRank);
        }
    }
}
...
```

There is no change to the functionality in Listing 8-9. It just has the switch to the consolidated data-access code. In the sections that follow, we'll build up that class to add other data operations.

Performing Other Data Operations

Now that we have consolidated the code that accesses the data model, we can add pages to our web application to handle other data operations. In the following sections, you will learn how to create, modify, and delete data from the database using the Entity Framework.

Adding Data

Adding new data using the entity data model is a four-step process:

- Create a new instance of the entity class that represents rows of the table of interest.

- Set values for the parameters of the entity object we created.

- Add the object to the collection of similar objects maintained by the entity context.

- Call the SaveChanges method to write the change to the database.

Because we have consolidated our data-access code, these four steps will be split between the page code-behind class and our consolidated DataAccess class. Listing 8-11 shows the method to add to DataAccess.

Listing 8-11. Handling adding data in the DataAccess class

```
...
public static void AddEvent(TrainingDataEntities contextParam,
    DateTime timeParam, string athleteParam, string typeParam,
    TimeSpan swimTimeParam, TimeSpan cycleTimeParam, TimeSpan runTimeParam) {

        // create the new entity object
        Event newEvent = new Event() {
            // set the date value in the event object
            Date = timeParam,
            // set the athlete and event type
            Athlete = athleteParam,
            Type = typeParam,
            // set the times
            SwimTime = swimTimeParam,
            CycleTime = cycleTimeParam,
            RunTime = runTimeParam,
            // calculate and set the overall time
            OverallTime = swimTimeParam + cycleTimeParam + runTimeParam
        };
```

```
    // add the Event object to the Events collection
    contextParam.Events.AddObject(newEvent);
    // save the change to the database
    contextParam.SaveChanges();
}
...
```

The AddEvent method demonstrates all four steps of the creating process. The Event object is created and the parameter values set in a single step. The values are set from the method parameters.

The Event object is added to the entity data model using the AddObject method of the Events property of the context object. Each of the context object properties that represents a database table has an AddObject method that takes an instance of the appropriate entity class as a parameter.

The changes are not applied to the database until the SaveChanges method of the context object is called. A single call to SaveChanges updates any pending changes that you have made to the entity data model, so you can batch up your database operations if preferred.

■ **Tip**   Notice that we did not provide a value for the primary key column, ID, in Listing 8-11. We configured this column as an identity key, meaning that SQL Server will generate the key automatically when we don't provide a value. If can be very hard to produce unique primary keys when there are multiple requests being processed simultaneously. The identity key feature removes this difficulty.

To make use of this new method, we can add another web page, called AddEvent.aspx, to the example project. I won't waste space showing the page markup, because the layout is pretty simple (check the download that accompanies this book for the details), as shown in Figure 8-15.

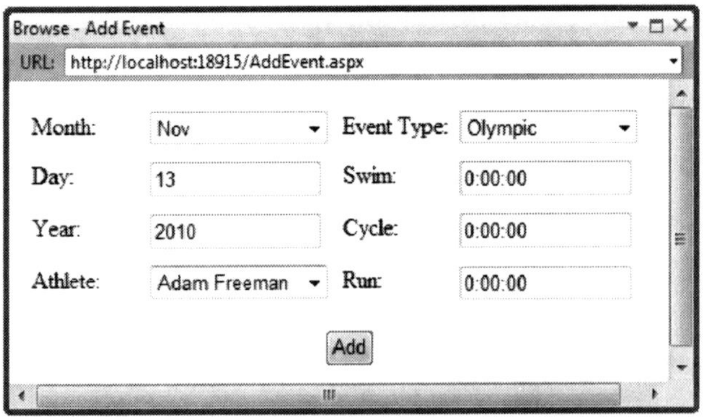

Figure 8-15. The AddEvent.aspx page

The users provide details of the event they want to add to the database by picking from the drop-down lists of HTML select elements and entering values in the input elements. Some of the default values are set by the code-behind class, which is shown in Listing 8-12.

Listing 8-12. *The AddEvent.aspx.cs code-behind file*

```
using System;
using System.Globalization;

namespace DataApp {

    public partial class AddEvent : System.Web.UI.Page {

        protected void Page_Load(object sender, EventArgs e) {

            using (TrainingDataEntities context = new TrainingDataEntities()) {

                // do the setup - placed in a separate method for clarity
                if (ViewState["setupComplete"] == null) {
                    PerformPageSetup(context);
                    ViewState["setupComplete"] = true;
                }

                if (IsPostBack) {
                    try {

                        // get the elements of the date
                        int day = int.Parse(dayText.Value);
                        int month = monthSelect.SelectedIndex + 1;
                        int year = int.Parse(yearText.Value);

                        // add a new event to the database
                        DataAccess.AddEvent(context,
                            new DateTime(year, month, day),
                            athleteSelect.Value,
                            eventTypeSelect.Value,
                            TimeSpan.Parse(swimText.Value),
                            TimeSpan.Parse(cycleText.Value),
                            TimeSpan.Parse(runText.Value)
                            );

                        // transfer the user to the list page
                        Response.Redirect("ListEvents.aspx");

                    } catch (FormatException) {
                        // set the error text
                        errorDiv.InnerText = "Cannot parse inputs";
                    }
                }
            }
        }
    }
}
```

```csharp
private void PerformPageSetup(TrainingDataEntities context) {

    // get the current culture info
    DateTimeFormatInfo formatInfo = CultureInfo.CurrentCulture.DateTimeFormat;

    // populate the month select element
    monthSelect.Items.Clear();
    for (int i = 1; i < 13; i++) {
        monthSelect.Items.Add(formatInfo.GetAbbreviatedMonthName(i));
    }

    // get the current date and use it to select a month and set the day and year
    DateTime now = DateTime.Now;
    monthSelect.SelectedIndex = now.Month - 1;
    dayText.Value = now.Day.ToString();
    yearText.Value = now.Year.ToString();

    // populate the athlete names
    athleteSelect.Items.Clear();
    foreach (string name in DataAccess.GetAthleteNames(context)) {
        athleteSelect.Items.Add(name);
    }

    // populate the event types
    eventTypeSelect.Items.Clear();
    foreach (string name in DataAccess.GetEventTypeNames(context)) {
        eventTypeSelect.Items.Add(name);
    }
}
}
}
```

The PerformPageSetup method in Listing 8-12 provides the content and the select elements, as well as the default values for the input elements in the page. This method is called only if the view state for the page doesn't contain a specific key (see Chapter 6 for more information about using view state).

We are more interested in the rest of the Page_Load method, where we parse the values provided by the user and call the AddEvent method defined in the DataAccess class. If there are any problems in parsing the inputs, the user is shown a simple error message (see Chapter 7 for details on more useful error-handling techniques). If there are no errors, the AddEvent page redirects the user to the ListEvents page once the DataAccess.AddEvent method returns, so that the newly added record can be viewed.

Updating and Deleting Data

To update data using the entity data model, you query for the object that represents the row you want to change, assign a new value to one or more of the properties, and call the SaveChanges method. Listing 8-13 shows the methods to add to the DataAccess class to handle updates.

Listing 8-13. *Handling update operations*

```
public static void UpdateEvent(TrainingDataEntities contextParam, int keyParam,
    DateTime dateParam, string athleteParam, string typeParam, TimeSpan swimTimeParam,
    TimeSpan cycleTimeParam, TimeSpan runTimeParam) {

    // query for the event with the specified key
    Event targetEvent = GetEventByID(contextParam, keyParam);

    // set the parameter values for the event
    if (targetEvent != null) {
        // update the event object properties
        targetEvent.Date = dateParam;
        targetEvent.Athlete = athleteParam;
        targetEvent.Type = typeParam;
        targetEvent.SwimTime = swimTimeParam;
        targetEvent.CycleTime = cycleTimeParam;
        targetEvent.RunTime = runTimeParam;
        targetEvent.OverallTime = swimTimeParam + cycleTimeParam + runTimeParam;
        // save the changes
        contextParam.SaveChanges();
    }
}

public static Event GetEventByID(TrainingDataEntities contextParam, int keyParam) {
    // query for the ID
    IEnumerable<Event> results = contextParam.Events
                                    .Where(e => e.ID == keyParam).Select(e => e);
    // as the ID is a primary key, there will be zero or one results
    return results.Count() == 1 ? results.First() : null;
}
```

As parameters, the UpdateEvent method takes a primary key value (which identifies the event object that is to be updated) and a set of values that correspond to the properties defined by the Event entity class. The GetEventByID method is called to query for the target event object, the parameter values are used to update the event properties, and then the SaveChanges method is called to write the changes to the database. The SQL statement that applies the change is generated and executed automatically by the Entity Framework.

To delete data from the database using the entity data model, you must locate the entity object that represents the row that you want to delete, and then call the DeleteObject method on the context object property that corresponds to the appropriate table. In this case, we would call Events.DeleteObject and pass the Event instance that represents the data we want removed as a parameter. The DeleteObject method is the counterpart to the AddObject method covered in the previous section. Listing 8-14 shows the method to add to the DataAccess class to support deleting event data.

Listing 8-14. Handling delete operations

```
public static void DeleteEventByID(TrainingDataEntities contextParam, int keyParam) {
    // query for the object that has the specified key
    Event targetEvent = GetEventByID(contextParam, keyParam);

    // if there is a result from the query, perform a delete
    if (targetEvent != null) {
        contextParam.Events.DeleteObject(targetEvent);
        contextParam.SaveChanges();
    }
}
```

The DeleteEventByID method calls the GetEventByID method to query for the Event object that has the primary key passed as the keyParam parameter, which is then passed to the Events.DeleteObject method of the context object. Finally, the SaveChanges method is called. Delete operations, like additions and updates, are not written to the database until this method is called.

Implementing Page Support for Updating and Deleting Data

Now that we have methods in the DataAccess class to handle updates and deletions, building the pages to support updating and deleting triathlon events is pretty simple. We can use one page to handle both operations.

■ **Tip**   There is sufficient similarity between the page functions required for adding, updating, and deleting content that a single page could be used for all of them. The decision as to how much functionality should be included in a single page will be influenced by the specifics of each project. In this chapter, I wanted to introduce key concepts gradually, but in a real project, I would have used a single page.

The page that will handle these operations is called UpdateOrDeleteEvent.aspx. To begin, we will add features to the ListEvents.aspx page, so that the user can choose to edit or delete an event from the list, as shown in Figure 8-16.

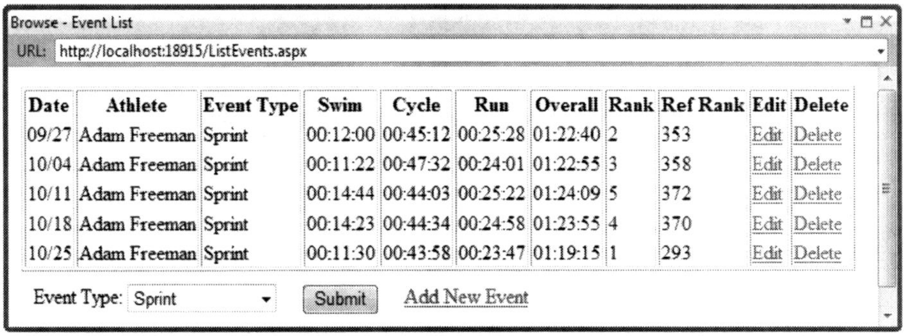

Figure 8-16. Adding edit and delete support to the ListEvents.aspx page

The additional column definitions are shown in Listing 8-15. (Notice that we add a static link to the AddEvent.aspx page as well, just to round out the functionality of our example web application.)

Listing 8-15. Adding to the ListEvents.aspx page

```
...
    <th>Rank</th>
    <th>Ref Rank</th>
    <th>Edit</th>
    <th>Delete</th>
</tr>
...
```

To populate these new columns, we use a new method in the ListEvents.aspx.cs code-behind class, named CreateLinkTableCell. This method embeds an HtmlAnchor control inside an HtmlCellTable control. The primary key of the event and the mode (edit or delete) are set as query string parameters. The CreateLinkTableCell method is shown in Listing 8-16.

Listing 8-16. The ListEvents.aspx.cs CreateLinkTableCell method

```
private HtmlTableCell CreateLinkTableCell(string urlParam, string textParam, int idParam,
string modeParam) {
    // create the anchor
    HtmlAnchor anchor = new HtmlAnchor() {
        HRef = string.Format("{0}?id={1}&mode={2}", urlParam, idParam, modeParam),
        InnerText = textParam};
    // add the anchor to a new cell
    HtmlTableCell cell = new HtmlTableCell();
    cell.Controls.Add(anchor);
    // return the cell
    return cell;
}
```

This method is called from within the ProcessEvent method, as follows:

```
row.Cells.Add(CreateLinkTableCell("/UpdateOrDeleteEvent.aspx", "Edit", eventParam.ID,
    "edit"));
row.Cells.Add(CreateLinkTableCell("/UpdateOrDeleteEvent.aspx", "Delete", eventParam.ID,
    "delete"));
```

■ **Note** For the fairly simple additions, I am now showing just the change fragments. At this point, you are familiar with the basic workings of the page file and the code-behind class, so the changes should be clear. You can see the changes applied to the entire example in the code download for this chapter.

The markup for the UpdateOrDeleteEvent.aspx page is very similar to the AddEvent.aspx page, but with the addition of two hidden input elements, as shown in Listing 8-17.

Listing 8-17. The UpdateOrDelete.aspx page

```
...
<input type="hidden" id="keyInput" runat="server" />
<input type="hidden" id="modeInput" runat="server" />
...
```

The hidden input elements are used to distinguish between update and delete operations when the form is posted by the user. The code-behind class for the UpdateOrDeleteEvent.aspx page is shown in Listing 8-18. There is nothing new in this class, other than the use of the methods defined in the DataAccess class to update and delete data.

Listing 8-18. The UpdateOrDeleteEvent.aspx.cs code-behind class

```
using System;
using System.Globalization;
using System.Web.UI.HtmlControls;

namespace DataApp {

    public partial class UpdateEvent : System.Web.UI.Page {

        protected void Page_Load(object sender, EventArgs e) {

            using (TrainingDataEntities context = new TrainingDataEntities()) {

                // do the setup - placed in a separate method for clarity
                if (ViewState["setupComplete"] == null) {
                    PerformPageSetup(context);
                    ViewState["setupComplete"] = true;
                }

                if (!IsPostBack) {
```

```
// make sure we have query string values for the key and
// the mode and can obtain the corresponding Event object
// if not, then push the user back towards the list page
string mode;
int eventID;
Event targetEvent;

if ((mode = Request.QueryString["mode"]) != null
    && int.TryParse(Request.QueryString["id"], out eventID)
    && (targetEvent = DataAccess.GetEventByID(context,
        eventID)) != null) {

    // set the hidden fields in the form
    this.modeInput.Value = mode;
    this.keyInput.Value = eventID.ToString();

    // use the property values of the event to populate page controls
    monthSelect.SelectedIndex = targetEvent.Date.Month - 1;
    dayText.Value = targetEvent.Date.Day.ToString();
    yearText.Value = targetEvent.Date.Year.ToString();

    // set the selected index for the the athlete and event controls
    SetSelectIndex(athleteSelect, targetEvent.Athlete);
    SetSelectIndex(eventTypeSelect, targetEvent.Type);

    // set the times
    swimText.Value = targetEvent.SwimTime.ToString();
    cycleText.Value = targetEvent.CycleTime.ToString();
    runText.Value = targetEvent.RunTime.ToString();

    // if we are in delete mode, then disable the HTML controls
    if (mode == "delete") {
        monthSelect.Disabled = true;
        dayText.Disabled = true;
        yearText.Disabled = true;
        athleteSelect.Disabled = true;
        eventTypeSelect.Disabled = true;
        swimText.Disabled = true;
        cycleText.Disabled = true;
        runText.Disabled = true;
    }

    // set the button text based on the mode
    button.Value = mode == "edit" ? "Save" : "Delete";
```

```
                } else {
                    // we have a problem - just send the user back to the list
                    Response.Redirect("/ListEvents.aspx");
                }

            } else {
                if (modeInput.Value == "edit") {
                    // this is an edit request that requires an update
                    DataAccess.UpdateEvent(context, int.Parse(keyInput.Value),
                        new DateTime(
                            int.Parse(yearText.Value),
                            monthSelect.SelectedIndex + 1,
                            int.Parse(dayText.Value)),
                        athleteSelect.Value,
                        eventTypeSelect.Value,
                        TimeSpan.Parse(swimText.Value),
                        TimeSpan.Parse(cycleText.Value),
                        TimeSpan.Parse(runText.Value));

                } else {
                    // this is a delete request
                    DataAccess.DeleteEventByID(context, int.Parse(keyInput.Value));
                }

                // return the user to the list
                Response.Redirect("ListEvents.aspx");
            }
        }
    }
}

private void SetSelectIndex(HtmlSelect selectParam, string targetValue) {
    for (int i = 0; i < selectParam.Items.Count; i++) {
        if (selectParam.Items[i].Text == targetValue) {
            selectParam.SelectedIndex = i;
            break;
        }
    }
}

private void PerformPageSetup(TrainingDataEntities context) {

    // get the current culture info
    DateTimeFormatInfo formatInfo = CultureInfo.CurrentCulture.DateTimeFormat;

    // populate the month select element
    monthSelect.Items.Clear();
    for (int i = 1; i < 13; i++) {
        monthSelect.Items.Add(formatInfo.GetAbbreviatedMonthName(i));
    }
```

```
                // get the current date and use it to select a month and set the day and year
                DateTime now = DateTime.Now;
                monthSelect.SelectedIndex = now.Month - 1;
                dayText.Value = now.Day.ToString();
                yearText.Value = now.Year.ToString();

                // populate the athlete names
                athleteSelect.Items.Clear();
                foreach (string name in DataAccess.GetAthleteNames(context)) {
                    athleteSelect.Items.Add(name);
                }

                // populate the event types
                eventTypeSelect.Items.Clear();
                foreach (string name in DataAccess.GetEventTypeNames(context)) {
                    eventTypeSelect.Items.Add(name);
                }
            }
        }
    }
}
```

When the page is invoked in edit mode, the details of the event are displayed and can be changed, as shown in Figure 8-17. Clicking the Save button updates the corresponding row in the Events table in the database.

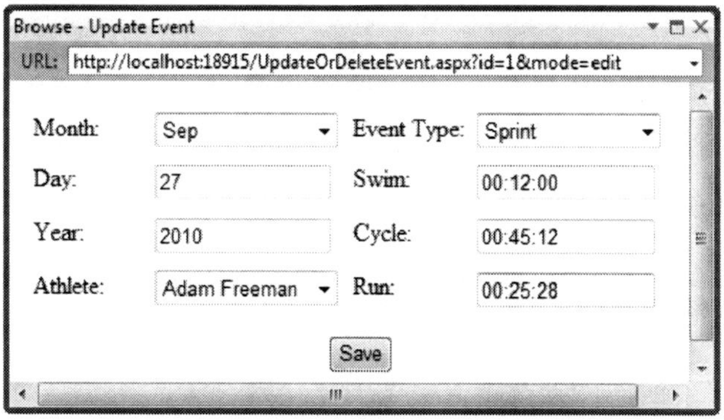

Figure 8-17. Editing an event

When the UpdateOrDeleteEvent.aspx page is invoked in delete mode, the details of the event are still displayed, but the HTML input elements are disabled, and the user cannot change the values, as shown in Figure 8-18.

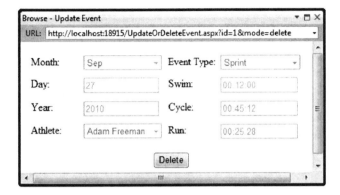

Figure 8-18. *Deleting an event*

When the operation is completed, the user is redirected to the ListEvents.aspx page, which will reflect the user's changes.

Managing Concurrency

The Entity Framework uses an *optimistic concurrency model* by default. In this case, *optimistic* means that we cross our fingers and hope that we don't get overlapping page requests that lead to conflicting data changes. One request leads to a change to the data and updates the database. A moment later, the second request leads to a different change to the *same* data and performs an update. When the second update is applied, the original changes are lost, and because the first request has completed, we have no way to signal to the users that their modifications have been overwritten.

We can partially address this problem by enabling concurrency checking on individual fields in the data model. This is still optimistic concurrency, because no data is locked in the database, but it does mean that you will know when someone else has made changes to data that you intend to modify.

WHY LOCKING MAKES THINGS WORSE

You might be tempted to deal with overlapping conflicting data changes by locking regions of the database. Don't do it! Web applications are so poorly suited to locking that the most common result of using locking is that the application grinds to a halt.

Locking data for the duration of a page request doesn't solve the problem. Neither the first nor second request will signal the problem. The effect of the lock will be to serialize the updates and nothing more. If you use locks that span multiple requests, you will find that the disconnected, stateless nature of web requests runs counter to the persistent, exclusive nature of database locks.

If a user walks away from her PC before she has finished the sequence of requests you are expecting, you will be left with an orphaned lock that will prevent other users from updating that region of the database. If you expire the locks to prevent this from happening, you force your users to send requests at a fast pace, which is counter to the web application experience they are used to. Either way, database locks should never be used in a web application without a lot of careful thought and testing.

To enable concurrency checking, follow these steps:

1. Open the data model file, TrainingDataModel.edmx.

2. Right-click the property that you want to modify and select Properties from the pop-up menu.

3. Change the value of the Concurrency Mode property to Fixed, as shown in Figure 8-19.

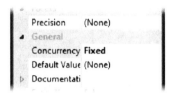

Figure 8-19. *Enabling concurrency checking*

There is no convenient way to enable concurrency checking for multiple properties. You must select them individually and apply the changes one by one. For this example, enable checking on all of the properties of the Event object.

Once you have enabled concurrency checking, the SaveChanges method of the context object will throw a System.Data.OptimisticConcurrencyException if the data you are attempting to modify has been changed since you queried the data model to obtain the entity object. For most web applications, the best way of dealing with a concurrency conflict is to alert the user who initiated the second request that his changes cannot be applied. This is largely because, by definition, the first request will already have completed.

Summary

In this chapter, you have seen how to use the Entity Framework and LINQ to bring data into your web applications without dealing directly with SQL. We created an example application that performed each of the CRUD operations, allowing a user to see the list of events in the sample database, add new events, and modify and delete existing events. There are alternatives to the Entity Framework, but I like the way that it allows me to work with regular C# objects, and without mixing SQL and C# in the same code files. I also like the close integration with LINQ, which provides a natural way to query for data.

The Entity Framework isn't everyone's preferred approach, but it is one of the major investment areas for Microsoft, and it supports such a wide range of databases that it is a good place to start when considering the data-access technology for your web application projects.

Both the Entity Framework and LINQ are worthy of books in their own right. If you want a complete guide to LINQ, I suggest the book I wrote with Joe Rattz, *Pro LINQ in C# 2010* (Apress, 2010). For the Entity Framework, I recommend *Pro Entity Framework 4.0* by Scott Klein (Apress, 2010). I also like *Entity Framework 4.0 Recipes* by Larry Tenny and Zeeshan Hirani (Apress, 2010).

CHAPTER 9

Styling Content

Our focus has been on the key ASP.NET technology building blocks so far in this book. The examples we have created have allowed us to explore each essential feature in turn, but they all have one thing in common—they look terrible.

Users' expectations for the appearance and richness of a web application have increased sharply in recent years, and even the simplest web application is expected to have a minimum of gloss and sparkle. In this chapter, we will look at the features that ASP.NET provides to style content, ranging from applying a constant appearance to all of the pages in an application to providing rich user interactions.

It is easy to dismiss styling as needless chrome, but do so at your peril. Consistent cues as to the behavior of your interface elements, clear signposting of progress through processes, and overall coherence in appearance and function will help your users navigate your application.

It is equally easy to get carried away; there is a repressed designer deep inside most programmers. A good question to ask oneself is, does my interface look like a Vegas slot machine? If the answer is yes, then you may have added more bells and whistles than is strictly essential; such interfaces induce fatigue and frustration in users, especially when it forms part of their daily workflow.

One area we will explore in this chapter is using JavaScript to style content. If you were a programming during the browser wars of the late 1990s, you may have a poor impression of JavaScript, which has been dogged by a checkered past. Inconsistent implementations, odd notational forms, and an ill-chosen name have all played their part in tarnishing the reputation of JavaScript. Fortunately, most of these problems have been resolved—partly through better browser support and partly through the development of libraries that smooth out any remaining inconsistencies and simplify the more awkward parts of the programming model.

Many JavaScript libraries are available, but the one that is most closely associated with ASP.NET is *jQuery*. Microsoft has embraced jQuery by contributing functionality, adding support for editing jQuery in Visual Studio, and including the jQuery library in some of the ASP.NET project templates. For most purposes, jQuery *is* JavaScript for ASP.NET projects. In this chapter, I'll give you a crash course in using jQuery, but I don't have the space to provide a comprehensive tutorial. If you want more detailed information, then I recommend *jQuery in Action* by Bear Bibeault and Yehuda Katz (published by Manning) and *jQuery Recipes* by B.M. Harwani (published by Apress).

Creating the Project

For this chapter, we will start with a project created from the Visual Studio ASP.NET Web Application template, as shown in Figure 9-1.

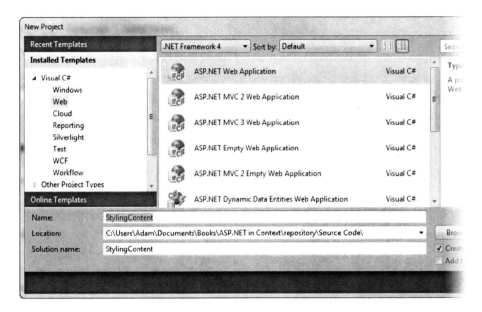

Figure 9-1. *Using the ASP.NET Web Application project template*

Select the template, set the name of the project to Styling Content, and click the OK button to create the project. We are going to use the data model and consolidated access class `DataAccess` from Chapter 8, so follow the steps to create the model and copy the code file from that project (don't forget to change the namespace). Alternatively, you can download the ready-to-go project as part of the download that accompanies this book, available from Apress.com.

Using ASP.NET Master Pages

The first approach to styling we will explore is the ASP.NET *master page* feature, which lets us apply a common design to pages using a system of templates. The master page feature is the reason we created an ASP.NET Web Application project, instead of the ASP.NET Empty Web Application we have relied on so far; when using this type of project, Visual Studio creates some default pages that use the master page feature. If you open the `Default.aspx` file and look at the markup, you will see that it has a different structure from the web pages we have seen so far, as illustrated by Listing 9-1.

Listing 9-1. *The Default.aspx file*

```
<%@ Page Title="Home Page" Language="C#" MasterPageFile="~/Site.master" AutoEventWireup="true"
    CodeBehind="Default.aspx.cs" Inherits="StylingContent._Default" %>

<asp:Content ID="HeaderContent" runat="server" ContentPlaceHolderID="HeadContent">
</asp:Content>
```

```
<asp:Content ID="BodyContent" runat="server" ContentPlaceHolderID="MainContent">
    <h2>
        Welcome to ASP.NET!
    </h2>
    <p>
        To learn more about ASP.NET visit <a href="http://www.asp.net" title="ASP.NET↵
Website">www.asp.net</a>.
    </p>
    <p>
        You can also find <a href="http://go.microsoft.com/fwlink/?LinkID=↵
152368&amp;clcid=0x409"
            title="MSDN ASP.NET Docs">documentation on ASP.NET at MSDN</a>.
    </p>
</asp:Content>
```

The most obvious change is the use of the asp:Content elements and the fact that the markup for this page is no longer a complete HTML page. The second change is the addition of the MasterPageFile attribute to the Page directive. Listing 9-2 shows the Site.Master file that this attribute specifies.

Listing 9-2. *The Site.Master file*

```
<%@ Master Language="C#" AutoEventWireup="true" CodeBehind="Site.master.cs"
Inherits="StylingContent.SiteMaster" %>

<!DOCTYPE html PUBLIC "-//W3C//DTD XHTML 1.0 Strict//EN"↵
 "http://www.w3.org/TR/xhtml1/DTD/xhtml1-strict.dtd">
<html xmlns="http://www.w3.org/1999/xhtml" xml:lang="en">
<head runat="server">
    <title></title>
    <link href="~/Styles/Site.css" rel="stylesheet" type="text/css" />
    <asp:ContentPlaceHolder ID="HeadContent" runat="server">
    </asp:ContentPlaceHolder>
</head>
<body>
    <form runat="server">
    <div class="page">
        <div class="header">
            <div class="title">
                <h1>
                    My ASP.NET Application
                </h1>
            </div>
            <div class="loginDisplay">
                <asp:LoginView ID="HeadLoginView" runat="server" EnableViewState="false">
                    <AnonymousTemplate>
                        [ <a href="~/Account/Login.aspx" ID="HeadLoginStatus"
                            runat="server">Log In</a> ]
                    </AnonymousTemplate>
```

```
            <LoggedInTemplate>
                Welcome <span class="bold"><asp:LoginName ID="HeadLoginName"
                runat="server" /></span>!
                [ <asp:LoginStatus ID="HeadLoginStatus" runat="server"
                  LogoutAction="Redirect" LogoutText="Log Out" LogoutPageUrl="~/"/> ]
            </LoggedInTemplate>
        </asp:LoginView>
    </div>
    <div class="clear hideSkiplink">
        <asp:Menu ID="NavigationMenu" runat="server" CssClass="menu"
          EnableViewState="false" IncludeStyleBlock="false"
          Orientation="Horizontal">
            <Items>
                <asp:MenuItem NavigateUrl="~/Default.aspx" Text="Home"/>
                <asp:MenuItem NavigateUrl="~/About.aspx" Text="About"/>
            </Items>
        </asp:Menu>
    </div>
</div>
<div class="main">
    <asp:ContentPlaceHolder ID="MainContent" runat="server"/>
</div>
<div class="clear">
</div>
</div>
<div class="footer">

</div>
</form>
</body>
</html>
```

The items we care about in relation to master pages are the asp:ContentPlaceHolder elements, which are shown in bold.

■ **Note** The other new elements in Listing 9-2 (asp:LoginView, AnonymousTemplate, LoggedInTemplate, asp:Menu and asp:MenuItem) are part of Web Forms, which we begin to look at in Chapter 13.

A master page is a template whose content is combined with the content of a page to provide a consistent style across some or all of the pages in an ASP.NET web application. The master page contains a number of asp:ContentPlaceHolder elements, like this one:

```
<asp:ContentPlaceHolder ID="MainContent" runat="server"/>
```

The ID attribute corresponds to an asp:Content element in the web page file, like this one from Default.aspx:

```
<asp:Content ID="BodyContent" runat="server" ContentPlaceHolderID="MainContent">
```

Note that the ContentPlaceHolderID attribute value in the page corresponds to the value of the ID element in the asp:ContentPlaceHolder element in the master page. When you request a web page that uses a master page, the result is the combination of the two sets of content. ASP.NET starts by processing the master page, and each time it encounters an asp:ContentPlaceHolder element, it looks for a corresponding asp:Content element in the web page and inserts the contents of the element into the output. If you view the Default.aspx web page in the example project, you can see how contents of the asp:Content elements are combined with the master page, as shown in Figure 9-2.

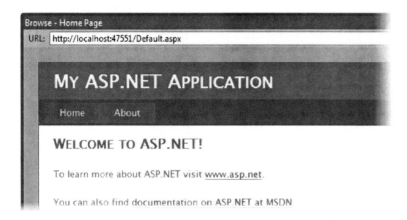

Figure 9-2. *The effect of using the standard ASP.NET master page*

In Figure 9-2 you can see how the HTML from the asp:Content element in the web page has been combined with the master page. The effect is applied to any web page that uses the same master page. The project that Visual Studio created for us contains an additional web page—About.aspx. If you view this page, either from within Visual Studio or by clicking the About link shown in the header in Figure 9-2, you can see the consistent styling that a master page offers, as illustrated in Figure 9-3.

Browse - About Us

URL: http://localhost:47551/About.aspx

MY ASP.NET APPLICATION

Home   About

ABOUT

Put content here.

Figure 9-3. *Consistent styling across pages*

▪ **Tip**   You can have more than one master page in a project, which allows you to apply consistent styling to groups of related pages without having one overarching standard template.

Customizing Master Pages

The default master page that Visual Studio created for us is perfectly serviceable, but most projects create their master pages from scratch. We are going to do the same thing, but the main reason for us to do this is to have something simpler that we can work with to explore the master pages features. Listing 9-3 shows my simplified Site.Master file.

Listing 9-3. *Simplifying the master page*

```
<%@ Master Language="C#" AutoEventWireup="true" CodeBehind="Site.master.cs"
 Inherits="StylingContent.SiteMaster" %>

<!DOCTYPE html PUBLIC "-//W3C//DTD XHTML 1.0 Strict//EN" "http://www.w3.org/TR/xhtml1/DTD↵
/xhtml1-strict.dtd">
<html xmlns="http://www.w3.org/1999/xhtml" xml:lang="en">
<head runat="server">
    <link href="/Styles/Site.css" rel="stylesheet" type="text/css" />
    <asp:ContentPlaceHolder ID="HeadContent" runat="server"/>
</head>
<body>
    <form runat="server">

    <div class="page">

        <div class="header" id="headerDiv" runat="server">
            <div class="title">
                <img src="Images/triathlon.png" alt="Triathlon Icon" />
                <h1>Triathlon Training Data</h1>
            </div>
        </div>

        <div class="main">
            <asp:ContentPlaceHolder ID="MainContent" runat="server"/>
        </div>

        <div class="clear" />

        <div class="footer" id="footerDiv" runat="server">
            <h2><span id="eventCountSpan" runat="server">???</span> Events,
            <span id="mileCountSpan" runat="server">???</span> Miles,
            <span id="hourCountSpan" runat="server">???</span></h2>
        </div>
    </div>
```

```
    </form>
</body>
</html>
```

Like the default that Visual Studio created for us, this master page has two asp:ContentPlaceHolder elements, for the header (HeadContent) and for the main part of the page (MainContent). There is a link to the CSS file, /Styles/Site.css, which contains the styles that are applied at the master page. Because the result of using a master page is an HTML response that combines the web page and master page content, the CSS styles that you define or reference in the master page can also be applied to web page elements.

WORKING WITH CSS

Perhaps the most obvious way of styling content is to use Cascading Style Sheets (CSS). Most of the examples so far in this book have relied on CSS in some way to control the layout of HTML elements or their appearance.

CSS is a nice approach to styling content, not least because it separates the definition of the styles from the content to which they are applied. With regard to ASP.NET applications, there are so many different ways to define CSS styles that it can be difficult to figure out which ones are being applied. As with a regular web page, an ASP.NET web page can define an external style sheet and define styles in the head element of the page and inline for individual elements. In this chapter, we'll see some further options— defining styles and style sheets in a master page, setting styles programmatically in the code-behind class, and using JavaScript. It may sound like a trivial issue, but it is important to have a clearly defined and understood approach to CSS in your web application; otherwise, as your project grows, various approaches will be used in different ways, and you'll end up spending time trying to debug style issues by figuring out which styles are being overridden and where the overrides come from. As a rule of thumb, the fewer sources of CSS you rely on, the better your development experience will be.

At the end of the master page is a div element that contains a footer for the page, as follows:

```
<div class="footer">
    <h2><span id="eventCountSpan" runat="server">???</span> Events,
    <span id="mileCountSpan" runat="server">???</span> Miles,
    <span id="hourCountSpan" runat="server">???</span></h2>
</div>
```

Master pages are not just static content—they are ASP.NET pages, too, meaning that they can have code-behind files and contain dynamic content. Visual Studio creates a code-behind file automatically for master pages with the same naming scheme so that the code-behind file for Site.Master is Site.Master.cs. Listing 9-4 shows the code-behind file I have created to populate the master page footer.

Listing 9-4. *Generating dynamic code in a master page*

```
using System;

namespace StylingContent {

    public partial class SiteMaster : System.Web.UI.MasterPage {

        protected void Page_Load(object sender, EventArgs e) {

            using (TrainingDataEntities context = new TrainingDataEntities()) {
                // get the total data from the database
                DataTotals totals = DataAccess.GetDataTotals(context);
                // use the totals to update the span contents for the footer
                eventCountSpan.InnerText = totals.EventTotal.ToString();
                mileCountSpan.InnerText = string.Format("{0:F1}", totals.MileTotal);
                hourCountSpan.InnerText = string.Format("{0} Hours and {1} Minutes",
                    totals.TimeTotal.Hours, totals.TimeTotal.Minutes); ;

            }
        }
    }
}
```

The statements in the Page_Load method rely on the GetDataTotals method, which I have added to the DataAccess class. The type that the GetDataTotals method returns is a simple struct called DataTotals, defined as follows:

```
public struct DataTotals {
    public int EventTotal;
    public float MileTotal;
    public TimeSpan TimeTotal;
}
```

I use the struct fields to set the InnerText properties of the span elements in the master page footer. Figure 9-4 shows the result, without any page content—in other words, just the elements from the master page (I created this page by removing the contents of the Default.aspx file).

Figure 9-4. *Dynamically generating a footer in a master page*

Using a Master Page in a Web Page

Once we have created a suitable master page, we can create web pages that have asp:Content elements to match the master page asp:ContentPlaceHolder elements. To start with, I have re-created the ListEvents.aspx page from Chapter 8 using this approach. The easiest way to use a master page is to ensure that you select the template called Web Form using Master Page, as shown in Figure 9-5.

Figure 9-5. *Adding a new web page using a master page*

When you use this template, Visual Studio prompts you to select the master page that you want to associate with the new web page, as shown in Figure 9-6; there is only one master page in our example project, but large-scale projects can have multiple master pages for different functional areas of the web application.

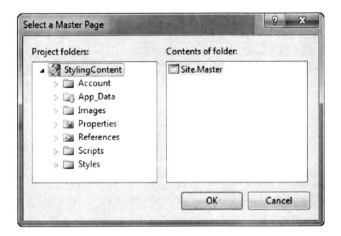

Figure 9-6. *Selecting the master page*

When you select a master page, the web page is created with asp:Content elements that correspond to the asp:ContentPlaceHolder elements in the master. Listing 9-5 shows the web page that Visual Studio created for me when I created the ListEvents.aspx page.

Listing 9-5. *A skeletal web page*

```
<%@ Page Title="" Language="C#" MasterPageFile="~/Site.Master" AutoEventWireup="true"
CodeBehind="AddEvent.aspx.cs" Inherits="StylingContent.AddEvent" %>

<asp:Content ID="Content1" ContentPlaceHolderID="HeadContent" runat="server">
</asp:Content>

<asp:Content ID="Content2" ContentPlaceHolderID="MainContent" runat="server">
</asp:Content>
```

From this point, I simply added the markup required for the page to each of the asp:Content elements, bearing in mind that some of the page structure will come from the master page. Listing 9-6 shows the ListEvents.aspx page from the previous chapter, modified to work with the master page from Listing 9-3.

Listing 9-6. *A web page that uses a master page*

```
<%@ Page Title="Triathlon Events" Language="C#" MasterPageFile="~/Site.master"
AutoEventWireup="true"
    CodeBehind="Default.aspx.cs" Inherits="StylingContent._Default" %>

<asp:Content ID="HeaderContent" runat="server" ContentPlaceHolderID="HeadContent">
    <link href="/Styles/Page.css" rel="stylesheet" type="text/css" />
</asp:Content>

<asp:Content ID="BodyContent" runat="server" ContentPlaceHolderID="MainContent">
  <table id="resultsTable" runat="server" rules="cols">
```

```
        <tr>
            <th>Date</th>
            <th>Athlete</th>
            <th>Event Type</th>
            <th>Swim</th>
            <th>Cycle</th>
            <th>Run</th>
            <th>Overall</th>
            <th>Rank</th>
            <th>Ref Rank</th>
            <th>Edit</th>
            <th>Delete</th>
        </tr>
    </table>

    <div class="standardDiv">
        <label>Event Type:</label>
        <select id="eventSelector" runat="server">
            <option>All</option>
        </select>
    </div>

    <div class="standardDiv">
        <input type="submit" value="Submit" />
    </div>

    <div class="standardDiv">
        <a href="AddEvent.aspx">Add New Event</a>
    </div>
</asp:Content>
```

In the HeadContent section, I have imported a CSS file called Styles/Page.css. This file will be inserted into the head element of the overall result, allowing me to specify local CSS styles to either complement or override those in the master page. In the MainContent section, I have added the table that makes up most of the page display.

▪ **Tip**   You can change the master page that a web page uses by setting a value for the Page.MasterPageFile property in the handler for the Page.PreInit event. See Chapter 5 for details of page events.

Figure 9-7 shows the finished result. I copied the code-behind class in its entirety, modifying only the namespace to match the new project name for this chapter.

Figure 9-7. *A web page using a master page*

If you look at the HTML for this page in the browser, you will see that ASP.NET has changed the value of the id attribute for the HTML elements. As an example, the table element, which is defined in ListEvents.aspx like this:

```
<table id="resultsTable" runat="server" rules="cols">
```

appears in the HTML of the rendered page like this:

```
<table id="MainContent_resultsTable" rules="cols">
```

The name of the content region, MainContent in this case, has been prepended to the id value, separated with an underscore. This ensures that controls that are defined using the same id in the master page and the web page have unique identifiers. I did not have to modify the original code-behind class; the ASP.NET server remaps the id values so that we don't have to worry about the modification. This is a useful feature for the code-behind file, but—as you'll see later in this chapter—this causes a minor problem when it comes to using JavaScript.

Of course, the benefit of master pages arises when they are applied to multiple web pages in a project, and as we create additional web pages that use master pages, we see consistent styling in our application. I have re-created the AddEvent.aspx page from Chapter 8 to use the master page. Figure 9-8 shows the result.

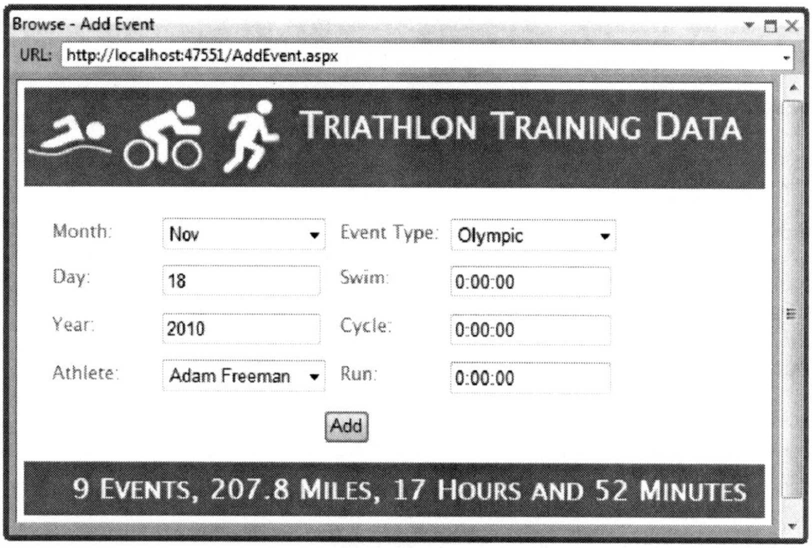

Figure 9-8. *Consistent styles across pages*

We have been able to get a consistent style across these pages very simply using master pages. I have not had to change a single line of the code files that we created in Chapter 8, and refactoring the markup to fit inside the asp:Content elements is very simple.

Managing a Master Page from a Web Page

Often, your application will require styling that is broadly visually consistent and yet that is distinct in some way to indicate a particular kind of operation—for example, to make it clear that a particular page will delete, rather than update, a database record. There are a number of ways to achieve this, but one approach that I like is to configure the HTML controls of the master page from within a web page.

You can access the master page from a web page by using the Master property, which returns an instance of the System.Web.UI.MasterPage class. You can then call the FindControl method on the MasterPage to locate an HTML control by name and work with it as you would any other HTML control, as shown in Listing 9-7.

Listing 9-7. *Configuring a master page control*

```
if (mode == "delete") {
    monthSelect.Disabled = true;
    dayText.Disabled = true;
    yearText.Disabled = true;
    athleteSelect.Disabled = true;
    eventTypeSelect.Disabled = true;
    swimText.Disabled = true;
    cycleText.Disabled = true;
    runText.Disabled = true;
```

```
foreach (string controlID in new string[] { "titleDiv", "footerDiv" }) {
    HtmlControl ctrl = Master.FindControl(controlID) as HtmlControl;
    if (ctrl != null) {
        ctrl.Style["background"] = "#980000";
    }
}
}
```

I have re-created the UpdateOrDeleteEvent.aspx page from Chapter 8, updating it to work with the master page in the example project for this chapter. This page operates differently based on whether the user intends to update or delete a triathlon event. The fragment shown in Listing 9-7 disables the input controls in the HTML form when we have been asked to delete an event—the additions I have made for this chapter are shown in bold. I find the HTML controls that represent div elements for the title and footer sections of the master page, cast them to HTMLContol objects, and then override the CSS background value.

In this way, the page retains the consistent overall style but changes the color of the master elements when the user is about to perform a delete operation. You can see the appearance of the page in the update and delete modes in Figure 9-9.

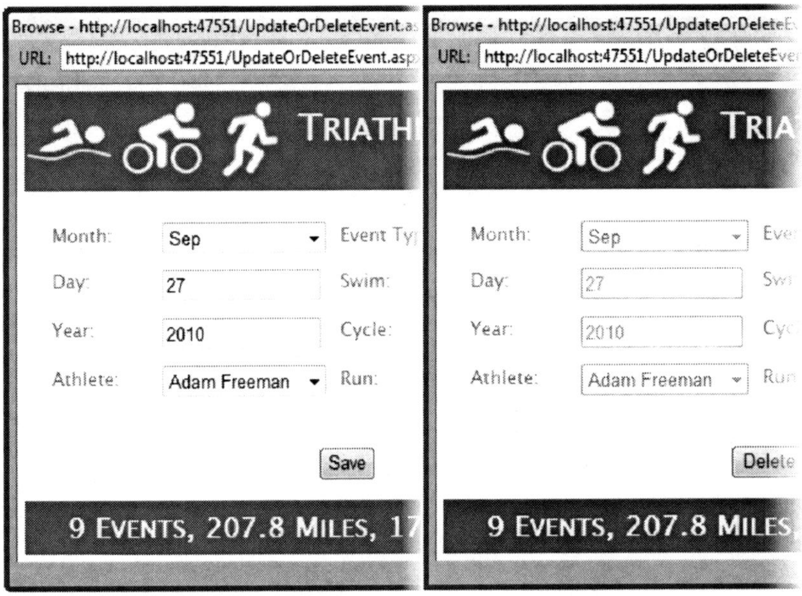

Figure 9-9. *Changing style elements in the master page*

Master pages are a simple and flexible way of enforcing a consistent style across the pages of your application. With them, you can increase the visual appeal of your pages with very little effort and establish the foundation for consistent interaction for your users.

Working with jQuery

When we created the example project using the ASP.NET Web Application template, Visual Studio automatically added support for jQuery. You can see this by opening the Scripts folder in the Solution Explorer window, which will contain three files, as illustrated in Figure 9-10.

Figure 9-10. *The jQuery files in an ASP.NET project*

The jQuery-1.4.1-vsdoc.js file provides support for Visual Studio IntelliSense for jQuery expressions, allowing Visual Studio to offer suggestions for completing your jQuery statements as you type in the code editor. The jQuery-1.4.1.js file contains the jQuery library; the contents of this file are uncompressed, which makes it useful for reading the source code and debugging any problems you encounter. The jQuery-1.4.1.min.js file is the compressed version of the library, which is intended to minimize the amount of data transferred to a browser. This is the file you would typically use in production.

UPDATING JQUERY IN A PROJECT

You can see from the names of the files in the Scripts folder that Visual Studio has provided us with version 1.4.1 of jQuery. Versions of Visual Studio appear less often than versions of jQuery, so you'll often find that jQuery has moved on. If you want the latest versions of jQuery, you can get them from jQuery.com.

As I write this, the current version is 1.4.4, which offers performance improvements and fixes some bugs. By the time you read this, newer versions will certainly have appeared. The –vsdoc file doesn't always get produced immediately, but I find that you can simply rename the latest file available as long as you don't mind not having IntelliSense support for any new functions that have been added.

Styling Content with jQuery

To get started with jQuery, we have to add the library to our page. The simplest way to do this is to drag the appropriate file from the Scripts folder to the head element of your page or master page. I have added the jQuery library to the Site.Master file of the example project so that it will be available in all the pages in the project. Listing 9-8 shows the addition that Visual Studio has made.

Listing 9-8. *Adding the jQuery library to a master page*

```
...
<head runat="server">
    <link href="/Styles/Site.css" rel="stylesheet" type="text/css" />
    <script src="Scripts/jquery-1.4.1.min.js" type="text/javascript"></script>
    <asp:ContentPlaceHolder ID="HeadContent" runat="server"/>
</head>
...
```

DELIVERING JQUERY VIA CDN

If you are delivering your web application via the Internet, you can use the Microsoft content delivery network (CDN) to access the jQuery library to your clients. Rather than have your ASP.NET servers transfer the library file, Microsoft will deliver the same content from a server located close to each user. This is a service that Microsoft makes available without charge. The benefit of such an approach is a more responsive web application for your users and a reduced bandwidth demand from your servers. You can get details of how this free service operates at www.asp.net/ajaxlibrary/cdn.ashx.

The CDN approach isn't suitable for applications that are delivered to users within an intranet because it causes all the browsers to go to the Internet to get the jQuery library, rather than access the ASP.NET server, which is generally closer and faster and has lower bandwidth costs.

The next step is to add a script element to the web page that will style the content, as illustrated by Listing 9-9. I have added this script statement to the ListEvents.aspx page.

Listing 9-9. *Styling content with jQuery*

```
<script type="text/javascript">
    $(document).ready(function () {

        $('td a').addClass('tableLink').css('text-decoration', 'none');

        $('td').filter(function () {
            return $(this).text() == 1;
        }).css({ 'color': 'green', 'font-weight': 'bold' });

    });
</script>
```

There is a lot packed into this script, but it gives us a foundation for understanding how to use jQuery to style content. We'll pick the script apart and look at each piece in turn.

A Simple jQuery Example

We'll start with the simpler of the two styling statements in the script, which is this one:

```
$('td a').addClass('tableLink').css('text-decoration', 'none');
```

The first step in most jQuery operations is to select the elements in the HTML that you want to work with. We do this by specifying a jQuery selector within parentheses, prepended with a dollar sign ($(<selector>)). jQuery supports a very wide range of selectors, including the CSS selectors. Table 9-1 describes the most commonly used selectors.

Table 9-1. *Commonly Used jQuery/CSS Selectors*

Selector	Description
$('div')	Selects all the div elements in the HTML
$('#myID')	Selects all the HTML elements of any type that have an ID attribute value of myID
$('.myClass')	Selects all the HTML elements that have a class attribute value of myClass
$('div h1')	Selects all the h1 elements that are contained within div elements

The selector in our statement, $('td a'), selects all the a elements contained within td elements. In the ListEvents.aspx page, this means that all the Edit and Delete links will be selected.

▨ **Note** jQuery complements the CSS selectors with some of its own; in fact, there are so many different ways to select elements using jQuery that the most difficult aspect is picking the model you prefer. I tend to rely on element types and classes, as shown in Table 9-1, but fall back on some of the other options for more complex selections. There are too many options to list here, but I recommend you consult the documentation available at jQuery.com. It is comprehensive, and every approach is explained with a useful example.

Once we have selected our target elements, we can apply styling. This statement applies two styles to the Edit and Delete links—the first using the jQuery addClass function, as shown in bold:

$('td a').**addClass('tableLink').**css('text-decoration', 'none');

The addClass function, as its name suggests, adds a class to the selected elements; in this case, the class is called tableLink and is defined as follows in the Styles/Page.css file:

a.tableLink { color: Red;}

I then call the css function, which lets me specify a value for a particular CSS property. I have specified a value of none for the text-decoration property. So, to summarize, my jQuery statement selects all the a elements that are contained within a td element, applies the tableLink CSS class, and sets the text-decoration property value to none. jQuery has a number of functions that make working with CSS very simple. Table 9-2 describes the most commonly used ones.

Table 9-2. *jQuery CSS-Related Functions*

Function	Description
addClass()	Adds a class to the selected elements
removeClass()	Removes a class from the selected elements
toggleClass()	Adds a class to each element that doesn't already have it and removes it from each element that does
css()	Sets one or more CSS properties

A More Complex Example

The second statement in the script is a little more complex, but it demonstrates the flexibility of jQuery. Here is the statement:

```
$('td').filter(function () {
    return $(this).text() == 1;
}).css({ 'color': 'green', 'font-weight': 'bold' });
```

The first part of the statement is the initial selector, $('td'), which selects all the td elements in the HTML. I then use the filter function to find those elements within the select that have text of 1.

The text function returns the text contained within an HTML element. I pass an anonymous function (created using function()) to the text function that is used to evaluate each of the selected elements. For each of the elements that passes through the filter, I use the css function to set new values for the color and font-weight properties, making the text in the element green and bold.

The jQuery Wrapper

The remaining part of the script is the jQuery wrapper, which looks like this:

```
$(document).ready(function () {
    // other jQuery statements
});
```

By default, a browser executes a script as soon as it is encountered, which presents the risk that we will apply our styling before all of the HTML elements have been loaded from the server. The wrapper, which is a common jQuery technique, prevents our script from being executed until all of the HTML is available.

The selector $(document) applies to the entire document, and the ready function is an event that is invoked when the HTML has been loaded for the page. jQuery has extensive support for managing JavaScript events, of which you'll see more in Chapter 10. We create an anonymous function that contains our other jQuery statements, and in doing so, we know that they won't be executed until the entire document is available.

When added to the ListEvents.aspx page, the jQuery script has the effect of formatting the rankings, which consist of 1 and the links to the Edit and Delete functions—you can see the effect in Figure 9-11.

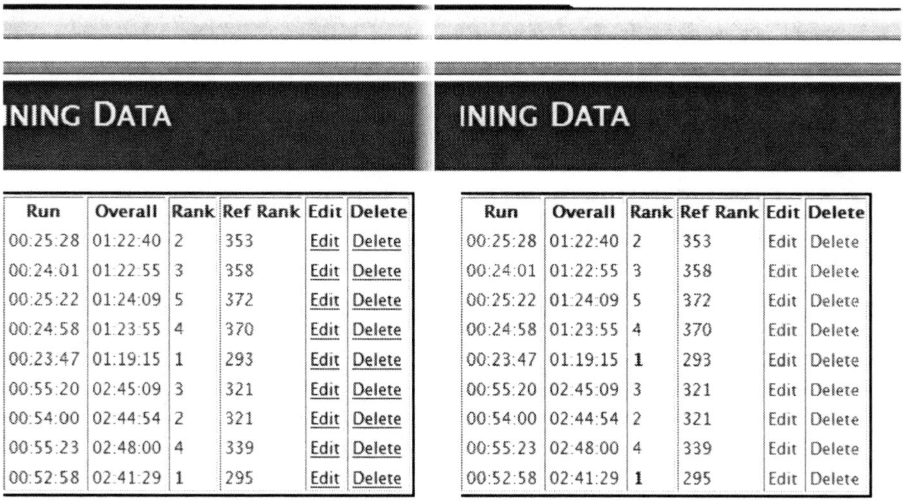

Figure 9-11. *The effect of the jQuery styling*

Using Other Common jQuery Styling Techniques

You can see from the previous example that using jQuery to style content is simple. You simply select some elements and then apply the class or style you want. In this section, I'll demonstrate three common styling techniques that rely on useful jQuery features to achieve a given style.

Styling Tables

Despite the limitations of the HTML table tag, tables remain a key component of many web applications, especially corporate applications. One of the most common ways to improve the readability of tables is to apply colors to alternate rows and a separate color to the table header row. Listing 9-10 demonstrates how to achieve this style using jQuery.

Listing 9-10. *Styling the header and selected rows of a table*

```
$(document).ready(function () {

    $('tr:has(th)').css({ 'background-color': '#007F7F', 'color': '#ffffff' });
    $('tr:has(td):even').css('background-color', "#11B1B1");

});
```

The selectors in this example use the :has selection modifier, which selects elements of the specified type that contain one or more elements of the type passed to the :has modifier. So, from the example, $('tr:has(th)') selects all the tr elements that contain one or more th elements. If you study the composition of the ListEvents.aspx page, you can see this will select the header row of the table.

The second selector works in the same way, selecting the tr elements that contain one or more td elements. This consists of all the rows that are not headers. The second statement further restricts the selection by using the :even modifier, which selects the even-numbered items in the selection (jQuery is zero-based, so the selection sequence for :even is 0, 2, 4, and so on). Both statements use the css function to set the background color for the rows they select. You can see the effect in Figure 9-12.

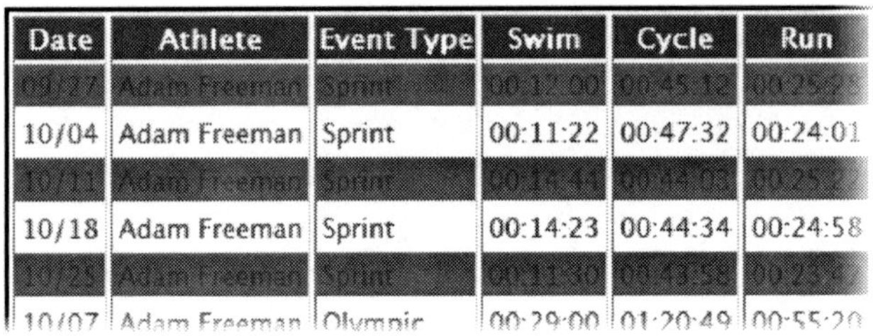

Figure 9-12. Header and alternate row coloring in a table

I mentioned earlier that you can create the same selections in different ways, and table rows are an ideal basis to provide a demonstration. Listing 9-11 shows a different way to achieve the effect shown in Figure 9-12.

Listing 9-11. An alternative approach to applying coloring to a table

```
$(document).ready(function () {
    $('tr').first().css({ 'background-color': '#007F7F', 'color': '#ffffff' });
    $('tr:odd').css('background-color', "#11B1B1");
});
```

The first statement selects all tr elements and then uses the first function to select only the first one that has been selected. In the ListEvents.aspx page, this will be the header row. The second statement selects all the tr elements as well but uses the :odd modifier to restrict the selection to the odd-numbered elements (once again, jQuery uses zero-based counting so that the first item in a selection is actually even).

Modifying Headers

The jQuery library contains some useful selectors and selection modifiers that make common selections simple and easy. One such modifier is :headers, which selects all header elements such as h1, h2, h3, and so on. Of course, we could select each type of header individually, but this can be a convenient way to apply a consistent style to all the headers in a page. Listing 9-12 contains a simple demonstration, which I have added to the Site.master page so that it will affect all of the pages in our example application.

Listing 9-12. Applying a style to all header elements

```
$(document).ready(function () {
    $(':header').css('text-decoration', 'underline');
});
```

A selection modifier applies to all elements when it is used on its own, as in Listing 9-12; this means that the selector $(':header') will first select all the elements in the document and then restrict that selection to those elements that are headers. The statement in the script underlines the text in header elements; you can see the result of this in Figure 9-13.

Figure 9-13. *Styling all header elements*

It is important to realize that the jQuery statements are executed by the browser, which isn't able to distinguish between HTML elements that come from the master page and those that come from the web page. As a consequence, using a jQuery modifier such as :header affects *all* the header elements in the rendered HTML, even though I added the script to the master page.

Changing the Content of Elements

When we looked at master pages, we saw how we could use the page code-behind file to modify the content elements contained in the master page. This allowed us to preserve the overall visual consistency for our web application and yet indicate to the user that the action they were about to perform had a different impact.

The key to the previous example was detecting when the page was being used in delete, rather than edit mode. This was expressed by the value of a hidden input element in the HTML form. Based on the mode, we changed the color of the header and footer for the page. We can use jQuery to achieve the same effect. Listing 9-13 shows the jQuery script, which I added to the UpdateOrDeleteEvent.aspx page. Rather than repeat the same modifications, we will change the text of the header and footer so that we display a warning to the user.

Listing 9-13. *Changing the header and footer based on the value of a hidden form field*

```
$(document).ready(function () {
    if ($('#<%=modeInput.ClientID%>').val() == 'delete') {
        $('#titleDiv h1').text('Delete Event');
        $('#footerDiv').html("<h2>Caution: Events cannot be restored</h2>");
    }
});
```

The first part of this script selects the hidden input field in the form and tests the value to determine whether the page is being used to edit or delete an event.

DEALING WITH CLIENT-SIDE IDS

As I mentioned earlier in the chapter, ASP.NET will rewrite the value of the ID attribute when a master page is used (and when an element has a runat value of server) to ensure that every element on a rendered page can be uniquely identified. This means that an element like this from the UpdateOrDeleteEvent.aspx file:

```
<input type="hidden" id="modeInput" runat="server" />
```

will result in an element like this in the rendered HTML sent to the browser:

```
<input name="ctl00$MainContent$modeInput" type="hidden" id="MainContent_modeInput"
value="edit" />
```

There are two changes of note. The ID value has been changed from modeInput to MainContent_modeInput, and a name attribute has been added. When we write our server-side code, ASP.NET hides this rewriting from us, and we can refer to the control as modeInput. When we are writing client-side code, we have to deal with the rewritten values in order to identify an element. There are two approaches to doing this. The first is to specify the rewritten name explicitly, like this:

```
if ($('#MainContent_modeInput').val() == 'delete') {
```

This approach is simple, but brittle—if you change the name of the content element in the master and web pages, then your jQuery script won't work as you expected. The better approach is to use a code block, which you first saw in Chapter 4, and read the value of the HTML control's ClientID property, like this:

```
if ($('#<%=modeInput.ClientID%>').val() == 'delete') {
```

The code block is shown in bold. I must admit that I tend to use the first approach more often than the second, even though I know it is problematic when there are changes. As an aside, we can access the value of the name attribute using the same approach but via the UniqueID property; you'll see an example of this in the next chapter.

The val function returns the value of the input element. If the value is delete, then the statements inside the if block are executed. If the value is not delete, then we are being asked to edit an event, and our style change is not required. The first statement in the if block is as follows:

```
$('#titleDiv h1').text('Delete Event');
```

The selector finds the elements with an ID of titleDiv and then selects the h1 elements that they contain. We have only one titleDiv element, and it contains only one h1 element, so the effect of our changes will be limited to a single element. The text function sets the text for the selected elements; in this case, the text is set to Delete Event.

The second statement in the if block demonstrates a different way to achieve the same effect, although this time applied to the page footer:

```
$('#footerDiv').html("<h2>Caution: Events cannot be restored</h2>");
```

The selector matches elements with an ID of footerDiv and then uses the html function to set the content of the element, including the h2 element. The html function is similar to the text element, except that it doesn't escape HTML structure characters. The relationship between the text and html jQuery functions is similar to the relationship between the InnerHtml and InnerText properties of the HTML control classes that you saw in Chapters 4 and 5. Of course, we could have set the footer in the same way as the header, like this:

```
$('#footerDiv h2').text("Caution: Events cannot be restored");
```

but I wanted to demonstrate that you can set or replace the contents of an entire element using the jQuery html function. Figure 9-14 demonstrates the effect of the script.

Figure 9-14. *Selectively applying styles to the header and footer of a page*

Notice that the text in the header and footer are underlined. This is because the script I applied to the master page in Listing 9-12 is still there. When the page is rendered, the script in the master page is included in the HTML along with the script defined in the .aspx page file. Here is the head element that is sent to the browser:

```
<head>
    <link href="/Styles/Site.css" rel="stylesheet" type="text/css" />
    <script src="Scripts/jquery-1.4.1.min.js" type="text/javascript"></script>

    <link href="/Styles/Page.css" rel="stylesheet" type="text/css" />

        <script type="text/javascript">
            $(document).ready(function () {
                if ($('#<%=modeInput.ClientID%>').val() == 'delete') {
                    $('#footerDiv h2').text("Caution: Events cannot be restored");
                    $('#titleDiv h1').text('Delete Event');
                }

            });

    </script>
```

```
<script type="text/javascript">
    $(document).ready(function () {
        $(':header').css('text-decoration', 'underline');
    });
</script>
<title></title>
</head>
```

It pays to be cautious when you have scripts defined in the master and web pages. You should ensure that they don't conflict with one another and that they are defined in the order that you want them to be executed in. In this example, you can see that the script defined in the master page appears *after* the script in the .aspx web page. If we look at the head element of the Site.Master page, we can see why this has happened:

```
<head runat="server">
    <link href="/Styles/Site.css" rel="stylesheet" type="text/css" />
    <script src="Scripts/jquery-1.4.1.min.js" type="text/javascript"></script>
    <asp:ContentPlaceHolder ID="HeadContent" runat="server"/>
    <script type="text/javascript">
        $(document).ready(function () {
            $(':header').css('text-decoration', 'underline');
        });
    </script>
</head>
```

The asp:ContentPlaceHolder element, shown in bold, appears after the jQuery library has been imported but before the local script is defined. There is nothing wrong with this approach unless you are relying on scripts being executed in order.

Summary

In this chapter, we have seen two key features for styling content. The first was master pages, which provides a simple and elegant system for defining consistent styles across some or all of the pages in a web application. I tend to switch to master pages in a project only when I have fleshed out the core features, and I am always struck by the immediate visual impact that consistent thematic elements bring to a web application. We could achieve the same effect in each page, but the master page system is almost effortless and avoids the problem of maintaining styles that are duplicated in every page.

The second technique we explored was the use of jQuery. The jQuery library is an essential tool to the ASP.NET programmer. It is easy to fall into the trap of believing that all of the magic in an ASP.NET application happens at the server, but that's a mistake. The scope of your application includes the browser, and we can do a lot in the browser to improve the experience that our users receive. The key to this is JavaScript—and, in particular, jQuery.

This is the first time in this book that we have encountered jQuery, but we will see it again in the next chapter when we look at user interactions and once more in Chapter 11 when we explore Ajax. The message to take from this is that although it is possible to build ASP.NET applications without using jQuery, it really doesn't make a lot of sense to do so, and realizing that the span of ASP.NET includes the browser will open up new vistas of development features.

CHAPTER 10

Adding Interactivity

The technologies that underpin a web application were not designed for stateful user interactions. The fact that we can build credible web applications at all is because of a lot of clever tricks and techniques built in to frameworks like ASP.NET. Web applications are like a magic trick; we form sessions from a series of stateless network requests, we hide essential information in the HTML we generate, and we express complex data relationships using simple markup.

By and large, everything works well enough to maintain the illusion, and we can make a fair stab at re-creating the experience of a traditional deployed application. But our weakest area—that which threatens to expose our web application as a façade—is the look and feel of our web pages. Standard HTML looks terrible, and every significant action in a web page causes a form POST, which can be slow. In a deployed application, the user experiences rich controls and sees a response to an action almost immediately. It can be hard to compete with that immediacy in a web application if you are sending the input from the user to the remote server for processing.

Fortunately, you can take steps to make your web applications more reactive and responsive, and you'll look at the most useful ones in this chapter. You'll return to jQuery, which you first saw in Chapter 9, and use JavaScript to explore different ways to enhance a web application.

No example in this chapter requires breaking changes for users who disable JavaScript in their browsers. By this I mean that you are going to use JavaScript to enhance the experience for users who enable it, but you'll maintain basic functions for those who don't. Most users leave JavaScript enabled, but a surprisingly large minority have it disabled, and the bias toward non-JavaScript clients increases sharply when you are targeting users in medium and large corporations. If you are targeting users in corporations in conservative markets—banking, insurance, government, and so on—then you must lower your expectations and expect to deal with client machines that disable most features and use obsolete versions of browsers. It is important, therefore, that you keep your target audience in mind and preserve functionality for every class of user you expect to support.

Creating the Project

In this chapter, we'll build directly on the web application that we built in Chapter 9, where we applied master pages and jQuery styles to the pages that let us view, add , edit, and delete triathlon events in the sample database.

Improving Client Interactions with jQuery

In the previous chapter, you saw how jQuery can be used to apply styling to elements in the HTML that you produce from the ASP.NET server. jQuery also includes a nice event system, which you can use to improve the interactions that users have with your applications.

Responding to Events

The HTML form element, the backbone of most web applications, was designed to collect information from a user, who would then click a submit button to send the data to the server. As the idea of the form has been stretched to give the user control over increasingly complex applications, the requirement for a distinct click of a button to move things along has become increasingly odd and redundant. You can see a good example of this in the ListEvents.aspx page, which presents the user with the ability to filter the displayed events by event type, as shown in Figure 10-1.

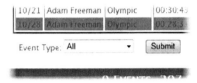

Figure 10-1. *The separate selection and button elements*

The user has to select the type of event they want to see from the drop-down list (All, Olympic, or Sprint) and then click the Submit button to have the selection take effect. You can improve on this by using the jQuery event system, as shown in Listing 10-1.

Listing 10-1. *Using jQuery events*

```
$(document).ready(function() {

    // respond to selections to filter the content and submit the form
    $('#<%=eventSelector.ClientID %>').change(function () {
        $('form').submit();
    });
    // hide the submit button
    $('input:submit').hide();

});
```

The jQuery event system is based upon the underlying JavaScript events, but the events are used in conjunction with the jQuery selectors. In Listing 10-1, the first part of the script, aside from the wrapper discussed in Chapter 9, is as follows:

```
$('#<%=eventSelector.ClientID %>').change(function () {
    // other statement
});
```

The selector finds the element with the ID assigned to the eventSelector element. As you can see from the ID value we are looking for, we are working with an .aspx web page that is associated with a master page (see the previous chapter for details).

Although jQuery selectors will match multiple elements, there is only one such HTML element with the ID you are looking for because ASP.NET makes the ID attribute values unique; it is the select element that presents the user with the drop-down list of event types. The call to the .change function allows us to register a function that will be invoked when the user changes the selected value. The second key statement in Listing 10-1 is what we want to happen when the user makes a selection:

```
$('form').submit();
```

The statement selects the HTML form elements (again, we know that there is only one in our page) and calls the submit function. When we call a jQuery event function with arguments, we register statements to be invoked when the event is triggered, but when we call the same function without argument, we invoke the event—in this case, we cause the form to be submitted to the ASP.NET server for processing. The last part of the script is this statement:

```
$('input:submit').hide();
```

The selector for this statement selects all of the input elements, and the :submit modifier then filters the selection for those whose type attribute is submit. There is one such element in the HTML, and it is the button the user has to click to submit the form.

The hide function does just what its name suggests; it hides the selected elements from the display. In the case of this example, we want to hide the submit button because it is no longer required. We want to include it in the page, just in case the user has disabled JavaScript, but we know that if our script has been executed, we can remove the button to avoid duplication and to avoid confusing the user. You can see the visual effect of this script by viewing the modified ListEvents.aspx page, also illustrated by Figure 10-2.

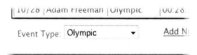

Figure 10-2. *Removing redundant HTML elements*

Now when the user makes a selection from the drop-down menu, the form is submitted to the server automatically, and the filtered data is returned and displayed—all without the user having to click a separate button.

Filtering Data at the Client

We can improve on the previous example by using jQuery to filter the rows in the events table. This means we don't have to make a request to the server to get a filtered set of data. Listing 10-2 shows a script that filters the data in the table without submitting the form to the server for processing.

Listing 10-2. *Filtering table rows*

```
$(document).ready(function () {
    // hide the submit button
    $('input:submit').hide();

    // respond to selections to filter the content and filter the content
    $('#<%=eventSelector.ClientID%>').change(function () {

        var selectedOption =
        $('#<%=eventSelector.ClientID%>').find('option:selected').text();

        if (selectedOption == 'All') {
            // ensure all rows are visible
            $('tr:has(td)').show();
        } else {
            $('tr:has(td)').hide();
            $("td:nth-child(3):contains('" + selectedOption + "')").parent().show();
        }
    });
});
```

We start by hiding the submit button again. We aren't going to need it in this example, not least because we are not going submit the form at all. We then add a function to be called when the user selects an option from the drop-down list:

```
$('#<%=eventSelector.ClientID%>').change(function () {
    // statements
});
```

This is the same approach that we took in the previous example. Inside the function, we get the text value of the selected item, as follows:

```
var selectedOption = $('#<%=eventSelector.ClientID%>').find('option:selected').text();
```

The selector in this statement matches the select control by ID. The find function is called to get the option elements contained within the select control, combined with the :selected modifier, which matches only selected elements. The result of this is the option element that the user has selected—the text function returns the label of the selected option element. Now that we know what the user is filtering for, we can respond accordingly:

```
if (selectedOption == 'All') {
    $('tr:has(td)').show();
} else {
    $('tr:has(td)').hide();
    $("td:nth-child(3):contains('" + selectedOption + "')").parent().show();
}
```

If the user has selected All, we select all tr elements that contain at least one td element. This gives us all the rows in the table except the header row. We call the show function to make sure all the rows are visible, which undoes the effect of any previous filtering. If the user has selected another option, then we hide all the rows so that nothing is visible and then select the rows we want to be visible again:

```
$("td:nth-child(3):contains('" + selectedOption + "')").parent().show();
```

The selector `td:nth-child(3)` selects all `td` elements that are the third child of their parent nodes. jQuery uses zero-based arrays in all functions except this one, which is one-based, which means that the third column in our table consists of children that are the third child of their parents. The `:contains` modifier restricts the selection to those elements that also contain the text that we are filtering on.

The result of the selector is the set of `td` elements that contain the target event type. We want to work with entire rows, which we can do with the `parent` function, which will return the `tr` for each selected `td`. The last step is to call `show` on each row to make it visible to the user. The result of this script is that the user can filter the content by event type without returning to the server for the filtered data. Figure 10-3 shows the resulting page.

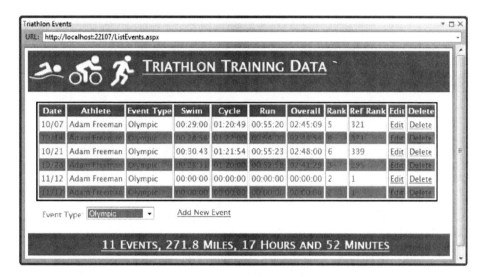

Figure 10-3. *Filtering table rows*

The approach works only for small sets of data and simple filters. Transferring large amounts of data to the browser can take longer than making requests for filtered subsets of the data. Further, we won't get any changes to the database until we reload the page. This is fine if we are the only user, because the add, edit, and delete operations end with the `ListEvents.aspx` page being loaded again. That said, there are many situations where the example shown in this section can be used. Not all projects work with large amounts of data, and not being able to see the latest updates from other users can be acceptable.

Replacing Links with Buttons

Users typically associate buttons with actions, not hyperlinks. In our `ListEvents.aspx` page, we present the user with hyperlinks to click if they want to add, edit, or delete an event. We can use jQuery to replace these links with regular buttons, as demonstrated by Listing 10-3.

Listing 10-3. Replacing hyperlinks with buttons

```
$(document).ready(function () {
    var counter = 0;
    // select all of the links in the page
    $('a').each(function () {
        var labelText = $(this).text();
        var targetURL = $(this).attr('href');
        var buttonID = 'newButton' + counter++;

        // create the button
        $(this).replaceWith("<button id='" + buttonID + "'>" + labelText + "</button>");

        // select the newly created button and bind to it
        $('#' + buttonID).click(function () {
            window.location = targetURL;
            return false;
        });
    });
});
```

This script starts by defining a variable called counter. We'll come back to this in a moment. We then select all the a elements and call the each function. This means the statements in the anonymous function we have created will be performed for each selected element, which is the equivalent of a C# foreach loop.

We create three variables each time the loop executes. The labelText variable is assigned the text from the a element (using the text function), and the targetURL is assigned the value of the href attribute (using the attr function). The final variable, buttonID, increments the value of counter and appends it to newButton. This creates a unique value for each element that we select and process.

The heart of this script is the replaceWith function, which replaces one HTML element with another. This is a helpful function because it lets us select all the a elements and then replace them with button elements, like this:

```
$(this).replaceWith("<button id='" + buttonID + "'>" + labelText + "</button>");
```

This function isn't quite as helpful as it could be, because it doesn't return the new element that we have created. This means we can't chain a call to the click function to register a handler function for when the button is clicked.

This means we have to select the button once we have created it, which is why we have assigned each button a unique id value. Here are the statements that select the newly created button and supply a function to be executed when the button is clicked:

```
$('#' + buttonID).click(function () {
    window.location = targetURL;
    return false;
});
```

The call to window.location uses the value of the href attribute from the original link to load the target page. Notice that we return false from this function. This stops the default browser handling of the event being performed (which is to submit the form that contains the button) and stops the event from being passed up the hierarchy of HTML elements for further processing.

Figure 10-4 shows the result of this script. You can see that all the links have been replaced with buttons. I have disabled the alternate-row coloring for this example; the combination of the coloring and the buttons creates an optical illusion where the buttons in alternate rows appear to be different sizes.

Figure 10-4. *Replacing hyperlinks with buttons*

When our goal is to create a web application that looks and behaves like a regular Windows application, simple changes like this can have a significant beneficial effect.

Improving Table Row Interactions

Tables are hard to read; long lists of similar information are hard to process. In this example, we are going to add two new interactions to the table in the `ListEvents.aspx` page to make it easier to work with. The first change will be to highlight the row when the mouse passes over it. This is a common technique to help users keep track of their progress in reviewing tables of data. The second change will be to allow the user to edit an event by clicking its row in the table. Listing 10-4 shows the jQuery script to enable both changes.

Listing 10-4. *Improving user interactions with table rows*

```
$(document).ready(function () {

    $('tr:has(td)').hover(
        function () {
            $(this).find('td').css({ 'background-color': '#007F7F', 'color': '#ffffff' });
        },
        function () {
            $(this).find('td').css({ 'background-color': '', 'color': '' });
```

```
    }).click(function () {
        $(this).find('td button:contains("Edit")').click();
    });
});
```

The key to highlighting rows is the hover event, which takes two functions as arguments. The first function is performed when the mouse first enters the screen space occupied by the element, and the second function is performed when the mouse leaves that area.

We bind to the event for each row (tr) that contains td elements. Once again, we don't want to change the header row. For the functions, we find the set of td elements that the affected row contains and use the css function to set and unset the CSS background-color and color properties. We would need to have defined a CSS class and then used the addClass and removeClass functions, but I found that the built-in browser in Visual Studio 2010 didn't change the row styles in response to these functions—that's why we set and unset the values directly.

The last part of this script chains a call to the click function for each selected tr element, providing a function to be called when the user clicks a row. The function that is called contains a single statement:

```
$(this).find('td button:contains("Edit")').click();
```

This statement finds the button element that contains the text *Edit* and is with a td element, within the tr element that triggered the click event. This is the edit button we created for the row in the previous example. Calling the click function without an argument invokes the event, just as though the user had clicked the button. This statement relies on the event handler we defined when we replaced the hyperlinks with buttons. If we are still using hyperlinks, we could achieve the same effect with this statement:

```
document.location = $(this).find('td a:contains("Edit")').attr('href');
```

This statement finds the a element that contains the text *Edit* and that is contained within a td element and then uses the JavaScript document.location feature to load the page specified by the value of the href attribute.

Validating Forms

One of the most effective ways to improve the way your users interact with your web application is to validate the contents of forms before they are submitted for processing. Immediate feedback, especially when something is wrong, can ease frustration and make a web application feel more responsive and more like a deployed Windows program.

We could handle the validation ourselves by using jQuery to bind functions to various events and parse the contents of the input elements in a form, but a neater approach is to use the jQuery extension library, which builds on the core jQuery features and provides a ready-made and flexible system for form validation. The compressed library is only 7KB and adds very little to the overhead of a project, and, like the base jQuery library, you can use the Microsoft CDN service to deliver the validation library to your clients. See the previous chapter for details of the CDN.

Installing the Validation Library

Download the validation library from http://jquery.bassistance.de, after which you can decompress the file and copy the jQuery.validate.min.js file to the Scripts folder of your ASP.NET project. Right-click the Scripts folder in the Visual Studio Solution Explorer window and select Add ➤ Existing Item from the pop-up menu. Then select the jQuery.validate.min.js file and click the Add button.

Once the library file appears in the Solution Explorer window, you can drag it to the web page or master page where you want to use it, or you can manually add a script element like this:

```
<script src="/Scripts/jquery.validate.min.js" type="text/javascript"></script>
```

Performing Validation

Once we have imported the validation library, we can add a script to validate the contents of a form. Listing 10-5 illustrated such a script, which I have added to the AddEvent.aspx page.

Listing 10-5. A form validation script

```
$(document).ready(function () {

    $('form').validate({
        errorLabelContainer: '#<%=errorDiv.ClientID%>',
        wrapper: 'li',
        rules: {
            <%=yearText.UniqueID %>: {
                required: true,
                range: [2010, 2012]
            }
        },
        messages: {
            <%=yearText.UniqueID %>: "Please enter a year from 2010 to 2012"
        }
    });
});
```

The form validation library is built on top of jQuery, so the selector and other features you saw in previous examples are all available for our use. We start by selecting the form element in the page and calling the validate function, like this:

```
$('form').validate({
    // other statements
});
```

This call sets up the validation on our form element. When the user submits the form, the contents of the form will be validated for us. The parameters to the validate function specify what validation should be performed and how any errors should be displayed. Like jQuery itself, the validation library is very flexible and has lots of different ways of achieve the same outcome. The approach we'll take is one that doesn't require changes to the HTML elements in the page. The first argument specifies where we want error messages to be displayed:

```
errorLabelContainer: '#<%=errorDiv.ClientID%>',
```

The errorLabelContainer parameter specifies the element that we want to use to display any error messages. Our AddEvent.aspx page contains a div with the ID errorDiv that we used for displaying errors in Chapter 7. I have specified this element, taking into account the way that ASP.NET rewrites the ID values when master pages are used. The next parameter specifies the element that should be used to wrap each error message:

```
wrapper: 'li',
```

213

Using the li element means that each error will be displayed as a bullet point, giving some structure to the display if there is more than one validation problem. The rules parameter specifies the validation that will be performed:

```
rules: {
    <%=yearText.UniqueID %>: {
        required: true,
        range: [2010, 2012]
    }
},
```

There is only one rule in this listing, and it applies to the yearText input element, where the user sets the year in which the event took place. Validation rules are applied based on the name attribute of an input element, which is unfortunate, because ASP.NET inserts these automatically so that it can keep track of form data. An element definition like this in the AddEvent.aspx file:

```
<input class="inputText" type="text" id="yearText" runat="server" />
```

ends up like this in the rendered HTML:

```
<input name="ctl00$MainContent$yearText" type="text" id="MainContent_yearText"
class="inputText" value="2010" />
```

The value attribute is set by the code-behind file, but the name attribute is created by the ASP.NET server and is beyond our control. To get the value of the name attribute, we can call the yearText.UniqueID property, which will return the name that ASP.NET generates, which, in this case, ctl00$MainContent$yearText. The rest of the rule specifies the constraints that are applied to the input element. There are two in this example:

```
required: true,
range: [2010, 2012]
```

Setting the required rule to true ensures that the user provides a value in the input field. The range rule takes a JavaScript array that specifies the lower and upper acceptable values. These rules are applied together, which means that we require the user to provide a year value that is between 2010 and 2012, inclusive.

The last part of our script tells the validation library what message we want the user to see when they have not supplied a value or when the value is outside the range that we have set:

```
messages: {
    <%=yearText.UniqueID %>: "Please enter a year from 2010 to 2012"
}
```

We specify the name of the element that the message applies to, using a code block to deal with the way that ASP.NET generates values for the name attribute and a text string to display to the user.

If you add this script to the AddEvent.aspx web page and then view it in the browser, you can see the effect of the validation, as shown in Figure 10-5. Clear the text box for the year or enter a value that is outside the range and click the Add button.

Figure 10-5. Validating a form

Nothing happened until the Add button is clicked, but once it is, the validation is performed, and the error message is displayed to the user. The validator now goes into *live* mode and validates the content every time you click a key, giving immediate feedback as you resolve the problem. Once you have entered a value that meets the criteria set in the validation rule, the error disappears, and you can click the Add button once again to submit the form and create the event in the database.

■ **Caution** Client-side form validation is a complement to, not a replacement for, server-side validation. You cannot rely on the user using a browser with JavaScript enabled. In extreme cases, you might find that your users are submitting form data programmatically (that is, not using a browser at all) or are trying to deliberately subvert your application by sending the server bad values. Client-side validation is a nice way to improve your users' experience, but it doesn't relieve you of the burden of checking the data again when it reaches the server.

The required and range rules are built in to the jQuery form validation library. Table 10-1 explains these and other built-in rules.

Table 10-1. *Useful Built-in Form Validation Rules*

Rule	Description
`required: true;`	A value is required.
`minlength: length;`	The value must contain at least length characters.
`maxlength: length`	The value must contain no more than length characters.
`rangelength: [minLen, maxLen]`	The value must contain at least `minLen` and no more than `maxLen` characters.
`min: minVal`	The value must be at least as large as `minVal`.
`max: maxVal`	The value must be at least as large as `maxVal`.
`range: [minVal, maxVal]`	The value must be between `minVal` and `maxVal`.
`email: true`	The value must be a valid e-mail address.
`url: true`	The value must be a URL.
`date: true`	The value must be a valid JavaScript date.
`number: true`	The value must be a decimal number.
`digits: true`	The value must contain only digits.
`creditcard: true`	The value must contain a credit card number.

Creating a Custom Validation Rule

The built-in form validation rules are useful for most situations, but not every format of input is supported. We can address this by defining custom rules, also known as *custom methods*. To demonstrate this feature, we will create a method to validate the inputs for the time taken for each stage of the triathlon, where we want the user to enter a value that we can parse into a C# System.TimeSpan, such as 2:34:12, representing two hours, thirty-four minutes, and twelve seconds. Listing 10-6 shows the additions to the validation script that define and apply such a method.

Listing 10-6. *Adding a simple custom validation rule*

```
$(document).ready(function () {

    $.validator.addMethod(
        'timespan',
        function (value, element) {
            return value != '0:00:00' && value.match(/[0-9]:[0-5][0-9]:[0-5][0-9]/);
        });

    $('form').validate({
        errorLabelContainer: '#<%=errorDiv.ClientID%>',
        wrapper: 'li',
        rules: {
            <%=yearText.UniqueID %>: {
                required: true,
                range: [2010, 2012]
            },
            <%=swimText.UniqueID %>: {
                timespan: true
            },
            <%=cycleText.UniqueID %>: {
                timespan: true
            },
            <%=runText.UniqueID %>: {
                timespan:true
            }
        },
        messages: {
            <%=yearText.UniqueID %>: "Please enter a year from 2010 to 2012",
            <%=swimText.UniqueID %>: "Please enter a swim time such as 1:34:52",
            <%=cycleText.UniqueID %>: "Please enter a cycle time such as 1:34:52",
            <%=runText.UniqueID %>: "Please enter a run time such as 1:34:52"
        }
    });
});
```

I have marked the additions to the script in bold. The first part defines a new method that we will use to validate time spans, as follows:

```
$.validator.addMethod(
    'timespan',
    function (value, element) {
        return value != '0:00:00' && value.match(/[0-9]:[0-5][0-9]:[0-5][0-9]/);
    }
);
```

We add new validation methods by calling the `$.validator.addMethod` function, which takes two parameters. The first is the name for the new method, and the second is a function that is used to evaluate whatever the user has entered into the `input` element. The function returns `true` if the user input is acceptable and `false` otherwise. In the example, I have given the new method the name `timespan`. The function checks to see that the user has not left the default value (0:00:00) and that the input matches a regular expression, which enforces a pattern that I can parse to a `TimeSpan` at the server.

The next step is to apply this method in the `rules` parameter to the `validate` function, like this:

```
...
<%=yearText.UniqueID %>: {
    required: true,
    range: [2010, 2012]
},
<%=swimText.UniqueID %>: {
    timespan: true
},
...
```

We apply the new method in the same way as we would the built-in ones. In this fragment, I have applied the rule to the swimText input, using a code block to get the `UniqueID` property of the HTML control. As you can see in Listing 10-6, I have applied the rule to each of the three time inputs in the form. This is a relatively verbose set of statements. The validation library does provide a more elegant approach that uses the `class` attribute to associate rules with `form` elements, but I prefer this approach because it doesn't require modification to the HTML part of the page. (And, as an aside, I find it more reliable inside the Visual Studio browser—not that anyone uses the browser in production, but I find it convenient for testing.)

The final stage is to define the messages that we want the user to see when the input doesn't satisfy the custom rule, which follows the same format as the existing message in the script:

```
...
<%=yearText.UniqueID %>: "Please enter a year from 2010 to 2012",
<%=swimText.UniqueID %>: "Please enter a swim time such as 1:34:52",
...
```

The validation library will now check the contents of the three time-related input elements and apply our new rule, warning the user if the content isn't what we need. This is in addition to the rule we defined previously, so the user will end up with multiple errors when there are multiple problems, as illustrated by Figure 10-6.

Figure 10-6. *Applying a custom validation rule*

You can see from Figure 10-6 that none of the values supplied for the swim, cycle, and run times match the format we require and that, as a consequence, an error message regarding each input is displayed. The input for the year is out of range, and you can see that the errors resulting from different rules and methods are displayed seamlessly together.

Validating Associated Inputs

Not all inputs in a form exist in isolation. For example, the validity of the day of the month depends on the month that has been selected. We want to make sure that the user doesn't submit a form where the date is February 31, for example. Listing 10-7 shows the additions to the jQuery script.

Listing 10-7. Adding a validation rule that associates two HTML elements

```
<script type="text/javascript">
$(document).ready(function () {

    var daysInMonth = new Array(31, 28, 31, 30, 31, 30, 31, 31, 30, 31, 30, 31);

    maxDaysInMonth = function () {
        return daysInMonth[$('#<%=monthSelect.ClientID%> option:selected').index()];
    }

    $.validator.addMethod(
        'timespan',
        function (value, element) {
            return value != '0:00:00' && value.match(/[0-9]:[0-5][0-9]:[0-5][0-9]/);
        });

    $('form').validate({
        errorLabelContainer: '#<%=errorDiv.ClientID%>',
        wrapper: 'li',
        rules: {
            <%=yearText.UniqueID %>: {
                required: true,
                range: [2010, 2012]
            },
            <%=swimText.UniqueID %>: {
                timespan: true
            },
            <%=cycleText.UniqueID %>: {
                timespan: true
            },
            <%=runText.UniqueID %>: {
                timespan:true
            },
            <%=dayText.UniqueID %>: {
                required:true,
                range: function() { return [1, maxDaysInMonth()] }
            }
        },
```

```
        messages: {
            <%=yearText.UniqueID %>: "Please enter a year from 2010 to 2012",
            <%=swimText.UniqueID %>: "Please enter a swim time such as 1:34:52",
            <%=cycleText.UniqueID %>: "Please enter a cycle time such as 1:34:52",
            <%=runText.UniqueID %>: "Please enter a run time such as 1:34:52",
            <%=dayText.UniqueID %>: {
                required: "Please enter a day",
                range: jQuery.format("Please enter a day between 1 and {1}")
            }
        }
    });

    $('#<%=monthSelect.ClientID %>').change(function() {
        $('#<%=dayText.ClientID %>').valid();
    });
});
```

```
</script>
```

We start these additions by defining a function that will return the number of days in the month that is currently selected in the monthSelect element:

```
var daysInMonth = new Array(31, 28, 31, 30, 31, 30, 31, 31, 30, 31, 30, 31);

maxDaysInMonth = function () {
    return daysInMonth[$('#<%=monthSelect.ClientID%> option:selected').index()];
}
```

This is standard stuff. I define an array that contains the number of days in each month and a function called maxDaysInMonth that gets the selection option element from within the select element and then calls the index function to get its position in the set of options available, which in then is used to return a value from the daysInMonth array.

This function is used in the rule that is applied to the dayText element, as follows:

```
...
<%=runText.UniqueID %>: {
    timespan:true
},
<%=dayText.UniqueID %>: {
    required:true,
    range: function() { return [1, maxDaysInMonth()] }
}
...
```

There are two parts to the rule, which is shown in bold. The first part is the standard require rule, meaning that we want to the user to provide a value. The second part uses the range rule, but the range is generated dynamically using a function that calls the maxDaysInMonth function. This means that when the form is validated, the acceptable range for the day value is driven by the currently selected month, preventing the user from entering dates that don't exist. (I have omitted handling leap years because we can take an example too far, but you get the idea.)

Next, we define the messages that the user will see if the newly added rule isn't satisfied during validation. I have used a couple of more advanced features for the messages for this rule:

```
...
<%=dayText.UniqueID %>:  {
    required: "Please enter a day",
    range: jQuery.format("Please enter a day between 1 and {1}")
}
...
```

The first feature is the ability to define different messages for each of the rules applied to an input element. For the dayText element, we defined required and range rules, and you can see from the listing that I have created different messages to be displayed for each of these rules.

The second feature is the ability to create messages that contain contextual information about the rule to which they respond. If you specify your message using a call to jQuery.format, you can refer to the parameters of your rule as {0}, {1}, and so on, just as you would when using the C# composite formatting feature. The meaning and number of these parameters varies between rules, but for the range rule, parameter 0 is the low-range bound and parameter 1 is the high-range bound. You can see the parameters for the built-in functions in Table 10-1.

The last addition to the script helps the user by giving the validation a more dynamic feel:

```
$('#<%=monthSelect.ClientID %>').change(function() {
    $('#<%=dayText.ClientID %>').valid();
});
```

We create a handler for the change function of the month select element, which calls the valid function on the dayText element. The valid function performs form validation on the selected element. This allows the user to fix a date problem by selecting a different month. If the user selects Feb from the list of months, enters 30 in the day input, and clicks Add, they will see an error. They can correct this error by entering a lower value or, thanks to previous fragment, selecting another month—at which time the day field is revalidated using the newly selected month as the basis for the range rule. Figure 10-7 shows the effect of this rule.

Figure 10-7. *Associating elements to create validation rules*

By using the validation library and core jQuery features, we have been able to create a validation rule in which the acceptable range of inputs for one element is driven by the currently selected value of another element.

Using jQuery UI

The scope and features of JavaScript libraries have exploded in recent years, and a good example of this is jQuery UI, which is a user interface toolkit built by the jQuery team on top of the core jQuery library. A good JavaScript UI toolkit such as jQuery UI allows us to build web applications that have more dynamic user controls and to further extend the visual theme of our pages.

The jQuery UI library has a lot of features—everything including drag and drop; special effects for making elements and widgets move, pulse, and flash on and off; and, of course, a set of rich widgets for improving user interactions.

This chapter will focus on enhancements that are simple, have a high impact, and are applicable to our example web application. I have picked examples that draw in the features of the core jQuery library as well. When you combine jQuery and jQuery UI, you can create some truly useful enhancements.

For full details of what jQuery UI can do, I recommend the comprehensive and clear documentation on jQueryUI.com. If you want more of a tutorial approach, then I recommend Dan Wellman's book *jQuery UI*, published by Packt Publishing.

Installing jQuery UI

You can download jQuery UI from jQueryUI.com. The link for the download is on the main page, and you get a zip file that contains everything you need. One of the strengths of jQuery UI is its strong support for visual themes, and a nice touch on the jQueryUI.com web site is the ability to create a custom download that contains only the UI elements you intend to use and a visual theme created to your specification, as illustrated in Figure 10-8.

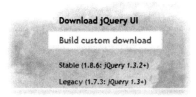

Figure 10-8. *Selecting the standard or custom jQuery UI downloads*

If you select the custom download option, you will be presented with a series of options to include or exclude individual widgets and special effects. You can also select a preconfigured visual theme or create a custom theme. When I downloaded jQuery UI for this chapter, I specified a custom theme to complement the appearance of the master pages we created in Chapter 9. The theme is expressed using CSS, and you can use the CSS classes throughout your project. (However, I have not done so for the example application, choosing instead to pick a theme using the same colors as in the master pages.)

Adding jQuery UI to your web application project is the same process irrespective of whether you chose the standard build or a custom build. You'll end up with a zip file that contains the library, the CSS styles, and documentation. Here are the steps you'll need to follow once you have decompressed the zip archive:

1. Copy the `jquery-ui-1.8.6.custom.min.js` file from the `js` directory of the zip file to the `Scripts` folder in your project.

2. Copy the `jquery-ui-1.8.6.custom.css` file and the `images` directory from the `css` directory of the zip file to the `Styles` folder in your project.

3. Add the jQuery UI library to your project by right-clicking the `Scripts` folder in the Visual Studio Solution Explorer window, selecting Add ➤ Existing Item from the pop-up menu, selecting the `jquery-ui-1.8.6.custom.min.js` file, and clicking the Add button.

4. Add the CSS themes to your project by right-clicking the `Styles` folder in the Visual Studio Solution Explorer window, selecting Add ➤ Existing Item from the pop-up menu, selecting the `jquery-ui-1.8.6.custom.css` file, and clicking the Add button.

The names of the files you download may differ; version numbers change as new releases are published, and the location of the CSS file and images directory varies slightly depending on which approach you have taken to create the download file.

The `images` directory is referenced by the CSS file, which is why we have copied it to the `Styles` folder rather than the `images` folder. If you are keen to keep different kinds of files together, you can move the images and replace the references to their location in the CSS file, but doing so means that you'll have to keep making these changes each time you install a new version of jQuery UI. I find it simpler to leave them in the CSS directory.

Once you have copied the files into place, you can add jQuery UI to a page by dragging the JavaScript library and the CSS file and dropping it on the page. Alternatively, you can manually add the required elements, as follows:

```
<script src="Scripts/jquery-ui-1.8.6.custom.min.js" type="text/javascript"></script>
<link href="Styles/jquery-ui-1.8.6.custom.css" rel="stylesheet" type="text/css" />
```

Creating a Better Button

The first thing we'll do with jQuery UI is to create better buttons. If you view the AddEvent.aspx page, you'll see that we are using the default HTML input button, as shown in Figure 10-9.

Figure 10-9. *The default form button*

We can use jQuery UI to create a button, which is consistent with the visual theme for our web application. Listing 10-8 provides a demonstration.

Listing 10-8. *Using the jQuery UI button feature*

```
<script type="text/javascript">

    $(document).ready(function () {

        $('input:submit').button().css({ 'width': 75, 'height': 35 });

        // create a cancel button
        $('input:submit').parent().append('<button>Cancel</button>')
            .find('button').button().css({ 'width': 75, 'height': 35 })
            .click(function() {document.location = '/ListEvents.aspx'});
    });

</script>
```

The script in Listing 10-8 is largely core jQuery. In fact, there are only two calls to a jQuery UI feature, which I have marked in bold—the call to the button function. The first statement selects the input button in the HTML form and converts it to a jQuery UI button:

```
$('input:submit').button().css({ 'width': 75, 'height': 35 });
```

That's all there is to it. A call to button causes jQuery UI to rewrite the HTML document so that we end up with something that is visual consistent. The effect of clicking the button is preserved, which in the case of the AddEvent.aspx page means that the input values are validated, and if everything is OK, the form is submitted to the ASP.NET server for processing.

The rest of the script demonstrates how to create a button programmatically. We can improve users' interaction with this page by providing a cancel button that takes them back to the ListEvents.aspx page when clicked. Here is the jQuery/jQuery UI script that creates such a button:

```
$('input:submit').parent().append('<button>Cancel</button>')
    .find('button').button().css({ 'width': 75, 'height': 35 })
    .click(function() {document.location = '/ListEvents.aspx'});
```

This statement selects the submit button in the form and then selects the parent and appends new HTML that defines a button with the text *Cancel*. This button is a peer to the submit button in the HTML document because we have added it to the parent.

Having created the new button element, we have to select it again (because the append function returns the element you appended content to, not the content) and then call the button function to have jQuery UI work its magic.

Both statements tweak the CSS for the jQuery UI buttons so that they are the same width and my preferred height, and I have added a handler for the click function of the Cancel button, which will load the ListEvents.aspx page. You can see the result of this script in Figure 10-10.

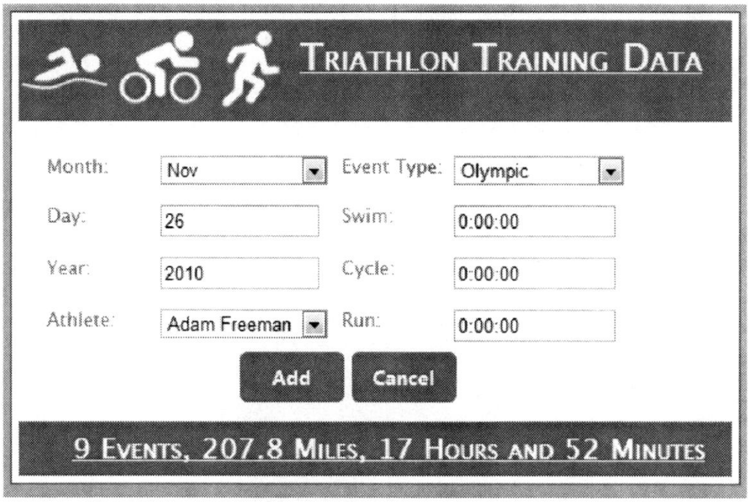

Figure 10-10. Using the jQuery UI button feature

⬛ **Note** The screenshots in this section are taken from Google Chrome and not the Visual Studio built-in browser, which doesn't display the rounded edges of the buttons correctly. Internet Explorer, up to and including version 8, doesn't implement this CSS feature and falls back to displaying square corners.

The jQuery UI button function can also be used to create themed buttons from hyperlinks. Listing 10-9 contains a simple demonstration, which I have applied to the ListEvents.aspx page.

Listing 10-9. Adding jQuery UI buttons to the ListEvents.aspx page

```
<script type="text/javascript">
    $(document).ready(function () {
        $('a').button().css('color', '#ffffff');
        $('td a').css('font-size', 'smaller');
    });
</script>
```

The same basic pattern applies to this example—select the targets, call the button function, and then tweak the CSS to fine-tune the appearance. In Listing 10-9, I select all the a elements, make them into buttons, and then set the CSS color property to override the styling defined for the a element in the Site.css file, as follows:

```
$('a').button().css('color', '#ffffff');
```

The a elements in the ListEvents.aspx file are in two groups. There is the Add Event link toward the bottom of the page that loads the AddEvent.aspx page, and the Edit and Delete links are contained in the HTML table, which allow the user to modify or remove an event from the database. We want the buttons in the table to be slightly smaller. To do this, we can modify the a elements so that they have a smaller font size, like this:

```
$('td a').css('font-size', 'smaller');
```

The appearance of the jQuery UI button is driven by the element the button function was applied to, so changing the size of the font for an a element reduces the display size of the jQuery UI button associated with it. You can see the effect of the script in Listing 10-9 in Figure 10-11.

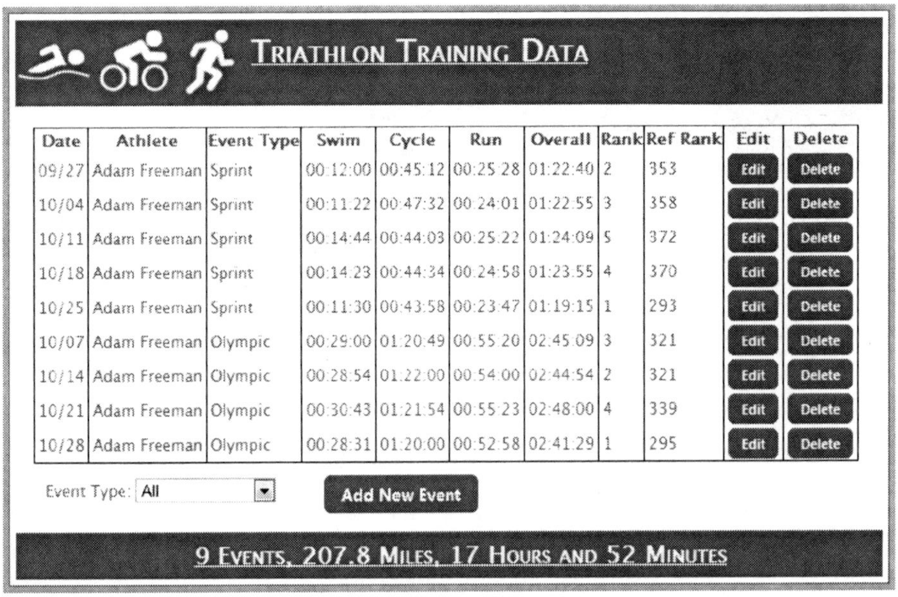

Figure 10-11. jQuery UI buttons applied to the ListEvents.aspx page

We have barely scratched the surface of the jQuery UI button feature. You can use it to create radio buttons, checkboxes, toolbars, buttons with icons, buttons with drop-down lists, and much more.

CREATING A BETTER SELECT ELEMENT

One omission from the jQuery UI feature set is a replacement for the select element. You can see from Figure 10-11 that the select that we use to filter events is out of keeping with the other parts of the interface.

We can remedy this by using the jQuery UI autocomplete feature. One of the examples for this feature on the jQuery UI web site demonstrates how to make a themed combo box, which fits nicely as a replacement for a select element.

The code required to demonstrate this feature is too long for this chapter, but I have included a jQuery script, called combobox.js, in the sample project for this part of the chapter. The script is based on the web site example, but I have added simple features to make it more useful in the example project. For example, the text input is readonly, and I expose the button and input elements using ID attributes so that they can be styled with CSS. You can see the effect of adding this feature to the ListEvents.aspx page in Figure 10-12.

Figure 10-12. *Adding a replacement for the select element*

Here are the statements that add the combo box to the ListEvents.aspx web page:

```
$(document).ready(function () {
    $("#<%=eventSelector.ClientID %>").combobox();
    $('#comboBoxInput').css('height', $('#comboBoxButton').height() - 2).width('100px');
});
```

The combobox function converts the select element to the combo box. The second statement tweaks the CSS to make the control narrower than it would be normally and to make the input and the button the same height.

Making Selecting Dates Easier

The next jQuery UI example focuses on making it easier for the user to select a date. The AddEvent.aspx page in the example web application presents three inputs for the user: a select for the month and text boxes for the year and the day. We will switch from this approach to use one of the most widely used jQuery UI controls—the date picker. The date picker presents the user with a pop-up calendar from which a date can be selected. This is simpler for the user and means that we can be sure the date is properly formatted. Listing 10-10 shows the script that introduces the date picker to the AddEvent.aspx web page.

Listing 10-10. *Using the jQuery UI date picker*

```
<script type="text/javascript">

    $(document).ready(function () {

        // get the three fields we are working with
        var dayField = $('#<%=dayText.ClientID %>');
        var monthField = $('#<%=monthSelect.ClientID %>');
        var yearField = $('#<%=yearText.ClientID %>');

        // get the parent that contains the date fields and add a new label and field
        var parentDiv = $(dayField).parent().parent();
        // insert the new field and label
        parentDiv.prepend('<div class="elementDiv"><div class="labelDiv">Date:</div>' +
            '<input class="inputText" type="text" id="dateText"/></div>');

        // set the intial value of the combined field
        $('#dateText').val(jQuery.format('{0}/{1}/{2}',
            $(monthField).find('option:selected').index(),
            dayField.val(), yearField.val()));

        // hide the original fields
        dayField.parent().hide();
        monthField.parent().hide();
        yearField.parent().hide();

        // move the event type input to the left-most column
        parentDiv.append($('#<%=eventTypeSelect.ClientID %>').parent().remove());

        // register a date picker on the field
        $('#dateText').datepicker({
            changeMonth: true,
            changeYear: true,
            yearRange: '2010:2012',
            selectOtherMonths: true,
            selectOtherYears: true,
            onClose: function (dateText, instance) {
                // get the selected date and split it
                var dateElements = $(this).val().split('/');
                monthField.find('option[index=' + (dateElements[0] -1)
                    + ']').attr('selected', 'selected');
```

```
                dayField.val(dateElements[1]);
                yearField.val(dateElements[2]);
            }
        });
    });

</script>
```

The first part of the script is preparation for the date picker, which involves reworking the page structure so that there is a single input that contains the entire date. To do this, we insert a new group of elements so that there is a new input as a peer to the existing three:

```
var parentDiv = $(dayField).parent().parent();
parentDiv.prepend('<div class="elementDiv"><div class="labelDiv">Date:</div>' +
            '<input class="inputText" type="text" id="dateText"/></div>');
```

We set the value of this new field using the values of the existing field, which the ASP.NET server will have set to today's date when rendering the page:

```
$('#dateText').val(jQuery.format('{0}/{1}/{2}',
    $(monthField).find('option:selected').index(),
        dayField.val(), yearField.val()));
```

As described earlier, the jQuery format function works similarly to the C# composite formatting feature, where values passed as parameters are inserted into a string in place of escaped indices, such as {0} and {1}.

The next step is to hide the original three date inputs. We don't want to remove them from the document, because they are an important part of the form, but we don't want the user to be able to see them any more:

```
dayField.parent().hide();
monthField.parent().hide();
yearField.parent().hide();
```

This leaves us with an odd layout. We have two inputs in the left column and four in the right. We can use jQuery to move one of the inputs on the right to the left, like this:

```
parentDiv.append($('#<%=eventTypeSelect.ClientID %>').parent().remove());
```

This statement selects the select element for the event type, calls the parent function to select the containing element, and removes it from its current position. The remove function returns the element that was removed and was passed to the append function, which inserts the element as the last content item in the target. You can see the effect of this page restructuring in Figure 10-13.

Figure 10-13. *Restructuring a page in preparation for the jQuery UI date picker*

Now that we have restructured the page, we can add the date picker control, which we do by calling the datepicker function on the input we want it to control, like this:

```
$('#dateText').datepicker({
    changeMonth: true,
    changeYear: true,
    yearRange: '2010:2012',
    selectOtherMonths: true,
    selectOtherYears: true,
    onClose: function (dateText, instance) {
        // get the selected date and split it
        var dateElements = $(this).val().split('/');
        monthField.find('option[index=' + (dateElements[0] -1)
            + ']').attr('selected', 'selected');
        dayField.val(dateElements[1]);
        yearField.val(dateElements[2]);
    }
});
```

Like most jQuery UI controls, the date picker has many configuration options. The options we have chosen allow the user to change the year and month and limit the range of dates that can be selected to between 2010 and 2012. You may recall that 2010 to 2012 is the range we checked for when we implemented form validation earlier in the chapter. Setting this constraint ensures that the user can't select a date with the picker that we later reject for being out of range.

The most important option for our purposes is onClose, which allows us to specify a function that will be called when the user has selected a date. The previous function gets the value from the combined date input, splits it, and uses the results to set the values of the original, now hidden, form elements. In this way, we have added the date picker without making any changes to the underlying HTML. When the user clicks or focuses on the date input, the date picker window will pop up, as shown in Figure 10-14.

Figure 10-14. *The jQuery UI date picker control*

I am very fond of jQuery and jQuery UI and of the examples in this chapter, but this one is my favorite. It shows the flexibility that jQuery gives you in making your pages easier to use without penalizing users without JavaScript. We created new elements, hid old ones, moved yet others around the page, and used the event mechanism to map between a unified date picker and the three separate inputs that the ASP.NET server expects—and we did all of this without changing any of the page HTML.

Adding Context with Tabs

The last jQuery UI feature we will look at involves adding tabs to our pages so that the user has an immediate sense of the area of the web application they are using and has a simple way to switch between them.

Using Basic jQuery UI Tabs

I will start by showing a simple example, using the generic tabs behavior. Tabs, like all jQuery UI features, are endlessly configurable, but a solid and basic demonstration of how they work is a good place to start.

To begin, I have created a new web page in the example project called `Performance.aspx`, which displays the best times and rankings in the database. Listing 10-10 shows the contents of `Performance.aspx`.

Listing 10-10. *The Performance.aspx web page*

```
<%@ Page Title="" Language="C#" MasterPageFile="~/Site.Master" AutoEventWireup="true"
CodeBehind="Performance.aspx.cs" Inherits="StylingContent.Performance" %>

<asp:Content ID="Content1" ContentPlaceHolderID="HeadContent" runat="server">
    <link href="Styles/Page.css" rel="stylesheet" type="text/css" />
</asp:Content>

<asp:Content ID="Content2" ContentPlaceHolderID="MainContent" runat="server">
```

```
<div id="sprintData">
    <table class="centerTable">
        <colgroup>
            <col/>
            <col width="100px" />
        </colgroup>
        <tr><th colspan="4">Sprint Results</th></tr>
        <tr>
            <td>Best Swim Time:</td><td id="sprintSwimTime" runat="server"/>
            <td>Best Swim Rank:</td><td id="sprintSwimRank" runat="server"/>
        </tr>
        <tr>
            <td>Best Cycle Time:</td><td id="sprintCycleTime" runat="server"/>
            <td>Best Cycle Rank:</td><td id="sprintCycleRank" runat="server"/>
        </tr>
        <tr>
            <td>Best Run Time:</td><td id="sprintRunTime" runat="server"/>
            <td>Best Run Rank:</td><td id="sprintRunRank" runat="server"/>
        </tr>
        <tr>
            <td>Best Overall Time:</td><td id="sprintOverallTime" runat="server"/>
            <td>Best Overall Rank:</td><td id="sprintOverallRank" runat="server"/>
        </tr>
    </table>
</div>

<p />

<div id="olympicData">
    <table class="centerTable">
        <colgroup>
            <col />
            <col width="100px" />
        </colgroup>
        <tr><th colspan="4">Olympic Results</th></tr>
        <tr>
            <td>Best Swim Time:</td><td id="olympicSwimTime" runat="server"/>
            <td>Best Swim Rank:</td><td id="olympicSwimRank" runat="server"/>
        </tr>
        <tr>
            <td>Best Cycle Time:</td><td id="olympicCycleTime" runat="server"/>
            <td>Best Cycle Rank:</td><td id="olympicCycleRank" runat="server"/>
        </tr>
        <tr>
            <td>Best Run Time:</td><td id="olympicRunTime" runat="server"/>
            <td>Best Run Rank:</td><td id="olympicRunRank" runat="server"/>
        </tr>
```

```
        <tr>
            <td>Best Overall Time:</td><td id="olympicOverallTime" runat="server"/>
            <td>Best Overall Rank:</td><td id="olympicOverallRank" runat="server"/>
        </tr>
    </table>
</div>

</asp:Content>
```

This page has a simple layout. There are two tables, which display the best times and ranks for the sprint and Olympic triathlon distances. The code-behind class populates the cells of the table using methods that I have added to the DataAccess class. I have not listed the class or the changes to DataAccess because they are not germane to this example, but you can see the details in the code download that accompanies this book, available without charge from Apress.com. You can see how the Performance.aspx page appears in Figure 10-15.

Figure 10-15. *The Performance.aspx page without tabs*

To add tabs to this page, we need to add an element to the page to create a home for the tabs to reside:

```
...
<asp:Content ID="Content2" ContentPlaceHolderID="MainContent" runat="server">

    <div id="tabsDiv"></div>

    <div id="sprintData">
...
```

The additional element is shown in bold—an empty div with an ID of tabsDiv. Once we have the new element, we can add a script to the page to create the tabs, as shown in Listing 10-11.

Listing 10-11. Adding tabs with a script

```
<script type="text/javascript">

    $(document).ready(function () {
        $('#tabsDiv').tabs()
            .tabs("add", "#sprintData", "Sprint Triathlon")
            .tabs("add", "#olympicData", "Olympic Triathlon");

        $('.main').hide();
        $('th').text("Results");

    });
</script>
```

We enable the tabs feature by calling the tabs function on the div element we created previously and use the tabs method on the result to add each tab. When creating individual tabs, we specify the add function, the section of the page that should be displayed by this tab, and the tab's label, like this:

```
.tabs("add", "#sprintData", "Sprint Triathlon")
```

▨ **Tip**   The jQuery UI tabs feature can also load the contents of tabs from the server using Ajax. See Chapter 11 for details of how to create and use Ajax services.

You can see the effect of the tabs in Figure 10-16. The unselected tab highlights when the mouse moves over it, and clicking the tab switches the content so that the other table is displayed.

Figure 10-16. *The effect of adding tabs to the Performance.aspx page*

Using Tabs with Master Pages

Adding tabs to a web application so that different pages are associated with different tabs requires more effort. The problem comes because the approach taken by ASP.NET master pages and jQuery UI are quite different; melding them together requires a little effort and patience.

What we need to do is introduce tabs into the master page and create a mapping between the pages of our application and the tab they should be associated with. When we click a tab, the appropriate page will be loaded, and the change will be reflected in the selected tab. As with the previous tab example, we begin by adding a div that will hold the tabs. However, in this case, we must apply it to the master page file, Site.master:

```
...
<div class="header">
    <div class="title" id="titleDiv" runat="server">
        <img src="Images/triathlon.png" alt="Triathlon Icon" />
        <h1>Triathlon Training Data</h1>
    </div>
</div>

<div id="masterTabsDiv"><ul></ul></div>

<div class="main">
    <asp:ContentPlaceHolder ID="MainContent" runat="server"/>
</div>
...
```

The new element is in bold, and Listing 10-12 shows the script that creates the tabs. This script is more complicated than the previous example because we are, in essence, going to use the CSS and layout features of jQuery UI tabs but override the way that tabs are selected so that we control the mapping of tabs to pages.

Listing 10-12. *Adding tabs through master pages*

```javascript
<script type="text/javascript">

    $(document).ready(function () {

        var pages = [
            ['Events', "/ListEvents.aspx", "/AddEvent.aspx", "UpdateOrDeleteEvent.aspx"],
            ['Performance', "/Performance.aspx"]
        ];

        var myPage = '<%=Request.Path %>';
        var tabsDiv = $('#masterTabsDiv');

        tabsDiv.tabs({
            select: function (event, ui) {
                document.location = pages[ui.index][1];
                return false;
            }
        });

        var indexToSelect = 0;

        for (var i = 0; i < pages.length; i++) {
            for (j = 0; j < pages[i].length; j++) {
                if (pages[i][j] == myPage) {
                    indexToSelect = i;
                    break;
                }
            }
            tabsDiv.tabs("add", '#main', pages[i][0]);
        }

        tabsDiv.find('li').removeClass('ui-tabs-selected ui-state-active');
        tabsDiv.find('li').eq(indexToSelect).addClass('ui-tabs-selected ui-state-active');
    });

</script>
```

To best understand this example, it helps to see the finished result, which is shown in Figure 10-17. The tabs appear below the header but above the main body of the page. There are two tabs (Events and Performance), and clicking a tab takes you to a corresponding page (Events.aspx and Performance.aspx, respectively).

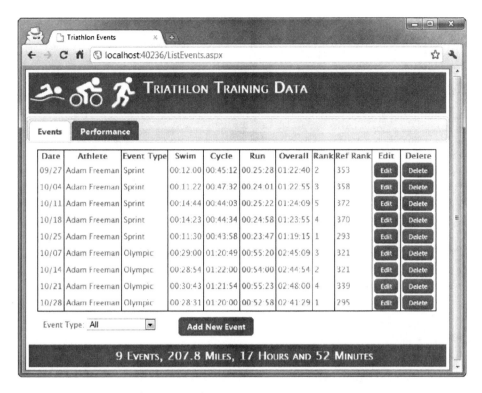

Figure 10-17. *Adding tabs using master pages*

Returning to the jQuery script, we begin by defining a mapping between the labels for the tabs and the pages that will be displayed using them, as follows:

```
var pages = [
    ['Events', "/ListEvents.aspx", "/AddEvent.aspx", "UpdateOrDeleteEvent.aspx"],
    ['Performance', "/Performance.aspx"]
];
```

The pages variable is an array of arrays. The first item in each inner array is the tab label, and the remaining items represent the pages that the label will be used for. What I want is for all the pages that are related by function to be displayed using the same tab. For example, the ListEvents.aspx, AddEvents.aspx, and UpdateOrDeleteEvent.aspx pages are all related to events and so—for visual consistency—we want the Events tab to be selected when any of these pages are being viewed.

Next, we define a couple of useful variables. myPage contains the path of the current page, which we obtain using a code block to read the Request.Path property. The tabsDiv is the div element we created to hold the tabs and that we need to refer to several times in the script:

```
var myPage = '<%=Request.Path %>';
var tabsDiv = $('#masterTabsDiv');
```

We use the second of these variables to call the tabs function, which creates the tabs using the div element we created for this purpose. We set an option that defines a custom handler that will be called when the user clicks a tab:

```
tabsDiv.tabs({
    select: function (event, ui) {
        document.location = pages[ui.index][1];
        return false;
    }
});
```

We want some nonstandard behavior here. When the user clicks a tab, we want to load the first page from the appropriate pages array. For example, if the user clicks the Events tab, we want to load the ListEvents.aspx page, and clicking the Performance tab will load the Performance.aspx page. We load the page using the standard document.location JavaScript property and return false from our custom function to prevent the default tabs event handling code from being used.

The remaining code creates the tabs from the page arrays and works out which of the tabs should be highlighted given the path of the current page. This requires some diligent searching through arrays:

```
var indexToSelect = 0;

for (var i = 0; i < pages.length; i++) {
    for (j = 0; j < pages[i].length; j++) {
        if (pages[i][j] == myPage) {
            indexToSelect = i;
            break;
        }
    }
    tabsDiv.tabs("add", '#main', pages[i][0]);
}

tabsDiv.find('li').removeClass('ui-tabs-selected ui-state-active');
tabsDiv.find('li').eq(indexToSelect).addClass('ui-tabs-selected ui-state-active');
```

The tab is highlighted by manually controlling the use of two CSS classes. This is not pretty and comes as a consequence of wanting the appearance, but not the event handling, from the tabs feature.

The advantage of this approach is that is hasn't introduced any breaking changes for non-JavaScript users. The pages can be viewed and used without the tabs. The drawback of this approach is that the mapping between tabs and pages must be maintained manually. We could add a hidden element to each page that indicated which tab it should be associated with, but we would still require details of which pages should be viewed when a tab is clicked, so I prefer to have the map be comprehensive. Just be aware that if you create a page, it will be associated with the first tab in the list if you forget to update the map in the master page.

Summary

In this chapter we have seen how to use jQuery and jQuery UI to improve the way that the user interacts with the pages in our application. Our focus has been on substantial improvements that improve feedback, responsiveness, or navigation or that build on concepts that users are generally familiar with, such as date pickers. There is room in web applications for enhancements that are purely adornments—often referred to as *chrome*—but my view is that these should be kept to a reasonable minimum and shouldn't get in the way of enhancements that improve usability.

Although JavaScript has suffered from a poor history and reputation, it is fair to say that libraries such as jQuery and jQuery UI provide huge improvements in consistency and utility. However, I admit that there are some wrinkles in getting jQuery to place well with ASP.NET. I hope that this chapter has shown you that the scope of your ASP.NET applications includes the client—a notion that is reinforced by Microsoft embracing jQuery.

CHAPTER 11

Working with Ajax

Asynchronous JavaScript and XML (Ajax) is a key tool in creating professional web applications. In essence, Ajax allows you to send and receive data to and from the server without reloading the web page. There are lots of different ways of integrating Ajax into an ASP.NET web application, and in this chapter you will continue using jQuery.

The jQuery library makes the client end of Ajax development simple to create and manage. You'll also use some jQuery plug-ins to make more complex tasks easier to implement. There are three main examples in this chapter, and through them you'll see how to perform different kinds of Ajax operation in the client and how to create the services to support them in the ASP.NET server.

Getting Started with Ajax

We are going to start our exploration of Ajax by modifying the Performance.aspx page so that the performance data is retrieved using Ajax. To make the Ajax interactions more obvious, we are going to add a select element to the page, which will let us select the data for the different athletes in the sample database. You can see the finished product in Figure 11-1. When the user selects a name from the drop-down menu, the appropriate data is loaded asynchronously from the ASP.NET server.

Figure 11-1. *Adding Ajax to the Performance.aspx page*

We will explore Ajax by building on the project that we used in Chapter 10. For this chapter, I have tidied up the project slightly, removing some of the jQuery scripts that we introduced and changing the project name and namespace declarations. Otherwise, the project is as we left it, with the data model, styling, and interaction improvements we created previously. I have included this project in the code download that accompanies this book; you can download the code from Apress.com.

Adding the Web Service

The best place to start with Ajax is at the server, by creating a *web service*. This term has been heavily abused in recent years and can mean many things. For the purposes of this book, a web service responds to requests with data that can be easily parsed and processed by JavaScript. Our goal is to create something that is as simple and elegant as possible. If your experience of web services brings up memories of impenetrable SOAP envelopes, UDDI registries, and WSDL documents, then relax—the world of Ajax web services is more laissez-faire.

The best way to add a web services to an ASP.NET web application is to use the *Windows Communications Foundation* (WCF). WCF is a .NET Framework library used for creating a wide range of network services, and it takes care of pretty much everything we need simply and quickly. WCF is a huge framework, with some very sophisticated features. We will be using only one aspect of WCF in this chapter. If you want more information about the broader capabilities of WCF, then I recommend Nishith Pathak's book *Pro WCF*, published by Apress.

■ **Note** ASP.NET includes support for its own variety of web services, known as ASMX services, which can be identified by files with the .asmx extension. This kind of web service has now been superseded by the WCF web services that we will use in this chapter.

To add a web service, in Visual Studio select Project ➤ Add New Item and select the Ajax-enabled WCF Service template, as shown in Figure 11-2.

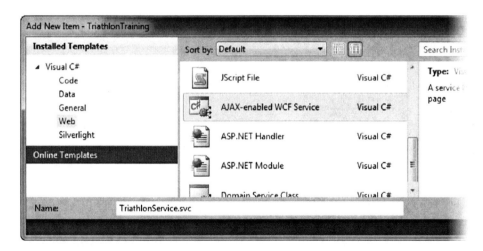

Figure 11-2. *Adding an Ajax WCF service*

Set the name for the service to be TriathlonService.svc, as shown in the figure, and click Add to create the item. Some new assembly references will be added to the project, and you will see that TriathlonService.svc has been added too. Right-click this item and select View Markup from the menu to open this file for editing. Listing 11-1 shows the contents of TriathlonService.svc.

Listing 11-1. The TriathlonService.svc file

```
<%@ ServiceHost Language="C#" Debug="true" Service="TriathlonTraining.TriathlonService"
CodeBehind="TriathlonService.svc.cs" %>
```

You can see that WCF web services follow the same format as the web pages and master pages in having a directive and a code-behind file. The directive for a web service is ServiceHost, and the code-behind class is TriathlonTraining.TriathlonService. Listing 11-2 shows the code-behind class.

Listing 11-2. The TriathlonService.svc.cs code-behind class

```csharp
using System.ServiceModel;
using System.ServiceModel.Activation;
using System.ServiceModel.Web;

namespace TriathlonTraining {

    [ServiceContract]
    [AspNetCompatibilityRequirements(RequirementsMode
        = AspNetCompatibilityRequirementsMode.Allowed)]
    public class TriathlonService {

        [OperationContract]
        [WebGet]
        public PerformanceReport GetPerformanceData(string athlete) {
            using (TrainingDataEntities context = new TrainingDataEntities()) {

                System.Threading.Thread.Sleep(2000);

                // get the times
                Event sprintTimes
                    = DataAccess.GetBestTimes(context, athlete, "Sprint");
                Event olympicTimes
                    = DataAccess.GetBestTimes(context, athlete, "Olympic");
                // get the rankings
                RankingSet sprintRanks
                    = DataAccess.GetReferenceRanking(context, sprintTimes);
                RankingSet olympicRanks
                    = DataAccess.GetReferenceRanking(context, olympicTimes);

                // create populate and return the result
                return new PerformanceReport() {

                    sprintSwimTime = sprintTimes.SwimTime.ToString(),
                    sprintCycleTime = sprintTimes.CycleTime.ToString(),
                    sprintRunTime = sprintTimes.RunTime.ToString(),
                    sprintOverallTime = sprintTimes.OverallTime.ToString(),
                    olympicSwimTime = olympicTimes.SwimTime.ToString(),
                    olympicCycleTime = olympicTimes.CycleTime.ToString(),
                    olympicRunTime = olympicTimes.RunTime.ToString(),
                    olympicOverallTime = olympicTimes.OverallTime.ToString(),
```

```
                    sprintSwimRank = sprintRanks.SwimRank,
                    sprintCycleRank = sprintRanks.CycleRank,
                    sprintRunRank = sprintRanks.RunRank,
                    sprintOverallRank = sprintRanks.OverallRank,
                    olympicSwimRank = olympicRanks.SwimRank,
                    olympicCycleRank = olympicRanks.CycleRank,
                    olympicRunRank = olympicRanks.RunRank,
                    olympicOverallRank = olympicRanks.OverallRank
                };
            }
        }
    }

    public class PerformanceReport {
        // times
        public string sprintSwimTime, olympicSwimTime;
        public string sprintCycleTime, olympicCycleTime;
        public string sprintRunTime, olympicRunTime;
        public string sprintOverallTime, olympicOverallTime;
        // ranks
        public int sprintSwimRank, olympicSwimRank;
        public int sprintCycleRank, olympicCycleRank;
        public int sprintRunRank, olympicRunRank;
        public int sprintOverallRank, olympicOverallRank;
    }
}
```

The goal in Listing 11-2 is to create a mechanism by which we can respond to requests for performance data for an athlete. I'll break down the code in Listing 11-2 so you can make sense of what is going on. Let's start with the class declaration:

```
[ServiceContract]
[AspNetCompatibilityRequirements(RequirementsMode
    = AspNetCompatibilityRequirementsMode.Allowed)]
public class TriathlonService {
```

WCF web services are defined using standard C# classes, annotated by attributes. The ServiceContract attribute tells WCF that this class contains a web service. The AspNetCompatibilityRequirements attribute tells WCF that we want to run this service as part of ASP.NET. Both of these attributes must be applied to the web service code-behind class for WCF to work the way we want.

■ **Note** The AspNetCompatibilityRequirements attribute enables the use of the HttpContext.Current property within your web service code, which means you can get information about the request and configure the response as shown in Chapter 5. For most web services, you won't need this feature, but it can be handy if you need detailed information the request.

Our code-behind class contains one method, which is declared as follows:

```
[OperationContract]
[WebGet]
public PerformanceReport GetPerformanceData(string athlete) {
```

The method is called GetPerformanceData and takes a string parameter, which is the name of the athlete for whom to retrieve data. The OperationContract attribute tells WCF that this method should be included as part of the web service; any method that you want your Ajax clients to access should be annotated with the OperationContract method.

The WebGet attribute tells WCF that we want our Ajax clients to be able to access the service by making HTTP GET requests. You'll see how to deal with other HTTP methods in the "Using Ajax to Post an HTML Form" section later in this chapter.

The body of the GetPerformanceData method retrieves the data from the database by using the DataAccess class and the Entity Framework data model (discussed in Chapter 8) and uses the data to populate and return an instance of the PerformanceReport class as the method result. The PerformanceReport class is as follows:

```
public class PerformanceReport {
    // times
    public string sprintSwimTime, olympicSwimTime;
    public string sprintCycleTime, olympicCycleTime;
    public string sprintRunTime, olympicRunTime;
    public string sprintOverallTime, olympicOverallTime;
    // ranks
    public int sprintSwimRank, olympicSwimRank;
    public int sprintCycleRank, olympicCycleRank;
    public int sprintRunRank, olympicRunRank;
    public int sprintOverallRank, olympicOverallRank;
}
```

Some care is required when deciding what data type a method in a web service should return. In the PerformanceReport class, I have created fields for each data item that will be returned to the Ajax client. Notice that I have broken the camel case convention for the field names. You'll see why in the "Adding the Ajax Script" section of this chapter.

You'll see other approaches, such as returning arrays of objects, in later examples. Most C# objects can be serialized and used directly as results, but doing this can make processing the data in the Ajax client awkward and slow. Taking the time to create additional data types that are easy to work with is usually the best approach.

■ **Caution** The way that the Entity Framework represents foreign-key relationships using navigation properties means that WCF can't serialize entity objects. If you are working with entity objects that have navigation properties (and most do), then you will need to create an intermediate data type that can be serialized and sent to the Ajax client.

There is one statement in the GetPerformanceData method that bears particular note:

System.Threading.Thread.Sleep(2000);

This call to the Thread.Sleep method stops the execution of the web service for two seconds. I have added this so that you can clearly see that Ajax is being used. Ajax operations can occur too quickly for the human eye to detect when the browser and ASP.NET server are on the same computer. To that end, I have introduced an artificial delay. As you might imagine, you should not add such statements to production web services.

And with that, we have defined our web service. We have created a pretty standard C# class that contains a pretty standard C# method. The only unusual aspects are the WCF attributes and the attention that is required when deciding on the result type from the web service methods.

Testing the Web Service

At this point, I like to test my web services using a browser. This is easy if your web service supports the GET method. The first step is to select the service file in the Solution Explorer window (PerformanceService.svc in this case) and right-click and select View In Browser from the pop-up menu.

What you will see is the web page telling you that there is no metadata available and providing instructions to enable it. You can ignore this. We selected View In Browser so that the ASP.NET server would load our WCF web service. The only information we need from the metadata web page is the URL. It will be similar to the one shown in Figure 11-3.

Figure 11-3. Getting the web service URL from the metadata instruction page

You can see from Figure 11-3 that the base URL for my service is http://localhost:40236/TriathlonService.svc. To test the GetPerformance method, we add the method name to the base URL and provide the method parameters in the query string, like this:

http://localhost:40236/TriathlonService.svc/GetPerformanceData?athlete=Adam%20Freeman

This URL references the GetPerformanceData method and sets the athlete parameter to Adam Freeman. Note that I have replaced the space between Adam and Freeman with %20 to create a legal query string.

■ **Note** The standard web service URLs have the virtue of being derived from the service file name and the method name, but they are long, ugly, and hard to remember. You can change them using the routing features described in Chapter 12.

You can type this URL into a browser to test the web service. I mentioned in an earlier chapter that I like to use the Google Chrome browser. One of the reasons is that it will display the result of calling our web service method in the main browser window, while Internet Explorer and Firefox require the data to be downloaded to a file and then viewed using a text editor. If you are testing and tweaking a web service, being able to see the data directly can be very helpful.

DEBUGGING WEB SERVICES

It can be tricky to debug Ajax and WCF web services working together. I use three different techniques when I have a problem. The first is to apply the following attribute to my web service class:

```
[ServiceBehavior(IncludeExceptionDetailInFaults = true)]
```

This attribute tells WCF to include details of exceptions in the result when a problem arises. This is useful for detecting problems in the code statements in my web service methods, especially when you are testing using a browser. The second approach I take is to add the following to my Web.Config file:

```
<system.diagnostics>
    <sources>
        <source name="System.ServiceModel" switchValue="Information, ActivityTracing"
            propagateActivity="true">
        <listeners>
            <add name="sdt" type="System.Diagnostics.XmlWriterTraceListener"
                initializeData="Trace.debug"  />
        </listeners>
    </source>
    </sources>
</system.diagnostics>
```

This configuration enables WCF request tracing. A file called Trace.debug will be created in your project directory, and detailed information about each request will be appended to it. This is the way to find problems when WCF takes issue with the data you are trying to return or when parsing a request from your Ajax client. You can view the tracing information using the SvcTraceViewer.exe tool, which can be found in C:\Program Files\Microsoft SDKs\Windows\v7.0A\Bin (if you are using the 32-bit version of Windows 7) or C:\Program Files (x86)\Microsoft SDKs\Windows\v7.0A\Bin (if you are using the 64-bit version of Windows 7). The location will vary if you use older versions of Windows. Be careful to disable this option before you deploy, and bear in mind that the trace file will grow every time you make a request. It is very easy to generate huge files during a mammoth debugging session.

The final approach I take to debugging, and the one I tend to find the most useful overall, is to sniff the HTTP requests that pass between the Ajax client and the server. There are lots of different ways to do this, but I like to use Fiddler, an excellent Windows program that can be downloaded from www.fiddler2.com.

Whichever browser you choose, you will either see or download data that is similar to that shown in Listing 11-3, formatted for legibility.

Listing 11-3. The data returned from the GetPerformance web service method

```
{"d":{"__type":"PerformanceReport:#TriathlonTraining",
    "olympicCycleRank":300, "olympicCycleTime":"01:20:00",
    "olympicOverallRank":295, "olympicOverallTime":"02:41:29",
    "olympicRunRank":339, "olympicRunTime":"00:52:58",
    "olympicSwimRank":280, "olympicSwimTime":"00:28:31",
    "sprintCycleRank":325, "sprintCycleTime":"00:43:58",
    "sprintOverallRank":293, "sprintOverallTime":"01:19:15",
    "sprintRunRank":366, "sprintRunTime":"00:23:47",
    "sprintSwimRank":417, "sprintSwimTime":"00:11:22"
}}
```

The data shown in Listing 11-3 is in the JavaScript Object Notation (JSON) format, one lightweight alternative to XML in web services. Although JSON originated in the JavaScript world, it has become very widely supported in other languages. It doesn't have the formal structure and self-describing nature of XML, but it is more compact and easier to work with in most situations.

The data in Listing 11-3 is one of two forms of JSON, a collection of name/value pairs. You'll see the other kind—an array of objects—in the "Using Data Templates" section later in this chapter. The TriathlonService WCF service has serialized our result as JSON data, using the names of the fields in the PerformanceReport class as the names in the name/value pairs.

The entire block of performance data is encapsulated in an element named d. This is a security measure applied by WCF to prevent web services generating content that can be interpreted as JavaScript. WCF also includes details of the C# type that was serialized to produce the data, in this case, the PerformanceReport class from the TriathlonTraining namespace.

Preparing the ASP.NET Web Page

The next stage in our process is to update the Performance.aspx web page and code-behind class. In the web page, we are going to add the select element that will allow the user to choose an athlete, as shown in Listing 11-4.

Listing 11-4. Modifying the Performance.aspx page

```
<%@ Page Title="Performance Data" Language="C#" MasterPageFile="~/Site.Master"
AutoEventWireup="true" CodeBehind="Performance.aspx.cs"
Inherits="TriathlonTraining.Performance" %>

<asp:Content ID="Content1" ContentPlaceHolderID="HeadContent" runat="server">
    <link href="Styles/Page.css" rel="stylesheet" type="text/css" />
</asp:Content>

<asp:Content ID="Content2" ContentPlaceHolderID="MainContent" runat="server">
```

```html
<div style="width:100%; text-align:center; padding-bottom:10px">
    <label for="athleteSelector">Athlete:</label>
    <select id="athleteSelector" runat="server">
    </select>
</div>

<div id="sprintData">

    <table class="centerTable">
        <colgroup>
            <col/>
            <col width="100px"/>
        </colgroup>
        <tr><th colspan="4">Sprint Results</th></tr>
        <tr>
            <td>Best Swim Time:</td><td id="sprintSwimTime" class="dataElement"/>
            <td>Best Swim Rank:</td><td id="sprintSwimRank" class="dataElement"/>
        </tr>
        <tr>
            <td>Best Cycle Time:</td><td id="sprintCycleTime" class="dataElement"/>
            <td>Best Cycle Rank:</td><td id="sprintCycleRank" class="dataElement"/>
        </tr>
        <tr>
            <td>Best Run Time:</td><td id="sprintRunTime" class="dataElement"/>
            <td>Best Run Rank:</td><td id="sprintRunRank" class="dataElement"/>
        </tr>
        <tr>
            <td>Best Overall Time:</td><td id="sprintOverallTime" class="dataElement"/>
            <td>Best Overall Rank:</td><td id="sprintOverallRank" class="dataElement"/>
        </tr>
    </table>
</div>

<p />

<div id="olympicData">
    <table class="centerTable">
        <colgroup>
            <col />
            <col width="100px" />
        </colgroup>
        <tr><th colspan="4">Olympic Results</th></tr>
        <tr>
            <td>Best Swim Time:</td><td id="olympicSwimTime" class="dataElement"/>
            <td>Best Swim Rank:</td><td id="olympicSwimRank" class="dataElement"/>
        </tr>
        <tr>
            <td>Best Cycle Time:</td><td id="olympicCycleTime" class="dataElement"/>
            <td>Best Cycle Rank:</td><td id="olympicCycleRank" class="dataElement"/>
        </tr>
        <tr>
```

```
        <td>Best Run Time:</td><td id="olympicRunTime" class="dataElement"/>
        <td>Best Run Rank:</td><td id="olympicRunRank" class="dataElement"/>
     </tr>
      <tr>
        <td>Best Overall Time:</td><td id="olympicOverallTime" class="dataElement"/>
        <td>Best Overall Rank:</td><td id="olympicOverallRank" class="dataElement"/>
     </tr>
   </table>
  </div>

  <p />
</asp:Content>
```

The additions for the select element are shown in bold. If you compare the HTML in Listing 11-4 with the original web page (shown in Listing 10-10 of Chapter 10), you will see that I have also removed the runat attribute from the td elements that hold the performance data and added the dataElement class. Removing the runat attribute makes the elements easier to select using jQuery, because we don't have to deal with the ID rewriting by using code blocks and the ClientID control property. Adding the dataElement class allows us to select all the td elements that hold data using a single jQuery statement, which will be useful when we come to write the Ajax script in the next section of this chapter. The changes to the web page require matching changes to the code-behind class, which is shown in Listing 11-5.

Listing 11-5. *Modifying the Performance.aspx.cs code-behind file*

```
using System;

namespace TriathlonTraining {

    public partial class Performance : System.Web.UI.Page {

        protected void Page_Load(object sender, EventArgs e) {

            using (TrainingDataEntities context = new TrainingDataEntities()) {
                athleteSelector.Items.Clear();
                foreach (string name in DataAccess.GetAthleteNames(context)) {
                    athleteSelector.Items.Add(name);
                }
            }
        }
    }
}
```

The code-behind class is greatly simplified because the performance data will be obtained via Ajax. The only responsibility of the code-behind class is to create the option items containing the athlete names for the select element (we could do this by Ajax as well, but I want to keep the example as simple as possible).

Adding the Ajax Script

If you view the Performance.aspx web page in a browser, you'll see something similar to Figure 11-4. The structure of the page and the select element are present, but there is no performance data.

Figure 11-4. *The Performance.aspx web page without the data*

At this point we can add our jQuery Ajax script. Because we are using jQuery, we can reuse the techniques we learned in earlier chapters for using selectors and events. Listing 11-6 shows the jQuery script for the Performance.aspx page.

Listing 11-6. *A jQuery Ajax script*

```
<script type="text/javascript">

    var GetSelectedAthlete = function () {
        return $('#<%=athleteSelector.ClientID %> option:selected').text();
    }

    $(document).ready(function () {

        $('#<%=athleteSelector.ClientID %>').change(function () {
            GetData();
        });

        GetData();
    });

    var GetData = function () {
```

```
        $.ajax({
            url: '/TriathlonService.svc/GetPerformanceData',
            data: { 'athlete': GetSelectedAthlete()},
            cache: false,
            beforeSend: function () {
                $('td.dataElement').text("---");
            },
            success: function (data) {
                for (var key in data.d) {
                    $('#' + key).text(data.d[key]);
                }
            }
        });
    };
</script>
```

This script starts by defining a function that will get the selected value from the select element:

```
var GetSelectedAthlete = function () {
    return $('#<%=athleteSelector.ClientID %> option:selected').text();
}
```

The select element is the only one with a runat attribute in the page, so we have to use a code block to correctly select it based on its ID attribute. The next part of the script registers for change events in the select element and gets the initial data:

```
$(document).ready(function () {

    $('#<%=athleteSelector.ClientID %>').change(function () {
        GetData();
    });

    GetData();
});
```

The GetData function is our Ajax function. We call it to get the initial data to display and then in response to the change event on the select element, when the user selects a new name from the list.

The heart of the script is the GetData function, which is as follows:

```
var GetData = function () {

    $.ajax({
        url: '/TriathlonService.svc/GetPerformanceData',
        data: { 'athlete': GetSelectedAthlete()},
        cache: false,
        beforeSend: function () {
            $('td.dataElement').text("---");
        },
```

```
        success: function (data) {
            for (var key in data.d) {
                $('#' + key).text(data.d[key]);
            }
        }
    });
};
```

GetData is a wrapper around the jQuery .ajax function, which performs Ajax operations. By placing our Ajax request in a function, we can call it from multiple points in the code without having to duplicate the options.

The options we have passed to the .ajax function are a mix of settings and callbacks. The url option sets the URL to which the request will be sent.

The data option sets the parameter names and values that will added to the URL as a query string. This information will be safely encoded, so we don't have to worry, for example, about replacing spaces with %20 as we did when we tested the web service using a browser. In this case, we set the athlete parameter to be the value returned from the GetSelectedAthlete function.

Setting the cache option to false prevents the data returned from an Ajax request from being cached by the web browser. Some browsers, notably Internet Explorer, will reuse previously returned data, while others, including Chrome and Firefox, will request fresh data from the server every time. When developing with Ajax, it is most useful to prevent caching. If you don't, changes in the data that your web service generates will not be displayed in the browser, causing endless confusion (well, for me at least). I tend to disable caching in production services as well, preferring the additional server workload to avoid having to manage stale data, but for projects where the Ajax data is largely static, caching can be a good idea. Table 11-1 shows the most important options that the jQuery .ajax function supports.

Table 11-1. Options for the jQuery .ajax Function

Option	Example	Description
cache	cache: false	Sets the browser cache policy for the Ajax data (see earlier discussion for details).
data	data: {'name' : 'value', 'otherName' : 'otherValue')	Sets the parameter data for an Ajax request (see earlier discussion for an example).
dataType	dataType: json	Specifies the kind of data that will be returned from the web service. If you don't specify this option, jQuery will guess based on the format of the data.
password	password: mySecretWord	Sets a password for authentication. See Chapter 13 for details.
timeout	timeout: 5000	Sets a period of time (in milliseconds) before a request is considered to have timed out.
username	username: myName	Sets a username for authentication. See Chapter 13 for details.

Our script also contains two callbacks. Here is the first:

```
beforeSend: function () {
    $('td.dataElement').text("---");
},
```

The specified function is called just before jQuery makes the Ajax request to the web service, in response to the beforeSend event. We can use this opportunity to select all the td elements in the dataElement class and change their content to --- so that it is obvious an Ajax request is about to start. You might choose not to do this in a real project, but I want to highlight the Ajax process, much like adding the Thread.Sleep call to the web service class. The second callback is as follows:

```
success: function (data) {
    for (var key in data.d) {
        $('#' + key).text(data.d[key]);
    }
}
```

This function is invoked in response to the success event, indicating that data has been obtained from the web service successfully. The parameter, which I have called data, is the JSON object. For our example, this is the data shown in Listing 11-3.

We use a for loop to enumerate through the set of names from the name/value pairs; note that we do this on data.d to accommodate that WCF web services deliver all data as a name/value pair where the name is d.

As each name is enumerated, we select the HTML element that has a matching ID attribute and use the text function to set its content to the JSON data associated with the name. When I mentioned designing the result type of the web service method with ease of processing in mind, this is what I meant. We set the fields of the PerformanceReport class so that they matched the corresponding HTML element, allowing us to process the data in a single, simple for loop.

SETTING DATA VALUES MANUALLY

It isn't always possible to dovetail the HTML and the JSON data like this. Sometimes you will have to work with legacy pages or legacy web services. If that had been the case in the example, I could have selected individual HTML elements and retrieved the appropriate JSON data value, like this:

```
...
$('#sprintSwimTime').text(data.d.sprintSwimTime);
$('#sprintCycleTime').text(data.d.sprintCycleTime);
...
```

This would have to be repeated for each data element, which can make for a verbose jQuery script. An alternative approach is to use data templates, which we will see later in this chapter.

Table 11-2 details the jQuery callback options.

Table 11-2. Callback Options for the jQuery .ajax Function

Callback	Parameters	Description
beforeSend	XMLHttpRequest	Called before the request is made.
complete	XMLHttpRequest, status	Called when the Ajax request is complete, irrespective of whether the request succeeded. The status parameter will be one of the following: success, notmodified, error, timeout, or parsererror. This callback is invoked after the error or success callbacks.
error	XMLHttpRequest, status, error	Called when a request has failed. The status parameter will be timeout, error, notmodified, or parsererror.
success	data, status, XMLHttpRequest	Called when a request is made successfully. The data parameter contains the data from the server.

The beforeSend callback will always be invoked first, followed by either success or error and, finally, complete.

■ **Note** All the .ajax callbacks have an XMLHttpRequest parameter. This is the standard JavaScript object for making HTTP requests to web servers. You rarely need to work directly with this object when using jQuery Ajax.

Testing the Ajax Functionality

We now have all the pieces in place for our first use of Ajax: the WCF web service that generates performance data expressed using JSON, the ASP.NET web page that has placeholders to display the data, and a jQuery script that bridges the two by requesting the data and placing it in the page. If you view Performance.aspx in a web browser, you will see the effect of the Ajax functionality, which we have exaggerated by adding a call to Thread.Sleep in the web service class and by clearing the data through the beforeSend callback. When the page first loads and when you select a new name from the drop-down list, you will see the data clear and then be refreshed a few seconds later, as shown in Figure 11-5.

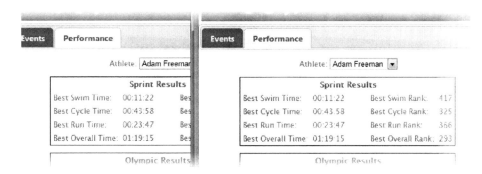

Figure 11-5. Loading data via Ajax

Using Data Templates

Often the data returned from a web service is an array of similar items. This is especially true when dealing with tables. In this section, we will create a web service that generates the content for the table in the ListEvents.aspx page, obtain the data using Ajax, and then use a jQuery extension created by Microsoft to integrate the data into the page.

Creating the Web Service

We can extend our existing web service to support the ListEvents.aspx page by adding another method to the service code-behind class and decorating it with the same attributes we used in the previous example. Listing 11-7 shows these additions; I have removed the bodies from the existing method and result type for brevity.

Listing 11-7. Adding a method to the web service

```
using System.Collections.Generic;
using System.ServiceModel;
using System.ServiceModel.Activation;
using System.ServiceModel.Web;

namespace TriathlonTraining {

    [ServiceContract]
    [AspNetCompatibilityRequirements(RequirementsMode
        = AspNetCompatibilityRequirementsMode.Allowed)]
    public class TriathlonService {

        [OperationContract]
        [WebGet]
        public IEnumerable<EventItem> GetEventData(string type) {
```

257

```
        List<EventItem> results = new List<EventItem>();

        using (TrainingDataEntities context = new TrainingDataEntities()) {

            IEnumerable<Event> events = (type == null || type == "All")
                ? DataAccess.GetAllEvents(context)
                    : DataAccess.GetEventsByType(context, type);

            foreach (Event e in events) {
                results.Add(new EventItem() {
                    Key = e.ID,
                    Date = e.Date.ToString("MM/dd"),
                    Athlete = e.Athlete,
                    EventType = e.Type,
                    SwimTime = e.SwimTime.ToString(),
                    CycleTime = e.CycleTime.ToString(),
                    RunTime = e.RunTime.ToString(),
                    OverallTime = e.OverallTime.ToString(),
                    Rank = DataAccess.GetPersonalRanking(context, e).OverallRank,
                    ReferenceRank = DataAccess
                        .GetReferenceRanking(context, e).OverallRank
                });
            }
        }
        return results;
    }


    [OperationContract]
    [WebGet]
    public PerformanceReport GetPerformanceData(string athlete) {
        // statements removed for brevity
    }
}

public class EventItem {
    public int Key;
    public string Date;
    public string Athlete;
    public string EventType;
    public string SwimTime, CycleTime, RunTime, OverallTime;
    public int Rank, ReferenceRank;
}

public class PerformanceReport {
    // fields removed for brevity
}
}
```

The GetEventData method takes a string parameter specifying the type of event data that is required. I have applied the WebGet and OperationContract attributes to the GetEventData method so that WCF will publish the method as part of the web service and allow access using the HTTP GET method.

The event data is obtained from the DataAccess class, and the result of the method is an IEnumerable<EventItem>, where EventItem is a class created to contain the result. Once again, I have added a type specifically for representing the data to the Ajax client to avoid the problems of serializing entity objects that have navigation properties.

Testing the Web Service

We can test the new method we have added to the web service by changing the method name in the URL and adding the appropriate parameters, like this:

```
http://localhost:40236/TriathlonService.svc/GetEventData?type=All
```

Returning a strongly typed IEnumerable from a web service method causes WCF to return the data to the Ajax client as a JSON array, part of which is shown in Listing 11-8, formatted for legibility.

Listing 11-8. *A JSON array*

```
{"d":
    [{"__type":"EventItem:#TriathlonTraining",
        "Athlete":"Adam Freeman",
        "CycleTime":"00:45:12",
        "Date":"09\/27",
        "EventType":"Sprint",
        "Key":1,
        "OverallTime":"01:22:40",
        "Rank":2,
        "ReferenceRank":353,
        "RunTime":"00:25:28",
        "SwimTime":"00:12:00"},
    {"__type":"EventItem:#TriathlonTraining",
        "Athlete":"Adam Freeman",
        "CycleTime":"00:47:32",
        "Date":"10\/04",
        "EventType":"Sprint",
        "Key":2,
        "OverallTime":"01:22:55",
        "Rank":3,
        "ReferenceRank":358,
        "RunTime":"00:24:01",
        "SwimTime":"00:11:22"},
    ...
]}
```

You can see that the result data is an array of sets of name/value pairs, all encapsulated with the d element that WCF adds.

Preparing the ASP.NET Web Page

The key change we made to ListEvents.aspx was to remove the runat attribute from the HTML table element. Removing the runat attribute means that we don't have to use a code block to refer to the ID attribute value in the jQuery script. We have also moved existing scripts that create buttons from hyperlinks and highlight a row as the mouse passes over it to an external file called Scripts/ ListEventsScripts.js (we'll return to this file later). Listing 11-9 shows the modified ListEvents.aspx file.

Listing 11-9. The modified ListEvents.aspx page

```
<%@ Page Title="Triathlon Events" Language="C#" MasterPageFile="~/Site.Master"
AutoEventWireup="true"
    CodeBehind="ListEvents.aspx.cs" Inherits="TriathlonTraining.ListEvents" %>

<asp:Content ID="HeaderContent" runat="server" ContentPlaceHolderID="HeadContent">
    <link href="/Styles/Page.css" rel="stylesheet" type="text/css" />
    <script src="Scripts/ListEventsScripts.js" type="text/javascript"></script>
</asp:Content>

<asp:Content ID="BodyContent" runat="server" ContentPlaceHolderID="MainContent">
  <table id="resultsTable" rules="cols">
        <tr>
            <th>Date</th>
            <th>Athlete</th>
            <th>Event Type</th>
            <th>Swim</th>
            <th>Cycle</th>
            <th>Run</th>
            <th>Overall</th>
            <th>Rank</th>
            <th>Ref Rank</th>
            <th>Edit</th>
            <th>Delete</th>
        </tr>
    </table>

    <div class="standardDiv">
        <label for="eventSelector">Event Type:</label>
        <select id="eventSelector" runat="server">
            <option>All</option>
        </select>
    </div>

    <div class="standardDiv">
        <input type="submit" value="Submit" />
    </div>
```

```
    <div class="standardDiv">
        <a href="AddEvent.aspx">Add New Event</a>
    </div>

</asp:Content>
```

Adding the Ajax Script

To make the JSON data easier to process, we are going to use a jQuery plug-in developed by Microsoft, called *jQuery Templates*. At the time of writing, the Templates plug-in has been released as a beta, so you might find that some details have changed, but the overarching principles will remain valid.

To begin, download the latest version of the jQuery Templates plug-in from https://github.com/jquery/jquery-tmpl and copy the jQuery.tmpl.min.js file to the Scripts directory in your project. Add the file to the project by right-clicking the Scripts folder in the Solution Explorer window, selecting Add Existing Item, selecting the jQuery.tmpl.min.js file, and clicking the Add button. Drag the newly added file from the Solution Explorer window to the other script elements in the ListEvents.aspx file, or add the following entry manually:

```
<script src="Scripts/jquery.tmpl.min.js" type="text/javascript"/>
```

Our next step is to add a data template. This is a special script addition that tells jQuery Templates what HTML should be generated for each element in the JSON array. Listing 11-10 shows the template I have created for this example.

Listing 11-10. *A jQuery template*

```
<script id="eventTemplate" type="text/x-jquery-tmpl">
    <tr>
        <td>${Date}</td>
        <td>${Athlete}</td>
        <td>${EventType}</td>
        <td>${SwimTime}</td>
        <td>${CycleTime}</td>
        <td>${RunTime}</td>
        <td>${OverallTime}</td>
        <td>${Rank}</td>
        <td>${ReferenceRank}</td>
        <td><a href="/UpdateOrDeleteEvent.aspx?id=${Key}&mode=Edit">Edit</a></td>
        <td><a href="/UpdateOrDeleteEvent.aspx?id=${Key}&mode=Delete">Delete</a></td>
    </tr>
</script>
```

Creating a template is a simple task. Create a script element in your web page, and assign it an ID so that you can refer to it later using jQuery. Set the type of the script to text/x-query-tmpl. This is the type that the template engine looks for, and it prevents the browser from trying to execute the script as though it contained JavaScript statements.

Inside the script element, we define the HTML we want to be created for each item in the JSON data result. In this case, we want to create a tr item that contains multiple td elements. To insert a data value, we wrap the name of the object property in braces ({}) and a $ prefix. For example, to include the value of the Athlete property, we refer to it as ${Athlete}, and when the template plug-in encounters this reference, it will insert the corresponding value from the JSON object. This will be repeated for each object in the JSON data array.

The final step is to create a jQuery script that uses Ajax to retrieve the data from the web service and apply the template. Listing 11-11 contains this script.

Listing 11-11. *Applying a template using jQuery*

```
<script type="text/javascript">

    $(document).ready(function () {
        $('#<%=eventSelector.ClientID %>').change(function () {
            GetData();
        });

        GetData();
    });

    var GetSelectedEventType = function () {
        return $('#<%=eventSelector.ClientID %> option:selected').text();
    }

    var GetData = function () {
        $.ajax({
            url: '/TriathlonService.svc/GetEventData',
            data: { 'type': GetSelectedEventType() },
            cache: false,
            success: function (data) {
                $('tr:has(td)').remove();
                $('#eventTemplate').tmpl(data.d).appendTo('#resultsTable');
                prettyTable();
            }
        });
    };
</script>
```

You will notice that this script is very similar to the previous example. We have changed the url property to call the GetEventData method and the data property to set the parameters for the method. In addition, we have removed the handler for the beforeSend event and changed the handler for the success event. The first line in the success function removes all tr elements that contain td element:

```
$('tr:has(td)').remove();
```

We remove the elements because when the template is applied to the data, new rows will be added to the table. The critical line in the script is this one, which applies the template to the data:

```
$('#eventTemplate').tmpl(data.d).appendTo('#resultsTable');
```

This statement uses a jQuery selector to select the template script and call the tmpl function. This is the central function of the template plug-in and applies the template to the data. The result of the tmpl function is the HTML generated by the script, which we add to the table using the appendTo function.

The final line in the success event handler calls the function prettyTable. This is the name of the function I have defined in the external ListEventsScripts.js file, which is shown in Listing 11-12.

Listing 11-12. *The ListEventsScripts.js file*

```
(function ($) {
    prettyTable = function () {
        $('table a').button().css('color', '#ffffff');
        $('td a').css('font-size', 'smaller');

        $('tr:has(td)').hover(
            function () {
                $(this).find('td')
                    .css({ 'background-color': '#007F7F',
                        'color': '#ffffff'
                    });
            },
            function () {
                $(this).find('td')
                    .css({ 'background-color': '',
                        'color': ''
                    });
            }
        ).click(function () {
            document.location = $(this).find('a:contains("Edit")').attr('href');
        });
    }
})(jQuery);
```

When the data was included in the HTML by the code-behind class, we could apply our styles and event handlers to the table rows by binding to the document.ready events. Now that the HTML elements that hold the data are re-created each time the user selects an event type, we must put the style and event statements in a function and then call this function each time we process new data from our Ajax call. The function in Listing 11-12 is called prettyTable, and it is called from the success event handler of the .ajax function.

Testing the Ajax Functionality

All that remains for this example is to view the ListEvents.aspx page in a browser. We have not added any deliberate delays or visual cues to indicate that data is being loaded via Ajax, so you might not be able to see any significant differences from the previous approach if you are using a particular fast computer for development. Nonetheless, when the page first loads and when you select a value from the drop-down list thereafter, the jQuery script queries the web service for data and then uses the jQuery Templates plug-in to create the rows of the table.

■ **Note** The jQuery Templates plug-in has a wide range of features, and this example has only scratched the surface of what kinds of templates can be created. If you are working with arrays of data, especially if those arrays are destined for tables, then I recommend exploring the features of this useful extension. You can render HTML from JSON data arrays manually, but using templates is an easier and more elegant solution.

Using Ajax to Post an HTML Form

The previous examples used the HTTP GET method, but we can as easily post data with Ajax, too. This is most commonly done to submit form data. The principal benefit of posting data with Ajax is that the page doesn't have to be reloaded, providing a smoother experience for the user. In this section, we'll start by building a regular ASP.NET form-based web page and then extend it to work with Ajax in different ways. This example will also demonstrate that Ajax isn't all about web services (although, in fairness, it often is, so I'll finish this section by showing you how to post to a web service).

Creating the Web Page

We will start by creating a simple form-based ASP.NET web page, called Calculator.aspx. This page uses a form to re-create the simple calculator that we first used in Chapter 6, where we convert time spent swimming and the length of the pool into values useful for my triathlon training diary. Listing 11-13 shows the content of Calculator.aspx.

Listing 11-13. The Calculator.aspx page

```
<%@ Page Title="" Language="C#" MasterPageFile="~/Site.Master" AutoEventWireup="true"
CodeBehind="Calculator.aspx.cs" Inherits="TriathlonTraining.Calculator" %>

<asp:Content ID="Content1" ContentPlaceHolderID="HeadContent" runat="server">
    <link href="Styles/Page.css" rel="stylesheet" type="text/css" />
    <style type="text/css">
        div.labelDiv { float: left; width: 100px; padding-right:2px; text-align:right}
        span.result {color:Black; padding-left:2px; text-align:left}
        div.result { width:auto; float:left; text-align:left; margin-left:30px;display:none}
    </style>

    <script type="text/javascript">
        $(document).ready(function () {
            $(':submit').button().css('color', '#ffffff');
        });
    </script>

</asp:Content>

<asp:Content ID="Content2" ContentPlaceHolderID="MainContent" runat="server">

    <div style="float:left">

        <div style="width:auto; float:left; text-align:right">
            <div class="elementDiv">
                <div class="labelDiv">Laps:</div>
                <input class="textinput" id="lapsInput"
                    type="text" runat="server" value="80"/>
            </div>
```

```
                <div class="elementDiv">
                    <div class="labelDiv">Pool Length:</div>
                    <input class="textinput" id="lengthInput"
                        type="text" runat="server" value="20"/>
                </div>
                <div class="elementDiv">
                    <div class="labelDiv">Minutes:</div>
                    <input class="textinput" id="minsInput"
                        type="text" runat="server" value="60"/>
                </div>
                <div class="elementDiv">
                    <div class="labelDiv">Calories/Hour:</div>
                    <input class="textinput" id="calsInput"
                        type="text" runat="server" value="1070" />
                </div>
            </div>

            <div class="result" id="resultsDiv" runat="server">
                <div style="text-align:center;color:Black">Results</div>
                <div class="elementDiv">
                    <div class="labelDiv">Distance:</div>
                    <span class="result" id="distanceResult" runat="server">??</span> miles
                </div>
                <div class="elementDiv">
                    <div class="labelDiv">Calories:</div>
                    <span class="result" id="caloriesResult" runat="server">??</span>
                </div>
                <div class="elementDiv">
                    <div class="labelDiv">Pace:</div>
                    <span class="result" id="paceResult" runat="server">??</span> seconds/lap
                </div>
                 <div class="elementDiv">
                    <div class="labelDiv">Source:</div>
                    <span class="result" id="sourceResult" runat="server">??</span>
                </div>
            </div>

            <div style="clear:both; text-align:center; padding:5px">
                <input type="submit" value="Calculate" />
            </div>
        </div>
    </asp:Content>
```

This page has three main areas. The first is a series of input elements through which the user enters the values for the calculation. The second area displays the results of the calculation. This area is hidden initially and then displayed when the calculation has been performed. The last area contains the submit button for the form, which I have prettified using jQuery UI (see Chapter 10 for details of how this works). Figure 11-6 shows the completed page displaying the results of a calculation.

***Figure 11-6.** The Calculator.aspx page*

Notice that the results area contains details of how the data was obtained. The Non-AJAX value is added by the code-behind class to show that the data was obtained through a regular page request. Listing 11-14 shows the code-behind class.

***Listing 11-14.** The Calculator.aspx.cs code-behind file*

```
using System;
using System.Collections.Generic;

namespace TriathlonTraining {
    public partial class Calculator : System.Web.UI.Page {

        private const float metersToMiles = 0.00062137119223733f;
        private const float minsPerHour = 60f;

        protected void Page_Load(object sender, EventArgs e) {

            if (IsPostBack) {

                // set the visibilty of the results div
                resultsDiv.Style.Add("display", "block");
```

```
            // parse the input values
            int laps = int.Parse(lapsInput.Value);
            int length = int.Parse(lengthInput.Value);
            int minutes = int.Parse(minsInput.Value);
            int calories = int.Parse(calsInput.Value);

            // perform the calculation and set the result values
            string distanceResultString
                = ((laps * length) * metersToMiles).ToString("F2");
            string caloriesResultString
                = ((minutes/ minsPerHour) * calories).ToString("F0");
            string paceResultString
                = ((minutes * minsPerHour) / laps).ToString("F0");

            distanceResult.InnerText = distanceResultString;
            caloriesResult.InnerText = caloriesResultString;
            paceResult.InnerText = paceResultString;
            sourceResult.InnerText = "Non-AJAX";
        }
    }
  }
}
```

The code-behind class shows the hidden results area, parses the input values, performs the calculation, and puts the result values into the appropriate HTML controls.

■ **Note** I have omitted any kind of form validation or error handling in order to keep this example focused on Ajax. For a real project, it is essential that you validate the input and response to the user if there is a problem. You can find details of error handling in Chapter 7, server-side validation in Chapter 6, and client-side validation in Chapter 10.

The final addition we have to make is to the Site.Master master page, so that the Calculator.aspx page is included in the jQuery UI tabs we added in Chapter 10. Listing 11-15 shows the required addition.

Listing 11-15. Adding a page to the Site.master tabs collection

```
var pages = [
    ['Events', "/ListEvents.aspx", "/AddEvent.aspx", "UpdateOrDeleteEvent.aspx"],
    ['Performance', "/Performance.aspx"],
    ['Calculator', "/Calculator.aspx"]
];
```

The addition for the Calculator.aspx page is shown in bold. See Chapter 10 for a reminder of the master page tabs script. If you load the Calculator.aspx page and submit the form, you will see the results with the source of the data listed as Non-AJAX. This is the base from which we start.

Adding Ajax Posting

The simplest way to handle posting a form using jQuery is, as you might expect by now, to use a plug-in. The jQuery Form plug-in does everything we require and is available for download at http://jquery. malsup.com/form. For this example, we require the jquery.form.js file, which you can download from the web site or find in the code download that accompanies this book. Place the file in the Scripts folder of your project and add it as an existing item in the Visual Studio Solution Explorer window, as we have done for the other jQuery extension we have used. Drag the JavaScript file to the Calculator.aspx page or add the following script element manually to add the forms plug-in:

```
<script src="Scripts/jquery.form.js" type="text/javascript"/>
```

We can now add a jQuery script to the Calculator.aspx page that will submit the form asynchronously; Listing 11-16 shows this script.

Listing 11-16. *Submitting a form using Ajax*

```
<script type="text/javascript">

    $(document).ready(function () {

        $('form').ajaxForm({
            success: function (data) {

                $('#<%=distanceResult.ClientID%>').text($(data)
                    .find('#<%=distanceResult.ClientID%>').text());
                $('#<%=caloriesResult.ClientID%>').text($(data)
                    .find('#<%=caloriesResult.ClientID%>').text());
                $('#<%=paceResult.ClientID%>').text($(data)
                    .find('#<%=paceResult.ClientID%>').text());

                $('#<%=resultsDiv.ClientID%>').show();
                $('#<%=sourceResult.ClientID%>').text('AJAX (HTML)');

            }
        });
    });

</script>
```

All we have to do to enable Ajax posting is to select our form element and call the ajaxForm function. One of the options you can pass to the .jaxForm function is a function that will be called if the POST is successful, just as we did when we used the built-in jQuery Ajax support for GET requests.

Remember that we are posting our form data back to the Calculator.aspx page, which means that the result of the operation will be HTML. To ASP.NET, the POST request doesn't look any different, and so we receive a rendered Calculator.aspx web page with the results embedded in the HTML content. This is passed as the parameter to our success function. The first three statements in this function select the contents of the result elements in the HTML that the server has sent and use them to populate the same items in the existing page. Here is the first of these statements, formatted to make its purpose a little clearer:

```
$('#<%=distanceResult.ClientID%>').text(
```

```
    $(data).find('#<%=distanceResult.ClientID%>').text()
);
```

The outer selector finds the element in the current page, while the inner selector finds the same element in the data parameter. This process is repeated for each of the three result elements. The remaining statements make the results panel visible and set the source indicator to AJAX (HTML). Once you add this script to the Calculator.aspx page, clicking the Calculate button causes the calculation to be performed using an Ajax post, avoiding the need to reload the page. You can see the changed source value in Figure 11-7.

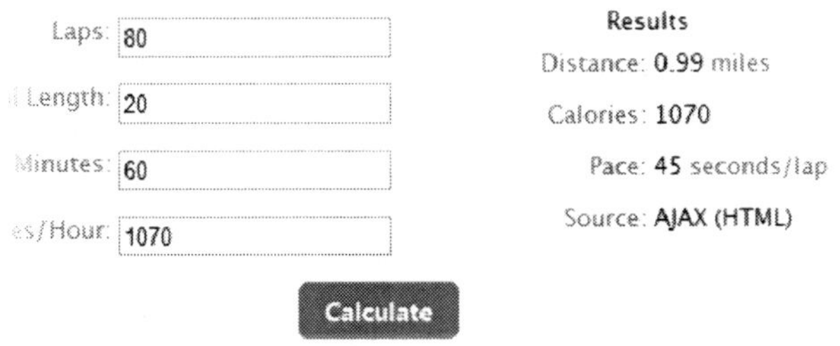

Figure 11-7. *Obtaining an HTML result with Ajax*

Notice that we didn't need to provide a handler for the click event of the form submit button; this was done automatically when we called the ajaxForm function.

Switching to JSON

The nice thing about the previous example is that it is a client-only solution. The problem is that we are transferring an entire web page in order to extract three numeric values, which is extremely inefficient. However, we can adapt the code-behind class of our Calculator.aspx page to return a JSON result that contains only the data we need. Listing 11-17 shows the required modifications to Calculator.aspx.cs.

Listing 11-17. *Adding JSON support to an ASP.NET web page*

```
using System;
using System.Collections.Generic;
using System.Runtime.Serialization.Json;

namespace TriathlonTraining {
    public partial class Calculator : System.Web.UI.Page {
```

```
    private const float metersToMiles = 0.00062137119223733f;
    private const float minsPerHour = 60f;

    protected void Page_Load(object sender, EventArgs e) {

        if (IsPostBack) {

            // set the visibilty of the results div
            resultsDiv.Style.Add("display", "block");

            // parse the input values
            int laps = int.Parse(lapsInput.Value);
            int length = int.Parse(lengthInput.Value);
            int minutes = int.Parse(minsInput.Value);
            int calories = int.Parse(calsInput.Value);

            // perform the calculation and set the result values
            string distanceResultString
                = ((laps * length) * metersToMiles).ToString("F2");
            string caloriesResultString
                = ((minutes/ minsPerHour) * calories).ToString("F0");
            string paceResultString
                = ((minutes * minsPerHour) / laps).ToString("F0");

            if (Request.Form["resultFormat"] == "JSON") {

                JSONCalculationResult calcResult = new JSONCalculationResult() {
                    distance = distanceResultString,
                    calories = caloriesResultString,
                    pace = paceResultString
                };

                DataContractJsonSerializer serializer
                    = new DataContractJsonSerializer(calcResult.GetType());
                serializer.WriteObject(Response.OutputStream, calcResult);

                Response.ContentType = "application/JSON";
                Response.End();

            } else {
                distanceResult.InnerText = distanceResultString;
                caloriesResult.InnerText = caloriesResultString;
                paceResult.InnerText = paceResultString;
                sourceResult.InnerText = "Non-AJAX";
            }
        }
    }
}
```

```
[Serializable]
public class JSONCalculationResult {
    public string distance;
    public string calories;
    public string pace;
}
```
}

The changes to the code-behind class are shown in bold. The class now checks to see whether there is a form element in the POST request called resultFormat with a value of JSON. If there is, an instance of the JSONCalculationResult class is created and populated with the three result values. This object is then passed to an instance of the DataContractJsonSerializer class, which converts the JSONCalculationResult object to JSON format and writes it to the output stream that returns data to the Ajax client. The Response context object is used to set the content type header for the response to the client, and the End method terminates the page rendering process. This prevents the contents of the HTML elements and controls from being included in the data sent back to the client.

To take advantage of this new JSON page capability, we need the cooperation of the Ajax client script. We need to add the resultFormat field to our form data. Listing 11-18 shows the changes required.

Listing 11-18. *Cooperating with the JSON-enabled code-behind class*

```
<script type="text/javascript">

    $(document).ready(function () {

        $('form').ajaxForm({
            data: { 'resultFormat': 'JSON' },
            dataType: 'json',
            success: function (data) {
                $('#<%=distanceResult.ClientID%>').text(data['distance']);
                $('#<%=caloriesResult.ClientID%>').text(data['calories']);
                $('#<%=paceResult.ClientID%>').text(data['pace']);

                $('#<%=resultsDiv.ClientID%>').show();
                $('#<%=sourceResult.ClientID%>').text('AJAX (JSON)');
            }
        });
    });

</script>
```

The changes in Listing 11-18 are shown in bold. The data option for the ajaxForm function allows us to provide additional data to include in the form data, and I have used this to create the resultFormat value that triggers the JSON result in the code-behind class.

We have to tell the form plug-in that the result of the POST will be JSON data, which we do using the dataType option:

```
dataType: 'json',
```

The three statements that extracted values from the HTML result have been updated to deal with the JSON data, as follows:

```
$('#<%=distanceResult.ClientID%>').text(data['distance']);
```

Notice that we don't have to deal with the d wrapper that is added when we use a WCF service. We can obtain each property from the JSON object directly. The final change is the value for the source indicator, which is set to Ajax (JSON). When you apply these changes to your project, submitting the form retrieves the data as JSON. Non-JavaScript-enabled clients can still use the regular form mechanism, albeit the page will be reloaded as part of this process. You can see the changed source information in Figure 11-8.

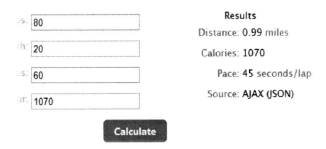

Figure 11-8. *Obtaining JSON data from an ASP.NET web page*

Using Ajax to POST to a Web Service

Although you can POST data to a web page, a small amount of additional work will let us post to a WCF web service method. In this section, we'll add a method to our web service that will perform the calculation and revise our jQuery script. Listing 11-19 shows the addition to the TriathlonService.svc code-behind class.

Listing 11-19. *Adding a calculation method to the web service*

```
[OperationContract]
[WebInvoke]
public JSONCalculationResult PerformCalculation(int laps, int length, int mins, int cals) {

    const float metersToMiles = 0.00062137119223733f;
    const float minsPerHour = 60f;
```

```
    return new JSONCalculationResult() {
        distance = ((laps * length) * metersToMiles).ToString("F2"),
        calories = ((mins / minsPerHour) * cals).ToString("F0"),
        pace = ((mins* minsPerHour) / laps).ToString("F0")
    };
}
```

This method, called `PerformCalculation`, uses the `JSONCalculationResult` class that we created in the previous example. The most significant feature of this method is the use of the `WebInvoke` attribute, which enables `POST` operations. This is the counterpart to the `WebGet` attribute, which enabled `GET` operations. In all other respects, this method operates just like the others in our web service. Listing 11-20 shows the changes that are required to our jQuery script to use the newly added `PerformCalculation` method.

Listing 11-20. *Using jQuery to POST to a web service*

```
<script type="text/javascript">

    var GetFormData = function () {
        return {
            'laps': $('#<%=lapsInput.ClientID%>').val(),
            'length': $('#<%=lengthInput.ClientID%>').val(),
            'mins': $('#<%=minsInput.ClientID%>').val(),
            'cals': $('#<%=calsInput.ClientID%>').val()
        }
    };

    $(document).ready(function () {

        $(':submit').click(function () {
            $.ajax({
                url: '/TriathlonService.svc/PerformCalculation',
                type: 'POST',
                contentType: 'application/json',
                data: JSON.stringify(GetFormData()),
                cache: false,
                success: function (data) {
                    $('#<%=distanceResult.ClientID%>').text(data.d['distance']);
                    $('#<%=caloriesResult.ClientID%>').text(data.d['calories']);
                    $('#<%=paceResult.ClientID%>').text(data.d['pace']);

                    $('#<%=resultsDiv.ClientID%>').show();
                    $('#<%=sourceResult.ClientID%>').text('AJAX (WCF)');
                }
            });
            return false;
        });
    });
</script>
```

We are not going to use the form plug-in to handle our POST operations. WCF web services can't receive form-encoded data easily, and the jQuery forms plug-in can't generate JSON data easily; so, the simplest path is to use the built-in jQuery Ajax features directly. This is not as bad as it sounds. We start with a function that obtains the values that the user has entered into the form input elements:

```
var GetFormData = function () {
    return {
        'laps': $('#<%=lapsInput.ClientID%>').val(),
        'length': $('#<%=lengthInput.ClientID%>').val(),
        'mins': $('#<%=minsInput.ClientID%>').val(),
        'cals': $('#<%=calsInput.ClientID%>').val()
    }
};
```

The only point of note for this function is that we need to use the code blocks to get the ClientID values. We could remove the runat attributes from the input elements, but then the non-JavaScript form function would be disrupted.

The rest of the script registers a handler for when the submit button is clicked. We didn't need to do this when using the form plug-in, but since we are handling the operation using the built-in jQuery functions, we need to register with the click event. The click handler makes a call to the ajax function, which performs our Ajax operation:

```
$.ajax({
    url: '/TriathlonService.svc/PerformCalculation',
    type: 'POST',
    contentType: 'application/json',
    data: JSON.stringify(GetFormData()),
    cache: false,
    success: function (data) {
        $('#<%=distanceResult.ClientID%>').text(data.d['distance']);
        $('#<%=caloriesResult.ClientID%>').text(data.d['calories']);
        $('#<%=paceResult.ClientID%>').text(data.d['pace']);

        $('#<%=resultsDiv.ClientID%>').show();
        $('#<%=sourceResult.ClientID%>').text('AJAX (WCF)');
    }
});
```

The url option specifies the target of our POST operation, which in this case is the newly added PerformCalculation method of our existing web service. The type option specifies the HTTP method to use—in this case, POST. The data option specifies the data to include in the POST operation, which I have set to be the result of the GetFormData, converted to JSON data using the JavaScript function JSON.stringify.

■ **Caution** A limitation of this script is that the JSON.stringify function, which converts an object into a JSON string, is not supported on older versions of Internet Explorer, which includes the Visual Studio built-in browser. A more widely supported approach is to use (yet) another jQuery plug-in that will generate JSON for you. I recommend Doug Crockford's JSON plug-in, which you can get from https://github.com/douglascrockford/JSON-js.

The cache option prevents browsers from caching the result of calling the web service, and the handler for the success event processes the JSON result to extract the data and display the results. Since we are using a WCF web service, we have to take into account the d wrapper once more. The source information is set to AJAX (WCF) to indicate that we got the data asynchronously from a WCF web service.

Notice that we return false at the end of the click event handler. This is so that the default handler, which would submit the form, isn't called. Figure 11-9 shows the page display resulting from these changes.

Figure 11-9. *Getting the data asynchronously from a WCF web service*

Summary

In this chapter, we have seen three different approaches to Ajax using jQuery and ASP.NET or WCF. Ajax is one of the key building blocks for rich web applications, and users' expectations of load times and efficiency are strongly influenced by the widespread use of this technique.

Of course, if you have users who cannot, or will not, use JavaScript, then Ajax isn't as appealing, but as the calculator demonstrations in this chapter have shown, it is possible to build web applications and pages that degrade gracefully and that will still function when JavaScript isn't available.

CHAPTER 12

Working with Routes

In our examples to this point, there has been a direct correlation between the name we give a page and the URL that is used to access it. For example, if we create a new web page called `MyPage.aspx` in the root directory of our Visual Studio ASP.NET project, then the URL that we would use to access it on our development machine would be something like this:

`http://localhost:1234/MyPage.aspx`

If we move the web page into a directory called `Pages`, then the URL becomes as follows:

`http://localhost:1234/Pages/MyPage.aspx`

Similarly, when we deploy our web application to our production server (deployment is the topic of Chapter 14), the URL will still be directly related to the location of the page file in our application directory, in other words, something like this:

`http://myserver.mydomain.com/Pages/MyPage.aspx`

This model isn't always convenient. A change in the location of a page file requires any URLs that point to the page to be updated, and it exposes the structure of your application to your users. The ASP.NET *routing* feature lets you create abstractions between the URLs that access your pages and the pages themselves and, in doing so, lets you create URLs that your users will find easier to access directly. In this chapter, we'll explore how routes work and how you can use them to add flexibility to your web application.

Note Routes are strictly optional in an ASP.NET web application, unless you are using the MVC or Dynamic Data framework, in which case they are an important part of the structure of an application.

Preparing the Project

Routes are typically defined in the global application class, which you first saw in Chapter 5. To add a global application class to our ongoing example, select Project ➤ Add New Item in Visual Studio, pick the Global Application Class template, and click the Add button. A new item, `Global.asax`, will be created in the project.

The convention for managing routes is to add a method to `Global.asax` called `RegisterRoutes` and call this method from the `Application_Start` method. Listing 12-1 shows these changes applied the `Global.asax` class, with the other methods removed for brevity (we won't be using the other methods in this chapter).

Listing 12-1. *Adding the RegisterRoutes method to the global application class*

```
using System;
using System.Web.Routing;

namespace TriathlonTraining {
    public class Global : System.Web.HttpApplication {

        protected void Application_Start(object sender, EventArgs e) {

            RegisterRoutes(RouteTable.Routes);
        }

        public static void RegisterRoutes(RouteCollection routes) {

            // routes will go here
        }
    }
}
```

The `RegisterRoutes` method accepts an instance of the `System.Web.Routing.RouteCollection` class as a parameter. The `Application_Start` method obtains such an object through the `RouteTable.Routes` property, which is part of the `HttpApplication` class, the base for global application classes.

■ **Tip**   I find that the ASP.NET development server doesn't reliably detect changes to the `Global.asax` file and recompile automatically. I recommend you use the Visual Studio Build menu to make explicitly recompile when you make changes to routes.

Working with Routes

At the heart of the ASP.NET routing feature is the idea of a URL pattern. When a URL is requested, the routing feature compares a list of patterns that you have provided and tries to match one of them to what has been requested. Here is an example of a routing URL:

`/App/{page}/Action/{name}`

URL patterns work on segments of a URL. A segment is a section of a URL delimited by the `/` character. Each segment in a pattern is represented by a literal value or a variable. Variables are expressed using braces ({ and }). In the previous pattern, there are four segments; two of the segments are literal (`App` and `Action`), and two are variables (`page` and `name`).

For a URL to match a URL pattern, there must be the same number of segments in the requested URL, and the URL pattern *and* the literal segments in the pattern must match the corresponding segments in the URL. For example, the following will match the example pattern:

```
/App/Default/Action/Edit
/App/Products/Action/Buy
```

A pattern will not match a URL if there are more or less segments than are in the pattern or the segments in the URL do not match the literal segments in the pattern. Here are some examples of URLs that won't match the pattern:

```
/App/Default/Action/Edit/Products
/WebApp/Products
/WebApp/Default/Action/Edit
```

The first URL won't match because it has too many segments, and the second has too few. The third URL won't match because the first segment in the URL (WebApp) is different from the literal value in the first segment in the pattern (App).

By contrast, it doesn't matter what is in the segment of a URL that corresponds to the variable segments in a pattern. However, we can restrict the range of acceptable variables values to narrow the focus of a pattern (we'll see how to do this in the "Applying Constraints to Routing Variables" section later in the chapter). In the following sections, we'll see how to use URL patterns to create ASP.NET routes that have different effects.

Creating an Alias for a URL

The first thing we will do with a route is create an alias URL for one of our pages so that we can request the ListEvents.aspx page using the URL /Events. Listing 12-2 shows the statement that creates this mapping.

Listing 12-2. Creating a URL alias

```csharp
using System;
using System.Web.Routing;

namespace TriathlonTraining {
    public class Global : System.Web.HttpApplication {

        protected void Application_Start(object sender, EventArgs e) {

            RegisterRoutes(RouteTable.Routes);
        }

        public static void RegisterRoutes(RouteCollection routes) {

            routes.MapPageRoute("myRoute", "Events", "~/ListEvents.aspx");

        }
    }
}
```

The route created in Listing 12-2 is shown in bold. Routes are created by calling the MapPageRoute method of the RouteCollection class (which is the parameter accepted by our RegisterRoutes method). There are three parameters to the MapPageRoute method.

The first parameter is the name that we want the route to be known by. This is purely for our use and doesn't change the behavior of the route. I have chosen myRoute, but any string value is acceptable, and it is quite common to specify an empty string ("") to assign no name to a route.

The second parameter is the URL pattern. We are starting with a very simple example; it has one segment, which is a literal value. It will match only if the requested URL is Events. There can be only one segment, and there are no variables involved.

The third and final parameter is the physical page we want the route to use when the pattern matches a URL. In this case, I have chosen the ListEvents.aspx page.

▪ **Note** Notice that the real page name in Listing 12-2 is prefixed with ~/. A tilde (~) represents the root of our web application as opposed to just /, which represents the root of the server. This is an important distinction when multiple web applications are deployed to the same server. When using routes, the real page must be specified relative to the application root.

To test the route, start the Visual Studio ASP.NET development server and request the URL /Events. The easiest way to do this is to right-click one of the existing .aspx web pages and select View in Browser from the pop-up menu. This will ensure that the global application class is compiled and that the server is started. When the page is displayed, edit the URL in the browser to the desired URL. If, for example, you viewed the Calculator.aspx page, the URL in the browser will be something similar to this:

http://localhost:16892/Calculator.aspx

To test the newly added route, change the URL in the browser to the following:

http://localhost:16892/Events

Routing a URL doesn't cause the browser to be redirected. Instead, the browser requests the /Events URL and receives the contents of the ListEvents.aspx page without being aware that the route exists. You can see this by examining the URL displayed by the browser, as shown in Figure 12-1.

Figure 12-1. The routed URL displayed by a browser

The closest equivalent to this is the **Server.Transfer** method you saw in Chapter 5, but the routing system is more convenient and, as we will see, has some additional features.

USING RELATIVE URLS WITH ASP.NET ROUTING

When using routed URLs, references to other resources, such as images, external script files, and CSS, must be fully qualified. For example, if you drag a JavaScript file from the Scripts folder onto an .aspx page, Visual Studio will create a script element like this:

```
<script src="Scripts/jquery-1.4.1.min.js" type="text/javascript"></script>
```

This reference will be properly resolved when a page is requested using a routed URL; we must specify the location absolutely, like this:

```
<script src="/Scripts/jquery-1.4.1.min.js" type="text/javascript"></script>
```

or relative to the root of the web application like this:

```
<script src="~/Scripts/jquery-1.4.1.min.js" type="text/javascript"></script>
```

If you start using routes and find that images are not displayed or that your scripts generate unexpected errors, this is the likely cause of the problem.

Adding a route doesn't stop requests directed at the page from working. You can still request ListEvents.aspx even though there is a route related to this page defined in the global application class. See the "Disabling Nonrouted URLs" section later in this chapter for details of how to prevent direct requests for .aspx files from working.

Understanding Route Ordering

Routes are evaluated in the order which they are added. Once a match is made, no further routes are checked. As a demonstration, Listing 12-3 shows a route I have added before the one from the earlier example.

Listing 12-3. Adding a route

```
public static void RegisterRoutes(RouteCollection routes) {

    routes.MapPageRoute("myGeneralRoute", "{mode}", "~/Calculator.aspx");

    routes.MapPageRoute("myRoute", "Events", "~/ListEvents.aspx");
}
```

The new route is shown in bold. It has one segment, and it is a variable, which means that this pattern will match any URL that contains one segment, including /Events. If you request the /Events URL using the web browser, you will see that the Calculator.aspx page is displayed. The second route is never evaluated. This means you should define routes that are more specific before you define those that are more general.

▨ **Note** If you are observant, you will have noticed that when a route leads to the `Calculator.aspx` page being displayed, the tabs that we added to the master page in Chapter 10 do not work correctly. This is because the jQuery script that handles the tabs relies on the `Request.Path` property to work out which tab should be highlighted, and this property returns the requested URL when a route has led to the page being displayed. I'll show you how to fix the tabs in the "Fixing the Master Page Tabs" section later in this chapter.

If we reversed the order of the two routes in Listing 12-3, like this:

```
routes.MapPageRoute("myRoute", "Events", "~/ListEvents.aspx");
routes.MapPageRoute("myGeneralRoute", "{mode}", "~/Calculator.aspx");
```

then `/Events` results in the `ListEvents.aspx` page being displayed, and any other one-segment URL will result in the `Calculator.aspx` page being displayed.

▨ **Note** We won't be using the `myGeneralRoute` defined in Listing 12-3 again, so you should remove it from your project; otherwise, it will interfere with later examples.

Working with Route Variables

You have seen how literals and values are used to match a URL pattern. The reason that we gave the variables names such as `mode`, `page`, and `name` is that ASP.NET makes the contents of each variable URL segment available to us when rendering our page, using the name we gave to the variable. Listing 12-4 adds a route for the `ListEvents.aspx` page to `Global.asax` that has a variable segment.

Listing 12-4. *A variable segment route*

```
public static void RegisterRoutes(RouteCollection routes) {

    routes.MapPageRoute("calcRoute", "Calculator", "~/Calculator.aspx");
    routes.MapPageRoute("myRoute", "Events", "~/ListEvents.aspx");

    routes.MapPageRoute("", "Events/{eventType}", "~/ListEvents.aspx");
}
```

The pattern for this new route will match any two-segment URL where the first segment is `Events`. We are going to use the pattern variable to create a *composable URL,* where the user shortcuts navigating through the web application by using URL segments. Until now, if we want to list all the `Sprint` triathlon events, we have to do the following:

1. Request the `ListEvents.aspx` web page.

2. Wait for the Ajax script to load and display all of the events.

3. Select Sprint from the drop-down menu of the `select` control.

4. Wait for the Ajax script to load and display the sprint events.

This isn't a huge hardship, but it presents a couple of problems. First, we ship more data around and process more requests that we need to process. Our web service processes an initial request for all the data and a subsequent request for just the sprint data. Second, we make the user jump through hoops. They already know what data they want to see, but we show them everything and only then allow them to apply a filter.

Our composable URL will let the user see just the events they want without having to navigate using the web page. When the user requests the URL `/Events/Sprint`, we will show them just the sprint events, and when the user requests the URL `/Events/Olympic`, we will show them just the Olympic data.

The type of event that the user wants to see will be contained in the second segment variable called `eventType`. Listing 12-5 shows how we can access this variable from within the `ListEvent.aspx` code-behind class.

Listing 12-5. *Accessing routing values from the code-behind class*

```
using System;

namespace TriathlonTraining {
    public partial class ListEvents : System.Web.UI.Page {
        protected void Page_Load(object sender, EventArgs e) {

            // create the entity data model context object
            using (TrainingDataEntities context = new TrainingDataEntities()) {

                // populate the select control if needed
                if (ViewState["setupComplete"] == null) {
                    foreach (string name in DataAccess.GetEventTypeNames(context)) {
                        eventSelector.Items.Add(name);
                    }
                    ViewState["setupComplete"] = true;
                }

                // get the value of the route data variable
                object specifiedSport = RouteData.Values["eventType"];
                if (specifiedSport != null) {
                    // get the list item that contains the selected event type
                    eventSelector.Items
                        .FindByText(specifiedSport.ToString()).Selected = true;
                }
            }
        }
    }
}
```

The routing-specific additions to the class are shown in bold. We can access the routing configuration through the `Page.RouteData` property, which returns a `System.Web.Routing.RouteData` object. The `RouteData` object contains information about the route that has led to this page being invoked, and we can get to the URL pattern variable using the `Values` property, so that this statement:

```
object specifiedSport = RouteData.Values["eventType"];
```

returns the contents of the URL segment that corresponds to the `eventType` variable in the URL pattern.

All we have to do to enable our composable URL is to ensure that the appropriate option element is selected in the `select` element. We do that using the `FindByText` method on the collection of list items that is returned by the `Items` property of the `HtmlSelect` HTML control class. That's all we have to do because the Ajax script that we added to the `ListEvents.aspx` page requests its data from the server based on the selected item in the `select` element. By preselecting the `Sprint` item, say, in the code-behind class, we ensure that the client-side jQuery script will ask for only the `Sprint` items in its initial request.

■ **Tip**   Some caution is required when working with the URL segment variables, because the user can also request the `ListEvents.aspx` page directly, in which case there will be no `eventType` variable. That's why the test in Listing 12-5 makes sure that we have successfully retrieved a value from the `RouteData.Values` collection. Note that when we do manage to obtain a value, we get an `object` that then has to be converted to a `string` before we can use it to select an item.

To test the effect of this route, start the ASP.NET development web server and request the `/Events/Sprint` URL. You will see only the `Sprint` type events shown in the list, as illustrated by Figure 12-2.

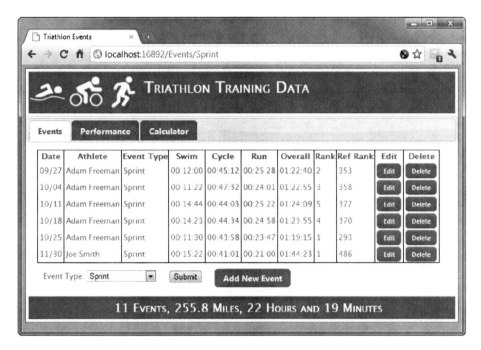

Figure 12-2. *Using a composable URL*

Notice that the **select** element correctly shows the event type. This is a nice consequence of using the HTML of the page as the bridge between ASP.NET and jQuery Ajax. If you request the URL **/Events/Olympic**, you will see just the Olympic events, and, of course, the **select** element still works as before, so you can change the kind of event that is displayed by selecting a new value from the drop-down list.

Supplying Default Values for Routing Variables

We now have two routes that relate to the **ListEvents.aspx** page. The first deals with the single-segment URL **/Events**, and the second deals with the two-segment **/Events/Sprint** (or other event type) URL. When you request the first URL, you see all of the events, and when you request the second URL, you see only the events that match the type you have specified.

We can combine these two routes and preserve the same behavior by using the default variable value feature. Listing 12-6 shows the combined route in the global application class.

Listing 12-6. *Using default URL parameter values*

```
public static void RegisterRoutes(RouteCollection routes) {

    routes.MapPageRoute("calcRoute", "Calculator", "~/Calculator.aspx");

    routes.MapPageRoute("", "Events/{eventType}",
        "~/ListEvents.aspx",
```

```
        true,
        new RouteValueDictionary() {
            {"eventType", "All"}
        });
}
```

The new route is shown in bold; it has two additional parameters. The first, a **bool** value, tells the routing system if it should check to see whether the user is authorized to access the page file. I cover authentication and authorization in Chapter 13, but in general setting this parameter to **true** is a sensible practice.

The second parameter is the one we are interested in for this chapter. It is a `System.Web.Routing.RouteValueDictionary` object containing the default values we want applied to the variable routing segments.

There is only one default value in Listing 12-6 because there is only one variable segment in the route URL pattern. You can see that I have specified a default value of `All`. Specifying default values widens the range of URLs that will match the pattern. If a variable segment has been omitted from a URL but a default value for the variable has been specified, the URL will match, and the routing system will assign the default value to the variable. For the rule in Listing 12-6, this means that when we request the URL `/Events`, it is as though we had really requested `/Events/All`, because the default value is applied.

Using default values doesn't affect the page or the code-behind class; it just broadens the scope of the URL pattern match and simplifies our set of routes.

Applying Constraints to Routing Variables

One problem with the previous example is that we don't check the pattern variable to ensure that it matches an event type that we recognize. To see what I mean, change the URL in the browser to `/Events/IronMan`, and you'll see an exception thrown by the page. One way to fix this is to constrain the URL pattern so that it matches only for certain variable values. Listing 12-7 shows the revised route.

Listing 12-7. *Restricting a URL through variable value constraints*

```
public static void RegisterRoutes(RouteCollection routes) {

    routes.MapPageRoute("calcRoute", "Calculator", "~/Calculator.aspx");
    routes.MapPageRoute("", "Events/{eventType}",
        "~/ListEvents.aspx",
        true,
        new RouteValueDictionary() {{"eventType", "All"}},

        new RouteValueDictionary() {{"eventType", "All|Sprint|Olympic"}}
    );
}
```

I have passed an additional parameter to the `MapPageRoute` method in Listing 12-7, which is another `RouteValueDictionary` object. Instead of default values, this one provides regular expressions that are used to limit the set of acceptable variable values when they are supplied. We want to support only three values, which can be expressed literally and combined using the bar character (|), but any valid regular expression can be specified.

Listing 12-7 specifies literal values that would be better obtained from the database through the `DataAccess` class and the Entity Framework data model. I listed them literally to make the example clearer, but it would be more sensible to build the constraint string programmatically, as shown in Listing 12-8.

Listing 12-8. *Creating a variable value constraint programmatically*

```
public static void RegisterRoutes(RouteCollection routes) {

    routes.MapPageRoute("calcRoute", "Calculator", "~/Calculator.aspx");

    using (TrainingDataEntities context = new TrainingDataEntities()) {
        string[] eventTypes = DataAccess.GetEventTypeNames(context);
        StringBuilder builder = new StringBuilder("All");
        for (int i = 0; i < eventTypes.Length; i++) {
            builder.Append('|').Append(eventTypes[i]);
        }

        routes.MapPageRoute("", "Events/{eventType}",
            "~/ListEvents.aspx",
            true,
            new RouteValueDictionary() {{"eventType", "All"}},
            new RouteValueDictionary() {{"eventType", builder.ToString()}}
        );
    }
}
```

Irrespective of whether you list your constraints literally or generate them programmatically, when the user provides a value for a variable segment that doesn't match the corresponding regular expression, a "not found" exception will be thrown, represented as an HTTP 404 error. See Chapter 7 for details of how to ASP.NET handle errors elegantly and in ways that won't confuse the user.

However, if you want to constrain the range of values and rely on a default value if there is no match, then we can add a second route. Remember that routes are evaluated in the order that are added and that we put less specific rules after more specific ones. Listing 12-9 shows the addition of a fallback route.

Listing 12-9. *Using a second route as a fallback*

```
public static void RegisterRoutes(RouteCollection routes) {

    routes.MapPageRoute("calcRoute", "Calculator", "~/Calculator.aspx");

    using (TrainingDataEntities context = new TrainingDataEntities()) {
        string[] eventTypes = DataAccess.GetEventTypeNames(context);
        StringBuilder builder = new StringBuilder("All");
        for (int i = 0; i < eventTypes.Length; i++) {
            builder.Append('|').Append(eventTypes[i]);
        }
```

```
        routes.MapPageRoute("", "Events/{eventType}",
            "~/ListEvents.aspx",
            true,
            new RouteValueDictionary() { { "eventType", "All" } },
            new RouteValueDictionary() { { "eventType", builder.ToString() } } }
        );
    }


    routes.MapPageRoute("", "Events/{placeholder}",
        "~/ListEvents.aspx",
        true,
        new RouteValueDictionary() { { "eventType", "All" } });

}
```

This is a sleight-of-hand trick that relies on the implementation of the routing system. It probably shouldn't work this way, and it might change in future versions of ASP.NET. However, it works in ASP.NET version 4 and is quite handy. The URL pattern of the new rule, which is marked in bold, will match a two-segment URL where the first segment in Events. This is the same as the previous route, but because routes are evaluated in order, it will match only if the second segment of the requested URL has failed the constraint check of the first Events route. The trick is to specify a variable name that we then ignore and to provide a default value for the variable that we care about. In this case, we match a variable called placeholder and supply a value for eventType. Even though eventType is not a variable URL segment, the routing system passes on the default value to the code-behind class. In this way, we create a behavior for URLs such as /Events/IronMan. They become equivalent to requesting /Events/All. Some care must be taken when using this approach, because it may not be what the user expects, but when it is appropriate to the style of your web application, it can be preferable to displaying an error page.

Routing Patterns with Variable Segments

We can specify routes with a variable number of segments by marking the last variable segment with an asterisk (*). Listing 12-10 provides a demonstration.

Listing 12-10. A route with a variable number of segments

```
public static void RegisterRoutes(RouteCollection routes) {

    routes.MapPageRoute("calcRoute", "Calculator", "~/Calculator.aspx");


    routes.MapPageRoute("variableCalcRoute",
        "Calculator/{firstVal}/{secondVal}/{*otherVals}",
        "~/Calculator.aspx");

    using (TrainingDataEntities context = new TrainingDataEntities()) {
        string[] eventTypes = DataAccess.GetEventTypeNames(context);
        StringBuilder builder = new StringBuilder("All");
        for (int i = 0; i < eventTypes.Length; i++) {
            builder.Append('|').Append(eventTypes[i]);
        }
```

```
        routes.MapPageRoute("", "Events/{eventType}",
            "~/ListEvents.aspx",
            true,
            new RouteValueDictionary() { { "eventType", "All" } },
            new RouteValueDictionary() { { "eventType", builder.ToString() } }
        );
    }

    routes.MapPageRoute("", "Events/{placeholder}",
        "~/ListEvents.aspx",
        true,
        new RouteValueDictionary() { { "eventType", "All" } });
}
```

The pattern for this route will match any URL that starts with /Calculator and has at least two other segments. If there are more than two segments, then their values will be assigned to the otherVals variable as a single string, so that if we requested the URL /Calculator/1/2/3/4, then firstVal would be 1, secondVal would be 2, and otherVals would be 3/4. We can use this feature to allow the user to perform calculations through the Calculator.aspx page, supplying a variable number of values to work with and relying on the default values in the page where values are not specified in the URL. Listing 12-11 shows how to do this in the Calculator.aspx code-behind class.

Listing 12-11. *Performing calculations via a routed URL*

```
...
if (IsPostBack || RouteData.Values.Count > 0) {

    if (RouteData.Values.Count > 0) {
        // we know that we have at least two values to process
        lapsInput.Value = RouteData.Values["firstVal"].ToString();
        lengthInput.Value = RouteData.Values["secondVal"].ToString();
        // see if we have a variable length item
        if (RouteData.Values["otherVals"] != null) {
            string[] additionalValues = RouteData.Values["otherVals"].ToString().Split('/');
            minsInput.Value = additionalValues[0];
            if (additionalValues.Length > 1) {
                calsInput.Value = additionalValues[1];
            }
        }
    }
}
....
```

Whereas the calculation would have been performed only if the request to the page was a POST, it is now also performed if there are routing variable values available. When this is the case, I set the Value properties of the appropriate input elements so that they reflect the routed URL variables and will be used in the calculation. I know that if there is routing data, there will be at least two variables (otherwise the route would not have matched the URL), and I check to see whether additional segments are present by checking for otherVals. When the user requests a URL such as /Calculator/100/50 or /Calculator/100/50/75/1000, the URL segments are used in the calculation, as shown in Figure 12-3.

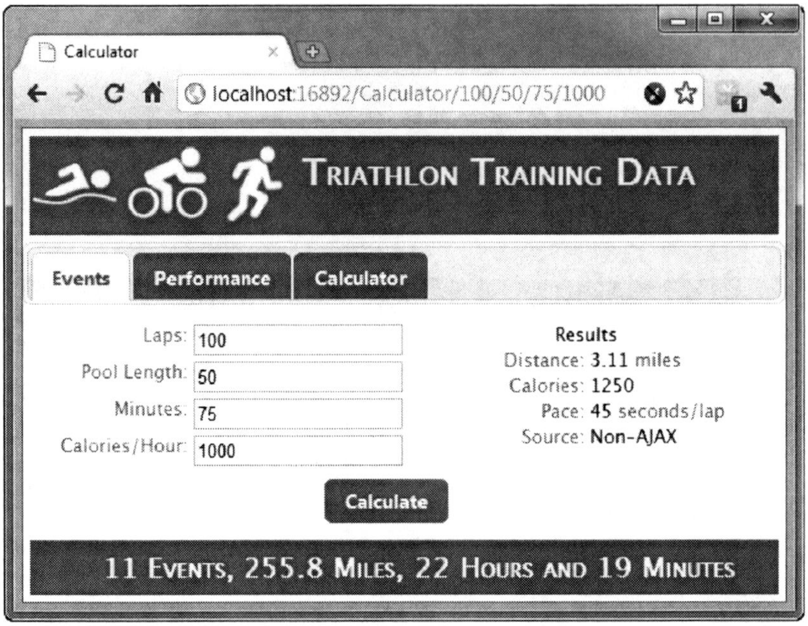

Figure 12-3. *Working with a URL that has a variable number of segments*

Disabling Nonrouted URLs

By default, the routed URLs coexist alongside regular URLs, meaning that we can get to the
`Calculator.aspx` page by requesting either /Calculator.aspx or /Calculator. We can disable requests for
the `.aspx` pages by name by adding two statements to the global application class, as shown in Listing
12-12.

Listing 12-12. *Disabling direct requests for web pages*

```
...
public static void RegisterRoutes(RouteCollection routes) {

    routes.RouteExistingFiles = true;
    routes.MapPageRoute("files", "{filename}.aspx/{*catchall}", "~/NoPage.aspx");

    routes.MapPageRoute("calcRoute", "Calculator", "~/Calculator.aspx");
...
```

The statements are shown in bold. The first enables routing when requests are for files on disk:

```
routes.RouteExistingFiles = true;
```

This means that if a URL is requested that matches a route *and* that is for a file in the web application, then the route takes precedence. By default, the standard URL handler is used in this situation, even if there is a matching route. The second statement adds a route whose pattern matches requests for .aspx files:

```
routes.MapPageRoute("files", "{filename}.aspx/{*catchall}", "~/NoPage.aspx");
```

The URL pattern matches any request for an .aspx file that has any number of additional segments. When such a request is made, the route matches, and the request is passed to the page NoPage.aspx.

At this point, we have a choice. We can create a page called NoPage.aspx and use the routing data to display a helpful message to the user explaining that we don't support direct requests for web page files. Or we can create a page that tries to figure out what routed URL should be used and transfers the request as seamlessly as possible, so if we had received a request for /ListEvents.aspx, we would transfer or redirect the user to /Events instead. The third option is to *not* create the file; when the route matches a URL, a standard "not found" exception will occur, and we can handle it like any request for a page that doesn't exist. See Chapter 7 for different approaches to doing this.

▪ **Caution** Be sure to remove the statements in Listing 12-12 from your project for the examples in the following sections. We are not ready to disable all direct requests for pages.

Using Routed URLs in Web Pages

To embrace routed URLs fully, we need to ensure that we include the routed versions of URLs in our web pages. We can do this several ways, and we can do it directly in the web page using a code block or in the code-behind file. In the following sections, I'll explain the different options.

Creating Routed URLs in a Web Page

We'll start with the ListEvents.aspx page, which contains an a element whose href attribute refers to the AddEvent.aspx page. Even when you use a routed URL to get to the ListEvents.aspx page, clicking the Add New Event link (or button, thanks to the jQuery UI we added in Chapter 10), we see the real name of the page in the browser, as illustrated by Figure 12-4.

Figure 12-4. The browser displaying the name of the AddEvent.aspx page

Our goal in this section is to have the browser display a routed URL, as part of our composable URL scheme. We start by defining a route for the AddEvents.aspx page, shown in Listing 12-13.

Listing 12-13. Adding a route for the AddEvent.aspx page

```
public static void RegisterRoutes(RouteCollection routes) {

    routes.MapPageRoute("calcRoute", "Calculator", "~/Calculator.aspx");
    routes.MapPageRoute("variableCalcRoute",
        "Calculator/{firstVal}/{secondVal}/{*otherVals}",
        "~/Calculator.aspx");


    routes.MapPageRoute("addRoute", "Events/Add", "~/AddEvent.aspx");


    using (TrainingDataEntities context = new TrainingDataEntities()) {
        string[] eventTypes = DataAccess.GetEventTypeNames(context);
        StringBuilder builder = new StringBuilder("All");
        for (int i = 0; i < eventTypes.Length; i++) {
            builder.Append('|').Append(eventTypes[i]);
        }

        routes.MapPageRoute("", "Events/{eventType}",
            "~/ListEvents.aspx",
            true,
            new RouteValueDictionary() { { "eventType", "All" } },
            new RouteValueDictionary() { { "eventType", builder.ToString() } }
        );
    }

    routes.MapPageRoute("", "Events/{placeholder}",
        "~/ListEvents.aspx",
        true,
        new RouteValueDictionary() { { "eventType", "All" } });
}
```

The new route has a two-segment literal pattern and will match only the URL /Events/Add. Notice that I have added this route before the others that work with the /Events prefix. This is a more specific URL than the others and so must be placed first. I have used the /Events prefix to further expand our composable URL theme.

Our next step is to update the reference to the AddEvents.aspx page from the ListEvents.aspx page; toward the end of the page you'll see a section as follows:

```
...
<div class="standardDiv">
    <a href="AddEvent.aspx">Add New Event</a>
</div>
...
```

The a element has an href attribute that is hardwired to the AddEvent.aspx page. To change to a routed URL, we need to replace the a element with an asp:HyperLink element, as shown in Listing 12-14.

Listing 12-14. Embedding a routed URL in a web page

```
...
<div class="standardDiv">
    <asp:HyperLink id="addLink" runat="server"
    NavigateUrl="<%$RouteUrl:RouteName=addRoute %>">Add New Event</asp:HyperLink>
</div>
...
```

The asp:HyperLink element refers to the System.Web.UI.WebControls.HyperLink class, which is a representation of the HTML a element but with convenience features implemented at the server, such as displaying images. We aren't really interested in these features, but the use of this control does let us use the code-block expression syntax for the NavigateUrl attribute, like this:

```
<%$RouteUrl:RouteName=addRoute %>
```

Notice the $ character after the <%. This indicates we are using an expression. Expressions consist of a keyword and a set of property names and values. In this case, the keyword is RouteUrl, and we have provided a value for the RouteName property. I don't like the asp:HyperLink class, and I tend to avoid the expression code blocks, but if we want to include a routed URL in our web page, this is how to do it.

The RouteName property specifies the name of route that we want to use to generate the routed URL. The addRoute value is the name we gave to the route we added in Listing 12-13. There are no variable segments in this route, so we don't need to provide any information. If you view the modified ListEvents.aspx page in the browser and look at the rendered HTML source, you'll see that our expression block has been converted into a routed URL, like this:

```
...
<div class="standardDiv">
    <a id="MainContent_addLink" href="/Events/Add">Add New Event</a>
</div>
...
```

The asp:HyperLink has been rendered as an a element, with the NavigationUrl attribute being expressed as the href attribute. Our RouteUrl expression has been converted into the routed URL /Events/Add. We can't just put the expression code block in our code without an even uglier sequence of elements. If we wanted to stick with our HTML a element and write the value of the routed URL directly into the href attribute, we have to use the asp:Literal element, like this:

```
<a href="<asp:Literal runat="server" Text="<%$RouteUrl:RouteName=addRoute%>" />">Add New
Event</a>
```

Creating Routed URLs in Code-Behind Classes

I love the fact we can get routed URLs, but I don't like either syntax style. I prefer to generate routed URLs from the code-behind class. The result is identical, but I find the style and syntax preferable. To demonstrate the code-behind approach, we must first change the link in the ListEvents.aspx page back to an a element, albeit one we can refer to from the code-behind class, like this:

```
...
<div class="standardDiv">

    <a id="addEventAnchor" runat="server">Add New Event</a>

</div>
...
```

We can now set the value of the `href` attribute programmatically, as demonstrated by Listing 12-15.

Listing 12-15. *Generating a routed URL programmatically*

```
using System;
using System.Web.Routing;

namespace TriathlonTraining {
    public partial class ListEvents : System.Web.UI.Page {
        protected void Page_Load(object sender, EventArgs e) {


            // set the href attribute of the anchor to be the routed URL
            addEventAnchor.HRef
                = RouteTable.Routes.GetVirtualPath(null, "addRoute", null).VirtualPath;


            // other statements removed for brevity
        }
    }
}
```

The statement shown in bold gets the set of defined routes using the `RouteTable.Routes` property and calls the `GetVirtualPath` method. We never need to provide a value for the first parameter, and the second parameter is the name of the route for which we want to generate a URL. The third parameter is the topic of the next section. The `GetVirtualPath` method returns a `VirtualPathData` object. We have no interest in this object other than that the `VirtualPath` property returns the URL we are looking for. If you display the `ListEvents.aspx` page after you have applied these changes, you can see the following in the HTML sent to the browser:

```
...
<div class="standardDiv">
    <a href="/Events/Add" id="MainContent_addEventAnchor">Add New Event</a>
</div>
...
```

Once again, we have a URL that will be matched by the route we named, in this case `/Events/Add`.

Creating Routed URLs Using Parameter Values

We can also create routed URLs that contain values for variable segments. To demonstrate this, we will create a route that deals with the `UpdateOrDeleteEvent.aspx` page and then generate routed URLs for that page that will be included in the Edit and Delete links/buttons of the `ListEvents.aspx` page. Listing 12-16 shows the new route.

Listing 12-16. Adding a route for the UpdateOrDelete.aspx page

```
public static void RegisterRoutes(RouteCollection routes) {

    routes.MapPageRoute("calcRoute", "Calculator", "~/Calculator.aspx");

    routes.MapPageRoute("variableCalcRoute",
        "Calculator/{firstVal}/{secondVal}/{*otherVals}",
        "~/Calculator.aspx");

    routes.MapPageRoute("addRoute", "Events/Add", "~/AddEvent.aspx");

    routes.MapPageRoute("editOrDelete",
        "Events/{mode}/{id}",
        "~/UpdateOrDeleteEvent.aspx",
        true,
        new RouteValueDictionary() {{"id", "1"}},,
        new RouteValueDictionary() { { "mode", "Edit|Delete"}});

    using (TrainingDataEntities context = new TrainingDataEntities()) {
        string[] eventTypes = DataAccess.GetEventTypeNames(context);
        StringBuilder builder = new StringBuilder("All");
        for (int i = 0; i < eventTypes.Length; i++) {
            builder.Append('|').Append(eventTypes[i]);
        }

        routes.MapPageRoute("", "Events/{eventType}",
            "~/ListEvents.aspx",
            true,
            new RouteValueDictionary() { { "eventType", "All" } },
            new RouteValueDictionary() { { "eventType", builder.ToString() } }
        );
    }

    routes.MapPageRoute("", "Events/{placeholder}",
        "~/ListEvents.aspx",
        true,
        new RouteValueDictionary() { { "eventType", "All" } });
}
```

The URL pattern for the new route, shown in bold, has three segments, two of which are variable. A default value is provided for the id variable, and constraints are provided for the mode variable. The mode variable must be Edit or Delete. I have not provided a constraint for the id variable. The reason for this will become clear shortly. If the user enters the URL /Events/Edit/1 or /Events/Delete/2, they will be able to edit or delete the events with a primary key value of 1 and 2, respectively.

Adding Route Variable Support in the Code-Behind Class

Having defined the route, we need to add support for handling the route variables in the UpdateOrDeleteEvent.aspx code-behind class. This page already accepts values for mode and id from the query string, and we want to preserve this so we can continue to refer to the page directly, in addition to via a routed URL. Listing 12-17 shows a method I have added to code-behind class.

Listing 12-17. Revising the UpdateOrDelete.aspx class

```
private string GetQueryStringOrRouteValue(string key) {

    string result = Request.QueryString[key];
    if (result == null && RouteData.Values[key] != null) {
        result = RouteData.Values[key].ToString();
    }
    return result;
}
```

This method checks to see whether a key exists in the request query string and, if not, tries to locate it in the set of routing variables. I have modified the class to use this method when determining how it has been called, like this:

```
...
string mode;
int eventID;
Event targetEvent;

if ((mode = GetQueryStringOrRouteValue("mode").ToLower()) != null
    && int.TryParse(GetQueryStringOrRouteValue("id"), out eventID)
    && (targetEvent = DataAccess.GetEventByID(context,
        eventID)) != null) {

    // set the hidden fields in the form
    this.modeInput.Value = mode;
    this.keyInput.Value = eventID.ToString();
...
```

■ **Note** I have only listed these fragments because the code-behind class for the UpdateOrDeleteEvent.aspx page is lengthy and has no bearing on the use of routing URLs beyond what I have shown here. You can see the whole class, including these modifications, by downloading the code that accompanies this book, freely available at Apress.com.

These small changes add support for getting the value for the mode and eventID code-behind class variables from the routing data without breaking the existing support for doing the same from the query string.

Adding the Routed URLs to the ListEvents.aspx Page

We generate a routed URL with variable segments by providing a set of name/value pairs. For example, to generate a routed URL for the UpdateOrDelete.aspx page in a code-behind class, we could use the code in Listing 12-18.

Listing 12-18. *Generating a routed URL with parameters in a code-behind class*

```
string routedUrl = RouteTable.Routes.GetVirtualPath(null, "editOrDelete",
    new RouteValueDictionary() {
        {"mode", "edit"},
        {"id", "5"}}).VirtualPath;
```

We simply pass an instance of the RouteValueDictionary class to the GetVirtualPath method, where the dictionary contains the segment variable names and the values for them. The previous statement would assign the following URL to the routedURL variable:

```
/Events/edit/5
```

A similar approach works for inline expressions, such as the one shown in Listing 12-19.

■ **Caution** Be careful when specifying values for segment variables. If the values you provide do not match the constraints in the route, you will get back an empty string (""), and your link or button won't function.

Listing 12-19. *Generating a routed URL with parameters inline*

```
<asp:HyperLink id="delLink" runat="server" NavigateUrl="<%$RouteUrl:RouteName=editOrDelete,
mode=Delete, id=4 %>Delete</asp:HyperLink>
```

In this example, we provide the values as a comma-separated name=value series following the route name. This markup generates the following HTML:

```
<a id="MainContent_delLink" href="/Events/Delete/4">Delete</a>
```

■ **Caution** You can omit the route name and just supply the names and values for the variable segments. The routing system will try to figure out which route should be used based on the limited information it has. It is an elegant feature when it works, but I find it unpredictable and prefer to give my routes names and then refer to them when generating routed URLs.

Things are slightly more complex to get these routed URLs in the ListEvents.aspx page because the event data is obtained using Ajax and the jQuery Templates plug-in. One of the values that we want as a URL segment is expressed as a data template item, like this:

```
<a href="/UpdateOrDeleteEvent.aspx?id=${Key}&mode=Edit">Edit</a>
```

This is where we might start generating the URLs:

```
<asp:HyperLink id="addLink" runat="server" NavigateUrl="<%$RouteUrl:RouteName=editOrDelete,
mode=Delete, id=${Key} %>">Edit</asp:HyperLink>
```

This is the same format we used before, but we have set the value of the id variable to ${Key}, which is the data template item. We would hope that this element is rendered as follows:

```
<a id="HeadContent_addLink" href="/Events/Delete/${Key}">Edit</a>
```

Unfortunately, the routing system tries to be helpful and encodes our parameter values so that they don't contain any characters that are illegal in a URL. What we actually get back is this:

```
<a id="HeadContent_addLink" href="/Events/Delete/%24%7BKey%7D">Edit</a>
```

I have highlighted the problem in bold. We lost our dollar and brace characters, which means that the jQuery template plug-in doesn't recognize a template item to be processed and we get a useless URL. Sadly, this is what happens when we bring disparate technologies like this together. For the most part, jQuery and ASP.NET can get along with only the most minor accommodations, but every now and again the design assumptions of one technology conflict with the design assumptions of the other.

We can fix this problem in a number of ways. The first would be to write our own handler for the routing system that doesn't encode the URL parameters automatically. This seems like overkill to me, especially since most of the time encoding the parameters is the kind of behavior that will save us time and avoid bugs.

The second approach would be to modify the jQuery template plug-in so that it recognizes a different syntax. I don't like this idea, because it means we create our own branch of the jQuery code and have to apply the same set of changes each time we want to move to a new version.

The approach that I have settled on when I encountered this on a real project was to compromise and mess around with the element syntax to get the URL format that I needed. This is how we would do the same in this case:

```
<a href="
    <asp:Literal runat="server"
        Text="<%$RouteUrl:RouteName=editOrDelete, mode=Edit%>"/>/${Key}">
    Edit
</a>
```

The asp:Literal element lets us access the RouteURL expression and just leaves the text behind when it is rendered. I use this element to create a partial URL, providing a value for the mode parameter only, so I end up with something like this:

```
/Events/Edit
```

I then cheat slightly and define the rest of the URL literally, which allows me to specify the template item, like this /${Key}. When this text is combined with the result of the asp:Literal element, we get the URL format we need:

```
/Events/Edit/${Key}
```

This is a format that the jQuery template plug-in can recognize, and when the data is obtained via Ajax, the template is applied correctly. The compromise in this example is that I have created a brittle dependency between the data template and the route URL pattern. I can't change the route without also changing the template. This is not ideal, but I find it preferable to the alternatives. Ideally, a better approach will emerge as the jQuery plug-in and ASP.NET continue to mature. Listing 12-20 shows these modifications applied to the data template in the ListEvents.aspx page.

Listing 12-20. Using routed URLs in a jQuery data template

```
<script id="eventTemplate" type="text/x-jquery-tmpl">
    <tr>
        <td>${Date}</td>
        <td>${Athlete}</td>
        <td>${EventType}</td>
        <td>${SwimTime}</td>
        <td>${CycleTime}</td>
        <td>${RunTime}</td>
        <td>${OverallTime}</td>
        <td>${Rank}</td>
        <td>${ReferenceRank}</td>
        <td>
            <a href="<asp:Literal runat="server" Text="<%$RouteUrl:RouteName=editOrDelete,
mode=Edit%>"/>/${Key}">Edit</a>
        </td>
        <td>
            <a href="<asp:Literal runat="server" Text="<%$RouteUrl:RouteName=editOrDelete,
mode=Delete%>"/>/${Key}">Delete</a>
        </td>
    </tr>
</script>
```

These changes mean that when you click the Edit or Delete button in the table in the ListEvents.aspx page, a routed URL is used to load the UpdateOrDeleteEvent.aspx page, as shown in Figure 12-5.

Figure 12-5. Using routed URLs for the UpdateOrDeleteEvent.aspx page

Redirecting Using Routed URLs

Everywhere that we can refer to a page by its name, we can do the same using a routed URL. A good example is when we want to redirect the browser to a different URL. In the UpdateOrDelete.aspx page, we do this when we have parameters that we can't process, and we do it like this:

```
Response.Redirect("ListEvents.aspx");
```

The `HttpResponse` class, an instance of which is returned by the `Page.Response` property, defines the `RedirectToRoute` method, which handles the redirect by generating a routed URL. We can use the method by specifying a rule name, like this:

```
Response.RedirectToRoute("default");
```

and if we need to provide values for variable segments, then we can do so by passing in an instance of `RouteValueDictionary`, just as we did for the previous examples:

```
Response.RedirectToRoute("default", new RouteValueDictionary() {{"variable", "value"}} );
```

Fixing the Master Page Tabs

Earlier in the chapter, we added a route for the `Calculator.aspx` class, and when we viewed the page using the routed URL, you may have noticed that the tabs that we added to the master page in Chapter 10 didn't work properly, as shown in Figure 12-6.

Figure 12-6. *The URL and the tab highlighting don't match.*

You can see that the URL is for the `Calculator` page but that the `Events` table is the one that is highlighted. The reason for this is that we used a map in the jQuery script to associate each tab with the pages that it represents, like this:

```
var pages = [
    ['Events', "/ListEvents.aspx", "/AddEvent.aspx", "UpdateOrDeleteEvent.aspx"],
    ['Performance', "/Performance.aspx"],
    ['Calculator', "/Calculator.aspx"]
];

var myPage = '<%=Request.Path%>';

var tabsDiv = $('#masterTabsDiv');
```

```
tabsDiv.tabs({
    select: function (event, ui) {
        document.location = pages[ui.index][1];
        return false;
    }
});
```

We then use the value of the `Request.Path` property to figure out which page is being displayed and select the appropriate tab. If the `Path` value doesn't correspond to a value in the `pages` map, then the first tab remains highlighted by default. When we use a routed URL, the `Path` property contains the routed URL rather than the page name, and so there is no match and the Events tab remains highlighted.

Fixing this is not straightforward. ASP.NET doesn't provide us with a feature that lets us get the physical page on disk. We could try to create a mapping between routes and events, but that is tricky when using composable URLs that have default values, and the routing system doesn't provide us with convenient access to the information we'd need anyway. We could move the tabs out of the master page and into each web page, which would make the problem slightly easier to solve, but doing that would require lots of duplication and require the mapping of tabs to pages to be maintained in each and every page.

To solve this problem, I ended up relying on the way that the routing feature is implemented. This is another case of a slight-of-hand trick that works with the current version of ASP.NET but that may not be so successful in the future. When we add a route in the global application class like this:

```
routes.MapPageRoute("calcRoute", "Calculator", "~/Calculator.aspx");
```

we are calling the `RouteCollection.MapPageRoute` method, which creates a `Route` object and passes it to the `RouteCollection.Add` method. One of the parameters to the constructor of the `Route` object is an implementation of the `IRouteHandler` interface. When we use the `MapPageRoute`, that implementation is the `System.Web.Routing.PageRouteHandler` (it is this class that was helpfully encoding our jQuery template items earlier), and this class has a `VirtualPath` property that returns the page we provided to the `MapPageRoute` method, in this case `~/Calculator.aspx`.

Putting this all together, we can create a method that retrieves the page associated with a route, as shown in Listing 12-21.

Listing 12-21. *Determining the current page*

```
protected string GetRealPageName() {
    RouteData routes = RouteTable.Routes.GetRouteData(new HttpContextWrapper(this.Context));
    if (routes != null && routes.RouteHandler is PageRouteHandler) {
        PageRouteHandler handler = (PageRouteHandler)routes.RouteHandler;
        int charIndex = handler.VirtualPath.IndexOf('/');
        return handler.VirtualPath.Substring(charIndex);
    } else {
        return Request.Path;
    }
}
```

We can apply this method either as a code block in the `Site.Master` page or in the code-behind class. I prefer the code-behind class, but it requires an additional statement to be added to the `Page_Load` method. You can see the method and the additional statement in Listing 12-22.

Listing 12-22. Adding the GetRealPageName method to the Site.Master code-behind class

```
using System;
using System.Web.Routing;
using System.Web;

namespace TriathlonTraining {
    public partial class Site : System.Web.UI.MasterPage {

        protected void Page_Load(object sender, EventArgs e) {

            DataBind();

            using (TrainingDataEntities context = new TrainingDataEntities()) {
                // get the total data from the database
                DataTotals totals = DataAccess.GetDataTotals(context);
                // use the totals to update the span contents for the footer
                eventCountSpan.InnerText = totals.EventTotal.ToString();
                mileCountSpan.InnerText = string.Format("{0:F1}", totals.MileTotal);
                hourCountSpan.InnerText = string.Format("{0} Hours and {1} Minutes",
                    totals.TimeTotal.Hours, totals.TimeTotal.Minutes);
            }
        }

        protected string GetRealPageName() {
            RouteData routes
                = RouteTable.Routes.GetRouteData(new HttpContextWrapper(this.Context));
            if (routes != null && routes.RouteHandler is PageRouteHandler) {
                PageRouteHandler handler = (PageRouteHandler)routes.RouteHandler;
                int charIndex = handler.VirtualPath.IndexOf('/');
                return handler.VirtualPath.Substring(charIndex);
            } else {
                return Request.Path;
            }
        }
    }
}
```

The changes to the code-behind class are shown in bold. The addition of the method and the using statements to import the namespaces for the method are obvious. The important addition is the call to the DataBind method. Data binding allows a page to refer to members of the code-behind class. It is a feature we will see in more depth when we come to look at MVC and Web Forms. In this example, it allows us to call the GetRealPageName method from the jQuery script in the Site.Master file, like this:

```
...
var pages = [
    ['Events', "/ListEvents.aspx", "/AddEvent.aspx", "UpdateOrDeleteEvent.aspx"],
    ['Performance', "/Performance.aspx"],
    ['Calculator', "/Calculator.aspx"]
];

var myPage = '<%=GetRealPageName()%>';

var tabsDiv = $('#masterTabsDiv');
...
```

Now we get the name of the page being rendered even when a routed URL is used, and this value is placed in the myPage JavaScript variable and fixes the highlighting problem.

The other issue we have to fix is that when the user clicks a tab, a request is made using a nonrouted URL. The simplest way to address this is to create routes for each of the pages that correspond to the names of the tabs, as shown in Listing 12-22.

Listing 12-22. Adding routes to support the master page tabs

```
public static void RegisterRoutes(RouteCollection routes) {

    routes.MapPageRoute("", "Events", "~/ListEvents.aspx");
    routes.MapPageRoute("", "Performance", "~/Performance.aspx");
    routes.MapPageRoute("", "Calculator", "~/Calculator.aspx");
...
```

Lastly, we have to update the part of the jQuery script that handles the select event for the jQuery UI tabs function. The change is simply to set the index for the second dimension of the pages array to 0 so that the name of the tab is used for the URL, like this:

```
...
tabsDiv.tabs({
    select: function (event, ui) {
        document.location = pages[ui.index][0];
        return false;
    }
});
...
```

We could add code blocks to get RouteURL expressions in the script, as we did in earlier examples, but I like this approach, which feels neater and simpler. With these changes applied to the Site.Master and Site.Master.cs files, our tabs work once more, as illustrated by Figure 12-7. You can see that the Calculator tab is highlighted and that the URL is a routed one.

Figure 12-7. *Fixing the master page tabs*

Routing URLs to Web Services

The standard URL format for WCF web services is not very elegant. Here is an example from the Ajax script in the `ListEvents.aspx` page:

```
url: '/TriathlonService.svc/GetEventData',
```

We can use the routing feature to improve the URLs of the web service. However, what we can do is much more limited than for web pages. In essence, we can replace the name of the web service file (`Triathlon.svc`) with something else. We can't use routing to change the name of the web service method (`GetEventData` in this case), and we can't use variable segments in the routed URL.

To begin, we must add a reference to the `System.ServiceModel.Activation` assembly. In Visual Studio, select Project ➤ Add Reference, click the .NET tab, and select `System.ServiceModel.Activation` from the list, as shown in Figure 12-8.

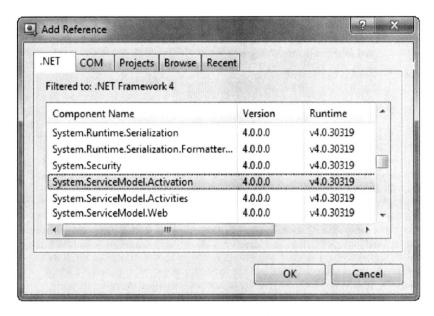

Figure 12-8. *Adding a reference to the System.ServiceModel.Activation assembly*

Click the OK button to add the assembly reference and dismiss the dialog box. The way we add a route for a web service is different from the previous examples, as shown in Listing 12-23.

Listing 12-23. *Adding a route for a web service*

```
public static void RegisterRoutes(RouteCollection routes) {

    routes.Add(new ServiceRoute("WS", new WebServiceHostFactory(),
        typeof(TriathlonService)));

    routes.MapPageRoute("", "Events", "~/ListEvents.aspx");
    routes.MapPageRoute("", "Performance", "~/Performance.aspx");
    routes.MapPageRoute("", "Calculator", "~/Calculator.aspx");
...
```

We call the Add method of the `RouteCollection` class, passing in an instance of the `System.ServiceModel.Activation.ServiceRoute` class. The constructor parameters to `ServiceRoute` are the URL pattern, a new instance of `System.ServiceModel.Activation.WebServiceHostFactory`, and the type of the web service class. (In our example, we have only one web service, and the class is called Triathlon service; see Chapter 11 for details of creating and using web services in an ASP.NET web application.)

Once this rule is in place, we can modify the Ajax script in the `ListEvents.aspx` page to use the routed URL, like this:

```
url: '/WS/GetEventData',
```

You cannot put variable segments into a URL pattern for a route for a web service. This means that the routed URL isn't composable. For example, if we want to use a `GET` request to call the `GetEventData` method in the web service, we still have to use a query string to encode the method parameters, like this:

```
http://localhost:16892/WS/GetEventData?type=Olympic
```

Summary

In this chapter, we explored the ASP.NET routing feature and saw how we can use it to create composable URLs for our web applications. We created simple patterns that act as aliases for `.aspx` web pages, saw how to add variable segments and access their values from inside code-behind classes, and learned how to provide default values and constraints for these variables.

We also saw that some care is required to get routed URLs to work with jQuery. The ASP.NET syntax for referencing URLs is ugly and verbose, and the classes that implement the routing policy do helpful things that conflict with the helpful things that jQuery tries to do. Nonetheless, with a little work we were able to use routed URLs in jQuery data templates and fix the jQuery UI tabs we added to the master page so that they work properly when routed URLs are used. We also saw how to apply routes to WCF web services, although the function is limited. I included this feature for completeness, but I rarely use it since the benefits are so scant and my web services are usually consumed by Ajax clients that don't reveal the web service URLs to the user.

An ASP.NET web application doesn't need to use routed URLs, but enabling them can do a lot to improve the experience of users, especially those who are more experienced and have encountered the idea of composable URLs previously. Routed URLs are an essential component of the MVC Framework, which we turn to in Chapter 22.

PART III

Using Web Forms

Now that you've seen the core of the ASP.NET framework, we can turn our attention to the first of the higher-level toolkits that are built upon it: Web Forms. As you'll learn, Web Forms is a much misunderstood technology that can be surprisingly useful in the right circumstances. In the chapters that follow, I'll show you how Web Forms works, explain how it relates to the core ASP.NET framework, and give some general guidance about when Web Forms should be used.

Putting Web Forms in Context

The core idea behind ASP.NET Web Forms is to make web application development as similar to Windows application development as possible. To make sense of this, we need to go back in time.

Visual Basic (VB) was all the rage when the first version of ASP.NET was released. Web applications were relatively new. In Web Forms, Microsoft created a web application tool kit that aimed to hide the complexity of web technology from the programmer (much as VB used to hide much of the complexity of Windows from the traditional application programmer).

ASP.NET Web Forms has been a success—a huge success. So many Web Forms applications exist in the world that there is no sensible way to count them. Just lately, Web Forms has become unfashionable, and attention has turned to the MVC framework, which I describe in Part IV of this book.

I am a big fan of the MVC framework, but to dismiss Web Forms out of hand is a mistake. There is a lot to love in ASP.NET Web Forms, and sometimes Web Forms is simply a better choice than MVC, as you'll learn in this chapter. Web Forms does have some issues, which you'll also learn about in this chapter. So, you should read through this chapter before dismissing Web Forms and turning to the MVC chapters.

Understanding Web Forms

I must start this section with a confession: the distinction I have made between the core ASP.NET features in Part II of this book and the Web Forms features in this part is somewhat arbitrary. ASP.NET and Web Forms were developed and delivered together, and they are very tightly integrated. Figure 13-1 shows how I have drawn the dividing line.

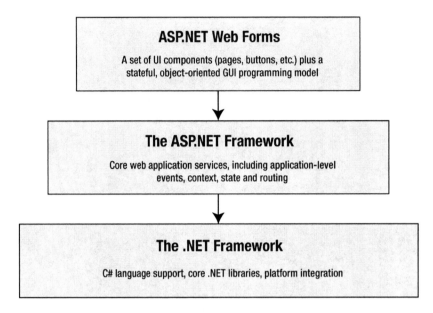

Figure 13-1. *Cutting the ASP.NET Web Forms cake*

The ASP.NET framework builds on the .NET Framework to provide web application services, whereas Web Forms builds on the ASP.NET framework to make the web application development experience as much like Windows Forms as possible. Windows Forms is the original .NET technology for building Windows client applications, although it has been eclipsed in recent years by the Windows Presentation Foundation (WPF), XAML and other new approaches (although, like Web Forms, Windows Forms continues to be actively developed and used, especially in corporate environments).

Web Forms is essentially a set of user interface controls that build on the core ASP.NET framework state and event features to simulate the stateful and event-driven Windows Forms equivalents. (As you'll see, there are some controls that do not present a user interface element to the user, but by and large, the emphasis is on the interface.) If you have done any Windows Forms development, you'll recognize key themes when we look at the Visual Studio support for Web Forms in Chapter 14.

The Web Forms Design Philosophy

Web Forms tries to abstract away two key technologies that underpin web applications: HTTP and HTML. This made some degree of sense when Web Forms was being developed, because these technologies were not widely understood or adopted by developers.

The problem with HTTP is that it is stateless. To hide this from the programmer, the Web Forms controls use the view state feature described in Chapter 6 to push their state into the web page using hidden HTML input elements. The problem with HTML is that it is a markup language and it doesn't naturally fit into the drag-and-drop development model that developers are used to employing. To address this, Microsoft created the design tools that we'll look at in Chapter 14.

These ideas may seem odd now, but that's because we have become used to HTTP and HTML over the past few years. At the time, this strategy seemed reasonable. Microsoft was late to see the Internet as a competitive opportunity. A key strategy to regain lost time was to protect its developer market share by making the process of writing a web application as similar as possible to what developers already knew—the pre-.NET era VB (a product so remarkably successful that people *still* use it to develop applications, even though Microsoft released the final version in 1998 and stopped supporting the development tools in 2005).

■ **Note** It wasn't the old VB *language* that Microsoft wanted to preserve, but rather the application development experience. The power behind the VB 6 product was how quickly and simply Windows programs could be created. In Web Forms, Microsoft tried to join this experience to the more modern .NET languages, such as C#.

In short, the design philosophy behind Web Forms was to make the scary Internet go away. If you imagine Microsoft placating nervous developers and soothingly repeating, "There, there, nothing to worry about. You already have the skills you need," then you have captured the origins of Web Forms.

As you'll see, this has led to some problems, but let me reiterate that there is some value in this approach. You don't always *need* (or want) to get into HTTP and HTML to build web applications, and for those situations, Web Forms can make a lot of sense.

The Web Forms Architecture

ASP.NET Web Forms follows an architectural pattern known as the *smart user interface* (smart UI). In general terms, to build a smart UI application, developers construct a user interface, usually by dragging a set of *components* or *controls* onto a design surface or canvas. The controls report interactions with the user by emitting events for button presses, keystrokes, mouse movements, and so on. The developer adds code to respond to these events in a series of *event handlers*, which are small blocks of code that are called when a specific event on a specific component is emitted. In this approach, we end up with the kind of pattern shown in Figure 13-2.

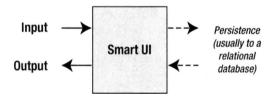

Figure 13-2. *The smart UI architecture*

This is the basic pattern used for a lot of development methodologies. Your application receives some kind of input (a user clicking a button, for example), an event is raised inside to reflect the input, and you respond by changing the internal state of the application and producing some kind of output (changing the display of another control, for example). Along the way, you might read or write data from some kind of persistence mechanism, usually a database. You can see how the smart UI maps to Web Forms in Figure 13-3.

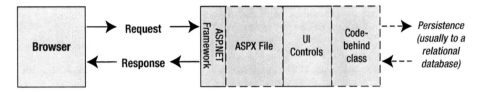

Figure 13-3. *Expressing Web Forms in terms of the smart UI architectural pattern*

The input in this case is a request from the user's browser. The request is received by the ASP.NET framework, and then passed to an `.aspx` file for processing. This is the same kind of `.aspx` file that we used in Part II of this book, but the markup contains references to the Web Forms controls.

The code-behind class contains your programming logic. You can read and alter the state of each control by using a set of properties, and can respond to the events that are raised by the controls.

You have already seen each of the key building blocks when we looked at the core ASP.NET framework features. You have seen how `.aspx` files work, and learned how to create code-behind classes and use them to respond to events reflecting changes in the application state. As you'll see, the addition of the more complex controls is an extension of these base features.

Understanding Web Forms Strengths

There is a lot to like in Web Forms. Each of the following sections describes one of the strengths of this technology.

Fast to Build, Simple to Use

Web Forms is one of the quickest ways to create web applications. With a little experience, it is possible to have a simple web application up and running in just a few minutes.

The Web Forms support in Visual Studio is pretty good (although not perfect, as I'll explain in Chapter 14), and you can go from a conceptual sketch to a professional-looking, fully functioning application in a remarkably short period of time.

Easy to Recruit Talent

Web Forms is a very widely used technology. Although the spotlight may have shifted toward the MVC framework, most ASP.NET development work is being done using Web Forms.

An informal survey by Microsoft suggests that around 90% of ASP.NET development projects are using Web Forms. The availability of developer talent can be a key technology differentiator, and there is no shortage of developer experience with Web Forms. Furthermore, the simplicity of Web Forms means that a little talent goes a long way. If you are running a development team of … shall we say, *mixed abilities*, even the weakest developer can be reasonably productive with Web Forms. There are relatively few new concepts to learn, and the similarity to other forms of drag-and-drop development puts even the most change-resistant developer at ease.

Ignores the Low-Level Details

The Web Forms abstraction means that you can focus on application development, without needing to worry too much about the specifics of *web* application development.

Web Forms is ideal for developing applications that are delivered over the Web, but that are not deeply connected to the underlying web technologies. This includes most corporate intranet applications, which expose some part of a database or some steps in a workflow process and just happen to be deployed using a browser. In these situations, web applications are selected to make deployment simpler and cheaper, not because there is any intrinsic advantage in web technology.

Corporations, especially large corporations, struggle to manage the cost and timeliness of deployment and updates, and they value the centralization that web applications give them. We would see the death of the intranet web application if there were an alternative set of technologies that offered the same benefits at a lower cost.

Actively Developed, Widely Supported

Given all of the attention that the MVC framework has attracted, you might conclude that Web Forms is dead. Microsoft is still investing in Web Forms technology; it just hasn't been that good at telling people about that.

Part of the problem is that Web Forms is an *in-band* .NET technology, meaning that releases of Web Forms are tied to releases of the .NET Framework. The .NET Framework doesn't change that often, which gives Web Forms the appearance of being a slow-moving technology when compared to the MVC framework, which is an *out-of-band* technology. MVC framework releases are *not* tied to the .NET Framework, and the MVC team makes more frequent releases.

■ **Note** Whether you see frequent new releases as a positive is a matter of perspective. I really like the MVC framework, but I get frustrated with the scattergun releases. It is hard to get a sense of direction for the MVC framework, and it is very difficult to create a technology baseline for a project when you depend on external libraries that create dependencies on fast-moving releases.

Web Forms is also extensively supported by third parties, especially in the area of controls. Some excellent control libraries are available, and a vibrant market has created a multitude of price points (including free) and license models. Google "Web Forms Controls," and you'll see what I mean.

Understanding Web Forms Weaknesses

Of course, Web Forms isn't a perfect technology, and there can be problems when Web Forms is applied in an unsuitable situation. The following sections describe some of the common problems that are associated with Web Forms.

Poor Maintainability

Although you can get results quickly with Web Forms, you can also dig a deep hole for yourself if your application has any complexity. Smart UI applications are notoriously difficult to maintain over the long-term, and Web Forms applications are no exception. In my experience, most complex Web Forms projects end up as a mass of code, where a single change causes cascades of unexpected behaviors and bugs.

The root of this problem is that the Web Forms architecture encourages the developer to mix together the code that handles the interface, the code that manages the data, and the code that applies the application's business logic. Eventually, these functions start to bleed together, and unraveling these tightly woven relationships to affect changes can be problematic.

This merging of functions breaks a common design principle known as the *separation of concerns*. The idea behind the separation of concerns is that you can build better applications by breaking your applications into functional areas and limiting the blurring of responsibility among them. This is a one of the key ideas in the design behind the MVC framework, as you will see in Part IV of this book.

For the most part, Web Forms applications have *poor* separation of concerns, and one outcome of this is that large or complex Web Forms applications can be difficult to maintain. This does not need to be the case, of course, but it requires serious discipline and planning to create a complex Web Forms application that is easy to extend and maintain—so much effort that I have rarely seen it done. The calm and thoughtful approach to building a Web Forms applications with good separation of concerns is at odds with the urgency and diffused sense of responsibility that underpin most large development projects.

Poor Unit Testability

Another issue that arises from poor separation of concerns is that Web Forms makes it difficult to perform unit testing. The widespread practice of unit testing occurred after the initial design of Web Forms, and the tightly integrated nature of smart UI technology makes it difficult to isolate and test a unit of code in isolation. You will be disappointed with Web Forms if unit testing is an important part of your development process.

Bandwidth-Heavy View State

A common criticism of Web Forms is that it can demand a lot of bandwidth. This is because of the way that the user interface state is stored in the HTML using hidden `input` elements. In ASP.NET 4, the Microsoft development team has done a lot to improve this situation. The overall size of the view state is reduced, and, as you saw in Chapter 6, you are able to disable view state for individual controls.

However, the amount of view state data that must be shipped between the browser and the server can be significant. This is rarely an issue in corporate intranet applications, but can be a problem on the public Internet, where bandwidth isn't free and connectivity varies.

Inflexibility

The abstraction layer that Web Forms creates is very good, until you need to step outside it or use it in ways that it wasn't originally intended to be used. If you want to get more involved with the HTTP and HTML aspects of a web application, Web Forms isn't the right technology to use. It is not that you can't get access to details of the request, the response, or the markup—you can. But it is difficult, and Web

Forms has some very rigid expectations, especially in terms of the way that form data is received and processed from browsers.

Low Developer Mindshare

The MVC framework really has stolen all of the attention away from Web Forms. Not only is this a shame, but it can also cause a problem. Although there are a lot of experienced Web Forms developers around, many of them are angling to work with the MVC framework.

Back in the heady days of the late 1990s, I used to make a living by rescuing skunk works Java projects. Java was *the* hot technology in those days, and most programmers were worried about being rendered obsolete if they didn't get some Java skills. Perfectly capable C programmers, working on projects that were ideally suited to being written in C, would start using Java instead, often without telling anyone. It would become apparent that critical application components had been written in Java, hadn't been well written, and hadn't been tested at all.

If you are embarking on a new Web Forms project, I urge you to make time to win the commitment of the developers and managers to the technology. If you don't, you run the risk of starting a Web Forms project and finishing with a weird kind of hybrid.

Deciding When to Use Web Forms

There is no absolute right or wrong in software—only the degree to which a given technology is an appropriate solution to a particular kind of problem. The Web Forms strengths that I described are strengths only in the right context, just as the weaknesses are only problems when Web Forms is used in the wrong kinds of situations.

There is a sweet spot that brings together all of the benefits that Web Forms offers and minimizes the drawbacks. Web Forms can be extremely useful if you have a project with the following requirements:

- Speed of development

- Intranet deployment

- Short life or low expectations of change

If you use Web Forms in these situations, you will get the very best from the technology. The convenience and the simplicity of Web Forms will be emphasized, and the inflexibility and separation of concerns issues will be minimized.

If you use Web Forms outside the sweet spot, things can be different, and there quickly comes a point when an alternative approach, such as the MVC framework, can be more useful. (Although, as you'll learn later in this book, the MVC framework isn't without its own problems and has its own sweet spot, too.)

Summary

This chapter outlined the context in which Web Forms exists—an abstraction layer designed to replicate the classic VB developer experience, albeit allied to a modern language such as C#.

Like any tool, Web Forms does some things well and other things not so well. If you use Web Forms for the kinds of projects it was intended for, you can get great results. But you can encounter some significant problems if you try to take it places that it really doesn't want to go.

In summary, don't dismiss Web Forms out of hand. It has a lot to offer in the right circumstances, is widely used and supported, and receives significant investment from Microsoft.

CHAPTER 14

Working with the Web Forms Designer

This chapter introduces the design tools that Visual Studio provides for developing Web Forms. If you have used any kind of rapid application development (RAD) tool or drag-and-drop designer, then you will recognize the basic themes that run throughout the Web Forms tooling.

You might get the impression in this chapter that I am not a fan of the Web Forms design tools. There is a degree of truth to this. I am uncomfortable with the idea of trying to hide away the details of HTML and HTTP when developing a web application, especially when this abstraction goes only so far. That said, I do like the way that the tools are tightly integrated with one another, even if they fall short of their original goal. The tools are smart and helpful, and they can be very convenient. In short, I like the tools, but I prefer to use them to aid me in using HTML and related technologies, rather than expecting them to hide the complexity.

Creating a Simple Web Forms Project

The best place to start exploring the Visual Studio Web Forms tools is to create a simple web application, as follows:

1. Create a new project in Visual Studio using the ASP.NET Empty Web Application template, as shown in Figure 14-1. I have called the project WebFormsApp.

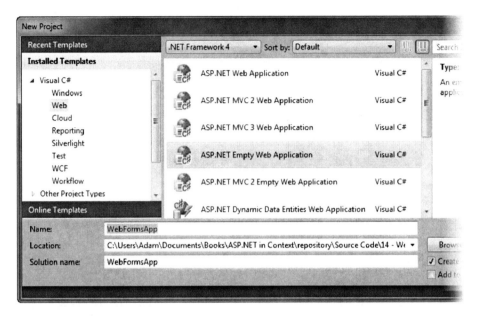

Figure 14-1. Creating the WebFormsApp ASP.NET project

2. Right-click the project in the Solution Explorer window and select Add ➤ New Item to open the Add New Item dialog.

3. Select the Web Form template and set the name of the new item to be Default.aspx, as shown in Figure 14-2.

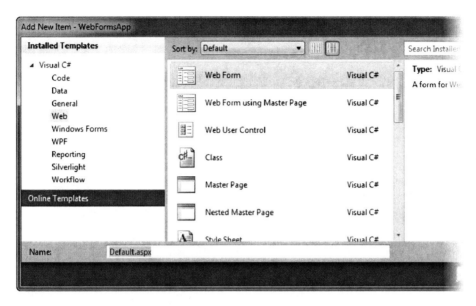

Figure 14-2. *Adding a Web Form to the project*

4.   Click the Add button to create the new Web Form in the project. A new item called `Default.aspx` will be displayed in the Solution Explorer window, and the editor for the item will be opened.

If this seems oddly familiar, it is because this is the same starting point we launched in Chapter 4, albeit by a more direct path. Web Forms is so tightly integrated into the ASP.NET framework that even the terminology has become intermingled. An ASP.NET `.aspx` page is called a *Web Form*, even if it doesn't use any of the Web Forms UI controls.

■ **Note**   I think that Microsoft did a disservice by blurring the lines between Web Forms and the broader ASP.NET framework. The ASP.NET framework is a flexible, powerful platform, which can be used to create different kinds of web applications using various development techniques, only one of which is Web Forms. I sigh with frustration when I think of all of the missed opportunities when project teams have decided not to use the ASP.NET framework for a project just because one part of it—Web Forms—wasn't quite what they were looking for.

Using the Design Surface

When you added the Web Form to the project, the editor opened automatically. This editor offers three views, and the one that we want to work with is the design view. At the bottom of the editor page is a toolbar. Click the Design button, as shown in Figure 14-3. This displays the *design surface*, which is the key element of the drag-and-drop designer feature. You can see the design surface highlighted in Figure 14-4.

Figure 14-3. *Switching to the design view*

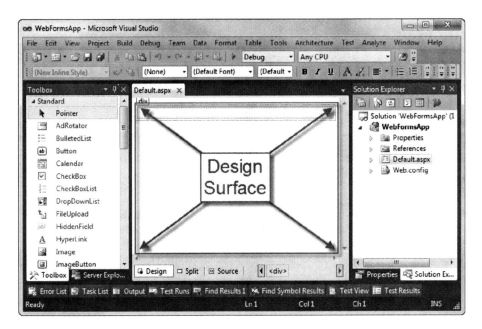

Figure 14-4. *The Visual Studio design surface*

In order to have some user interface (UI) controls that we can drag-and-drop, we need the Toolbox window. Visual Studio may have opened this window automatically, but if not, select View ➤ Toolbox. In Figure 14-4, the Toolbox window is to the left of the design surface.

Adding Controls to the Design Surface

To use the Web Forms controls, you simply drag what you want from the Toolbox window and drop it in the location you want in the design surface. To get some experience with the design surface, we will re-create the swimming calculator application from Chapter 6. As a reminder, Figure 14-5 shows that application.

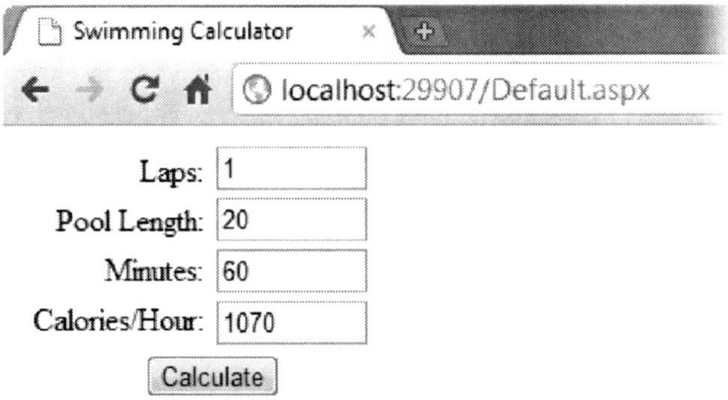

Laps: 1
Pool Length: 20
Minutes: 60
Calories/Hour: 1070

Calculate

Figure 14-5. *The swimming calculator web application from Chapter 6*

To start, we need a label and a text box . Conveniently, these are represented by the Label and TextBox controls in the Toolbox window. Drag a Label from the Toolbox and release it over the design surface. Repeat the process for a TextBox. Your design surface should look similar to the one shown in Figure 14-6.

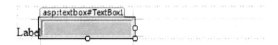

Figure 14-6. *Adding UI controls to the design surface*

You can see that we are already getting somewhere. But if we repeat this process for the next row of controls, we will encounter the first problem with the design surface, as shown in Figure 14-7.

Figure 14-7. *Adding other controls to the design surface*

If you have used a drag-and-drop design tool before, you probably positioned the second Label control under the first one and released the mouse. When you dropped the control, it was positioned on the same line as the existing controls, to the right.

This is one example of where the abstraction of the Web Forms design surface doesn't quite work. We need to look at the underlying web technologies—in this case, HTML—to figure out what is happening.

You can see exactly what is going on by viewing the page in a browser, so the ASP.NET framework renders the UI controls to HTML. Right-click `Default.aspx` in the Solution Explorer window and select View in Browser from the pop-up menu. Once the page has been rendered in the browser, view the HTML markup.

■ **Note** The steps required to view the HTML for a page differ slightly between browsers, although they all follow the same pattern. Right-click the web page and select one of the items from the pop-up menu. For Google Chrome and Mozilla Firefox, the menu item is called View Page Source. For Microsoft Internet Explorer, the menu item is simply View Source. Firefox and Internet Explorer display the HTML markup in a separate window. Chrome opens a new tab in the existing window.

The HTML for our `Default.aspx` page is shown in Listing 14-1.

Listing 14-1. *The HTML generated for a page created with the design surface*

```
<!DOCTYPE html PUBLIC "-//W3C//DTD XHTML 1.0 Transitional//EN"
"http://www.w3.org/TR/xhtml1/DTD/xhtml1-transitional.dtd">
<html xmlns="http://www.w3.org/1999/xhtml">
<head>
    <title>
    </title>
</head>
<body>
    <form method="post" action="Default.aspx" id="form1">
        <div class="aspNetHidden">
            <input type="hidden" name="__VIEWSTATE" id="__VIEWSTATE"
                value="/wEPDwULLTE5NTc4MjA0OTJkZPvWsOFKDBYDIB3YLyNoCH1/6p+UOSDMSkXs9+J+W/4a" />
        </div>
        <div class="aspNetHidden">                <input type="hidden" name="__EVENTVALIDATION"↵
  id="__EVENTVALIDATION"
            value="/wEWAwKOp9CaCQLsObLrBgLsOfbZDHtJq92pLoksPAuKly67VmMIiANC6mkjdfrQtPGOgA/e" />
        </div>
        <span id="Label1">Label</span>
        <input name="TextBox1" type="text" id="TextBox1" />
        <span id="Label2">Label</span>
        <input name="TextBox2" type="text" id="TextBox2" />
    </form>
</body>
</html>
```

The Label controls have been rendered as `span` elements, and the TextBox controls have been rendered as `input` elements whose `type` is `text`. The issue is that the HTML elements have been added sequentially to the markup, and there is no structure to control the layout.

■ **Note** Don't worry too much about the mapping of Web Forms UI controls to HTML at the moment. We'll come back to this in Chapter 15, which provides a more complete list.

Using Absolute Control Positioning

You can control the layout of UI controls in a few ways, one of which I like a lot less than the others. Let's start with the one that makes me uncomfortable.

Select Tools ➤ Options and expand the HTML Designer element. Select the CSS Styling item in the list of the left side of the window and check the option labeled "Change positioning to absolute for controls added using Toolbox, paste or drag and drop," as shown in Figure 14-8. This feature enables the absolute positioning of controls on the HTML page, effectively re-creating the traditional design surface behavior and ignoring the usual HTML approach to layouts.

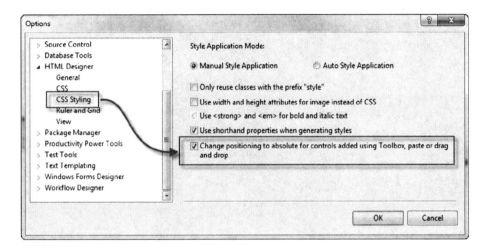

Figure 14-8. *Enabling absolute control positioning*

With this option enabled, controls that you drag from the Toolbox will be positioned exactly where you place them, using CSS styles. Listing 14-2 shows an example of the HTML that is generated using this approach. The style attributes added to each HTML element are shown in bold.

Listing 14-2. *The HTML generated for controls that are positioned absolutely*

```
...
<span id="Label1" style="z-index: 1; left: 24px; top: 28px; position: absolute; height:⏎
25px">Label</span>
<input name="TextBox1" type="text" id="TextBox1" style="z-index: 1; left: 140px; top: 33px;⏎
position: absolute" />
...
```

You can see that the positions are specified down to the pixel. I dislike this process because it creates HTML that doesn't work the way that the user expects. As an example, the HTML controls don't move when the user resizes the browser window, which can make for a frustrating experience if you overestimate or underestimate the size of the user's computer display.

■ **Note** Don't forget to disable the absolute control positioning option in Visual Studio for the rest of this chapter. We won't be using it again.

Letting the Design Surface Add Layout Elements

The next best approach is to move the controls to where we want them, and let the design surface add some HTML elements to support the layout.

Click a control on the design surface, and a small tab that identifies the control appears, as shown in Figure 14-9. You can drag this tab to reposition the control elsewhere on the design surface. When you select the Label control, as shown in the figure, and drag downward, you will see a caret appear, hinting that the control can be added on a new line. If you release the control, it will occupy a new position, as shown in Figure 14-10.

Figure 14-9. *Selecting a Web Forms control*

Figure 14-10. *Moving a Web Forms control to a new relative position*

If you select a TextBox control and drag its tab, you can position it on the second row as well, as shown in Figure 14-11.

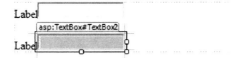

Figure 14-11. *Arranging multiple controls*

To understand what the design surface is doing, you need to view the Web Forms page in the browser and look at the HTML markup again. Listing 14-3 shows the markup for the design shown in Figure 14-11.

Listing 14-3. *The HTML markup generated for relatively positioned controls*

```
...
    <span id="Label1">Label</span>
    <input name="TextBox1" type="text" id="TextBox1" />
    <p>
    <span id="Label2">Label</span>
    <input name="TextBox2" type="text" id="TextBox2" />
    </p>
...
```

A paragraph (p) element has been added to the HTML to introduce some structure to the page. This is a big improvement over absolute positioning, but it still is not ideal. There is nothing intrinsically wrong with using a p element to add structure to an HTML page, but I don't like the designer tools making that decision for me. I want to be able to select from the many other choices for structuring an HTML page.

Dragging Web Forms UI controls by their tabs lets you control the rough position on the page relative to other controls, but it doesn't let you fine-tune the layout. You can handle this using the UI controls' properties, as you'll learn later in this chapter.

Using the Split View

As you've seen, using the design surface means ceding a degree of control over the basic structure of the page. HTML might have been a strange and unusual technology back when Web Forms was conceived, but it certainly isn't now. So, let's find a way to take back some control over the page markup.

When I use the design surface, I use the split view. You can switch to this view by using the Split button at the bottom of the design surface window, as shown in Figure 14-12.

Figure 14-12. *Selecting the split view*

The split view shows the design surface *and* the source window, so that you can see the page markup, as shown in Figure 14-13. The reason I like working with this view is that I can get the benefits of using the Web Forms UI controls (such as the support for properties and events that I'll show you shortly), without needing to give up control of the page markup. Figure 14-13 shows the Visual Studio split view.

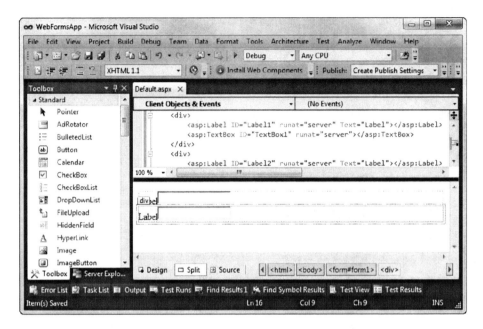

Figure 14-13. *The Visual Studio split view*

Remove the four controls from the design surface and add a pair of **div** elements so that your markup matches Listing 14-4. You can do this by typing directly into the source window or by dragging a Div control from the HTML section of the Toolbox window.

Listing 14-4. *Directly adding page structure via the source window*

```
<html xmlns="http://www.w3.org/1999/xhtml">
<head runat="server">
    <title></title>
</head>
<body>
    <form id="form1" runat="server">
    <div></div>
    <div></div>
    </form>
</body>
</html>
```

From the Toolbox, drag a Label control and drop it on the source window, so that the caret is between the first set of **div** elements, as shown in Figure 14-14. When you release the mouse, the source code will be updated to include the Label control inside the first **div** element, as shown in Listing 14-5.

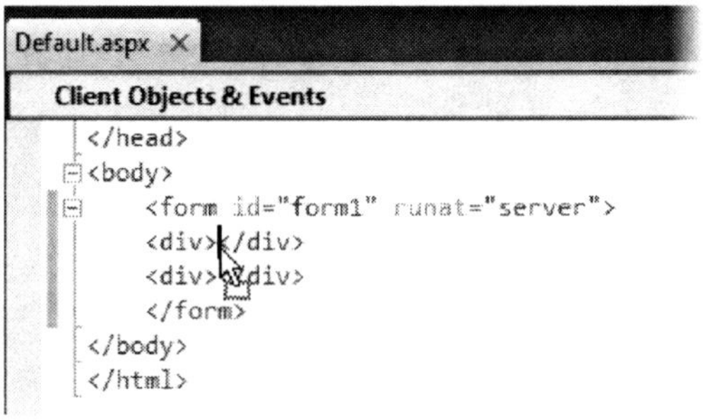

Figure 14-14. *Dragging a control to the source window*

Listing 14-5. *Adding a List control to the source window*

```
...
<body>
    <form id="form1" runat="server">
    <div>
        <asp:Label ID="Label1" runat="server" Text="Label"></asp:Label>
    </div>
    <div></div>
    </form>
</body>
...
```

The Web Forms UI controls are represented by special elements that are prefixed with asp:. In the listing, you can see that the Label control is represented by the asp:Label element. These are not standard HTML elements; they are rendered to standard HTML during the compilation process.

When you edit the markup in the source window, you will see a message displayed at the top of the design surface telling you that the view is out of sync. By working directly with the markup, you are using the design surface as a preview of your web page. This preview won't be updated until you save the web page or click the message displayed on the design surface.

■ **Tip**   If you scroll down the Toolbox window, you will see a section called HTML, which contains a set of items that represent the HTML controls that we worked with in Part II of this book. If you don't want to type in elements such as div, for example, you can drag a Div item from this section of the Toolbox to the design surface or the source window.

The source view and the design surface are nicely integrated. For example, when you select an element in the source view, it is selected in the design surface and vice versa. You can continue to drag UI controls from the Toolbox to create the UI you want for your web application. You can also cut and paste sections of the markup in the source view or controls in the design surface. The new elements will automatically be assigned unique ID attribute values. Listing 14-6 shows the markup that we need for our swimming calculator.

Listing 14-6. *The basic markup for the swimming calculator example*

```
...
<body>
    <form id="form1" runat="server">
    <div>
        <asp:Label ID="Label1" runat="server" Text="Label"></asp:Label>
        <asp:TextBox ID="TextBox1" runat="server"></asp:TextBox>
    </div>
    <div>
        <asp:Label ID="Label2" runat="server" Text="Label"></asp:Label>
        <asp:TextBox ID="TextBox2" runat="server"></asp:TextBox>
    </div>
        <div>
        <asp:Label ID="Label3" runat="server" Text="Label"></asp:Label>
        <asp:TextBox ID="TextBox3" runat="server"></asp:TextBox>
    </div>
    <div>
        <asp:Label ID="Label4" runat="server" Text="Label"></asp:Label>
        <asp:TextBox ID="TextBox4" runat="server"></asp:TextBox>
    </div>
    <div>
        <asp:Button ID="Button1" runat="server" Text="Button" />
    </div>
    <asp:TextBox ID="TextBox5" runat="server"></asp:TextBox>
    </form>
</body>
...
```

The design surface will give you a preview of how your web application will appear. If you have created the markup shown in the listing, the design surface should look similar to Figure 14-15. The appearance is pretty basic, but we'll sort that out shortly.

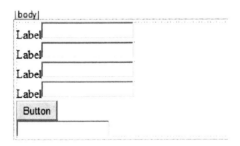

Figure 14-15. *The design surface view of the markup shown in Listing 14-6*

By mixing regular HTML elements and Web Forms UI controls, we are able to get the best of both worlds, although we must give up on part of the basic abstraction that Web Forms aims for. My belief is that this abstraction doesn't make sense any more, but some nice Web Forms features can make using the controls worthwhile. These issues really relate to the other big part of the abstraction, which is to keep HTTP hidden away. We'll come back to this topic later in the chapter.

Configuring UI Controls Using Properties

One of the features that the designer does well is configuring UI controls using properties. If you have used most any drag-and-drop development tool, you will be familiar with this concept: the appearance and basic behavior of a control are configured by setting values for a range of properties.

If the Properties window isn't already open, select View ➤ Properties Window. The window usually appears at the right side of the Visual Studio window. You might need to bring the window to the front using the tab at the bottom of the window. Visual Studio often gives preference to the Solution Explorer window by default.

Select the first Label control on the design surface (or click the corresponding element in the source window), and the Properties window will update to display the control's properties. By default, the properties are grouped by function, but you can click the A-Z button at the top of the Properties window to order them by name. You might find this easier when trying to locate specific properties as we work through this chapter.

We will start by changing the text that the Label controls display, configuring the TextBox that will hold the results of the calculation, and changing the text in the Button. Table 14-1 identifies the controls by their ID attribute and the property changes required for each.

Table 14-1. *Setting Web Forms UI Control Properties*

Control ID	Property	Value
Label1	Text	Laps:
Label2	Text	Pool Length:
Label3	Text	Minutes:
Label4	Text	Calories/Hour:
TextBox5	BorderStyle ReadOnly TextMode Rows	None True MultiLine 3
Button1	Text	Calculate

The Properties window makes it easy to see the changes by showing any value that is not the default in bold text, as you can see in Figure 14-16.

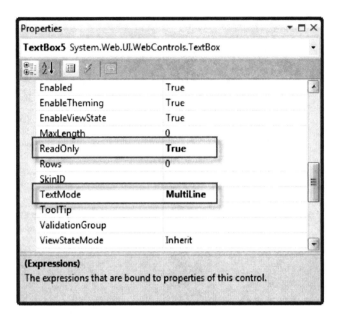

Figure 14-16. *Nondefault values highlighted in the Properties window*

You can see the effect of setting these properties by looking at the markup that is generated. As an example, Listing 14-7 shows the changes caused by setting the properties on the results TextBox control.

Listing 14-7. *The markup for the results TextBox control after property changes are applied*

```
<asp:TextBox ID="TextBox5" runat="server" BorderStyle="None" ReadOnly="True"
    TextMode="MultiLine" Rows="3"></asp:TextBox>
```

You can see that the property values are expressed at element attributes. However, these are special Web Forms attributes, rather than regular HTML attributes. During the rendering process, when the HTML is generated from the Web Form, these attributes are converted to regular HTML that any browser can understand. Listing 14-8 shows the HTML that is rendered for the `asp:TextBox` element shown in Listing 14-7.

Listing 14-8. *The HTML rendered for a Web Forms UI control*

```
<textarea name="TextBox5" rows="2" cols="20" readonly="readonly"
    rows="3" id="TextBox5" style="border-style:None;">
</textarea>
```

Some of the attributes have direct mapping. For example, `ReadOnly` is rendered as the `readonly` attribute. Others are indirect. For example, the `BorderStyle` attribute is rendered as a value for the `border-style` CSS property, which is set by using the `style` attribute.

◼ **Tip** The source window supports IntelliSense for the Web Forms UI controls. If you place your cursor inside one of the UI control elements and press the spacebar, Visual Studio will display a pop-up menu of attributes and will also offer suggestions for suitable values.

Once the properties shown in Table 14-1 have been applied to the Web Forms controls, the design surface should look similar to the one shown in Figure 14-17.

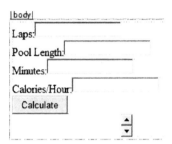

Figure 14-17. *Applying property values to the sample controls*

Using CSS with Web Forms UI Controls

We have the basic structure of our page in place, but the Web Forms design tools don't give us fine control over the layout unless we enable the absolute positioning option, which I *really* don't like. Instead, we will use CSS.

Visual Studio provides some basic tools for creating and managing CSS styles. You don't need to use these tools, but they are convenient and easy to apply, and they are visually and behaviorally consistent with the rest of Visual Studio.

◼ **Note** CSS is a broad topic. Here, we'll just cover some examples of its use with ASP.NET in Visual Studio. To learn more about CSS, I recommend reading *Pro CSS Techniques* by Jeff Croft, Ian Lloyd, and Dan Rubin (Apress, 2006).

Using the New Style Dialog

To begin, we are going to define the styles that we will later apply to the controls. Select View ➤ Manage CSS Styles to open the Manage Styles window.

At the top of the Manage Styles window is a button called New Style, which is marked in Figure 14-18. Clicking this button opens the New Style dialog, which provides a structured approach to defining CSS styles.

Figure 14-18. Click the New Style button to open the New Style dialog

In the New Style dialog, the major CSS properties are grouped into categories, there is a nice preview of what effect the style will have, and the CSS properties and their values are displayed for reference.

To start, we will create a simple style that will apply to all of the input elements. Set the Selector option to input and set the Define in option to New style sheet. In the Box category, you will find the margin settings. Set the margin to 5 pixels. Be sure to leave the Same for all checkbox checked. Figure 14-19 shows the settings for this style.

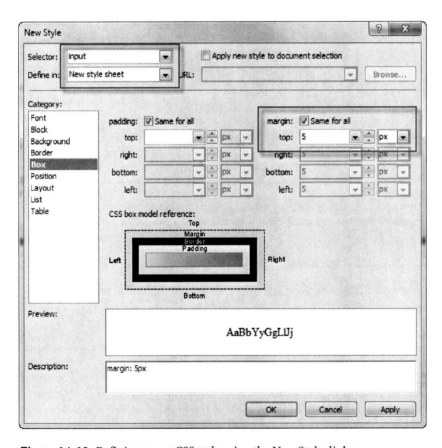

Figure 14-19. Defining a new CSS style using the New Style dialog

You can see from the Description area at the bottom of the dialog that the CSS for the option we have chosen is `margin:5px`. Click the OK button to create the style. Since we selected the option to place the style in a new style sheet, you will be prompted to attach the style sheet to the current page. Click the Yes button to continue.

If you look at the Solution Explorer window, you will see that an item called `StyleSheet1.css` has been added to the project. This is the CSS style sheet, the contents of which are shown in Listing 14-9.

Listing 14-9. *Creating a CSS style*

```
body {
}

input
{
    margin: 5px;
}
```

This style adds some spacing around all of the `input` elements on the page. The design tools create perfectly standard CSS styles (the **body** style is created by default; we won't be using it in this example). Since we chose to link the newly created style sheet to our web page, Visual Studio added a reference to `Stylesheet1.css` in our markup, as shown in Listing 14-10.

Listing 14-10. *Automatically added reference to a CSS style sheet*

```
...
<html xmlns="http://www.w3.org/1999/xhtml">
<head runat="server">
    <title></title>
    <link href="StyleSheet1.css" rel="stylesheet" type="text/css" />
</head>
<body>
...
```

Using the New Style dialog, create a second style with the selector **span** in the same style sheet, using the properties and values shown in Table 14-2.

Table 14-2. *CSS Properties and Values for the span CSS style*

Category	Property	Value
Block	text-align	Right
Box	margin	5px
Position	Width	100px
	height	20px
Layout	Float	Left
	clear	Left

This style is applied to all of the span elements in the page. It adds some spacing, makes all of the span elements the same size, and aligns the text to the right. Once you have created the style, the design surface shows the effect it has, as shown in Figure 14-20.

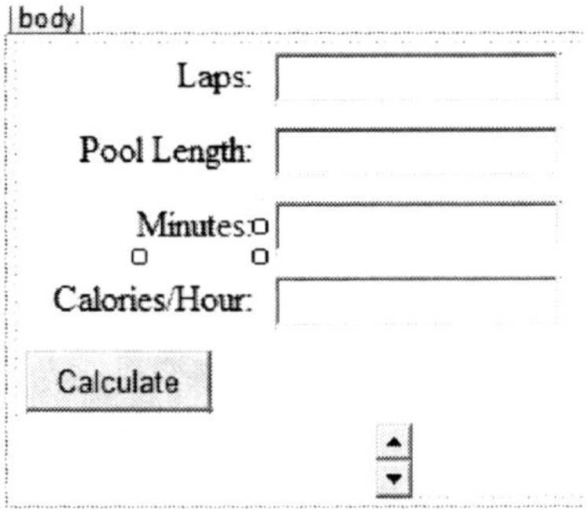

Figure 14-20. *The effect of defining a CSS style shown in the design surface*

Note that we have defined a style that selects span elements, and it has been automatically applied to the asp:Label UI controls on the page. The Web Forms design tools are clever enough to know which HTML elements each UI control is rendered to and close the loop between the UI controls and the HTML.

The two styles we have defined have selectors that are automatically applied to elements on the page, meaning that we didn't need to change the markup to apply the styles.

Create a new style whose selector is .results (note the leading period) and that has the property values shown in Table 14-3.

Table 14-3. *CSS Properties and Values for the .results CSS style*

Category	Property	Value
Font	font-weight color	Bold #FF0000
Box	margin	10px

Once you have defined the style, select the TextBox control at the bottom of the page (the one on which we set the TextMode property to MultiLine earlier). Then right-click the .results style in the Manage Styles window and select Apply Style from the pop-up menu. The markup for the TextBox will be updated, as shown in Listing 14-11.

Listing 14-11. *The effect of applying a CSS style to a Web Forms control*

```
...
<asp:TextBox ID="TextBox5" runat="server" BorderStyle="None" ReadOnly="True"
        TextMode="MultiLine" CssClass="results"></asp:TextBox>
...
```

The markup has been updated to add the `CssClass` attribute. This will be converted to the HTML `class` attribute when the page is rendered, as shown in Listing 14-12.

Listing 14-12. *The effect of the Web Forms CssClass attribute*

```
...
<textarea name="TextBox5" rows="2" cols="20" readonly="readonly" id="TextBox5" rows="3"
    class="results" style="border-style:None;"></textarea>...
```

Note that CSS properties specified directly on an element using the `style` attribute take precedence over those that are set through the `class` attribute. This means that control properties such as `BorderStyle` that are expressed using CSS take precedence over CSS class styles. For our example, if we had set the `border-style` property in the `results` class, our value would be ignored, because the `BorderStyle` control property generates a value for the same CSS property and attaches it directly to the element.

Using the CSS Properties Tool

The New Style dialog supports the most commonly used CSS properties, but it is far from comprehensive. You can get more fine-grained control using the CSS Properties window, which can be opened from the Visual Studio View menu. Visual Studio tends to open the CSS Properties window in the same place that it opens the Manage Styles window, but we need to use them together, so take a moment to move one of the windows, as shown in Figure 14-21.

Figure 14-21. *Using the Manage Styles and CSS Properties windows together*

Select one of the styles, such as `.results`, in the Manage Styles window, and the CSS Properties window will display the details of the style. There is a much more comprehensive set of properties available, far beyond what is available in the New Style dialog. The CSS properties can be displayed in groups or alphabetically, and those properties for which values have been set are highlighted in the list to make them easy to spot.

You can also use the CSS Properties window to apply CSS to individual elements. Simply select a control on the design surface or click the corresponding markup in the source window, and the CSS Properties window will display the CSS that applies to the element. The information displayed shows which CSS classes apply to the selected element, and any changes you make are applied to the class that defines the CSS class.

As noted earlier, you don't need to use the design tools to manage CSS. You can, instead, create your classes and apply styles manually, as we have done in previous chapters. To complete our set of CSS modifications, Listing 14-13 shows how we can apply a regular HTML `style` attribute to the markup of a Web Forms UI control.

Listing 14-13. Adding a style attribute to a Web Forms UI control

```
...
<asp:Button ID="Button1" runat="server" Text="Calculate" style="margin-left:100px"/>
...
```

The Web Forms tools are smart enough to merge `style` attributes when you combine your own styles and use a UI control property that is rendered using CSS, such as the `BorderStyle` property we set for one of the TextBox controls. The effects of the styles we have created and applied are shown in Figure 14-22.

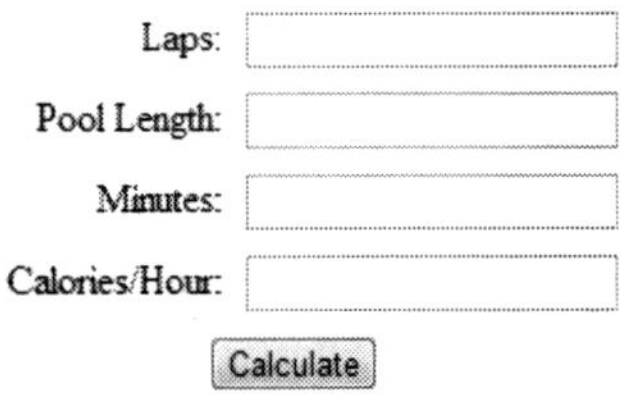

Figure 14-22. Applying CSS to the Web Forms page

Creating UI Control Event Handlers

In Chapter 5, you saw how the ASP.NET framework supports a set of application-level events. You can implement specific methods that are called when your web application enters various states. You also saw how page events can be used to achieve a similar effect as an individual page enters different states.

The Web Forms UI controls implement events that work in a similar fashion, but focused on individual controls. All Web Forms UI controls implement the same set of core events, which is then supplemented with events specific to individual control types. The core events are described in Table 14-4.

Table 14-4. *Events Common to All Web Forms UI Controls*

Event	Description
Init	Invoked when the control is initialized. This is the first step in the control's life cycle.
Load	Invoked when the control is loaded into the page.
PreRender	Invoked after the control has been loaded, but before it is rendered to HTML.
Unload	Invoked after the control has been rendered.
Disposed	Invoked when the control is released from the server's memory. This is the last step in the control's life cycle.
DataBinding	Invoked when the control is bound to a data source. Chapter 18 explains how Web Forms controls can be used with data sources.

These events correspond to the page-level events introduced in Chapter 5, but apply to a specific control. The additional events available differ from control to control.

To complete our example, we will implement a method that will be called when the user clicks the Calculate button on the web page.

Open the Properties window in Visual Studio and select the Button control on the design surface (or click the markup in the source window). At the top of the Properties window is a pair of buttons that let you toggle between the set of properties available for a control and the set of events it implements, as shown in Figure 14-23 (the Events button is highlighted).

Figure 14-23. *The buttons at the top of the Properties window*

Click the Events button to display the events that are implemented by the selected Web Forms UI control. In this case, the Button control is selected, and as shown in Figure 14-24, this control implements two additional events: Click and Command.

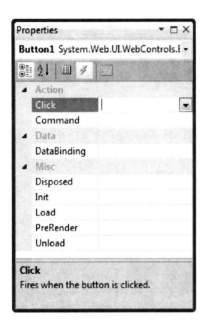

Figure 14-24. The events implemented by the Web Forms Button control

Both the Click and Command events are invoked when the Button control is clicked. The difference is that the Command event makes it easier to implement a single handler method that can process events from multiple controls, potentially of different types. Since we need to handle events from only a single control, we are going to work with the Click event.

Double-click the empty box to the left of the Click event name, and Visual Studio will create a new method in the code-behind file for our page. We can use this method to handle the event, as shown in Listing 14-14.

■ **Note** We are only interested in the process of creating events in this chapter, since our focus is on the Visual Studio tools that support Web Forms. We'll look at events in more detail in the following chapter.

Listing 14-14. Handling the Click event from the Button control

```
protected void Button1_Click(object sender, EventArgs e) {

    // define the int values that will hold the values from the input elements
    int laps, length, mins, cals;
```

```
    // try to get the values from the form elements as ints
    if (int.TryParse(TextBox1.Text, out laps)
        && int.TryParse(TextBox2.Text, out length)
        && int.TryParse(TextBox3.Text, out mins)
        && int.TryParse(TextBox4.Text, out cals)) {

        // perform the calculation
        SwimCalcResult calcResult
            = SwimCalc.PerformCalculation(laps, length, mins, cals);

        // compose the results
        StringBuilder stringBuilder = new StringBuilder();
        stringBuilder.AppendFormat("Distance: {0:F2} miles\n",
            calcResult.Distance);
        stringBuilder.AppendFormat("Calories Burned: {0:F0}\n",
            calcResult.Calories);
        stringBuilder.AppendFormat("Pace : {0:F0} sec/lap\n",
            calcResult.Pace);

        // set the results text
        TextBox5.Text = stringBuilder.ToString();
    }
}
```

I've copied this code from Chapter 6 and adapted it to the default control names that Visual Studio assigned as we dragged controls from the Toolbox. Visual Studio adds to the markup for the control, indicating which method will be used to handle the event, as shown in Listing 14-15.

Listing 14-15. Additions to the markup for a control to register an event handler

```
...
<div>
    <asp:Button ID="Button1" runat="server" Text="Calculate"
        style="margin-left:100px" onclick="Button1_Click"/>
</div>
...
```

The calculations are performed by a class called SwimCalc and represented by a struct called SwimCalcResult. These are shown in Listing 14-16.

Listing 14-16. Performing the swimming calculations

```
public struct SwimCalcResult {
    public float Distance;
    public float Calories;
    public float Pace;
}

public class SwimCalc {
    private const float metersToMiles = 0.00062137119223733f;
    private const float minsPerHour = 60f;
```

```
public static SwimCalcResult PerformCalculation(int lapsParam, int lengthParam,
    int minsParam, int calsPerHourParam) {

    // validate the parameter values - we need all values to be greater than zero
    foreach (int paramValue in new[] {lapsParam, lengthParam,
        minsParam, calsPerHourParam}) {

        if (paramValue < 1) {
            // this is not a value we can work with
            throw new ArgumentOutOfRangeException();
        }
    }

    // create the result
    SwimCalcResult result = new SwimCalcResult();

    result.Distance = (lapsParam * lengthParam) * metersToMiles;
    result.Calories = (minsParam / minsPerHour) * calsPerHourParam;
    result.Pace = (minsParam * minsPerHour) / lapsParam;

    // return the result
    return result;
}
}
```

You can see the effect of handling this event by running the application. Right-click the **Default.aspx** item in the Solution Explorer and select View in Browser. Enter some numeric values into the text boxes and click the Calculate button. You can see how the application is rendered in Figure 14-25.

Figure 14-25. *The web application displayed in a browser*

Notice that we don't need to handle the form post in the `Page_Load` method, as we did in Chapter 6. The Web Forms UI control event system takes care of this for us, and calls the `Click` event of the button when the form is received.

Using the control-level events doesn't preclude us from using the application- and page-level events. As a demonstration, We can add the statements shown in Listing 14-17 to the `Page_Load` method in the `Default.aspx.cs` code-behind file. These simply set default values for the TextBox controls when the page is loaded.

Listing 14-17. *Using the page-level Load event*

```
protected void Page_Load(object sender, EventArgs e) {
    if (!IsPostBack) {
        TextBox1.Text = "1";
        TextBox2.Text = "20";
        TextBox3.Text = "60";
        TextBox4.Text = "1070";
    }
}
```

We check the value of the `IsPostBack` property to ensure that we don't overwrite the values that the user has entered into the TextBox controls when the form is posted back to the ASP.NET server, and set the contents of the controls using the `Text` property.

Summary

In this chapter, you have seen how Visual Studio provides a set of design tools to aid in the creation of Web Forms applications. We used the design surface and the source window to create a simple interface, and employed the CSS tools to style controls. We also used the design tools to wire up an event handling method, obviating the need to handle form posts directly.

You have seen that the Web Forms abstraction is *leaky*, meaning that you must have at least some knowledge of the underlying web technologies in order to use the Web Forms UI controls. This is particularly true when it comes to styling, in which a knowledge of CSS is essential. The design tools make using CSS a smoother experience, but you still need to know what CSS is, what the properties do, and how they might be rendered by a browser.

To my mind, the value in the Web Forms design tools comes when we set aside the idea of abstraction and consider the design tools as developer productivity aids. The tight integration, the ability to mix regular HTML and Web Forms elements, the nicely packaged CSS, and the property/event support are all useful and helpful.

CHAPTER 15

Working with Web Forms Controls

Now that you've seen the Visual Studio tools for working with the Web Form controls, we'll look at the controls themselves. In this chapter, we'll start to explore which controls are available, how they work, and how they are rendered to HTML for the browser.

There are a lot of Web Forms controls. So many, in fact, that I can't cover them all in a single chapter. We are going to start with the basic controls—the ones that are the most commonly used. Later chapters will explain how the more advanced controls work. For example, we will look at the data controls in Chapters18 and 19, and the Web Forms support for authentication in Chapter 34.

As you read through this chapter, you will note that I hold some of the Web Forms controls in higher regard than others. As a general rule, I have more time and respect for the basic controls (the first set that I describe). The more complex controls tend to generate copious amounts of HTML, JavaScript, and CSS, and produce HTML that is hard to read and debug. To be fair, these controls were created at a time when developers didn't generally *want* to read or debug their HTML, but times have changed and the output from some of these controls is a little dated. I have made suggestions for alternatives for the most offending controls, typically involving a few lines of jQuery.

Getting to Know the Basic Web Forms Controls

The basic Web Forms controls are the ones that directly correspond to regular HTML elements. The controls we used in the previous chapter were examples of basic controls. The Label control was rendered to a span element, and the TextBox and Button controls were rendered to input elements whose type values were text and submit, respectively.

You could work directly with the HTML elements, but the value of the Web Forms controls is that you can benefit from the Web Forms property and event support. With this support, you can configure controls using property sheets and to respond to events when the user interacts with the controls.

Table 15-1 shows a list of the basic Web Forms controls and the HTML elements that they are rendered as.

Table 15-1. *The Basic Web Forms Controls*

Control	Corresponding HTML Element
BulletedList	`<ul>` and `<ol>`
Button	`<input type="submit">`
CheckBox	`<input type="checkbox">`
CheckBoxList	A table that contains `<input type="checkbox">` elements
DropDownList	`<select>`
HyperLink	`<a>`
Image	`<img>`
ImageButton	`<input type="image">`
Label	`<span>`
LinkButton	`<a>` with JavaScript to post the form
ListBox	`<select>`
Panel	`<div>`
RadioButton	`<input type="radio">`
RadioButtonList	A table that contains `<input type="radio">` elements
Table	`<table>`
TextBox	`<input type="text">`

As I mentioned in the previous chapter, you don't need to use these controls, but there are some benefits in doing so. The most obvious is the integration with the Web Forms design tools, allowing you to easily configure the controls using property sheets, and to create and register event-handling methods. You can see examples of both of these activities in Chapter 14. Another benefit is that you can work with these controls programmatically.

▪ **Note** Web Forms includes some controls for performing Ajax operations. Web programming has moved on since these controls were first designed and written, and they are cumbersome and fiddly to use. I haven't covered them in this chapter because I don't think they should be used any more. Given that Microsoft has embraced jQuery, I recommend you use the techniques described in Chapter 11.

Working with Controls Programmatically

Working with Web Forms controls programmatically can be more natural than working with the corresponding HTML elements directly, even the simplest of controls, such as Panel. As Table 15-1 shows, the Panel control renders to the div element.

For the purposes of comparison, we'll look at the same programmatic task using the Web Forms controls and the HTML element. Listing 15-1 contains the contents of Default.aspx, which I have added to a new, Empty ASP.NET project.

Listing 15-1. *A simple ASPX page*

```
<%@ Page Language="C#" AutoEventWireup="true" CodeBehind="Default.aspx.cs"
Inherits="WebApp.Default" %>

<!DOCTYPE html PUBLIC "-//W3C//DTD XHTML 1.0 Transitional//EN" ↵
  "http://www.w3.org/TR/xhtml1/DTD/xhtml1-transitional.dtd">

<html xmlns="http://www.w3.org/1999/xhtml">
<head runat="server">
<title>Control Demo</title>
</head>
<body>
<form id="form1" runat="server">

<div id="myDiv" runat="server"></div>
<p/>
<asp:Panel ID="myPanel" runat="server"></asp:Panel>
<p/>
<div id="results" runat="server" />

</form>
</body>
</html>
```

This simple page contains a div element called myDiv and a Panel control called myPanel. These will be the focus of this example. There is an additional div element called results, which we'll use to provide the user with some feedback. Listing 15-2 shows the code-behind file, Default.aspx.cs.

Listing 15-2. The code-behind file for the sample web page

```
using System;
using System.Drawing;
using System.Web.UI;
using System.Web.UI.WebControls;

namespace WebApp {
    public partial class Default : System.Web.UI.Page {

        protected void Page_Load(object sender, EventArgs e) {

            Button myDivButton = new Button();
            myDivButton.Text = "Press Me!";
            myDivButton.Click += new EventHandler(myDivButton_Click);

            myDiv.Controls.Add(myDivButton);
            myDiv.Attributes.CssStyle.Add(HtmlTextWriterStyle.BackgroundColor, "Bisque");

            Button myPanelButton = new Button();
            myPanelButton.Text = "Press Me!";
            myPanelButton.Click += new EventHandler(myPanelButton_Click);

            myPanel.Controls.Add(myPanelButton);
            myPanel.BackColor = Color.Bisque;
        }

        void myPanelButton_Click(object sender, EventArgs e) {
            results.InnerText = "The panel button was pressed";
        }

        void myDivButton_Click(object sender, EventArgs e) {
            results.InnerText = "The div button was pressed";
        }
    }
}
```

We have performed the same two tasks on both the div element and the Panel control. We added a Button to each of them, and set the background color. You can see that the process of adding the Button as a child control is identical. We obtain the collection of child controls through the `Controls` property and call the **Add** method, passing in the Button as a parameter.

The process of setting a CSS property is slightly different. The div element is represented by the `HtmlGenericControl` class, which forces us to set the background by adding a new value to the `CssStyle` collection, which we access through the `Attributes` set:

```
myDiv.Attributes.CssStyle.Add(HtmlTextWriterStyle.BackgroundColor, "Bisque");
```

By contrast, the Panel control has a property that sets the CSS property directly, as follows:

```
myPanel.BackColor = Color.Bisque;
```

We don't need to provide the color we want as a string, and we don't need to navigate through a set of properties to set the value.

When working with a Web Forms control, you have programmatic access to all of the properties Visual Studio shows in the Properties window when you use the design surface. Whichever technique you choose, you end up with the same HTML, as shown in Listing 15-3.

Listing 15-3. *The HTML rendered from the div element and the Web Forms Panel control*

```
...
<div id="myDiv" style="background-color:Bisque;">
<input type="submit" name="ctl02" value="Press Me!" />
</div>
<p/>
<div id="myPanel" style="background-color:Bisque;"><input type="submit" name="ctl03"↵
 value="Press Me!" />
</div>
...
```

The difference is slight, but the Web Forms control packages the process of setting the CSS property in a neater way. How much value this offers is a matter of personal preference.

Using List-Based Controls

Some of the basic controls are concerned with managing lists of items. A good example is BulletedList, which can be used to produce ul and ol elements.

To demonstrate the BulletedList control and how Web Forms handles lists, create a new project using the Empty ASP.NET Application template, add a page called `Default.aspx`, and drag a BulletedList control from the Toolbox to the design surface. The markup that this generates is shown in Listing 15-4.

Listing 15-4. *The default markup for a Web Forms BulletedList control*

```
...
<asp:BulletedList ID="BulletedList1" runat="server">
</asp:BulletedList>
...
```

Having created the control, we then need to add some items to the list. We can do this using the design tools, by adding elements to the markup, or programmatically.

■ **Note** The BulletedList control also supports data binding, where the items that are displayed in the list are obtained from a data source such as a database. See Chapters18 and 19 for details on using data with Web Forms controls.

To use the design tools, click the control in the design surface. You will see a small arrow appear on the right edge of the control. Click the arrow and select Edit Items, as shown in Figure 15-1.

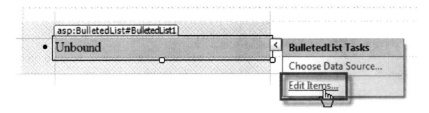

Figure 15-1. *Preparing to add items to the BulletedList control*

The ListItem Collection Editor dialog will be displayed. To add an item to the list, click the Add button and set values for the **Text** and **Value** properties, as shown in Figure 15-2 (these properties can have the same value).

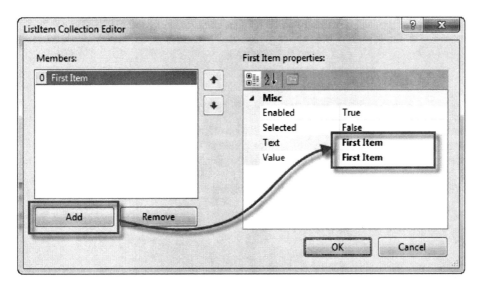

Figure 15-2. *Adding an item to the list*

Repeat this process until you have created a few items, and then click the OK button to dismiss the dialog. For this demonstration, I created four items, imaginatively called First Item, Second Item, Third Item, and Fourth Item. Listing 15-5 shows the markup that adding the items produces.

Listing 15-5. *The markup of a BulletedList control to which items have been added*

```
<asp:BulletedList ID="BulletedList1" runat="server">
<asp:ListItem>First Item</asp:ListItem>
<asp:ListItem>Second Item</asp:ListItem>
<asp:ListItem>Third Item</asp:ListItem>
<asp:ListItem>Fourth Item</asp:ListItem>
</asp:BulletedList>
```

As an alternative to using the design tools, you can simply create the items in the source window. As you can see from the listing, items are expressed using the `asp:ListItem` element. If you don't want the `Text` and `Value` properties to be the same, you can use the `Value` attribute, like this:

```
<asp:ListItem Value="Second Item Value">Second Item</asp:ListItem>
```

The final option for adding the list items is to do so programmatically, as shown in Listing 15-6. I have placed these statements in the `Page_Load` method (described in Chapter 5).

Listing 15-6. *Adding items to a list*

```
using System;
using System.Web.UI.WebControls;

namespace WebApp {
    public partial class Default : System.Web.UI.Page {

        protected void Page_Load(object sender, EventArgs e) {

            string[] textValues = {"First Item", "Second Item",
                                    "Third Item", "Fourth Item"};

            foreach (string str in textValues) {
                BulletedList1.Items.Add(new ListItem(str));
            }
        }
    }
}
```

Now that we have created and populated the list, you can see how it renders. Listing 15-7 shows the HTML that is rendered by the markup in Listing 15-5.

Listing 15-7. *The HTML markup rendered from a BulletedList control*

```
...
<ul id="BulletedList1">
<li>First Item</li>
<li>Second Item</li>
<li>Third Item</li>
<li>Fourth Item</li>
</ul>...
```

By default, the BulletedList control is rendered as an unordered list using the ul element. The items contained by the list are rendered as list items using the `li` element. You can vary the kind of list that is rendered using the `BulletStyle` attribute, as shown in Listing 15-8.

Listing 15-8. *Using the BulletStyle attribute to render a different kind of list*

```
<asp:BulletedList ID="BulletedList1" runat="server" BulletStyle="Numbered">
```

The `BulletStyle` attribute is set using one of the values from the `BulletStyle` enumeration. The `Numbered` value used in Listing 15-8 causes the list to be rendered as an ordered list, using the ol element, as shown in Listing 15-9.

Listing 15-9. *Rendering a BulletedList to an HTML ordered list*

```
...
<ol id="BulletedList1" style="list-style-type:decimal;">
<li>First Item</li>
<li>Second Item</li>
<li>Third Item</li>
<li>Fourth Item</li>
</ol>
...
```

The other values in the `BulletStyle` enumeration allow you to specify the bullet used for list items. Table 15-2 describes the most commonly used `BulletStyle` values, including the kind of HTML list to which they render.

Table 15-2. *Values from the BulletStyle Enumeration*

Value	HTML List Element	Bullet Style
Numbered	ol	Decimal numbers (1, 2, 3, …)
LowerAlpha	ol	Lowercase letters (a, b, c, …)
UpperAlpha	ol	Uppercase letters (A, B, C, …)
LowerRoman	ol	Lowercase Roman numerals (i, ii, iii, …)
UpperRoman	ol	Uppercase Roman numerals (I, II, III, …)
Disc	ul	Filled circle shapes
Circle	ul	Empty circle shapes
Square	ul	Filled square shapes

The BulletedList is a single control that can be used to render different HTML elements. A variation on this theme comes from the ListBox and DropDownList controls, which are distinct controls that render to the *same* HTML element, with a minor configuration change. Listing 15-10 shows markup that uses these two controls.

Listing 15-10. *Using the Web Forms ListBox and DropDownList controls*

```
...
<asp:ListBox ID="ListBox1" runat="server">
<asp:ListItem>First Item</asp:ListItem>
<asp:ListItem>Second Item</asp:ListItem>
<asp:ListItem>Third Item</asp:ListItem>
</asp:ListBox>
```

```
<asp:DropDownList ID="DropDownList1" runat="server">
<asp:ListItem>First Item</asp:ListItem>
<asp:ListItem>Second Item</asp:ListItem>
<asp:ListItem>Third Item</asp:ListItem>
</asp:DropDownList>
...
```

Both controls use the `asp:ListItem` element to define the items they contain. This is as you saw with the BulletedList control and is a consistently used pattern with Web Forms controls. When we render the controls, we get the HTML shown in Listing 15-11.

Listing 15-11. *The HTML rendered by a ListBox control and a DropDownList control*

```
...
<select size="4" name="ListBox1" id="ListBox1"><option value="First Item">First Item</option>
<option value="Second Item">Second Item</option>
<option value="Third Item">Third Item</option>
</select>
<select name="DropDownList1" id="DropDownList1"><option value="First Item">First Item</option>
<option value="Second Item">Second Item</option><option value="Third Item">Third Item</option>
</select>
...
```

The difference in the HTML is minor—just one property, which I have highlighted in bold. The visual difference is striking, as Figure 15-3 shows. The ListBox is on the left.

Figure 15-3. *A ListBox and a DropDownBox displayed by the browser*

It may seem odd to have two controls that do essentially the same thing . The difference is in the mapping between the HTML element and the properties that the controls support. The DropDownList control allows the programmer to determine which single list item has been selected using the `SelectedIndex` method. The ListBox control generates a `select` element that allows multiple selections. To determine the selections in a ListBox control, you need to enumerate the `ListItem` objects available via the `Items` property and check the `Selected` property of each one.

Using Controls that Produce JavaScript

Some Web Forms controls add JavaScript to the page when they are rendered. A good example of this from the set of basic controls is LinkButton, which generates a hyperlink using the anchor (`a`) element and some JavaScript when rendered.

The JavaScript is required because the LinkButton control produces a link that causes the HTML `form` to be posted, which is something that regular links don't do. Listing 15-12 shows the markup for a simple LinkButton.

Listing 15-12. The markup for a Web Forms LinkButton

```
<asp:LinkButton ID="LinkButton1" runat="server">Press Me</asp:LinkButton>
```

Listing 15-13 shows the script and HTML element that are generated when a LinkButton is rendered.

Listing 15-13. The HTML and JavaScript rendered by a LinkButton control

```
...
<script type="text/javascript">
//<![CDATA[
var theForm = document.forms['form1'];
if (!theForm) {
    theForm = document.form1;
}
function __doPostBack(eventTarget, eventArgument) {
    if (!theForm.onsubmit || (theForm.onsubmit() != false)) {
        theForm.__EVENTTARGET.value = eventTarget;
        theForm.__EVENTARGUMENT.value = eventArgument;
        theForm.submit();
    }
}
//]]>
</script>...
<a id="LinkButton1" href="javascript:__doPostBack('LinkButton1','')">Press Me</a>
...
```

The href attribute of the anchor element is set so that the __doPostBack function of the script is called when the user clicks the link. This function posts the form. The properties supported by the LinkButton control allow you to configure where the form is posted. By default, it posts back to the URL from which the page originates.

There are two potential issues to be aware of when using JavaScript:

- These controls will not perform properly if the user has disabled JavaScript. For example, the LinkButton will not post the form if JavaScript is not enabled. The hyperlink is rendered, and the user can click it, but the form will never be posted.

- When using additional JavaScript on the same page, you must take care to ensure that the scripts that you add do not conflict with the ones generated by the Web Forms controls. Problems usually arise when an additional script binds to the same events as a Web Forms control script, which leads to duplicate actions or inconsistent results.

You will see more use of JavaScript as we look at some of the specialized Web Forms controls.

Understanding When Control Events Are Triggered

In the previous chapter, you saw how to use the design tools to create a method to handle a control event, and how the tools take care of registering the method with the control in the markup.

The Web Forms events can be confusing if you are used to handling events in Windows applications written using Windows Forms or WPF. The issue is when the events are triggered. Listing 15-14 shows the markup for a page that contains a TextBox control. This control defines the TextChanged event, which is called when the text in the box changes.

Listing 15-14. A simple page containing a Web Forms TextBox control

```
<body>
<form id="form1" runat="server">

<asp:TextBox ID="TextBox1" runat="server"
        ontextchanged="TextBox1_TextChanged">Original Text</asp:TextBox>

<asp:Button ID="Button1" runat="server" Text="Submit" />

<div id="result" runat="server" />
</form>
</body>
```

Here, I have registered an event handler method for the TextChanged event, as shown in Listing 15-15.

Listing 15-15. A handler for the TextBox.TextChanged event

```
using System;

namespace WebApp {
    public partial class Default : System.Web.UI.Page {

        protected void TextBox1_TextChanged(object sender, EventArgs e) {
            result.InnerText = "Event was triggered - text has changed";
        }
    }
}
```

When the TextChanged event is triggered, the handler method changes the text contained within the div element that has the ID result. Figure 15-4 shows how the application is displayed by the browser.

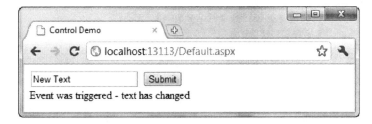

Figure 15-4. The example application displayed by the browser

If I were using Web Forms or WPF, I would expect the TextChanged event to fire every time there was a change to the text in the TextBox. But, of course, this is a web application, and the event-handling code is executed on the ASP.NET server. This is model is entirely different from that of a regular Windows application, and it means that the event is not triggered until the form is submitted to the server.

■ **Note** If the user has performed actions that trigger multiple events for which you have registered handlers, then your methods will be called in quick succession when the form is next posted. You don't need to worry about making sure that your methods are thread-safe. The ASP.NET framework makes sure that the methods are called sequentially. You must not make any assumptions about the relative order in which your methods are called.

You can alter the behavior of the Web Forms controls using the AutoPostBack property. When this property is true, the control adds JavaScript to the rendered page that posts the form back to the server when the user interacts with the control. Listing 15-16 shows the change to the markup.

Listing 15-16. Using the AutoPostBack property with a TextBox control

```
<body>
<form id="form1" runat="server">

<asp:TextBox ID="TextBox1" runat="server"
        ontextchanged="TextBox1_TextChanged" AutoPostBack="True">Original Text</asp:TextBox>

<asp:Button ID="Button1" runat="server" Text="Submit" />

<div id="result" runat="server" />
</form>
</body>
```

Here is the HTML that is rendered when the AutoPostBack property is set to true on a TextBox control:

```
...
<input name="TextBox1" type="text" value="Original Text2"
onchange="javascript:setTimeout('__doPostBack('TextBox1','')', 0)"
onkeypress="if (WebForm_TextBoxKeyHandler(event) == false) return false;"
id="TextBox1" />
...
```

You can see that JavaScript handlers have been added for the change and keypress events. When the user presses Enter or navigates away from the input element (either by using the Tab key or clicking another element), the form will be posted to the server. The server will then invoke the handler method.

I have marked a call to the WebForm_TextBoxKeyHandler function in bold. Not only does the AutoPostBack property add JavaScript to the HTML element, but it also defines a reference to some supporting functions, like this:

```
<script src="/WebResource.axd?d=-cv-A_Wv9AbWwOHgj5GO4XDxeo6QCOVCHG8AkjuS
lhaahAPRDofIgRz4OWdKq2g7OgsBB4fOhZHzN2QoifIRpt4dKnmEGJfjNH7Dt3IGZk1&amp;
t=634358667871704093" type="text/javascript"></script>
```

`WebResource.axd` is a mechanism that allows resources contained within a .NET assembly to be requested through the ASP.NET server. It doesn't concern us directly, other than to note that there is a fair amount of JavaScript code returned from the server.

The `AutoPostBack` property should be used with caution. The entire form is posted back to the server when the state of the control changes. If you create a page that contains multiple elements that rely on `AutoPostBack`, then the browser will be making a lot of trips back to the server. Not only will this increase the load on the server, but it can also be extremely frustrating for the user.

When contemplating using `AutoPostBack`, think about whether the problem can be more elegantly solved using jQuery. If the objective is to validate the data that the user has entered, then the jQuery validation library is worth considering. See Chapter10 for details and examples. To re-create the effect of using `AutoPostBack` in the example, you can use a simple jQuery script like the one in Listing 15-17.

Listing 15-17. *Replacing AutoPostBack with a jQuery script*

```
<script type="text/javascript">

    $(document).ready(function () {
        $('#<%=TextBox1.ClientID%>')
            .change(function () {
                $('#result').text("Event was triggered - text has changed");
            });
    });
</script>
```

Aside from being more responsive and reducing the load on your server, using a jQuery script like this separates the script from the HTML, which makes a page easier to read and therefore maintain.

Understanding Bubble Events

A special kind of event, known as a *bubble event*, propagates up through the hierarchy of controls in a page until one of the controls (or the page itself) processes the event.

Bubble events are most commonly encountered with the Button control and its close relatives, ImageButton and LinkButton. These implement the `IButtonCommand` interface, which allows a parent control to receive *command events* that bubble up from child controls without needing to register for events with individual control instances. An example helps illustrate this behavior. Listing 15-18 shows three buttons on a page called `Bubble.aspx`.

Listing 15-18. *Using the button command feature to bubble events*

```
<%@ Page Language="C#" AutoEventWireup="true" CodeBehind="Bubble.aspx.cs"
Inherits="WebApp.Bubble" %>

<!DOCTYPE html PUBLIC "-//W3C//DTD XHTML 1.0 Transitional//EN"
  "http://www.w3.org/TR/xhtml1/DTD/xhtml1-transitional.dtd">
```

```
<html xmlns="http://www.w3.org/1999/xhtml">
<head runat="server">
<title></title>
</head>
<body>
<form id="form1" runat="server">
<div>

<asp:Button ID="Button1" runat="server" Text="Button 1"
            CommandName="MyCommand" CommandArgument="MyCommandArg"/>
<asp:Button ID="Button2" runat="server" Text="Button 2"
            CommandName="MyCommand" CommandArgument="MyCommandArg"/>
<asp:Button ID="Button3" runat="server" Text="Button 3"
            CommandName="MyCommand" CommandArgument="MyOtherCommandArg"/>

<div>
<asp:Label ID="Label1" runat="server" Text=""></asp:Label>
</div>
</div>
</form>
</body>
</html>
```

For each button, we have set values for the CommandName and the CommandArgument attributes. When these buttons are clicked, they emit a bubble event, which ASP.NET passes to the next highest control in the page hierarchy. That control can process the event, but if it doesn't, then the event is passed to the next highest control, and this continues until the event has been handled or the event bubbles up to the page itself.

In this example, we have not created a control hierarchy, so the event bubbles up directly to the page. You can see how to handle the event in the code-behind class, shown in Listing 15-19.

Listing 15-19. Handling bubble events

```
using System;
using System.Web.UI.WebControls;

namespace WebApp {
    public partial class Bubble : System.Web.UI.Page {
        protected void Page_Load(object sender, EventArgs e) {

        }

        protected override bool OnBubbleEvent(object source, EventArgs args) {
            if (args is CommandEventArgs) {
                CommandEventArgs ce = (CommandEventArgs)args;

                Label1.Text = String.Format("Command Name: {0}, Command Argument: {1}",
                    ce.CommandName, ce.CommandArgument);

                return true;
            }
```

```
                return false;
            }
        }
}
```

We override the `OnBubbleEvent` method to handle bubble events and test the type of `EventArgs` parameter the method receives to check for `CommandEventArgs` objects. This is our cue that the bubble event we are dealing with is a command event from one of the buttons. The values that we assigned to the `CommandName` and `CommandArgument` attributes are available as properties with the same names in the `CommandEventArgs` class. By reading these values, we can determine which action our web application should perform in response to the button being pressed. When implementing the `OnBubbleEvent` method, we return `true` if we have handled the method and it should not be bubbled any further; otherwise, we return `false`.

Notice that we receive these events without needing to register with the Button controls directly, and that multiple buttons can have the same values for the `CommandName` and `CommandArgument` attributes. This is useful because it allows us to have controls in different parts of the user interface that perform the same action.

Button commands and bubble events are most commonly used with the data controls, which are described in Chapter 19.

Using the Navigation Controls

One of the sections of the Toolbox is called Navigation. It contains a set of three controls that can be used to help a user navigate around an application. We'll look at how to use each of these controls in this section.

Using the Menu Control

The Menu control is used to create JavaScript-powered menus. Listing 15-20 shows how to use this control in markup.

Listing 15-20. *Using the Web Forms Menu control*

```
...
<asp:Menu ID="Menu1" runat="server" onmenuitemclick="Menu1_MenuItemClick">
<Items>
<asp:MenuItem Text="First Menu Item">
<asp:MenuItem Text="Inner Item 1" />
<asp:MenuItem Text="Inner Item 2" />
</asp:MenuItem>

<asp:MenuItem Text="Second Menu Item"/>
```

```
<asp:MenuItem Text="Third Menu Item">
<asp:MenuItem Text="Inner Item 3" Enabled="false"/>
<asp:MenuItem Text="Inner Item 4" />
</asp:MenuItem>
</Items>
</asp:Menu>
...
```

The Menu control requires a nested `Items` element, to which we add one or more MenuItem controls. The `MenuItem.Text` property sets the label that will be used for a menu item, and each MenuItem control can itself contain further MenuItem controls to created nested menus. Individual MenuItems can be enabled or disabled. For example, in the listing, the `Enabled` attribute for `Inner Item 3` is set to `false`.

The Menu control defines the `MenuItemClick` event, which is triggered when the user clicks a menu item. The entire form is posted back to the server in order to trigger the event. Listing 15-21 shows a simple implementation of a handler method for the `MenuItemClick` event.

Listing 15-21. *Handling the Menu.MenuItemClick event*

```
using System;
using System.Web.UI.WebControls;

namespace WebApp {
    public partial class Default : System.Web.UI.Page {

        protected void Menu1_MenuItemClick(object sender, MenuEventArgs e) {
            results.InnerText = "Selected Menu Item: " + e.Item.Text;
        }
    }
}
```

We can determine which `MenuItem` control the user has selected using the `Item` property of the `MenuEventArgs` object that is passed as a parameter to our handler method. In the listing, we set the contents of a `div` element to show which item has been selected. Figure 15-5 shows how the menu is rendered in the browser.

Figure 15-5. *The default rendering for a Menu control*

We can change the direction in which the menu items are displayed by setting the `Orientation` property to `Horizontal`. You can see the effect this has in Figure 15-6.

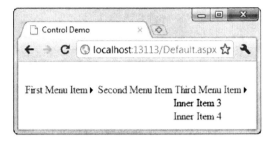

Figure 15-6. *Rendering a horizontal menu*

The way that the Menu control is rendered by default is pretty raw and unsuitable for most projects. Fortunately, a lot of formatting options are available, and we'll go over the basics of formatting here.

The simplest way to apply styling is to select the control on the design surface, click the arrow that appears on the right edge, and select Auto Format from the pop-up menu, as shown in Figure 15-7.

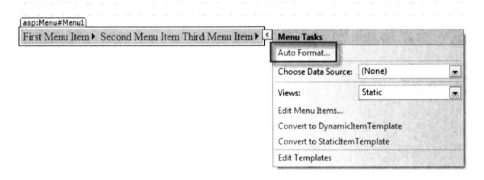

Figure 15-7. *Selecting the Auto Format feature for a Menu control*

The AutoFormat window will open, allowing you to select from a set of predefined styles, as shown in Figure 15-8. A preview of the style is shown as each item is selected. In the figure, I have selected the Classic style. Click OK to apply the style and close the window.

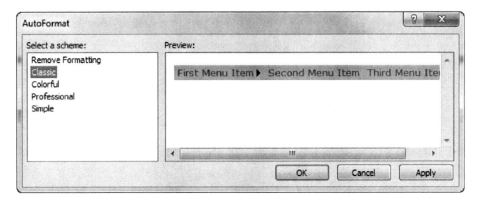

Figure 15-8. *Selecting a predefined style using AutoFormat*

Selecting a style causes the Menu control to render some CSS styles in the HTML sent to the browser. You can see these styles in Listing 15-22. These styles have the effect shown in Figure 15-9.

Listing 15-22. *The CSS styles generated by autoformatting a Menu control*

```
<style type="text/css">
    #Menu1 { background-color:#B5C7DE; }
    #Menu1 img.icon { border-style:none;vertical-align:middle; }
    #Menu1 img.separator { border-style:none;display:block; }
    #Menu1 ul { list-style:none;margin:0;padding:0;width:auto; }
    #Menu1 ul.dynamic { background-color:#B5C7DE;z-index:1;margin-left:2px; }
    #Menu1 a { color:#284E98;font-family:Verdana;font-size:0.8em;text-decoration:none;↲
white-space:nowrap;display:block; }
    #Menu1 a.static { padding:2px 5px 2px 5px;text-decoration:none; }
    #Menu1 a.popout { background-image:url↲
("/WebResource.axd?d=vzxUDvR806S1v2C7xQ92C1TBR168KAoOp4awUZyWOWHlwWcrVf2sGt354Rs7jwb5m↲
-Hvse2euzON_cyypRDS6H106AslJud01SOOV4XE-3Y1&t=634358667871704093");background-repeat:↲
no-repeat;background-position:right center;padding-right:14px; }
    #Menu1 a.dynamic { padding:2px 5px 2px 5px;text-decoration:none; }
    #Menu1 a.static.selected { background-color:#507CD1;text-decoration:none; }
    #Menu1 a.dynamic.selected { background-color:#507CD1;text-decoration:none; }
    #Menu1 a.static.highlighted { color:White;background-color:#284E98; }
    #Menu1 a.dynamic.highlighted { color:White;background-color:#284E98; }</style>
```

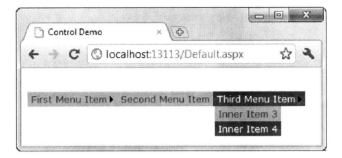

Figure 15-9. *The effect of a style on a Menu control displayed in the browser*

If you want to create a custom style, you can do so using the extensive set of properties that the Menu control supports. You can see these in the Layout section of the property sheet. The control differentiates between *static* and *dynamic* menu items, as follows:

- Static menu items are the ones that are always displayed (typically the top level of MenuItem controls.

- Dynamic items are the ones that are popped up using JavaScript.

If you prefer to handle the styling yourself, you can use the default rendering and define the styles shown in Listing 15-20. Or you can use the handy CSS classes that are included in the HTML that the Menu control renders.

I haven't shown you the HTML that is produced because it is pretty messy, but one nice feature is that you can target elements in the menu using classes. Each level of menu is assigned a `levelX` class, where *X* is the level of nesting. The top-level menu items are assigned to `level1`, the first set of nested items is `level2`, and so on. You can even change which classes are assigned to each level. See MSDN for details.

Using the TreeView Control

The TreeView control uses JavaScript and the HTML `table` element to re-create a Windows style tree view. Listing 15-23 shows how this control can be used.

Listing 15-23. *Using the Windows Forms TreeView control*

```
...
<asp:TreeView ID="TreeView1" runat="server"
ShowCheckBoxes="All"
    ShowLines="True">
<Nodes>
<asp:TreeNode Text="First Item" Value="First Item">
<asp:TreeNode Text="Child Node 1" Value="Child Node 1"></asp:TreeNode>
<asp:TreeNode Text="Child Node 2" Value="Child Node 2"></asp:TreeNode>
</asp:TreeNode>
<asp:TreeNode Checked="True" Text="Second Item" Value="Second Item" />
<asp:TreeNode Checked="True" Text="Third Item" Value="Third Item">
<asp:TreeNode Text="Child Node 1" Value="Child Node 3"></asp:TreeNode>
```

```
<asp:TreeNode Text="Child Node 2" Value="Child Node 4"></asp:TreeNode>
</asp:TreeNode>
</Nodes>
</asp:TreeView>
```
...

To build the structure of the tree, we add a `Nodes` element and populate it with TreeNode controls, which can be nested to create additional depth. Figure 15-10 shows how this control is rendered in the browser.

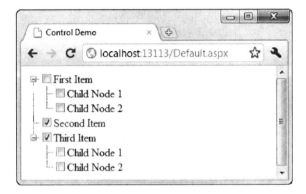

Figure 15-10. *Rendering the TreeView control to HTML*

TreeView is another control that has a lot of configuration options. The most useful options are described in Table 15-3.

Table 15-3. *Useful Configuration Properties for the TreeView Control*

Property	Default Value	Description
NodeIndent	20	Specifies the number of pixels that child nodes are indented from their parents
ShowExpandCollapse	True	Specifies whether the + and – icons are shown for expanding and collapsing parts of the tree
ShowLines	False	Specifies whether the lines connecting nodes are drawn
ShowCheckBoxes	None	Specifies if checkboxes are displayed next to nodes; checkboxes can be disabled, shown for all nodes, root nodes, parent nodes or leaf nodes
EnableClientScript	True	Specifies if JavaScript is used to manage the tree view

The name of the `EnableClientScript` property is misleading. The TreeView control always requires JavaScript to be enabled on the client. The difference is that when `EnableClientScript` is `true`, the opening and closing of nodes in the tree are handled at the client. When `EnableClientScript` is `false`, the same actions cause the entire form to be posted back to the server. Changes in the layout are handled by rendering different HTML back to the client. Since it is not possible to use the TreeView control on a browser that has JavaScript disabled, I recommend that you leave `EnableClientScript` set to `true` in order to reduce the number of requests the browser must make to the server.

■ **Tip**   The same developer responsible for the excellent jQuery validation library that we used in Chapter 10 has produced a jQuery plug-in that creates tree views. You can get further details at `http://plugins.jquery.com/project/treeview`.

The TreeView control defines the set of events described in Table 15-4.

***Table 15-4.** Events Defined by the TreeView Control*

Event	Description
SelectedNodeChanged	Triggered when the user clicks a tree node
TreeNodeCheckChange	Triggered when the user checks or unchecks one or more nodes
TreeNodeExpanded TreeNodeCollapsed	Triggered when the user expands or collapses nodes

Creating handlers for these events changes the way that the TreeView control operates. When no handler methods are registered and the `EnableClientScript` property is `true`, the TreeView control tries to handle some of its operations on the client. Opening and closing nodes, for example, are done using JavaScript and don't call the server.

When events are being handled, the TreeView control calls back to the server each time the user interacts with the control, posting the entire form as it does so. The exception is when the user checks or unchecks a node, which doesn't cause an event to be triggered until the form is next posted back by some other event or control.

It is a bit of a mess, to be honest. The TreeView control is perfectly usable if you don't need events, but I would suggest using the jQuery alternative (available at `http://plugins.jquery.com/project/treeview`), if events are important.

Using Site Maps

Site maps are a useful means for giving users a sense of where they are in the structure of your application. To define a site map, your project needs a file that expresses the structure of your pages. You add this file by using the Visual Studio Site Map template. The default name for this file is `Web.sitemap`. Listing 15-24 shows a simple `Web.sitemap` file.

Listing 15-24. *A simple Web.sitemap file*

```
<?xml version="1.0" encoding="utf-8" ?>
<siteMap xmlns="http://schemas.microsoft.com/AspNet/SiteMap-File-1.0" >
<siteMapNode url="~/Main.aspx" title="Triathlon">
<siteMapNode url="~/Data.aspx" title="Race Data">
<siteMapNode url="~/Default.aspx" title="Lastest Data"  description="" />
</siteMapNode>
<siteMapNode url="~/People.aspx" title="Athletes">
<siteMapNode url="~/Adam.aspx" title="Adam Freeman"  description="" />
<siteMapNode url="~/Joe.aspx" title="Joe Smith"  description="" />
</siteMapNode>
</siteMapNode>
</siteMap>
```

We use the `siteMap` element to create a hierarchy of `.aspx` pages, so that the `Default.aspx` page is a child of `Data.aspx`, which in turn is a child of `Main.aspx`. When using a site map file, you are expressing a relationship between pages that is different from the way that the pages are organized on the disk. This is how you want your users to think about your application, not how your application is constructed.

Using the SiteMapPath Control

To give the users a sense of context, we use the Web Forms SiteMapPath control, as shown in Listing 15-25.

Listing 15-25. *Using a SiteMapPath control*

```
...
<body>
<form id="form1" runat="server">
<asp:SiteMapPath ID="SiteMapPath1" runat="server">
</asp:SiteMapPath>
</form>
</body>
...
```

This control is rendered to a series of hyperlinks, as shown in Figure 15-11.

Figure 15-11. *The default appearance of the SiteMapPath control*

Each of the links takes the user to a page one step higher in the hierarchy described in the `Web.sitemap` file. Not only does this give users a sense of where there are in the application, but it also gives them a simple mechanism for navigation.

▓ **Caution** The site map will display links for pages that do not exist. For example, if you download the source code that accompanies this chapter, you will find that only the `Default.aspx` page exists. This is fine for a simple example, but for a real application, it is essential to ensure that all of the pages that you refer to in a site map exist. Otherwise, users will be presented with a `404 - Not Found` error when they click a navigation link.

Like the other controls covered in this section, the default rendering is not especially attractive, but is useful if you want to apply styling with jQuery. If not, you can configure the appearance using either the AutoFormat feature (which works similar to the one for the Menu control. as described earlier in the chapter) or by setting values for the Styles group of properties on the property sheet.

Using Other Controls to Display Site Maps

You can use the other navigation controls to display site maps as well. These rely on the Web Forms data-binding feature, which is discussed in Chapters 18 and 19. Without going into the details of how this feature works, Listing 15-26 shows how to use a Menu control and a TreeView control to display the site map by setting a value for the `DataSourceID` property.

Listing 15-26. Using a Menu and a TreeView to display a site map

```
<body>
<form id="form1" runat="server">

<asp:SiteMapDataSource ID="SiteMapDataSource1" Runat="server" />

<asp:TreeView ID="TreeView1" runat="server" DataSourceID="SiteMapDataSource1"/>

<p />

<asp:Menu ID="Menu1" runat="server" DataSourceID="SiteMapDataSource1"
        Orientation="Horizontal"/>

</form>
</body>
...
```

In order to use this feature, we need to add a `SiteMapDataSource` element to the page, as marked in bold in the listing. Don't worry about what this does at the moment. We'll come back to the topic of data sources in Chapter 18. For the moment, you can simply copy this line into your markup.

To have a TreeView or Menu control display the site map, you set the `DataSourceID` property to the ID value for the `SiteMapDataSource` element. In this example, the ID is `SiteMapDataSource1`. You can see how the site map is displayed in Figure 15-12.

Figure 15-12. *A site map displayed by TreeView and Menu controls*

One very neat feature of these controls relates to authentication. In Chapter 34, I'll show you how to require your users to identify themselves to your application and how to restrict access to pages based on that identity. When displaying a site map in a TreeView or Menu control, these restrictions are taken into account, meaning that a user sees only those parts of the site map to which they have been granted access. It is a small and clever feature that highlights the integration between Web Forms and the underlying ASP.NET platform.

Using Other Web Forms Controls

Web Forms includes some interesting, yet less widely used, controls in addition to the basic and navigation controls. The following sections provide a brief overview of each of them.

■ **Note** You'll quickly realize that I don't like some of these controls. They produce HTML that is inelegant and relies heavily on inline scripting. If you want to use Web Forms throughout your application, then these controls can be useful. But I believe that there are simpler and more elegant approaches available for some of these controls, as long as you are willing to poke holes in the Web Forms abstraction and embrace tools such as jQuery.

Using the Calendar Control

The Calendar control provides a mechanism for allowing a user to select a date. You can use the control's properties to set the initial date that is displayed and to apply styling to every aspect of the rendered HTML. You can see an example of the Calendar control in Figure 15-13.

Figure 15-13. *The Calendar control displayed in a browser*

I don't like this control. The HTML and JavaScript that it generates is horrendous—a mass of inline styles and event handlers that makes reading and debugging the HTML impossible. I strongly suggest that you use the jQuery UI calendar instead. It has more features, is much more elegant, and leaves your HTML readable. See Chapter 10 for details and examples.

Using the PlaceHolder Control

The PlaceHolder control is an oddity in that it doesn't render any HTML. This control exists so that you can pragmatically add other controls at a specific place in the page. Listing 15-27 shows the PlaceHolder control declared as markup.

Listing 15-27. *Using the Web Forms PlaceHolder control*

```
...
<body>
<form id="form1" runat="server">
    This is the text before the placeholder
<asp:PlaceHolder ID="PlaceHolder1" runat="server"></asp:PlaceHolder>
    This is the text after the placeholder
</form>
</body>
</html>
...
```

You see the PlaceHolder control surrounded by some literal text. Listing 15-28 shows how we can use this control in the Page_Load method of the code-behind class.

Listing 15-28. Using the PlaceHolder control to add controls programmatically

```
using System;
using System.Web.UI.WebControls;

namespace WebApp {
    public partial class Default : System.Web.UI.Page {

        public void Page_Load() {

            Button myButton = new Button();
            myButton.Text = "Press Me!";

            PlaceHolder1.Controls.Add(myButton);
        }
    }
}
```

When the page is rendered, we add a new Button control to the PlaceHolder control, producing the output shown in Figure 15-14.

Figure 15-14. Using a PlaceHolder control

We could achieve the same effect using a regular HTML element such as div, but this is a tidier approach because the PlaceHolder control doesn't generate any HTML itself. If you choose not to add any controls to the PlaceHolder, then nothing is added to the page. If you use a div element and don't add any controls, you are left with an empty div element.

How much you value this feature depends on how much control you like to have over your HTML. I like a lot of control, as you might have guessed by now.

Using the Wizard Control

The Wizard control is used to create Windows-style wizards that take users through a process in a series of steps—the sort of wizard that is commonly used to install Windows applications, for example. Listing 15-29 shows the markup for a simple three-step wizard.

Listing 15-29. *Using the Web Forms Wizard control*

```
...
<body>
<form id="form1" runat="server">

<asp:Wizard ID="Wizard1" runat="server" ActiveStepIndex="0">
<WizardSteps>
<asp:WizardStep ID="WizardStep1" runat="server" Title="Step 1">
<asp:Label ID="Label1" runat="server" Text="First Name:"></asp:Label>
<asp:TextBox ID="TextBox1" runat="server"></asp:TextBox>
</asp:WizardStep>
<asp:WizardStep ID="WizardStep2" runat="server" Title="Step 2">
<asp:Label ID="Label2" runat="server" Text="Surname:"></asp:Label>
<asp:TextBox ID="TextBox2" runat="server"></asp:TextBox>
</asp:WizardStep>
<asp:WizardStep ID="WizardStep3" runat="server" Title="Step 3">
<asp:Label ID="Label3" runat="server" Text="Email Address:"></asp:Label>
<asp:TextBox ID="TextBox3" runat="server"></asp:TextBox>
</asp:WizardStep>
</WizardSteps>
</asp:Wizard>

</form>
</body>
...
```

You define each step using the `WizardStep` element. These steps contain the controls that you want to be displayed at each stage in the process. In this simple example, we ask the users for their first name, surname, and e-mail address. You can see the progression from step to step in Figure 15-15. The Wizard control has extensive support for styling, and I have applied some basic styles to the control shown in the figure.

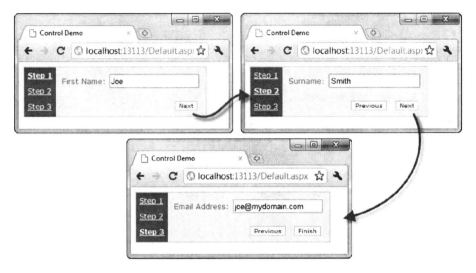

Figure 15-15. *Using the Wizard control*

This is another Web Forms control that I don't like using. It generates a lot of barely readable HTML, CSS, and script. I prefer to use the jQuery FormToWizard plug-in, which has many nice features and integrates nicely with the rest of jQuery. You can see a demonstration and get the plug-in at http://www.jankoatwarpspeed.com/post/2009/09/28/webform-wizard-jquery.aspx.

Using the MultiView Control

The MultiView control lets you assemble different collections of controls using **View** elements and display any one of them to the user. This is usually done programmatically to selectively reveal part of the user interface based on some input to the user. Listing 15-30 shows the markup for a simple MultiView control.

Listing 15-30. *Using the Windows Forms MultiView control*

```
...
<body>
<form id="form1" runat="server">

<asp:Button ID="Button1" runat="server" Text="Cycle" onclick="Button1_Click" />

<asp:MultiView ID="MultiView1" runat="server">
<asp:View ID="View1" runat="server">
<asp:Label ID="Label1" runat="server" Text="First Name:"></asp:Label>
<asp:TextBox ID="TextBox1" runat="server"></asp:TextBox>
</asp:View>
<asp:View ID="View2" runat="server">
<asp:Label ID="Label2" runat="server" Text="Surname:"></asp:Label>
<asp:TextBox ID="TextBox2" runat="server"></asp:TextBox>
```

```
</asp:View>
<asp:View ID="View3" runat="server">
<asp:Label ID="Label3" runat="server" Text="Email Address:"></asp:Label>
<asp:TextBox ID="TextBox3" runat="server"></asp:TextBox>
</asp:View>
</asp:MultiView>

</form>
</body>
...
```

The view that a MultiView control displays is controlled using the `ActiveViewIndex` property. The default value is -1, meaning that *none* of the views is displayed. You will notice that Listing 15-30 includes a Button control. The handler for the `Click` event cycles through the available views. You can see the code for this method in Listing 15-31.

Listing 15-31. *Setting the active view for a MultiView control*

```csharp
using System;
using System.Web.UI.WebControls;

namespace WebApp {
    public partial class Default : System.Web.UI.Page {

        protected void Button1_Click(object sender, EventArgs e) {
            MultiView1.ActiveViewIndex = (MultiView1.ActiveViewIndex + 1) % 3;
        }
    }
}
```

This code simply cycles through the views, but you can select views on any criteria at all. Figure 15-16 shows the effect of clicking the button in the example.

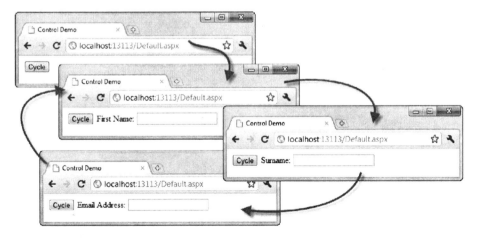

Figure 15-16. *Cycling through a MultiView*

The MultiView control requires that the form be posted to the server in order for the displayed view to be changed. This can be useful sometimes, depending on what your views contain. For a simple scenario like our example, we can achieve the same effect using a little jQuery, as shown in Listing 15-32.

Listing 15-32. Using jQuery to replace a MultiView control

```
<%@ Page Language="C#" AutoEventWireup="true" CodeBehind="jQueryView.aspx.cs"
Inherits="WebApp.jQueryView" %>

<!DOCTYPE html PUBLIC "-//W3C//DTD XHTML 1.0 Transitional//EN"
"http://www.w3.org/TR/xhtml1/DTD/xhtml1-transitional.dtd">

<html xmlns="http://www.w3.org/1999/xhtml">
<head runat="server">
<title></title>
<script src="Scripts/jquery-1.4.1.js" type="text/javascript"></script>
<script type="text/javascript">

        $(document).ready(function () {
            var counter = 0;
            $('#cycleButton').click(function () {
                counter = (counter + 1) % 4;
                $('.view').hide();
                $('#View' + counter).show();
                return false;
            }).click();

        });

</script>
</head>
<body>
<form id="form1" runat="server">

<input id="cycleButton" type="submit" value="Cycle" />

<div ID="View1" class="view">
<asp:Label ID="Label1" runat="server" Text="First Name:"></asp:Label>
<asp:TextBox ID="TextBox1" runat="server"></asp:TextBox>
</div>
<div ID="View2" class="view">
<asp:Label ID="Label2" runat="server" Text="Surname:"></asp:Label>
<asp:TextBox ID="TextBox2" runat="server"></asp:TextBox>
</div>
<div ID="View3" class="view">
<asp:Label ID="Label3" runat="server" Text="Email Address:"></asp:Label>
<asp:TextBox ID="TextBox3" runat="server"></asp:TextBox>
</div>
```

```
</form>
</body>
</html>
```

The script in this listing preserves the behavior of not displaying any controls at first. It does this by creating a selector (`#View0`) that doesn't match any elements in the page.

Summary

This chapter has given you a tour of the core Web Forms controls. You've seen how they work and how they are transformed to HTML.

The basic Web Forms controls are the ones that I tend to use most frequently. They provide support for the design tools and control events, without generating a lot of JavaScript and inline styles. Some of the controls are at the opposite end of this spectrum; I rarely use the Calendar or Wizard controls, for example.

In the next chapter, we'll look at the options available for customizing controls to get exactly the behavior you want. This provides all of the benefits of the Web Controls tools and events *and* gives you a lot more control over the HTML that is generated.

Customizing Web Forms Controls

Although Web Forms includes a comprehensive set of built-in controls, there are times when they are not what you want. Sometimes, they won't generate the HTML you are looking for, and other times there won't be a control that suits your needs at all. This chapter introduces four different techniques for customizing Web Forms controls.

Creating a User Control

The first kind of customization we will look at is *user controls*, which are like markup templates that you can reuse in different pages. By contrast, the controls you saw in the previous chapter were all *server controls*. The differences between these types of controls will become apparent as we proceed. I'll show you how to customize server controls and create new ones later in this chapter.

User controls can be helpful when you have a block of markup that you want to use throughout your web application, such as a set of labels and text boxes that gather a user's name and e-mail address. Rather than re-create the markup required for this multiple times, you can create a user control.

To demonstrate how user controls work, we'll create one that contains the now familiar swimming-conversion calculator.

To begin, in Visual Studio, select Project ➤ Add New Item and select the Web User Control template, as shown in Figure 16-1. I have named my user control SwimCals.ascx. Notice that the file name extension for user controls is different from the .aspx files we have been working with so far.

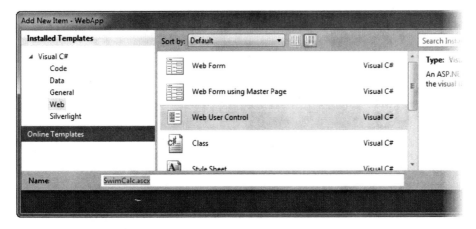

Figure 16-1. *Creating a user control*

When you choose to create the new user control, Visual Studio opens the source window, and the Toolbox window displays all of the Web Forms controls, just as if you were creating a new page. You use the same controls and techniques to create a user control, but focus on just the markup that you want to reuse across your application. Listing 16-1 shows the markup to add to `SwimCalc.ascx`.

Listing 16-1. *The markup for the SwimCalc user control*

```
<%@ Control Language="C#" AutoEventWireup="true" CodeBehind="SwimCalc.ascx.cs"↵
 Inherits="WebApp.SwimCalc" %>

<style type="text/css">
    span.swimcalc
    {
        text-align:right; margin:5px; width:100px;
        height:20px; float:left; clear:left;
    }

    input.swimcalcInput
    {
        margin:5px;
    }
</style>
<div>
<asp:Label CssClass="swimcalc" ID="Label1" runat="server" Text="Laps:"></asp:Label>
<asp:TextBox CssClass="swimcalcInput" ID="LapsText" runat="server">1</asp:TextBox>
</div>
<div>
<asp:Label CssClass="swimcalc" ID="Label2" runat="server" Text="Length:"></asp:Label>
<asp:TextBox CssClass="swimcalcInput" ID="LengthText" runat="server">20</asp:TextBox>
</div>
<div>
<asp:Label CssClass="swimcalc" ID="Label3" runat="server" Text="Minutes:"></asp:Label>
```

```
<asp:TextBox CssClass="swimcalcInput" ID="MinText" runat="server">60</asp:TextBox>
</div>
<div>
<asp:Label CssClass="swimcalc" ID="Label4" runat="server" Text="Cals/Hr:"></asp:Label>
<asp:TextBox CssClass="swimcalcInput" ID="CalsText" runat="server">1070</asp:TextBox>
</div>
```

There are a few points to note about this listing. The first is that there is no form defined. This is because ASP.NET allows us to create only one form per page, and since we are going to employ our user control within regular .aspx pages, there will already be a form defined. Similarly, we have not added any kind of submit button. The expectation is that the page in which the user control is embedded will provide the mechanism to submit the form to the ASP.NET server.

Note also that we have defined the CSS styles we want applied to the elements inline. Using CSS with user controls can be tricky, because the styles can spill onto other elements when the HTML is rendered. I usually avoid using CSS in user controls and rely on the page-level styling to achieve the effects I require. However, if control-specific styling is essential, make your CSS class names as specific as possible to reduce the scope in which they are applied.

Adding Events to User Controls

User controls wouldn't be that useful if they were just fragments of markup. Fortunately, you can add more functionality. One of the most useful things you can do is define events. In the case of our swimming calculator control, a useful event might indicate when a calculation has been performed, which happens whenever the user changes the values entered into the TextBox controls.

User controls have code-behind classes, just like pages and the controls you saw in the previous chapter. Listing 16-2 shows the code to add to the Swimcalc.ascx.cs code-behind file to define and implement the new event.

Listing 16-2. *Defining a new event in a user control*

```
using System;
using System.Linq;
using System.Web.UI;

namespace WebApp {

    public class SwimCalcEventArgs : EventArgs {
        private SwimCalcResult result;

        public SwimCalcEventArgs(SwimCalcResult res) {
            result = res;
        }

        public float Distance { get { return result.Distance; } }
        public float CalsBurned { get { return result.Calories; } }
        public float Pace { get { return result.Pace; } }
    }
```

```
public partial class SwimCalc : System.Web.UI.UserControl {
    public event EventHandler<SwimCalcEventArgs> CalcPerformed;
    private float[] lastInputs;

    protected void Page_Load(object sender, EventArgs e) {

        // define the int values that will hold the values from the input elements
        int laps, length, mins, cals;

        // try to get the values from the form elements as ints
        if (int.TryParse(LapsText.Text, out laps)
            && int.TryParse(LengthText.Text, out length)
            && int.TryParse(MinText.Text, out mins)
            && int.TryParse(CalsText.Text, out cals)) {

            float[] newinputs = new float[] { laps, length, mins, cals };

            // perform the calculation only if one of the inputs has changed
            if (lastInputs == null || !lastInputs.SequenceEqual(newinputs)) {

                // perform the calculation
                SwimCalcResult result
                    = SwimCalculator.PerformCalculation(laps, length, mins, cals);
                // invoke the event
                OnCalcPerformed(new SwimCalcEventArgs(result));
                // update the set of inputs reflecting the last calculation
                lastInputs = newinputs;
            }
        }
    }

    protected virtual void OnCalcPerformed(SwimCalcEventArgs args) {
        EventHandler<SwimCalcEventArgs> handler = CalcPerformed;
        if (handler != null) {
            handler(this, args);
        }
    }

    protected override void OnInit(EventArgs e) {
        base.OnInit(e);
        Page.RegisterRequiresControlState(this);
    }

    protected override void LoadControlState(object savedState) {
        if (savedState != null) {
            lastInputs = (float[])savedState;
        }
    }
```

```
        protected override object SaveControlState() {
            return lastInputs;
        }
    }
}
```

There is a fair amount of code in the listing just to define an event, but most of it is plumbing that we require just to get started. I'll run through the listing in sections.

We start by defining the SwimCalcEventArgs class, which is derived from EventArgs and will be the type that is passed to the methods that handle our event:

```
public class SwimCalcEventArgs : EventArgs {
    private SwimCalcResult result;

    public SwimCalcEventArgs(SwimCalcResult res) {
        result = res;
    }

    public float Distance { get { return result.Distance; } }
    public float CalsBurned { get { return result.Calories; } }
    public float Pace { get { return result.Pace; } }
}
```

We have reused the classes that handle the actual calculation from earlier chapters. The calculation result is expressed using the SwimCalcResult struct. In order to make the details of the calculation result available through the EventArgs class, we have defined a constructor for SwimCalcEventArgs that takes an instance of SwimCalcResult as a parameter. Individual values from the result are exposed through the Distance, CalsBurned, and Pace properties.

The SwimCalc class is the code-behind class for the user control. We have defined the event, called CalcPerformed, using the standard C# event handler pattern, and a private field called lastInputs. The private field is an array of float values that represents the data from the user that was used to calculate the last result:

```
public partial class SwimCalc : System.Web.UI.UserControl {
    public event EventHandler<SwimCalcEventArgs> CalcPerformed;
    private float[] lastInputs;
...
```

We are going to use the last set of data inputs to restrict the number of times we invoke the CalcPerformed event. Rather than perform the calculation every time the form is posted back to the server, we will do the calculation and invoke the event only when the user changes one of the data values. You'll see how to manage this shortly.

Most of the action takes place in the Page_Load method, which will be invoked when our user control is loaded. This will happen once when the page is first loaded, and then again each time the user posts the form back to the server. The interesting part happens after we have parsed the values from the TextBox controls:

```
float[] newinputs = new float[] { laps, length, mins, cals };

// perform the calculation only if one of the inputs has changed
if (lastInputs == null || !lastInputs.SequenceEqual(newinputs)) {
```

```
        // perform the calculation
        SwimCalcResult result
            = SwimCalculator.PerformCalculation(laps, length, mins, cals);
        // invoke the event
        OnCalcPerformed(new SwimCalcEventArgs(result));
        // update the set of inputs reflecting the last calculation
        lastInputs = newinputs;
}
```

We create an array of the float values containing the values read from the TextBox controls. If there are no previous values available, or if they differ from the values that we just read, then we perform the calculation and call the OnCalcPerformed method to invoke the event, which follows the standard event-handler pattern.

One key action that we take in the Page_Load method is to assign the array containing the most recent data values to the lastInputs field. In order for our strategy to send events only when the input data has changed, we need some way of storing the values that we have been working with between requests. We could use the session or view state features, as described in Chapter 6, but these can be disabled on a per-page basis, which makes them unreliable as a means for storing data essential for the operation of a control. Instead, we have used *control state*, which cannot be disabled in the same way.

There are two stages to implementing control state. The first is to register for the feature with the page that contains our control. We do this by overriding the OnInit method and calling the Page.RegisterRequiresControlState method, like this:

```
protected override void OnInit(EventArgs e) {
    base.OnInit(e);
    Page.RegisterRequiresControlState(this);
}
```

We then need to override the LoadControlState and SaveControlState methods in order to save and load the data we require. Here are the implementations from the example:

```
protected override void LoadControlState(object savedState) {
    if (savedState != null) {
        lastInputs = (float[])savedState;
    }
}

protected override object SaveControlState() {
    return lastInputs;
}
```

The LoadControlState method passes an object as a parameter. We are responsible for converting this into the type that we require (which is an array of float values in this example). This method will be called at the start of the control's life cycle, ensuring that the data is available when the Page_Load method is called. In the example, we assign the values read from the control state to the lastInputs field, which is how we make comparisons across requests. In the SaveControlState, we return an object that represents the state we want stored. This can be any data at all, but as a rule, you should store as little data as possible.

We have now added an event to our user control, which will be invoked whenever a new calculation result is generated.

Adding Properties to User Controls

In addition to events, you can define properties for your user control, and then set these properties using markup or the Web Forms design tools. As a demonstration, we will add a `bool` property called `EnableTextBoxAutoPostBack` to our swimming calculator control. When this property is `true`, we will enable the `AutoPostBack` feature on the TextBox controls contained in our user control so that changing the contents of any of them will cause the form to post back (and so lead to a new calculation being performed). Listing 16-3 shows the additions to the code-behind class to implement the property.

Listing 16-3. *Adding a property to a user control*

```
public partial class SwimCalc : System.Web.UI.UserControl {
    public event EventHandler<SwimCalcEventArgs> CalcPerformed;
    private float[] lastInputs;

    [DefaultValue(false)]
    [Category("Behavior")]
    public bool EnableTextBoxAutoPostBack { get; set; }

    protected void Page_Load(object sender, EventArgs e) {

        // configure the TextBoxes based on the property value
        foreach (TextBox tb in new [] {LapsText, LengthText, MinText, CalsText}) {
            tb.AutoPostBack = EnableTextBoxAutoPostBack;
        }

        ...rest of class as shown in Listing 16-2...

    }
}
```

We have defined an automatically implemented property in the normal way, and then annotated it with the `DefaultValue` and `Category` attributes. These attributes help support the property in the source window and the property sheet for the user control. The default value is the one that will be displayed in the property sheet by default, and the `Category` attribute allows us to specify where in the sheet our property will be displayed. Here, we have chosen the Behavior category.

We act on the value of the property in the `Page_Load` method, setting the value of the `AutoPostBack` property on each of the TextBox controls to match the value of the property. The property value is set before the `Page_Load` method is is invoked.

Using User Controls in Pages

The process for using a user control in an `.aspx` page is reasonably straightforward. Listing 16-4 shows the `Default.aspx` page, which uses the `SwimCalc.ascx` control we created in the previous sections.

Listing 16-4. *Using a user control*

```
<%@ Page Language="C#" AutoEventWireup="true" CodeBehind="Default.aspx.cs"↩
 Inherits="WebApp.Default" %>
<%@ Register Src="~/SwimCalc.ascx" TagName="Calc" TagPrefix="Custom" %>

<!DOCTYPE html PUBLIC "-//W3C//DTD XHTML 1.0 Transitional//EN"↩
 "http://www.w3.org/TR/xhtml1/DTD/xhtml1-transitional.dtd">

<html xmlns="http://www.w3.org/1999/xhtml">
<head runat="server">
<title>Control Demo</title>
</head>
<body>
<form id="form1" runat="server">

<div>
<Custom:Calc ID="calc" runat="server"
            OnCalcPerformed="HandleCalcPerformed"
            EnableTextBoxAutoPostBack="true"/>

<asp:Button ID="Button1" runat="server" Text="Button"
            style="margin-left:110px"/>
</div>

<asp:TextBox ID="TextBox1" runat="server" TextMode="MultiLine"
        Rows="5" ReadOnly="True" BorderStyle="None"
        style="margin-left:60px; margin-top:20px"/>

</form>
</body>
</html>
```

Before we can use the control, we must add a `Register` directive to the page to bring our control into the page scope, like this:

```
<%@ Register Src="~/SwimCalc.ascx" TagName="Calc" TagPrefix="Custom" %>
```

The `Src` attribute specifies the control that you want to use. The `TagName` is the name that you will use to refer to the control in the markup. The `TagPrefix` attribute specifies the prefix that you must prepend to the `TagName` value. You can see how the `TagName` and `TagPrefix` attributes are used in the markup for the control, as follows:

```
<Custom:Calc ID="calc" runat="server"
    OnCalcPerformed="HandleCalcPerformed"
    EnableTextBoxAutoPostBack="true"/>
```

User controls can be used only through the source window and are not supported by the design surface. You can set a value for the `EnableTextBoxAutoPostBack` property directly in the markup, as we did in Listing 16-4, or by setting a value in the property sheet, as shown in Figure 16-2.

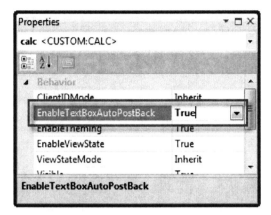

Figure 16-2. *Setting a user control property using the property sheet*

We register a handler for the `CalcPerformed` event by setting `OnCalcPerformed` to the name of a suitable method in the code-behind class for the page. In this case, the method is called `HandleCalcPerformed`, as shown in Listing 16-5.

Listing 16-5. *Handling the user control event*

```
using System.Text;

namespace WebApp {
    public partial class Default : System.Web.UI.Page {

        protected void HandleCalcPerformed(object sender, SwimCalcEventArgs e) {

            // compose the results
            StringBuilder stringBuilder = new StringBuilder();
            stringBuilder.AppendFormat("Distance: {0:F2} miles\n", e.Distance);
            stringBuilder.AppendFormat("Calories Burned: {0:F0}\n", e.CalsBurned);
            stringBuilder.AppendFormat("Pace : {0:F0} sec/lap\n", e.Pace);

            // set the results text
            TextBox1.Text = stringBuilder.ToString();
        }
    }
}
```

You can see how the `Default.aspx` page containing the user control is rendered in Figure 16-3.

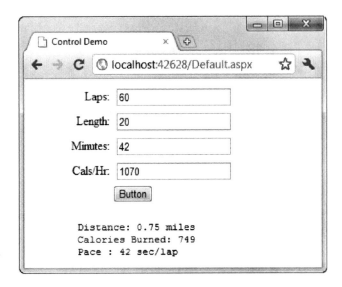

Figure 16-3. Rendering the user control as part of a page

Using Control Templates

Some of the built-in Web Forms controls support *templates*, which you can use to alter the way that they are rendered to HTML. To demonstrate the template feature, we will look at the SiteMapPath control.

To set the baseline, Listing 16-6 shows the `Web.sitemap` file we will be using, which is the same one that we used in Chapter 15.

Listing 16-6. A simple site map

```
<?xml version="1.0" encoding="utf-8" ?>
<siteMap xmlns="http://schemas.microsoft.com/AspNet/SiteMap-File-1.0" >
<siteMapNode url="~/Main.aspx" title="Triathlon">
<siteMapNode url="~/Data.aspx" title="Race Data">
<siteMapNode url="~/Default.aspx" title="Lastest Data"  description="" />
</siteMapNode>
<siteMapNode url="~/People.aspx" title="Athletes">
<siteMapNode url="~/Adam.aspx" title="Adam Freeman"  description="" />
<siteMapNode url="~/Joe.aspx" title="Joe Smith"  description="" />
</siteMapNode>
</siteMapNode>
</siteMap>
```

Listing 16-7 shows the markup for a SiteMapPath control. To create this markup, simply drag the control from the Toolbox and release it on the source window.

Listing 16-7. *Using the SiteMapPath control*

```
...
<body>
<form id="form1" runat="server">

<asp:SiteMapPath ID="SiteMapPath1" runat="server">
</asp:SiteMapPath>

</form>
</body>
...
```

When we render the markup, the control uses the site map to produce the HTML shown in Listing 16-8.

Listing 16-8. *The default HTML produced by the SiteMapPath control*

```
<span id="SiteMapPath1">
<a href="#SiteMapPath1_SkipLink">
<img alt="Skip Navigation Links" height="0"
width="0" src="/WebResource.axd?d=SQXK" style="border-width:0px;" />
</a>
<span><a href="/Main.aspx">Triathlon</a></span><span>&gt; </span>
<span><a href="/Data.aspx">Race Data</a></span><span>&gt; </span>
<span>Lastest Data</span>
<a id="SiteMapPath1_SkipLink"></a></span>
```

I've tidied up this HTML to make it easier to read. At the start and end of the HTML, you'll see links with references to **SkipLink.** These are hints for screen readers to make web pages more accessible.

I've marked the section that interests us in regard to templates: a set of **span** elements. The first two **span** elements contain links to other pages, and the last one is a literal reference to the current page. As you might have guessed, I rendered the HTML from the **Default.aspx** page. Figure 16-4 shows how the browser displays the HTML.

Figure 16-4. *The default appearance of the SiteMapPath control*

Now that we are set up and you've seen the default rendering, we can start to work with the control templates. A template controls the appearance of one part of the control. Each template-enabled control supports a different set of templates. The SiteMapPath control supports the set of templates shown in Table 16-1.

Table 16-1. *The Templates Supported by the SiteMapPath Control*

Template	Description
NodeTemplate	The template that is applied to all nodes in the path, subject to the RootNodeTemplate and CurrentNodeTemplate
RootNodeTemplate	The template used specifically for the root node in the path; overrides the NodeTemplate
CurrentNodeTemplate	The template used specifically for the node in the path representing the current page; overrides the NodeTemplate
PathSeparatorTemplate	The template used for the separator between nodes in the path

You can define a template using the design tools or directly in the markup—the end result is the same. If you are new to using control templates, the design tools are the easiest way to start.

We'll begin with the simplest template that the SiteMapPath defines: the PathSeparator template.

Using the PathSeparator Template

To open the template, select the control on the design surface, click the arrow that appears on the right edge, and select Edit Templates, as shown in Figure 16-5.

Figure 16-5. *Starting the design tool template editing process*

The design surface display will change to show the current template, which will be blank because we have yet to define any. Select PathSeparatorTemplate from the Display drop-down list, as shown in Figure 16-6.

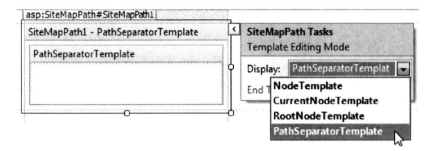

Figure 16-6. *Selecting the template for the path separator*

You can now drag controls or enter markup into the empty space to define the template. For this example, we are going to use an image, so I created a project folder called Content and added an image called path_separator.gif. To use the image as the path separator, simply drag it from the Solution Explorer to the template area. You will be prompted to provide details for the link, as shown in Figure 16-7. Click OK, and the image will be used as the template, as shown in Figure 16-8.

Figure 16-7. *Providing accessibility information for the path separator image*

Figure 16-8. *Using an image as the site map path separator*

As you can see, we used a simple arrow image. When working with the template in the design surface, you can drag any control or enter any text, and Visual Studio will take care of creating the markup for the template. You can see the modified markup for the SiteMapPath control in Listing 16-9.

Listing 16-9. The effect of defining a template for the SiteMapPath path separator

```
<asp:SiteMapPath ID="SiteMapPath1" runat="server">
<PathSeparatorTemplate>
<img alt="Path Separator" class="style1" src="Content/path_separator.gif" />
</PathSeparatorTemplate>
</asp:SiteMapPath>
```

As with our previous example, you don't need to use the design tools. You can enter the markup directly, creating an element for the template name (in this case `PathSeparatorTemplate`, as listed in Table 16-1).

Figure 16-9 shows the effect of this template when the SiteMapPath control is rendered to HTML and displayed in the browser.

Figure 16-9. The SiteMapPath control with a path separator template

Using the Other Control Templates

To use the other templates, you need to use an aspect of the data-binding feature that is the topic of Chapters 18 and 19. Listing 16-10 shows the markup for the `RootNodeTemplate`, which involves a new kind of ASP.NET tag.

Listing 16-10. Markup for the RootNodeTemplate using data-binding tags

```
<RootNodeTemplate>
<div class="nodeStyle" style="background-image:url('Content/back_1.png')">
<a class="textStyle" href='<%# Eval("Url") %>'><%# Eval("Title") %></a>
</div>
</RootNodeTemplate>
```

When we created a template for the path separator, we could work with just markup. but when creating a template for a node in the site map path, we need some way of including information from the site map into the HTML that we generate. We do this using the `<%# Eval("`*term*`")%>` tag, where *term* is one of `Url`, `Title`, or `Description`. I am not going to explain this expression until Chapters 18 and 19; for the moment, it is enough to know that this incantation will produce information about a node in the map.

Listing 16-11 shows a SiteMapPath control for which I have defined all four templates. Notice that I have left the `PathSeparatorTemplate` empty. This is because I don't require any separator between the nodes in the path.

Listing 16-11. Using all of the templates of the SiteMapPath control

```
<%@ Page Language="C#" AutoEventWireup="true" CodeBehind="Default.aspx.cs"↵
 Inherits="WebApp.Default" %>

<!DOCTYPE html PUBLIC "-//W3C//DTD XHTML 1.0 Transitional//EN"↵
 "http://www.w3.org/TR/xhtml1/DTD/xhtml1-transitional.dtd">

<html xmlns="http://www.w3.org/1999/xhtml">
<head runat="server">
<title>Control Demo</title>
<style type="text/css">
        .nodeStyle
        {
            background-repeat:repeat-x; float: left;
            min-height:51px;
        }
        .textStyle
        {
            padding: 15px 15px 15px 30px;
            vertical-align: middle;
            float: left; clear: left;
            text-decoration: none;
            font-weight: bold; font-size: large;
            color: #FFFFFF;
        }
</style>
</head>
<body>
<form id="form1" runat="server">
<asp:SiteMapPath ID="SiteMapPath1" runat="server">
<PathSeparatorTemplate>
<!-- left empty: path separator not required -->
</PathSeparatorTemplate>
<RootNodeTemplate>
<div class="nodeStyle" style="background-image:url('Content/back_1.png')">
<a class="textStyle" href='<%# Eval("Url") %>'><%# Eval("Title") %></a>
</div>
</RootNodeTemplate>
<NodeTemplate>
<div class="nodeStyle" style="background-image:url('Content/back_2.png')">
<a class="textStyle" href='<%# Eval("Url") %>'><%# Eval("Title") %></a>
</div>
</NodeTemplate>
<CurrentNodeTemplate>
<div class="nodeStyle"
                    style="background-image:url('Content/back_final.png');">
<a class="textStyle" style="color:#801100"
                    href='<%# Eval("Url") %>'><%# Eval("Title") %></a>
</div>
<div class="nodeStyle" style="background:#801100; width:2px" />
```

```
    </CurrentNodeTemplate>
  </asp:SiteMapPath>
  </form>
</body>
</html>
```

For each of the different templates, I used HTML elements to specify the layout. I could have just as easily used Web Forms controls—it doesn't really matter which technique you use to create the contents of the template.

The effect of these templates is shown in Figure 16-10. As you can see, a small amount of work on the templates for a control can transform its appearance.

Figure 16-10. *Applying templates to the SiteMapPath control*

■ **Note**   To keep this example simple, I accepted some limitations in the site map path that is displayed. The images I created work only for paths that have three nodes, and there is a limit to the length of the `Title` attribute that will display properly.

Not all of the Web Forms control support templates, and those that do tend to be the more complicated ones. Of the controls you have seen so far, the Menu, SiteMapPath, and Wizard controls support templates. Many of the other template-enabled controls, such as GridView and ListView, are rich data controls, which are described in Chapter 20.

Using Control Adapters

Control templates are useful, but they are not supported by all controls, and they allow us to change only certain aspects of a control's appearance. An alternative approach is to use a control adapter.

Creating a Control Adapter

A *control adapter* is a mechanism designed to deal with differences between browsers, but we can co-opt it to gain wider influence over a control. To demonstrate creating and using a control adapter, we will use the RadioButtonList control. Listing 16-12 shows some markup that uses this control in a page.

Listing 16-12. *Using the RadioButtonList control*

```
<%@ Page Language="C#" AutoEventWireup="true" CodeBehind="Default.aspx.cs"
Inherits="WebApp.Default" %>

<!DOCTYPE html PUBLIC "-//W3C//DTD XHTML 1.0 Transitional//EN"↵
 "http://www.w3.org/TR/xhtml1/DTD/xhtml1-transitional.dtd">

<html xmlns="http://www.w3.org/1999/xhtml">
<head runat="server">
<title>Control Demo</title>
</head>
<body>
<form id="form1" runat="server">

<asp:RadioButtonList ID="RadioButtonList1" runat="server">
<asp:ListItem>First Item</asp:ListItem>
<asp:ListItem>Second Item</asp:ListItem>
<asp:ListItem>Third Item</asp:ListItem>
</asp:RadioButtonList>

</form>
</body>
</html>
```

The RadioButtonList is a simple control that takes a set of list items and creates a series of radio buttons from them, as illustrated in Figure 16-11.

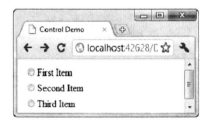

Figure 16-11. *A RadioButtonList displayed in the browser*

By default, the RadioButtonListControl uses an HTML `table` element to handle the layout of the checkboxes. Listing 16-13 shows the HTML produced by the control in Listing 16-12.

Listing 16-13. *The HTML generated by a RadioButtonListControl*

```
<table id="RadioButtonList1"><tr><td>
<input id="RadioButtonList1_0" type="radio" name="RadioButtonList1"
value="First Item" />
<label for="RadioButtonList1_0">First Item</label>
</td></tr>
<tr>
```

```
<td>
<input id="RadioButtonList1_1" type="radio" name="RadioButtonList1"
value="Second Item" />
<label for="RadioButtonList1_1">Second Item</label>
</td></tr>
<tr><td>
<input id="RadioButtonList1_2" type="radio" name="RadioButtonList1"
value="Third Item" />
<label for="RadioButtonList1_2">Third Item</label>
</td>
</tr>
</table>
```

We are going to use a control adapter to take over the rendering process for the control and change the HTML that is generated. The first step is to implement our rendering code in a class that is derived from the WebControlAdapter class, which can be found in the System.Web.UI.WebControls.Adapters namespace. Listing 16-14 shows the adapter implementation.

Listing 16-14. An adapter for the RadioButtonList control

```
using System.Web.UI;
using System.Web.UI.WebControls;
using System.Web.UI.WebControls.Adapters;

namespace WebApp {
    public class RadioButtonListAdaptor : WebControlAdapter {

        protected override void RenderBeginTag(HtmlTextWriter writer) {
            writer.AddStyleAttribute(HtmlTextWriterStyle.BorderStyle, "solid");
            writer.AddStyleAttribute(HtmlTextWriterStyle.BorderColor, "black");
            writer.AddStyleAttribute(HtmlTextWriterStyle.BorderWidth, "thin");
            writer.AddStyleAttribute(HtmlTextWriterStyle.Width, "150px");
            writer.AddAttribute(HtmlTextWriterAttribute.Id, Control.ID);
            writer.AddAttribute(HtmlTextWriterAttribute.Name, Control.ID);
            writer.RenderBeginTag(HtmlTextWriterTag.Div);
        }

        protected override void RenderEndTag(HtmlTextWriter writer) {
            writer.RenderEndTag();
        }

        protected override void RenderContents(HtmlTextWriter writer) {

            RadioButtonList rblist = Control as RadioButtonList;
            if (rblist != null) {
                int counter = 0;
                foreach (ListItem item in rblist.Items) {

                    // open the div element
                    writer.RenderBeginTag(HtmlTextWriterTag.Div);
```

```
                // set the attributes for the input element
                writer.AddAttribute(HtmlTextWriterAttribute.Id, Control.ID
                    + "_" + counter);
                writer.AddAttribute(HtmlTextWriterAttribute.Name, Control.ID);
                writer.AddAttribute(HtmlTextWriterAttribute.Type, "radio");
                writer.AddAttribute(HtmlTextWriterAttribute.Value, item.Value);
                if (item.Selected) {
                    writer.AddAttribute(HtmlTextWriterAttribute.Checked, "checked");
                }
                // write the input element
                writer.RenderBeginTag(HtmlTextWriterTag.Input);
                writer.RenderEndTag();

                // write the label element
                writer.RenderBeginTag(HtmlTextWriterTag.Label);
                writer.Write(item.Text);
                writer.RenderEndTag();

                // close the div element
                writer.RenderEndTag();

                // register the value as an expected data item
                Page.ClientScript.RegisterForEventValidation(Control.ID, item.Value);

                // increment the counter
                counter++;
            }
        }
    }
}
```

To create a control adapter, we must override three methods from the WebControlAdapter class: RenderBeginTag, RenderEndTag, and RenderContents. The names give clues as to the purpose of each of these methods.

The RenderBeginTag method is called in order to produce the opening tag for your element. Neither ASP.NET nor Web Forms cares which element you produce—you can do anything you want. Our example uses a set of div elements to lay out the checkboxes. You can see how to open the tag for this in the RenderBeginTag method:

```
protected override void RenderBeginTag(HtmlTextWriter writer) {
    writer.AddStyleAttribute(HtmlTextWriterStyle.BorderStyle, "solid");
    writer.AddStyleAttribute(HtmlTextWriterStyle.BorderColor, "black");
    writer.AddStyleAttribute(HtmlTextWriterStyle.BorderWidth, "thin");
    writer.AddStyleAttribute(HtmlTextWriterStyle.Width, "150px");
    writer.AddAttribute(HtmlTextWriterAttribute.Id, Control.ID);
    writer.AddAttribute(HtmlTextWriterAttribute.Name, Control.ID);
    writer.RenderBeginTag(HtmlTextWriterTag.Div);
}
```

We are passed an `HtmlTextWriter` object in order to render our HTML. Producing an element using the `HtmlTextWriter` class is a two-step process: render the element for the control itself, and then render each of the `ListItems` that the control contains.

First, we specify the attributes and styles that we want the element to have using the `AddAttribute` and `AddStyleAttribute` methods. There are enumerations available to help you specify the names of the attributes and styles (`HtmlTextWriterAttribute` and `HtmlTextWriterStyle`, respectively), or you can specify the names as strings. In the `RenderBeginTag` method, we have set some styles just to help differentiate our adapted control from the regular output—after all, a set of checkboxes laid out in a `table` element looks pretty similar to a set of checkboxes laid our using `div` elements.

The three critical statements are shown in bold. We must set the `ID` and `Name` attributes if we want to be able to post requests back to the server. We can get details about the control we are adapting through the `Control` property that we inherited from the `WebControlAdapter` class. In this case, we have used the `Control.ID` property to set the values for the `ID` and `Name` attributes.

The third statement in bold is the one that renders the begin tag of the element and the attributes we have specified—a call to `HtmlTextWriter.RenderBeginTag`. You can specify the tag you want to create by selecting a value from the `HtmlTextWriterTag` enumeration or by specifying it as a string.

The counterpart to the `RenderBeginTag` method in the adapter is `RenderEndTag`, as follows:

```
protected override void RenderEndTag(HtmlTextWriter writer) {
    writer.RenderEndTag();
}
```

The `HtmlTextWriter` class keeps track of which elements are currently open, and when we call the `RenderEndTag` method, it produces whichever tag is required. Taken together, the `RenderBeginTag` and `RenderEndTag` methods in the control adapter produce the following HTML:

```
<div id="RadioButtonList1" name="RadioButtonList1"
    style="border-style:solid;border-color:black;border-width:thin;width:150px;">
</div>
```

Now that we have rendered the element for the control itself, we need to render each of the `ListItems` that the control contains. We do this by overriding the `RenderContents` method. Once again, you are passed an `HtmlTextWriter` object as a parameter, and you can choose to use it to produce any HTML that you require. For the demonstration adapter, we want to create the following HTML for each list item:

```
<div><input id="<item_ID>" name="<item_Name>" type="radio" value="First Item" />
<label>First Item</label>
</div>
```

As the listing shows, we cast the `Control` property to the `RadioButtonList` type, and then use a `foreach` loop to process each `ListItem` contained in the `Items` collection. Creating the tags for the `div`, `input`, and `label` elements is all very straightforward, but there are a couple of points to note.

The first point is that the `ID` attribute for every element we add to the page must be unique. To achieve this, we create a variable called `counter` and append its value to the `Control.ID` property for each `ListItem`, like this:

```
writer.AddAttribute(HtmlTextWriterAttribute.Id, Control.ID + "_" + counter);
```

This means that if the parent control has an ID of `RadioButtonList1`, then the sequence of IDs for the individual `input` elements will be `RadioButtonList1_1`, `RadioButtonList1_2`, `RadioButtonList1_3`, and so on.

We also need to assign a name to each `input` control, and this must be the same name that we used when we created the top-level `div` element, like this:

```
writer.AddAttribute(HtmlTextWriterAttribute.Name, Control.ID);
```

By reusing the name, we ensure that posting back the form to the server triggers the Web Forms control events properly. If we generate different name values, then the input elements won't be associated with the RadioButtonList control.

When you use a control adapter, you are solely responsible for implementing the control properties. In the example adapter, we ensure that ListItems are checked by reading the ListItem.Selected property, like this:

```
if (item.Selected) {
    writer.AddAttribute(HtmlTextWriterAttribute.Checked, "checked");
}
```

The last point to note is that when creating an adapter, we need to register all of the possible values that might be posted back to the server, like this:

```
Page.ClientScript.RegisterForEventValidation(Control.ID, item.Value);
```

If we don't do this, then the ASP.NET framework will assume that the user is trying to forge a request and will report an error. The preceding statement adds the value of the ListItem being processed to the set of expected results.

The HTML generated by the control adapter is shown in Listing 16-15.

***Listing 16-15.** The HTML generated by the example control adapter*

```
<div id="RadioButtonList1" name="RadioButtonList1"
    style="border-style:solid;border-color:black;border-width:thin;width:150px;">

<div><input id="RadioButtonList1_0" name="RadioButtonList1" type="radio"
            value="First Item" />
<label>First Item</label>
</div>
<div><input id="RadioButtonList1_1" name="RadioButtonList1" type="radio"
            value="Second Item" checked="checked" />
<label>Second Item</label>
</div>
<div>
<input id="RadioButtonList1_2" name="RadioButtonList1" type="radio"
            value="Third Item" />
<label>Third Item</label>
</div>
</div>
```

Creating a Browser File

Before we can generate the preceding HTML, we need to tell the ASP.NET framework that we want to associate the adapter with the control. We do this by creating a *browser file*. In Visual Studio, select Project ➤ Add New Item and select the Browser File template, as shown in Figure 16-12.

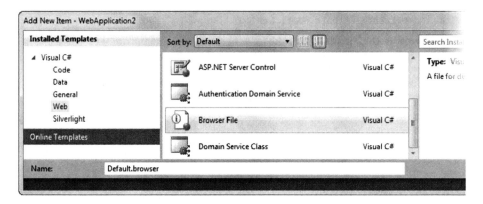

Figure 16-12. *Using the Browser File template*

Name the new item **Default.browser** and click the Add button. Visual Studio will prompt you to create the **App_Browsers** folder and place the new item there, as shown in Figure 16-13. Click the Yes button.

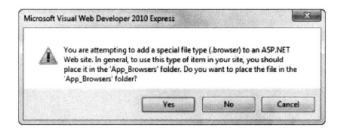

Figure 16-13. *Putting the browser file into the App_Browsers folder*

Browser files are used to identify and define the capabilities of different kinds of browsers. This feature used to be essential in building a web application, because different browsers supported different technologies. These days, browsers are more standards-based, and JavaScript libraries smooth out minor differences in scripting engines. The main use is to differentiate between desktop and mobile browsers, but even this is less common as mobile browsers gain features.

One feature of browser files is to register adapters. The original idea was that you could render a control for a given browser without using the elements it didn't implement properly. I don't recommend using this feature, but you can use a browser file to register an adapter for *all* browsers. Listing 16-16 shows how you can do this using the **Default.browser** file we added to the project.

Listing 16-16. Registering a control adapter for all browsers

```
<browsers>
<browser refID="Default">
<controlAdapters>
<adapter
        controlType="System.Web.UI.WebControls.RadioButtonList"
        adapterType="WebApp.RadioButtonListAdaptor"/>
</controlAdapters>
</browser>
</browsers>
```

In this file, I created a browser definition for the browser Default, which is the identifier for all browsers. I then created an adapter element whose controlType specifies the control I want to adapt and whose adapterType specifies the adapter I want to use. Both attributes require fully qualified class names, and you'll find that most Web Forms controls are in the System.Web.UI.WebControls namespace.

Once we have registered our control adapter, it will be used to render HTML whenever the control is used. You can see how the browser displays this HTML in Figure 16-14.

Figure 16-14. The adapted control displayed in the browser

The control doesn't look much different now that it has been adapted, but you can see the new border surrounding the control. And, of course, if you look at the HTML that the browser is displaying, you will see that the radio buttons are laid out using div elements, rather than a table.

Creating Custom Controls

You've seen how a user control can group together and extend existing Web Forms controls, and how to use adapters to take responsibility for the HTML that a control renders. But if you want to create an entirely new kind of element, then you need to create a *custom server control*.

Most of the time, user controls or control adapters will allow you to achieve the effect you require, so creating a server control is a pretty unusual thing to do.

In order to demonstrate the process of building a custom control, we will create one that neatly displays the results of the swimming calculation performed earlier in the chapter. This is something that could easily be done as a user control, but we'll do it as a server control instead.

To get started, select Project ➤ Add New Item and choose the ASP.NET Server Control template, as shown in Figure 16-15. Set the name of the new item to be `ResultsControl.cs` and click the Add button.

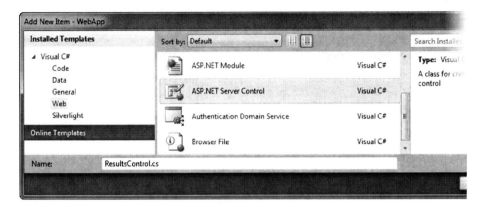

Figure 16-15. *Creating a custom server control*

Visual Studio will create the item and open it for editing. Notice that there is no design surface—server controls are just C# class files. Visual Studio creates a helpful template for a custom server control, but for this example, we are going to strip out everything that we don't need so that we start with the class shown in Listing 16-17, and then build it back up again.

Listing 16-17. *The empty custom server control class*

```
using System.Web.UI;
using System.Web.UI.WebControls;

namespace WebApp {
    public class ResultsControl : WebControl {

        protected override void RenderContents(HtmlTextWriter output) {

        }
    }
}
```

Our custom server control class is derived from `WebControl`, which is the base class for all of the Web Forms UI controls.

Adding Properties to a Custom Server Control

Our first task is to add properties to our control. These are the properties that we will configure using the Properties window or programmatically when we come to use the control later. Our custom control will have three properties: the distance, the number of calories burned, and the pace. Listing 16-18 shows how to define these properties.

Listing 16-18. Adding properties to a custom server control

```
using System.Web.UI;
using System.Web.UI.WebControls;
using System.ComponentModel;

namespace WebApp {

    public class ResultsControl : WebControl {

        [Category("Appearance")]
        [DefaultValue("0")]
        public string Distance { get; set; }

        [Category("Appearance")]
        [DefaultValue("0")]
        public string Calories { get; set; }

        [Category("Appearance")]
        [DefaultValue("0")]
        public string Pace { get; set; }

        [Browsable(false)]
        public override Color BackColor { get; set; }
        [Browsable(false)]
        public override Color ForeColor { get; set; }

        protected override void RenderContents(HtmlTextWriter output) {

        }
    }
}
```

You can see that we followed the same approach that we used to add properties to our user control earlier in the chapter. We used the `Category` attribute to set the group in which the property will be displayed, and the `DefaultValue` attribute to set a default value for each property.

When you derive from `WebControl`, you inherit a set of basic properties. If they don't have any meaning for your custom control, you can hide them by applying the `Browsable` attribute, passing in `false` as the parameter. In the listing, we have hidden the `BackColor` and `ForeColor` properties; these will not appear in the Properties window.

Rendering the Output of a Custom Server Control

The next step is to produce the HTML for our control. This is done using the `RenderContents` method, which works just like the methods we used when creating a control adapter. Listing 16-19 shows the implementation of the `RenderContents` method for the example control.

Listing 16-19. Implementing the RenderContents method for a custom server control

```
protected override void RenderContents(HtmlTextWriter output) {

    if (!string.IsNullOrEmpty(CssClass)) {
        output.AddAttribute(HtmlTextWriterAttribute.Class, CssClass);
    }
    output.RenderBeginTag("div");

    output.RenderBeginTag("div");
    output.Write(string.Format("Distance: {0}", Distance));
    output.RenderEndTag();

    output.RenderBeginTag("div");
    output.Write(string.Format("Calories: {0}", Calories));
    output.RenderEndTag();

    output.RenderBeginTag("div");
    output.Write(string.Format("Pace: {0}", Pace));
    output.RenderEndTag();

    output.RenderEndTag();
}
```

As with control adapters, when you render the output, you are responsible for taking care of handling any properties that the control implements. The statements that support the CssClass property are marked in bold. This is one of the properties that we inherit from the base WebControl class, and it is translated into the class attribute in the HTML. We have ignored the other properties we inherited, but in a real project, you should either render suitable HTML to support them or use the Browsable attribute to hide them from the user. The rest of the HTML that we generate in the RenderContents method is simple: an overall div element that contains nested div elements for each of the data values.

Adding the Custom Control to the Toolbox

Custom server controls can be added to the Visual Studio Toolbox window—something that isn't true for user controls. The ToolboxData attribute specifies the markup that will be added to the page when you drag your custom control from the Toolbox onto the design surface or source window.

Before we can add our example control to the toolbox, we need to define the format of the markup that dragging the control onto the design surface or source window will produce. We do this using the ToolboxData attribute, which we apply to the class, as shown in Listing 16-20.

Listing 16-20. Defining the markup for a custom control

```
using System.ComponentModel;
using System.Drawing;
using System.Web.UI;
using System.Web.UI.WebControls;
```

```
namespace WebApp {

    [ToolboxData("<{0}:ResultsControl runat=server></{0}:ResultsControl>")]
    public class ResultsControl : WebControl {

        [Category("Appearance")]
        [DefaultValue("0")]
        public string Distance { get; set; }
```

...

The parameter for the `ToolboxData` attribute is the markup we want for our control. The composite formatting parameter {0} will be replaced with a tag prefix, which we'll define shortly.

To add the control to the Toolbox, right-click the group in which you want the control to appear and select Choose Items from the pop-up menu. The Choose Toolbox Items dialog box appears. Select the .NET Framework Components tab and click the Browse button. Select the assembly produced by the current project. It will usually be in the `bin` directory of the project. Mine is called `WebApp.dll` because I named my web application project `WebApp`. A new entry will appear in the component list, as shown in Figure 16-16. Click OK to dismiss the dialog, and the control will appear in the section of the Toolbox you selected, as shown in Figure 16-17.

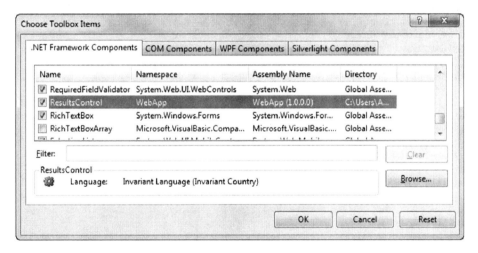

Figure 16-16. Adding a custom control to the Toolbox

■ **Tip**   Although in this example, we created the custom control inside the project where we intend to use it, we could also have created the control in a separate project, and then import its assembly in the same way. If you obtain controls from a third party, this is usually how they are packaged and distributed.

Figure 16-17. *The custom control displayed in the Toolbox*

Once the control has been added to the Toolbox, you can use it like any other Web Forms control. Listing 16-21 shows the markup created when we drag the custom control onto the page that we used earlier for the user control.

Listing 16-21. *Using a custom control on a page*

```
<%@ Page Language="C#" AutoEventWireup="true" CodeBehind="Default.aspx.cs"
Inherits="WebApp.Default" %>

<%@ Register Assembly="WebApp" Namespace="WebApp" TagPrefix="cc1" %>
<%@ Register Src="~/SwimCalc.ascx" TagName="Calc" TagPrefix="Custom" %>

<!DOCTYPE html PUBLIC "-//W3C//DTD XHTML 1.0 Transitional//EN"
 "http://www.w3.org/TR/xhtml1/DTD/xhtml1-transitional.dtd">

<html xmlns="http://www.w3.org/1999/xhtml">
<head runat="server">
<title>Control Demo</title>
</head>
<body>
<form id="form1" runat="server">

<div>
<Custom:Calc ID="calc" runat="server"
            OnCalcPerformed="HandleCalcPerformed"
            EnableTextBoxAutoPostBack="true"/>

<asp:Button ID="Button1" runat="server" Text="Button"
            style="margin-left:110px"/>
</div>
```

```
<cc1:ResultsControl ID="ResultsControl1" runat="server" />

</form>
</body>
</html>
```

When you release the control, Visual Studio adds a `Register` directive to specify a tag prefix (`cc1` in this case) and tell ASP.NET where it can find the control (in the namespace called `WebApp`, in an assembly also called `WebApp`). If you want to use the control without the Toolbox, then you will need to add this directive to each page where the custom control is required.

All that remains is to set the properties of the control programmatically, which is done in the code-behind class for the page, as shown in Listing 16-22.

Listing 16-22. Setting the properties for the custom control

```
using System.Text;

namespace WebApp {
    public partial class Default : System.Web.UI.Page {

        protected void HandleCalcPerformed(object sender, SwimCalcEventArgs e) {
            ResultsControl1.Distance = e.Distance.ToString("F0");
            ResultsControl1.Calories = e.CalsBurned.ToString("F0");
            ResultsControl1.Pace = e.Pace.ToString("F0");
        }
    }
}
```

The method shown is the handler for the event emitted from the user control we created earlier in the chapter. Figure 16-18 shows the custom control displayed by the browser.

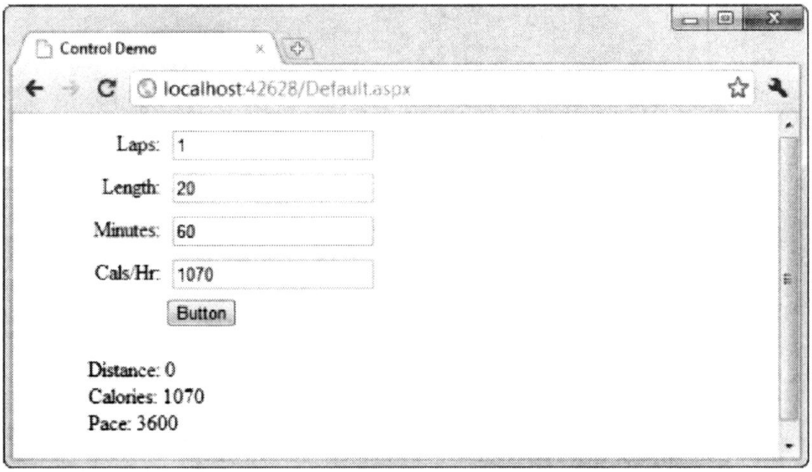

Figure 16-18. A simple custom control

Summary

This chapter showed you four ways to customize the Web Forms control system: user controls, control templates, control adapters, and custom controls. Each has its benefits and drawbacks, but you can use these features to get fine-grained control over the HTML that is emitted and the properties and events that are defined—all while still getting the benefits of the Web Forms design tools.

CHAPTER 17

Validating Form Data

Most web applications use HTML forms to gather some kind of data from the user. This can range from simple data such as a name and password to complex data that is critical to business processes. As web application developers, we are responsible for taking the data that the user provides and making sense of it. Users are human, and they can make mistakes or misread instructions. The process of checking the inputs we receive is called *validation*. This chapter describes the set of Web Forms controls that support validation.

Performing Manual Validation

We are going to start by demonstrating the problem that validation solves: preventing the user from entering nonsensical data into form fields. To do this, we will use the swimming calculator example again. Listing 17-1 contains the markup for the `Default.aspx` page, added to a Visual Studio project created using the Empty ASP.NET Application template.

Listing 17-1. The markup for Default.aspx

```
<%@ Page Language="C#" AutoEventWireup="true" CodeBehind="Default.aspx.cs"
Inherits="WebFormsApp.Default" %>

<!DOCTYPE html PUBLIC "-//W3C//DTD XHTML 1.0 Transitional//EN"
 "http://www.w3.org/TR/xhtml1/DTD/xhtml1-transitional.dtd">

<html xmlns="http://www.w3.org/1999/xhtml">
<head runat="server">
<title></title>
<link href="StyleSheet1.css" rel="stylesheet" type="text/css" />

</head>
<body>
<form id="form1" runat="server">
<div>
<asp:Label ID="Label1" runat="server" Text="Laps:" CssClass="label"/>
<asp:TextBox ID="TextBox1" runat="server"></asp:TextBox>
</div>
<div>
```

```
<asp:Label ID="Label2" runat="server" Text="Pool Length:" CssClass="label"/>
<asp:TextBox ID="TextBox2" runat="server"></asp:TextBox>
</div>
<div>
<asp:Label ID="Label3" runat="server" Text="Minutes:" CssClass="label"/>
<asp:TextBox ID="TextBox3" runat="server"></asp:TextBox>
</div>
<div>
<asp:Label ID="Label4" runat="server" Text="Calories/Hour:" CssClass="label"/>
<asp:TextBox ID="TextBox4" runat="server"></asp:TextBox>
</div>
<div style="clear:left">
<asp:Button ID="Button1" runat="server" Text="Calculate"
          style="margin-left:100px" onclick="Button1_Click"/>
</div>
<div class="results">
<asp:TextBox ID="TextBox5" runat="server" BorderStyle="None" ReadOnly="True"
          TextMode="MultiLine" Rows="4" Columns="30"></asp:TextBox>
</div>
</form>
</body>
</html>
```

We have gone back to a simpler version of this markup. We don't need the control customizations described in the previous chapter. Figure 17-1 shows how this markup is displayed in the browser.

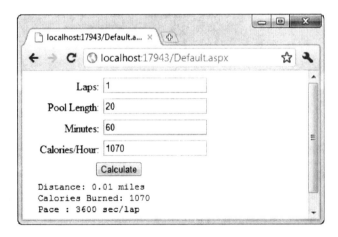

Figure 17-1. *The swimming calculator application*

Almost every web application that requires data from a user needs to perform some kind of validation. Users will type pretty much anything into a form, and this makes us responsible for two things:

- Ensuring that the data is the kind of data we expect and can work with

- Helping the user figure out what the problem is when the data isn't valid

Listing 17-2 demonstrates how to perform some basic validation on the data received in the swimming calculator application.

Listing 17-2. *Processing data in the swimming calculator application*

```
using System;
using System.Text;

namespace WebFormsApp {

    public partial class Default : System.Web.UI.Page {

        protected void Page_Load(object sender, EventArgs e) {
            if (!IsPostBack) {
                TextBox1.Text = "1";
                TextBox2.Text = "20";
                TextBox3.Text = "60";
                TextBox4.Text = "1070";
            }
        }

        protected void Button1_Click(object sender, EventArgs e) {

            // define the int values that will hold the values from the input elements
            int laps, length, mins, cals;

            // try to get the values from the form elements as ints
            if (int.TryParse(TextBox1.Text, out laps)
                && int.TryParse(TextBox2.Text, out length)
                && int.TryParse(TextBox3.Text, out mins)
                && int.TryParse(TextBox4.Text, out cals)) {

                // perform the calculation
                SwimCalcResult calcResult
                    = SwimCalc.PerformCalculation(laps, length, mins, cals);

                // compose the results
                StringBuilder stringBuilder = new StringBuilder();
                stringBuilder.AppendFormat("Distance: {0:F2} miles\n",
                    calcResult.Distance);
```

```
            stringBuilder.AppendFormat("Calories Burned: {0:F0}\n",
                calcResult.Calories);
            stringBuilder.AppendFormat("Pace : {0:F0} sec/lap\n",
                calcResult.Pace);

            // set the results text
            TextBox5.Text = stringBuilder.ToString();
        } else {
            TextBox5.Text = "";
        }
    }
  }
}
```

This approach is known as *manual validation*. We take the values from the input elements in the form and perform explicit checks or conversions to make sure that we have usable data.

This discharges one of our responsibilities. We want only integer values from the user, and we use the int.TryParseInt method to convert the string values from the TextBox controls into int values. If any of the calls to TryParseInt fail, then we assume that the user hasn't provided valid data, and we don't perform the calculation.

Unfortunately, this is a pretty dumb approach, and it doesn't take into account the fact that users may not think the way that we do. What if a user doesn't know that we assume the pool length is in meters and enters 25m in the text box? That value isn't an integer, and so we discard the data and don't perform the calculation.

Worse still, we don't provide the user with any feedback when there is a problem. Remember that the point at which your user must spend time figuring out what's wrong is the point at which you have lost a customer.

There is yet another problem: the validation logic is spread around the application. The class that performs the calculation, called SwimCalc, contains the statements shown in Listing 17-3.

Listing 17-3. *Dispersed validation statements*

```
...
// validate the parameter values - we need all values to be greater than zero
foreach (int paramValue in new[] {lapsParam, lengthParam, minsParam, calsPerHourParam}) {

    if (paramValue < 1) {
        // this is not a value we can work with
        throw new ArgumentOutOfRangeException();
    }
}
...
```

Values that pass the test in the code-behind class (such as -50, which is a valid integer value) are rejected in the SwimCalc class because we want to perform calculations with only positive values.

If we need to change the validation logic in our application, we need to hunt around looking for all of the code that applies some kind of restriction, which presents a maintenance problem for web applications of even modest complexity. And, of course, the user doesn't get any useful feedback here either. If you enter -50 into one of the TextBox controls, an exception is thrown, causing an error page (see Chapter 7 for details on how ASP.NET deals with exceptions).

Performing Automatic Validation

ASP.NET Web Forms contains a set of controls that you can use to perform *automatic* data validation. You use these controls to specify one or more rules that define valid data, and if these rules are broken, the user is shown an error message explaining what went wrong. These controls also let you consolidate your validation rules in a single place, which makes maintaining them a lot simpler. You can see the controls in the Validation section of the Toolbox window, as shown in Figure 17-2.

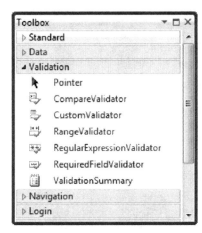

Figure 17-2. *The Web Forms validation controls*

When you use a validation control, you position it where you want the error message to appear. Usually, this is somewhere close to the form element where the user will enter the data , which is the TextBox control in our example.

As a quick demonstration of using the validation controls, Listing 17-4 shows how to apply validation to one of the TextBox controls in the markup for Default.aspx.

Listing 17-4. *Using validation controls*

```
...
<form id="form1" runat="server">
<div>
<asp:Label ID="Label1" runat="server" Text="Laps:" CssClass="label"/>
<asp:TextBox ID="TextBox1" runat="server"></asp:TextBox>
<asp:RangeValidator ID="RangeValidator1" runat="server"
  ControlToValidate="TextBox1"
        ErrorMessage="Enter a number of laps between 1 and 200"
        MaximumValue="200"
        MinimumValue="1"
        Type="Integer"
        CssClass="validation"
        Display="Dynamic"/>
```

```
<asp:RequiredFieldValidator ID="RequiredFieldValidator1" runat="server"
  ControlToValidate="TextBox1"
        ErrorMessage="Enter a number of laps"
        CssClass="validation"
        Display="Dynamic"/>
</div>
...
```

There is a lot happening in these two elements, so let's break things down bit by bit. First, the fact there *are* two elements is important. We can apply multiple validation controls to the same input control. The two validation controls used here are RangeValidator, which ensures that the submitted value is in a specified range, and RequiredFieldValidator, which ensures that the user has supplied a value. A value is considered to be valid only if it passes the rules contained in *all* of the validation controls that have been applied. In this case, the user is required to supply a value *and* that value must be in the defined range.

Validation controls have two essential attributes (we'll come back to the other properties later):

- `ControlToValidate` specifies to which control the validation rules will be applied. For both validation controls, Listing 17-4 specifies `TextBox1`, which is the TextBox control used to gather the number of laps that have been swum.

- `ErrorMessage` is the message that will be displayed to the users if the data they enter fails to meet the rule specified by the validation control.

These validation controls add JavaScript to the page, so that the validation rules are applied at the client when the form is about to be posted or if the focus changes from the TextBox control. If any of the validation rules have been broken, the error message for the appropriate validation control is displayed to the user, and the user won't be able to post the form to the server until the problem has been resolved. Figure 17-3 shows the error messages for the two validation controls in Listing 17-4.

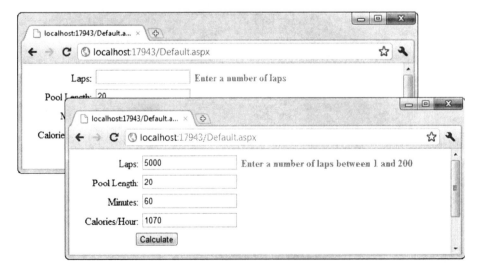

Figure 17-3. *Validation controls displaying their error messages*

Now that you've seen a quick demonstration of how to use validation, we can dig into the details and look at the different options available.

Understanding the Validation Controls

Web Forms includes four core validation controls that you can combine to create validation rules. I say *combine* because most validation rules tend to require more than one validation control to enforce.

As an example, consider the simple example in the previous section. If we had used just the RangeValidator control, the user could pass validation by entering a value between 1 and 200, or without entering any value at all. RangeValidator checks a value only if a user enters one, and so we need to use RequiredFieldValidator as well. Table 17-1 describes the four core validation controls.

Table 17-1. *The Web Forms Validation Controls*

Control	Properties	Description
RequiredFieldValidator	None	Requires that the user has entered a value

CompareValidator	`ValueToCompare`
	`ControlToCompare`
	`Type`
	`Operator`
		Compares the value the user has entered to another control or a specific value

RegularExpressionValidator	`ValidationExpression`	Ensures that the value entered by the user matches the regular expression defined by the `ValidationExpression` property

RangeValidator	`MinimumValue`
	`MaximumValue`
	`Value`
		Ensures that the value entered by the user is within the range bounded by the `MinimumValue` and `MaximumValue` properties

Three of these controls define properties that you use to specify the validation rule. In the following sections, I'll show you each control and demonstrate how these properties are used.

Requiring a Value

The simplest validation control is RequiredFieldValidator. This control does not have any configuration properties. To pass validation, the user only needs to enter a value.

The RequiredFieldValidator control takes no view about the aptness of the data entered, and cares only that there is *something* in the field. You can see an example of this control being used in Listing 17-4.

Accepting a Range of Values

As demonstrated in Listing 17-4, the RangeValidator control ensures that the data entered by the user falls within a specified range. In the example, we required a value between 1 and 200. The `MinimumValue` and `MaximumValue` properties set the inclusive bounds for the range. Here is the markup from the earlier listing:

```
<asp:RangeValidator ID="RangeValidator1" runat="server"
    ControlToValidate="TextBox1"
    ErrorMessage="Enter a number of laps between 1 and 200"
    MaximumValue="200"
    MinimumValue="1"
    Type="Integer"
    CssClass="validation"
    Display="Dynamic" />
```

A common problem with the RangeValidator control is to omit the property I have marked in bold: `Type`. The RangeValidator control doesn't infer the kind of data you are working with from the `MinimumValue` and `MaximumValue` properties, and so you must provide a hint to the control through the `Type` property. If you omit the `Type` property, then the RangeValidator control assumes you are working with strings, and this can lead to some odd results, as shown in Figure 17-4.

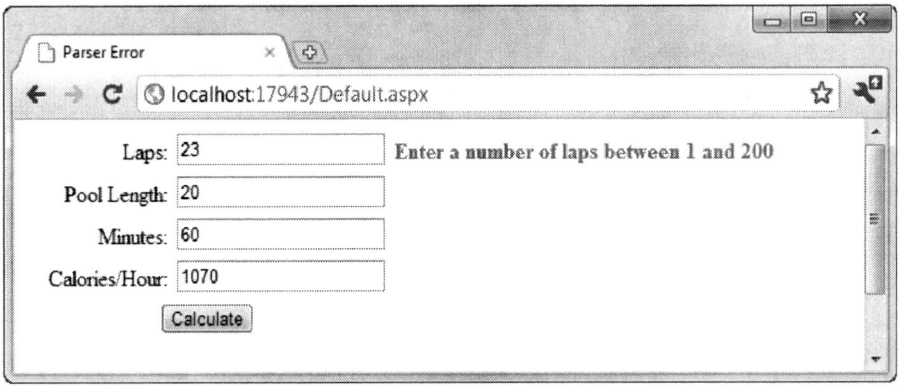

Figure 17-4. *A common error with the RangeValidator control*

You can see that the user has entered a value of 23 into the text box, but is still being shown the error message by the RangeValidator control. As you may have guessed, the validation control is comparing string values alphabetically, and the string `23` is alphabetically greater than the string `200`.

If you every find yourself staring at a range error message like this one, the odds are that you have forgotten to set the `Type` property. (I speak from bitter experience—I *always* forget to set the `Type`, and it *always* takes me a moment to remember this.)

The `Type` property can be set to one of the following values:

- `Currency`
- `Date`
- `Double`
- `Integer`
- `String`

The RangeValidator control tries to convert the data to the specified type before checking whether it falls into the range. If the data cannot be converted, then the error will be displayed. This can cause problems when checking Date ranges. Dates are notoriously difficult to deal with because of the wide range of formats and conventions that are used around the world. A problem can easily arise when the date format used by the server and the date format used by the user are different. There is no good solution to this problem, but at the very least, you should specify the format that you expect the date to be in, such as (*mm/dd/yy* or *dd/mm/yy*) in order to give the user a hint.

■ **Note** The rules defined by validation controls are evaluated independently, which means that you cannot use multiple RangeValidator controls to specify noncontiguous ranges. In order to achieve this effect, you must create a custom validation control. See the "Creating a Custom Validation Function" section later in this chapter for details.

Validating Against a Specific Value

The CompareValidator control allows you to compare the data that the user has entered against a value you have specified. Listing 17-5 shows this validation control applied to the TextBox control that collects the length of the pool from the user in our example.

Listing 17-5. Applying the CompareValidator control

```
...
<div>
<asp:Label ID="Label2" runat="server" Text="Pool Length:" CssClass="label"/>
<asp:TextBox ID="TextBox2" runat="server"></asp:TextBox>
<asp:CompareValidator ID="CompareValidator1" runat="server"
        ControlToValidate="TextBox2"
        ErrorMessage="Enter a value less than 50"
        ValueToCompare="50"
        Operator="LessThan"
        Type="Integer"
        CssClass="validation"/>
</div>
...
```

Once again, we use the ControlToValidate and ErrorMessage properties to specify the Web Forms control we want to work with and the message that will be displayed to the user if validation fails.

The ValueToCompare property lets us provide a value that we want to compare the entered data against, and the Operator property lets us specify how that comparison should be made. This property can be one of the following values:

- Equal

- NotEqual

- GreaterThan

- GreaterThanEqual

- LessThen

- LessThanEqual

- DataTypeCheck

The CompareValidator control tries to convert the data value into the data type specified by the Type property, and then uses the Operator to make the comparison against the value specified by ValueToCompare. When the DataTypeCheck operator is selected, only the conversion to the specified Type value is performed; the ValueToCompare property is ignored. The valid values for the Type property are the same as for the RangeValidator control, as described in the previous section.

■ **Caution** Do not use a CompareValidator control unless you are able to accept and process the full range of data values that will pass validation. For example, in Listing 17-5, we specify that we will accept any value that is less than 50 for the length of the pool, but if you enter -50, you will see some odd results. What we really needed here was a range of 1-50, which we could have achieved using the RangeValidator control.

The CompareValidator control can also be used to compare the value the user has entered to the value in another control, effectively creating a relationship between two controls. Listing 17-6 provides a demonstration.

Listing 17-6. Using the CompareValidator to make comparisons between controls

```
...
<div>
<asp:Label ID="Label2" runat="server" Text="Pool Length:" CssClass="label"/>
<asp:TextBox ID="TextBox2" runat="server"></asp:TextBox>
<asp:CompareValidator ID="CompareValidator1" runat="server"
        ControlToValidate="TextBox2"
        ErrorMessage="Enter a value more than the number of minutes"
        Operator="GreaterThan"
        Type="Integer"
        ControlToCompare="TextBox3"
        CssClass="validation"/>
</div>
...
```

The ControlToCompare property specifies which control we want to reference. In this listing, we have changed the operator, making the validation rule that TextBox2 must contain an integer value that is greater than the value in TextBox3. You can see the effect of this rule in Figure 17-5.

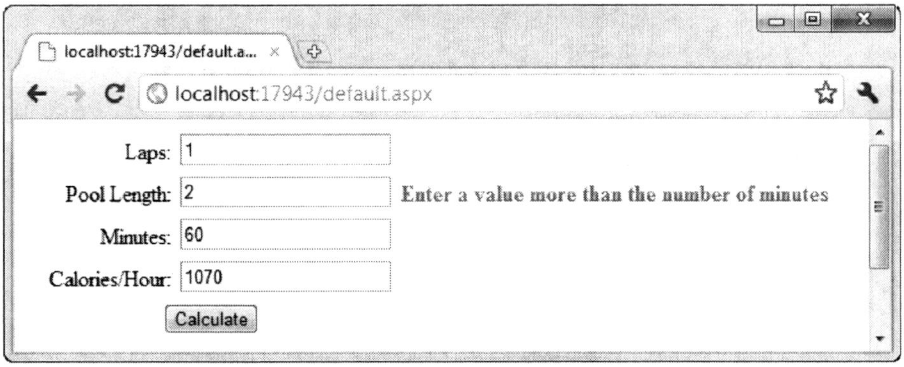

Figure 17-5. *Validating one control based on the contents of another*

Validating Using a Regular Expression

The last of the validation controls, RegularExpressionValidator, lets you validate a data item using a regular expression. Listing 17-7 provides a simple demonstration.

Listing 17-7. *Using the RegularExpressionValidator control*

```
...
<div>
<asp:Label ID="Label4" runat="server" Text="Calories/Hour:" CssClass="label"/>
<asp:TextBox ID="TextBox4" runat="server"></asp:TextBox>
<asp:RegularExpressionValidator ID="RegularExpressionValidator1" runat="server"
    ControlToValidate="TextBox4"
    ErrorMessage="Enter a 4-digit number that starts with 1"
    ValidationExpression="1\d\d\d"
    CssClass="validation"/>
</div>
...
```

As with the other validation controls, the `ControlToValidate` property specifies the control that will be validated, and the `ErrorMessage` property specifies the message to show to the user if validation fails. The RegularExpressionValidator control also defines the `ValidationExpression` property, which specifies the regular expression to match against. The expression we used in the example will match any four-digit number where the first digit is 1.

Styling and Positioning Validation Messages

By default, the HTML that is produced by the validation controls is pretty basic, as shown in Listing 17-8.

Listing 17-8. The HTML generated by a validation control

```
<span id="RequiredFieldValidator1" style="display: none;">Enter a number of laps</span>
```

The error messages are expressed as span elements, and they are hidden from the user initially. If validation changes, then the JavaScript that the validation control adds to the page shows the span element to the user, revealing the error message. You can style the error messages that you display to the user either by setting a value for the CssClass property or by setting individual style properties in the property sheet. For all of the examples so far in this chapter, we have applied the validation CSS class. Listing 17-9 shows the definition of this class.

Listing 17-9. A simple CSS class applied to validation controls

```
.validation
{
    margin:5px;
    font-weight:bold;
    color:Red;
    float:left;
}
```

The CSS properties make sure that the text is displayed along with the other elements on the page and that the errors are clearly shown (in this case, as bold, red text).

Remember that when you add a validation control to the page, you are really selecting where the error message will be displayed. The validation control doesn't need to be placed near the control that is being validated, although that is a common convention.

Using Static and Dynamic Layout

The validation controls implement a property called Display, which can be set to one of three values: None, Static, or Dynamic. This property affects the way that the validation control is laid out when the page is rendered to HTML.

The None value means that the control doesn't display an error message. We'll come back to this option when we look at validation summaries shortly. The Static value means that the validation error takes space on the page, even when no error is being shown to the user. Listing 17-10 shows the HTML generated by a RequiredFieldValidator control using the Static value.

Listing 17-10. HTML rendered by a validation control using the Static value for the Display property

```
<span id="RequiredFieldValidator1" style="visibility:hidden;">Enter a number of laps</span>
```

The Dynamic value uses a different technique to hide the error message, so that it doesn't occupy space on the page until it is shown. You can see the HTML for this setting in Listing 17-11.

Listing 17-11. HTML rendered by a validation control using the Dynamic value for the Display property

```
<span id="RequiredFieldValidator1" style="display:none;">Enter a number of laps</span>
```

The difference in the HTML may be minor, but the effect can be significant, as you can see in Figure 17-6.

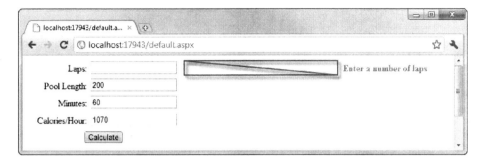

Figure 17-6. *The effect of the Static Display value*

In the figure, there is a validation control that has not been triggered but is still occupying space on the page because it uses the `Static` value. I have outlined the space it uses. A second validation control *is* displaying its error message, but that message is shifted off to the right by the first control. Figure 17-7 shows the same situation, but with the first validation control configured to use the `Dynamic` value instead.

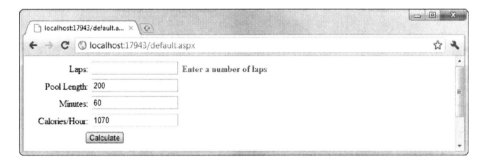

Figure 17-7. *The effect of the Dynamic Display value*

Obviously, the `Dynamic` value makes more sense for the layout of the example application, but this isn't always the case. The value that makes the most sense for a project depends on how you lay out the other controls.

Using a Validation Summary

If the user submits a form with a number of validation issues, the error messages can be overwhelming, as shown in Figure 17-8. Of the four data controls, errors are displayed on three of them. In longer forms, it can be hard to figure out which fields are causing the problem.

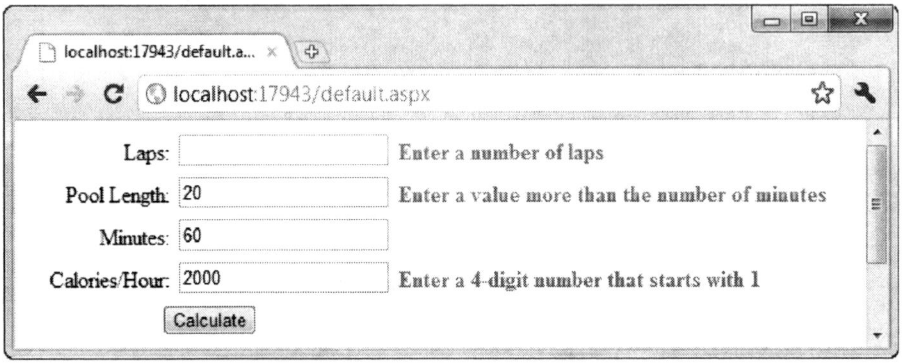

Figure 17-8. *Individual error messages on controls*

An alternative approach is to use a validation summary, which is achieved with the ValidationSummary control, as shown in Listing 17-12.

Listing 17-12. *Using the ValidationSummary control*

```
...
<body>
<form id="form1" runat="server">

<asp:ValidationSummary ID="ValidationSummary1" runat="server"
      HeaderText="Please correct the following errors:"
        ShowMessageBox="False"
        DisplayMode="BulletList"
        ShowSummary="True"
        CssClass="validation" />

<div>
<asp:Label ID="Label1" runat="server" Text="Laps:" CssClass="label"/>
<asp:TextBox ID="TextBox1" runat="server"></asp:TextBox>
<asp:RangeValidator ID="RangeValidator1" runat="server"
          ErrorMessage="Enter a number of laps between 1 and 200"
          ControlToValidate="TextBox1"
          MaximumValue="200"
          MinimumValue="1"
          Type="Integer"
          CssClass="validation"
          Display="Dynamic"/>
<asp:RequiredFieldValidator ID="RequiredFieldValidator1" runat="server"
          ErrorMessage="Enter a number of laps"
          ControlToValidate="TextBox1"
          CssClass="validation"
          Display="Dynamic"/>
</div>
...
```

418

When there are validation errors, they are shown in the ValidationSummary control, which we have positioned at the top of the page, as shown in Figure 17-9.

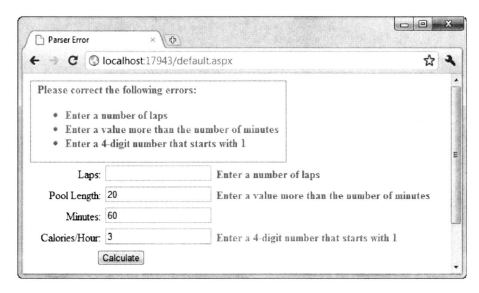

Figure 17-9. *Using the ValidationSummary control*

You don't need to take any steps to associate the ValidationSummary control with the individual validation controls, because Web Forms takes care of this automatically.

Coordinating the Validation Controls and the Validation Summary

Although we have a nice summary at the top of the page, we haven't addressed the fact that the errors are overwhelming. We can do that by setting the Text property of the individual validation controls to an asterisk (*) or similar character. The ErrorMessage property will be displayed in the validation summary, and the value of the Text property will be shown by the control itself. Listing 17-13 shows how to apply this property to a control.

Listing 17-13. Using the ErrorMessage and Text properties together on a validation control

```
<asp:RequiredFieldValidator ID="RequiredFieldValidator1" runat="server"
    ErrorMessage="Enter a number of laps"
    Text="*"
    ControlToValidate="TextBox1"
    CssClass="validation"
    Display="Dynamic"/>
```

The effect of applying this change to all of the validation controls can be seen in Figure 17-10. Now the summary details the problems that the user must address, and the individual controls provide a guide as to where those problems have occurred.

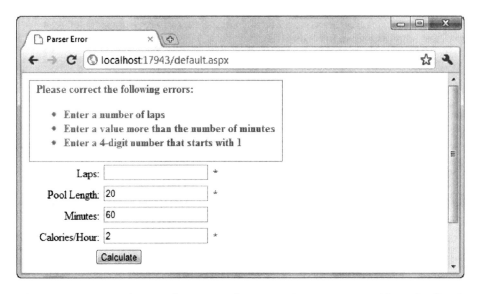

Figure 17-10. Using the Text character to draw attention to an error without duplicating the message

Configuring the ValidationSummary Control

The ValidationSummary control supports a small number of properties, which you can use to alter the way you present validation errors to the user. One of these properties is ShowMessageBox. If you set this property to true, the error messages will be displayed to the user using an alert box, as shown in Figure 17-11.

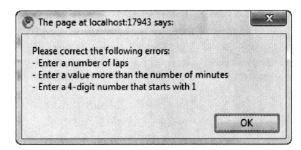

Figure 17-11. Displaying validation errors in an message box

If you use the ShowMessageBox property, you can set ShowSummary to false to prevent the validation errors from being duplicated on the web page; by default, the user will see the errors in both locations.

You can change the way that the summary is displayed on the web page by using the `DisplayMode` property, which can be set to `BulletList`, `List`, or `SingleParagraph`. The effect of the `BulletList` value can be seen in Figure 17-10—each validation error is shown as a bulleted list item. The effect of the `List` value is shown in Figure 17-12. The `SingleParagraph` value displays the validation errors without using a list, as shown in Figure 17-13.

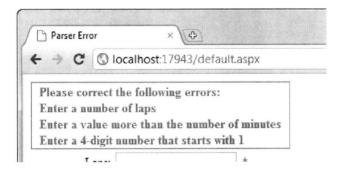

Figure 17-12. *Using the List value for the DisplayMode property*

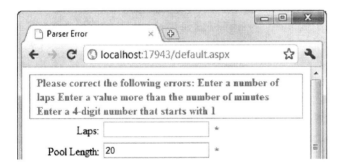

Figure 17-13. *Using the SingleParagraph value for the DisplayMode property*

Using Server-Side Validation

So far, the Web Forms validation support has been remarkably similar to the jQuery validation support demonstrated in Chapter 10. In fact, the Web Forms validation system has a significant advantage, which is that the validation performed using JavaScript on the client is performed again on the server when the user posts the form.

In Chapter 10, I warned you that relying on client-side validation alone is a dangerous thing to do. Not only does this preclude validation when JavaScript is disabled in the browser, but you also make it very easy for someone to forge a request and send you bad data values, causing problems in your application. Figure 17-14 shows the validation at work when JavaScript is disabled in the browser, meaning that the validation was performed by the server. It looks the same as when validation is done in the client.

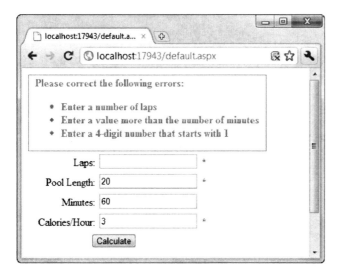

Figure 17-14. *Validation performed at the server*

You don't need to take any additional steps to enable server-side validation. It is done automatically, even when client-side validation has been performed as well—a very useful feature.

▪ **Note** You can disable client-side validation by setting the `EnableClientScript` property to `false` on your validation controls. Validation will not be performed until the form is posted back to the server. This is generally not a good idea, since you lose the immediacy of feedback that client-side validation provides to the user.

If you have looked at the JavaScript added to the page by the validation controls, you will see that it is a mess and nowhere as elegant as the jQuery approach we used in Chapter 10. You might be tempted to rely on the Web Forms validation controls for server-side validation and jQuery to handle client-side validation. You can certainly do this, but it is hard to get consistent results, both in terms of the validation and in the appearance of the error messages displayed to the user. This approach also creates maintenance overhead, so that changes to validation logic must be made in two places. As ugly as the JavaScript emitted by the Web Forms validation controls can be, it is better than the alternative.

The MVC framework, which is described in Part IV of this book, has a much more elegant approach to this problem. Microsoft has hinted that it will follow this model in future versions of Web Forms.

Creating a Custom Validation Function

If the built-in validation controls (shown earlier in Table 17-1) don't match your validation needs, you can create custom validation functions using the CustomValidator control. Listing 17-14 shows the CustomValidator control applied to the TextBox control that collects the number of minutes from the user.

Listing 17-14. Using the CustomValidator control

```
...
<div>
<asp:Label ID="Label3" runat="server" Text="Minutes:" CssClass="label"/>
<asp:TextBox ID="TextBox3" runat="server"></asp:TextBox>
<asp:CustomValidator ID="CustomValidator1" runat="server"
        ControlToValidate="TextBox3"
        ErrorMessage="Enter a whole number of minutes that is less than 50"
        Text="*"
        onservervalidate="CustomValidator1_ServerValidate"
        ClientValidationFunction="CustomValidation"
        CssClass="validation"
        />
</div>
...
```

This custom validation ensures that the value supplied by the user is an integer that is less than 50. This could be achieved using the built-in controls, but it provides a simple example of how to create custom validation logic.

For custom validation, you need to implement your validation logic twice: once in C# so that it can be applied at the server, and once in JavaScript so that it can be applied in the client. You implement server-side validation by handling the `ServerValidate` event, which is called when the form is posted back to the server. Listing 17-15 shows the method used to handle this event in our example, which is defined in the code-behind class for the page that contains the CustomValidator control.

Listing 17-15. Defining custom validation logic by handling the ServerValidate event

```
...
protected void CustomValidator1_ServerValidate(object src, ServerValidateEventArgs args){
    int convertedValue;
    args.IsValid = int.TryParse(args.Value, out convertedValue) && convertedValue < 50;
}
...
```

Our handler method is passed an object representing the source of the event (which is the CustomValidator control) and a `ServerValidateEventArgs` object. We obtain the value that the user has supplied by reading the `ServerValidateEventArgs.Value` property and indicate whether the value passed validation by setting a value for the `ServerValidateEventArgs.IsValid` property. A value of `true` means that the value is valid; `false` means that the value is invalid. In the example, we try to parse the value supplied by the user to an `int`; if that succeeds, then we also check to see that the value is less than 50. We associate our handler method with the event in the usual way: either by using the event list in the Properties window or by manually adding the following to the markup for the CustomValidator control:

```
onservervalidate="CustomValidator1_ServerValidate"
```

If you want to support client-side validation, then you must duplicate your logic in JavaScript. The first step toward client-side validation is to define the validation function. Listing 17-16 shows the script for this example.

Listing 17-16. *Implementing the JavaScript validation function*

```
...
<script type="text/javascript">
    function CustomValidation(oSrc, args) {
        var iVal = parseInt(args.Value);
        args.IsValid = (parseFloat(args.Value) == iVal) && iVal < 50;
    }
</script>
...
```

The JavaScript function is as similar as possible to the C# equivalent. We are passed two parameters that represent the source of the event and the event arguments. We get the value entered by the user through the `args.Value` property, and use the `args.IsValid` property to report on the success of our validation. Checking for integer values in JavaScript is a little different from doing so in C#, but the code in Listing 17-16 should be self-evident.

It doesn't matter where you define the JavaScript function, as long as it will be available in the page. This means that you can share a set of common validation functions by creating a script file or by defining functions in a master page (see Chapter 9 for details about master pages). For this example, we have added the `script` element to the `head` section of `Default.aspx`.

We associate our JavaScript function with the CustomValidator control through the `ClientValidationFunction` property, like this:

```
ClientValidationFunction="CustomValidation"
```

And that's it. We have created custom validation logic, which is applied at both the server and client. You can see the effect of this in Figure 17-15.

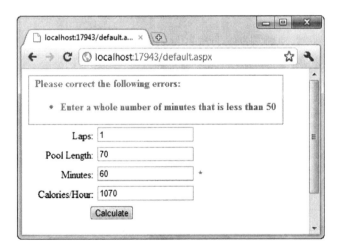

Figure 17-15. *The error message produced by a custom validation control*

Implementing client-side support is optional, but you will confuse the user if you do not implement it but *do* use client validation for other validation controls. This is because some errors will be caught by the client, and then others will be flagged by the server after the form has posted. Anything you can do to make validation as immediate as possible will improve the user's experience and perception of your web application.

Summary

This chapter covered the set of Web Forms controls that support validation. We started with an overview of how validation works and the validation models that the built-in controls provide. We then looked at how to style the error messages displayed to the user and how to group messages together using a validation summary. We finished by implementing some custom validation logic that can be applied at both the client and the server.

CHAPTER 18

Using Web Forms Data Sources

One of the key strengths of Web Forms is the ease with which you can display and manipulate data in a web application. In this chapter, we are going to look at one of the key enablers for the Web Forms data features: *data sources*.

You use data sources to being data into your application. Web Forms includes some built-in data source controls to make this a simple process for a wide range of data types. You can work as easily with objects created in memory as you can with those in SQL databases. I'll introduce the most useful data source controls and also demonstrate how to work without them to get some advanced results.

A Quick Example of Using Data Source Controls

You need three items to work with the Web Forms data controls: some data, a data source control, and a data-bound UI control.

To begin, create a new Visual Studio project named WebApp using the Empty ASP.NET Application template and add a new Web Form called Default.aspx. All of the examples in this chapter will be added to this page.

Creating the Data

You can use a range of different data types with Web Forms, but we are going to start with the simplest—some objects contained in a class. In the code-behind file, Default.aspx.cs, define a new data type called Fruit and create an array of Fruit objects in the Default code-behind class, as shown in Listing 18-1.

Listing 18-1. Creating some data

```
using System;

namespace WebApp {

    public class Fruit {
        public string Name { get; set; }
        public string Color { get; set; }
    }
```

```
public partial class Default : System.Web.UI.Page {
    public Fruit[] FruitDataArray = new[] {
        new Fruit() {Name = "Apple", Color = "Green"},
        new Fruit() {Name = "Banana", Color = "Yellow"},
        new Fruit() {Name = "Cherry", Color = "Red"},
        new Fruit() {Name = "Plum", Color = "Red"}
    };

    protected void Page_Load(object sender, EventArgs e) {

    }
}
}
```

The Fruit class defines two public properties: Name and Color. The Default class defines an array of Fruit objects called FruitDataArray, which we have populated with details of some example fruits.

Creating the Data Source

When we use the term *data source control*, we are really referring to a special kind of Web Forms control that acts as an adapter between a particular kind of data and a data-bound Web Forms UI control. As you'll see later, there are different kinds of data sources available to deal with different kinds of data. For this example, we will use the LinqDataSource control. One of the features of this control is that it can work with arrays of objects, such as the one we created in the code-behind class.

You can create the control by dragging it from the Visual Studio Toolbox to the design surface or source window. The data source controls, including LinqDataSource, can be found in the Data section. Drop the control so that it appears between the body tags. Your markup should look similar to Listing 18-2.

Listing 18-2. Adding a LinqDataSource control to a page

```
<%@ Page Language="C#" AutoEventWireup="true" CodeBehind="Default.aspx.cs"
Inherits="WebApp.Default" %>

<!DOCTYPE html PUBLIC "-//W3C//DTD XHTML 1.0 Transitional//EN"
  "http://www.w3.org/TR/xhtml1/DTD/xhtml1-transitional.dtd">

<html xmlns="http://www.w3.org/1999/xhtml">
<head runat="server">
<title>Data Demo</title>
</head>
<body>
<form id="form1" runat="server">
<div>

</div>
</form>
```

```
<asp:LinqDataSource ID="LinqDataSource1" runat="server">
</asp:LinqDataSource>
</body>
</html>
```

It doesn't matter where you place the control, but I tend to put mine at the bottom of the page so that my data sources are somewhat apart from my UI controls.

After you have created the data source, you must configure it. You can do this directly from the markup, but for this example, we are going to use the nice UI available from the design surface.

Select the data source in the design surface, click the small arrow that appears, and then select Configure Data Source from the menu, as shown in Figure 18-1.

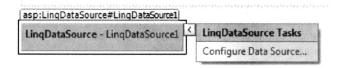

Figure 18-1. *Choosing to configure the data source*

The Configure Data Source wizard opens, as shown in Figure 18-2. From this first screen, you select the source of the data. The same wizard is used in different situations, so the terminology doesn't make complete sense when working with a set of objects defined in a class.

Figure 18-2. *Starting the Configure Data Source wizard*

Note If you don't see any entries in the drop-down menu, cancel the wizard, rebuild the project, and start configuring the data source control again.

The Choose your context object menu contains a list of data sources that the current control can support. In our case, we can choose from two items, which represent the two classes we have defined in the project so far: `WebApp.Default` and `WebApp.Fruit`. These are the fully qualified names of the classes. We called the example project `WebApp` when we created it, so Visual Studio automatically assigned the classes to the `WebApp` namespace. Select `WebApp.Default` (which is where we defined the array of `Fruit` objects), and then click the Next button.

The next screen, shown in Figure 18-3, lets us select the data and the fields that we want to work with. The LinqDataSource control applies a LINQ query to an enumeration of C# objects. The Table drop-down menu shows a list of all the suitable enumerations that were found in the `Default` class. Select `FruitDataArray` to work with the data we defined earlier.

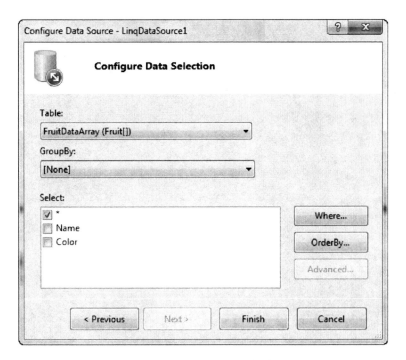

Figure 18-3. *Selecting the data and the data fields*

The Select area displays the fields available in the selected data. Our example object has only the `Name` and `Color` properties. Check the * option, as shown in Figure 18-3, to include both of these in the data source. The GroupBy menu and the Where and OrderBy buttons allow you to filter the data, which we'll discuss later in the chapter. For the moment, ignore these options. Click the Finish button to complete the setup of the data source control. The markup in the source window will be updated, as shown in Listing 18-3.

Listing 18-3. *The effect of using the Configure Data Source wizard on the data source control*

```
...
<asp:LinqDataSource ID="LinqDataSource1" runat="server"
    ContextTypeName="WebApp.Default"
    EntityTypeName=""
    TableName="FruitDataArray">
</asp:LinqDataSource>
...
```

We now have the data and the data source. The data source control can act as a bridge between the data defined in the `Default` class and one of the Web Forms data-bound UI controls.

Creating the UI Control

One of the nice features of Web Forms is the number of controls that are data-bound, including some of the controls introduced in Chapter 15. This means that you can take some pretty basic controls and associate them with a data source so that their contents are derived from your data.

As a simple example, we will use the DropDownList control. Drag the control from the Toolbox window to the design surface or to the source window, so that the markup of the page looks like Listing 18-4.

Listing 18-4. *Adding a DropDownList control to the page*

```
<%@ Page Language="C#" AutoEventWireup="true" CodeBehind="Default.aspx.cs"
Inherits="WebApp.Default" %>

<!DOCTYPE html PUBLIC "-//W3C//DTD XHTML 1.0 Transitional//EN"
 "http://www.w3.org/TR/xhtml1/DTD/xhtml1-transitional.dtd">

<html xmlns="http://www.w3.org/1999/xhtml">
<head runat="server">
<title>Data Demo</title>
</head>
<body>

<form id="form1" runat="server">
<div>
<asp:DropDownList ID="DropDownList1" runat="server">
</asp:DropDownList>
</div>
</form>
```

```
<asp:LinqDataSource ID="LinqDataSource1" runat="server"
        ContextTypeName="WebApp.Default" EntityTypeName="" TableName="FruitDataArray">
</asp:LinqDataSource>
</body>
</html>
```

Select the DropDownList control on the design surface, click the arrow that appears, and select Choose Data Source from the pop-up menu, as shown in Figure 18-4. This opens the Data Source Configuration wizard, which allows you to select the data source control and data fields to use in the UI control, as shown in Figure 18-5.

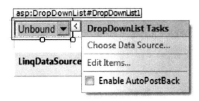

Figure 18-4. Choosing to configure a UI control

Figure 18-5. Selecting the data source and data fields

We have added only one data source control to our page, so the menu for the Select a data source option contains only one item. It also contains an option to create a new data source. I like to create the data source and then the UI control, but you can do it the other way around if you prefer.

For a DropDownList control, you need to select two values: the field to display to the user and the field that will be selected as the value. Since we have only two fields in our `Fruit` class, select `Name` for the display field and `Color` for the value field. (Note that you can use the same field for both options.) Click the OK button to dismiss the wizard. The markup will be updated as shown in Listing 18-5.

Listing 18-5. *The markup for a data-bound DropDownList control*

```
<%@ Page Language="C#" AutoEventWireup="true" CodeBehind="Default.aspx.cs"
Inherits="WebApp.Default" %>

<!DOCTYPE html PUBLIC "-//W3C//DTD XHTML 1.0 Transitional//EN"
 "http://www.w3.org/TR/xhtml1/DTD/xhtml1-transitional.dtd">

<html xmlns="http://www.w3.org/1999/xhtml">
<head runat="server">
<title>Data Demo</title>
</head>
<body>
<form id="form1" runat="server">
<div>

<asp:DropDownList ID="DropDownList1" runat="server"
          DataSourceID="LinqDataSource1"
          DataTextField="Name"
          DataValueField="Color">
</asp:DropDownList>
</div>
</form>
<asp:LinqDataSource ID="LinqDataSource1" runat="server"
        ContextTypeName="WebApp.Default" EntityTypeName="" TableName="FruitDataArray">
</asp:LinqDataSource>
</body>
</html>
```

We have now bound the UI control to the data source control. If you view the `Default.aspx` page in a browser, you will see a drop-down list populated with the names of our fruit, as shown in Figure 18-6.

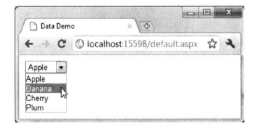

Figure 18-6. *A data-bound drop-down list*

If you look at the HTML that the browser is displaying, you can see how Web Forms has mapped the data we defined when the control was rendered, as shown in Listing 18-6.

Listing 18-6. *The HTML rendered by a data-bound DropDownList control*

```
...
<select name="DropDownList1" id="DropDownList1">
<option value="Green">Apple</option>
<option value="Yellow">Banana</option>
<option value="Red">Cherry</option>
<option value="Red">Plum</option>
</select>...
```

You can see what I meant when I said how easy it is to add data to a Web Forms application. Admittedly, the example in this section is pretty simple, but as you will see, the basic pattern remains the same even when you're working with more complex data and controls.

Working with Data Sources

Web Forms includes a set of data source controls that operate on a range of different types of data. This range runs from simple collections of .NET objects through to the Entity Framework. The complete set is described in Table 18-1.

Table 18-1. *Web Forms Data Source Controls*

Control	Description
AccessDataSource	Operates on Microsoft Access databases
EntityDataSource	Operates on Entity Framework data contexts
LinqDataSource	Acts as a bridge between LINQ and LINQ data objects
ObjectDataSource	Uses .NET reflection to support third-party business object systems
SiteMapDataSource	Operates on ASP.NET site maps (see Chapter 15 for examples)
SqlDataSource	Operates on a SQL database using ADO.NET
XmlDataSource	Operates on an XML document

For our purposes, three of these controls are particularly interesting: LinqDataSource, SqlDataSource, and EntityDataSource. We'll start with EntityDataSource because it provides a simple mechanism for achieving a very common goal: integrating data from a database into a web application.

The other data sources are perfectly functional, but the ones I describe are the most likely to be useful in projects. I'll show you how to use the XmlDataSource control in Chapter 19, although I find it easier to work with XML using the technique described in this chapter, relying on LINQ. The SiteMapDataSource control was covered in Chapter 15.

Using the Entity Framework Data Source

In Chapter 8, you saw how to use the Entity Framework to access a SQL Server database. As you will recall, the Entity Framework lets you work with databases without needing to write SQL code. Instead, you use .NET objects, which is a more natural mechanism when writing C# applications.

The EntityDataSource control is the Web Forms data source control for working with the Entity Framework. To demonstrate using this control, we will use the `TrainingData` database from Chapter 8. Before we can start, we need to create the Entity Framework context. To do this, turn to Chapter 8 and follow the instructions for creating the data model.

Once the Entity Framework data model has been added to the project, we can use the EntityDataSource control. Drag the control to the source window, and you will see markup similar to that shown in Listing 18-7.

Listing 18-7. *Adding an EntityDataSource control to a page*

```
<%@ Page Language="C#" AutoEventWireup="true" CodeBehind="Default.aspx.cs"
Inherits="WebApp.Default" %>

<!DOCTYPE html PUBLIC "-//W3C//DTD XHTML 1.0 Transitional//EN"
 "http://www.w3.org/TR/xhtml1/DTD/xhtml1-transitional.dtd">

<html xmlns="http://www.w3.org/1999/xhtml">
<head runat="server">
<title>Data Demo</title>
</head>
<body>

<form id="form1" runat="server">
<div>

</div>
</form>
<asp:EntityDataSource ID="EntityDataSource1" runat="server">
</asp:EntityDataSource>
</body>
</html>
```

For this example, we've removed the LinqDataSource and DropDownList controls from the page to avoid confusion.

Next, select the new data source on the design surface, click the arrow that appears, and select Configure Data Source. If you have followed the instructions in Chapter 8, when the Configure Data Source wizard starts, you will have an entry available under the Name Connection menu. This is the database connection string that was added to the `Web.config` file. Select that connection string, and the value for the `DefaultContainerName` will be updated to `TrainingDataEntities`, which is the name of the data model that we created. Figure 18-7 shows the entries. Click Next to continue.

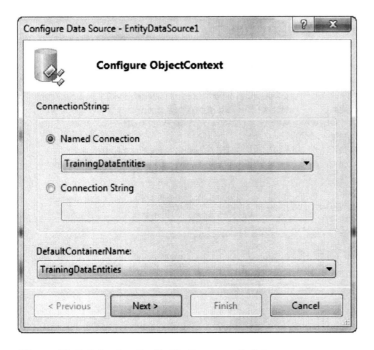

Figure 18-7. Selecting the Entity Framework data source

The wizard to will move to the screen for configuring the data selection. The EntitySetName drop-down menu lists all of the entity types that are available, and these correspond to the objects we created to represent the tables in the database in Chapter 8: Athletes, Events, EventTypes, and ReferenceTimes. Select the Athletes option, and the main part of the display will be populated with the properties of the Athlete class that the Entity Framework created for us, as shown in Figure 18-8.

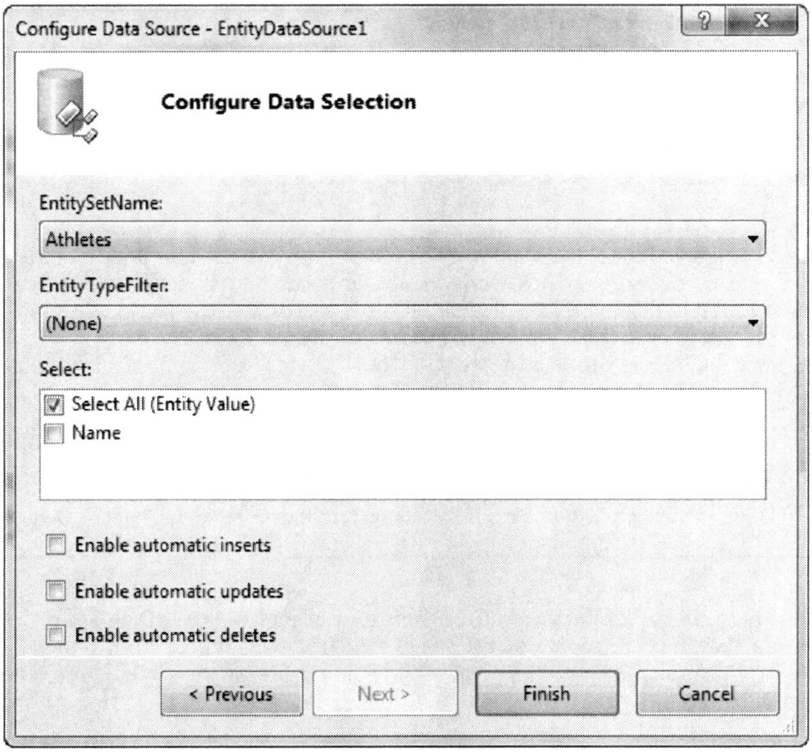

Figure 18-8. *Selecting the entities and properties used in the data source*

We can choose all of the properties or be more selective and check only those items we want to display on the page. There is only one property in the Athlete class, so it doesn't make any difference in this example, but in general, you should select only the properties that are required for the display to minimize the amount of data that is loaded.

Click Finish to dismiss the wizard and update the markup for the data source control, as shown in Listing 18-8.

Listing 18-8. *The configured EntityDataSource control*

```
...
<body>

<form id="form1" runat="server">
<div>

</div>
</form>
```

```
<asp:EntityDataSource ID="EntityDataSource1" runat="server"
       ConnectionString="name=TrainingDataEntities"
       DefaultContainerName="TrainingDataEntities" EnableFlattening="False"
       EntitySetName="Athletes">
</asp:EntityDataSource>

</body>
...
```

Once you have created and configured the EntityDataSource control, you can use it to populate the contents of a data-bound control as we did previously. Given the tabular nature of databases, the EntityDataSource control is often used to display data in a grid (I'll show you how to use a grid in the "Using the LINQ Data Source" section later in the chapter). For this example, we'll use the DropDownList control again, since it suits the simple `Athlete` data set.

■ **Tip**   Some of the Web Forms data controls support features that work only when the data in the data source is sorted. To enable sorting on an EntityDataSource control, set the `AutoGenerateWhereClause` property to `true`.

Drag a DropDownList control from the Toolbox, click the arrow, and select Configure Data Source from the pop-up menu. Using the Select a data source menu, select the EntityDataSource control that we just created, and select the `Name` property for both the display and value fields, as shown in Figure 18-9. Click OK to dismiss the wizard.

Figure 18-9. *Selecting the data properties for the control*

If you prefer to work directly with the markup, then you need to add the element shown in Listing 18-9.

Listing 18-9. *Configuring a DropDownList control to work with an EntityDataSource*

```
<form id="form1" runat="server">
<div>
<asp:DropDownList ID="DropDownList1" runat="server"
        DataSourceID="EntityDataSource1" DataTextField="Name" DataValueField="Name">
</asp:DropDownList>
</div>
</form>
```

When you view the page that contains these controls, you see a drop-down list populated with the values taken from the `Athletes` table in the database.

Using the SQL Data Source

The `SqlDataSource` control accesses data from a relational database using SQL directly. I like working with the Entity Framework, but if you prefer SQL, then this is the data source for you. In this section, I'll show you how to set up a `SqlDataSource` control to query the `TrainingData` database.

Start by dragging a SqlDataSource control from the Toolbox to the design surface, clicking the arrow button, and selecting Configure Data Source from the pop-up menu. You will see the dialog shown in Figure 18-10. Select a connection from the drop-down list or create a new one using the New Connection dialog. In the figure, I have selected the `TrainingData` database, which is running on my database server, `Titan`. One you have selected or configured your connection, click the Next button to continue.

Figure 18-10. *Selecting the data connection*

Next, you can choose to save the connection string for the database in the `Web.config` file for your project or as a property of the SqlDataSource control in the page. I recommend choosing the `Web.config` option, as shown in Figure 18-11, because it makes deployment to a production server easier. We'll cover this in more detail in Chapter 33. Click the Next button to move to the next page.

Figure 18-11. *Saving the connection string*

You can now select the table or store procedure that will generate the data for the data source. For this example, select the `Athletes` table, as shown in Figure 18-12.

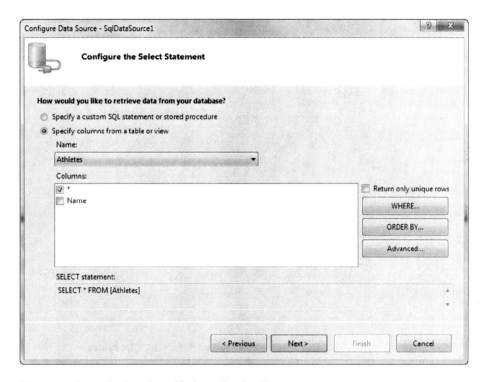

Figure 18-12. *Selecting the table from the database*

Some of the data controls introduced in Chapters 19 and 20 support features that work only when the data in the data source is sorted. To enable this, click the ORDER BY button to open the Add ORDER BY Clause dialog. Select the field that the data should be sorted by, as shown in Figure 18-13, and then click OK to return to the wizard.

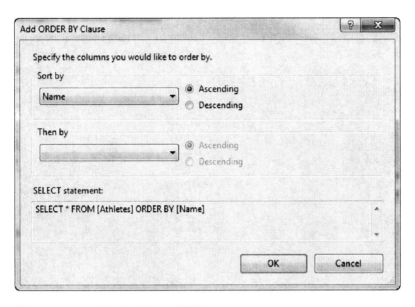

Figure 18-13. *Selecting the sort field*

Clicking the WHERE button opens a dialog that allows you to filter the data in the table. Some of the data controls support editing data. To implement this feature, you must click the Advanced button and check the option to create `INSERT`, `UPDATE`, and `DELETE` statements, as shown in Figure 18-14. Click the OK button to return to the wizard.

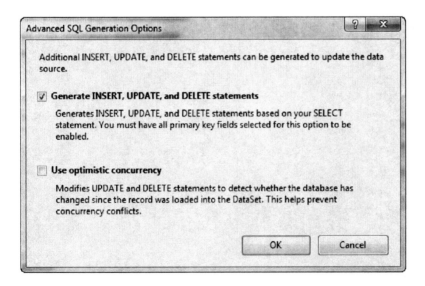

Figure 18-14. *Generating the SQL statements required to modify data*

Now, click the Next button to advance to the next screen. At this point, you can test the query that that will be used to retrieve data from the database.

Once you are satisfied that everything is OK, click the Finish button to close the wizard and update the markup for the data source. Listing 18-10 shows the markup that was generated.

Listing 18-10. *The markup for a SqlDataSource control*

```
<asp:SqlDataSource ID="SqlDataSource1" runat="server"
    ConnectionString="<%$ ConnectionStrings:TrainingDataConnectionString %>"
    DeleteCommand="DELETE FROM [Athletes] WHERE [Name] = @Name"
    InsertCommand="INSERT INTO [Athletes] ([Name]) VALUES (@Name)"
    SelectCommand="SELECT * FROM [Athletes] ORDER BY [Name]">
<DeleteParameters>
<asp:Parameter Name="Name" Type="String" />
</DeleteParameters>
<InsertParameters>
<asp:Parameter Name="Name" Type="String" />
</InsertParameters>
</asp:SqlDataSource>
```

After configuring the SqlDataSource control, you can use it in the same way as we used the EntitySourceControl control earlier. For example, here is the markup to populate a DropDownList control with the data from the database:

```
<asp:DropDownList ID="DropDownList2" runat="server"
    DataSourceID="SqlDataSource1" DataTextField="Name"
    DataValueField="Name" AutoPostBack="True">
</asp:DropDownList>
```

You need to change only the value of the DataSourceID property. The data source system abstracts all of the other differences away.

Using the LINQ Data Source

You already saw the LinqDataSource control in action at the start of the chapter, but this is a very flexible control that can do a lot more than process a set of .NET objects. In this section, you'll see some of the other uses of this control.

Before we get started, you should know that I *love* LINQ, the .NET Language Integrated Query feature. I think it is one of the best features of the .NET Framework, and it is a key reason I write in C#. If you are not familiar with LINQ, then I suggest you read the book I wrote with Joe Rattz, *Pro LINQ: Language Integrated Query in C# 2010* (Apress, 2010).

The LinqDataSource control provides a way to apply LINQ to any LINQ-compatible data source. LINQ likes to work with strongly typed IEnumerable sequences, and so any such sequence is valid data for the LinqDataSource control.

Populating a List Box with Data from a Database Table

One of the ways that you can use LINQ is to query an Entity Framework data model, just as we did using the EntityDataSource control previously. To demonstrate this, we are going to populate a UI control with data from the Events database table, via the data model we created earlier.

Start by dragging a LinqDataSource control from the Toolbox to the design surface, clicking the arrow button, and selecting Configure Data Source from the pop-up menu. Our project now contains an Entity Framework data model, and the LinqDataSource control detects the classes that the model created and puts them in the drop-down menu, as shown in Figure 18-15.

Figure 18-15. *Selecting the Entity Framework class*

We don't want to use the individual entity classes. These don't contain any data that the LinqDataSource control can work with because they are just the definitions of the set of properties that correspond to the columns in each underlying database table. Instead, we want the WebApp.TrainingDataEntities item, which is at the bottom of the list. This class contains sequences of entity objects that represent the data in the database. After choosing this item, click Next.

Once again, you can choose the type and properties that you want to work with, For this example, select Events from the Table drop-down list, and leave the GroupBy menu set to None. Select the Date, OverallTime, and Type properties, as shown in Figure 18-16.

Figure 18-16. *Selecting the database table*

Because we are dealing with LINQ, we can query and filter the data. For this example, click the Where button. This displays the dialog shown in Figure 18-17, where you can select data records that match filters you define. In the figure, I have created a filter that will select only `Event` objects where the `Athlete` property is `Adam Freeman`. To do this, select `Athlete` from the Column menu, the equality operator (==) from the Operator menu, and None from the Source menu (we'll come back to the Source menu in a moment). When you select None, the Value text box appears. Enter `Adam Freeman` and click the Add button. This adds the `where` clause to the LINQ expression. Click the OK button to dismiss the dialog.

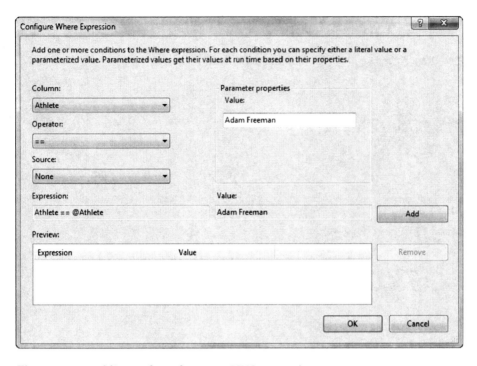

Figure 18-17. *Adding a where clause to a LINQ expression*

Click the Finish button to close the wizard and update the control markup, which is shown in Listing 18-11.

Listing 18-11. *The markup for a LinqDataSource that uses a where clause*

```
...
<body>

<form id="form1" runat="server">
<div>
<asp:DropDownList ID="DropDownList1" runat="server"
            DataSourceID="EntityDataSource1" DataTextField="Name" DataValueField="Name">
</asp:DropDownList>
</div>
</form>

<asp:EntityDataSource ID="EntityDataSource1" runat="server"
        ConnectionString="name=TrainingDataEntities"
        DefaultContainerName="TrainingDataEntities" EnableFlattening="False"
        EntitySetName="Athletes">
</asp:EntityDataSource>
```

```
<asp:LinqDataSource ID="LinqDataSource1" runat="server"
        ContextTypeName="WebApp.TrainingDataEntities" EntityTypeName="" TableName="Events"
        Where="Athlete == @Athlete"
Select="new (Date, Type, OverallTime)">
<WhereParameters>
<asp:Parameter DefaultValue="Adam Freeman" Name="Athlete" Type="String" />
</WhereParameters>
</asp:LinqDataSource>
</body>
...
```

We've left the other controls on the page this time, because we are going to use them again later. Notice that you can have multiple data source controls happily coexisting in the same page. In this case, both controls use the same underlying database, but this does not need to be the case, and you can bring data from a wide range of data sources into a page.

You can see how our selections in the configuration wizard are reflected in LINQ-like additions to the markup. We selected specific properties from the Event class, and they appear in a Select attribute like this:

```
Select="new (Date, Type, OverallTime)"
```

The where clause we defined appears in a Where attribute like this:

```
Where="Athlete == @Athlete"
```

The @Athlete reference is to the WhereParameters element, which contains a corresponding Parameter element, like this:

```
<asp:Parameter DefaultValue="Adam Freeman" Name="Athlete" Type="String" />
```

You can see the LINQ query in the attributes of the LinqDataSource element. To use this query, we need to add a UI control. This time, we will use the ListView control. Drag a ListView from the Toolbox to the design surface, click the arrow, and select LinqDataSource1 from the Choose Data Source drop-down menu, as shown in Figure 18-18.

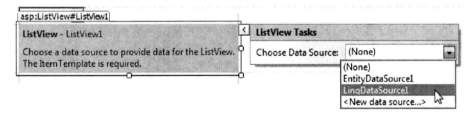

Figure 18-18. Selecting a data source for the ListView control

As soon as LinqDataSource1 is selected from the list, the contents of the pop-up menu change to those shown in Figure 18-19.

447

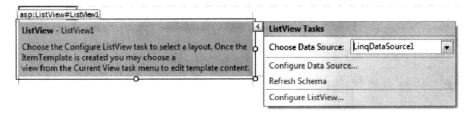

Figure 18-19. *The updated pop-up menu*

Click the Configure ListView item to open the Configure ListView dialog, as shown in Figure 18-20. The ListView control won't work until you tell it how to display the data, which you do through this window. The Select a Layout list shows the different ways that the ListView control can display data, and the Select a Style list shows some built-in styles that can be applied to the data.

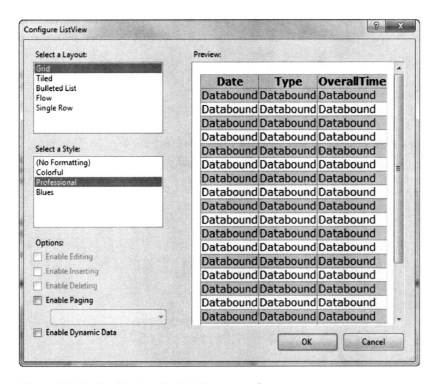

Figure 18-20. *Configuring the ListView control*

We are going to use the Grid layout and the Professional formatting option. Make sure these are selected, and then click the OK button. Ignore the Enable Paging and Enable Dynamic Data options; we won't be using these.

After you close the Configure ListView dialog, the markup for the ListView control will be updated. A lot of new elements are added. The ListView control works using a set of templates, and they require a number of elements to express.

Viewing the Default.aspx page in the browser shows the result of our configuration, which is a list of all of the records from the Events database table where the value of the Athlete column/property is Adam Freeman, as shown in Figure 18-21.

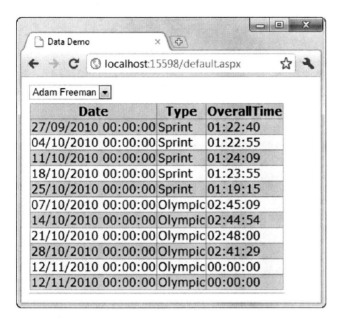

Figure 18-21. Showing data in a ListView control that has been obtained from a LinqDataSource

---

■ **Tip**   You can change the appearance of a ListView control using the templates it defines. See Chapter 16 for more information about the control template system.

Obtaining a LINQ Query Parameter from Another Control

Our page now contains a DropDownList control that shows the set of Athlete names, and a ListView that displays the details of events performed by a specified athlete. Using the magic of the LinqDataSource control, we can easily connect the drop-down menu and the list, so that we can select whose events are displayed.

To do this, select the LinqDataSource control on the design surface, click the arrow, and select Configure Data Source from the pop-up menu. Click the Next button to skip over selecting the source of the data and arrive at the screen where you select properties and define clauses. Click the Where button to open the Configure Where Expression dialog.

First of all, we need to delete the existing `where` clause. Select the `Athlete==@Athlete` expression from the list at the bottom of the page and click the Remove button. We now have an empty `where` clause.

To add the new `where` clause, select `Athlete` from the Column menu. This is the entity class property that we want to use. Select the equality operator (`==`) from the Operator menu. This is the comparison we require. Select Control from the Source menu. This is where we deviate from our previous `where` clause. Instead of defining a static value, we are telling the LinqDataSource control that we want it to get a value from another control on the same page. Select `DropDownList1` from the Control ID menu, and enter `Adam Freeman` in the Default Value field. This is the value that will be used when no value is available from the other control. Figure 18-22 shows the completed configuration.

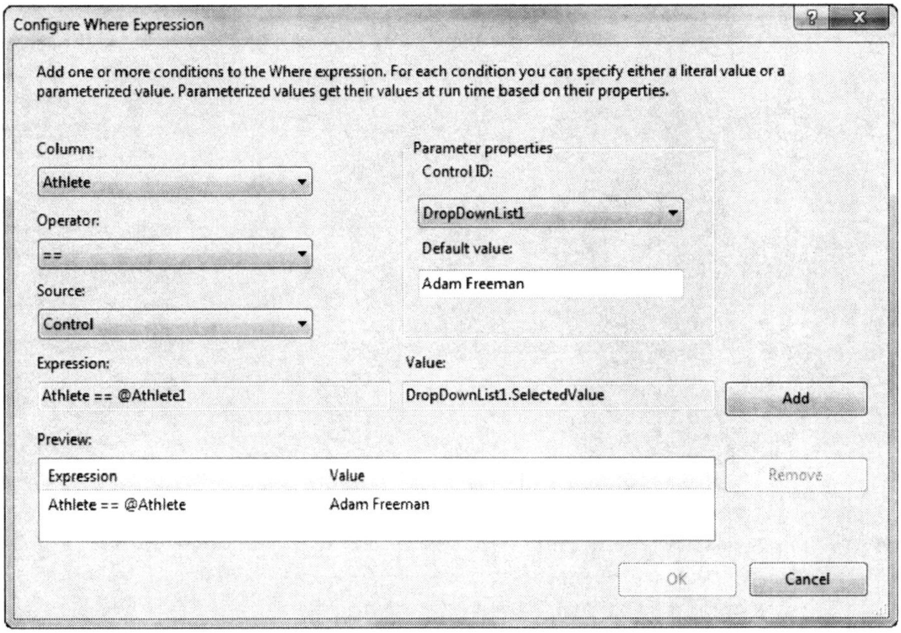

Figure 18-22. Adding a control-derived where clause to a LinqDataSource

Click the Add button to create the `where` clause, click the OK button to close the Configure Where Expression dialog, and then click Finish to close the Configure Data Source wizard. The updated markup for the LinqDataSource control is shown in Listing 18-12.

Listing 18-12. Obtaining a value from another control in a LinqDataSource

```
...
<asp:LinqDataSource ID="LinqDataSource1" runat="server"
    ContextTypeName="WebApp.TrainingDataEntities" EntityTypeName="" TableName="Events"
    Where="Athlete == @Athlete1"
    Select="new (Date, Type, OverallTime)">
<WhereParameters>
```

```
<asp:ControlParameter ControlID="DropDownList1" DefaultValue="Adam Freeman"
        Name="Athlete1" PropertyName="SelectedValue" Type="String" />
</WhereParameters>
</asp:LinqDataSource>
```
...

We need to do one more thing to make this work, and that is to enable the **AutoPostBack** feature on the DropDownList control so that when we select a new value, the page will be updated and rendered using the new data. Here is the addition to the markup for the control:

```
<asp:DropDownList ID="DropDownList1" runat="server"
    DataSourceID="EntityDataSource1" DataTextField="Name"
    DataValueField="Name" AutoPostBack="True">
</asp:DropDownList>
```

Once these changes are in place, you can select a name in the drop-down list, and the events that person has participated in will be displayed in the list, as shown in Figure 18-23.

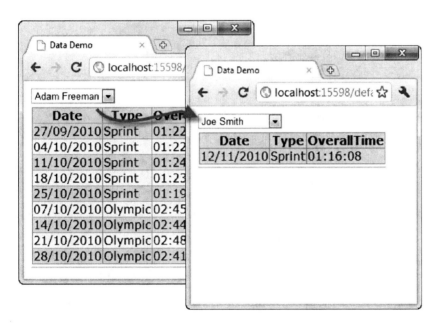

Figure 18-23. *Changing the contents of a ListView control by changing a property in the data source*

As an aside, I cheated slightly to create the HTML displayed in Figure 18-23. By default, the ListView control displays dates in their full format, such as 28/10/2010 00:00:00. In order to get to the short date format, I replaced all the instances of this tag:

```
<%# Eval("Date") %>
```

with this one:

```
<%# Eval("Date", "{0:d}") %>
```

in the templates for the `ListView` control. This causes the value of the date to be formatted using the short date template. You'll learn more about the data controls and their appearance in Chapters 19 and 20.

Using LINQ Queries As Data Sources

The `LinqDataSource` control supports only the basic LINQ clauses, such as `select`, `where`, and `orderby`. As I mentioned earlier, the `LinqDataSource` control will operate on any strongly typed `IEnumerable` sequence. One consequence of this is the ability to use the results from LINQ queries defined in code as the source for the data. Listing 18-13 shows a LINQ query defined in the `Default.aspx.cs` code-behind file.

Listing 18-13. *Defining a LINQ query*

```
using System;
using System.Collections.Generic;
using System.Linq;

namespace WebApp {

    public partial class Default : System.Web.UI.Page {
        public IEnumerable<LinqWrapper> AthleteNames
                = new TrainingDataEntities().Events
                    .Select(ev => new LinqWrapper() { Name = ev.Athlete });

        protected void Page_Load(object src, EventArgs e) {

        }
    }

    public class LinqWrapper {
        public string Name { get; set; }
    }
}
```

The `AthleteNames` field contains the results of a LINQ query to the Entity Framework data model that selects all of the `Athlete` properties from the `Event` entity objects. We can use this field as the data for a LinqDataSource control, which can in turn populate the DropDownList control. At the moment, this query doesn't do anything that we couldn't achieve using the LinqDataSource control directly on the data model, but bear with me for a moment. There are some problems in the listing, which I will point out after we finish the setup.

Add a new LinqDataSource control to the page, click the arrow, and select Configure Data Source. Choose `WebApp.Default` as the context object on the first page of the wizard, and select `AthleteNames` from the Table menu on the second page. Click Finish to close the wizard and update the markup, which should be as shown in Listing 18-14.

Listing 18-14. Creating a LinqDataSource that is backed by a LINQ query

```
...
<asp:LinqDataSource ID="LinqDataSource2" runat="server"
    ContextTypeName="WebApp.Default" EntityTypeName="" TableName="AthleteNames">
</asp:LinqDataSource>
...
```

To associate the new LinqDataSource control with the list, select the DropDownList control on the design surface, click the arrow, and select Choose Data Source from the pop-up menu. Select the new data source control from the drop-down menu, and ensure that both the data fields are set to Name (they should be populated automatically), as shown in Figure 18-24. Then click OK. This updates the markup, as shown in Listing 18-15.

Figure 18-24. Selecting the new LinqDataSource

Listing 18-15. The updated DropDownList markup

```
...
<asp:DropDownList ID="DropDownList1" runat="server"
    DataSourceID="LinqDataSource2" DataTextField="Name"
    DataValueField="Name" AutoPostBack="True">
</asp:DropDownList>
...
```

Now when you view the page, the data drop-down menu is obtained from the results of the LINQ query. We can remove the EntityDataSource control from the page, since it isn't being used any more.

Using Query Results As Data Sources

As I mentioned earlier, there are a few things that are not ideal about this example. The first is that we have needed to define the LINQ query as we define the `AthleteName` field. We must do this because Web Forms data sources are initialized before any of the page events are invoked, and assigning a value to the field in the `Page_PreInit` or `Page_Init` methods is too late to be useful (see Chapter 5 for information about these events).

Not only is this an ugly approach, but it means that we can't change the nature of the LINQ query in response to the state of the page, which we would ideally do in the `Page_Load` method.

The second problem is that we need to create a helper class called `LinqWrapper`. The controls we are using assume that they are working with a set of result objects that contain properties, one or more of which will be used in the page display. Suppose we had written the query like this:

```
public IEnumerable<string> AthleteNames
    = new TrainingDataEntities().Events
    .Select(ev => ev.Athlete);
```

Then the results would be a sequence of `string` values, and the data controls allow us to select a property only from the `string` class, not the string itself. This is fine if you want to generate a list of string lengths, but not much help otherwise. To get around this, we project the `Athlete` property into a simple helper class with a property called `Name`. This exposes the `string` value in a way that the data controls can work with.

We can solve both of these problems by using the results of our LINQ query as a data source and *not* using one of the built-in data source controls. Such an approach means that we lose the design surface support for creating and configuring data sources, but it gives us a lot of freedom in return.

The first step is to change the markup of the DropDownList control so that it no longer references the LinqDataSource control, as shown in Listing 18-16.

Listing 18-16. Removing the data source reference in a DropDownList control

```
...
<asp:DropDownList ID="DropDownList1" runat="server" AutoPostBack="True">
...
```

Now we can change our code-behind class to use the new technique, as shown in Listing 18-17.

Listing 18-17. Using the results of a LINQ query as a data source

```
using System;
using System.Collections.Generic;
using System.Linq;

namespace WebApp {

    public partial class Default : System.Web.UI.Page {

        protected void Page_Load(object src, EventArgs e) {
```

```
if (!IsPostBack) {
var results = new TrainingDataEntities().Events
        .Select(ev => ev.Athlete);
DropDownList1.DataSource = results;
            DropDownList1.DataBind();
}
        }
    }
}
```

We define the query and use the results to set the DataSource property of the DropDownList control. This tells the control that it should obtain its data from the sequence of objects that the query generates. When doing this, it is essential to call the DataBind method—the results won't be displayed if you forget.

The last problem to fix is repetition of data. When we were using the EntityDataSource control, we were reading the names from the Athletes table, where each name is unique. Now that we are reading the names from the Events table, we get data duplication in the drop-down list, as shown in Figure 18-25.

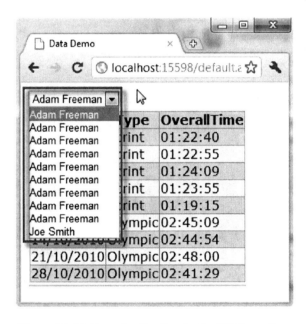

Figure 18-25. *Data duplication in the LINQ results*

This is a pretty simple problem to solve, but it neatly demonstrates that we can use all of the LINQ features, including those not easily supported through the LinqDataSource control. To solve this issue, we simply use the LINQ Distinct method, as shown in Listing 18-18.

Listing 18-18. Removing data duplication from the LINQ results

```
using System;
using System.Collections.Generic;
using System.Linq;

namespace WebApp {

    public partial class Default : System.Web.UI.Page {

        protected void Page_Load(object src, EventArgs e) {


        if (!IsPostBack) {
                var results = new TrainingDataEntities().Events
                    .Select(ev => ev.Athlete)
                    .Distinct();
                DropDownList1.DataSource = results;
                DropDownList1.DataBind();
                }
            }
        }
}
```

And we've fixed all of our problems. We can adapt the query programmatically (because we define it in the Page_Load method), we don't need to use helper classes, and we can use the full range of LINQ features (because we are no longer using the data source controls).

Using LINQ with XML

The fact that we can use LINQ results as data sources makes it very easy to work with XML data. The LINQ support for XML is excellent, and I find it more flexible and easier to use than any other XML-processing API. Listing 18-19 shows how to use LINQ to process XML data to populate a drop-down list.

Listing 18-19. Using LINQ to XML to populate a Web Form control

```
using System;
using System.Collections.Generic;
using System.Linq;
using System.Xml.Linq;

namespace WebApp {

    public partial class Default : System.Web.UI.Page {

        protected void Page_Load(object src, EventArgs e) {

            string xmlDataString = @"<Athletes>
```

```
<Athlete>
<Name>Adam Freeman</Name>
<City>London</City>
</Athlete>
<Athlete>
<Name>Joe Smith</Name>
<City>New York</City>
</Athlete>
</Athletes>";

        if (!IsPostBack) {

            var results = XDocument.Parse(xmlDataString)
                .Descendants("Name")
                .Select(elem => elem.Value);

            DropDownList1.DataSource = results;
            DropDownList1.DataBind();
        }
    }
  }
}
```

For simplicity, I have defined the XML using a string. The data is a simple structure where the name of each person is contained in a Name element. A simple LINQ query extracts the names into a result sequence, which is then used as the data source for the UI control.

Summary

This chapter demonstrated how to make data accessible to Web Forms UI controls. We looked at two main approaches. The first was to use the data source controls, which provide a design-surface-enabled approach to obtaining and preparing data. The second approach was to use the code-behind class to perform LINQ requests and use the query results as data sources directly. This is the most flexible approach, but it doesn't fit as neatly into the Visual Studio design tools.

In the next chapter, we'll take a close look at the basic Web Forms controls that are capable of using data sources and set the foundation for exploring the more complex controls covered in Chapter 20.

CHAPTER 19

Using Web Forms Data Binding

Data binding is the process of populating the content of a Web Forms control with the data contained in a data source. A Web Forms control that can be used in this way is known as a *data-bound control*, and the most useful way to explain how the data-bound controls work is to break them into three categories: basic, navigation, and rich data controls.

As you'll learn in this chapter, performing data binding with the basic and navigation controls is pretty straightforward. Using the rich data controls is much more complex. So, before we tackle them in the next chapter, we are going to spend some time looking behind the scenes to see the techniques that the data controls use. The more you understand about how the rich data controls function, the fewer problems you will have when using them in a development project.

Data Binding with Basic Web Forms Controls

Of the basic controls introduced in Chapter 15, five are frequently used for data binding:

- BulletedList

- CheckBoxList

- DropDownList

- ListBox

- RadioButtonList

In Chapter 18, you saw how to populate the DropDownList control with a data source, and the other controls work in much the same way. What all these controls have in common is that you can use them to *display* data elements; they don't provide the ability to edit that data.

You use these controls to enrich the UI of your web application. You don't need to require the user to type in values when you can load them from a database, for example.

Listing 19-1 shows the markup for a page that contains all five of the data-bound controls and a `LinqDataSource` control that uses a data model derived from the training database, just as we used in Chapter 18 (and initially created in Chapter 8). This example uses the `EventType` entity object, which has a property called `Name`.

Listing 19-1. The basic data-bound controls on a single page

```
<%@ Page Language="C#" AutoEventWireup="true" CodeBehind="Default.aspx.cs"↩
 Inherits="WebApp.Default" %>

<!DOCTYPE html PUBLIC "-//W3C//DTD XHTML 1.0 Transitional//EN"↩
 "http://www.w3.org/TR/xhtml1/DTD/xhtml1-transitional.dtd">

<html xmlns="http://www.w3.org/1999/xhtml">
<head runat="server">
<title></title>
<style type="text/css">
        .dataitem  {margin:10px; width:140px; float:left;}
        code {vertical-align:top; margin-bottom:5px;clear:both;}
</style>
</head>
<body>
<form id="form1" runat="server">
<div>
<div class="dataitem">
<code>BulletedList</code>
<asp:BulletedList ID="BulletedList1" runat="server"
                DataSourceID="LinqDataSource1" DataTextField="Name" DataValueField="Name"/>
</div>
<div class="dataitem">
<code>CheckBoxList</code>
<asp:CheckBoxList ID="CheckBoxList1" runat="server"
                DataSourceID="LinqDataSource1" DataTextField="Name" DataValueField="Name"/>
</div>
<div class="dataitem">
<code>DropDownList</code>
<asp:DropDownList ID="DropDownList1" runat="server"
                DataSourceID="LinqDataSource1" DataTextField="Name" DataValueField="Name"/>
</div>
<div class="dataitem">
<code>ListBox</code>
<asp:ListBox ID="ListBox1" runat="server" DataSourceID="LinqDataSource1"
                DataTextField="Name" DataValueField="Name"/>
</div>
<div class="dataitem">
<code>RadioButtonList</code>
<asp:RadioButtonList ID="RadioButtonList1" runat="server"
                DataSourceID="LinqDataSource1" DataTextField="Name" DataValueField="Name"/>
</div>
</div>
</form>
<asp:LinqDataSource ID="LinqDataSource1" runat="server"
        ContextTypeName="WebApp.TrainingDataEntities" EntityTypeName=""
        TableName="EventTypes">
</asp:LinqDataSource>
```

```
</body>
</html>
```

You can see that the markup for each control is the same in regard to data binding. The `DataSourceID`, `DataTextField`, and `DataValueField` attributes determine the data source control and the data type properties that will be used. Figure 19-1 shows this page displayed in a browser.

Figure 19-1. *The basic data-bound controls*

These controls all use the same wizard screens to select the values for the three data-binding properties (as you saw in Chapter 18). And as also discussed in Chapter 18, you can programmatically use the results of a LINQ query as a data source by relying on the `DataSource` property and the `DataBind` method.

Using the Navigation Controls

The Menu and `TreeView` navigation controls both support data binding, but only to hierarchical data. This means that you can use them with site map files (as discussed in Chapter 15) or with XML documents.

In this section, I'll show you how to use these controls with XML. This is a slightly different approach from the one in the previous chapter, because we want to preserve the hierarchical structure of the XML document, rather than use LINQ to extract specific values.

To begin, create a new project using the Visual Studio `Empty ASP.NET Application` template and add a new XML file called `Data.xml`. The contents of this file are shown in Listing 19-2. Create the special ASP.NET folder `App_Data` and place the XML file within it.

Listing 19-2. *The source XML data*

```
<?xml version="1.0" encoding="utf-8" ?>
<Athletes>
<Athlete Rank="Winner">
<name>Joe Smith</name>
<city>New York</city>
</Athlete>
<Athlete Rank="Runner-Up">
<name>Adam Freeman</name>
<city>London</city>
</Athlete>
</Athletes>
```

This is a simple piece of XML, but it has a hierarchical nature, which we will display in the navigation controls.

Add a new Web Form to the page called `Default.aspx` and drag an `XmlDataSource` control to the page's design surface. Select the control on the surface, click the arrow button, and select `Configure Data Source` from the pop-up menu.

In the Configure Data Source dialog, the `Data file` text box allows you to select the XML file that you will work with, which is `~/App_Data/Data.xml` in this example. You can also specify a transformation that will be applied to the XML (which we won't be using) and an `XPath` expression to select only part of the file. In this case, we specify `/Athletes/Athlete` so that we get a set of top-level `Athlete` nodes without the enclosing `Athletes` element. Figure 19-2 shows the completed dialog.

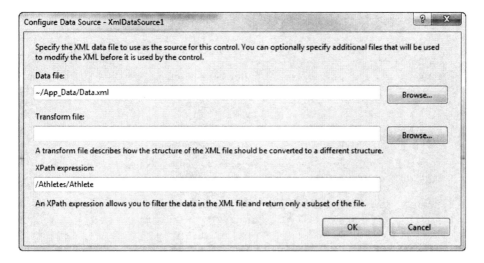

Figure 19-2. *Configuring an XmlDataSource control*

The markup for the configured `XmlDataSource` control is shown in Listing 19-3.

Listing 19-3. *The markup for the configured XmlDataSource control*

```
...
<asp:XmlDataSource ID="XmlDataSource1" runat="server"
DataFile="~/App_Data/Data.xml" XPath="/Athletes/Athlete"></asp:XmlDataSource>
...
```

We can now add a `TreeView` control. Drag one to the design surface, select it, click the arrow button, and select XmlDataSource from the Choose Data Source drop-down menu. The default behavior of the TreeView control isn't that useful. As you can see in Figure 19-3, it displays the names of the XML elements.

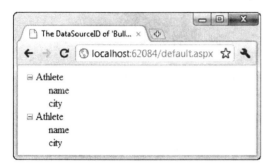

Figure 19-3. *The default behavior of the TreeView control*

To get something useful from this control, select the `Edit TreeNode Databindings` menu item, as shown in Figure 19-4.

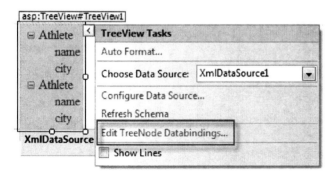

Figure 19-4. *Editing the tree node bindings*

Figure 19-5 shows the TreeView DataBindings Editor dialog that appears. You need to tell the `TreeView` control what to display for each of the nodes in the `Available data bindings` text box (at the top left of the dialog). For each of `Athlete`, `name`, and `city`, select the node, click the `Add` button, and change the value of the `TextField` property as follows:

463

- For the Athlete item, select Rank for the TextField property. This tells the TreeView that each time it finds an Athlete element in the XML data, we want it to display the value of the Rank attribute.

- For the name and city items, set the TextField value to #InnerText (see Figure 19-5). This tells the control we want to display the text contained by the name and city items when it encounters them.

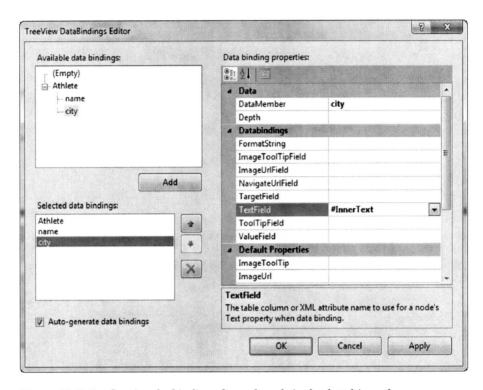

Figure 19-5. Configuring the bindings for each node in the data hierarchy

Click the OK button to close the dialog and update the markup, which can be seen in Listing 19-4.

Listing 19-4. The markup for a configured TreeView control

```
...
<asp:TreeView ID="TreeView1" runat="server" DataSourceID="XmlDataSource1">
<DataBindings>
<asp:TreeNodeBinding DataMember="Athlete" TextField="Rank" />
<asp:TreeNodeBinding DataMember="name" TextField="#InnerText" />
```

```
<asp:TreeNodeBinding DataMember="city" TextField="#InnerText" />
</DataBindings>
</asp:TreeView>
```
...

Now when we display the page, the `TreeView` control processes the XML data, finds the XML elements we have specified using the `TreeNodeBinding` elements in the markup, and displays the appropriate data, as shown in Figure 19-6.

Figure 19-6. *Displaying the correctly configured TreeView control in the browser*

You follow the same process for the `Menu` control. I won't repeat the wizard sequence, but Listing 19-5 shows the markup for a `Menu` control that uses the same `XmlDataSource` control as the `TreeView` example.

Listing 19-5. *Data binding to XML with a Menu control*

```
<asp:Menu ID="Menu1" runat="server" BackColor="#B5C7DE"
    DataSourceID="XmlDataSource1" DynamicHorizontalOffset="2" Font-Names="Verdana"
    Font-Size="0.8em" ForeColor="#284E98" Orientation="Horizontal"
    StaticSubMenuIndent="10px">
<DataBindings>
<asp:MenuItemBinding DataMember="Athlete" TextField="Rank" />
<asp:MenuItemBinding DataMember="name" TextField="#InnerText" />
<asp:MenuItemBinding DataMember="city" TextField="#InnerText" />
</DataBindings>
<DynamicHoverStyle BackColor="#284E98" ForeColor="White" />
<DynamicMenuItemStyle HorizontalPadding="5px" VerticalPadding="2px" />
<DynamicMenuStyle BackColor="#B5C7DE" />
<DynamicSelectedStyle BackColor="#507CD1" />
<StaticHoverStyle BackColor="#284E98" ForeColor="White" />
<StaticMenuItemStyle HorizontalPadding="5px" VerticalPadding="2px" />
<StaticSelectedStyle BackColor="#507CD1" />
</asp:Menu>
```

We've applied some styling to this menu as well, but you can clearly see the way that the `MenuItemBinding` elements correspond to the `TreeNodeBinding` elements from the previous example. Figure 19-7 shows the `Menu` control as it is displayed in the browser (the data doesn't lend itself to use in a menu, but you get the idea).

Figure 19-7. *Binding a Menu control to XML data*

Creating Data-Bound Templates

Before we look at the rich data controls in the next chapter, it is worth examining some of the underlying mechanisms that these controls employ—in particular, the way that the control templates work. These templates follow the same approach as the ones described in Chapter 16, but they are known as *data-bound templates*, because they include values from the data you introduce to your project.

Getting a handle on the different types of templates makes understanding the rich data controls easier. Along the way, you'll see two of the simpler rich data controls and use them to create templates that render HTML containing data values.

To get started, you need to create a data source. Create a new project using the Visual Studio Empty ASP.NET Application template, and create a Web Form called `Default.aspx`. Add the Entity Framework data model for the `TrainingData` database, following the steps outlined in Chapter 8. Create an EntityDataSource control, and when configuring it, select the `Events` table as the source of the data. Listing 19-6 shows the markup for `Default.aspx` for this example.

Listing 19-6. *Preparing the Default.aspx page*

```
<%@ Page Language="C#" AutoEventWireup="true" CodeBehind="Default.aspx.cs"
Inherits="WebApp.Default" %>

<!DOCTYPE html PUBLIC "-//W3C//DTD XHTML 1.0 Transitional//EN"
  "http://www.w3.org/TR/xhtml1/DTD/xhtml1-transitional.dtd">

<html xmlns="http://www.w3.org/1999/xhtml">
<head runat="server">
<title>Data Controls</title>
</head>
<body>
<form id="form1" runat="server">
<div>
```

```
</div>
</form>
<asp:EntityDataSource ID="EntityDataSource1" runat="server"
        ConnectionString="name=TrainingDataEntities"
        DefaultContainerName="TrainingDataEntities" EnableFlattening="False"
        EntitySetName="Events">
</asp:EntityDataSource>
</body>
</html>
```

This is our baseline project. We can now add controls to this page and define templates for them.

Creating Read-Only Templates

We are going to start by adding a Repeater control to the page. The Repeater control uses templates to generate the same HTML for each item in the data source. The data is read-only, and the Repeater control doesn't support data editing.

Drag a Repeater from the Toolbox and drop it onto the page. Select the control on the design surface, click the arrow button, and select the EntityDataSource that we just created from the Choose Data Source drop-down menu. We need to define the Repeater template in the source window, since the design tools don't provide the graphical support you saw in Chapter 16 for the Repeater control.

The most important Repeater template is ItemTemplate, which is how you define the markup that will be displayed for each data item. Listing 19-7 shows the addition of the Repeater control to the Default.aspx page and the definition of a simple ItemTemplate.

Listing 19-7. *Adding and configuring a Repeater control*

```
<%@ Page Language="C#" AutoEventWireup="true" CodeBehind="Default.aspx.cs"
Inherits="WebApp.Default" %>

<!DOCTYPE html PUBLIC "-//W3C//DTD XHTML 1.0 Transitional//EN" ↵
 "http://www.w3.org/TR/xhtml1/DTD/xhtml1-transitional.dtd">

<html xmlns="http://www.w3.org/1999/xhtml">
<head runat="server">
<title>Data Controls</title>
</head>
<body>
<form id="form1" runat="server">
<div>
<asp:Repeater ID="Repeater1" runat="server" DataSourceID="EntityDataSource1">
<ItemTemplate>
<div>
<asp:Label ID="Label1" runat="server" Text="Date:"/>
<asp:Label ID="Label2" runat="server"
```

```
Text='<%# Eval("Date", "{0:d}") %>'/>
</div>
</ItemTemplate>
</asp:Repeater>
</div>
</form>
<asp:EntityDataSource ID="EntityDataSource1" runat="server"
        ConnectionString="name=TrainingDataEntities"
        DefaultContainerName="TrainingDataEntities" EnableFlattening="False"
        EntitySetName="Events">
</asp:EntityDataSource>
</body>
</html>
```

Whatever you put between the start and end `ItemTemplate` tags will be rendered for each data item that the data source provides—in our case, for each `Event` entity object. We can mix pure HTML, HTML controls, and Web Forms controls freely. In the example, we have placed two Label controls inside a regular `div` element.

The key part of the template is the way that we set the `Text` attribute for the second Label control, like this:

```
Text='<%# Eval("Date", "{0:d}") %>'
```

Tags that start with `<%#` are called *single-value data-binding expressions*. These tags retrieve a data value from some part of your application and insert it into the HTML when the page is rendered.

■ **Note** Notice that we needed to use single quotes (') to open and close the value for the `Text` attribute. This is because we must use double-quotes (") to delineate the parameters of the `Eval` method.

These tags can retrieve the value of any field, property, or method in your page or code-behind class. For example, if our code-behind class contained a property called `Name` and a method called `GetTime`, we could access the value of each using the following data-binding expression tags:

```
<%# Name %>
<%# GetTime() %>
```

The binding expression in Listing 19-7 calls the `Page.Eval` method, which retrieves a value for the property name you specify—in this case, `Date`. The `Eval` method takes an optional second parameter, which is a composite formatting string that will be applied to the data value. We have specified `{0:d}`, which will extract just the date part from a `DateTime` value.

When you use data-binding expressions in a rich data control like Repeater, you don't need to worry about *which* data item is being processed. The control takes care of this for you, and your call to `Eval` will return the appropriate value for the current data item.

When you display the page in the browser, the template is applied to each data item, and the value of the `Date` property is added to the HTML, as shown in Figure 19-8.

Figure 19-8. *Using a data-binding expression in a Repeater control template*

A template can contain as many data-binding expressions as you require. I have shown only one in this example, but it is a simple matter to add markup for the other properties in the Event entity class, following the same format that we used for the Date property.

The Repeater control also supports a number of other templates, including one for the header. I can create a little grid using this template and some CSS. The markup for this is shown in Listing 19-8.

Listing 19-8. *Multiple data bindings in a Repeater control template*

```
<%@ Page Language="C#" AutoEventWireup="true" CodeBehind="Default.aspx.cs"
Inherits="WebApp.Default" %>

<!DOCTYPE html PUBLIC "-//W3C//DTD XHTML 1.0 Transitional//EN"
  "http://www.w3.org/TR/xhtml1/DTD/xhtml1-transitional.dtd">

<html xmlns="http://www.w3.org/1999/xhtml">
<head runat="server">
<title>Data Controls</title>
<style type="text/css">
        span { width:100px; float:left; margin:5px; }
        div.data  { clear:both; }
</style>
</head>
<body>
<form id="form1" runat="server">
<div>
<asp:Repeater ID="Repeater1" runat="server" DataSourceID="EntityDataSource1">
<ItemTemplate>
<div class="data">
<asp:Label ID="Label1" runat="server" Text='<%# Eval("Date", "{0:d}") %>'/>
<asp:Label ID="Label2" runat="server" Text='<%# Eval("Type") %>'/>
<asp:Label ID="Label3" runat="server" Text='<%# Eval("OverallTime") %>'/>
</div>
</ItemTemplate>
<HeaderTemplate>
<div class="data">
```

```
<asp:Label ID="Label4" runat="server" Text="Date"/>
<asp:Label ID="Label5" runat="server" Text="Type"/>
<asp:Label ID="Label6" runat="server" Text="Time"/>
</div>
</HeaderTemplate>
</asp:Repeater>
</div>
</form>
<asp:EntityDataSource ID="EntityDataSource1" runat="server"
        ConnectionString="name=TrainingDataEntities"
        DefaultContainerName="TrainingDataEntities" EnableFlattening="False"
        EntitySetName="Events">
</asp:EntityDataSource>
</body>
</html>
```

For this example, I didn't need to use the formatting parameter when calling the `Eval` method for the `Type` and `OverallTime` properties because I am happy to display the data values "as is." Figure 19-9 shows the simple grid effect.

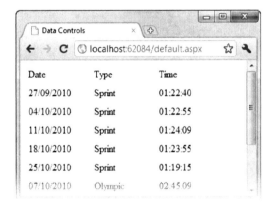

Figure 19-9. *Applying a simple grid effect by using data-binding in a control templates*

Using Data Item Containers

When the data-binding system renders your template, you have access to a property called `Container`. This is a class that implements the `IDataItemContainer` interface and is used by the data-bound control to represent a data item. The `IDataItemContainer` interface defines three properties that can be useful in templates, as described in Table 19-1.

Table 19-1. *IDataItemContainer Properties*

Property	Description
DataItem	Gets the current data item that is being processed
DataItemIndex	Gets the index of the current item in the overall data sequence
DisplayIndex	Gets the index of the current item in the current page

We'll return to the `DisplayIndex` property when we look at paging templates later in the chapter, but we can put the others to good use in the current example. Listing 19-9 shows these properties applied in the Repeater template.

Listing 19-9. *Using the IDataItemContainer properties*

```
<%@ Page Language="C#" AutoEventWireup="true" CodeBehind="Default.aspx.cs"
Inherits="WebApp.Default" %>
<%@ Import Namespace="WebApp" %>

<!DOCTYPE html PUBLIC "-//W3C//DTD XHTML 1.0 Transitional//EN"
 "http://www.w3.org/TR/xhtml1/DTD/xhtml1-transitional.dtd">

<html xmlns="http://www.w3.org/1999/xhtml">
<head runat="server">
<title>Data Controls</title>
<style type="text/css">
        span { width:100px; float:left; margin:5px; }
        div.data  { clear:both; }
        td.button {text-align:center}
</style>
</head>
<body>
<form id="form1" runat="server">
<div>

<asp:Repeater ID="Repeater1" runat="server" DataSourceID="EntityDataSource1">
<ItemTemplate>
<div class="data">
<asp:Label ID="Label1" runat="server"
                Text='<%# ((IDataItemContainer)Container).DataItemIndex + 1 %>'/>
<asp:Label ID="Label2" runat="server"
                Text='<%# Eval("Date", "{0:d}") %>'/>
<asp:Label ID="Label3" runat="server"
                Text='<%# ((Event)Container.DataItem).Type %>'/>
<asp:Label ID="Label4" runat="server"
                Text='<%# DataBinder.Eval(Container.DataItem, "OverallTime") %>'/>
</div>
</ItemTemplate>
<HeaderTemplate>
```

```
<div class="data">
<asp:Label ID="Label5" runat="server" Text="#"/>
<asp:Label ID="Label6" runat="server" Text="Date"/>
<asp:Label ID="Label7" runat="server" Text="Type"/>
<asp:Label ID="Label8" runat="server" Text="Time"/>
</div>
</HeaderTemplate>
</asp:Repeater>
</div>
</form>
<asp:EntityDataSource ID="EntityDataSource1" runat="server"
        ConnectionString="name=TrainingDataEntities"
        DefaultContainerName="TrainingDataEntities" EnableFlattening="False"
        EntitySetName="Events" EnableDelete="True" EnableInsert="True"
        EnableUpdate="True">
</asp:EntityDataSource>
</body>
</html>
```

The `Container` property returns an object that implements the `IDataItemContainer` interface, which means that we can add a column to our simple grid that shows the index into the data sequence for each data item, like this:

```
<asp:Label ID="Label1" runat="server"
    Text='<%#((IDataItemContainer)Container).DataItemIndex + 1 %>'/>
```

We needed to cast to `IDataItemContainer` in order to access the `DataItemIndex` property. For some reason, the class that the Repeater control uses as the `IDataItemContainer` hides the `DataItemIndex` property. It does, however, implement an equivalent `ItemIndex` property, so we can get the same result by using this expression:

```
<asp:Label ID="Label1" runat="server" Text='<%# Container.ItemIndex + 1 %>'/>
```

Notice that in both cases, we can add an integer value in the expression. The index is zero-based, but by performing a calculation in the expression, we are able to generate a numerical sequence that beings with 1.

The other two new binding expressions in Listing 19-9 show how to access the `DataItem` property. We can ignore the `Eval` method and simply cast the value of the `DataItem` property as an object, like this:

```
<asp:Label ID="Label3" runat="server" Text='<%# ((Event)Container.DataItem).Type %>'/>
```

To make this expression work, we add a directive to the page to import the namespace that contains the `Event` class:

```
<%@ Import Namespace="WebApp" %>
```

Alternatively, we can pass the `DataItem` value and the name of the property we require to the static `DataBinder.Eval` method, like this:

```
<asp:Label ID="Label4" runat="server"
    Text='<%# DataBinder.Eval(Container.DataItem, "OverallTime") %>'/>
```

You can see the HTML generated by the new template in Figure 19-10. As you might expect, the data looks the same, with the exception of the new numeric column.

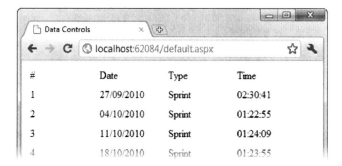

Figure 19-10. Obtaining data values through the IDataItemContainer interface

There is endless Internet discussion about which of these techniques offers the best performance. This debate misses the point. If you are worrying about performance over convenience when using data binding, then Web Forms is probably not the best platform for your project. My advice is to use whichever approach you prefer. If performance is an issue, then consider switching to the MVC framework, which gives you all the opportunities you could wish for to obsess and fine-tune performance (see Part IV of this book for details on the MVC framework).

Creating Editor Templates

The `Eval` method creates a *one-way binding*, meaning that you read the data value but you can't edit it. In this section, I'll show you how to use *two-way bindings*, with which you can read *and* edit the values. But before we can start working with this type of binding, we need to modify the data source to support modifying the data values.

Select the EntityDataSource control on the design surface, click the arrow button, and select Configure Data Source from the pop-up menu. Click the Next button to advance through the wizard, and then check the Enable automatic inserts, Enable automatic updates, and Enable automatic deletes options, as shown in Figure 19-11. Click Finish to close the wizard and update the markup for the data source control.

Figure 19-11. Enabling the data source control options for modifying data

473

The Repeater control doesn't support editing data, so we are going to use another rich data control: FormView. The FormView control generates markup for a single data item, rather than for each item in a sequence.

Remove the Repeater control from the page and drag a FormView control from the Toolbox to replace it. Select the control, click the arrow button, and select the EntityDataSource control from the drop-down list. When you select the data source, Visual Studio will generate a set of templates for the FormView control. We are going to delete those and start over so we can build up the markup gradually. Remove the markup from the FormView control until it looks like the one shown in Listing 19-10.

Listing 19-10. *The starting point for the FormView control markup*

```
...
<asp:FormView ID="FormView1" runat="server"
DataKeyNames="ID"
    DataSourceID="EntityDataSource1">
</asp:FormView>
...
```

The addition to the control markup is the DataKeyNames attribute, which specifies the data keys. We need to set this so that the FormView and EntityDataSource controls can work together properly to modify data in the data model and the database. The primary key is ID for the Events table. We can now add an ItemTemplate element to the FormView control, which will render a read-only view of the data. Listing 19-11 shows this template.

Listing 19-11. *Adding an ItemTemplate to the FormView control*

```
<asp:FormView ID="FormView1" runat="server"
    DataKeyNames="ID"
    DataSourceID="EntityDataSource1">
<ItemTemplate>
<tr>
<td><asp:Label ID="Label1" runat="server" Text="Date:"/></td>
<td><asp:Label ID="Label2" runat="server"
                Text='<%# Eval("Date", "{0:d}") %>'/></td>
</tr>
<tr>
<td><asp:Label ID="Label3" runat="server" Text="Type:"/></td>
<td><asp:Label ID="Label4" runat="server"
                Text='<%# Eval("Type") %>'/></td>
</tr>
<tr>
<td><asp:Label ID="Label5" runat="server" Text="Time:"/></td>
<td><asp:Label ID="Label6" runat="server"
                Text='<%# Eval("OverallTime") %>'/></td>
</tr>
<tr>
<td colspan="2" class="button">
<asp:Button ID="Button1" runat="server"
                Text="Edit Record" CommandName="Edit" />
```

```
</td>
</tr>
</ItemTemplate>
</asp:FormView>
```

By default, the FormView control generates an outer HTML table, and we use the templates to create table rows with the tr and td elements. We can disable this behavior using the RenderOuterTable property, but we'll leave it enabled, since it suits our needs for this simple example. Within the ItemTemplate, we have defined a tr element for each of the Date, Type, and OverallTime properties, and this row contains one static and one data-bound Label control. Each label is contained in its own td element, and the data-bound Label's content is set using the Eval method introduced in the previous example.

At the end of the template, we have defined a table row that contains one cell, which in turn contains a Button control. This is how we will switch from the read-only to the editable data view. The Button control is specified with the CommandName property (described in Chapter 15), which allows us to add as many buttons as we like to the template, and for the FormView control to be able to respond to them without needing to discover and register for events with individual controls.

In this case, the command is Edit. This is the cue to the FormView control to switch to the markup defined in the EditItemTemplate element. Listing 19-12 shows the addition of this template to the FormView control.

Listing 19-12. Adding the EditItemTemplate to the FormView control

```
<asp:FormView ID="FormView1" runat="server"
    DataKeyNames="ID"
    DataSourceID="EntityDataSource1">

<ItemTemplate>
        <!-- elements removed for clarity -->
</ItemTemplate>
<EditItemTemplate>
<tr>
<td><asp:Label ID="Label1" runat="server" Text="Date:"/></td>
<td>
<asp:TextBox ID="TextBox1" runat="server"
                Text='<%# Bind("Date", "{0:d}") %>'/>
</td>
</tr>
<tr>
<td><asp:Label ID="Label2" runat="server" Text="Type:"/></td>
<td><asp:TextBox ID="TextBox2" runat="server"
            Text='<%# Bind("Type") %>'/>
</td>
</tr>
<tr>
<td><asp:Label ID="Label3" runat="server" Text="Time:"/></td>
<td>
<asp:TextBox ID="TextBox3" runat="server"
                Text='<%# Bind("OverallTime") %>'/>
</td>
</tr>
```

```
<tr>
<td class="button">
<asp:Button ID="Button1" runat="server"
               Text="Save Change" CommandName="Update" />
</td>
<td class="button">
<asp:Button ID="Button2" runat="server"
               Text="Cancel" CommandName="Cancel" />
</td>
</tr>
</EditItemTemplate>
</asp:FormView>
```

This is a long setup for what is actually a simple change. We need to define an entirely new template for editing a data item, but the parts we care about are the data-binding expressions, such as this one:

```
<asp:TextBox ID="TextBox3" runat="server" Text='<%# Bind("OverallTime") %>'/>
```

We replace the call to the `Eval` method with a call to `Bind`. This creates a two-way binding, so that changes made to the data value will cause updates to the underlying data model and database. Naturally, we need to use this kind of binding with a Web Forms control that allows the user to edit the value. In this case. we have used a TextBox control.

We need to create a mechanism that will post the form and tell the FormView control what we want it to do with the data. To do this, we used the `CommandName` feature again. The `CommandName` value of `Update` tells the control that we want to save any changes that the user has made and push them to the database as an update. The `Cancel` value tells the control to discard any changes. After either button has been clicked, the FormView control reverts back to displaying the content defined in the ItemTemplate.

■ **Tip** The FormView control supports other `CommandName` values and templates. You can see the complete set in the templates that Visual Studio generates when you select a data source for the FormView control.

The effect of these templates and commands is shown in Figure 19-12. When you click the Edit button, the EditItemTemplate is displayed so that we can edit the data values. Click the Save Changes button, and the data is updated and redisplayed using the ItemTemplate.

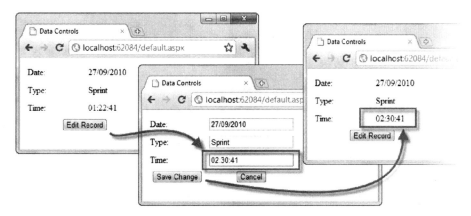

Figure 19-12. *Using two-way data bindings to edit data*

Using Paging

You can use *paging* to allow the user to move through the data when there are more items than you can reasonably display. This can be because you are using a control that lists data (such as Repeater), and you don't want the list to go on forever, or because a control can display only one record (such as FormView), and you want the user to be able to select which record is displayed. Some of the data controls support paging directly, while others require you to take a slightly longer route to achieve the same effect.

Using a Paging-Enabled Control

A good example of a control that has built-in support for paging is FormView. This control displays only one data item or record at a time, but the addition of paging allows the user to decide *which* record that will be. Enabling paging is simple: just set the AllowPaging attribute to True, as shown in Listing 19-13. (I have omitted the contents of the templates from this listing to make it easier to read.)

Listing 19-13. *Enabling paging in the FormView control*

```
<asp:FormView ID="FormView1" runat="server"
    DataKeyNames="ID"
    DataSourceID="EntityDataSource1"
    AllowPaging="True">
<PagerSettings Mode="Numeric" />
<ItemTemplate>
    ... elements removed for clarity ...
</ItemTemplate>
<EditItemTemplate>
        ... elements removed for clarity ...
</EditItemTemplate>
</asp:FormView>
```

We have added a `PageSettings` element, which we can use to configure the default paging template that the FormView controls. The `Mode` attribute lets you select one of four settings: `Numeric`, `NumericFirstLast`, `NextPrevious`, or `NextPreviousFirstLast`. These modes differ in the HTML elements that are presented to the user for navigation between records. Figure 19-3 shows the `Numeric` mode.

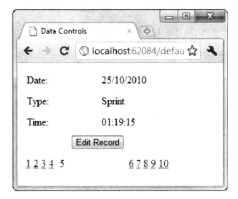

Figure 19-13. *The Numeric paging mode of the FormView contol*

The FormView control generates a set of links that take the user to the data record at the indicated index. The appearance of the paging elements is pretty basic, but the FormView control defines a set of properties that let you apply styling.

■ **Tip**   The order in which data items appear is determined by the data source. In the case of the EntityDataSource control, this is usually the order in which the records appear in the database table that is behind the data model. This isn't always the case, however. If the order in which data items appears is important in your project, then you should use a LinqDataSource control and apply an `OrderBy` clause.

We can ignore the built-in paging templates and define our own using the `PagerTemplate` element, as shown in Listing 19-14.

Listing 19-14. *Defining a paging template for the FormView control*

```
...
<asp:FormView ID="FormView1" runat="server"
    DataKeyNames="ID"
    DataSourceID="EntityDataSource1"
    AllowPaging="True">
<PagerTemplate>
<table>
<tr>
<td>
```

```
<asp:Button ID="Button3" runat="server" Text="First"
CommandName="Page" CommandArgument="First" />
</td>
<td>
<asp:Button ID="Button4" runat="server" Text="Prev"
CommandName="Page" CommandArgument="Prev"/>
</td>
<td>
<%# Container.PageIndex + 1 %> of <%# Container.PageCount %>
</td>
<td>
<asp:Button ID="Button5" runat="server" Text="Next"
CommandName="Page" CommandArgument="Next"/>
</td>
<td>
<asp:Button ID="Button6" runat="server" Text="Last"
CommandName="Page" CommandArgument="Last"/>
</td>
</tr>
</table>
</PagerTemplate>
<ItemTemplate>
        ... elements removed for clarity ...
</ItemTemplate>
<EditItemTemplate>
        ... elements removed for clarity ...
</EditItemTemplate>
</asp:FormView>
...
```

Unlike the main templates, the FormView control doesn't render an outer table, so if you want that style of layout, you must do it yourself.

When creating the buttons (either using the Button control or one of the other similar controls such as LinkButton), we use the CommandName and CommandArgument attributes to tell the FormView control what to do when the button is pressed. In the paging template, the CommandName must be Page, and the supported CommandArgument values are First, Last, Prev, and Next. These buttons give the user control over which data record it displayed by the FormView control.

We can go further and use data binding to give the user a sense of context in the data, like this:

```
<%# Container.PageIndex + 1 %> of <%# Container.PageCount %>
```

Unlike the Repeater control, which uses a separate class to implement the IDataItemContainer interface, the FormView control implements this interface directly. This means that we can refer to the PageIndex and PageCount properties defined by the FormView class to get details of which page is being displayed and how many pages there are. Obviously, this will be different when using controls that display multiple records.

Using the PagedDataSource Control

You can still add paging to controls that don't otherwise support it by using the PagedDataSource control. This approach takes a little more effort and, as you'll see, it has a serious drawback. Adding paging in this way isn't appropriate for most projects, because it is a simple matter to use a control that *does* support paging. I have included this section to give a more complete view on how Web Forms data binding can be used.

■ **Caution** The PagedDataSource control is part of the System.Web.UI.WebControls namespace (like the other data source controls) but isn't documented anywhere by Microsoft. This means that using the PagedDataSource control requires some trial and error.

To demonstrate manually adding paging, add a new page to the project called Pager.aspx and give it a Repeater control. Listing 19-15 shows the markup for the page.

Listing 19-15. The Pager.aspx page markup

```
<%@ Page Language="C#" AutoEventWireup="true" CodeBehind="Pager.aspx.cs"
Inherits="WebApp.Pager" %>

<!DOCTYPE html PUBLIC "-//W3C//DTD XHTML 1.0 Transitional//EN"↵
 "http://www.w3.org/TR/xhtml1/DTD/xhtml1-transitional.dtd">

<html xmlns="http://www.w3.org/1999/xhtml">
<head runat="server">
<title></title>
<style type="text/css">
        span { width:100px; float:left; margin:5px; }
        div.data  { clear:both; }
        td.button {text-align:center}
</style>
</head>
<body>
<form id="form1" runat="server">
<div>
<asp:Repeater ID="Repeater1" runat="server">
<ItemTemplate>
<div class="data">
<asp:Label ID="Label1" runat="server" Text='<%# Eval("Date", "{0:d}") %>'/>
<asp:Label ID="Label2" runat="server" Text='<%# Eval("Type") %>'/>
<asp:Label ID="Label3" runat="server" Text='<%# Eval("OverallTime") %>'/>
</div>
</ItemTemplate>
<HeaderTemplate>
<div class="data">
<asp:Label ID="Label4" runat="server" Text="Date"/>
<asp:Label ID="Label5" runat="server" Text="Type"/>
<asp:Label ID="Label6" runat="server" Text="Time"/>
</div>
```

```
</HeaderTemplate>
</asp:Repeater>

<div style="clear:both">
<table>
<tr>
<td>
<asp:Button ID="Button1" runat="server" Text="Prev" CommandName="Prev"/>
</td>
<td style="text-align:center">
<asp:Label ID="PagerLabel" runat="server" Text="Label"></asp:Label>
</td>
<td>
<asp:Button ID="Button2" runat="server" Text="Next" CommandName="Next"/>
</td>
</tr>
</table>
</div>
</div>
</form>
</body>
</html>
```

When using the PagedDataSource control, we are responsible for creating the interface elements for the user to navigate through the data. For this example, we have defined two Button controls that will move to the next and previous record, and a Label control that will provide context to the user. Notice that we don't define the data source in the markup. We must do this programmatically in the code-behind class. Listing 19-16 shows the code-behind class for the `Pager.aspx` page.

Listing 19-16. *The Pager code-behind class*

```
using System;
using System.Linq;
using System.Web.UI.WebControls;

namespace WebApp {
    public partial class Pager : System.Web.UI.Page {
        private PagedDataSource DataSource;

        protected void Page_Load(object sender, EventArgs e) {

            DataSource = new PagedDataSource();
            DataSource.AllowPaging = true;
            DataSource.DataSource = new TrainingDataEntities().Events.ToArray();
            DataSource.PageSize = 1;

            Repeater1.DataSource = DataSource;
```

```
            if (!IsPostBack) {
                DoCommonPrep();
                ViewState["page_index"] = 0;
            }
        }

        private void DoCommonPrep() {
            Button1.Enabled = !DataSource.IsFirstPage;
            Button2.Enabled = !DataSource.IsLastPage;
            Repeater1.DataBind();
            PagerLabel.Text = String.Format("{0} of {1}",
                DataSource.CurrentPageIndex + 1,
                DataSource.DataSourceCount);
        }

        protected override bool OnBubbleEvent(object source, EventArgs args) {

            if (args is CommandEventArgs) {

                int page_index = int.Parse(ViewState["page_index"].ToString());

                switch (((CommandEventArgs)args).CommandName) {
                    case "Prev":
                        DataSource.CurrentPageIndex = Math.Max(page_index - 1, 0);
                        break;
                    case "Next":
                        DataSource.CurrentPageIndex = Math.Min(page_index + 1,
                            DataSource.DataSourceCount -1);
                        break;
                }

                DoCommonPrep();
                ViewState["page_index"] = DataSource.CurrentPageIndex;
                return true;
            }
            return false;
        }
    }
}
```

This is quite a different approach to the ones you have seen so far, so I'll break down the class and walk through what's going on in stages. We begin with the Page_Load method:

```
...
public partial class Pager : System.Web.UI.Page {
    private PagedDataSource DataSource;

    protected void Page_Load(object sender, EventArgs e) {

        DataSource = new PagedDataSource();
        DataSource.AllowPaging = true;
```

```
        DataSource.DataSource = new TrainingDataEntities().Events.ToArray();
        DataSource.PageSize = 1;

        Repeater1.DataSource = DataSource;

        if (!IsPostBack) {
            DoCommonPrep();
            ViewState["page_index"] = 0;
        }
    }
...
```

In this method, we start by creating and configuring a PagedDataSource control. This control acts as an intermediary between our data and the Repeater control. As far as the Repeater control is concerned, PagedDataSource is a standard data source control that contains only one data item. We explicitly change which item the PagedDataSource control presents to the Repeater control, and so create the effect of paging through the data.

Setting the `AllowPaging` property to `true` enables the paging behavior. The `PageSize` property allows us to set how many data items the PagedDataSource control will present to the Repeater control at any one time. In this case, it's one item, so that we can create an effect similar to the one that we achieved with the FormView control.

The `DataSource` property allows us to tell the PagedDataSource control where to obtain its data items, and this is where we hit the drawback of this approach. The PagedDataSource control works only with data sequences that implement the `ICollection` interface. This is so that it can determine how many records there are and figure out the number of pages. This is not an approach that works well with the Entity Framework, which tries to defer making queries to the database until the data is required. It doesn't implement the `ICollection` interface because it is unable to tell in advance how many records from the database will be returned from a query.

To get around this, we must force the Entity Framework to retrieve the data from the database in such a way that it can be used by the PagedDataSource control. The easiest way to do this is by calling the `ToArray` method. The problem is that we end up loading all of the rows from the `Events` database table, even though we intend to display only one row to the user. This is an incredible waste of resources and should be used with care.

Returning to the `Page_Load` method, once we have created and configured the PagedDataSource control, we set it as the data source of the Repeater control using the `DataSource` property.

If the request we are processing is not a postback (caused by one of the navigation buttons being pressed), then we need to perform some further configuration. We call the `DoCommonPrep` method and set a value in the view state to indicate the index of the data record being displayed. The `DoCommonPrep` method contains some actions that we need to perform, irrespective of whether the page is being set up for the initial view or updated because the user has pressed one of the buttons. Here is the method:

```
private void DoCommonPrep() {
    Button1.Enabled = !DataSource.IsFirstPage;
    Button2.Enabled = !DataSource.IsLastPage;
    Repeater1.DataBind();
    PagerLabel.Text = String.Format("{0} of {1}",
        DataSource.CurrentPageIndex + 1,
        DataSource.DataSourceCount);
}
```

The PagedDataSource control defines the `IsFirstPage` and `IsLastPage` methods which return **true** if the current page being displayed is the first or last page, respectively. We use these properties to disable the Button controls when pressing them would advance the display to a record that is beyond the bounds of the data sequence.

The call to the `DataBind` method is required to ensure that the Repeater control displays the data item that the PagedDataSource control presents; without this, no data at all would be displayed. Then we set the contents of the Label control to display a context string to the user using the `CurrentPageIndex`, and we set the `DataSourceCount` property to display the index of the current page and the total number of pages available. Since we are displaying only one record at a time, the `DataSourceCount` property effectively reports the number of data items that have been retrieved from the database.

Finally, we override the `OnBubbleEvent` method to handle the bubble events that are emitted by the Button controls. In this method, we increase or decrease the `CurrentPageIndex` property to tell the PagedDataSource control which data item should be displayed and set the view data values in preparation for further updates.

You can see the effect of paging in this way in Figure 19-14.

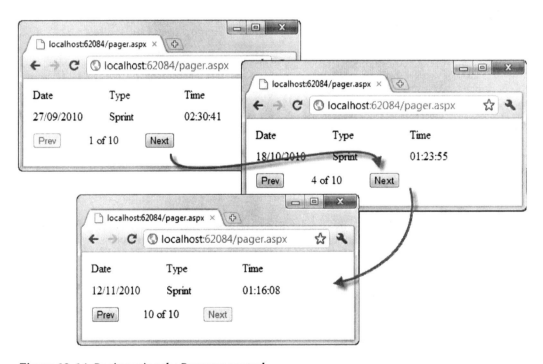

Figure 19-14. Paging using the Repeater control

Fixing the Data-Loading Problem

We don't really want to load all of the `Events` records to then discard most of them. We can improve the situation by using *custom paging*. This is where you take responsibility for providing the

PagedDataSource control with only the record it needs to pass to the Repeater control and giving it
information about how many records there are in total. Listing 19-17 shows how custom paging is done.

Listing 19-17. Custom paging with a PagedDataSource control

```
using System;
using System.Linq;
using System.Web.UI.WebControls;

namespace WebApp {
    public partial class Pager : System.Web.UI.Page {
        private PagedDataSource DataSource;
        private TrainingDataEntities Entities;

        protected void Page_Load(object sender, EventArgs e) {

            Entities = new TrainingDataEntities();

            DataSource = new PagedDataSource();
            DataSource.AllowPaging = true;
            DataSource.AllowCustomPaging = true;
            DataSource.PageSize = 1;
            DataSource.VirtualCount = Entities.Events.Count();

            Repeater1.DataSource = DataSource;

            if (!IsPostBack) {
                DoCommonPrep();
                ViewState["page_index"] = 0;
            }
        }

        private void DoCommonPrep() {

            DataSource.DataSource = Entities.Events
                .OrderBy(item => item.ID)
                .Skip(DataSource.CurrentPageIndex)
                .Take(1);

            Repeater1.DataBind();

            Button1.Enabled = !DataSource.IsFirstPage;
            Button2.Enabled = !DataSource.IsLastPage;

            PagerLabel.Text = String.Format("{0} of {1}",
                DataSource.CurrentPageIndex + 1,
                DataSource.DataSourceCount);
        }
```

485

```
        protected override bool OnBubbleEvent(object source, EventArgs args) {

            if (args is CommandEventArgs) {

                int page_index = int.Parse(ViewState["page_index"].ToString());

                switch (((CommandEventArgs)args).CommandName) {
                    case "Prev":
                        DataSource.CurrentPageIndex = Math.Max(page_index - 1, 0);
                        break;
                    case "Next":
                        DataSource.CurrentPageIndex = Math.Min(page_index + 1,
                            DataSource.VirtualCount - 1);
                        break;
                }

                DoCommonPrep();
                ViewState["page_index"] = DataSource.CurrentPageIndex;
                return true;
            }
            return false;
        }
    }
}
```

Let's go through the class again and examine the changes, starting with the Page_Load method:

```
...
public partial class Pager : System.Web.UI.Page {
    private PagedDataSource DataSource;
    private TrainingDataEntities Entities;

    protected void Page_Load(object sender, EventArgs e) {

        Entities = new TrainingDataEntities();

        DataSource = new PagedDataSource();
        DataSource.AllowPaging = true;
        DataSource.AllowCustomPaging = true;
        DataSource.PageSize = 1;
        DataSource.VirtualCount = Entities.Events.Count();

        Repeater1.DataSource = DataSource;

        if (!IsPostBack) {
            DoCommonPrep();
            ViewState["page_index"] = 0;
        }
    }
...
```

As you'll see, we need to refer to the entity data model at two points in the class, so we have moved the `TrainingDataEntities` object to be a class field. When configuring the PagedDataSource control, we have made two changes:

- The first is to set the `AllowCustomPaging` property to `true`, which simply enables the custom paging feature.

- The second is to set the value of the `VirtualCount` property. When using custom paging, the PagedDataSource control doesn't have any idea of how many items there are, so we need to provide a value through the `VirtualCount` property. This allows the control to calculate values for other properties, such as `IsFirstPage` and `CurrentPageCount`.

To determine how many `Event` records there are, we call the `Count` method on the `Events` collection of the `TrainingDataEntities` object. The Entity Framework is smart enough to use the SQL `COUNT` function, rather than loading all of the data and then counting the objects that are created.

Let's move on to the `DoCommonPrep` method:

```
private void DoCommonPrep() {

    DataSource.DataSource = Entities.Events
        .OrderBy(item => item.ID)
        .Skip(DataSource.CurrentPageIndex)
        .Take(1);

    Repeater1.DataBind();

    Button1.Enabled = !DataSource.IsFirstPage;
    Button2.Enabled = !DataSource.IsLastPage;

    PagerLabel.Text = String.Format("{0} of {1}",
        DataSource.CurrentPageIndex + 1,
        DataSource.DataSourceCount);
}
```

The big difference here is that we set the `DataSource` property of the PagedDataSource control using a LINQ query.

In order to select a single `Event` object from the overall sequence of `Event` objects, we use the `Skip` and `Take` methods, which are standard LINQ extension methods. These methods can be used on Entity Framework data models only in conjunction with the `OrderBy` method, so we order the objects using the `ID` property, and then select the one that we want to display. Once again, the Entity Framework is smart enough not to load all of the data when we use the `Skip` and `Take` methods. It creates a SQL query that retrieves just the record we require.

We don't need to worry about adding the `ToArray` call to the end of this query, since the PagedDataSource control doesn't try to count the items. It knows that it is being given a subset and relies on the `VirtualCount` property instead.

The last change occurs in the `OnBubbleEvent` method, where we use the `VirtualCount` property to make sure that we don't advance outside the bounds of the data items:

```
...
case "Next":
    DataSource.CurrentPageIndex = Math.Min(page_index + 1,DataSource.VirtualCount - 1);
    break;
...
```

The problem we have here is that the `DataSourceCount` property returns -1 until the `DataBind` method is called, but we can't call `DataBind` until we have worked out where the user wants to navigate. So, we read the `VirtualCount` property, which we already set in the `Page_Load` method (safe in the knowledge that `Page_Load` is called before `OnBubbleEvent` when the form is posted to the server).

With these changes, we have drastically reduced the amount of data that we retrieve from the database, most of which we were discarding. However, we have done this by making two separate requests to the database each time the web page is loaded. This is a compromise that may not be ideal for every project.

Summary

In this chapter, you have seen how to use data binding with the basic controls and how the navigation controls can be used with hierarchical data such as XML. This chapter also laid the foundation for the next chapter by looking at how to use data binding in templates to display data and allow the user to page through data.

CHAPTER 20

Using the Rich Data Controls

The previous chapter showed how to use data binding on the simpler Web Forms controls. Now, it's time to look at the more sophisticated and feature-rich controls. Most of the problems that programmers encounter with these controls arise from how the data is bound to the control. I hope that our exploration of this process in the previous chapter will help minimize these problems.

In this chapter, I'll introduce you to each of the Web Forms rich data controls and give you a demonstration of its capabilities and usage. We'll finish this chapter with a rich data control that is slightly different from the others: the Chart control, which allows you to generate professional-looking charts and graphs.

Putting the Rich Data Controls in Context

Web Forms provides seven built-in rich data controls. These controls can be useful when you are working with data and want to use the Web Forms data-binding features.

As we go through each control, you will start to notice some overlapping functions. Different controls can display data in similar ways, or support templates in such a way that you can easily create the same effect. Most of the time, it doesn't matter which control you use, so just pick the one that you like the best. But there are some differences in their use, and to help put these controls in context, I have summarized them in Table 20-1, including whether the controls support built-in paging and the ability to modify as well as display data.

Table 20-1. *The Built-in Web Forms Rich Data Controls*

Control	Description	Edit Data	Page Data
DetailsView	Displays a single data record	Yes	Yes
ListView	Displays groups of items using a set of related templates	Yes	Yes
GridView	Displays multiple data items in a grid	Yes	Yes
FormView	Displays a single data record	Yes	Yes
Repeater	Generates HTML for each item in a data source	No	No

Continued

Control	Description	Edit Data	Page Data
DataList	Generates table or flow views for multiple items	Yes	No
Chart	Creates graphs and charts from data	N/A	N/A

You may notice that I don't list the entire markup that adding and configuring a control generates in the examples in this chapter. This is because the amount of markup can be significant. For example, adding a ListView control and selecting some basic configuration options can generate around 300 lines of markup as Visual Studio adds the default templates to the page. Instead, I'll show you the way that the controls appear on the page and tell you about the different ways that you can change that appearance. If you want the full markup for each example, you can find it in the free source-code download that accompanies this book, available from Apress.com.

These controls share common approaches to displaying and editing data, and responding to user actions. Rather than duplicate this information for each, I have included it with the control that best represents the technique. You will find that other similar controls will use the same approach.

Using the DetailsView Control

The DetailsView control displays a single data record at a time and supports paging to allow the user to select which record that is. The DetailsView control is similar in purpose to the FormView control, although, as you'll see, it is somewhat less flexible.

The easiest way to configure a DetailsView control is through the design surface, as shown in Figure 20-1.

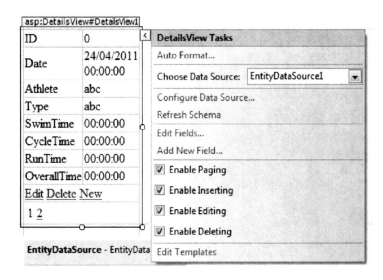

***Figure 20-1.** Using the design surface to configure the DetailsView control*

Using the design surface, you can enable paging between controls and the ability to insert, delete, and edit the individual data items. The DetailsView control supports the templates described in Table 20-2.

Table 20-2. *The DetailsView Templates*

Template	Description
HeaderTemplate	A template for the area immediately above the data fields
FooterTemplate	A template for the area immediately below the data fields, but above the paging area
PageTemplate	A template for the paging controls
EmptyDataTemplate	A template that is displayed when there is no data

You can use these templates to provide some basic styling for the control. The DetailsView control renders an outer HTML `table` element, so when you use the templates, you need to generate only the content inside table row (`tr`) elements. Listing 20-1 shows our basic markup for a DetailsView control example.

Listing 20-1. *Basic markup for a DetailsView control*

```
...
<div>
<asp:DetailsView ID="DetailsView1" runat="server"
    AllowPaging="True" AutoGenerateRows="False" DataKeyNames="ID"
    DataSourceID="EntityDataSource1">

<HeaderTemplate>
<tr><td colspan="2" class="hf">Header</td></tr>
</HeaderTemplate>
<FooterTemplate>
<tr><td colspan="2" class="hf">Footer</td></tr>
</FooterTemplate>
<PagerTemplate>
<tr><td colspan="2" style="text-align:center">
<asp:Button ID="Button1" runat="server" Text="Prev"
            CommandName="Page" CommandArgument="Prev" />
<%# Container.PageIndex + 1 %> of <%# Container.PageCount %>
<asp:Button ID="Button2" runat="server" Text="Next"
            CommandName="Page" CommandArgument="Next" />
</td></tr>
</PagerTemplate>
```

```
<Fields>
        ... elements omitted...
</Fields>
</asp:DetailsView>
</div>
...
```

We added a simple header and footer, and replaced the built-in paging controls with a pair of buttons and some basic data binding to tell the users which record they are viewing and how many records are available. The navigation buttons follow the same command event pattern that you saw in the previous chapter. Figure 20-2 shows this control.

Figure 20-2. *The DetailsView control with some basic template changes*

The DetailsView control doesn't let us change the basic structure of the data layout shown in the figure, which is a top-to-bottom table with each row representing one of the data fields. We can, however, exert some control over how each field is displayed. We do this by configuring the BoundField elements that the control markup contains. A good starting point is to hide a field. In our example, we don't want the user to be able to see (or edit) the ID field. This is the primary key for the Event database table, and the values are generated automatically by the database. To hide this field, we use the Visible attribute, like this:

```
<asp:BoundField DataField="ID" HeaderText="ID" ReadOnly="True"
    SortExpression="ID" Visible="True" />
```

The `Visible` attribute determines if the field is displayed. If you want the field to be visible but not allow the user to edit or create new values, use the `InsertVisible` attribute instead.

We can change the way that a data field is rendered by using the `DataFormatString` attribute, as follows:

```
<asp:BoundField DataField="Date" HeaderText="Date" SortExpression="Date"
DataFormatString="{0:d}"/>
```

The `DataFormatString` attribute applies a standard .NET composite formatting string to the field value. In the case of this element, we have applied the short date format to the `Date` field. You can see the effect of both the `Visible` and `DataFormatString` attributes in Figure 20-3.

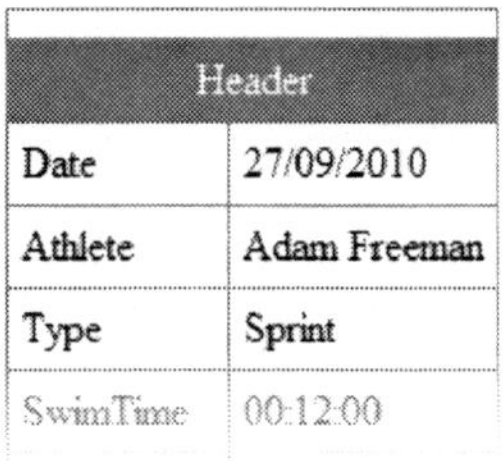

Header	
Date	27/09/2010
Athlete	Adam Freeman
Type	Sprint
SwimTime	00:12:00

Figure 20-3. *Hiding and formatting data fields*

If we want to go further, we can replace the `BoundField` element in the markup with a `TemplateField`. This element lets us define templates that are used when the field is displayed, allowing users to create a new item or edit an existing one. Listing 20-2 shows a `TemplateField` applied to the `Athlete` field.

Listing 20-2. *Using the TemplateField feature*

```
...
<asp:BoundField DataField="Date" HeaderText="Date" SortExpression="Date" ↵
 DataFormatString="{0:d}"/>
<asp:TemplateField HeaderText="Athlete" SortExpression="Athlete">
<ItemTemplate>
<asp:Label ID="Label1" runat="server" Text='<%# Eval("Athlete") %>'></asp:Label>
</ItemTemplate>
<EditItemTemplate>
<asp:DropDownList ID="DropDownList1" runat="server" DataSourceID="LinqDataSource1"
          SelectedValue='<%# Bind("Athlete") %>' DataTextField="Name"/>
</EditItemTemplate>
<InsertItemTemplate>
<asp:DropDownList ID="DropDownList1" runat="server" DataSourceID="LinqDataSource1"
          SelectedValue='<%# Bind("Athlete") %>' DataTextField="Name"/>
</InsertItemTemplate>
</asp:TemplateField>
<asp:BoundField DataField="Type" HeaderText="Type" SortExpression="Type" />
...
```

Within the `TemplateField` element, we define three templates. The ItemTemplate is used when the data item is displayed in the read-only view. We used some standard data binding in this template to set the contents of a Label control. The EditItemTemplate and the InsertItemTemplate are used when the user edits an existing item or starts to create a new item, respectively (the user initiates these actions by clicking the Edit or New button).

▨ **Note** The ItemTemplate is required, but you don't need to supply both the EditItemTemplate and InsertItemTemplate elements. If you omit the InsertItemTemplate, the EditItemTemplate will be used when the user creates a new record. If you omit the EditItemTemplate, then the ItemTemplate will be used when the user edits a record (which typically means that the user won't be able to change the value of that field).

In these templates, we have done something special. We started by adding a new data source that retrieves the values from the `Athletes` table, like this:

```
<asp:LinqDataSource ID="LinqDataSource1" runat="server"
    ContextTypeName="WebApp.TrainingDataEntities" EntityTypeName="" OrderBy="Name"
    Select="new (Name)" TableName="Athletes">
</asp:LinqDataSource>
```

We used a LinqDataSource control, but any data source would do, as long as we can get the Name values from the table. Within the `TemplateField` edit and insert templates, we define a DropDownList control that is data-bound to the new data source, like this:

```
<asp:DropDownList ID="DropDownList1" runat="server" DataSourceID="LinqDataSource1"
SelectedValue='<%# Bind("Athlete") %>' DataTextField="Name"/>
```

This means that the drop-down list will allow the user to select from the names defined in the `Athletes` table. The clever part—and this is an example of how Web Forms excels when it comes to making using data easy—is that we can then use data binding in the `SelectedValue` attribute to bind the DropDownList control to the `Athlete` field of the of the `Event` item being displayed by the DetailsView control. This allows us to neatly constrain the value that a user can provide for a data field, as shown in Figure 20-4.

Figure 20-4. *Using data binding to restrict the set of values a user can select*

Using the FormView Control

The FormView control is broadly similar in function to DetailsView, although the templates that are supported operate on the entire data item and not just individual fields. This means that you are not bound by the tabular layout that DetailsView enforces, but also means that you are responsible for every aspect of laying out and formatting the data fields. Table 20-3 describes the templates that the FormView control supports.

Table 20-3. *The FormView Templates*

Template	Description
ItemTemplate	Used to render the data item
InsertItemTemplate	User to render the HTML required to specify the fields for a new item
EditItemTemplate	Used to render the HTML required to edit an item
EmptyDataTemplate	Used when there are no items in the data source
HeaderTemplate	Used to insert content above the data item
FooterTemplate	Used to insert content following the data item
PagerTemplate	Used to render the paging controls

The FormView control renders an outer HTML `table` element, which means that you can define the templates in terms of table row (`tr`) elements. This tends to tie you to some close variant of the tabular form used by the DetailsView control, but if you want to do something different, you can disable the table by setting the `RenderOuterTable` attribute to `false`. You can see the basic appearance of the FormView control and the effect that some simple templates and a little CSS can create in Figure 20-5.

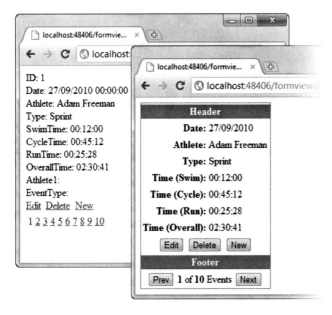

Figure 20-5. *Applying some simple styling and templates to the FormView control*

It should be obvious from the figure that I have never made much headway as a designer, but you can see it is possible to transform the appearance of the FormView control with modest effort. The templates that I created are included in the source-code download that accompanies this book (go to Apress.com to download the source code for free).

When creating the templates for the figure, I replaced the default LinkButton controls with regular Button controls. The FormView control relies on bubble events to respond to button presses to trigger different actions. Table 20-4 lists the `CommandName` and `CommandArgument` values that are supported in these templates.

Table 20-4. *The FormView CommandName and CommandArgument Values*

Template	CommandName	CommandArgument	Description
ItemTemplate	Edit	-	Displays the EditItemTemplate
ItemTemplate	Delete	-	Deletes the existing data item
ItemTemplate	New	-	Displays the InsertItemTemplate
EditItemTemplate	Update	-	Saves the changes to the item
EditItemTemplate	Cancel	-	Abandons the changes and displays the EditItemTemplate
InsertItemTemplate	Insert	-	Inserts a new item
InsertItemTemplate	Cancel	-	Displays the EditItemTemplate
PagingTemplate	Page	First	Moves to the first item in the data source
PagingTemplate	Page	Last	Moves to the last item in the data source
PagingTemplate	Page	Next	Moves to the next item
PagingTemplate	Page	Prev	Moves to the previous item
PagingTemplate	Page	\<integer\>	Moves to the item with the index specified by the integer value

The CommandName and CommandArguments are supported by most of the rich data controls and templates. If you are unsure of how to set up a bubble event in a template, the values in the table are a good place to start.

Using the Repeater Control

In Chapter 19, you saw how the Repeater control is used and how it can be combined with the PagedDataSource control to page through data, even though Repeater itself doesn't support paging. So, there isn't a great deal more to say about this control. Table 20-5 describes the templates that the Repeater control supports.

Table 20-5. *The Repeater Templates*

Template	Description
HeaderTemplate	A template for content added prior to the list of items
FooterTemplate	A template for content added following the list of items
ItemTemplate	A template rendered for each item in the data source
AlternatingItemTemplate	If defined, rendered for every other item in the data source
SeparatorTemplate	A template rendered between each item in the data source

Using the ListView Control

The ListView control displays multiple records and includes built-in template options to display those items in a grid, as a set of tiles, as a bulleted list, in a single row, or as a regular list. Figure 20-6 shows a ListView displaying the data from the Events database table using the built-in tile template scheme.

Figure 20-6. *The tile view of the ListView control*

You can use the built-in templates by selecting the ListView control, clicking the arrow button, and selecting Configure ListView from the pop-up menu. You can then choose the formatting to apply to the control, as shown in Figure 20-7.

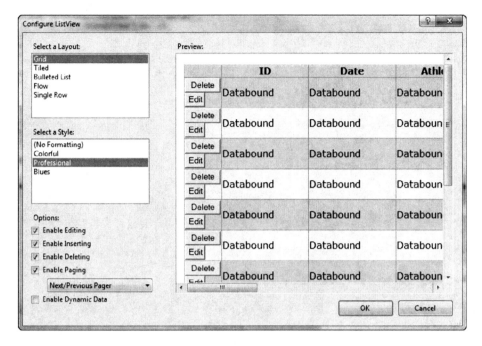

Figure 20-7. *Formatting a ListView control using the built-in template options*

When you select a layout from the Select a Layout list, Visual Studio will generate the templates required to support that appearance.

▓ **Note** If the Configure ListView menu item isn't visible, or not all of the options are available in the menu, the likely cause is that the data source isn't configured to sort the data item. See Chapter 18 for details on how to enable this feature.

Table 20-6 lists the templates that the ListView control supports.

Table 20-6. *The ListView Templates*

Template	Description
LayoutTemplate	The top-level template, with a placeholder for the group or item template
GroupTemplate	The template for a group of items
ItemTemplate	The template for a single item
GroupSeparatorTemplate	Used between groups of items
ItemSeparatorTemplate	Used between individual items
AlternatingItemTemplate	Used for odd-numbered items (typically for contrast)
SelectedItemTemplate	Used when an item is selected
EditItemtemplate	Used when an item is being edited
InsertItemTemplate	Used when a new item is being created
EmptyItemTemplate	Used when there are fewer items in a group than the maximum
EmptyDataTemplate	Used when there are no items in the data source

I don't like the built-in templates, because they produce enormous amounts of markup and I don't find them useful or visually appealing. That said, if we discard the built-in templates and write our own, we can take advantage of a useful feature of the ListView control, called *grouping*. This is where a specified number of data items is inserted into a nominated location in a template.

There are lot more templates available in the ListView control than in the other controls you have seen so far. The best way to understand how they fit together is to create an example Web Forms page that emphasizes the relationships between them. For the data items, we will use a sequence of easily recognized values. Create a new Web Forms page called **ListViewStructure.aspx** and define the values in the code-behind file, as shown in Listing 20-3.

Listing 20-3. *Defining some easily recognized data items*

```
using System;

namespace WebApp {
    public partial class ListViewStructure : System.Web.UI.Page {
        public StringAdapter[] DataItems = new[] {
            new StringAdapter {Name = "Item 01"}, new StringAdapter {Name = "Item 02"},
            new StringAdapter {Name = "Item 03"}, new StringAdapter {Name = "Item 04"},
            new StringAdapter {Name = "Item 05"}};
```

```
        protected void Page_Load(object sender, EventArgs e) {

        }
    }

    public class StringAdapter {
        public string Name { get; set; }
    }
}
```

We can then use this data as the basis for the LinqDataSource control and add a ListView control to the page, as shown in Listing 20-4.

Listing 20-4. *The starting point for the ListViewStructure page*

```
<%@ Page Language="C#" AutoEventWireup="true" CodeBehind="ListViewStructure.aspx.cs"
Inherits="WebApp.ListViewStructure" %>

<!DOCTYPE html PUBLIC "-//W3C//DTD XHTML 1.0 Transitional//EN"↵
 "http://www.w3.org/TR/xhtml1/DTD/xhtml1-transitional.dtd">

<html xmlns="http://www.w3.org/1999/xhtml">
<head runat="server">
<title></title>
<style type="text/css">
        .group {border: thin solid black; background-color:Gray;
color:White; padding:2px; text-align:center}
        .item {background-color:Aqua}
        .emptyitem {background-color:Fuchsia}
</style>
</head>
<body>
<form id="form1" runat="server">
<div>
<asp:ListView ID="ListView1" runat="server" DataSourceID="LinqDataSource1"
GroupItemCount="3">

... templates will go here...

</asp:ListView>
</div>
</form>
<asp:LinqDataSource ID="LinqDataSource1" runat="server"
        ContextTypeName="WebApp.ListViewStructure" EntityTypeName="" OrderBy="Name"
        Select="new (Name)" TableName="DataItems">
</asp:LinqDataSource>
</body>
</html>
```

Before we get started on the markup and the templates, Figure 20-8 shows our goal. We will lay out the items in a simple grid with three items per group.

Figure 20-8. *A simple grouped grid created using the ListView control*

I have marked two sections of the listing in bold. The first is GroupItemCount, which tells the ListView control how many data items should be placed in each group. You can see from the figure that we have three items per row. This is how GroupItemCount works, and you'll see the significance when we create the group template.

The second bold section indicates where we will add the templates as we create them. We are going to start with the LayoutTemplate, which is the template that the ListView control looks for first.

■ **Note** You can use the ListView control without group templates, and even without defining a LayoutTemplate element. All that it really requires is an ItemTemplate. But the real value of the ListView control is in how its templates work together. If you just want a simple list, there are other controls that are easier to work with, such as the DataList control, described later in this chapter.

Listing 20-5 shows the LayoutTemplate for this example.

Listing 20-5. *The LayoutTemplate example*

```
<LayoutTemplate>
<table border="1">
<tr><th colspan="3">LayoutTemplate</th></tr>
<tr ID="groupPlaceholder" runat="server"/>
</table>
</LayoutTemplate>
```

You have complete freedom to create any kind of layout you like. I have chosen a grid because it makes it easy to see the relationships among the templates.

To create the grid, we defined an HTML **table** element with a header. The ListView control relies on placeholder element with specific ID values to associate templates together. You can see that we have included a **tr** element with an ID of groupPlaceholder. This is the ID that the ListView control looks for when you are using the grouping feature. It doesn't matter what kind of element you use, because it will be replaced with the contents of the GroupTemplate, although you must use the **runat="server"** attribute so that ASP.NET can find the element and perform the substitution.

The contents of the GroupTemplate are rendered each time the ListView control has rendered the number of data items specified by the `GroupItemCount` attribute. In our case, this means that the GroupTemplate will be generated for every three data items. Listing 20-6 shows the GroupTemplate for this example.

Listing 20-6. *The GroupTemplate example*

```
<GroupTemplate>
<tr><th colspan="3" class="group">GroupTemplate</th></tr>
<tr><td ID="itemPlaceholder" runat="server"></td></tr>
</GroupTemplate>
```

Since we are using the HTML `table` element, we generate two table rows in each group. The first contains a header, just so we know where the groups appear in the page. The second contains another placeholder—this time for individual data items. The ListView control looks for an element that has an ID value of `itemPlaceholder` and replaces it with several copies of the contents of the ItemTemplate—in our case, three copies. Listing 20-7 shows the example ItemTemplate.

Listing 20-7. *The ItemTemplate example*

```
<ItemTemplate>
<td class="item"><%# Eval("Name") %></td>
</ItemTemplate>
```

This template doesn't need any placeholders. The ListView control simply renders the HTML the required number of times and uses the result to replace the placeholder in the group template. In our example, the ItemTemplate will be rendered three times per group, creating three `td` elements, which are inserted into the `tr` element defined in the group template.

The only other template we need for the moment is EmptyItemTemplate. The number of items in the data source won't always neatly align with the number of items in a group, so the ListView control renders the content of the EmptyItemTemplate whenever there is a shortfall. There are only five items in the data source for this example, so the ListView control needs to use the EmptyItemTemplate once to flesh out the second group. Listing 20-8 shows the EmptyItemTemplate for this example.

Listing 20-8. *The EmptyItemTemplate example*

```
<EmptyItemTemplate>
<td class="emptyitem">Empty</td>
</EmptyItemTemplate>
```

When these templates are used together, we get the result shown earlier in Figure 20-8: a simple grid with two groups, each containing three data items. Once you understand the relationship among these four templates, then the roles of the others become evident.

Paging with the ListView Control

There is no paging template for the ListView control. If you want to support paging, you must define the controls yourself in the LayoutTemplate. However, unlike some of the other controls, ListView relies on the DataPager control to handle paging, as opposed to bubble events. Listing 20-9 shows the LayoutTemplate updated to include a DataPager control.

Listing 20-9. Adding a DataPager control to a ListView LayoutTemplate

```
...
<asp:ListView ID="ListView1" runat="server" DataSourceID="LinqDataSource1"
    GroupItemCount="3">
<LayoutTemplate>
<table border="1">
<tr><th colspan="3">LayoutTemplate</th></tr>
<tr ID="groupPlaceholder" runat="server"/>
<tr><td colspan="3">
<asp:DataPager ID="DataPager1" runat="server" PageSize="3">
<Fields>
<asp:NextPreviousPagerField

                                ButtonType="Button"
                                ShowFirstPageButton="True"
                                ShowLastPageButton="True" />

</Fields>
</asp:DataPager>
</td></tr>
</table>
</LayoutTemplate>

<GroupTemplate>
<tr><th colspan="3" class="group">GroupTemplate</th></tr>
<tr><td ID="itemPlaceholder" runat="server"></td></tr>
</GroupTemplate>

<ItemTemplate>
<td class="item"><%# Eval("Name") %></td>
</ItemTemplate>

<EmptyItemTemplate>
<td class="emptyitem">Empty</td>
</EmptyItemTemplate>
</asp:ListView>
...
```

The PageSize attribute specifies how many items are included in each page. When used with a ListView control, this refers to the number of items, not the number of groups. The grouping is applied to each page, regardless of the number of items on the page. Figure 20-9 shows the effect of the paging control applied to the example.

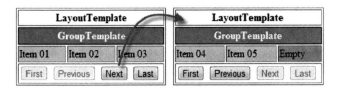

Figure 20-9. Paging with the ListView and DataPager controls

Sorting Data with the ListView Control

You can sort the order of the items displayed in the ListView control using buttons and bubble events in the LayoutTemplate. Listing 20-10 provides a demonstration.

Listing 20-10. *Using bubble events to sort data in a ListView control*

```
...
<LayoutTemplate>
<table border="1">
<tr><th colspan="3">LayoutTemplate</th></tr>
<tr ID="groupPlaceholder" runat="server"/>
<tr><td colspan="3" style="text-align:center">
<asp:Button ID="Button1" runat="server" Text="Sort Asc"
CommandName="Sort" CommandArgument="Name" />
<asp:Button ID="Button2" runat="server" Text="Sort Desc"
CommandName="Sort" CommandArgument="Name DESC" />
</td></tr>
</table>
</LayoutTemplate>
...
```

The CommandName to use for these buttons is Sort, and the CommandArgument is the name of the data field that the data should be sorted by. Data is sorted in ascending order by default, but you can perform a descending sort by appending DESC to the CommandArguement value, so that Name becomes Name DESC. You can see the effect of the item sort in Figure 20-10.

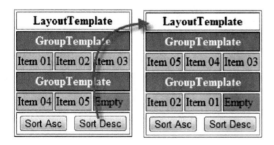

Figure 20-10. *Sorting data in a ListView control using bubble events*

Using the DataList Control

The DataList control is another template-based control, with the addition that you can specify different methods for repeating the templates to display all of the items. Table 20-7 describes the templates that the DataList control supports.

Table 20-7. *The DataList Templates*

Template	Description
ItemTemplate	Used to display individual data items
AlternatingItemTemplate	Used to display alternate data items
SelectedItemTemplate	Used to display an item when it has been selected
EditItemTemplate	Displayed when an item is being edited
HeaderTemplate	Displays a header above the data items
FooterTemplate	Displays a header below the data items
SeparatorTemplate	Used to add content or markup between data items

Listing 20-11 shows a DataList control with the ItemTemplate and AlternatingItem templates defined.

Listing 20-11. *The DataList control example*

```
<%@ Page Language="C#" AutoEventWireup="true" CodeBehind="DataListDemo.aspx.cs"
Inherits="WebApp.DataListDemo" %>

<!DOCTYPE html PUBLIC "-//W3C//DTD XHTML 1.0 Transitional//EN"
  "http://www.w3.org/TR/xhtml1/DTD/xhtml1-transitional.dtd">

<html xmlns="http://www.w3.org/1999/xhtml">
<head runat="server">
<title>DataList</title>
</head>
<body>
<form id="form1" runat="server">
<div>
<asp:DataList ID="DataList1" runat="server" DataKeyField="ID"
            DataSourceID="EntityDataSource1" RepeatColumns="3"
            RepeatDirection="Vertical" RepeatLayout="Table">

<ItemTemplate>
<table style="border:thin solid black">
<tr><td>Index:</td><td><%# Container.ItemIndex %></td></tr>
<tr><td>Date:</td><td><%# Eval("Date", "{0:d}") %></td></tr>
<tr><td>Time:</td><td><%# Eval("OverallTime") %></td></tr>
</table>

</ItemTemplate>
<AlternatingItemTemplate>
```

```
<table style="border:thin solid black; background-color:Gray; color:White">
<tr><td>Index:</td><td><%# Container.ItemIndex %></td></tr>
<tr><td>Date:</td><td><%# Eval("Date", "{0:d}") %></td></tr>
<tr><td>Time:</td><td><%# Eval("OverallTime") %></td></tr>
</table>
</AlternatingItemTemplate>
</asp:DataList>
</div>
</form>
<asp:EntityDataSource ID="EntityDataSource1" runat="server"
        ConnectionString="name=TrainingDataEntities"
        DefaultContainerName="TrainingDataEntities" EnableDelete="True"
        EnableFlattening="False" EnableInsert="True" EnableUpdate="True"
        EntitySetName="Events" AutoGenerateWhereClause="True">
</asp:EntityDataSource>
</body>
</html>
```

We render each item in an HTML `table` with rows that contain cells for a label and a data value. The data comes from the `TrainingData` database, and to keep things simple, we display only a couple of data fields. I have included the data item index in the templates to highlight the order in which the items are displayed. The DataList control supports two kinds of layout: `Table` and `Flow`. For each layout style, you can specify the layout direction (`Horizontal` or `Vertical`) and the number of columns that are used. In the example, we have configured the DataList control to use a vertical table with three columns:

```
<asp:DataList ID="DataList1" runat="server" DataKeyField="ID"
    DataSourceID="EntityDataSource1" RepeatColumns="3"
    RepeatDirection="Vertical" RepeatLayout="Table">
```

As you might expect, when the `RepeatDirection` attribute is set to `Vertical`, the data items are laid out so that they go down the column. You can see this on the left side of Figure 20-11. When `RepeatDirection` is set to `Horizontal`, the items are laid out across the rows.

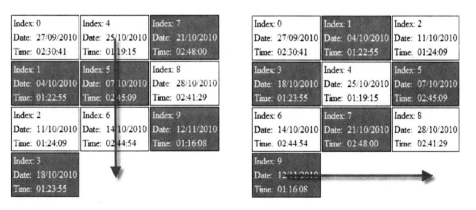

Figure 20-11. *Vertical and horizontal table layouts in a DataList control*

Using a Flow Layout

When you use the Table layout option, the DataList control creates an outer HTML table and places the contents of each ItemTemplate in a table cell (td) element. The number of td elements per table row (tr) element is controlled by the RepeatColumns attribute.

However, when you use the Flow layout, you get a different effect. Each data item is placed inside a span element. The RepeatColumns value is used to group span elements together, although this is done in such a way as to undermine the benefit of flowing items. After each RepeatColumns item is rendered, the DataList control inserts a br element. This means that if you apply a CSS style to the span element so that the span elements float on the page, you get the odd effect shown in Figure 20-12.

Figure 20-12. *The effect of br elements in the flow layout of a DataList when the CSS float value is used*

The control markup that generated Figure 20-12 is as follows:

```
...
<asp:DataList ID="DataList1" runat="server" DataKeyField="ID"
            DataSourceID="EntityDataSource1"  RepeatColumns="2"
            RepeatDirection="Horizontal" RepeatLayout="Flow">
...
```

After every two items, the DataList control inserts a br element. Some browsers render the HTML that the DataList control generates differently, as shown in the example in Figure 20-13.

Index: 0	Index: 1
Date: 27/09/2010	Date: 04/10/2010
Time: 02:30:41	Time: 01:22:55
Index: 2	Index: 3
Date: 11/10/2010	Date: 18/10/2010
Time: 01:24:09	Time: 01:23:55
Index: 4	Index: 5

Figure 20-13. *An alternate rendering of the DataList HTML*

This still isn't a flow layout. No matter how wide the browser window is, only two items across will be displayed. (As an aside, Figure 20-12 is from Internet Explorer, and Figure 20-13 is from Chrome.)

You can't disable the addition of the br elements, but you can set the value of the RepeatColumns value so high that it has no effect, like this:

```
...
<asp:DataList ID="DataList1" runat="server" DataKeyField="ID"
            DataSourceID="EntityDataSource1"  RepeatColumns="<%# int.MaxValue %>"
            RepeatDirection="Horizontal" RepeatLayout="Flow">
...
```

By setting the value of the RepeatColumns attribute to the maximum int value, you prevent the
DataList control from inserting br elements and get a true flow layout, where a row contains as many
items as will fit in the browser window, as shown in Figure 20-14.

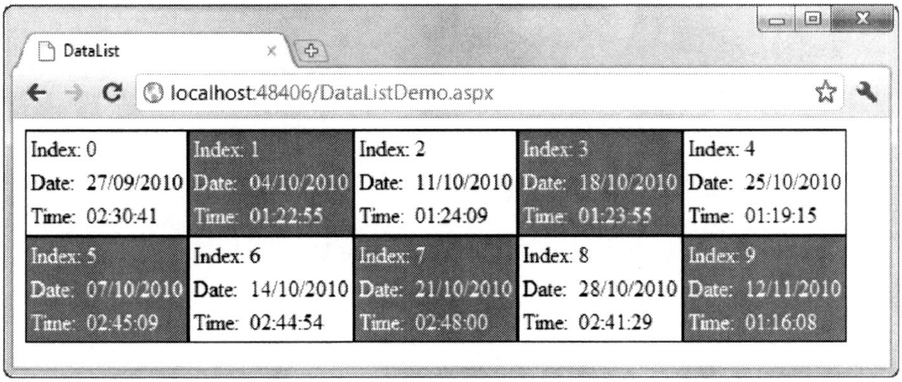

Figure 20-14. *A true flow layout from a DataList control*

Selecting Data Items

DataList is one of the Web Forms data controls that support *selecting* data items. In order to select a data
item, you need to add a Button control to the ItemTemplate and use a bubble event so that the DataList
control receives the command. In this case, the CommandName value must be select. Listing 20-12 shows
the markup for our example.

Listing 20-12. *Selecting DataList items*

```
...
<asp:DataList ID="DataList1" runat="server" DataKeyField="ID"
    DataSourceID="EntityDataSource1"  RepeatColumns="2"
    RepeatDirection="Horizontal" RepeatLayout="Flow"
onselectedindexchanged="DataList1_SelectedIndexChanged">

<ItemTemplate>
<table style="border:thin solid black">
<tr><td>Index:</td><td><%# Container.ItemIndex %></td></tr>
<tr><td>Date:</td><td><%# Eval("Date", "{0:d}") %></td></tr>
<tr><td>Time:</td><td><%# Eval("OverallTime") %></td></tr>
<tr><td colspan="2" style="text-align:center">
<asp:Button ID="Button1" runat="server" Text="Select" CommandName="select" />
```

```
</td></tr>
</table>
</ItemTemplate>

<SelectedItemTemplate>
<table style="border:thin solid black; background-color:Red; color:White">
<tr><td>Index:</td><td><%# Container.ItemIndex %></td></tr>
<tr><td>Date:</td><td><%# Eval("Date", "{0:d}") %></td></tr>
<tr><td>Time:</td><td><%# Eval("OverallTime") %></td></tr>
<tr><td colspan="2" style="text-align:center">
<asp:Button ID="Button1" runat="server" Text="Select"/>
</td></tr>
</table>
</SelectedItemTemplate>

</asp:DataList>
...
```

I've marked two sections of the listing in bold. The first registers a handler method for the SelectedIndexChanged method. The DataList control needs a helping hand to deal with items being selected, and so we must call the DataBind method when the event is invoked, like this:

```
using System;

namespace WebApp {
    public partial class DataListSelect : System.Web.UI.Page {
        protected void Page_Load(object sender, EventArgs e) {

        }

        protected void DataList1_SelectedIndexChanged(object sender, EventArgs e) {
            DataList1.DataBind();
        }
    }
}
```

The second highlighted part of the listing is the SelectedItemTemplate. This is used by the DataList control to render an item when it is selected. We have changed the styles for the selected item to make it easier to see, and we have omitted the CommandName attribute, since there is no need to reselect an item once it is selected. You can see the effect of selecting an item in Figure 20-15.

Figure 20-15. *Selecting an item with the DataList control*

Allowing the user to select an item is useful, but only if you then do something with the selection. You can extend the code in the handler method for the `SelectedIndexChanged` method to respond in a meaningful manner. The index of the selected item can be obtained through the `DataList.SelectedIndex` property, which will return -1 when there is no item selected.

Using the GridView Control

The GridView control displays data in a grid, just as the name suggests. The overall appearance is that of a table, with the field names forming the columns and the individual data items providing the rows. Figure 20-16 shows the basic appearance of a GridView control.

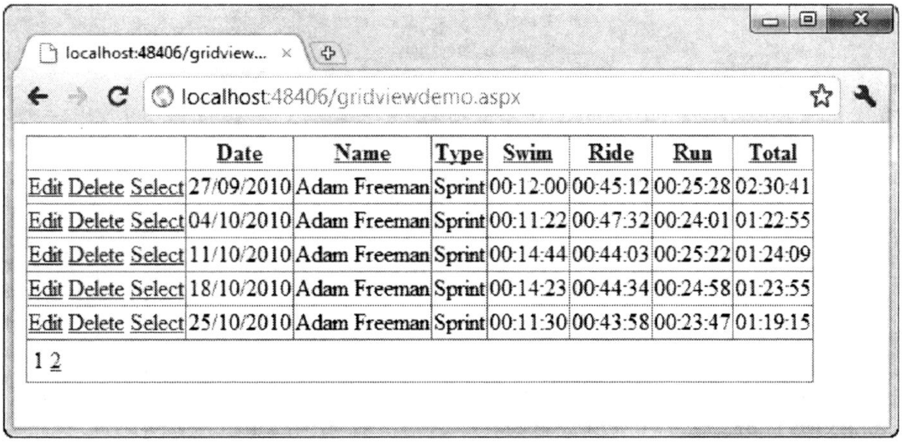

Figure 20-16. *The basic appearance of a GridView control*

The GridView control uses the same techniques that you have seen in earlier sections, so there isn't much new information to add. The GridView control uses the same `BoundField` elements that you saw in the DetailsView control, although they are contained in a `Columns` element, as shown in Listing 20-13.

Listing 20-13. *The BoundField elements in a GridView control*

```
<asp:GridView ID="GridView1" runat="server" AllowPaging="True"
    AllowSorting="True" AutoGenerateColumns="False" DataKeyNames="ID"
    DataSourceID="EntityDataSource1" PageSize="5">
<Columns>
<asp:CommandField ShowDeleteButton="True" ShowEditButton="True" ShowSelectButton="True"/>
<asp:BoundField DataField="ID" HeaderText="ID" ReadOnly="True" SortExpression="ID"
        Visible="false"/>
<asp:BoundField DataField="Date" HeaderText="Date" SortExpression="Date"
        DataFormatString="{0:d}"/>
<asp:BoundField DataField="Athlete" HeaderText="Name" SortExpression="Athlete" />
<asp:BoundField DataField="Type" HeaderText="Type" SortExpression="Type" />
<asp:BoundField DataField="SwimTime" HeaderText="Swim" SortExpression="SwimTime" />
<asp:BoundField DataField="CycleTime" HeaderText="Ride" SortExpression="CycleTime" />
<asp:BoundField DataField="RunTime" HeaderText="Run" SortExpression="RunTime" />
<asp:BoundField DataField="OverallTime" HeaderText="Total"
SortExpression="OverallTime" />
</Columns>
</asp:GridView>
```

You can see from the listing that I have applied some of the same attribute values as when we used the DetailsView control. I have hidden the ID field from the user with the `Visible` attribute, and formatted the `Date` field using the `DataFormatString` attribute.

Although the GridView control uses `BoundField` elements to render items, there is still template support for two aspects of the control. Table 20-8 describes the templates available.

Table 20-8. *The GridView Templates*

Template	Description
EmptyDataTemplate	Used when there are no items in the data source
PagerTemplate	Used to render the paging controls

Controlling Data Sorting

One particularly interesting attribute of the `BoundField` element is `SortExpression`. If the `AllowSorting` attribute in the main `GridView` element is set to `true`, the control will allow the user to sort the data by any of the displayed columns. In Figure 20-6, you can see that each of the column labels is a hyperlink. Clicking one of these links sorts the data based on that field.

For each column represented by a `BoundField` element, the `SortExpression` attribute specifies which of the data fields will be used to perform the sort operation. This does not need to be the same field as the column. For example, if you want the data to be sorted by the `ID` element when the user clicks the column header for the `Athlete` field, you could use the following markup:

```
<asp:BoundField DataField="Athlete" HeaderText="Name" SortExpression="ID" />
```

If you don't want the user to be able to sort a column, then simply omit the SortExpression attribute completely.

Configuring the Command Buttons

Like many of the Web Forms data controls, GridView relies on bubble events sent from buttons to perform actions. You don't have the freedom to define your own Button controls with GridView, because it doesn't support free-form item templates. Instead, you must rely on the CommandField control, which is defined like this:

```
<asp:CommandField ShowDeleteButton="True" ShowEditButton="True" ShowSelectButton="True"/>
```

ShowDeleteButton, ShowEditButton, and ShowSelectButton control the presence of the three link buttons in the leftmost column in Figure 20-16. You can switch to conventional buttons by setting the ButtonType attribute to Button, like this:

```
<asp:CommandField ShowDeleteButton="True" ShowEditButton="True"
ShowSelectButton="True" ButtonType="Button"/>
```

In all other respects, the GridView control responds to the standard set of CommandName and CommandArgument values described earlier in Table 20-4.

Creating Charts

The last rich data control we will discuss is Chart. It produces graphical representations of data, as opposed to the textual representations that you have seen from the other controls. The Chart control supports infinite configurability. Dozens of different chart types are available, countless color and style options exist, and it even offers support for three-dimensional charts.

In fact, there are so many configuration options that I am not even going to try to describe them. All I can do in this chapter is provide a single example as a starting point for you to explore the capabilities of the Chart control.

To begin, we need some data to plot. We are going to create a chart with two data series. The first will be the overall time taken (expressed in hours), and the second will be the total distance. This is not the most useful data to plot, but it is well suited for an example.

The first issue to resolve is that the Chart control is somewhat picky about the data types that it will work with. It's limited to the .NET intrinsic types: Double, Decimal, Single, int, long, uint, ulong, String, DateTime, short, and ushort. Specifically, it won't plot the TimeSpan values from the OverallTime field. To address this, we can create a LINQ query and project the values that we want into a wrapper class, as shown in Listing 20-14.

Listing 20-14. *Projecting event data values into a wrapper class*

```
using System;
using System.Collections.Generic;
using System.Linq;
```

513

```
namespace WebApp {
    public partial class ChartDemo : System.Web.UI.Page {
        public IEnumerable<EventWrapper> Results = new TrainingDataEntities().Events
            .Select(e => new {
                Date = e.Date,
                Time = e.OverallTime,
                Distance = e.EventType.SwimMiles
                    + e.EventType.CycleMiles + e.EventType.RunMiles
            })
            .ToArray()
            .Select(e => new EventWrapper() {
                Date = e.Date,
                Hours = e.Time.TotalHours,
                Distance = e.Distance
            });

        protected void Page_Load(object sender, EventArgs e) {
        }
    }

    public class EventWrapper {
        public DateTime Date { get; set; }
        public double Hours { get; set; }
        public float Distance { get; set; }
    }

}
```

This is a pretty ugly LINQ query because we want to read the value of the `TimeSpan.TotalHours` property, which is hard to do when using LINQ against an Entity Framework data model. For brevity, we create a sequence of anonymously typed objects containing the data fields that we require, and then convert the sequence to an array so that we can project the results into a series of `EventWrapper` objects, reading the `TotalHours` property as we do so.

Having created the data, we can add the data source, as shown in Listing 20-15.

***Listing 20-15.** Markup for the LinqDataSource control*

```
<%@ Page Language="C#" AutoEventWireup="true" CodeBehind="ChartDemo.aspx.cs"
Inherits="WebApp.ChartDemo" %>

<%@ Register Assembly="System.Web.DataVisualization, Version=4.0.0.0, Culture=neutral,⏎
PublicKeyToken=31bf3856ad364e35"
    Namespace="System.Web.UI.DataVisualization.Charting" TagPrefix="asp" %>

<!DOCTYPE html PUBLIC "-//W3C//DTD XHTML 1.0 Transitional//EN"⏎
 "http://www.w3.org/TR/xhtml1/DTD/xhtml1-transitional.dtd">

<html xmlns="http://www.w3.org/1999/xhtml">
<head runat="server">
<title>Chart</title>
</head>
```

```
<body>
<form id="form1" runat="server">
<div>

</div>
</form>
<asp:LinqDataSource ID="LinqDataSource1" runat="server"
        ContextTypeName="WebApp.ChartDemo" EntityTypeName="" OrderBy="Date"
        TableName="Results">
</asp:LinqDataSource>
</body>
</html>
```

It is now time to add the Chart control. Add the control to the page, select it on the design surface, click the arrow button, and select LinqDataSource from the Choose Data Source menu, as shown in Figure 20-17.

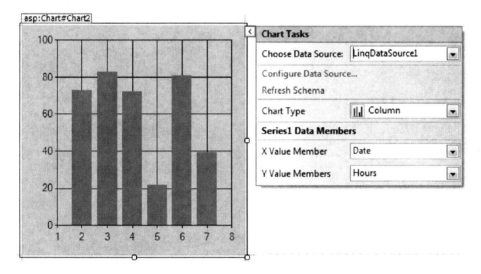

Figure 20-17. *Configuring the Chart control*

Once the data source is selected, we can choose which fields will be used for the x axis and y axis, and, of course, pick one of the many different types of charts available. For the moment, leave the chart type as Column, and select Date for the x axis and Hours for the y axis, as shown in Figure 20-17. We now have a basic chart, which Figure 20-18 shows in a browser.

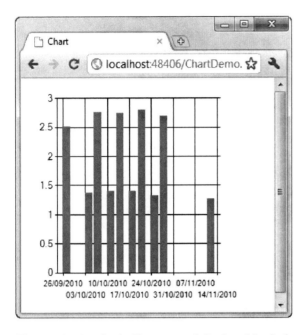

Figure 20-18. *A basic Chart control displayed in the browser*

At this point, a lot of programmers look at the result and give up on the Chart control. Sadly, others look at the result and call it a job done. I have seen countless projects that use charts that are this poor. With the Web Forms Chart control, however, this is just the start.

The markup in Listing 20-16 adds a second data series to the chart (the values of the Distance field) and a secondary y axis, and applies some basic styling.

Listing 20-16. *Formatting and styling a chart*

```
<asp:Chart ID="Chart1" runat="server" DataSourceID="LinqDataSource1"
    BackColor="Gray" BackSecondaryColor="WhiteSmoke"
    BackGradientStyle="DiagonalRight" BorderlineDashStyle="Solid"
    BorderlineColor="Gray" BorderSkin-SkinStyle="Emboss" Width="644px"
    Height="247px">
<Series>
<asp:Series Name="Times" XValueMember="Date" YValueMembers="Hours">
</asp:Series>
<asp:Series Name = "Distance" XValueMember="Date" YValueMembers="Distance"
ChartType="Spline" BorderWidth="3" ShadowOffset="2" Color="PaleVioletRed"
YAxisType="Secondary">
</asp:Series>
</Series>
<ChartAreas>
<asp:ChartArea Name="ChartArea1" BackColor="Wheat">
<AxisX>
<LabelStyle Format="MM-dd"/>
```

```
</AxisX>
<AxisY Title="Time" Interval="1"/>
<AxisY2 Title="Distance" Interval="10" Minimum="10" Maximum="40"/>
</asp:ChartArea>
</ChartAreas>
<Titles>
<asp:Title Text="Time & Distance" Font="Utopia, 16"/>
</Titles>
<BorderSkin SkinStyle="Emboss"></BorderSkin>
</asp:Chart>
```

As I've mentioned, the Chart control offers a lot of configuration options, and it can take some experimentation to find the most suitable appearance for your application, but the time can be well spent. Figure 20-19 shows the Chart control from the listing displayed in the browser.

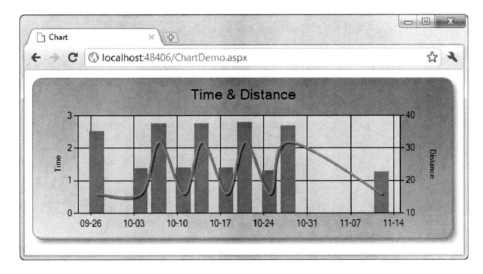

Figure 20-19. *Applying formatting to a chart*

We are still just scratching the surface of what this control can do. The Chart control can produce very high-quality results once it has been mastered. You can learn more about the capabilities of the Chart control on MSDN at this URL: `http://msdn.microsoft.com/en-us/library/dd456632.aspx`.

Summary

This chapter introduced the rich data controls. These controls are endlessly configurable and often overlap with the functionality of other controls in the set. All of the controls can bind to a wide variety of data sources, making it easy to display and manage data in a Web Forms application.

The only way to truly master these controls is to use them in real projects. It can be a frustrating and time-consuming process, but has the benefit of giving you a lot of flexibility as to how data is consumed by the application and displayed to the user.

CHAPTER 21

The Web Forms Triathlon App

In this chapter, we will complete our tour of Web Forms by using it to re-create the triathlon application that we saw in Part II of the book. In doing this, we can see some of the topics from earlier chapters put to concrete use and combined to create an application (albeit a simple one). As a reminder, Figure 21-1 shows the main page of the triathlon application.

Figure 21-1. *The triathlon web application from Part II of this book*

There are a couple of points to note as we build the application. The first is that I have deliberately not used jQuery, despite urging you to take advantage of its features in earlier chapters. I have done this because jQuery operates on the HTML that a web application generates, and when considering Web Forms, we are looking at the tools that generate that HTML. Adding jQuery would make for a better application but a worse example.

The second point to note is that there are many different ways to use Web Forms controls. Not only do the controls have overlapping functions and features, but the ability to mix Web Forms controls with HTML controls and static HTML gives a broad range of approaches to solve every problem. In this chapter, the approaches you will see are a mix of my personal preferences (favoring one kind of control over another or my preference for working with LINQ directly) and techniques that I want to demonstrate (such as displaying complex templates with the DataList control). You should not take these techniques as canon. Instead, use them as a starting point to develop your own style, prefer your own components, and obtain and process data in the manner that suits your projects best.

Creating the Project

We will start by creating the project and setting up the basics. Use the Visual Studio Empty ASP.NET Web Application template to create a project called TriathlonApp.

Adding the Data Model

Next, create an Entity Framework data model by following the steps laid out in Chapter 9. Don't forget to import the stored procedures, since we will use them in this project.

Adding Images and Styles

Since I won't be using jQuery to create the buttons for the pages the way we did in Chapter 10, I have created a set of images so we can achieve a similar appearance using the Web Forms ImageButton control. There is no easy way for you to create these button images, but they are available as part of the free source code download that accompanies this book and that is available from Apress.com. I created a project folder called Images and imported the image files.

To make styling the content with CSS easier, I created a Styles folder and copied the Site.css file that we used in earlier chapters. I won't list the styles here (and in fact, we won't use most of them), but you can see the contents in the source-code download.

Adding the Master Page and Web Forms Pages

We are going to use a master page to provide a consistent appearance across the pages in the application. You can learn more about master pages and how they work in Chapter 9. Add a new master page to the application and name it Site.master.

Now that we have created the master page, we can create the pages that will use it. Use the Web Form using Master Page template to create pages called Events.aspx, EventEditor.aspx, Calculator.aspx, and Performance.aspx. Select Site.master as the master page for all of these Web Forms pages.

Edit each of the ASPX pages so that it is obvious which is which from the content. Listing 21-1 shows the addition I have made to the Events.aspx page.

Listing 21-1. Differentiating the empty pages

```
<%@ Page Title="" Language="C#" MasterPageFile="~/Site.Master" AutoEventWireup="true"
CodeBehind="Events.aspx.cs" Inherits="TriathlonApp.Events" %>
<asp:Content ID="Content1" ContentPlaceHolderID="head" runat="server">
    <title>Triathlon Events</title>
</asp:Content>
<asp:Content ID="Content2" ContentPlaceHolderID="ContentPlaceHolder1" runat="server">
    <h2>This is the Events.aspx page</h2>
</asp:Content>
```

We are going to create the tabs to switch between pages before we work on the pages themselves, and these changes will make it easier for us to determine whether the tabs are working properly.

Checking the Project

If you have made all the additions that we need, then the Solution Explorer window for your project should look very similar to the one shown in Figure 21-2.

Figure 21-2. The Solution Explorer window for the example project

If you view one of the pages in the browser, then you should see what is shown in Figure 21-3.

Figure 21-3. *The starting point for the Events.aspx page*

It doesn't look like much at the moment, but we'll get to the point where it has some basic structure pretty quickly.

Building the Master Page

There are three elements in the master page for this project: the static image banner across the top of the page, the tabs that let the user select different pages in the application, and the footer that displays the totals across the bottom of the page. We'll tackle them in order of complexity, starting with the simplest.

Adding the Banner

The banner is a very simple addition to the page. It spans the page width and shows a simple image and some text. You can see the markup that defines the banner in Listing 21-2.

Listing 21-2. *Adding the banner to the master page*

```
<%@ Master Language="C#" AutoEventWireup="true" CodeBehind="Site.master.cs"
Inherits="TriathlonApp.Site" %>

<!DOCTYPE html PUBLIC "-//W3C//DTD XHTML 1.0 Transitional//EN"
 "http://www.w3.org/TR/xhtml1/DTD/xhtml1-transitional.dtd">

<html xmlns="http://www.w3.org/1999/xhtml">
<head runat="server">
    <title></title>
    <asp:ContentPlaceHolder ID="head" runat="server">
    </asp:ContentPlaceHolder>
    <link href="Styles/Site.css" rel="stylesheet" type="text/css" />
</head>
<body>
<div style="background-color:White">
<form id="form1" runat="server">
<div>
```

```
<div class="header">
    <div class="title" id="titleDiv" runat="server">
        <asp:Image ID="Image1" runat="server" ImageUrl="~/Images/triathlon.png" />
        <h1>Triathlon Training Data</h1>
    </div>
</div>

<div class="clear"></div>

<!-- tabs will go here -->

<asp:ContentPlaceHolder ID="ContentPlaceHolder1" runat="server">
</asp:ContentPlaceHolder>

<div class="clear"></div>

<-- footer will go here -->

</div>
</form>
</div>
</body>
</html>
```

I have added some basic structure to the page, but the most important additions are the ones that I have marked in bold. I have added a reference to the Site.css style sheet so that I can reference the CSS styles that it defines.

The banner itself includes an Image control. Usually, I wouldn't use this control unless I needed to change some aspect of the image programmatically in the code-behind class, but since we are looking at Web Forms and Web Forms controls, I thought I'd include it here.

I have also included a couple of comments to show where I'll add the markup for the tabs and the footer. This is so I don't have to duplicate the entire markup when we add new elements.

Adding the Footer

The footer is another simple addition. It just displays the total number of events, the total distance traveled, and the sum of the event times. It has no values beyond giving some visual consistency and polish to the application. Listing 21-3 shows the markup that supports the footer.

Listing 21-3. Adding the markup for the footer

```
...
<div class="clear"></div>

<div class="footer" id="footerDiv" runat="server">
    <h2>
        <asp:Label ID="footerLabel" runat="server"></asp:Label>
    </h2>
</div>
...
```

The key element is the Label control, which we'll use to display the summary, which we will calculate in the code-behind class, as shown in Listing 21-4.

Listing 21-4. *Populating the footer in the master page code-behind class*

```
using System;
using System.Linq;

namespace TriathlonApp {
    public partial class Site : System.Web.UI.MasterPage {

        protected void Page_Load(object sender, EventArgs e) {

            using (TrainingDataEntities entities = new TrainingDataEntities()) {

                int eventCount = entities.Events.Count();
                TimeSpan time = new TimeSpan();
                float distance = 0;

                foreach (EventType ev in entities.Events.Select(ev => ev.EventType)) {
                    distance += (ev.SwimMiles + ev.CycleMiles + ev.RunMiles);
                }

                foreach (TimeSpan ts in entities.Events.Select(ev => ev.OverallTime)) {
                    time += ts;
                }

                footerLabel.Text
                    = string.Format("{0} Events, {1:F1} Miles, {2} Hours and {3} Minutes",
                    eventCount.ToString(), distance, time.Hours, time.Minutes);
            }
        }
    }
}
```

I create a new Entity Framework context and use it to query for the information I require, which includes the number of events, the sum of the distances, and the total time. These kinds of queries are impossible to manage using data source controls, and you'll see that I switch between using data source controls and working with the data in the code-behind class throughout the project. After we have added the banner and the footer to the master page, the individual ASPX pages look like the one shown in Figure 21-4.

Figure 21-4. The effect of the banner and footer in the master page

Adding the Tabs

We are going to create a user control that will handle the tabs. This is an easy way to create a simple and reusable control and makes adding features such as custom events easy and convenient. You can learn more about user controls in Chapter 16.

Start by using the Web User Control template to add a new item to the project called TabButtons.ascx. Listing 21-5 shows the markup for this control.

Listing 21-5. The markup for the tabs user control

```
<%@ Control Language="C#" AutoEventWireup="true" CodeBehind="TabButtons.ascx.cs"
Inherits="TriathlonApp.TabButtons" %>

<style type="text/css">
    div.tabcontainer {float:left; clear:both; background-color:#ECE8DA;
                      width:100%; padding:5px}
    .tabbutton {margin: 2px 0px 2px 1px; float:left; z-index:2; position:relative }
    .tabstrip {margin: 2px 0px 2px 1px; width:100%; height:37px; position:absolute;
            left:0px; z-index:1; padding: 0 0px 0 5px}
</style>

<div class="tabcontainer">

    <asp:Image ID="Image1" runat="server"
        ImageUrl="~/Images/btn-backing-strip.png" CssClass="tabstrip" />

    <asp:ImageButton ID="EventButton" CssClass="tabbutton" runat="server" CommandName="Tab"
        CommandArgument="Events" ImageUrl="~/Images/btn-off-event.png" />
    <asp:ImageButton ID="PerfButton" CssClass="tabbutton" runat="server"
        CommandName="Tab" CommandArgument="Performance"
        ImageUrl="~/Images/btn-off-perf.png" />
```

```
    <asp:ImageButton ID="CalcButton" CssClass="tabbutton" runat="server"
        CommandName="Tab" CommandArgument="Calculator"
        ImageUrl="~/Images/btn-off-calc.png" />
</div>
```

I have modeled the appearance of this control as closely as possible to the tabs we created using jQuery in Chapter 10. There are three ImageButton controls representing the three tabs we require, and each is set to display the image that corresponds to the tab not being selected. There is also an Image control. I use this image and some CSS to create a bar that goes across the page to give a sense of continuity to the tab buttons.

We add the tab control to the master page in two parts. The first is to use the Register directive, as shown in Listing 21-6.

Listing 21-6. Registering a user control

```
<%@ Master Language="C#" AutoEventWireup="true" CodeBehind="Site.master.cs"↵
 Inherits="TriathlonApp.Site" %>
<%@ Register Src="~/TabButtons.ascx" TagName="TabButtonPanel" TagPrefix="Custom" %>
...
```

The second part is to add the markup for the control itself, as shown in Listing 21-7.

Listing 21-7. Adding the markup for the tab user control

```
...
<div>
    <Custom:TabButtonPanel ID="TabPanel" runat="server"
        OnTabSelectionChanged="HandleTabChange"/>
</div>
...
```

Notice that I have registered a handler for an event called TabSelectionChanged. This is defined in the code-behind class for the user control, which you can see in Listing 21-8.

Listing 21-8. The code-behind class for the tabs user control

```
using System;
using System.Web.UI.WebControls;

namespace TriathlonApp {

    public class TabSelectedEventArgs : EventArgs {
        public string SelectedTab { get; set; }
    }

    public partial class TabButtons : System.Web.UI.UserControl {
        public event EventHandler<TabSelectedEventArgs> TabSelectionChanged;
```

```
        protected void Page_Load(object sender, EventArgs e) {
            switch (Request.FilePath) {
                case "/Events.aspx":
                    EventButton.ImageUrl = "~/Images/btn-on-event.png";
                    break;
                case "/Performance.aspx":
                    PerfButton.ImageUrl = "~/Images/btn-on-perf.png";
                    break;
                case "/Calculator.aspx":
                    CalcButton.ImageUrl = "~/Images/btn-on-calc.png";
                    break;
            }
        }

        protected override bool OnBubbleEvent(object source, EventArgs args) {

            if (args is CommandEventArgs) {
                CommandEventArgs ce = (CommandEventArgs)args;
                if (ce.CommandName == "Tab" && TabSelectionChanged != null) {
                    TabSelectionChanged(this,
                            new TabSelectedEventArgs {
                                SelectedTab = ce.CommandArgument.ToString()
                            });
                    return true;
                }
            }
            return false;
        }
    }
}
```

In the Page_Load method, I used the Request.FilePath property to determine which page is being loaded and so change the ImageUrl property for the ImageButton control that represents the current page.

Each of the ImageButton controls is defined with a CommandName value of Tab and a CommandArgument value that represents the page the user wants to go to (Events, Performance, and Calculator). I have overridden the OnBubbleEvent method so that I can easily receive events from the ImageButton controls. In my implementation of this method, I invoke the TabSelectionChanged event defined at the head of the class. When invoking the event, I pass in a TabSelectedEventArgs object, which extends the base EventArgs class to add a property that indicates the page the user has selected.

All that remains is to implement the HandleTabChange method to handle the event emitted by the user control. I do this in the code-behind class for the master page so that I can separate the tabs from the actions that occur when they are selected. You can see the method implementation in Listing 21-9.

Listing 21-9. Implementing the handler for the user control event

```
using System;
using System.Linq;
```

```
namespace TriathlonApp {
    public partial class Site : System.Web.UI.MasterPage {

        protected void Page_Load(object sender, EventArgs e) {
            ...contents of this method shown previously...
        }

        protected void HandleTabChange(object sender, TabSelectedEventArgs e) {
            Response.Redirect(string.Format("~/{0}.aspx", e.SelectedTab));
        }
    }
}
```

This method is called when the user control emits its event, and I simply take the value from the `TabSelectedEventArgs` object and use it to redirect the user to the appropriate page. I could have easily done this simple task in the user control itself, but I like this kind of separation, and it provides a nice example of how user controls can be integrated into other parts of a Web Forms application.

If we view any of the ASPX pages now, the master page will include the tabs. If we click the tabs, the browser will be directed to the appropriate page. Since no page has any of its own content at the moment, we have to rely on the placeholder text that was added. You can see the transition between pages in Figure 21-5.

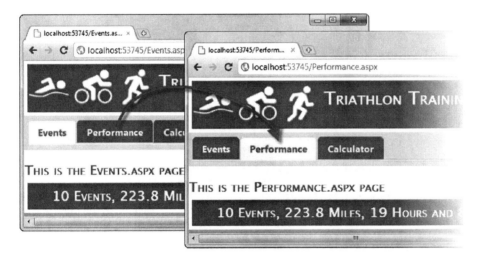

Figure 21-5. Moving between pages using the tabs user control

The main drawback of the approach that I have taken with the tabs is that the tabs themselves are hard-coded into the user control. A more flexible approach would be to specify the tabs and the pages that they correspond to using properties that we could set in the markup. Still, simplicity has its virtues, and this approach is entirely serviceable for our needs in this chapter.

Building the Events Page

Now that we have the master page in place, we can start to fill out the individual pages that make up the backbone of the application, starting with `Event.aspx`. This page displays a list of the events that are in the database, along with ranking information. The events can be filtered based on the event type. There is a button to click for adding a new event, and each individual event has buttons to edit or delete the record. Listing 21-10 shows the markup I added for this page to get started. It's just some basic CSS.

Listing 21-10. *The Events.aspx markup*

```
<%@ Page Title="" Language="C#" MasterPageFile="~/Site.Master" AutoEventWireup="true"
CodeBehind="Events.aspx.cs" Inherits="TriathlonApp.Events" %>

<asp:Content ID="Content1" ContentPlaceHolderID="head" runat="server">
    <title>Triathlon Events</title>
    <style type="text/css">
        .dataview { margin:0px;  border-spacing:0px; border:
            thin black solid; border-top: none}
        th { color:#696969; font-weight:bold; padding:0 5px 0 5px;
            border-top:thin black solid; padding-top:2px }
        .dataitem {padding: 0 5px 0 5px; margin:0px;display:table-cell}
        #eventselector {margin-top:10px}
    </style>
</asp:Content>
<asp:Content ID="Content2" ContentPlaceHolderID="ContentPlaceHolder1" runat="server">

    <div class="main">

    </div>
</asp:Content>
```

Adding the Event Table

The key control in this page is a DataList. There are other controls that I could have used to achieve the same effect, but I find that I generally use DataList instead of the others. This is just personal preference. For example, I prefer working with those data controls that used templates, as opposed to those that use `BoundField` elements, as GridView does. You can see the markup for the DataList in Listing 21-11.

Listing 21-11. *Adding the DataList control to the Events.aspx page*

```
...
<asp:DataList ID="DataList1" runat="server" CssClass="dataview" rules="cols"
        ExtractTemplateRows="True">
    <HeaderTemplate>
        <asp:Table ID="Table1" runat="server">
            <asp:TableHeaderRow>
            <asp:TableHeaderCell>Date</asp:TableHeaderCell>
            <asp:TableHeaderCell>Athlete</asp:TableHeaderCell>
            <asp:TableHeaderCell>Event Type</asp:TableHeaderCell>
```

```
                    <asp:TableHeaderCell>Swim</asp:TableHeaderCell>
                    <asp:TableHeaderCell>Cycle</asp:TableHeaderCell>
                    <asp:TableHeaderCell>Run</asp:TableHeaderCell>
                    <asp:TableHeaderCell>Overall</asp:TableHeaderCell>
                    <asp:TableHeaderCell>Rank</asp:TableHeaderCell>
                    <asp:TableHeaderCell>Ref Rank</asp:TableHeaderCell>
                    <asp:TableHeaderCell>Edit</asp:TableHeaderCell>
                    <asp:TableHeaderCell>Delete</asp:TableHeaderCell>
                    </asp:TableHeaderRow>
            </asp:Table>
    </HeaderTemplate>
    <ItemTemplate>
        <asp:Table ID="Table2" runat="server">
            <asp:TableRow>
            <asp:TableCell CssClass="dataitem"><%# Eval("Date",
                                            "{0:MM/dd}")%></asp:TableCell>
            <asp:TableCell CssClass="dataitem"><%# Eval("Athlete")%></asp:TableCell>
            <asp:TableCell CssClass="dataitem"><%# Eval("Type")%></asp:TableCell>
            <asp:TableCell CssClass="dataitem"><%# Eval("SwimTime")%></asp:TableCell>
            <asp:TableCell CssClass="dataitem"><%# Eval("CycleTime")%></asp:TableCell>
            <asp:TableCell CssClass="dataitem"><%# Eval("RunTime")%></asp:TableCell>
            <asp:TableCell CssClass="dataitem"><%# Eval("OverallTime")%></asp:TableCell>
            <asp:TableCell CssClass="dataitem"
                style="text-align:right"><%# Eval("PRank") %></asp:TableCell>
            <asp:TableCell CssClass="dataitem"
                style="text-align:right"><%# Eval("RRank") %></asp:TableCell>
            <asp:TableCell CssClass="dataitem"><asp:ImageButton ID="ImageButton1"
                runat="server" ImageUrl="~/Images/btn-edit-off.png" Height="25"
                PostBackUrl='<%# "~/EventEditor.aspx?mode=edit&id="
                    + Eval("ID") %>' /></asp:TableCell>
            <asp:TableCell CssClass="dataitem"><asp:ImageButton ID="ImageButton2"
                runat="server" ImageUrl="~/Images/btn-delete-off.png" Height="25"
                PostBackUrl='<%# "~/EventEditor.aspx?mode=delete&id="
                    + Eval("ID") %>'/></asp:TableCell>
            </asp:TableRow>
        </asp:Table>
    </ItemTemplate>
</asp:DataList>
...
```

The HeaderTemplate and the ItemTemplate both contain Table controls. This may seem like an odd thing to do, but notice that I have set the ExtractTemplateRows attribute to true, like this:

```
...
<asp:DataList ID="DataList1" runat="server" CssClass="dataview" rules="cols"
    ExtractTemplateRows="True">
...
```

This is a neat trick that DataList offers. By default, DataList renders an outer HTML table element and inserts the output from the ItemTemplate into a table cell (td) element, which in turn is inserted into a table row (tr) element. This is fine if you just want to display simple values. DataList creates a one-column table, and the contents of the ItemTemplate are displayed inside each row for that column.

■ **Tip**   You will notice that I have not added paging to the DataList control. This is for simplicity and because the application we are re-creating didn't page either. You can see examples of paging with the rich data controls in Chapter 20.

If we try to add our own `table` or `tr` elements to display more complex values, then we get an odd effect, as shown in Figure 21-6. Now each row of the one-column outer table contains a separate table, as does the `HeaderTemplate`, and they all size themselves to their contents.

Figure 21-6. *Embedding table elements in the DataList ItemTemplate*

A similar effect arises if we define our own `tr` elements in the templates. In both cases, any border defined for the DataList doesn't go right around the outer table and contains breaks in continuity. We can fix this by setting the `ExtractTemplateRows` attribute to `true` in the markup for the DataList control and by using Table controls in our `ItemTemplate` and `HeaderTemplate` definitions. The DataList control finds the individual `TableHeaderRow` and `TableRow` elements and adds them directly to the outer table, without wrapping them in any way. This means the HTML generated by the templates appears in the same table, and the border and alignments issues do not occur. The individual Table controls aren't rendered. They are just a convenient container so that DataList can find and extract the rows from the template.

Understanding the DataList Templates

Once we understand the purpose of the Table controls, the templates themselves are pretty simple. The HeaderTemplate defines a single header row that will provide a label for each column. The ItemTemplate uses standard data binding to express fields from the data items.

There are a couple of points to note in the ItemTemplate. The first is that I bind to values that are not in the Event object as defined in the Entity Framework data model, like this:

```
...<%# Eval("PRank") %>...
...<%# Eval("RRank") %>...
```

The data that we require for this control isn't obtainable directly from the database, which is why I have not used a data source control. Instead, I have used a LINQ query, which you'll see shortly. The second point of note is that the two ImageButton controls that are included in the ItemTemplate, like this:

```
<asp:ImageButton ID="ImageButton2" runat="server"
    ImageUrl="~/Images/btn-delete-off.png" Height="25"
    PostBackUrl='<%# "~/EventEditor.aspx?mode=delete&id=" + Eval("ID")%>'/>
```

I use the PostBackUrl attribute to specify that the EventEditor page be invoked when these buttons are clicked, using the query string to specify two parameters: mode, to differentiate between editing and deleting a record, and id, to specify the value of the ID field of the Entity object that we want to edit or delete. You'll see how I have implemented the EventEditor.aspx page later in this chapter.

Adding the Other UI Elements

We need to add two other UI elements to the Events.aspx page: the drop-down list that allows the user to filter the events by type and a button that starts the process for adding a new event to the database. You can see the markup for both of these in Listing 21-12.

Listing 21-12. *Adding the filter selector and the Add button*

```
...
<table id="eventselector">
    <tr>
    <td>Event Type:</td>
    <td>
        <asp:DropDownList ID="DropDownList1" runat="server" AutoPostBack="True" />
    </td>
    <td><asp:ImageButton ID="AddEventButton" runat="server"
        ImageUrl="~/Images/btn-add-event-off.png" Height="25"
        PostBackUrl="~/EventEditor.aspx?mode=add" /></td>
    </tr>
</table>
...
```

As you might imagine, I have used a DropDownList control for the first UI element. I have set the AutoPostBack attribute to true so that the form is posted back to the ASP.NET server as soon as the user selects a value.

The button is handled by another ImageButton control, also configured to post back to the `EventEditor` page, just like the Edit and Delete buttons in the DataList control. In this case, I use the query string to set the `mode` parameter to `add`, which is a signal to the `EventEditor.aspx` page that we want to create a new record.

Obtaining the Data and Configuring the Controls

I have not added any data source controls to the `Events.aspx` page. This is because the data required for the DataList and DropDownList controls cannot be obtained directly from a single database table, and I prefer to use LINQ whenever I have to manipulate data (as previously mentioned, I really like LINQ, and it doesn't take much of an excuse for me to use it). Listing 21-13 shows the queries I have used in the `Events.aspx` code-behind class.

Listing 21-13. *The Events code-behind class*

```
using System;
using System.Collections.Generic;
using System.Linq;

namespace TriathlonApp {
    public partial class Events : System.Web.UI.Page {

        protected void Page_Load(object sender, EventArgs args) {

            using (TrainingDataEntities entities = new TrainingDataEntities()) {

                if (!IsPostBack) {
                    DropDownList1.DataSource
                        = new[] { "All" }.Concat(entities.EventTypes.Select(e => e.Name));
                }

                string selectedEventType
                    = string.IsNullOrEmpty(DropDownList1.SelectedValue)
                        ? "All" : DropDownList1.SelectedValue;

                IEnumerable<Event> events = selectedEventType == "All" ?
                    entities.Events :
                        entities.Events.Where(e => e.Type == selectedEventType);

                DataList1.DataSource = events.Select(e => new {
                    e.ID,
                    e.Date,
                    e.Athlete,
                    e.Type,
                    e.SwimTime,
                    e.CycleTime,
                    e.RunTime,
                    e.OverallTime,
```

```
                    PRank = entities.GetPersonalRanking(e.Athlete, e.Type, e.SwimTime,
                        e.CycleTime, e.RunTime, e.OverallTime)
                        .Where(r => r.Activity == "Overall")
                        .Select(r => r.Pos).FirstOrDefault(),
                    RRank = entities.GetReferenceRanking(e.Type, e.SwimTime, e.CycleTime,
                        e.RunTime, e.OverallTime)
                        .Where(r => r.Activity == "Overall")
                        .Select(r => r.Pos).FirstOrDefault()
                });

            DataBind();
        }
    }
}
}
```

I start by setting the items in the DropDownList control. I do this only when the request isn't a postback to the server. This means the DropDownList control can use the view state feature to maintain the user's selected value when the page is updated. If I reset the data source each time the page was loaded, then either I would have to take care to preserve the selection or we would have to accept that the value displayed by the drop-down menu and the items shown by the DataList control would be uncoordinated.

I want to provide values for each of the records in the EventTypes table, plus a value that represents the entire set of events available, which I have expressed as All. To do this, I use the LINQ Concat method to combine two sequences, like this:

```
DropDownList1.DataSource = new[] { "All" }.Concat(entities.EventTypes.Select(e => e.Name));
```

The first sequence contains just the value All, and this is combined with the value of the Name field for each EventType object that the Entity Framework produces.

The next task is to use the selected value from the DropDownList control to select the Events we need to display. I do this in two stages. The first is to get the selected value, as follows:

```
string selectedEventType = string.IsNullOrEmpty(DropDownList1.SelectedValue)
    ? "All" : DropDownList1.SelectedValue;
```

When the page is first loaded, the DropDownList control won't have bound to the data items produced by the LINQ result, and so the SelectedValue property won't return a meaningful value. When this happens, I assume we need to display all the events and default to the All value.

I then use the selected value to perform a LINQ query, like this:

```
IEnumerable<Event> events = selectedEventType == "All" ?
    entities.Events :
    entities.Events.Where(e => e.Type == selectedEventType);
```

There is no All event type, so when this is the selected value, I use a different LINQ query. Otherwise, I use a standard where clause to filter the items contained in the database.

The next step is to project a sequence of anonymously typed object from the LINQ results and set them as the data source for the DataList control:

```
DataList1.DataSource = events.Select(e => new {
    e.ID,
    e.Date,
    e.Athlete,
    e.Type,
    e.SwimTime,
    e.CycleTime,
    e.RunTime,
    e.OverallTime,
    PRank = entities.GetPersonalRanking(e.Athlete, e.Type, e.SwimTime,
        e.CycleTime, e.RunTime, e.OverallTime)
        .Where(r => r.Activity == "Overall")
        .Select(r => r.Pos).FirstOrDefault(),
    RRank = entities.GetReferenceRanking(e.Type, e.SwimTime, e.CycleTime,
        e.RunTime, e.OverallTime)
        .Where(r => r.Activity == "Overall")
        .Select(r => r.Pos).FirstOrDefault()
});
```

I need to generate the values for the PRank and RRank fields that I bind to in the control templates. Unfortunately, these values are produced by calling stored procedures for each event record, which means we make one request for the required set of events and then two additional requests for each event that we are going to display.

This may seem needlessly inelegant, but it accurately reflects a dilemma that programmers often face. It is rare that the structure of a database completely matches the data we require for a page, and so we either have to make additional requests or modify the database in some way. In this case, I have elected to make the additional requests.

The final statement in the code-behind class is this one:

```
DataBind();
```

We don't have to call DataBind on each individual data-bound control on a page. We can instead invoke the method on the code-behind class, and it will ensure that the data controls are properly bound to their data sources. Once we have implemented the code-behind class, we can see how the Events.aspx page looks. It should be similar to Figure 21-7.

Figure 21-7. The populated Events.aspx page

The page shown in the figure is displaying only Olympic events, selected through the drop-down list.

Building the Event Editor Page

The Add New Event, Edit, and Delete buttons in the `Events.aspx` page all load the `EventEditor.aspx` page, providing context using the query string as to what actions are required. We can expect to deal with three types of URLs:

```
/EventEditor.aspx?mode=add
/EventEditor.aspx?mode=edit&id=3
/EventEditor.aspx?mode=delete&id=3
```

The first is the kind we can expect when the user wants to add a new event, and the others are for when the user wants to edit or delete an event, respectively. For this page, I have started by defining the data source controls, as shown in Listing 21-14.

Listing 21-14. The data source controls in the EventEditor.aspx page

```
<%@ Page Title="" Language="C#" MasterPageFile="~/Site.Master" AutoEventWireup="true"
CodeBehind="EventEditor.aspx.cs" Inherits="TriathlonApp.EventEditor" %>
<asp:Content ID="Content1" ContentPlaceHolderID="head" runat="server">
    <title>Event Editor</title>
    <style type="text/css">
        table.centerTable {border:thin solid black; margin: 10px auto 10px auto}
    </style>
</asp:Content>
```

```
<asp:Content ID="Content2" ContentPlaceHolderID="ContentPlaceHolder1" runat="server">

    <!-- other controls will go here -->

    <asp:EntityDataSource ID="EntityDataSource1" runat="server"
        ConnectionString="name=TrainingDataEntities"
        DefaultContainerName="TrainingDataEntities" EnableDelete="True"
        EnableFlattening="False" EnableInsert="True" EnableUpdate="True"
        EntitySetName="Events">
    </asp:EntityDataSource>
    <asp:EntityDataSource ID="EntityDataSource2" runat="server"
        ConnectionString="name=TrainingDataEntities"
        DefaultContainerName="TrainingDataEntities" EnableFlattening="False"
        EntitySetName="Athletes">
    </asp:EntityDataSource>
    <asp:EntityDataSource ID="EntityDataSource3" runat="server"
        ConnectionString="name=TrainingDataEntities"
        DefaultContainerName="TrainingDataEntities" EnableFlattening="False"
        EntitySetName="EventTypes" Select="it.[Name]">
    </asp:EntityDataSource>
</asp:Content>
```

There are three data source controls. The first retrieves the Event that we want to edit or delete and will be responsible for making changes to the database, including adding new records.

The second data source retrieves the contents of the Athletes table, and the third does the same for the EventTypes table. I will use both of these data source controls to populate DropDownList controls to constrain the range of values that the user can select when creating or editing a record.

The heavy lifting in this page is handled by a FormView control, the markup for which is shown in Listing 21-15.

Listing 21-15. *The markup for the FormView control*

```
<asp:FormView ID="FormView1" runat="server" DataSourceID="EntityDataSource1"
    RenderOuterTable="False" DefaultMode="Edit"
    onitemupdated="ItemChanged" DataKeyNames="ID"
    onitemdeleted="ItemChanged" oniteminserted="ItemChanged">
    <EditItemTemplate>
        <table class="centerTable">
            <colgroup>
            <col />
            <col width="100" />
            </colgroup>
        <tr><th colspan="4">Event Details</th></tr>
        <tr>
            <td>Date:</td>
            <td>
                <asp:TextBox ID="TextBox1" runat="server"
                    Text='<%# Bind("Date", "{0:d}") %>' />
            </td>
            <td>Swim Time:</td>
```

```
                <td>
                    <asp:TextBox ID="TextBox2" runat="server" Text='<%# Bind("SwimTime") %>'/>
                </td>
            </tr>
            <tr>
                <td>Athlete:</td>
                <td>
                    <asp:DropDownList ID="DropDownList1" runat="server"
                        DataSourceID="EntityDataSource2"
                        SelectedValue='<%# Bind("Athlete") %>' DataTextField="Name"/>
                </td>
                <td>Cycle Time:</td>
                <td>
                    <asp:TextBox ID="TextBox4" runat="server" Text='<%# Bind("CycleTime") %>'/>
                </td>
            </tr>
            <tr>
                <td>Event Type:</td>
                <td>
                    <asp:DropDownList ID="DropDownList2" runat="server"
                        DataSourceID="EntityDataSource3" SelectedValue='<%# Bind("Type") %>'
                        DataTextField="Name"/>
                </td>
                <td>Run Time:</td>
                <td>
                    <asp:TextBox ID="TextBox5" runat="server" Text='<%# Bind("RunTime") %>'/>
                </td>
            </tr>
            <tr>
                <td colspan="2" />
                <td>Overall Time:</td>
                <td>
                    <asp:TextBox ID="TextBox6" runat="server" Text='<%# Bind("OverallTime")%>'/>
                </td>
            </tr>
            <tr>
                <td colspan="4" style="text-align:center">
                    <asp:Button ID="EditButton" runat="server" Text="Update"
                        CommandName="Update"/>
                    <asp:Button ID="DeleteButton" runat="server" Text="Delete"
                        CommandName="Delete"/>
                </td>
            </tr>
            </table>
    </EditItemTemplate>
    <InsertItemTemplate>
        <table class="centerTable">
            <colgroup>
            <col />
            <col width="100" />
            </colgroup>
        <tr><th colspan="4">Event Details</th></tr>
```

```
            <tr>
                <td>Date:</td>
                <td>
                    <asp:TextBox ID="TextBox1" runat="server"
                        Text='<%# Bind("Date", "{0:d}") %>' />
                </td>
                <td>Swim Time:</td>
                <td>
                    <asp:TextBox ID="TextBox2" runat="server" Text='<%# Bind("SwimTime") %>'/>
                </td>
            </tr>
            <tr>
                <td>Athlete:</td>
                <td>
                    <asp:DropDownList ID="DropDownList1" runat="server" DataTextField="Name"
                        DataSourceID="EntityDataSource2" SelectedValue='<%# Bind("Athlete")%>'/>
                </td>
                <td>Cycle Time:</td>
                <td>
                    <asp:TextBox ID="TextBox4" runat="server" Text='<%# Bind("CycleTime") %>'/>
                </td>
            </tr>
            <tr>
                <td>Event Type:</td>
                <td>
                    <asp:DropDownList ID="DropDownList2" runat="server" DataTextField="Name"
                        DataSourceID="EntityDataSource3" SelectedValue='<%# Bind("Type") %>' />
                </td>
                <td>Run Time:</td>
                <td>
                    <asp:TextBox ID="TextBox5" runat="server" Text='<%# Bind("RunTime") %>'/>
                </td>
            </tr>
            <tr>
                <td colspan="2" />
                <td>Overall Time:</td>
                <td><asp:TextBox ID="TextBox6" runat="server"
                    Text='<%# Bind("OverallTime") %>'/>   </td>
            </tr>
            <tr><td colspan="4" style="text-align:center">
                <asp:Button ID="Button1" runat="server" Text="Create" CommandName="Insert"/>
            </td></tr>
            </table>
        </InsertItemTemplate>
</asp:FormView>
```

This is a lot of markup, but the result is pretty simple. I have defined InsertItemTemplate and EditItemTemplate elements. The InsertItemTemplate will be used when the user wants to create an event. The template defines a simple table layout and uses data binding to display the values of an event record. There are two DropDownList controls that bind to the data sources to restrict the user choice for the Athlete and Type fields.

■ **Note**   To keep the example simple, I have left out any validation of the form controls. I don't recommend that you do this in a real project. See Chapter 17 for details of the Web Forms validation controls and examples of their use.

This template also includes two Button controls, which use the `CommandName` values of `Update` and `Delete`. These cause the FormView control to push any changes the user has made to the database or delete the record entirely, depending on which button has been clicked.

The `InsertItemTemplate` is similar in structure to the `EditItemTemplate`, except that there is only one Button control and it has the `CommandName` value `Insert`. Notice that I have still used data binding for the individual fields, even though this is a new record and won't have any values to display. This is so that I can rely on the FormView control to pick up the values entered by the user and handle the insert operation automatically.

The FormView control is fussy about which `CommandName` values it will respond to, which is why I have essentially duplicated the same template. If we send a bubble event with the `Insert` value for the `CommandName` from the `EditItemTemplate`, the FormView control will ignore the action and do nothing.

Adding the Code-Behind Class

All that remains is to manage the FormView control in the code-behind class so that we respond to the parameter values supplied in the query string. Listing 21-16 shows the code-behind class.

Listing 21-16. The EventEditor code-behind class

```
using System;
using System.Web.UI.WebControls;

namespace TriathlonApp {
    public partial class EventEditor : System.Web.UI.Page {
        private string mode;

        protected void Page_Load(object sender, EventArgs e) {

            mode = Request.QueryString["mode"];
            string id =  Request.QueryString["id"];

            if (string.IsNullOrEmpty(mode)) {
                Response.Redirect("~/Events.aspx");
            } else {
                if (mode == "add") {
                    FormView1.ChangeMode(FormViewMode.Insert);
                } else if (mode == "edit" || mode == "delete") {
                    EntityDataSource1.Where = "it.ID = " + id;
                    FormView1.ChangeMode(FormViewMode.Edit);
                }
            }
        }
    }
}
```

```
        protected void ItemChanged(object sender, EventArgs e) {
            Response.Redirect("~/Events.aspx");
        }

        protected void Page_PreRender(object sender, EventArgs e) {
            if (mode == "edit" || mode == "delete") {
                FormView1.FindControl("EditButton").Visible = mode == "edit";
                FormView1.FindControl("DeleteButton").Visible = mode == "delete";
            }
        }
    }
}
```

I use the Page_Load method to get the values for the mode and id parameters and use them to configure the data control and the data source control. For the FormView control, I need to call the ChangeMode method to select either the Insert (for adding new records) or the Edits (for modifying or deleting records) mode. This ensures that the correct template is displayed and, critically, means that the FormView will respond to the bubble events that arise from the Button controls in the templates.

For the EntityDataSource control, I set the Where property to filter the data items so that only the item we want to work with is available, like this:

```
EntityDataSource1.Where = "it.ID = " + id;
```

When setting these properties, we are essentially defining LINQ queries, and it references the current item in the source sequence. This is equivalent to a query such as this:

```
new TrainingEntities().Events.Where(it => it.ID == id)
```

Note, however, that we don't use the C# equality operator (==) when setting the Where property on an EntityDataSource. Instead, we must use the assignment operator (==).

Handling the Control Events

In the markup for the FormView control, I register the ItemChanged method as the handler for the ItemUpdated, ItemInserted, and ItemDeleted events. This ensures that the ItemChanged method will be called whenever the user completes an operation using the FormView control. The implementation of this method is simple:

```
protected void ItemChanged(object sender, EventArgs e) {
    Response.Redirect("~/Events.aspx");
}
```

I simply use the Redirect method to return the user to the Events.aspx page.

Tweaking the Buttons

The remaining method in the code-behind class is Page_PreRender, which as you'll recall from Chapter 5, is called just before the page is rendered to HTML. Here is the implementation of the method:

```
protected void Page_PreRender(object sender, EventArgs e) {
    if (mode == "edit" || mode == "delete") {
        FormView1.FindControl("EditButton").Visible = mode == "edit";
        FormView1.FindControl("DeleteButton").Visible = mode == "delete";
    }
}
```

I set the visibility of the Button controls in the EditItemTemplate based on the mode parameter that we received as part of the query string. I do this so that the user sees only the button that is relevant to the action they are performing.

I have to do this in response to the PreRender event because the FormView control doesn't load the template until it has been data-bound, which occurs after the Load event. Once this has happened, we can use the FindControl method to locate the Button controls and set the Visible property. You can see the finished EventEditor.aspx page as it appears in the browser in Figure 21-8.

Figure 21-8. Editing an event using the EventEditor.aspx page

This page in particular demonstrates the strengths of Web Forms when it comes to working with data. We just selected the data we wanted using the data source control, set out templates for displaying the data in different ways, and defined some Button controls to trigger actions. We didn't have to deal with loading, updating, deleting, or adding records at all. Everything was handled for us.

Building the Performance Page

We have dealt with all the complex parts of this application. All that remain are a couple of pages that are largely similar to their Part II implementations. The Performance page is relatively simple; you can see the markup in Listing 21-17. I use a data source control to populate a DropDownList with the names of the athletes in the database and use individual Label controls in a regular HTML `table` to display data values. This is an approach I use often, using regular HTML for elements that don't change and Web Forms controls when I need to set a value in the code-behind class or when I want to receive and process events.

Listing 21-17. *The markup for the Performance.aspx page*

```
<%@ Page Title="" Language="C#" MasterPageFile="~/Site.Master" AutoEventWireup="true"
CodeBehind="Performance.aspx.cs" Inherits="TriathlonApp.Performance" %>

<asp:Content ID="Content1" ContentPlaceHolderID="head" runat="server">
    <title>Performance</title>
    <style type="text/css">
        table.centerTable {margin-left:auto;margin-right:auto;
                            border:thin solid black; margin-bottom:10px}
    </style>
</asp:Content>

<asp:Content ID="Content2" ContentPlaceHolderID="ContentPlaceHolder1" runat="server">

<div style="width:100%; text-align:center; padding:10px">
    <asp:Label ID="Label1" runat="server" Text="Athlete:"></asp:Label>
    <asp:DropDownList ID="DropDownList1" runat="server"
        DataSourceID="EntityDataSource1" DataTextField="Name" DataValueField="Name"
        AutoPostBack="True"/>
</div>

<table class="centerTable">
    <colgroup><col /><col width="100px" /><col /><col width="40px" /></colgroup>
    <tr><th colspan="4">Sprint Results</th></tr>
    <tr>
     <td>Best Swim Time:</td><td><asp:Label ID="sbstLabel" runat="server" Text="--"/></td>
     <td>Best Swim Rank:</td><td><asp:Label ID="sbsrLabel" runat="server" Text="--"/></td>
    </tr>
    <tr>
     <td>Best Cycle Time:</td><td><asp:Label ID="sbctLabel" runat="server" Text="--"/></td>
     <td>Best Cycle Rank:</td><td><asp:Label ID="sbcrLabel" runat="server" Text="--"/></td>
    </tr>
    <tr>
     <td>Best Run Time:</td>
     <td><asp:Label ID="sbrtLabel" runat="server" Text="--"/></td>
     <td>Best Run Rank:</td>
     <td><asp:Label ID="sbrrLabel" runat="server" Text="--"/></td>
    </tr>
```

```
    <tr>
     <td>Best Overall Time:</td><td><asp:Label ID="sbotLabel" runat="server" Text="--"/></td>
     <td>Best Overall Rank:</td><td><asp:Label ID="sborLabel" runat="server" Text="--"/></td>
    </tr>
</table>

<table class="centerTable">
    <colgroup><col /><col width="100px" /><col /><col width="40px" /></colgroup>
    <tr><th colspan="4">Olympic Results</th></tr>
    <tr>
     <td>Best Swim Time:</td><td><asp:Label ID="obstLabel" runat="server" Text="--"/></td>
     <td>Best Swim Rank:</td><td><asp:Label ID="obsrLabel" runat="server" Text="--"/> </td>
    </tr>
    <tr>
     <td>Best Cycle Time:</td><td><asp:Label ID="obctLabel" runat="server" Text="--"/></td>
     <td>Best Cycle Rank:</td><td><asp:Label ID="obcrLabel" runat="server" Text="--"/></td>
    </tr>
    <tr>
     <td>Best Run Time:</td><td><asp:Label ID="obrtLabel" runat="server" Text="--"/></td>
     <td>Best Run Rank:</td><td><asp:Label ID="obrrLabel" runat="server" Text="--"/></td>
    </tr>
    <tr>
     <td>Best Overall Time:</td><td><asp:Label ID="obotLabel" runat="server" Text="--"/></td>
     <td>Best Overall Rank:</td><td><asp:Label ID="oborLabel" runat="server" Text="--"/> </td>
    </tr>
</table>

<asp:EntityDataSource ID="EntityDataSource1" runat="server"
    ConnectionString="name=TrainingDataEntities"
    DefaultContainerName="TrainingDataEntities" EnableFlattening="False"
    EntitySetName="Athletes" Select="it.[Name]"/>
</asp:Content>
```

The data that I require for the two **table** elements requires some processing, so I use LINQ in the code-behind class, as shown in Listing 21-18.

Listing 21-18. *The Performance code-behind class*

```
using System;
using System.Collections.Generic;
using System.Linq;
using System.Web.UI.WebControls;

namespace TriathlonApp {
    public partial class Performance : System.Web.UI.Page {

        protected void Page_Load(object sender, EventArgs args) {

            using (TrainingDataEntities entities = new TrainingDataEntities()) {
```

```
        // get the selected athlete
        string athlete = DropDownList1.SelectedValue;
        if (string.IsNullOrEmpty(athlete)) {
            athlete = entities.Athletes.First().Name;
        }

        ProcessFieldSet(entities, athlete, "Sprint",
            new Label[] { sbstLabel, sbctLabel, sbrtLabel, sbotLabel },
            new Label[] { sbsrLabel, sbcrLabel, sbrrLabel, sborLabel });

        ProcessFieldSet(entities, athlete, "Olympic",
          new Label[] { obstLabel, obctLabel, obrtLabel, obotLabel },
          new Label[] { obsrLabel, obcrLabel, obrrLabel, oborLabel });
    }
}

private void ProcessFieldSet(TrainingDataEntities entities, string athlete,
    string eventType, Label[] personaLabels, Label[] overallLabels) {

    Event bestTimes = new Event();
    IEnumerable<Event> classEvents = entities.Events
        .Where(e => e.Athlete == athlete && e.Type == eventType);

    if (classEvents.Count() > 0) {

        bestTimes.SwimTime = classEvents.Select(e => e.SwimTime).Min();
        bestTimes.CycleTime = classEvents.Select(e => e.CycleTime).Min();
        bestTimes.RunTime = classEvents.Select(e => e.RunTime).Min();
        bestTimes.OverallTime = classEvents.Select(e => e.OverallTime).Min();

        personaLabels[0].Text = bestTimes.SwimTime.ToString();
        personaLabels[1].Text = bestTimes.CycleTime.ToString();
        personaLabels[2].Text = bestTimes.RunTime.ToString();
        personaLabels[3].Text = bestTimes.OverallTime.ToString();

        // get the ranking for the sprint events
        IEnumerable<Ranking> ranks = entities.GetReferenceRanking(eventType,
            bestTimes.SwimTime, bestTimes.CycleTime,
            bestTimes.RunTime, bestTimes.OverallTime);

        foreach (Ranking rank in ranks) {
            switch (rank.Activity) {
                case "Swim":
                    overallLabels[0].Text = rank.Pos.ToString();
                    break;
                case "Cycle":
                    overallLabels[1].Text = rank.Pos.ToString();
                    break;
                case "Run":
                    overallLabels[2].Text = rank.Pos.ToString();
                    break;
                case "Overall":
```

```
                        overallLabels[3].Text = rank.Pos.ToString();
                        break;
                }
            }

        } else {
            foreach (Label lab in personaLabels.Concat(overallLabels)) {
                lab.Text = "--";
            }
        }
    }
}
```

I am not going to go into the details of this code. There is nothing in this class that you haven't seen in earlier chapters because we don't require any of the special Web Forms features to process or display the data. You can see the completed Performance.aspx page as it is shown by the browser in Figure 21-9.

Figure 21-9. *The completed Performance.aspx page*

Building the Calculator Page

The remaining page is even simpler. However, for variety, I have used a Web Forms Table control, as shown in Listing 21-19.

Listing 21-19. The markup for the Calculator.aspx page

```
<%@ Page Title="" Language="C#" MasterPageFile="~/Site.Master" AutoEventWireup="true"
CodeBehind="Calculator.aspx.cs" Inherits="TriathlonApp.Calculator" %>

<asp:Content ID="Content1" ContentPlaceHolderID="head" runat="server">
    <title>Calculator</title>
    <style type="text/css">
        table.CalcTable {margin:20px;float:left}
    </style>
</asp:Content>

<asp:Content ID="Content2" ContentPlaceHolderID="ContentPlaceHolder1" runat="server">

<asp:Table ID="Table1" runat="server" CssClass="CalcTable">
    <asp:TableRow>
        <asp:TableCell>Laps:</asp:TableCell>
        <asp:TableCell>
            <asp:TextBox ID="LapsTextBox" runat="server">80</asp:TextBox>
        </asp:TableCell>
    </asp:TableRow>
    <asp:TableRow>
        <asp:TableCell>Pool Length:</asp:TableCell>
        <asp:TableCell>
            <asp:TextBox ID="LengthTextBox" runat="server">20</asp:TextBox>
        </asp:TableCell>
    </asp:TableRow>
    <asp:TableRow>
        <asp:TableCell>Minutes:</asp:TableCell>
        <asp:TableCell>
            <asp:TextBox ID="MinutesTextBox" runat="server">60</asp:TextBox>
        </asp:TableCell>
    </asp:TableRow>
    <asp:TableRow>
        <asp:TableCell>Calories/Hour:</asp:TableCell>
        <asp:TableCell>
            <asp:TextBox ID="CaloriesTextBox" runat="server">1070</asp:TextBox>
        </asp:TableCell>
    </asp:TableRow>
    <asp:TableFooterRow>
        <asp:TableCell ColumnSpan="2" HorizontalAlign="Center">
            <asp:ImageButton ID="CalculateButton" runat="server"
                ImageUrl="~/Images/btn-calculate-off.png" Height="25"/>
        </asp:TableCell>
    </asp:TableFooterRow>
</asp:Table>
```

```
<asp:Table ID="ResultsTable" runat="server" CssClass="CalcTable" Visible="False">
    <asp:TableHeaderRow>
        <asp:TableHeaderCell ColumnSpan="2">Results</asp:TableHeaderCell>
    </asp:TableHeaderRow>
    <asp:TableRow>
        <asp:TableCell>Distance:</asp:TableCell>
        <asp:TableCell><asp:Label ID="DistanceLabel" runat="server"
            ForeColor="Black" /> miles</asp:TableCell></asp:TableRow>
    <asp:TableRow>
        <asp:TableCell>Calories:</asp:TableCell>
        <asp:TableCell>
            <asp:Label ID="CalsLabel" runat="server" ForeColor="Black"/>
        </asp:TableCell>
    </asp:TableRow>
    <asp:TableRow>
        <asp:TableCell>Pace:</asp:TableCell>
        <asp:TableCell>
            <asp:Label ID="PaceLabel" runat="server" ForeColor="Black"/> seconds/lap
        </asp:TableCell>
    </asp:TableRow>
</asp:Table>

</asp:Content>
```

Once again, I have omitted any validation controls, but you should not do this in a real project. Listing 21-20 shows the code-behind class for the `Calculator.aspx` page. This is very similar to the implementation of the corresponding page in Part II of this book.

Listing 21-20. *The Calculator code-behind class*

```
using System;

namespace TriathlonApp {
    public partial class Calculator : System.Web.UI.Page {
        private const float metersToMiles = 0.00062137119223733f;
        private const float minsPerHour = 60f;

        protected void Page_Load(object sender, EventArgs e) {

            if (IsPostBack) {

                // parse the input values
                int laps = int.Parse(LapsTextBox.Text);
                int length = int.Parse(LengthTextBox.Text);
                int minutes = int.Parse(MinutesTextBox.Text);
                int calories = int.Parse(CaloriesTextBox.Text);

                // perform the calculation and set the result values
                DistanceLabel.Text = ((laps * length) * metersToMiles).ToString("F2");
                CalsLabel.Text = ((minutes / minsPerHour) * calories).ToString("F0");
                PaceLabel.Text = ((minutes * minsPerHour) / laps).ToString("F0");
```

```
            // make the results table visible
            ResultsTable.Visible = true;
        }
    }
  }
}
```

And with that class, we have completed the application, adding some key Web Forms features as covered in the previous chapters. You can see the completed `Calculator.aspx` page in Figure 21-10.

Figure 21-10. *The completed Calculator.aspx page*

Summary

In this chapter, we implemented the triathlon application using Web Forms controls and features. We saw the strengths and weaknesses of Web Forms in this simple application. The strengths are the speed and simplicity with which we can create pages that contain data and the ease with which we can manipulate that data to edit, delete, or add records to the underlying database. We also combined Web Forms controls with static HTML, something I tend to do often.

The weaknesses are equally evident, such as the little tweaks and tricks that are required to make the Web Forms controls behave as required and the limitations of the data source controls when it comes to complex data manipulations. Overall, however, the Web Forms controls do a solid job, and although it can take some trial and error to get the controls to do just as we want, the time is well-spent given the richness and flexibility of the results.

I return to the theme with which I opened this part of the book. Web Forms is slick, flexible, and feature-rich and can deliver great results when used on the right kind of project. Depending on the situation you face, it can be worth seeing past the shininess of the MVC framework and embracing the capable and useful Web Forms.

PART IV

Using the MVC Framework

The MVC framework is a relatively recent addition to ASP.NET and provides a very different and more modern approach to web application development compared to Web Forms. If you are familiar with Ruby on Rails, for example, you'll recognize a lot of common themes in the MVC framework.

In the chapters that follow, I'll show you how the MVC framework fits into the ASP.NET world, explain how to create application using the MVC framework, and demonstrate the strengths and weaknesses of this new technology.

CHAPTER 22

Putting MVC in Context

The MVC framework is a relatively new addition to ASP.NET, and it takes a very different approach to building web applications. The Web Forms system that you saw earlier has a lot to offer, but if you want to build a large-scale web application that was a long life cycle and that embodies current trends in web development, then you should consider using the MVC framework.

In this chapter, I'll give you a little context for the MVC framework and describe its main strengths and weaknesses.

What won't be apparent until we start building MVC framework applications in the coming chapters is just how much the *style* of programming with the MVC framework differs from Web Forms. Once the basics are mastered, the MVC framework offers a compelling approach to development that results in flexible and maintainable web applications.

Note There are limits to the amount of detail that I can include in this part of the book. I'll show you everything you need to know in order to effectively create and deploy MVC framework applications, but there isn't room for all the gory details. If you are interested in more in-depth details, including the extensive customizations that the MVC framework supports, I suggest the book I wrote with Steve Sanderson who is from the Microsoft Web Platform and Tools team (the people responsible for the MVC framework). The book is called *Pro ASP.NET MVC 3 Framework*, published by Apress.

Understanding Model-View-Controller

ASP.NET has been enormously successful, but in recent years new trends in web application development, especially Web Forms, have made the platform look a little outdated.

The days where the developer doesn't know about HTTP and HTML and doesn't *want* to know are past, and competing technologies such as Ruby on Rails have embraced the details of these technologies to create an entirely different approach to web application development, reinvigorating an old architectural pattern called *Model-View-Controller* (MVC).

The MVC pattern has been around since the late 1970s and comes back into fashion every now and again. The reason that MVC is back in the limelight now is that it fits very nicely with the stateless nature of HTTP requests and, with the right tools, can be used to build scalable and maintainable applications.

It is important to differentiate between the *MVC architecture pattern* and the *MVC framework*. The MVC architecture pattern is an abstract approach to developing applications. The MVC framework is a set of tools and technologies produced by Microsoft that embraces the MVC pattern in order to create a more modern, more Ruby-like development experience for web applications.

We are going to focus on the MVC framework rather than the pattern in this book, but the two dovetail together pretty closely anyway. As the name suggests, an application created using the MVC framework has three main parts:

- *Models*, which contain or represent the data that users work with. These can be simple *view models*, which just represent data being transferred between views and controllers, or *domain models*, which represent the data in a business domain as well as the operations, transformations, and rules for manipulating that data.

- *Views*, which are used to render some part of the model as a user interface.

- *Controllers*, which process incoming requests, perform operations on the model, and select views to render to the user.

■ **Note** You might find that some of these concepts are familiar even if you have not heard of MVC before. There are a couple of reasons why. The first is that even though the MVC pattern isn't universally known, the ideas that it contains have been widely adopted and adapted elsewhere, such as in other patterns, in best-practice guidance, and so on. The other reason is that much of MVC is just common sense, and many developers intuitively write code that incorporates some of the essential MVC concepts.

Understanding the Model

The most important part of an MVC application is the *domain model*. A domain is the universe that our application works in. In a banking application, for example, the domain includes everything in the bank that the application operates on. This might include accounts, the general ledger, and credit limits and balances for customers. The domain also includes all of the processes that can be performed on those things, such as the means by which credit limits are assessed, funds are transferred between accounts, and new accounts are created, for example.

When we write an application using the MVC framework, we create a software representation of the domain. This is the *domain model*. The domain model is a set of .NET types (classes, structs, and so on) that are known as the *domain types*, and the logic in the methods of these types represents the processes in the model. (To complete the nomenclature when we create an instance of a domain type, we create a new *domain object*.)

The logic in the model types is responsible for preserving the integrity and overall state of the domain model, such as making sure that all transactions are added to the ledger or making sure that a client doesn't withdraw more money than they are entitled to or more money than the bank has.

In most MVC applications, the domain model is persistent and long-lived, reflecting the nature of the domain being modeled. There are lots of different ways to make a domain model persistent, but the most common remains a relational database.

Models are also defined by what they are *not* responsible for; models don't deal with rendering UIs or processing requests. Those are the responsibilities of *views* and *controllers*, which I describe in a moment.

■ **Note** There is another kind of model, called a *view* (or *presentation*) model. These models are used to pass data between controllers and views. Chapter 28 shows some view models.

Understanding the Controller

The controller is responsible for processing incoming requests, performing operations on the domain model, and selecting the view that will be rendered in response to the request.

In the MVC framework, a controller is a class that is derived from System.Web.Mvc.Controller and that has a number of public methods, each of which represents an *action* that the controller will perform on the domain model. These are known as *action methods*. Each action method in a controller is associated with a URL, and when a request for that URL is received by the controller, the logic in the action method is executed, and the view that is selected by the action method is rendered and returned to the browser.

Understanding the View

In the MVC framework, the *view* is a template that is rendered to generate a response to a request, typically HTML to be sent to a browser, although we can also produce other kinds of data, including JSON and XML.

Views are the simplest part of the MVC triumvirate, although we do need to learn a new markup language, called *Razor*, to get the best from them. I introduce you to Razor in Chapter 25.

Understanding the Model, Controller, and View Interaction

The three parts of an MVC application have very clearly defined roles, and a key idea behind MVC is that we should not blur the lines between these roles. This means we don't process requests in the model, that we only use the view to render content, and that the glue between them is the controller. Figure 22-1 shows the interaction between the key components.

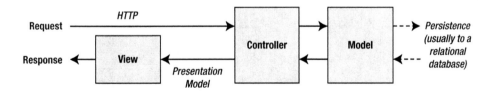

Figure 22-1. *The interactions in an MVC application*

Each piece of the MVC architecture is well-defined and self-contained. This is referred to as the *separation of concerns*. The logic that manipulates the data in the model is *only* contained in the model, the logic that displays data is *only* in the view, and the code that handles user requests and input is contained *only* in the controller.

Understanding MVC Framework Strengths

There is a lot to like when it comes to the MVC framework. In the following sections, I describe the key strengths of this technology.

Separation of Concerns

The main benefit of breaking our application into three separate *concerns* is that it makes programming easier and simplifies long-term maintenance.

I say that programming is easier because when coding, we only have to focus the responsibilities of the current concern, and we can ignore everything else. To return to our banking application, for example, if we were implementing the domain types for customer accounts, we just focus on accurately representing the domain and writing the logic that defines the processes that relate to accounts. We don't have to worry about how accounts are displayed to the user or how to handle requests from the browser that relate to accounts.

The long-term maintenance benefit arises because the functionality for a given feature should arise in only one concern, effectively isolating the rest of the application from change (or, at least, minimizing the amount of change in other concerns).

There are some responsibilities that affect all concerns, such as security or logging, for example. These are known as *cross-cutting concerns*. These concerns affect the entire application and can't be as easily separated. We'll see some examples of a cross-cutting concern in Chapter 34 when we look at authentication and authorization.

What constitutes a concern or a cross-cutting concern is often a matter of interpretation. In this book, we are focused more on the technology than the theory, so I am going to present examples that liberally interpret the pattern in order to emphasize the features of the MVC framework.

A WORD ON PATTERNS

Patterns can be incredibly useful when developing software. They express tried-and-tested ways of dealing with different kinds of problems, allowing the programmer to focus on implementation. By adopting a pattern, especially a widely used pattern, we can expect to create code that is more robust and easily understood by other programmers who are familiar with the pattern.

We can also expect to spend a lot of time arguing with other programmers about how true our code is to the intent of the pattern. As useful as they can be, patterns are incredibly divisive. Patterns are usually expressed in abstract terms, meaning that the programmer has to interpret some elements of the pattern to adapt them to a particular programming language and project. For some simple patterns, there are often implementations you can download and use, but for something as complex and far-reaching as MVC, there are choices and value judgments to be made. And this is where the trouble starts.

Like any topic that is subject to interpretation (such as politics, religion, and the tax code), different schools of thought emerge. Questions about the intent of the original pattern writers emerge, vicious critiques of implementations are advanced, and people put themselves forward as being one of the glorious few who understand what the pattern is really for.

If you think I am exaggerating, then just wait until you start a project that uses the MVC pattern. At least one of your colleagues will turn into someone who prefers to discuss the significance of the pattern, rather than applying it. If you are unlucky enough to have two such colleagues, then you can look forward to many hours of e-mail warfare. If you want to provoke actual violence, simply advance the view that pattern *X* is actually a derivation of pattern *Y* with some aspects of pattern *Z* roughly grafted on. Fisticuffs will ensue.

To my mind, patterns are just a *starting point*. Some smart people have figured out a nice, general approach for solving some software development problems. In the case of MVC, the pattern is about structuring an application so that it can be easily modified and maintained. But it doesn't matter how smart those people were. They didn't face the unique combination of technology, product, interpersonal, schedule, and financial constraints of your project. The best way to benefit from patterns is to take advantage of the fundamental approach but adapt it to suit your needs.

My advice is to try not to reason with pattern zealots. They have settled on their view, and there is nothing you can do to change it. Smile politely, back away slowly, and avoid all future conversations with that individual.

As an aside, you don't need to write in and complain to Apress if you have strongly held views on politics or religion (or the tax code for that matter) and don't like my equating these topics to software patterns. There is no need. I agree 100% with *your* view of the world, and I am referring to those *other* people—the ones who don't appreciate your unique wisdom and insight and charm. You are a wonderful person and quite possibly a genius, and I'll write a snippy e-mail on your behalf to anyone who doesn't think so.

Easy Testing

Unit testing has become extremely prevalent since ASP.NET was first developed, and the designers of the MVC framework have provided extensive support for unit testing individual aspects of an MVC application. An MVC framework can be unit tested with any one of a number of testing frameworks, including MSTest, which is part of the paid-for editions of Visual Studio.

Tight Control Over HTTP and HTML

The MVC framework gives the programmer very tight control over the HTML that is rendered to the browser and the way that HTTP requests are received and processed. This is an entirely different approach from the one you saw with Web Forms, which tries to hide the detail from the programmer and takes over the HTML. And since we are not using web controls, we don't have to worry about the bandwidth required to send the view state data around, and we are not limited to one HTML form per page.

One drawback of having absolute control is that we don't have access to the convenient Web Forms controls, but we can compensate for this by using libraries such as jQuery and jQuery UI, just as we saw in Part II of this book. In fact, as you'll see in Chapters 29 and 30, Microsoft has embraced jQuery in the MVC framework to provide some important functionality.

Open Source

The MVC framework is open source. Microsoft publishes the source code at http://aspnet.codeplex.com. There are limits placed on what you can do with that code, but I find it endlessly helpful in debugging MVC framework applications. Being able to trace requests all the way through the software stack is useful. Microsoft doesn't open the source code to the rest of the ASP.NET framework, but this is a good start, and I recommend you take a moment to download the source code.

Highly Configurable

Almost every aspect of the MVC framework can be replaced or supplemented with a custom implementation. We are not going to get into the details of advanced configuration in this book, but if there is any aspect of the MVC framework that doesn't work quite the way you want, then the odds are good that you can change it.

Built on ASP.NET

The MVC framework is built on the core ASP.NET platform, which means all the features that we saw in Part II of this book can be readily applied to MVC applications.

The Prettiest Girl at the Prom

The MVC framework has attracted a *lot* of attention, and that makes it easy to find programmers who want to work on MVC framework projects. It also means that there are burgeoning communities of MVC framework programmers on sites such as Stackoverflow.com who are able and willing to share their experiences and tips and tricks.

■ **Tip**   Of course, although a lot of programmers want to work on the MVC framework, there are not huge numbers that have any deep experience yet. Before selecting the MVC framework for a project, I suggest ensuring that you have the required skills available in your team. An inexperienced team can easily hit all of the shortcomings of the MVC framework without getting any of the benefits.

Understanding MVC Framework Weaknesses

The MVC framework isn't the prefect tool for every job. In the following sections, I describe some of the key drawbacks.

Lots of New Concepts to Learn

The approach taken by the MVC framework is very different from Web Forms, which means that there are a lot of new concepts to learn before you can write an effective MVC framework application. The concepts are not especially complex, but they are different, and they take time to master.

Projects Take Longer to Get Started

MVC framework projects require a lot more preparation than Web Forms projects, and this means that we don't get the "web app in an instant" buzz that Web Forms offers. It can take a while before we reach the point where we see a web page displayed in a browser, which means that for quick proof-of-concept apps, Web Forms remains the best option.

That initial setup pays dividends, however. It is just that it can take a while to get them. You'll get more of a feel of what I mean when we start building MVC framework applications in the coming chapters.

Discipline Is Required

The MVC framework is a robust and feature-filled platform, but some of the long-term benefits of adopting the MVC pattern require rigor and discipline in maintaining the separation of concerns. If you work in a team that lacks discipline, then you will be at risk of incurring some of the overhead associated with the MVC framework but not getting the long-term upside. This isn't important if you intent to embrace the MVC framework to replace Web Forms without also embracing the MVC pattern, but I don't recommend this approach. There is a lot to be gained by following the pattern when using the framework.

Rapidly Changing Platform

The MVC framework is not part of the main .NET Framework. It follows an *out-of-band* release schedule, making more frequent updates than the rest of ASP.NET. This is a mixed blessing. On one hand, bug fixes and new features arrive more rapidly, but on the other, it can be hard to keep up with the changes, especially in large projects.

Team Architecture Tension

I mentioned this already, but one of the biggest problems with the MVC framework is that the underlying pattern attracts pattern purists. I can't really blame Microsoft for this. After all, the MVC pattern is widely used and contains a lot of common sense, but there is something about a pattern-centric technology that brings out the pedant in some people. I am not suggesting you avoid the MVC framework, but I do think it worthwhile to prepare yourself for many months of debate about what features belong in different concerns and which concerns cross-cut.

Deciding When to Use the MVC Framework

As I said when introducing Web Forms, there isn't an absolute right or wrong in software. There is only the degree to which a solution suits a particular kind of problem. The MVC framework can bring significant benefits when applied to the right kind of problem. Here are the key requirements that I think best suit the MVC framework:

- Internet (as opposed to intranet) deployment

- Long life or high expectations of change

- Complex or volatile domain

If you are contemplating a project that hits this spot, then the MVC framework is likely to be a good choice. If not, then you might be better off using Web Forms or some other web application technology. I don't want to belabor the point, but I think that there is another point to add to the list:

- Disciplined team

Getting the best from the MVC framework means rigorously applying the principle of separation of concerns. If you have a team that lacks discipline and has a tendency to take shortcuts, be cautious.

Summary

This chapter has outlined the context in which the MVC framework exists, a recent addition to ASP.NET that reflects the current thinking, trends, and techniques for web application development. The MVC framework encompasses many of the best features from other web development tool sets, especially Ruby on Rails, and combines them with the core of ASP.NET and the .NET Framework. We can use our existing knowledge of C# and ASP.NET to create web applications in a thoroughly contemporary manner.

Don't worry if all of this seems too abstract. The relevance will become apparent as we apply the tools to create our first MVC framework application in the next chapter.

CHAPTER 23

A First MVC Application

There are a lot of new concepts to learn with the MVC framework, and the best way to get started is to build an application. In this chapter, we'll create a simple web application that allows athletes to register for triathlon competitions. We will then build on this example in later chapters as we dig into the details of the MVC framework.

This chapter is a quick MVC framework primer and a guide to the chapters that follow. I have included a lot of references to other chapters in this part of the book where individual concepts are further expanded and demonstrated. Don't worry if not everything in this chapter makes sense at first. There is a lot to take in, and it can take some time before clarity emerges.

Caution We will be using version 3 of the MVC framework in this book. Make sure you have installed the MVC Tools Update package as described in Chapter 3. Visual Studio will show different dialog options if you don't install the update, and the code-first feature shown in Chapter 24 will not be available.

Creating the Project

We start by creating a new project. We are going to continue the theme of previous examples by creating an application that will allow users to register for competitive events. To begin, create a new Visual Studio project using the ASP.NET MVC 3 Web Application template, as shown in Figure 23-1.

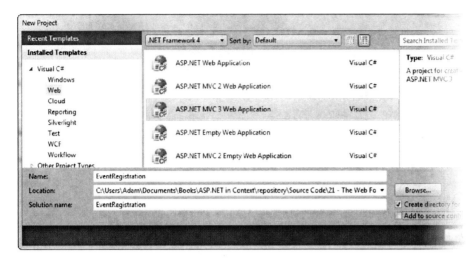

Figure 23-1. *Creating a new MVC framework project*

■ **Note** If you see project templates for MVC version 2 only, then you may have forgotten to apply some of the required Visual Studio updates. See Chapter 3 for details of the software required and installation instructions. You won't be able to follow the MVC version examples using MVC version 2.

I have called the project EventRegistration. Clicking the OK button brings up a new dialog that allows us to select different kinds of MVC project, as shown in Figure 23-2.

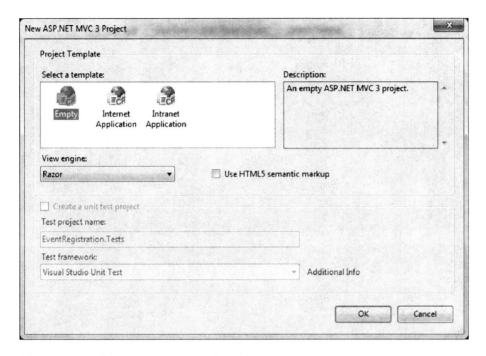

Figure 23-2. *Selecting a project template*

Three project templates are available: Empty, Internet Application, and Intranet Application. The Internet Application template creates some default items to get a project started. The Intranet Application template is very similar, except it assumes you want to authenticate users using an Active Directory/Domain controller. We are going to use the Empty template. I'll show you how to create equivalent items to the ones included in the other templates as we go along.

When you create a new MVC framework application, you can choose from different *view engines*. We are going to be using the Razor engine that was introduced with version 3 of the MVC framework. I'll explain more about view engines and Razor in Chapter 25. For the moment, just ensure that the Razor option is selected from the menu.

We can ignore the other options. The most recent update for the MVC framework has added some preliminary support for HTML5, but we are going to stick with HTML4 in this book (because HTML5 is still evolving and is a topic unto itself). Click OK to create the project. Visual Studio will busy itself and create the new project. Figure 23-3 shows the structure of the project.

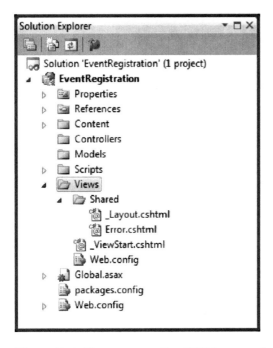

Figure 23-3. *The structure of an MVC framework project created with the Empty template*

The MVC framework uses a technique called *convention over configuration*. This means that when we want to add a new component to a project, we simply place it into the appropriate project folder. As long as we put the component in the place that the MVC framework looks for that component type, we don't have to rely on configuration files. We'll work through each of the folders and items in the project as we go through the chapters, but Table 23-1 provides a summary and a reference to the chapters where each is explained.

Table 23-1. *MVC Framework Project Structure*

Folder	Description	Chapter
Content	Contains static content, including images and CSS	
Controllers	Contains the controller classes	28
Models	Contains the model types	23 to 25, 28
Scripts	Contains the jQuery and other JavaScript library files	29 and 30
Views	Contains the views	25

The `Global.asax` and `Web.config` files play the same role as for any other ASP.NET project, although we add slightly different content for MVC framework projects.

■ **Note** Notice that there are two `Web.config` files: `~/Web.config` and `~/Views/Web.config`. The second one of these configures Razor, and it is rare that we need to make any changes to this file. Most of the time, we will modify the main `Web.config` file, as we would for other kinds of ASP.NET applications.

Creating the Domain Model

As I mentioned earlier, there are two kinds of model in an MVC framework: domain models and view models. It is common practice to create a separate class library project for the domain model and add it as a reference to the MVC framework project. The idea is that this helps enforce the separation between the domain model and the rest of the application. I usually take this approach on real projects, but to keep these examples simple, I am going to use the alternate approach of defining the model within the MVC framework project.

■ **Tip** Putting the domain model into a separate project can be a little frustrating if you are using Visual Web Developer 2010 Express. This is because you can open only one project at a time, unlike the commercial versions of Visual Studio that allow multiple projects to be opened within the context of a single solution. You can partially solve this by having two instances of Visual Web Developer open, one for each project, but it still makes for an awkward working style.

When including both kinds of model in a single project, I like to add some additional structure so it is clear which types are part of the domain model and which types are view models. The `Models` folder is the conventional home for model types in an MVC framework project, so use Visual Studio to create two new folders, `Models/Domain` and `Models/View`. You don't have to put your model classes in the `Models` folder. You can put them anywhere that suits you (including, as I say, in a separate project), but in this book, I am going to stick with the usual conventions.

■ **Note** Don't worry about view models at the moment. I'll explain them in Chapter 25. For the moment, it is enough to know that there are two kinds of model, and I want to be able to differentiate between them in the example project.

We are going to start by creating the types for our model. We are going to keep things simple and just have two domain classes, one to represent a competition and one to represent a registration for a competition. Both of these classes are added to the `Models/Domain` folder. Right-click this folder and select Add ➤ Class from the pop-up menu. The first class is called `Competition`, and the contents are shown in Listing 23-1.

Listing 23-1. *The Competition class*

```
using System;

namespace EventRegistration.Models.Domain {
    public class Competition {

        public string Name {get; set;}
        public string Location {get; set;}
        public DateTime Date {get; set;}
        public string EventType { get; set; }
    }
}
```

This is a very simple class. There are four properties, and we'll use the values of these properties to represent the details of different triathlon competitions. The other domain class is called `Registration` and is shown in Listing 23-2.

Listing 23-2. *The Registration class*

```
namespace EventRegistration.Models.Domain {
    public class Registration {

        public string Name { get; set; }
        public string HomeCity { get; set; }
        public int Age { get; set; }
        public Competition Competition {get; set;}
    }
}
```

This is another simple class. The `Name`, `Home`, and `Age` properties describe a registrant for a competition, and the `Competition` property references the competition they have registered for.

Creating the Repository

Most domain models are persistent, mostly using relational databases. We want to allow our controllers to be able to access our persistent domain model, but we will create a dependency between the controllers and the domain model if we include the code that retrieves and modifies data in the controller classes. The most common approach to ensuring separation is to use a *repository*, which is an abstract class or interface that provides the means to work with the persistent data but doesn't say anything about how the data is operated on. I prefer to use a C# interface to define repositories. Listing 23-3 shows the repository for the domain types, which I have called `IRepository`.

Listing 23-3. *The IRepository interface*

```
using System.Collections.Generic;
using System.Linq;

namespace EventRegistration.Models.Domain.Repository {
    public interface IRepository {

        IQueryable<Competition> Competitions { get; }

        void SaveCompetition(Competition comp);
    }
}
```

I like to add structure in my projects to my models to keep various elements separate, so I created a new folder, Models/Domain/Repository, and added the IRepository interface there. Only two members are defined in the interface at the moment. The first, the Competitions property, retrieves a sequence of Competition objects that we can use as the basis for LINQ queries. The other member, the SaveCompetition method, takes a Competition object that we want to be persisted. This could be a new instance or a modification of an existing one. This is the basic pattern for the way that repository will support domain types: a property to obtain a sequence of types and a method to save changes. We can repeat this pattern to add support for the Registration model type, as shown in Listing 23-4.

Listing 23-4. *Adding support for an additional model type*

```
using System.Collections.Generic;
using System.Linq;

namespace EventRegistration.Models.Domain.Repository {
    public interface IRepository {

        IQueryable<Competition> Competitions { get; }

        void SaveCompetition(Competition comp);

        IQueryable<Registration> Registrations { get; }

        void SaveRegistration(Registration reg);
    }
}
```

Creating a Dummy Repository Implementation

In Chapter 24, I'll show you how we can implement the repository so that our domain model objects are stored and retrieved from SQL Server. In the meantime, we need a stand-in, something that will let us simulate the database. To that end, we are going to create a dummy implementation of the repositories. I have created a class called DummyRepository in the Models/Domain/Repository folder, the contents of which are shown in Listing 23-5.

Listing 23-5. The dummy implementation of the repository

```
using System;
using System.Collections.Generic;
using System.Linq;

namespace EventRegistration.Models.Domain.Repository {
    public class DummyRepository : IRepository {
        private static List<Registration> registrations = new List<Registration>();
        private static List<Competition> competitions
            = new List<Competition>() {
                new Competition { Name= "London Lunge", EventType = "Sprint",
                    Location = "London", Date = new DateTime(2012, 4, 22)},
                new Competition { Name= "New York Nudge", EventType = "Olympic",
                    Location = "New York", Date =  new DateTime(2012, 5, 12), },
                new Competition { Name = "Paris Panic", EventType = "Sprint",
                    Location = "Paris" , Date = new DateTime(2012, 5, 16)}
            };


        public IQueryable<Competition> Competitions {
            get {
                return competitions.AsQueryable();
            }
        }

        public void SaveCompetition(Competition competition) {
            competitions.Add(competition);
        }

        public IQueryable<Registration> Registrations {
            get {
                return registrations.AsQueryable();
            }
        }

        public void SaveRegistration(Registration registration) {
            registrations.Add(registration);
        }
    }
}
```

I have created some limited persistence for our domain model classes using some static strongly typed Lists. As we'll see later, the MVC framework creates new instances of classes that it needs to service requests (much like core ASP.NET does), and so the static collections will give us a degree of persistence for as long as the application is running. I have also included some initial Competition objects in the dummy repository. This will keep us going until we create a real repository in Chapter 24.

Creating the Controller

Now that we have created a simple domain model, we can create a controller. To add a controller to the project, right-click the **Controllers** project folder, and select Add ➤ Controller from the pop-up menu. You'll see the Add Controller dialog, as shown in Figure 23-4.

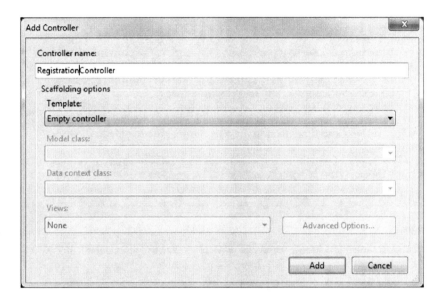

Figure 23-4. *The Add Controller dialog*

Change the Controller Name setting to RegistrationController. The convention is to give controller meaningful names, and we are going to use this controller to allow users to register for competitions. Ensure that the Template option is set to Empty controller. Visual Studio can create controllers using different templates. These templates can be a useful way to get started, but we are going to keep things simple and add what we need to an empty controller. Click Add to dismiss the dialog box and create the controller.

An MVC framework controller is a C# class, usually derived from **System.Web.Mvc.Controller**. Change the contents of the controller that Visual Studio just created so that it matches Listing 23-6.

Listing 23-6. *The RegistrationController class*

```
using System.Web.Mvc;
using EventRegistration.Models.Domain;

namespace EventRegistration.Controllers {

    public class RegistrationController : Controller {
```

```
        public ActionResult Index() {
            return View();
        }
    }
}
```

If you are looking at the listing with a sense of bewilderment, then don't worry. The MVC framework works in a very different way than the rest of ASP.NET, and seeing a controller for the first time can be jarring.

The core ASP.NET platform and Windows Forms work on a page basis. We create a file that represents a web page, and when the user requests that page, ASP.NET renders the content to produce HTML that is sent to the browser. There is a direct mapping between the pages that the user can request and the structure of our application. We can change the URLs using the routing features (as described in Chapter 27), but the structure of the web application is still based around pages.

The MVC framework doesn't have pages; it has only models, views, and controllers. The role of a controller is to process an HTTP request, update the state of the domain model to reflect the request, and then select a view that will be rendered and displayed to the user. Users are not able to directly request views, and as we'll see, views are not equivalent to pages.

Controllers have *action methods*, each of which performs some action that the application supports. There is one action method, called Index, in the RegistrationController class shown in the listing.

▓ **Tip**   The convention is that the Index method causes the initial display for the controller. However, this is just a convention, and you can call your action methods by any name and do anything you like in an action method called Index.

The user requests that the application perform one if its actions by requesting a URL that targets the corresponding action method in a controller. Here is an example of such a URL:

`http://<myserver>/Registration/Index`

This URL targets the Index action in the Registration controller. This corresponds to the Index *method* in the RegistrationController *class*. Notice that when we want to target the RegistrationController, we omit the Controller part of the class name and specify Registration. The MVC framework manages the correlation between the controller that has been requested and the class itself.

▓ **Note**   The URL form controller/action is the default for a new MVC framework application. I'll show you how to change this using routing in Chapter 27.

Action methods return an **ActionResult** object, which represents an instruction to the MVC framework as to what it should do next. In the listing, I have called the **View** method, which is a convenient way of telling the MVC framework to render a view. I have used the parameterless version of the **View** method, which tells the MVC framework to render the default view for the action method (we'll create this default view in a moment).

So, to put this together, when the MVC framework receives a request for the URL /Registration/ Index, it creates a new instance of our **RegistrationController** class and then calls the **Index** method. The **Index** method returns an **ActionResult** object that was created by calling the **View** method. The MVC framework takes this as an instruction to render the default view associated with the **Index** method and to return the result to the user.

Creating the View

The missing piece of our example application is the *view*. To create a view, right-click the **Index** action method and select Add View from the pop-up menu, as shown in Figure 23-5.

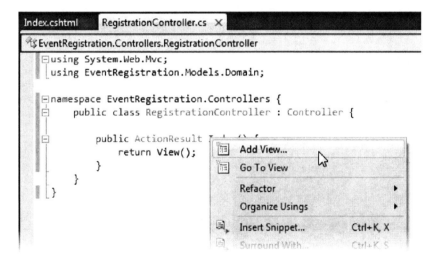

Figure 23-5. *Creating a view for an action method*

The Add View dialog will appear, as shown in Figure 23-6. This is our opportunity to configure the view.

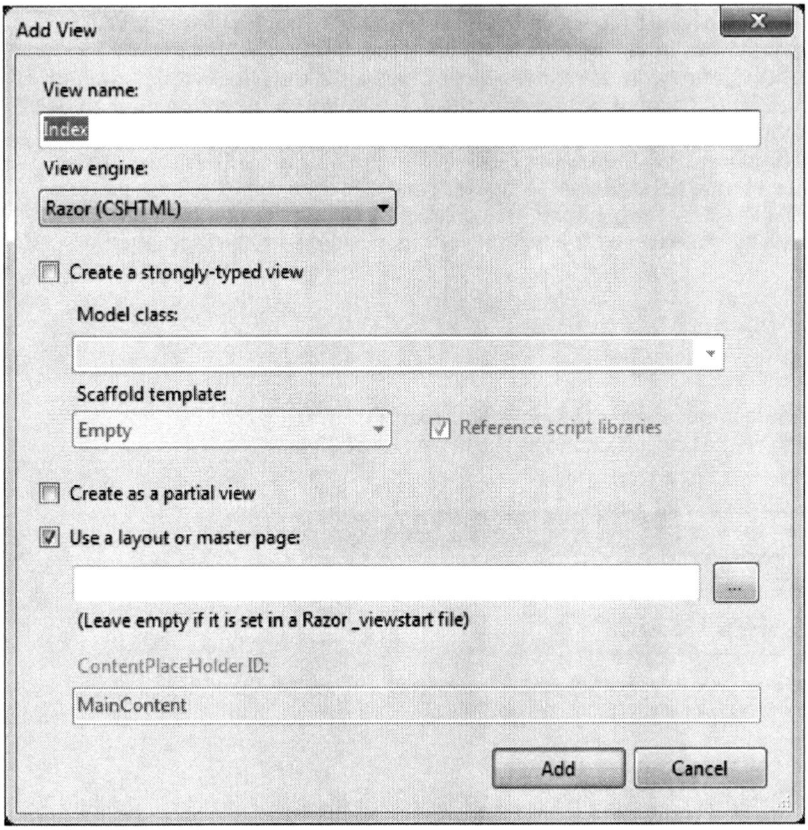

Figure 23-6. *The Add View dialog*

Visual Studio sets the view name to Index, which will make this the default view for the Index action method. Ensure that the options in the dialog match the figure. The "Create a strongly-typed view" option is unchecked, the "Create as a partial view" option is unchecked, and the "Use a layout or master page" is checked.

Click the Add button to create the view. If you look at the Solution Explorer window, you will see that Visual Studio has created a folder called Registration and added a file called Index.cshtml, as shown in Figure 23-7.

Figure 23-7. *The newly added view shown in the Solution Explorer window*

Multiple controllers can define an action called Index, so the Index.cshtml file is placed into the Registration folder to form the association between the view and the RegistrationController class. The .cshtml prefix indicates that this is a view that uses the Razor view engine and C# syntax. I introduce you to Razor properly in Chapter 25, but for the moment, update the contents of the view to match Listing 23-7.

Listing 23-7. *The Index.cshtml view*

```
@{
    ViewBag.Title = "Registration";
}

<style type="text/css">
    td[colspan] {text-align:center}
</style>

<h4>Registration</h4>

@using (Html.BeginForm()) {

    <table>
        <tr><td>Name:</td><td>@Html.Editor("Name")</td></tr>
        <tr><td>Age:</td><td>@Html.Editor("Age")</td></tr>
        <tr><td>City:</td><td>@Html.Editor("HomeCity")</td></tr>
        <tr><td>Competition:</td><td>@Html.Editor("CompetitionName")</td></tr>

        <tr><td colspan="2"><input type="submit" value="Register" /></td></tr>
    </table>
}
```

We use Razor tags to include instructions in views. In many ways, Razor is similar to the <% tags %> tags we have been using with the rest of ASP.NET. A Razor tag starts with the @ symbol, but there isn't a corresponding end tag. The Razor view engine, which is the MVC framework component that renders HTML from Razor views, is smart enough to figure everything out. (Well, usually smart enough. I'll show you how to give it a helping hand in Chapter 25.)

▨ **Tip** You can use the regular ASP.NET <% and %> tags in the MVC framework. Just change the View Engine selection in the Add View dialog shown in Figure 23-6. I recommend, however, that you use Razor. It doesn't take too much effort to learn the new syntax, and it provides a nice and expressive means of creating views. In this book, I only use Razor for MVC framework examples.

Notice that there are no design tools in an MVC framework project. We work directly with the HTML and Razor tags in the views and with C# code in the controllers and the domain model. This makes a lot of sense. The MVC framework expects us to control the HTML that our application produces, and the Web Forms style of design tool insulates the developer from the HTML.

You can see the structure of the HTML that the `Index.cshtml` view will render in the listing. Aside from the Razor tags, everything is raw HTML. I have used a `table` element to create a grid layout and defined several rows, each of which has two columns. In the left column are a series of literal labels. In the right column are a series of Razor calls in the form `@Html.Editor()`. These are calls to an *HTML helper method*. HTML helper methods, also referred to as *HTML helpers*, are convenience methods that we can use in views to help generate HTML. In this case, the `Editor` method creates an input element suitable for collecting a value from the user. The `Editor` method is actually quite sophisticated, and you'll learn more about it in Chapter 26.

The `@using` block that includes a call to the `Html.BeginForm` HTML helper creates an HTML form element that posts back to a URL that targets the controller and action method that caused the view to be rendered, in this case, the `Index` action in the `Registration` controller. This block:

```
@{
    ViewBag.Title = "Registration";
}
```

is a Razor block, which can contain multiple C# statements. This block sets the title for the HTML page sent to the user, using a feature called the `ViewBag`, which I'll introduce properly in Chapter 28. In general, the `ViewBag` lets us pass data from the controller to the view, but it has some additional features, such as allowing us to set the title.

Running the MVC Framework Application

We are ready to test our (very simple) application. Select Start Without Debugging from the Visual Studio Debug menu to compile the application and display it in the browser. The first thing that you'll see is a `404 - Not Found` error, like the one shown in Figure 23-8.

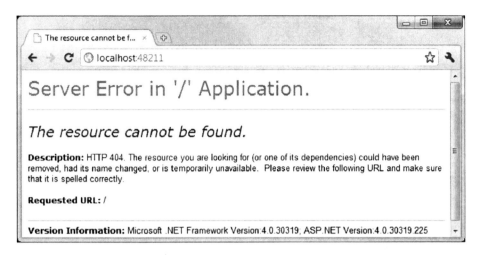

Figure 23-8. *The error shown when starting the MVC framework application from Visual Studio*

Our combination of controller and action method means that we have a target for the /Registration/Index method, but we haven't told the MVC framework what to do when the default URL (/) is requested, so we get an error. I'll show you how to configure the URLs for an application in Chapter 27.

For the moment, append /Registration/Index in the URL bar of your browser to target our action method. You'll see something very similar to Figure 23-9.

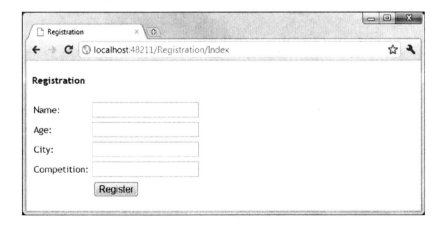

Figure 23-9. *The example MVC framework application displayed in a browser*

You can see the HTML that was rendered by the view in Listing 23-8.

Listing 23-8. *The HTML generated by the Index.cshtml view*

```html
<!DOCTYPE html>
<html>
<head>
    <title>Registration</title>
    <link href="/Content/Site.css" rel="stylesheet" type="text/css" />
    <script src="/Scripts/jquery-1.5.1.min.js" type="text/javascript"></script>
</head>
<body>
<style type="text/css">td[colspan] {text-align:center}</style>

<h4>Registration</h4>

<form action="/Registration/Index" method="post">
<table>
<tr>
    <td>Name:</td>
    <td>
        <input class="text-box single-line" id="Name" name="Name" type="text" value=""/>
    </td>
</tr>
    <tr>
    <td>Age:</td>
    <td>
        <input class="text-box single-line" id="Age" name="Age" type="text" value="" />
    </td>
</tr>
<tr>
    <td>City:</td>
    <td>
        <input class="text-box single-line" id="HomeCity" name="HomeCity"
            type="text" value="" />
    </td>
</tr>
<tr>
    <td>Competition:</td>
    <td>
        <input class="text-box single-line" id="CompetitionName" name="CompetitionName"
            type="text" value="" />
    </td>
</tr>
<tr>
    <td colspan="2"><input type="submit" value="Register" /></td>
</tr>
</table>
</form>
</body>
</html>
```

There are a few things to note about this HTML, in particular some things that are missing when compared to the HTML generated when using ASPX files. There is no view state data blob. This is because the MVC framework doesn't store state data in the HTML. And there are no mangled ID values. Because there are no controls, the MVC framework doesn't need to embed special meaning in HTML elements. This means that when we call an HTML helper like this:

```
<td>@Html.Editor("Name")</td>
```

we get HTML like this:

```
<td><input class="text-box single-line" id="Name" name="Name" type="text" value=""/></td>
```

The HTML helpers are just a convenient way to generate HTML. They don't include any special information in the HTML that they produce, and we can ignore them altogether and use static HTML if required.

Figure 23-10 recaps the sequence of events that led to the HTML being generated and displayed in the browser.

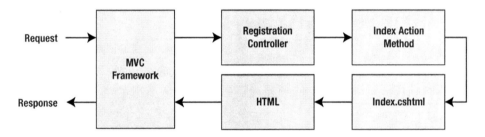

Figure 23-10. *The request processing path*

The MVC framework received a request for the URL **/Registration/Index**, which it interpreted as targeting the **Index** action method in the **RegistrationController** class. A new instance of the class was created, and the **Index** method was invoked. The **Index** method is very simple. It just returns an **ActionResult** object that tells the MVC framework to render the default view associated with the method. The framework finds the file **/Views/Registration/Index.cshtml** and processes it using the Razor view engine. Razor interprets the @ tags and replaces them with HTML that is combined with the static HTML already in the template. The combined HTML is returned to the browser, where it is displayed. I keep reiterating the relationship between the components because understanding the way that a request is processed is the key to understanding the MVC framework.

Finishing the Basic Features

We have something very basic in place. We can request a URL and get some HTML displayed, but that's about it. In the following sections, I'll show you how to add some more functionality to the application such that we start to see something useful emerge.

Using the Repositories

Our first enhancement will be to starting using the repositories so that we can work with the domain model in the controller. Listing 23-9 shows the changes to the `RegistrationController` class.

Listing 23-9. *Using the repositories in the RegistrationController class*

```
using System.Linq;
using System.Web.Mvc;
using EventRegistration.Models.Domain.Repository;

namespace EventRegistration.Controllers {

    public class RegistrationController : Controller {
        private IRepository repository;

        public RegistrationController() {
            repository = new DummyRepository();
        }

        public ActionResult Index() {
            ViewBag.Competitions = repository.Competitions.Select(e => e.Name);
            return View();
        }
    }
}
```

I have defined a new field for the repository using the interface we created earlier. I then create an instance of the `DummyRepository` class and assign it to the field, like this:

```
public RegistrationController() {
    repository = new DummyRepository();
}
```

If you are observant, you will have realized that I have done something very, very silly in the constructor. By creating an instance of the `DummyRepository` class directly, I have created a dependency between the controller and the repository implementation. Later in this chapter, I'll show you how to solve the issue of creating implementations of interfaces without directly instantiating the implementation. The other addition to the controller class is in the `Index` action method, where I added this statement:

```
ViewBag.Competitions = repository.Competitions.Select(e => e.Name);
```

The `ViewBag` is a feature that allows us to pass data from the controller to the view. The `ViewBag` property returns a *dynamic* object. If you are not familiar with the .NET support for dynamic types, this allows us to arbitrarily define new properties without defining them first. In the listing, there was no `Competitions` property until I assigned a value to it, at which point the property was created. The value I have assigned to the `ViewBag.Competitions` property is the sequence of `Name` values from the `Competition` repository.

I want to pass the names of the competitions to the view so that I can constrain the set of competitions that the user can choose from. As it stands, the user can enter any old string, which will cause problems later. Listing 23-10 shows the changes I have made to `Index.cshtml` to use this data.

Listing 23-10. Using the ViewBag to retrieve data passed from the controller

```
@{
    ViewBag.Title = "Registration";
}

<style type="text/css">
    td[colspan] {text-align:center}
</style>

<h4>Registration</h4>

@using (Html.BeginForm()) {

    <table>
        <tr><td>Name:</td><td>@Html.Editor("Name")</td></tr>
        <tr><td>Age:</td><td>@Html.Editor("Age")</td></tr>
        <tr><td>City:</td><td>@Html.Editor("HomeCity")</td></tr>

        <tr>
            <td>Competition:</td>
            <td>
                @Html.DropDownList("Competition", new SelectList(ViewBag.Competitions))
            </td>
        </tr>
        <tr><td colspan="2"><input type="submit" value="Register" /></td></tr>
    </table>
}
```

I have replaced the call to the `Html.Editor` helper with one to `Html.DropDownList`. As the name suggests, this helper generates a `select` element. The arguments are the value that will be used for the ID and `name` attributes of the `select` element and a `SelectList` object containing the set of values that will be used to create `option` elements. To create the `SelectList`, I use the set of competition names that I assigned to the `ViewBag.Competitions` property. The result of this change is the following URL:

```
<select id="Competition" name="Competition">
    <option>London Lunge</option>
    <option>New York Nudge</option>
    <option>Paris Panic</option>
</select>
```

We return to the `ViewBag` (and other forms of passing and preserving data) in Chapter 28. If you recompile the application and navigate to the `/Registration/Index` URL, you can see that the user is not able to select one of the competitions defined in the repository, as shown in Figure 23-11.

Figure 23-11. *The effect of using the Html.DropDownList HTML helper to render ViewBag data*

The flow of information is in one direction. We can pass data from the controller to the index, but not the other way around. There is a technique, called *child actions*, in which a view can call an action method. I'll show you how to do this in Chapter 28.

Handling the Form POST

Clicking the Register button in the browser doesn't do much at the moment. Any data the user has entered simply disappears. You can see why this is happening by looking at the form that our view generates:

```
<form action="/Registration/Index" method="post">
    ...
</form>
```

When we click the Register button, the browser posts the form to the URL specified in the action attribute of the `form` element, which in the example is `/Registration/Index`. Of course, this is the URL that targets our `Index` action method, which sets a value in the `ViewBag` and tells the MVC framework to render the `Index.cshtml` view.

To process the `form` post properly, we need to add another method to our controller, as shown in Listing 23-11.

Listing 23-11. *Handling the form post in the controller*

```
using System.Linq;
using System.Web.Mvc;
using EventRegistration.Models.Domain.Repository;
using EventRegistration.Models.Domain;

namespace EventRegistration.Controllers {

    public class RegistrationController : Controller {
        private IRepository repository;

        public RegistrationController() {
            repository = new DummyRepository();
        }
```

```
    public ActionResult Index() {
        ViewBag.Competitions = repository.Competitions.Select(e => e.Name);
        return View();
    }

    [HttpPost]
    public ActionResult Index(string name, string homecity, string age,
        string competition) {

        Registration registration = new Registration {
            Name = name, HomeCity = homecity, Age = int.Parse(age),
            Competition = repository.Competitions
                                .Where(e => e.Name == competition)
                                .FirstOrDefault()
        };

        repository.SaveRegistration(registration);

        return View("RegistrationComplete", registration);
    }
  }
}
```

Now that we have two `Index` methods, the MVC framework needs to know which one should be invoked in response to a request. We provide this information using a .NET attribute, like this:

```
...
[HttpPost]
public ActionResult Index(string name, string homecity, string age, string competition) {
...
```

The `HttpPost` attribute tells the MVC framework that we only want this method to be used to handle HTTP `POST` requests. When a request comes in, the MVC framework looks for the most specific match it can for the action method. For a `POST` request, this is our new method, and for `GET` requests this is our original method (because there are no methods that have the more specific `HttpGet` attribute).

The new `Index` method has parameters that match the input fields in the HTML that we generate from the `Index.cshtml` view. When the MVC framework receives the `POST` request, it obtains values from the form data and passes them to us through the parameters. Inside the method body, I use the parameter values to create a new `Registration` object. I set the values of the `Name`, `HomeCity`, and `Age` properties directly from the parameters and perform a simple LINQ query to get the `Competition` object from the repository whose `Name` property matches the value from the `select` control (which is passed to us through the `competition` method parameter). I then save the new `Registration` by calling the `SaveRegistration` method defined by the `IRepository` interface.

All that remains is to tell the MVC framework what it should do next. I call the `View` method to tell the MVC framework to render a view, and the arguments I specify are the name of the view that I want rendered (`RegistrationComplete`) and a *view model object*, which is the `Registration` object that we created from the request.

A view model is the main way in which we can pass data from the controller to the view. The convention is to a view model object to pass the main data item that the view is responsible for displaying and use the `ViewBag` to pass supporting data. This is just a convention, and we could use the `ViewBag` for everything, but if we did that, we'd miss out on *strongly typed views* and the convenience they can offer.

Let's create a strongly typed view now. Right-click anywhere in the new Index method and select Add View from the pop-up menu. Set the name of the view to be RegistrationComplete, as shown in Figure 23-12. This is the name of the view that I told the MVC framework to render in the new POST-only Index method.

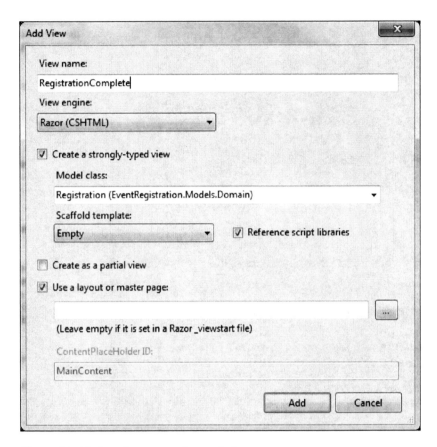

Figure 23-12. *Creating a strongly typed view*

Check the "Create a strongly-typed view" option and select Registration for the model class. Leave the other options as they are and click the Add button to create the view. Visual Studio will create a new file called RegistrationComplete.cshtml in the ~/Views/Registration folder. Edit the contents of this file to match Listing 23-12.

Listing 23-12. The strongly typed RegistrationComplete view

```
@model EventRegistration.Models.Domain.Registration

@{
    ViewBag.Title = "Registration Completed";
}

<h3>Registration Completed</h3>

@Model.Name has registered for the @Model.Competition.Name which will be held in
@Model.Competition.Location on @Model.Competition.Date.ToShortDateString()

<p />

<table>
    <tr><th colspan="2">Summary</th></tr>
    <tr><td>Competitor:</td><td>@Html.DisplayFor(m => m.Name)</td></tr>
    <tr><td>Age:</td><td>@Html.DisplayFor(m => m.Age)</td></tr>
    <tr><td>Home City:</td><td>@Html.DisplayFor(m => m.HomeCity)</td></tr>
    <tr><td>Competition Name:</td><td>@Html.DisplayFor(m => m.Competition.Name)</td></tr>
    <tr><td>Competition City:</td><td>@Html.DisplayFor(m => m.Competition.Location)</td></tr>
    <tr><td>Competition Date:</td><td>@Model.Competition.Date.ToShortDateString()</td></tr>
</table>
```

A strongly typed view has a @model declaration (with a lowercase m)to tell the MVC framework what the view model type is. In our case, this is a **Registration** object since this is the type we selected when we created the view. We can access the model object using the Razor @Model tag (with an uppercase M). Visual Studio uses the type information to provide IntelliSense support to help use select model members in our code.

I have used the model object in two different ways in the listing. The first explicitly uses the @Model tag, like this:

```
@Model.Name has registered...
```

This causes Razor to insert the value of the Name property of the model object into the HTML that will be sent to the browser. The other way I have used the model is with the helper method Html.DisplayFor like this:

```
<tr><td>Age:</td><td>@Html.DisplayFor(m => m.Age)</td></tr>
```

This is an example of a strongly typed helper. We use a lambda expression to select the property or other member from the model object, and the helper will render suitable HTML. The Html.DisplayFor helper generates read-only HTML. I'll show you why this can be useful (as compared with just writing the value as I did with the Name property) in Chapter 26.

Enhancing the Application

We've reached the point where we have something that functions. We can create new registrations, and they are stored in our dummy repository. Along the way, we have used the ViewBag and strongly typed views to pass data from the controller to the view, we have used helper methods to conveniently generate HTML for use in views, and we have read from and written to the repositories. In the following sections, we'll add some additional functions and features.

Using Model Binding

One of my favorite MVC features is *model binding*. It's a neat trick that makes it easier to process requests. When I added the action method to handle form posts, I defined a parameter for each of the input field values that I was interested in and used them to populate the properties of a new Registration object, like this:

```
...
[HttpPost]
public ActionResult Index(string name, string homecity, string age, string competition) {

    Registration registration = new Registration {
        Name = name, HomeCity = homecity, Age = int.Parse(age),
        Competition = repository.Competitions
            .Where(e => e.Name == competition)
            .FirstOrDefault()
    };
...
```

As part of this process, I had to parse the age parameter to an int to make sure the value that the user entered was suitable to be used for the Registration.Age property (if it is not, an exception will be thrown, and an error will be reported to the user). We can neatly side step this work by changing the method signature, as shown in Listing 23-13.

Listing 23-13. Using model binding in an action method

```
using System.Linq;
using System.Web.Mvc;
using EventRegistration.Models.Domain.Repository;
using EventRegistration.Models.Domain;

namespace EventRegistration.Controllers {

    public class RegistrationController : Controller {
        private IRepository repository;

        public RegistrationController() {
            repository = new DummyRepository();
        }

        public ActionResult Index() {
            ViewBag.Competitions = repository.Competitions.Select(e => e.Name);
            return View();
        }
```

```
[HttpPost]
public ActionResult Index(Registration registration, string competition) {

    registration.Competition = repository.Competitions
        .Where(e => e.Name == competition).FirstOrDefault();

    repository.SaveRegistration(registration);

    return View("RegistrationComplete", registration);
    }
  }
}
```

All we have to do is define a parameter of the type that we want to receive, and the MVC framework will try to create an instance and populate the properties from the request by looking for element names that match the property names of the type we have specified. And so, just like magic, our Index method is passed a Registration with the data the user has entered, well...almost. The MVC framework doesn't know how to turn the value of the competition select element into a Competition object in the repository. To deal with this, I still use my LINQ query, but in Chapter 29 I'll show you how to create a custom model binder to make the whole processes seamless.

▪ **Tip**   The model binding system also validates the data that the user has entered to make sure it can be converted to the types required by the action method parameter properties. I'll show you to take advantage of this in Chapter 29.

I like model binding because it eliminates one of the most tedious and error-prone parts of web application programming, grubbing around in the request data to find the values that the user has supplied and then parsing them to make sure that we can work with them. The MVC framework requires us to be intimately involved in the HTTP and HTML that our application deals with, but it does have some very handy features to make the experience more pleasant and robust.

Adding Dependency Injection

The RegistrationController class needs a way to create instances of the implementation class for the repository interface. The way I am doing it at the moment creates a direct dependency between the controller and the repository implementation, like this:

```
...
public RegistrationController() {
    repository = new DummyRepository();
}
...
```

I have created *tightly coupled components*. If I want to change the repository implementation in use, I have to find all the places that DummyRepository is instantiated and change them. What we'd like is *loosely coupled components*, where the controller depends on the repository interfaces and doesn't have any knowledge of the implementations in use.

585

Fortunately, we can do this by using a technique called *dependency injection* (DI). The MVC framework has extensive support for DI, most usefully through the **IDependencyResolver** interface, which is shown in Listing 23-14.

Listing 23-14. *The IDependencyResolver interface*

```
namespace System.Web.Mvc {
    using System.Collections.Generic;

    public interface IDependencyResolver {

        object GetService(Type serviceType);
        IEnumerable<object> GetServices(Type serviceType);
    }
}
```

We create a *dependency resolver* by implementing the **IDependencyResolver** interface and then register it with the MVC framework. The MVC framework will call one of the methods in our dependency resolver every time that it needs to create a new object. This gives us an opportunity to create and configure the required object and, in doing so, break dependencies between parts of the application. The best way to explain this is with a demonstration. First, we need to remove the dependency from the controller class, as shown in Listing 23-15.

Listing 23-15. *Removing the dependency from the controller class*

```
using System.Linq;
using System.Web.Mvc;
using EventRegistration.Models.Domain.Repository;
using EventRegistration.Models.Domain;

namespace EventRegistration.Controllers {

    public class RegistrationController : Controller {
        private IRepository repository;

        public RegistrationController(IRepository repo) {
            repository = repo;
        }

        public ActionResult Index() {
            ViewBag.Competitions = repository.Competitions.Select(e => e.Name);
            return View();
        }

        [HttpPost]
        public ActionResult Index(Registration registration, string competition) {

            registration.Competition = repository.Competitions
                .Where(e => e.Name == competition).FirstOrDefault();
```

```
        repository.SaveRegistration(registration);
        return View("RegistrationComplete", registration);
      }
    }
}
```

I've changed the constructor for the controller class so that it requires an **IRepository** parameter. The controller is no longer responsible for creating the implementation of the interface directly and is no longer dependent on the **DummyRepository** class. We can start using a different repository implementation without changing the controller code.

The next step is to create a dependency resolver that will *inject* the dependencies into the **RegistrationController** class as it is created. This is much simpler than it sounds. Create a new folder in the project called **Infrastructure**. This is where we will add classes that support the plumbing of the application and don't really fit anywhere else. Inside this folder, create a new class called **CustomDependencyResolver** and edit the class to match Listing 23-16.

Listing 23-16. *The CustomDependencyResolver class*

```
using System;
using System.Collections.Generic;
using System.Linq;
using System.Web.Mvc;
using EventRegistration.Controllers;
using EventRegistration.Models.Domain.Repository;

namespace EventRegistration.Infrastructure {
    public class CustomDependencyResolver : IDependencyResolver {

        public CustomDependencyResolver() {
        }

        public object GetService(Type serviceType) {

            if (serviceType == typeof(RegistrationController)) {
                DummyRepository dr = new DummyRepository();
                return new RegistrationController(dr);
            } else {
                return null;
            }
        }

        public IEnumerable<object> GetServices(Type serviceType) {
            return Enumerable.Empty<object>();
        }
    }
}
```

The MVC framework differentiates between *singly registered services* and *multiply registered services*. This just means that there are some parts of the MVC framework where only one class is responsible for performing an action and other parts where there can be multiple classes, each of which will be asked to perform the same action in turn. Controllers are examples of singly registered services. This is because there is only one type that can be used to service a request for **RegistrationController** itself. Multiply registered services are typically used when there are multiple implementations of the same interface or abstract class.

When the MVC framework wants to create a new instance of a singly registered service, it calls the GetService method, passing in the type that it wants instantiated. We check the type, and if the request is for a RegistrationController, we create a new instance and pass in an instance of the DummyRepository class to satisfy the constructor dependencies on the IRepository interface.

We don't want to take any special steps for other types, so we return null if the type requested from the GetService method isn't RegistrationController and return an empty enumeration when GetServices is called. This tells the MVC framework that we are not interested in the request and that the default mechanism for creating objects should be used.

Now we need to register our dependency resolver with the MVC framework. We do this in the Application_Start method of Global.asax, as shown in Listing 23-17.

Listing 23-17. Registering the dependency resolver

```
...
protected void Application_Start() {
    AreaRegistration.RegisterAllAreas();

    DependencyResolver.SetResolver(new CustomDependencyResolver());

    RegisterGlobalFilters(GlobalFilters.Filters);
    RegisterRoutes(RouteTable.Routes);
}
...
```

The static DependencyResolver.SetResolver method lets us register an implementation of the IDependencyResolver interface with the MVC framework, in this case, a new instance of our CustomDependencyResolver class.

If you select Debug ➤ Start Without Debugging in Visual Studio and navigate to /Registration/Index, you will see that the application works as before, except that behind the scenes we have broken the tight coupling between the controller class and the repository implementation.

Using a Dependency Injection Container

Our dependency resolver is useful, but it will be hard to maintain. Any changes to the constructor of the controller class require us to change the way that we create new instances in the resolver, and we need to maintain the resolver class so that it knows how to instantiate all the other classes we add to our project. We have solved the dependency injection problem but in a very manually and brittle way.

We need a *dependency injection controller* to make a more flexible and general solution. My favorite DI container is Ninject, which I asked you to download in Chapter 3. There are many DI containers available, including one called Unity from Microsoft, but I use Ninject because it is simple and reliable.

The first step is to add a reference to the Ninject assembly. Right-click the References item in the Solution Explorer window and select Add Reference from the pop-up menu. Select the Browse tab and navigate to the folder that contains Ninject and select Ninject.dll, as shown in Figure 23-13.

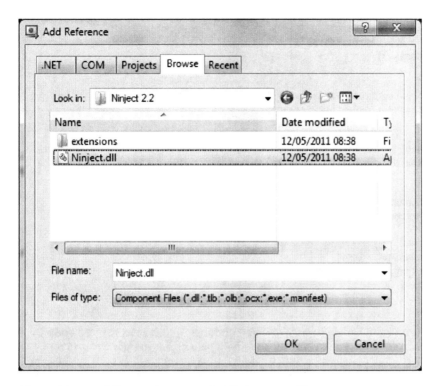

Figure 23-13. *Adding a reference to the Ninject assembly*

Click OK and Visual Studio will close the Add Reference dialog, expand the set of references in the Solution Explorer window, and add a new reference to Ninject. We can now modify the `CustomDependencyController` to use Ninject. Listing 23-18 shows the revised version of this class.

Listing 23-18. *The Ninject-enabled CustomDependencyResolver class*

```csharp
using System;
using System.Collections.Generic;
using System.Web.Mvc;
using EventRegistration.Models.Domain.Repository;
using Ninject;
using Ninject.Syntax;

namespace EventRegistration.Infrastructure {
    public class CustomDependencyResolver : IDependencyResolver {
        private IKernel ninjectKernel;
```

```
        public CustomDependencyResolver() {
            ninjectKernel = new StandardKernel();
            AddDefaultBindings();
        }

        public object GetService(Type serviceType) {
            return ninjectKernel.TryGet(serviceType);
        }

        public IEnumerable<object> GetServices(Type serviceType) {
            return ninjectKernel.GetAll(serviceType);
        }

        public IBindingToSyntax<T> Bind<T>() {
            return ninjectKernel.Bind<T>();
        }

        private void AddDefaultBindings() {
            Bind<IRepository>().To<DummyRepository>();
        }
    }
}
```

Ninject is a pretty flexible tool and can do a range of different things. In this case, Ninject works by inspecting the types that it is asked to instantiate and looking for dependencies in their constructors. When it sees that a class requires an interface as a constructor argument, it looks to a set of bindings to see which class it should create as the implementation of that interface and passes a new instance of that class to the constructor.

Ninject maintains the set of bindings using what it calls a *kernel*. I create the kernel in the dependency resolver's constructor like this:

```
public CustomDependencyResolver() {
    ninjectKernel = new StandardKernel();
    AddDefaultBindings();
}
```

I then call the AddDefaultBindings method so I can set up the implementations I want to use for various interfaces. Ninject uses a fluent API that relies on the C# generic typing features. Here is an example of creating a binding:

```
Bind<IRepository>().To<DummyRepository>();
```

This statement tells Ninject that when it receives a request to instantiate a class that has a constructor dependency on the IRepository interface, it should satisfy that dependency by creating a new instance of the DummyRepository class. The last change is to update the GetService and GetServices methods so that they call Ninject to get instances of the requested type.

> **Note** I have made the `Bind<T>` method public, which means that I can also define bindings elsewhere in the application. The most common place to do this is in `Global.asax` when the application starts. I like to do the bindings in the dependency resolver itself, but that's just personal preference.

The most important point to note about the listing is that there are no references to the `RegistrationController` class. Ninject works dynamically. It automatically detects dependencies so we don't have to tell it what to do for any specific class; we just ensure that we provide it with the bindings between our interfaces and their implementations.

> **Tip** Ninject offers some different options for how types are instantiated, which can be useful if you want more fine-grained control over how dependencies are resolved and injects. See the Ninject.org web site for details.

Summary

In this chapter, we created a simple web application using the MVC framework and saw the major architectural components: the model, the view, and the controller. There is more initial setup required with the MVC framework (as opposed to Web Forms, for example). Once the building blocks are in place, we can begin to add functionality more rapidly, as you'll see in the chapters that follow.

As I said at the start of the chapter, don't worry if not everything makes sense at this point. There are a lot of new concepts to learn with the MVC framework, and it can take a while to grasp them.

CHAPTER 24

Implementing a Persistent Repository

In this chapter, we are going to fix the most pressing problem in our example application—a lack of proper model persistence. To do this, we will use the Entity Framework again but in a different way to the approach we used previously.

In the earlier chapters, we relied on the Entity Framework to generate the classes that represented rows in our database tables. We don't really want to cede control of our model classes in an MVC framework, and our goal is to create a repository in such a way that our model classes are not persistence-aware. This approach has a couple of advantages. The first is that we don't have to update all of the references to our model classes if we change ORM technologies, and the second is that other programmers can't gain access to the underlying persistence features that the Entity Framework embeds in the classes it creates. Fortunately, version 4.1 of the Entity Framework makes this easy for us.

Note Version 4.1 of the Entity Framework is included in the MVC 3 Tools Update that I asked you to install in Chapter 2. If you haven't installed this update, then you should do so now.

The Entity Framework makes it easy for us to use our own model classes to represent rows in a database. We are going to use a feature called *code-first*, which lets us start with the model classes and associate them with a database. One of the main benefits of the code-first feature is that it can create the database for us from our model classes. This is a great idea, but I estimate than less than 5% of the projects I have worked on have the luxury of creating the databases from scratch. We have to work with an existing database in the vast majority of cases. Of course, in the weirdly artificial environment of a book, we don't have a database legacy, so we are going to create one. We are going to do this from scratch, unlike the earlier data examples, where I provided a prepared database as part of the source code download.

■ **Caution** Visual Web Developer doesn't have the features required to create a database. This is another of the ways in which Microsoft differentiates between the free and commercial editions of Visual Studio. You can create a database using the SQL Server Management Studio (which I mentioned in Chapter 2). The process is largely similar to the one for Visual Studio shown in this chapter. Alternatively, I have included this database in the source code download as well.

Creating the Database

Start by opening the Server Explorer window (available from Visual Studio's View menu). Right-click Data Connections and select Create New SQL Server Database from the pop-up menu; this will open the dialog shown in Figure 24-1.

Figure 24-1. *Creating a new database*

Enter the name of your database server and select the authentication options. In the figure, I am creating the new SQL Server Express database on my server, called Titan, and using the authentication support built into SQL Server. I have created an account called *adam* with a password also of *adam*. (Obviously, you shouldn't use such weak credentials in a real project.) If you have installed the database server on your development machine, then the server name should be .\SQLEXPRESS, and you should check the Use Windows Authentication option. Set the database name to Competitions, and click the OK button. The database will be created, and a new item will appear in the Data Connections section of the Server Explorer window.

Adding the Tables

If you expand the new connection in the Server Explorer window, you will see a Tables item. Right-click this and select Add New Table from the pop-up menu, as shown in Figure 24-2.

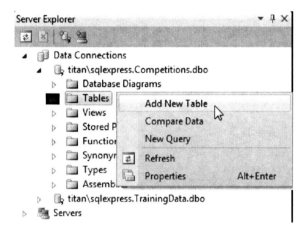

Figure 24-2. *Adding a new table to the database*

Visual Studio will open the table schema editor. We are going to start by creating a table for the Competition model types. Using the schema editor, enter details of the columns shown in Figure 24-3.

Column Name	Data Type	Allow Nulls
ID	int	☐
Name	varchar(100)	☐
Location	varchar(100)	☐
Date	date	☐
EventType	varchar(20)	☐
		☐

Figure 24-3. *The schema for the Competitions table*

Right-click the ID column and select Set Primary Key. This will add a small golden key next to the ID column, as shown in Figure 24-4.

Column Name	Data Type	Allow Nulls
ID	int	☐
Name	varchar(100)	☐
Location	varchar(100)	☐
Date	date	☐

Figure 24-4. *Setting the primary key for the table*

Right-click anywhere in the schema designer and select Properties from the pop-up menu. Change the value of the Identity Column property to ID. This tells SQL Server that it will be responsible for generating unique values for this column, which saves us a lot of work.

Press Ctrl+S to save the table and name it Competitions when prompted to do so. We can now repeat the process for other table we need, which we'll call `Registrations`. Figure 24-5 shows the schema for this table.

Column Name	Data Type	Allow Nulls
ID	int	☐
Name	varchar(MAX)	☐
HomeCity	varchar(MAX)	☐
Age	int	☐
CompetitionID	int	☐
		☐

Figure 24-5. *The schema for Registrations*

Once again, right-click the designer, select Properties, and change the Identity Column property to ID. Don't forget to make the ID column the primary key for the table so that the key is shown as in the figure.

Notice that not all of the columns that we have added to the tables correspond to properties in our domain model classes. We have added an ID column to both tables and a CompetitionID column to the `Competitions` table. There is usually additional data required to get the best from a database, and we have to accept this small burden in order to get persistence.

Defining the Foreign Key Relationship

The `Competition` property in the `Registration` domain model class creates a relationship between our two model types. We are going to replicate that relationship in the database using a foreign key to make things simpler later (and to demonstrate a cool Entity Framework trick).

Double-click the `Registrations` table in the Solution Explorer window to open the schema designer. Right-click and select Relationships from the pop-up menu; this will open the Foreign Key Relationships dialog. Click the Add button, and a new item will appear in the Selected Relationships list on the left of the screen. In the properties area, click the Tables and Columns Specification item, and click the ellipsis (...) button that appears, as shown in Figure 24-6.

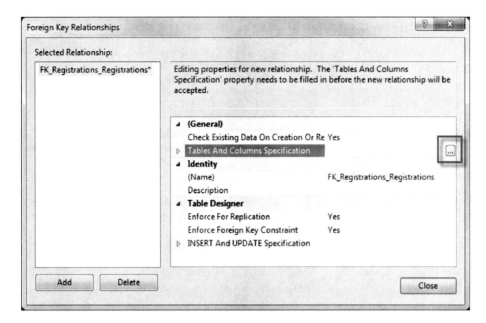

Figure 24-6. Defining the foreign key specification

The Tables and Columns dialog will open, as shown in Figure 24-7. Change the primary key table to Competitions, and select ID from the list of available fields. Select CompetitionID as the field for the Registrations table; you can see the required settings in the figure.

Figure 24-7. Setting the detail of the foreign key relationship

This relationship ensures that the CompetitionID column in the `Registrations` table will correspond to one of the defined ID values in the `Competitions` table. Click OK to dismiss the Tables and Columns dialog, and then click Close to dismiss the Foreign Key Relationships dialog. Finally, press Ctrl+S to save the changes to the tables.

Inserting the Seed Data

The last thing we are going to do is add some data to the `Competitions` table. We'll add the same set of competitions that we put in the `DummyRepository` class in the previous chapter; this will allow us to focus on the `RegistrationController` class without having to create the code and views required to populate the competitions as well.

Right-click the `Competitions` table in the Server Explorer, and select Show Table Data from the pop-up menu – the empty table is shown in Figure 24-8. Start adding data by clicking the Name column. We don't need to add values for the ID column because we asked SQL Server to generate unique values for us. You'll see those values being produced as you enter data.

	ID	Name	Location	Date	EventType
▶*	NULL	NULL	NULL	NULL	NULL

Figure 24-8. *Entering data into the table*

Enter values for the columns and tab between them until your table has the data shown in Figure 24-9.

	ID	Name	Location	Date	EventType
	1	London Lunge	London	22/04/2012	Sprint
	3	New York Nudge	New York	12/05/2012	Olympic
	4	Paris Panic	Paris	16/05/2012	Sprint
▶*	NULL	NULL	NULL	NULL	NULL

Figure 24-9. *Adding the seed data*

A unique value for the ID column will be generated, and the record will be saved each time you tab to a new row. You can see from the figure that the ID values in my table are not contiguous. This is because I deleted a record and then added two more. The values don't have to be in sequence; SQL Server will ensure that they are unique, however.

■ **Tip** Visual Studio will display the date values in the format for your locale. I live in the United Kingdom, where we use the format day/month/year. Your date values may be displayed differently if you live elsewhere.

Creating the Repository

The first step to creating a repository is to create a class that drives the Entity Framework to connect to our database and use our model types to represent records. There are lots of different ways to do this, but I like to use a separate class that I think of as an adapter between the repository class and the Entity Framework.

Creating the Entity Framework Adapter

Create a new class in the `Models/Domain/Repository` folder called `EFAdapter` and set its contents to match Listing 24-1.

Listing 24-1. The EFAdapter class

```
class EFAdapter : DbContext {

    public EFAdapter(string connectionName)
        : base(connectionName) {
        // do nothing
    }

    public DbSet<Competition> Competitions { get; set; }
    public DbSet<Registration> Registrations { get; set; }
}
```

This is the real magic of the new Entity Framework features. We create a class that is derived from `DbContext` and then define properties that tell the Entity Framework which domain types should be used to represent data from specific tables. For example, this property:

```
public DbSet<Registration> Registrations { get; set; }
```

tells the Entity Framework that rows in the `Registrations` table should be represented by the `Registration` model class. The constructor parameter lets me specify a connection string in the `Web.config` file that should be used to connect to the database. If I had not passed the parameter value to the base class constructor, then it would look for a connection string that has the same name as the derived class, which is `EFAdapter` in this case.

Creating the Repository Implementation

The next step is to define the repository class. Add a new class in the `Models/Domain/Repository` folder called `EFRepository`. Listing 24-2 shows the contents of this class.

Listing 24-2. The EFRepository class

```
using System.Data.Entity;
using System.Linq;

namespace EventRegistration.Models.Domain.Repository {
```

```
public class EFRepository : IRepository {
    private EFAdapter adapter = new EFAdapter("EFRepository");

    public IQueryable<Competition> Competitions {
        get {
            return adapter.Competitions;
        }
    }

    public IQueryable<Registration> Registrations {
        get {
            return adapter.Registrations;
        }
    }

    public void SaveRegistration(Registration reg) {
        if (reg.ID == 0) {
            adapter.Registrations.Add(reg);
            adapter.Entry(reg).Reference("Competition").Load();
        }
        adapter.SaveChanges();
    }

    public void SaveCompetition(Competition comp) {
        if (comp.ID == 0) {
            adapter.Competitions.Add(comp);
            adapter.Entry(comp).Collection("Registrations").Load();
        }
        adapter.SaveChanges();
    }
}
```

This class is pretty straightforward. It implements the repository interface by working with the properties of the EFAdapter class we created previously. The SaveXXX methods in this class test for newly created domain model objects by checking to see whether the ID property value is 0. We know this represents data that is not yet in the database because we set the ID column in both tables to be the identity column, meaning that any value that has been obtained from the database will have an ID value greater than 0. We need to use the Add method on the DbSet before calling the SaveChanges method in order to have the Entity Framework handle our data.

Defining the Connection String

Now we must define the connection string. In the EFRepository class, we define the EFAdapter field like this:

```
private EFAdapter adapter = new EFAdapter("EFRepository");
```

This means that the Entity Framework will be looking for a connection string with the name EFRepository. Listing 24-3 shows the connection string added to the Web.config file.

Listing 24-3. The connection string for the Competitions database

```
<configuration>
  <connectionStrings>
    <add name="EFRepository" connectionString="Data Source=TITAN\SQLEXPRESS;Initial
      Catalog=Competitions;Persist Security Info=True;User ID=adam;Password=adam"
      providerName="System.Data.SqlClient"/>
  </connectionStrings>
...
```

To find the connection string for your database, open the Server Explorer window and find the appropriate connection in the Data Connections items. Right-click the connection and select Properties from the pop-up window. One of the properties is Connection String, which you can use for your Web.config file. If, like me, you are using SQL Server authentication, the connection string will contain a string of asterisks for the password. You will need to replace this with the real password to allow the Entity Framework to make the connection.

■ **Tip**   This is not the same format of connection string that we saw when we created Entity Framework data models in Chapter 8. The connection string we need in this situation is the simpler kind shown in the listing.

Registering the Repository Class

The final step is to tell Ninject that it should use our new repository implementation to satisfy demands for the repository interface. Listing 24-4 shows the changes required to the AddDefaultBindings method of the CustomDependencyResolver class.

Listing 24-4. Registering the new repository implementation with Ninject

```
private void AddDefaultBindings() {
    Bind<IRepository>().To<EFRepository>().InRequestScope();
}
```

By default, Ninject creates a new object each time an implementation is requested. This is fine for most types of object, but it can cause some problems when using the Entity Framework. In particular, we can end up with situations where we try to mix and match objects from different repository implementation instances.

Ninject is aware of how ASP.NET works and can be configured to create a new instance for each web request. This is done by calling the InRequestScope method, as shown in the listing. Only one instance of the repository implementation class will be created per web request, irrespective of how many requests for an implementation are received. Instances are not shared between requests and are destroyed when the request has been processed.

Don't worry if this doesn't make sense at the moment. I'll show you an example of this problem in Chapter 29 when we look at model binding.

Preparing the Model

It would be perfect if we could add persistence to our domain model without having to change any of the classes, but that is rarely possible. There are two main reasons for this when persisting to a relational database—primary keys and relationships between tables, both of which usually require that we make some additions to our model classes. Listing 24-5 shows the required changes to the **Registration** class.

Listing 24-5. *Modifying the Registration model class to support persistence*

```
namespace EventRegistration.Models.Domain {

    public class Registration {

        public int ID { get; set; }
        public string Name { get; set; }
        public string HomeCity { get; set; }
        public int Age { get; set; }
        public int CompetitionID { get; set; }
        public virtual Competition Competition {get; set;}
    }
}
```

The ID property allows the Entity Framework to easily determine which record a given model object represents, and the CompetitionID property allows us to define a relationship between a registration and a competition in a way that makes sense to the database.

Notice that I have left the Competition property in the class. The Entity Framework is clever enough to recognize the implied foreign key relationship between the Registration and Competition classes. When we read a Registration object from the repository, the Entity Framework will create a Competition object with the appropriate data and use it to set the value of the Competition property. In Entity Framework terms, Competition is a navigation property, used to navigate through the model without having to make explicit queries to the database.

I have marked the Competition property with the **virtual** keyword. This tells the Entity Framework that I want to use *lazy loading*. With lazy loading, no value is assigned to the Competition property of a Registration object until I read its value, at which point the Entity Framework makes a database query, creates the appropriate Competition object, and assigns it to the property. All of this happens seamlessly, which makes it simple and convenient.

NEW MODEL OBJECTS AND USING EAGER LOADING

The lazy loading feature means that we don't load data from the database if we don't read the value of a navigation property, but we generate an additional database query the first time we *do* read it. The alternative is to use *eager loading*, where the navigation objects are loaded as part of the main query. We do this using the Include method in the repository implementation, like this:

```
public IQueryable<Registration> Registrations {
    get {
        return adapter.Registrations.Include("Competitions");
    }
}
```

The Entity Framework can only apply lazy loading or eager loading to objects that it created, and so when the model binding process creates a new Registration object, the Competition navigation property will return null when it is read. This is why I explicitly load the Competition object in the repository implementation when we save the object, like this:

```
adapter.Entry(reg).Reference("Competition").Load();
```

This step isn't needed if we save the object and then don't use it again, but it is good practice if we intend to pass the newly created model object to a view.

We need to make similar changes to the Competition class, as shown in Listing 24-6.

Listing 24-6. Modifying the Competition model class to support persistence

```
using System;
using System.Collections.Generic;

namespace EventRegistration.Models.Domain {
    public class Competition {

        public int ID { get; set; }
        public string Name {get; set;}
        public string Location {get; set;}
        public DateTime Date {get; set;}
        public string EventType { get; set; }
        public virtual ICollection<Registration> Registrations { get; set; }
    }
}
```

The ID property serves just the same purpose as the one in the Registration class. The Registrations property is something different. It is a nice bonus that comes from the cleverness of the Entity Framework.

■ **Caution** The ability to lazily load navigation objects based on foreign key relationships is a very cool feature, but there is a situation in which it doesn't work as expected. In Chapter 25, I'll show you what that problem is and how to address it.

This property represents the other end of the foreign key relationship. Each Competition record can be associated with multiple Registration records, and we can access those registrations by reading the Registrations property.

■ **Note** The new Entity Framework feature set is endless configurable, allowing complete control over the mapping of the database to the model objects. See the ADO.NET section of MSDN for further details.

Modifying the Controller and the Views

The changes that we made to the model classes are not all overhead. We can use these new properties to tidy up our controller and views. Let's start with the controller; Listing 24-7 shows the revised code.

Listing 24-7. Modifying the RegistrationController class

```
using System.Web.Mvc;
using EventRegistration.Models.Domain;
using EventRegistration.Models.Domain.Repository;

namespace EventRegistration.Controllers {

    public class RegistrationController : Controller {
        private IRepository repository;

        public RegistrationController(IRepository repo) {
            repository = repo;
        }

        public ActionResult Index() {
            ViewBag.Competitions = repository.Competitions;
            return View();
        }

        [HttpPost]
        public ActionResult Index(Registration registration) {
            repository.SaveRegistration(registration);
            return View("RegistrationComplete", registration);
        }
    }
}
```

I'll take you through the changes step by step. First, we have changed the `Index()` method, in other words, the version of the method that specifies no parameters. Here is the old version of this method:

```
public ActionResult Index() {
    ViewBag.Competitions = repository.Competitions.Select(e => e.Name);
    return View();
}
```

The old version uses the `ViewBag` to pass just the names of the competitions to the view. In the new version, we pass the entire `Competition` object, as follows:

```
public ActionResult Index() {
    ViewBag.Competitions = repository.Competitions;
    return View();
}
```

We do this because it allows us to render the select control in the view such that the data value we get back from the control is assigned to the `ControlID` property of the `Registration` object creating during the model binding process. Here's how the `select` control in `Index.cshtml` was rendered previously:

```
@Html.DropDownList("Competition", new SelectList(ViewBag.Competitions))
```

Listing 24-8 shows the modified version of Index.cshtml.

Listing 24-8. *Modifying Index.cshtml to render the select control differently*

```
@{
    ViewBag.Title = "Registration";
}

<style type="text/css">
    td[colspan] {text-align:center}
</style>

<h4>Registration</h4>

@using (Html.BeginForm()) {

    <table>
        <tr><td>Name:</td><td>@Html.Editor("Name")</td></tr>
        <tr><td>Age:</td><td>@Html.Editor("Age")</td></tr>
        <tr><td>City:</td><td>@Html.Editor("HomeCity")</td></tr>

        <tr>
            <td>Competition:</td>
            <td>
                @Html.DropDownList("CompetitionID",
                    new SelectList(ViewBag.Competitions, "ID", "Name"))
            </td>
        </tr>
        <tr><td colspan="2"><input type="submit" value="Register" /></td></tr>
    </table>
}
```

We use a different overload of the SelectList constructor that lets us specify the property that will be displayed to the user (Name) and the value that will be sent when the form is posted (ID). We also change the first parameter to the Html.DropDownList helper so that the ID assigned to the select element when the view is rendered matches the name of the new property in the Registration class.

You can see the effect of this change in the other version of the Index method—the one that takes parameters and processes POSTs. Here is the previous version:

```
[HttpPost]
public ActionResult Index(Registration registration, string competition) {

    registration.Competition = repository.Competitions
            .Where(e => e.Name == competition).FirstOrDefault();

    repository.SaveRegistration(registration);
    return View("RegistrationComplete", registration);
}
```

You can see that we had to use the value of the competition parameter to perform a LINQ query in order to associate the competition with the registration. Here is the new version of that method:

```
[HttpPost]
public ActionResult Index(Registration registration) {
    repository.SaveRegistration(registration);
    return View("RegistrationComplete", registration);
}
```

The LINQ query and the parameter are gone. The association between the registration and the competition is handled through the CompetitionID property, which is automatically assigned the value from the select control during model binding. With a couple of small changes, we can take advantage of the properties we added for persistence to create a simpler and tidier controller.

Summary

In this chapter, I have shown you how to use features of version 4.1 of the Entity Framework to add persistence to our domain model classes. We are able to do this with only minor modifications to the model classes themselves, and most importantly, the model classes are unaware of the persistence technology that is being used. We could move to a different technology with little effort, especially if the underlying data store remained a relational database.

CHAPTER 25

Working with Views

This chapter will cover another big building block in the MVC framework—views, the *V* in MVC. As I explained earlier, a *view* is a template that contains instructions that the MVC framework follows to generate a response to a request. The MVC framework uses a view engine to render a view into HTML. The engine we will use is called Razor; introduced in MVC 3, it's a more elegant alternative to the traditional ASP.NET <% and %> tags.

Creating the Action Method

Before we can start, we need to create a new action method that we'll work with as we investigate views. We are going to build on the example we have used in the past few chapters, and Listing 25-1 shows the RegistrationController class with a new action method.

Listing 25-1. Adding a new action method to the RegistrationController class

```
using System;
using System.Linq;
using System.Web.Mvc;
using EventRegistration.Models.Domain;
using EventRegistration.Models.Domain.Repository;

namespace EventRegistration.Controllers {

    public class RegistrationController : Controller {
        private IRepository repository;

        public RegistrationController(IRepository repo) {
            repository = repo;
        }

        public ActionResult Index() {
            ViewBag.Competitions = repository.Competitions;
            return View();
        }

        [HttpPost]
```

```
    public ActionResult Index(Registration registration) {
        repository.SaveRegistration(registration);
        return View("RegistrationComplete", registration);
    }

    public ActionResult List() {
        return View(repository.Registrations);
    }
}
}
```

This is a very simple action method; it just tells the MVC framework to render the default view and passes the sequence of Registration objects from the repository as the view model. To give us some data to work with, I have created the registrations shown in Table 25-1 in the database.

Table 25-1. *Registrations Created for the Examples in This Chapter*

Name	Home City	Age	Event Name
Joe Smith	New York	40	London Lunge
Joe Smith	New York	40	New York Nudge
Adam Freeman	London	39	London Lunge
Adam Freeman	London	39	Paris Panic
Anne Jones	Boston	51	London Lunge

Understanding the Location Search

Before we go any further, let's target the newly created action method. Start the application (by selecting either Debug ➤ Start Debugging or Debug ➤ Start Without Debugging in Visual Studio) and navigate to /Registration/List. You'll see an error message similar to the one shown in Figure 25-1.

Figure 25-1. *Searching for a view*

The MVC framework reports an error because it can't find the default view associated with the `List` action method. This is not a surprise because we have yet to create it. What's important is *where* the MVC framework looked for the view before reporting the error. You can see the list of locations in the figure.

When we return the result of the `View` method in an action, we tell the MVC framework we want to render a view. If we don't specify the view name, then the framework assumes we want to use a view with the same name as the action method, which is `List` in our case.

The MVC framework looks in two locations for our views—in the `Views/<controllername>` folder and in the `Views/Shared` folder. Including the name of the controller in the path that is used to find a view allows us to use meaningful view names without having to worry about colliding with views from other controllers. If we want to reuse a view in multiple controllers, then we can put it in the `Views/Shared` folder.

Note also that the MVC framework looks for four different file extensions in each location: `.aspx`, `.ascx`, `.cshtml`, and `.vbhtml`. These extensions specify which view engine should be used to render the view. The ASPX engine is used to process `.aspx` and `.ascx` files. These are views that use the traditional `<%` and `%>` tags for markup. We are interested in the `.cshtml` extension, which is a Razor view where the markup is C# (as opposed to `.vbhtml`, which is Razor with Visual Basic). We can mix and match views that use different view engines in a single project, although in this book I will be using only `.cshtml` views.

609

> ■ **Note** Views that use the ASPX view engine are *not* Web Forms pages. They are MVC views that use the <% and %> tags. The difference between an ASPX view and a Razor view is the format of the markup. As a simple example, calling an HTML helper with traditional tags (<%: Html.DisplayFor(e => e.Name) %>) is similar to performing the same task using Razor (@Html.DisplayFor(e => e.Name)).

Creating the View

Now we are ready to get started with the view. We can create a view in a couple of ways. The first is to expand the **Views** folder, right-click the folder that relates to our controller, and select Add ➤ View from the pop-up menu. The second, and usually more convenient, way is to right-click anywhere in the action method in the controller class and select Add View from the pop-up menu; it's more convenient because Visual Studio works out where the view should go and sets the name for the view to match the action method.

Choose one of these techniques to create a new view for the **List** method in the **RegistrationController** class. You can see the Add View dialog in Figure 25-2.

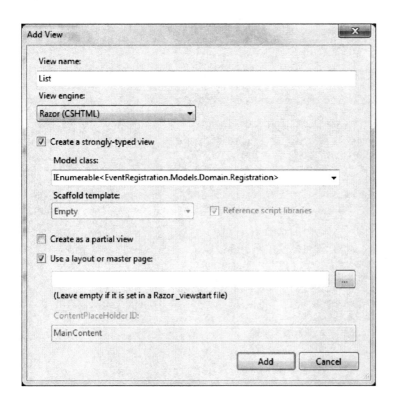

Figure 25-2. *The Add View dialog*

Ensure that the view name is List and the selected view engine is Razor (CSHTML). Select the "Create a strongly-typed view" option and set the model class to IEnumerable<EventRegistration .Models.Domain.Registration>. You will have to enter this manually because it won't be available in the drop-down list.

■ **Caution** It is important that the model class type matches the type of the object that the action method passes to the View method. You will encounter problems if they do not match.

Select the "Use a layout or master page" option (which I'll explain later) and click the Add button to create the view. Listing 25-2 shows the contents of the List.cshtml view that Visual Studio creates.

Listing 25-2. *The List.cshtml view*

```
@model IEnumerable<EventRegistration.Models.Domain.Registration>

@{
    ViewBag.Title = "List";
}

<h2>List</h2>
```

There isn't much to this view, but even so, it includes some important features. I'll explain what they are in the following sections and then demonstrate some additional Razor and view features.

Understanding Razor

In the following sections, I'll show you the different types of Razor tag, and along the way, we'll add some new functionality to our view. As you read these sections, remember where the view sits in the MVC model. The MVC framework has passed a request to an *action method* in a *controller*, and the controller has done whatever it needs to the *model* and has called the View method to tell the MVC framework to render a view. The view will be used to generate an HTML page that will be returned to the user's browser.

To maintain our separation of concerns, we want to focus on creating a template that renders the HTML we require. We don't want to do any heavy computation (that's the job of the controller), and we don't want to hold or represent any of the domain state (that's the job of the model).

Working with the Model Object

We selected the option for a strongly typed view when we created the List.cshtml view, which means we have declared the type of the view model object that the controller will pass to the view. This is an enumeration of Registration objects in our example. We define this type using the Razor @model tag (with a lowercase m), like this:

```
@model IEnumerable<EventRegistration.Models.Domain.Registration>
```

Notice that we have to specify the fully qualified name of the `Registration` class, including the namespace. This is because the MVC framework doesn't have any special knowledge about our example project. It can be tedious to have to refer to our model classes in this way, but we can tell Razor to look for classes in additional namespaces by editing the `~/Views/Web.config` file. This is the *other* `Web.config` file, not the main one for the application. This `Web.config` file configures Razor, and we can extend the set of places it looks for classes by adding items to the `namespaces` element, as shown in Listing 25-3.

Listing 25-3. Adding namespaces to the ~/Views/Web.config file

```
<configuration>
  ...
  <system.web.webPages.razor>
    <host factoryType="System.Web.Mvc.MvcWebRazorHostFactory, System.Web.Mvc,↵
Version=3.0.0.0, Culture=neutral, PublicKeyToken=31BF3856AD364E35" />
    <pages pageBaseType="System.Web.Mvc.WebViewPage">
      <namespaces>
        <add namespace="System.Web.Mvc" />
        <add namespace="System.Web.Mvc.Ajax" />
        <add namespace="System.Web.Mvc.Html" />
        <add namespace="System.Web.Routing" />
        <add namespace="EventRegistration.Models.Domain"/>
      </namespaces>
    </pages>
  </system.web.webPages.razor>
...
</configuration>
```

This allows us to omit the namespace from the `@model` directive, as shown in Listing 25-4.

Listing 25-4. Omitting the namespace from the @model directive

```
@model IEnumerable<Registration>

@{
    ViewBag.Title = "List";
}

<h2>List</h2>
```

We can refer to the model object using the `@Model` tag (uppercase letter M) and access fields, properties, and methods just as we would in a C# class. Listing 25-5 contains a simple example, which calls the `Count` method on our view model to report how many items there are in the collection.

Listing 25-5. Using the @Model tag

```
@model IEnumerable<Registration>

@{
    ViewBag.Title = "List";
}

<h4>There are @Model.Count() registrations</h4>
```

If we start the application and navigate to /Registration/List, we can see the effect of this tag, which is illustrated by Figure 25-3.

Figure 25-3. *The effect of using the model object*

This is a very simple example, but you can see that using a Razor tag in a view is similar to using the <% and %> tags in a Web Form. We can mix our tags with static HTML, CSS, and other web elements. These tags are then detected and evaluated when the view is rendered, and the output is included in the HTML sent to the client. I'll show you different (and more complex) ways of working with the model object while we look at different kinds of Razor tag shortly.

CHANGING THE VIEW MODEL TYPE

There is very little behind-the-scenes magic in the MVC framework. As an example, the only effect of selecting the option to create a strongly typed view is that the @model directive is added to the view file. There is no configuration file that records how a view was created or what the view model type is. This means we can easily change the type of the view model by changing the @model directive—or if we accidentally forget to check the strongly typed option, we can make a view strongly typed by adding an @model directive.

MVC views are compiled into classes in much the same way as I described for ASPX pages in Chapter 4, although the files are much harder to read. The effect of the @model directive is to change the generic type parameter of the base class, but the real benefit is that Visual Studio can use IntelliSense when we are editing the view to help us select members of the model object. Figure 25-4 shows what happened when I hit the period key after typing @Model in the view.

Figure 25-4. *IntelliSense support when editing a strongly typed view*

Using Dynamically Typed Views

Using an `@model` directive doesn't mean we *must* pass a view model from the controller to the view every time we render the view. It just means that when we do pass a view model, it will be of the type we specified.

If we omit the `@model` directive, we create a *dynamically typed* view, also referred to as *weakly typed*. These views are called *dynamic* because omitting the `@model` directive is equivalent to using a directive like this:

```
@model dynamic
```

Using a dynamically typed view doesn't mean we can't pass a view model object from the controller to the view. It just means that we haven't declared the view model type and so the MVC framework will treat our view model as though it were a dynamic object. Listing 25-6 shows a dynamic version of our `List.cshtml` view.

Listing 25-6. *A dynamic view*

```
@{
    ViewBag.Title = "List";
}

<h4>There are @Model.Count() registrations</h4>
```

If we try to render this view, we'll get an error telling us that the type `System.Data.Entity.DbSet<EventRegistration.Models.Domain.Registration>` does not contain a definition for `Count`. This is because when we apply the `Count` method to the enumeration, we are calling an extension method that is defined in the `System.Linq.Enumerable` class, and Razor can't make the association between the extension method and the view model. We can fix this in a few ways, but the simplest is to call the extension method directly, as shown in Listing 25-7.

Listing 25-7. *Calling an extension method directly in a dynamically typed view*

```
@{
    ViewBag.Title = "List";
}

<h4>There are @Enumerable.Count(Model) registrations</h4>
```

Another option is to take advantage of the dynamic support to send a view data object from the controller that already includes all the values we want. Listing 25-8 shows an example of doing this in the `List` action method of the `RegistrationController` class.

Listing 25-8. *Using a dynamic object as a view model object*

```
public ActionResult List() {

    dynamic dobj = new ExpandoObject();
    dobj.Data = repository.Registrations;
    dobj.ItemCount = repository.Registrations.Count();
    return View(dobj);
}
```

We can then access these dynamically defined properties in the view, as shown in Listing 25-9.

Listing 25-9. Accessing properties from a dynamic view model object

```
@{
    ViewBag.Title = "List";
}
```

```
<h4>There are @Model.ItemCount registrations</h4>
```

The choice between strongly and dynamically typed is a matter of personal preference. We lose IntelliSense support in a dynamically typed view, but we create an environment that is more in keeping with other dynamic web development languages, such as Ruby or even JavaScript. We can also use a single dynamic view to handle different kinds of view model type—although this requires care to make sure that we don't invoke nonexistent members. My preference is for strongly typed views, probably because I like strongly typed programming languages in general.

Inserting Other Values

We can insert any value into a view with a Razor @ tag, not properties and fields from the view model. After the model object, the most commonly used data comes from the ViewBag, which we briefly encountered in Chapter 23. In both the controller and the view, the ViewBag property returns a dynamic object that the controller can use to pass ancillary data to the view. Listing 25-10 gives an example of passing the current time to the view using the ViewBag.

Listing 25-10. Passing data to the view via the ViewBag

```
public ActionResult List() {

    ViewBag.Time = DateTime.Now;
    return View(repository.Registrations);
}
```

We can then access this data in the view, as shown in Listing 25-11.

▒ **Note** There is another way of passing data from the controller to the view, which is to use session state. I'll show you how to do this in Chapter 28.

Listing 25-11. Reading data from the ViewBag

```
@model IEnumerable<Registration>

@{
    ViewBag.Title = "List";
}
```

```
<h4>There are @Model.Count() registrations</h4>
```

```
<h6>This page was rendered at: @ViewBag.Time </h6>
```

■ **Note** Our view sets a value for the ViewBag.Title property, which may seem to contradict what I said about how information flows from the controller to the view. In fact, this is a neat trick to do with the Razor equivalent to master pages, called *layouts*. I explain how layouts work later in this chapter.

We can also call methods. You saw this earlier when we called an extension method directly, but we can call any static method using an @ tag. As an example, Listing 25-12 shows using the composite formatting feature to render just the time from the DateTime object passed to the view using the ViewBag.

Listing 25-12. Calling a static method in a view

```
@model IEnumerable<Registration>

@{
    ViewBag.Title = "List";
}
```

```
<h4>There are @Model.Count() registrations</h4>
```

```
<h6>This page was rendered at: @string.Format("{0:t}", ViewBag.Time) </h6>
```

There are no terminator tags in Razor. We just start with @, and Razor figures out when our directive ends. When using tags like the ones in this section, Razor assumes that the value of the field or property (or the result from the method) should be inserted into the HTML response. This means we can't call methods that return **void**, but I'll show you a different technique for this shortly.

Using Razor Conditional Tags

Razor supports a set of C# keywords that we can include in our views to create simple logic. Listing 25-13 provides a demonstration.

Listing 25-13. A Razor if tag

```
@model IEnumerable<Registration>

@{
    ViewBag.Title = "List";
}
```

```
@if (Model.Count() == 0) {
    <h4>There are no registrations</h4>
} else if (Model.Count() == 1) {
    <h4> There is one registration</h4>
} else {
    <h4>There are @Model.Count() registrations</h4>
}

<h6>This page was rendered at: @string.Format("{0:t}", ViewBag.Time) </h6>
```

The listing shows an `@if` statement, which is broadly similar to a regular C# `if` statement. There are a couple of points to note. The first is that we don't need to use the @ sign to access data values in the conditions so that we write the following:

```
} else if (Model.Count() == 1) {
```

and not the following:

```
} else if (@Model.Count() == 1) {
```

The second key point is to understand what Razor does with the contents of a block when it matches a condition. Razor processes each line in turn. If a line starts with the < character, Razor interprets this as a block of HTML that should be written to the output. If the line contains Razor @ tags, then they are evaluated, and their results are inserted into the HTML as normal.

If the line doesn't begin with an HTML tag, then Razor assumes that it is dealing with a C# statement and tries to execute the statement. This allows us to mix and match code and HTML in a single block, as demonstrated by Listing 25-14.

Listing 25-14. *Mixing HTML and C# statements in Razor @if statements*

```
@model IEnumerable<Registration>

@{
    ViewBag.Title = "List";
}

@if (Model.Count() == 0) {
    <h4>There are no registrations</h4>
} else if (Model.Count() == 1) {
    <h4> There is one registration</h4>
} else {
    <h4>There are @Model.Count() registrations</h4>
    DateTime nextMonth = DateTime.Now.AddMonths(1);
    string nextMonthName = string.Format("{0:MMMM}", nextMonth);
    <span>Next month will be: @nextMonthName</span>
}

<h6>This page was rendered at: @string.Format("{0:t}", ViewBag.Time) </h6>
```

In this listing, I have added a couple of C# statements to create and manipulate a `DateTime` object and a line of HTML that includes a Razor @ tag to display the result. You can see how this is rendered in Figure 25-5.

Figure 25-5. *Rendering a mix of HTML, Razor tags, and C# code*

We need to give Razor a hint when a line doesn't start with an HTML tag and isn't a C# statement, and one way of doing this is to prefix the line with the @: tag, as shown in Listing 25-15.

Listing 25-15. *Using the @: tag to indicate text content*

```
@model IEnumerable<Registration>

@{
    ViewBag.Title = "List";
}

<h4>
@switch (Model.Count()) {
    case 0:
        @:There are no registrations
        break;
    case 1:
        @:There is one registration
        break;
    default:
        @:There are @Model.Count() registrations
        break;
}
</h4>

<h6>This page was rendered at: @string.Format("{0:t}", ViewBag.Time) </h6>
```

I have used an @switch tag in this listing, which is another conditional statement that Razor supports. I have put the h4 HTML tags outside the @switch statement, which I use to insert just the text in between the open and close tags. Since each of these lines doesn't start with an HTML tag and isn't a C# statement, I have prefixed them with the special @: tag. When Razor encounters this tag, it processes the line for any further @ tags, evaluates them, and writes the results to the HTML response.

Prefixing lines with @: can be tedious if we have multiple lines to process. In such situations we can enclose these lines in a **text** element, as shown in Listing 25-16.

Listing 25-16. Using a text element as a hint to Razor

```
@model IEnumerable<EventRegistration.Models.Domain.Registration>

@{
    ViewBag.Title = "List";
}

<h4>
@switch (Model.Count()) {
    case 0:
        @:There are no registrations
        break;
    case 1:
        @:There is one registration
        break;
    default:
        <text>
            There are @Model.Count() registrations.
            The first of them is for @Model.First().Name at
            the @Model.First().Competition.Name event.
        </text>
        break;
}
</h4>

<h6>This page was rendered at: @string.Format("{0:t}", ViewBag.Time) </h6>
```

The **text** element doesn't add anything to the rendered HTML; it is just an instruction for Razor to process the contents as though each element were prefixed with the **@:** tag.

Iterating in a Razor View

In addition to **@if** and **@switch**, Razor supports two iterative tags that let us perform an activity repeatedly. The first one we'll look at is **@foreach**, which is demonstrated in Listing 25-17.

Listing 25-17. Using the @foreach tag

```
@model IEnumerable<EventRegistration.Models.Domain.Registration>

@{
    ViewBag.Title = "List";
}

<h4>
@switch (Model.Count()) {
    case 0:
        @:There are no registrations
        break;
```

```
    case 1:
        @:There is one registration
        break;
    default:
        @:There are @Model.Count() registrations.
        break;
}
</h4>

<table>
    <tr><th>Name</th><th>Age</th><th>Home City</th><th>Event</th></tr>
    @foreach (var item in Model) {
        <tr>
            <td>@item.Name</td>
            <td>@item.Age</td>
            <td>@item.HomeCity</td>
            <td>@item.Competition.Name</td>
        </tr>
    }
</table>
```

```
<h6>This page was rendered at: @string.Format("{0:t}", ViewBag.Time) </h6>
```

In this listing, I define a **table** element and use the **@foreach** tag to work through the sequence of **Registration** objects in the view model and generate a **tr** element for each of them. As with the **@if** and **@switch** tags, Razor assumes that lines that begin with an HTML tag should be added to the rendered output and other lines are C# statements to execute.

Fixing the Lazy Loading Iteration Problem

If you start the application and navigate to the **/Registration/List** URL, you'll find that the view shown in the listing won't render. Instead, you'll see an error message, like the one shown in Figure 25-6.

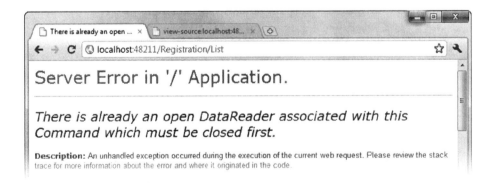

Figure 25-6. *An error message displayed when iterating through model items*

The error message isn't especially descriptive, but this problem is caused by an optimization that the Entity Framework makes when retrieving data, conflicting with the way that lazy loading and LINQ operate. It takes a little explanation to understand the interactions between these elements.

The first thing we need to know is that we are using LINQ to Entities to retrieve data from the repository. When we pass the value of the `Registrations` property from the repository implementation to the view, we are not passing the data items. We are passing a query that won't be evaluated and executed against the database until we start to access the results (this is known as *deferred execution* and is a key LINQ concept). This means that our database query isn't performed until the first iteration of the `@foreach` loop in the view.

The second thing we need to know is that the Entity Framework tries to optimize its connections to the database by allowing only one query at a time to be made over each connection. The results from one query must have been fully read from the database before another query is allowed to proceed.

The third thing we need to know is that the database query for a lazily loaded navigation property isn't executed until we try to read the value of the property.

Put these three things together, and we can see what is happening. The `@foreach` tag takes the first `Registration` object from the `IEnumerable` sequence. This triggers the database query, and the results are ready to be read from the connection. We start inserting values from the first object into the HTML, and all goes well until we access the `Competition` property, which causes a *second* query to be made to the database. But, as we know, the Entity Framework sets things up so that only one query can be active at a time. This is a problem because we have read only the first result from the original query and all of the other data is still there, blocking the connection. As a consequence, we get the error shown in the figure, and our view doesn't render.

We can fix this problem in a couple of different ways. The first is to force evaluation of the LINQ query. This will read all of the results from the database and leave the connection free for the navigation property requests. We can do that by calling the `ToArray` method on the model object, as shown in Listing 25-18.

Listing 25-18. *Forcing execution of the LINQ query*

```
...
<table>
    <tr><th>Name</th><th>Age</th><th>Home City</th><th>Event</th></tr>
    @foreach (var item in Model.ToArray()) {
        <tr>
            <td>@item.Name</td>
            <td>@item.Age</td>
            <td>@item.HomeCity</td>
            <td>@item.Competition.Name</td>
        </tr>
    }
</table>
...
```

As an alternative, we can disable the Entity Framework optimization by changing the database connection string, as shown in Listing 25-19.

Listing 25-19. Enabling concurrent result sets

```
...
<add name="EFRepository" connectionString="Data Source=TITAN\SQLEXPRESS;Initial
Catalog=Competitions;Persist Security Info=True;User ID=adam;Password=adam;
MultipleActiveResultSets=true"
...
```

You can see how the `table` element is rendered once either of these changes has been made in Figure 25-7. I prefer modifying the connection string, but that is just because it means I don't have to remember to force evaluation on each of my affected LINQ queries.

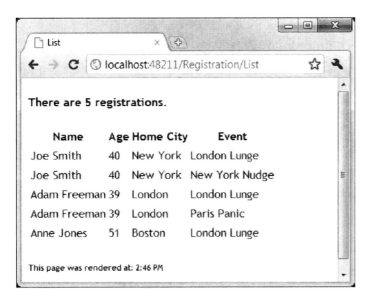

Figure 25-7. The rendered table element displayed in a browser

REDUCING THE DATABASE LOAD WITH AN UGLY LINQ QUERY

Neither of the fixes I just showed you is perfect. We know that we are going to access the `Competition` property for every `Registration` object in the database, which seems wasteful. In Chapter 24, I showed you how we can use the `Include` method to eagerly load navigation properties, but that is also problematic. The `Include` method is implemented by one of the Entity Framework classes, and if we expose that method through the repository interface, we start to leak details of how the repository is implemented (which will make things difficult if we ever move away from the Entity Framework as our persistent store). A workable, but ugly, alternative is to perform a two-stage LINQ query in the action method that causes the Entity Framework to load all of the `Registration` and `Competition` objects together, like this:

```
public ActionResult List() {

    ViewBag.Time = DateTime.Now;

    var results = repository.Registrations
        .Join(repository.Competitions, reg => reg.CompetitionID, comp => comp.ID,
        (reg, comp) => new { Reg = reg, Comp = comp })
        .ToArray()
        .Select(e => {
            e.Reg.Competition = e.Comp;
            return e.Reg;
        });

    return View(results);
}
```

The first part of the query is shown in bold; it performs a join operation that causes the Entity Framework to use a SQL JOIN to get all the data from the Registrations and Competitions tables in a single query. LINQ to Entities is very particular about what kinds of objects you can create as a result of a join, so I have projected the results into an anonymously typed object with properties for the Registration object and the associated Competition.

The second part of the query is as follows:

```
.ToArray()
.Select(e => {
    e.Reg.Competition = e.Comp;
    return e.Reg;
});
```

The call to the ToArray method forces the evaluation of the LINQ to Entities query and ensures that any further query operations performed on the data will be done using LINQ to Objects, which is more flexible when it comes to creating objects. The Select clause sets the Competition property of the Registration objects. The end result is an IEnumerable<Registration> where the Competition property of each Registration object is correctly populated.

If this looks like an ugly mess...well, it is. And it implicitly leaks knowledge of our repository implementation into our controller class. After all, we wouldn't use this kind of query if we didn't have prior knowledge of how the Entity Framework handles join requests (and we wouldn't need a two-part LINQ query if we didn't know the limitations of LINQ to Entity when it comes to creating new objects). If we changed repository implementations, we'd probably have to change this query in some way.

I have shown you this approach because it is useful, even if it erodes the separation of concerns slightly. I often see programmers twisting themselves in knots trying to maintain performance while preserving the integrity of the MVC pattern, but there are times when you have to make compromises. In this case, either we can accept a high number of requests to the database or we can blur the edges of our separation of concerns. The most appropriate approach depends on the details of each project.

Using the @for Tag

The other iterating tag is **@for**; it follows the same pattern as **@foreach** and works in a way that is broadly similar to its C# counterparts. Listing 25-20 shows the **@for** tag being used to construct the rows for the **table** element.

Listing 25-20. Using the @for tag

```
...
<table>
    <tr><th>Index</th><th>Name</th><th>Age</th><th>Home City</th><th>Event</th></tr>

    @for (int i = 0; i < Model.Count(); i++) {
        Registration item = Model.Skip(i).First();
        <tr>
            <td>@(i + 1)</td>
            <td>@item.Name</td>
            <td>@item.Age</td>
            <td>@item.HomeCity</td>
            <td>@item.Competition.Name</td>
        </tr>
    }
</table>
...
```

This is an inefficient example because I use the LINQ **Skip** extension method to scan through the enumeration of **Registration** objects for every iteration of the loop, but it shows how the **@for** tag works without requiring any other changes to the example project. You can see the effect of the index in Figure 25-8.

Figure 25-8. Adding an index column to the table

Notice how I display the index of the current item by using a regular C# statement in parentheses, like this:

```
<td>@(i + 1)</td>
```

Razor evaluates everything inside the parameters as a C# statement, producing the index numbers we can see in the figure. If I had instead done this:

```
<td>@i + 1</td>
```

then Razor would interpret only the expression as being @i, and we'd see the result shown in Figure 25-9.

Index	Name	Age	Home City	Event
0 + 1	Joe Smith	40	New York	London Lunge
1 + 1	Joe Smith	40	New York	New York Nudge
2 + 1	Adam Freeman	39	London	London Lunge
3 + 1	Adam Freeman	39	London	Paris Panic

Figure 25-9. *Leaving part of a C# expression outside the parentheses*

Defining a Code Block

We can improve on the @for example by using a *code block*. Listing 25-21 provides a demonstration.

Listing 25-21. *Using a Razor code block*

```
...
<table>
    <tr><th>Index</th><th>Name</th><th>Age</th><th>Home City</th><th>Event</th></tr>

    @{
        Registration[] regArray = Model.ToArray();
        int itemCount = regArray.Length;
    }

    @for (int i = 0; i < itemCount; i++) {
        <tr>
            <td>@(i + 1)</td>
            <td>@regArray[i].Name</td>
            <td>@regArray[i].Age</td>
            <td>@regArray[i].HomeCity</td>
            <td>@regArray[i].Competition.Name</td>
        </tr>
    }

</table>
...
```

We start a code block with the @{ and close it with }. Razor applies the same rules to code blocks as to its other tags. The line is added to the HTML response if it starts with an HTML element or the @: tag or is contained in a text element. Otherwise, the line is assumed to be a C# statement. In the example, I have defined a code block with two C# statements that define variables to make iterating through the model objects easier. Notice that once I define these variables, they are available for use in subsequent Razor tags.

We can tidy up the view by merging the code block and the @for tag, as shown in Listing 25-22.

Listing 25-22. *Merging a code block and an @for tag*

```
...
<table>
    <tr><th>Index</th><th>Name</th><th>Age</th><th>Home City</th><th>Event</th></tr>

    @{
        Registration[] regArray = Model.ToArray();
        int itemCount = regArray.Length;

        for (int i = 0; i < itemCount; i++) {
            <tr>
                <td>@(i + 1)</td>
                <td>@regArray[i].Name</td>
                <td>@regArray[i].Age</td>
                <td>@regArray[i].HomeCity</td>
                <td>@regArray[i].Competition.Name</td>
            </tr>
        }
    }

</table>
...
```

Notice that I have changed @for to simply for. We don't need to prefix lines with the @ sign if we want them to be interpreted as C# statements.

Creating an Inline HTML Helper

Razor supports the *inline HTML helpers,* which allows us to avoid repetition in our views by placing markup and tags into a reusable block. Listing 25-23 shows a simple inline helper.

■ **Note** Inline helpers are different from the HTML helper methods that we saw in Chapter 23, such as @Html.Editor. I'll show you the HTML helper methods in more detail in Chapter 26.

Listing 25-23. *A simple Razor inline HTML helper*

```
@model IEnumerable<EventRegistration.Models.Domain.Registration>

@{
    ViewBag.Title = "List";
}

@helper CreateOrdinal(int index) {

    switch (index.ToString().Last()) {
        case '1':
            @(index + "st");
            break;
        case '2':
            @(index + "nd");
            break;
        case '3':
            @(index + "rd");
            break;
        default:
            @(index + "th");
            break;
    }
}

<h4>
@switch (Model.Count()) {
    case 0:
        @:There are no registrations
        break;
    case 1:
        @:There is one registration
        break;
    default:
        @:There are @Model.Count() registrations.
        break;
}
</h4>

<table>
    <tr><th>Index</th><th>Name</th><th>Age</th><th>Home City</th><th>Event</th></tr>

    @{
        Registration[] regArray = Model.ToArray();
        int itemCount = regArray.Length;

        for (int i = 0; i < itemCount; i++) {
            <tr>
                <td>@CreateOrdinal(i + 1)</td>
                <td>@regArray[i].Name</td>
```

```
                    <td>@regArray[i].Age</td>
                    <td>@regArray[i].HomeCity</td>
                    <td>@regArray[i].Competition.Name</td>
                </tr>
            }
        }
```

```
</table>
```

```
<h6>This page was rendered at: @string.Format("{0:t}", ViewBag.Time) </h6>
```

The inline helper I have defined creates ordinal strings from integer values (1 becomes 1st, 2 becomes 2nd, and so on). It is adequate for our example but isn't sophisticated for use in a real project. For example, 11 becomes 11st, and it doesn't support localized formats. You can see that we define an inline helper using an @helper tag and specify a name and the parameters for the helper just as we would for a regular C# method:

```
@helper CreateOrdinal(int index) {
```

Notice that there is no return type. Razor evaluates each of the lines in the helper using its normal approach. We simply express the HTML that we want, rather than return a value to the caller. In the example helper, I use the @ tag to have Razor evaluate a C# string concatenation statement and emit the result to the HTML response. We invoke an inline helper using the standard @ tag, like this:

```
<td>@CreateOrdinal(i + 1)</td>
```

Inline helpers are fine for avoiding the repetition of simple markup, but for complex problems I prefer to create a custom HTML helper method. I'll show you how to do this in Chapter 26.

Working with Layouts

When we created the List.cshtml view, we checked the option to use a *layout*. You can see the option from the Add View dialog in Figure 25-10. Layouts are the Razor equivalent to the master pages you saw in Chapter 9. They serve the same purpose as master pages but work in a slightly different way.

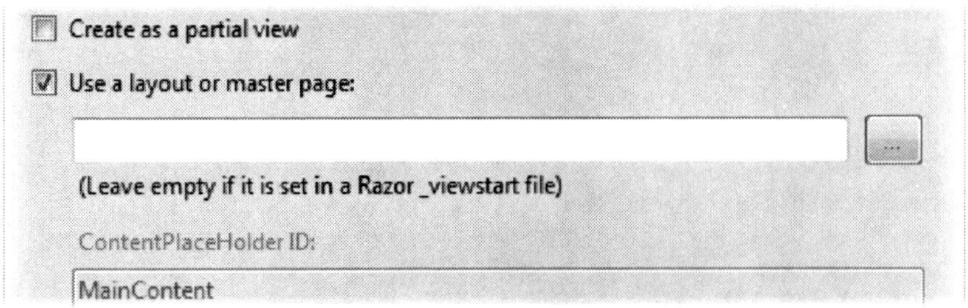

Figure 25-10. Setting the layout options when creating a view

We checked the option to use a layout, but we didn't specify one. If we look underneath the text box in the figure, we will see that it says "(Leave empty if it is set in a Razor _viewstart file)," and if we open the ~/Views/_ViewStart.cshtml file, we can see what the default layout for our project is. Listing 25-24 shows the contents of the _ViewStart.cshtml file.

Listing 25-24. The _ViewStart.cshtml file

```
@{
    Layout = "~/Views/Shared/_Layout.cshtml";
}
```

This file contains a Razor code block that sets a value for the Layout property. This property is defined in the base class that is used for all Razor views, System.Web.Mvc.WebViewPage. As you can see in the listing that the _ViewStart.cshtml file sets the Layout property to be ~/Views/Shared/_Layout.cshtml, the contents of which are shown in Listing 25-25.

■ **Note** You might be wondering about the significance of the leading underscores (_) in the names of these files. They are carried over from the WebMatrix product, which also uses Razor and won't serve content to users if the requested file starts with an underscore. There is no bearing on MVC framework applications.

Listing 25-25. The _Layout.cshtml file

```
<!DOCTYPE html>
<html>
<head>
    <title>@ViewBag.Title</title>
    <link href="@Url.Content("~/Content/Site.css")" rel="stylesheet" type="text/css" />
    <script src="@Url.Content("~/Scripts/jquery-1.5.1.min.js")"
        type="text/javascript"></script>
</head>

<body>
    @RenderBody()
</body>
</html>
```

This is a short file, but there is a lot going on. I'll walk through each aspect in the following sections.

Defining the Title

We have reached the point where I can finally reveal the reason for the code block that was added to the example view by Visual Studio:

```
@{
    ViewBag.Title = "List";
}
```

The code block in the view sets a value for the `Title` property in the `ViewBag`. Remember that the `ViewBag` is dynamic, and until that moment, there was no such property. In the layout, the `ViewBag.Title` property is used to set the title for the HTML document that will be returned to the user:

```
<title>@ViewBag.Title</title>
```

The `ViewBag` provides a nice mechanism by which we can pass data from the view to the layout. It is used for the `title` element by default, but we can add our own `ViewBag` properties and use them in the view.

Adding Content References

One of the most common uses for layouts is to add references for script and style files in a single location, rather than repeat the references in each view. The default layout adds references for jQuery and for the `Content/Site.css` style sheet:

```
<link href="@Url.Content("~/Content/Site.css")" rel="stylesheet" type="text/css" />
<script src="@Url.Content("~/Scripts/jquery-1.5.1.min.js")" type="text/javascript"></script>
```

Notice that to define references, we must use the `Url.Content` helper method. I'll explain what the URL helpers do in Chapter 27.

Inserting the View Contents

The last part of the layout is the call to the `RenderBody` method:

```
@RenderBody()
```

This is another method defined in the base class, and it inserts all the view into the response, except those parts that are in named sections. I'll explain Razor sections later in this chapter.

Defining a Different Layout

If we want to specify a layout for a view other than the default, then we can do it by setting the `Layout` property ourselves. Listing 25-26 shows the contents of a layout I have created in the `~/Views/Shared` folder called `CustomLayout.cshtml`. I created this file by right-clicking the `Views/Shared` folder in the project and selecting Add View.

Listing 25-26. A custom layout

```
<!DOCTYPE html>

<html>
<head>
    <title>@ViewBag.Title</title>
    <script src="@Url.Content("~/Scripts/jquery-1.5.1.min.js")"
        type="text/javascript"></script>
    <style type="text/css">
        table {border:thin solid black}
        th {background-color:Gray; color:White; padding: 5px; text-align:left}
```

```
        td {padding: 5px}
    </style>
    <script type="text/javascript">
        $(document).ready(function () {
            $('tr:even').css('background-color', '#CCCCCC');
        });
    </script>
</head>
<body>
    <div>
        @RenderBody()
    </div>
</body>
</html>
```

I have defined some new CSS styles and added a simple jQuery script to this layout. We can then use this layout by adding to the code block in the view, as shown in Listing 25-27.

Listing 25-27. *Using a nondefault layout in the List.cshtml view*

```
@model IEnumerable<EventRegistration.Models.Domain.Registration>

@{
    ViewBag.Title = "List";
    Layout = "~/Views/Shared/CustomLayout.cshtml";
}

@helper CreateOrdinal(int index) {
...
```

When we start the application and navigate to `/Registration/List`, we can see the effect that the custom layout has, as shown in Figure 25-11.

Figure 25-11. *The effect of a custom layout*

■ **Tip** We don't have to use a layout, but if we choose not to, then we are responsible for generating all of the elements that are required for an HTML document. If you don't want to use a layout, just set the value of the `Layout` property to `null` in your view.

Using Partial Views

Partial views are fragments of markup that we can insert into a view. They are more flexible than sections because we can use a partial view repeatedly. Partial views are usually kept in the `Views/Shared` folder. To create a partial view, right-click this folder and select Add ➤ View from the pop-up menu. Visual Studio will display the Add View dialog, as shown in Figure 25-12.

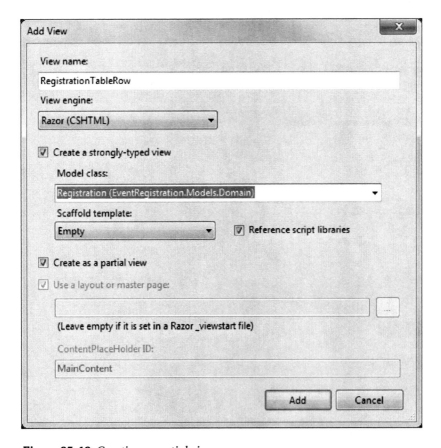

Figure 25-12. Creating a partial view

I have named the view RegistrationTableRow, checked the option to create a strongly typed view, and set the model class to be Registration. I have also selected the "Create as a partial view" option. Clicking the Add button creates the view, which initially contains only the @model tag, as follows:

```
@model EventRegistration.Models.Domain.Registration
```

I have added to the view, as shown in Listing 25-28.

Listing 25-28. *The RegistrationTableRow partial view*

```
@model EventRegistration.Models.Domain.Registration

<tr>
    <td>@Model.Name</td>
    <td>@Model.Age</td>
    <td>@Model.HomeCity</td>
    <td>@Model.Competition.Name</td>
</tr>
```

I have added the markup required to generate a table row for a Registration object. To use this view, we call the Html.Partial helper, as shown in Listing 25-29.

Listing 25-29. *Using a partial view*

```
@model IEnumerable<EventRegistration.Models.Domain.Registration>
@{
    ViewBag.Title = "List";
    Layout = "~/Views/Shared/CustomLayout.cshtml";
}

<h4>
@switch (Model.Count()) {
    case 0:
        @:There are no registrations
        break;
    case 1:
        @:There is one registration
        break;
    default:
        @:There are @Model.Count() registrations.
        break;
}
</h4>

<table>
    <tr><th>Name</th><th>Age</th><th>Home City</th><th>Event</th></tr>
```

```
    @foreach (Registration reg in Model) {
        @Html.Partial("RegistrationTableRow", reg)
    }
</table>

<h6>This page was rendered at: @string.Format("{0:t}", ViewBag.Time) </h6>
```

The parameters for the `Html.Partial` method are the name of the partial view and, optionally, the object that will be the view model. Each iteration of the @**foreach** loop causes the partial method to be rendered and inserted into the overall result to be set to the browser. The partial method is available for use in any view because we placed the partial method in the **Views/Shared** folder. For this example, it means that we can have a single, standardized approach to rendering a table row for a `Registration` object anywhere in the application.

■ **Note**   A related feature is child actions, which I described in Chapter 25. They allow us to invoke an action method from a view, which can offer additional flexibility as opposed to using a partial view.

Other View Features

To finish this chapter, I will show you some other features that Razor views support. These don't follow any single theme; they are just useful things to know that can make development easier.

Razor Sections

When I described the @RenderBody tag, I explained that it is used in a layout to insert the contents of the view, except those parts that are in a named section. Listing 25-30 shows the `List.cshtml` view reworked to include some sections.

Listing 25-30. Defining sections in a Razor view

```
@model IEnumerable<EventRegistration.Models.Domain.Registration>

@{
    ViewBag.Title = "List";
    Layout = "~/Views/Shared/CustomLayout.cshtml";
}

@section Header {

    <h4>
    @switch (Model.Count()) {
        case 0:
            @:There are no registrations
            break;
```

```
        case 1:
            @:There is one registration
            break;
        default:
            @:There are @Model.Count() registrations.
            break;
    }
    </h4>
}

<table>
    <tr><th>Name</th><th>Age</th><th>Home City</th><th>Event</th></tr>

    @foreach (Registration reg in Model) {
        @Html.Partial("RegistrationTableRow", reg)
    }
</table>

@section Footer {
    <h6>This page was rendered at: @string.Format("{0:t}", ViewBag.Time) </h6>
}
```

We define a section by using the @section tag and specifying a name. I have created two sections, one called Header and the other Footer. Everything from the opening brace ({) to the closing brace (}) is part of the section. We can then render the sections in the layout, as shown in Listing 25-31.

Listing 25-31. Rendering sections in a layout

```
<!DOCTYPE html>

<html>
<head>
    <title>ViewBag.Title</title>
</head>
<body>
    @RenderSection("Header")
    <hr />
    <div>
        @RenderBody()
    </div>
    <hr />
    @RenderSection("Footer")
</body>
</html>
```

I have added hr elements so that we can see where the sections have been added, as illustrated by Figure 25-13.

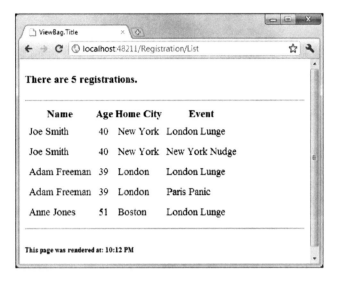

Figure 25-13. *Rendering sections in a layout*

There are some restrictions on the way that sections can be used; a layout *must* render each and every section defined in a view, and each section can be rendered only once. Razor will throw an exception if you do not follow these rules.

Razor Comments

Views in an MVC framework tend not to need much in the way of comments; my rule of thumb is that if the complexity of the view demands comments, then my separation of concerns isn't being properly maintained, and I push some of the data processing back into the controller.

Razor does support comments, but I find them most useful for disabling tags when chasing down bugs. Razor won't evaluate any content in a comment block nor will it pass the contents of that block to the client. A Razor comment block starts with @* and ends with *@. Listing 25-32 shows a comment applied to the List.cshtml view.

Listing 25-32. *Using a Razor comment block*

```
@model IEnumerable<EventRegistration.Models.Domain.Registration>

@{
    ViewBag.Title = "List";
    Layout = "~/Views/Shared/CustomLayout.cshtml";
}

@helper CreateOrdinal(int index) {

    @* This helper is not production-ready *@
```

```
    switch (index.ToString().Last()) {
        case '1':
            @(index + "st");
            break;
        case '2':
            @(index + "nd");
            break;
        case '3':
            @(index + "rd");
            break;
        default:
            @(index + "th");
            break;
    }
}
...
```

Using jQuery IntelliSense

Visual Studio provides support for IntelliSense in Razor views, and we can extend this to include support for jQuery. To do this, we need to add a reference to the `Script/ jquery-1.5.1-vsdoc.js` file, as shown in Listing 25-33.

Listing 25-33. *Adding support for jQuery IntelliSense in a Razor view*

```
@model IEnumerable<EventRegistration.Models.Domain.Registration>
<script src="../../Scripts/jquery-1.5.1-vsdoc.js" type="text/javascript"></script>
@{
    ViewBag.Title = "List";
    Layout = "~/Views/Shared/CustomLayout.cshtml";
}
```

You will notice that the script libraries in the `Scripts` folder contain jQuery 1.51. This upgrade was performed as part of the MVC Tools Update that you applied for the MVC framework.

This isn't a real script reference; it is just to support IntelliSense. Unfortunately, we need to add this reference for each view where we want to use IntelliSense for jQuery. Applying it to a layout doesn't enable IntelliSense in the view.

Enabling Compile-Time Checking

Our Razor views are not usually compiled until the application is used, but we can change this so that they are compiled alongside our regular C# classes. To do this, we have to edit the Visual Studio project file (the one that has the `.csproj` file extension). Open the file with a text editor, and you will see that this is an XML file. Find the `MvcBuildViews` element and set the value to `true`, like this:

```
...
<TargetFrameworkVersion>v4.0</TargetFrameworkVersion>
<MvcBuildViews>true</MvcBuildViews>
<UseIISExpress>false</UseIISExpress>
...
```

Now your views will be compiled when you build the project, and any errors will be reported in the Error List window, just like errors in regular classes are.

Summary

In this chapter, you have seen how Razor works and how Razor tags can be added to views to generate content. Razor is much easier to use than the old <% and %> tags, and it has made the MVC framework much more pleasant to use—so much so that I expect that ASP.NET version 5 will adopt Razor throughout the platform, including Web Forms.

In the next chapter, I'll show you how to go further with views by using the different kinds of helpers available.

CHAPTER 26

Using HTML Helpers and Templates

The previous chapter introduced you to Razor and showed you how you can create views in an MVC framework application to render results for a request. This chapter will show how to inject content into a view using helpers. Chapter 23 already touched on HTML helper methods, but this chapter will cover them in detail, show you some other kinds of helpers, and explain how templates fit into the picture.

Note The HTML helpers are not the only helpers in the MVC framework. Chapter 27 will show you the URL helpers, which are used to generate URLs in views, and Chapter 30 will explain the Ajax helpers, which are used to perform Ajax requests.

Creating an External Helper Method

Chapter 25 showed you how to use the @helper tag to create an internal helper. These are a useful way to avoid repetition, but they can be used only in the view in which they are defined, and they have a tendency to take over a view if they involve any significant amount of code.

The alternative is to create an external helper, which takes the form of a C# extension method. Listing 26-1 shows an example of an external helper that I have placed in a class called ExternalHelpers in the Infrastructure project folder. The MVC framework contains a set of built-in helper methods that cover most common requirements, but understanding how to build your own helps put everything in context.

Tip Helper methods are intended to make generating HTML simpler, but they are not compulsory. You can define the HTML elements you want and inject dynamic values using regular Razor @ tags.

Listing 26-1. Creating an external helper method

```
using System.Web.Mvc;

namespace EventRegistration.Infrastructure {

    public static class ExternalHelpers {

        public static string RegistrationCount(this HtmlHelper html, int i) {
            string result;
            switch (i) {
                case 0:
                    result = "There are no registrations";
                    break;
                case 1:
                    result = "There is one registration";
                    break;
                default:
                    result = string.Format("There are {0} registrations", i);
                    break;
            }
            return result;
        }
    }
}
```

The type that a helper extension method operates on is `System.Web.Mvc.HtmlHelper`. This is why the first parameter of the helper method is of this type, prefixed with the `this` keyword. Aside from this requirement, we can do whatever we want in the method in order to produce a value that can be inserted into the HTML. In this example, I have taken the `@switch` block from the `List.cshtml` view we created in the previous chapter and reproduced it in C#. Listing 26-2 shows how we can use this helper method.

Listing 26-2. Using an external helper method

```
@model IEnumerable<EventRegistration.Models.Domain.Registration>
@using EventRegistration.Infrastructure
@{
    ViewBag.Title = "List";
    Layout = "~/Views/Shared/CustomLayout.cshtml";
}

<h4>@Html.RegistrationCount(@Model.Count())</h4>

<table rules="cols">
    <tr><th>Name</th><th>Age</th><th>Home City</th><th>Event</th></tr>
```

```
    @foreach (Registration reg in Model) {
        @Html.Partial("RegistrationTableRow", reg)
    }
</table>

<h6>This page was rendered at: @string.Format("{0:t}", ViewBag.Time) </h6>
```

We have to bring the namespace that contains our helper class into context for the view. We do this by using the @using tag or by adding to the set of namespaces defined in the ~/Views/Web.config file as described in Chapter 25. Once that's done, we can call our external helper method by using @Html.MyMethodName and passing in arguments that match the parameters defined by the helper, like this:

```
@Html.RegistrationCount(@Model.Count())
```

The result generated by the method is encoded and inserted into the HTML rendered by the view. The key word here is *encoded*. The MVC framework encodes the values it gets from helper methods to make them safe to display. See the "Encoding Unsafe Data" sidebar for details.

ENCODING UNSAFE DATA

We have to be very careful when rendering data values to the user, especially values that we have collected from *other* users. Imagine that a nefarious user registers for a competition, but instead of entering their name, they enter a script element into the input field. Let's keep things simple and say that they enter the following:

```
<script>alert('Hello')</script>
```

When another user invokes the List action, the script element and its contents will be included in the HTML like this:

```
<tr>
    <td><script>alert('Hello')</script></td>
    <td>39</td>
    <td>London</td>
    <td>London Lunge</td>
</tr>
```

The browser encounters the script element when it displays the HTML and executes the script. In this simple example, a dialog box pops up, but most attacks of this kind are much more sophisticated and often include references to external script libraries that are used to gain access to data and functions of the application by making Ajax requests to remote servers. These are known as *cross-site scripting* (XSS) attacks because they allow scripts from one site to be executed in the context of another.

To help avoid XSS attacks, the MVC framework encodes data values inserted from HTML helper methods so that they can be displayed in the browser safely. This means that this string:

```
<script>alert('Hello')</script>
```

will be encoded like this:

```
&lt;script&gt;alert(&#39;Hello&#39;);  &lt;/script&gt;
```

before it is sent to the browser. This browser will display the string as regular text and not treat the string as a script. Be very careful when rendering unencoded content. Even though it might come from a trusted source today, future changes to your application can create an XSS vulnerability.

In the previous example, the content returned by the helper method was enclosed by an h4 element in the view. If we change the result from the RegistrationCount method:

```
return string.Format("<h4>{0}</h4>", result);
```

then we can see the effect of the encoding, as shown in Figure 26-1.

Figure 26-1. *The effect of Razor encoding a value that contains HTML elements*

To avoid this problem, we need to return an MvcHtmlString object, which indicates that we have taken care of making sure that the content is safe to display. Listing 26-3 shows how we can do this.

Listing 26-3. *Returning an MvcHtmlString from an external HTML helper method*

```
using System.Web.Mvc;

namespace EventRegistration.Infrastructure {

    public static class ExternalHelpers {

        public static MvcHtmlString RegistrationCount(this HtmlHelper html, int i) {
            string result;
            switch (i) {
                case 0:
                    result = "There are no registrations";
                    break;
                case 1:
                    result = "There is one registration";
                    break;
```

```
            default:
                result = string.Format("There are {0} registrations", i);
                break;
        }
        return new MvcHtmlString(string.Format("<h4>{0}</h4>", html.Encode(result)));
    }
    }
}
```

The important point to note about this listing is shown in bold. I call the Encode method of the HtmlHelper object to ensure that the data value is safe to display. This may seem like overkill since I am generating the value of the result field programmatically immediately prior to creating the MvcHtmlString, but it pays to be paranoid when it comes to making data safe to display.

■ **Tip** I can't overemphasize how important it is to get encoding in place when the method is first created. One day, if this were a real project, another programmer would come and modify this method so that the value of the result field was based on user input. The programmer is in a hurry, the ship date is approaching, and no one takes the time to make sure that the change doesn't create a scripting vulnerability. No one wants to have to explain to the CEO why all of the user data has been siphoned off, and no CEO I have met would ever say, "It's not your fault. I put so much pressure on your team to make the release window."

Using the Built-in Helper Methods

Now that we have seen how helper methods work, we can look at the built-in helpers that the MVC framework provides. We have already encountered some of these helpers in earlier examples, but this is the part of the book where we can look at them in depth.

■ **Note** The built-in helpers automatically encode data values to make them safe to display in a browser.

Creating Forms

One of the most frequently used helper methods is Html.BeginForm, which lets us create an HTML form element. This helper is used in a special way, as shown in Listing 26-4.

Listing 26-4. Using the Html.BeginForm helper

```
@using (Html.BeginForm()) {
    ...markup and tags for form go here...
}
```

We use this helper with the `@using` statement. This relies on an elegant trick involving the C# `IDisposable` interface so that when Razor gets to the end of the `@using` block, the call to the `Dispose` method generates the closing tags for the form. We put the input and submit elements we require inside the braces.

The `Html.BeginForm` helper has several overloaded versions. The one I have used in the listing posts the form back to the controller and action method that caused the form to be rendered. So, for example, if we generated a form in response to a request to the `Index` method of the `Registration` controller, submitting the form would target that same method. I showed you how to create an action method to handle a form post in Chapter 23. Other overloads allow us to target different controllers and action methods, as shown in Listing 26-5.

Listing 26-5. Using the Html.BeginForm helper to target a different action method

```
@using (Html.BeginForm("MyAction", "MyController")) {
    ...markup and tags for form go here...
}
```

I am not showing you the HTML that this helper generates deliberately. This is because the URL that the rendered `form` element targets depends on the application's routing configuration, which I describe in Chapter 27.

Using the Input Helper Methods

The `Html.BeginForm` helper doesn't generate any elements inside the form, but there are some helper methods that we can use to do this, called the *input helpers*. These helpers generate different elements that we can use to capture input from the user. Once again, we don't have to use these helpers. We can just define the HTML in the view directly, but they can be convenient and concise. Table 26-1 shows the set of input helpers, gives examples of their use, and shows the output that they generate.

Table 26-1. The Input HTML Helpers

HTML Element	Example

Checkbox	`Html.CheckBox("myCheckbox", false)`
	Output:
	`<input id="myCheckbox" name="myCheckbox" type="checkbox" value="true" />`
	`<input name="myCheckbox" type="hidden" value="false" />`

Hidden field	`Html.Hidden("myHidden", "val")` Output: `<input id="myHidden" name="myHidden" type="hidden" value="val" />`
Radio button	`Html.RadioButton("myRadiobutton", "val", true)` Output: `<input checked="checked" id="myRadiobutton" name="myRadiobutton" type="radio" value="val" />`
Password	`Html.Password("myPassword", "val")` Output: `<input id="myPassword" name="myPassword" type="password" value="val" />`

HTML Element	Example

Text area	`Html.TextArea("myTextarea", "val", 5, 20, null)`
	Output: `<textarea cols="20" id="myTextarea" name="myTextarea" rows="5">`
	`val</textarea>`

Text box	`Html.TextBox("myTextbox", "val")` Output: `<input id="myTextbox" name="myTextbox" type="text" value="val" />`

Notice that the checkbox helper (`Html.CheckBox`) renders *two* `input` elements. It renders a checkbox and then a hidden `input` of the same name. This is because browsers don't submit a value for checkboxes when they are not selected. Having the hidden control ensures that the MVC framework will get a value from the hidden field when this happens.

Defining HTML Attributes

One of the characteristics that these helper methods have in common is that they have an overload that takes an `object` as a parameter. We can use this to define attributes that will be added to the HTML element. Listing 26-6 shows a simple example.

Listing 26-6. *Defining additional HTML attributes for an input element*

```
@Html.TextBox("myTextbox", "val", new {
    @class = "myCSSclass",
    title = "MyTitle"
})
```

I have used the C# anonymous type feature to create an object with `class` and `title` properties. The properties are translated into attributes when the `input` element is rendered, like this:

```
<input class="myCSSclass" id="myTextbox" name="myTextbox" title="MyTitle"
    type="text" value="val" />
```

There is a slightly unfortunate clash between C# and HTML in this situation. The HTML attribute `class` clashes with the C# keyword `class`. To specify a `class` attribute in the anonymously typed object, we have to prefix the property name with an `@` character, as in `@class`. This is how we tell the C# compiler that we are using a keyword for a member name.

Inserting Data Values

The input helpers have a trick when it comes to inserting data values into the elements they render. We can, of course, use the model object as shown in Listing 26-7.

Listing 26-7. *Using a standard Razor syntax to insert a data value into an input*

```
@model EventRegistration.Models.Domain.Registration

@Html.TextBox("Name", Model.Name)
```

In this listing I have defined a view whose model object is a single `Registration`. I have provided two arguments to the `Html.TextBox` helper. The first is the value that I want used for the name and ID attributes, and the second is for the `value` attribute, which is the `Name` property of the model object. When this view is rendered, we see HTML like this:

```
<input id="Name" name="Name" type="text" value="Joe Smith" />
```

The trick happens when we use the overloaded version of the helper that takes a single `string` parameter, as shown in Listing 26-8.

Listing 26-8. *Using the single string parameter helper overload*

```
@model EventRegistration.Models.Domain.Registration

@Html.TextBox("Name")
```

When we render this view, we get the following HTML:

```
<input id="Name" name="Name" type="text" value="Joe Smith" />
```

We have given the helper a hint about what we want (`Name`), and it has figured out that there is a name property in the model object and used this as the basis to render the `input` element. This doesn't sound that clever, but the helper looks different places to find some data to display:

- `ViewBag.Name`
- `ViewData["Name"]`
- `@Model.Name`

The helper works its way down the list until it finds some data. In our case, the third and final item yielded a match. The second item on the list, `ViewData`, is a mechanism for passing data from the controller to the view and has been superseded by the `ViewBag`. I'll show you how `ViewData` works in Chapter 28.

We can make the helper work harder by providing a more complex hint, like this:

```
@Html.TextBox("Competition.Location")
```

The set of locations that the helper searches becomes longer:

- `ViewBag.DataValue. Competition.Location`
- `ViewBag.DataValue["Competition"].Location`
- `ViewBag.DataValue["Competition.Location"]`
- `ViewBag.DataValue["Competition"]["Location"]`
- `ViewData["DataValue.Competition.Location "]`
- `ViewData["DataValue"].Competition.Location`
- `ViewData["DataValue.Competition"].Location`

and so on. In my example, the helper finds a match in the `Location` property of the object returned by the `Competition` property of the `Registration` view model object. We get the following HTML:

```
<input id="Competition_Location" name="Competition.Location" type="text" value="London" />
```

I tend not to use this feature, but it can be helpful, and the performance overhead is generally negligible since there are usually just a couple of items in the ViewBag.

Using the Strongly Typed Input Helper Methods

For each of the HTML helpers described in Table 26-1, there is a corresponding *strongly typed helper*. The helpers can be used only in strongly typed views and work on lambda expressions. The value that is passed to the expression is the view model object. Table 26-2 describes the strongly typed helpers.

Table 26-2. *The Strongly Typed Input HTML Helpers*

HTML Element	Example

Checkbox	`Html.CheckBoxFor(x => x.IsApproved)`
	Output:
	`<input id="IsApproved" name="IsApproved" type="checkbox" value="true" />`
	`<input name="IsApproved" type="hidden" value="false" />`

Hidden field	`Html.HiddenFor(x => x.SomeProperty)`
	Output: `<input id="SomeProperty" name="SomeProperty" type="hidden"`
	`value="value" />`

Radio button	`Html.RadioButtonFor(x => x.IsApproved, "val")` Output: `<input id="IsApproved" name="IsApproved" type="radio" value="val" />`
Password	`Html.PasswordFor(x => x.Password)` Output: `<input id="Password" name="Password" type="password" />`

Text area	`Html.TextAreaFor(x => x.Bio, 5, 20, new{})`
	Output: `<textarea cols="20" id="Bio" name="Bio" rows="5">`
	`Bio value</textarea>`

Text box	`Html.TextBoxFor(x => x.Name)` Output: `<input id="Name" name="Name" type="text" value="Name value" />`

Listing 26-9 shows the Html.TextBoxFor helper in use in a view. I have used the lambda expression to select the Name property from the model object.

Listing 26-9. *Using a strongly typed helper*

```
@model EventRegistration.Models.Domain.Registration
```

```
@Html.TextBoxFor(x => x.Name)
```

The choice between using the basic helpers and the strongly typed helpers is largely a matter of preference. I tend to use them because it means I don't have to separately provide a value for the name and ID attributes and a data value. The strongly typed helpers use the property name to generate the HTML element. The output from the listing is something like this:

```
<input id="Name" name="Name" type="text" value="Joe Smith" />
```

It is important to use property names when rendering values that will be used by the model binding process, and using the strongly typed helpers ensures that this happens. If you have enabled compile-time view checking, then the compiler will report errors if you try to pass properties of an inappropriate type to the helpers, such as a property that is not a `bool` or a `bool?` (a nullable `bool`), to the `Html.CheckBoxFor` helper.

Creating select Elements

The built-in helpers for creating **select** elements work differently from the ones we have seen so far. Table 26-3 shows the set of available helpers, which are available as basic and strongly typed versions.

Table 26-3. *The HTML Helpers That Render select Elements*

HTML Element	Example

Drop-down list	`Html.DropDownList("myList", new SelectList(new [] {"A", "B"}), "Choose")`
	Output:
	`<select id="myList" name="myList">`
	`    <option value="">Choose</option>`
	`    <option>A</option>`
	`    <option>B</option>`
	`</select>`

Drop-down list	`Html.DropDownListFor(x => x.Gender, new SelectList(new [] {"M", "F"}))`
	Output:
	`<select id="Gender" name="Gender">`
	`    <option>M</option>`
	`    <option>F</option>`
	`</select>`

Multiselect	`Html.ListBox("myList", new MultiSelectList(new [] {"A", "B"}))`
	Output:
	`<select id="myList" multiple="multiple" name="myList">`
	`    <option>A</option>`
	`    <option>B</option>`
	`</select>`

Multiselect	`Html.ListBoxFor(x => x.Vals, new MultiSelectList(new [] {"A", "B"}))`
	Output:
	`<select id="Vals" multiple="multiple" name="Vals">`
	`    <option>A</option>`
	`    <option>B</option>`
	`</select>`

The `select` helpers take `SelectList` or `MultiSelectList` parameters. The difference between these classes is that the `MultiSelect` list has constructor options that let us specify that more than one item should be selected when the page is initially rendered. Both of these classes operate on `IEnumerable` sequences of objects. In Table 26-3, I used arrays that contained the list items we wanted displayed.

A nice feature of `SelectList` and `MultiSelectList` is that they will extract values from objects for the list items. Listing 26-10 provides an example.

Listing 26-10. *Selecting data and text values using a SelectList*

```
@model IEnumerable<EventRegistration.Models.Domain.Registration>

@Html.DropDownList("Name", new SelectList(Model, "Age", "Name"))
```

The model in this view is an enumeration of `Registration` objects, which I pass to the `SelectList` constructor, along with the names of the properties I want used for the `value` attribute and the inner text of the option elements (`Age` and `Name`, respectively). The HTML that this produces is as follows:

```
<select id="Name" name="Name"><option value="40">Joe Smith</option>
    <option value="40">Joe Smith</option>
    <option value="39">Adam Freeman</option>
    <option value="39">Adam Freeman</option>
    <option value="51">Anne Jones</option>
</select>
```

Using the Templated Helper Methods

The MVC framework includes a set of helpers that take a different approach to rendering HTML for data items. Rather than choosing the HTML element we want and then using the corresponding helper, we simply pass the data item to the helper and let it figure out which HTML element should be used. These are known as the *templated* helpers because the choice of HTML element is driven by a simple template system. Table 26-4 describes the templated helper methods.

Table 26-4. *The Templated Helper Methods*

Helper	Example	Description
Display DisplayFor	Html.Display("Name") Html.DisplayFor(x => x.Name)	Renders a read-only view of the specified property, choosing an HTML element according to the property's type and metadata
Editor EditorFor	Html.Editor("Name") Html.EditorFor(x => x. Name)	Renders an editor for the specified property, choosing an HTML element according to the property's type and metadata
Label LabelFor	Html.Label("Name") Html.LabelFor(x => x.Name)	Renders an HTML `<label>` element referring to the specified property

To demonstrate the templated view helpers, I have created a view model class called CompetitionSummary in the Models/View folder. I have more to say about view models in Chapter 28, but in short, a view model is a simple class that we use to pass data from the controller to the view. I have created a new class because I want to demonstrate working with a wider range of properties than is available in our model types. Listing 26-11 shows the CompetitionSummary class.

Listing 26-11. *The CompetitionSummary class*

```
using System;

namespace EventRegistration.Models.View {

    public class CompetitionSummary {
        public string Name { get; set; }
        public string City { get; set; }
        public DateTime Date { get; set; }
        public bool Approved { get; set; }
    }
}
```

I have also created a new controller, called CompetitionController, which is shown in Listing 26-12. This is a very simple controller whose Summary action method creates a CompetitionSummary object and uses it as a view model object for the default view.

Listing 26-12. *The CompetitionSummary*

```
using System.Web.Mvc;
using EventRegistration.Models.View;

namespace EventRegistration.Controllers {
    public class CompetitionController : Controller {

        public ActionResult Summary() {

            CompetitionSummary summary = new CompetitionSummary {
                Name = "Mass Mangler",
                City = "Boston",
                Date = new System.DateTime(2013, 1, 20),
                Approved = true
            };

            return View(summary);
        }
    }
}
```

To demonstrate the helpers, I have created a view by right-clicking the action method in Visual Studio and selecting Add View. I have called the view Summary and set the model object to be a CompetitionSummary. Following the pattern that I described in Chapter 25, Visual Studio created the view in the Views/Competition folder. I have created a table that shows the templated helpers being applied to the properties of the CompetitionSummary class, as shown in Listing 26-13.

Listing 26-13. *The Summary.cshtml view*

```
@model EventRegistration.Models.View.CompetitionSummary

<style type="text/css">
    td {padding: 5px}
    th {text-align:left}
</style>

<table >
    <tr><th>Label</th><th>Display</th><th>Editor</th></tr>
    <tr>
        <td>@Html.LabelFor(x => x.Name)</td>
        <td>@Html.DisplayFor(x => x.Name)</td>
        <td>@Html.EditorFor(x => x.Name)</td>
    </tr>
    <tr>
        <td>@Html.LabelFor(x => x.City)</td>
        <td>@Html.DisplayFor(x => x.City)</td>
        <td>@Html.EditorFor(x => x.City)</td>
    </tr>
    <tr>
        <td>@Html.LabelFor(x => x.Date)</td>
        <td>@Html.DisplayFor(x => x.Date)</td>
        <td>@Html.EditorFor(x => x.Date)</td>
    </tr>
    <tr>
        <td>@Html.LabelFor(x => x.Approved)</td>
        <td>@Html.DisplayFor(x => x.Approved)</td>
        <td>@Html.EditorFor(x => x.Approved)</td>
    </tr>
</table>
```

We can render this view by starting the application and requesting /Competition/Summary. Figure 26-2 shows the result.

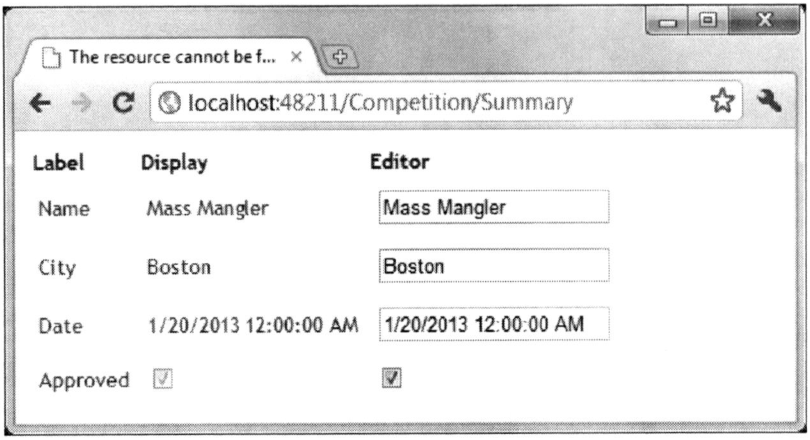

Figure 26-2. *The HTML rendered by the Summary view*

By looking at the HTML that is being displayed, you can see how the different templated helpers have rendered the properties. The `LabelFor` helper has just rendered a `label` element using the name of the property, like this:

```
<label for="Name">Name</label>
```

The `DisplayFor` helper has just emitted the string representations of the `Name`, `City`, and `Date` properties without any HTML elements at all. The `bool` property `Approved` has been handled differently, and a disable checkbox has been used. Here is the HTML:

```
<input checked="checked" class="check-box" disabled="disabled" type="checkbox" />
```

The `EditorFor` helper has rendered text boxes to allow the `Name`, `City`, and `Date` properties to be edited and set the contents of those text boxes to be the current values. The `bool` property has been handled using a checkbox again. As I mentioned previously, two checkbox elements are required to ensure that a value is posted back to the server. Here is the HTML:

```
<input checked="checked" class="check-box" id="Approved" name="Approved" type="checkbox"
    value="true" />
<input name="Approved" type="hidden" value="false" />
```

Customizing the Templated Helpers with Metadata

Aside from the fact that the `bool` property has been rendered using a checkbox, the templated helpers don't appear to be that impressive. And, in their default guise, they are not. To get the best from these helper methods, we need use metadata to describe how we want our model objects to be rendered.

Using Metadata for Labels

The first thing we can do is specify a value that will be used by the `LabelFor` helper, instead of the property name. We do this by applying the `DisplayName` attribute, as shown in Listing 26-14.

Listing 26-14. *Using the DisplayName attribute*

```
using System;
using System.ComponentModel;

namespace EventRegistration.Models.View {

    public class CompetitionSummary {

        [DisplayName("Event Name")]
        public string Name { get; set; }

        [DisplayName("Location")]
        public string City { get; set; }

        public DateTime Date { get; set; }
        public bool Approved { get; set; }
    }
}
```

In this listing, I have applied the `DisplayName` to define the values I want used for the `Name` and `City` properties. We can see the effect that this has on the rendered HTML in Figure 26-3.

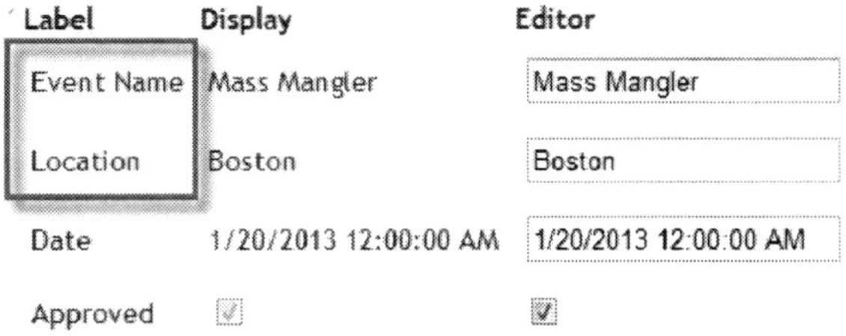

Figure 26-3. *Specifying values for the LabelForHelper to use*

Using Metadata for Formatting

Without metadata, the helpers don't have any guidance about how we want our properties to be handled. You can see this in the way that the `DateTime` property `Date` is rendered. This property represents a day, but it has been rendered as a day and a time. The helpers can't detect the implied meaning of a property, so we have to make it explicit. We do this using additional the `DataType` attribute, as demonstrated in Listing 26-15.

Listing 26-15. *Applying the DataType attribute*

```
using System;
using System.ComponentModel;
using System.ComponentModel.DataAnnotations;
```

```
namespace EventRegistration.Models.View {

    public class CompetitionSummary {

        [DisplayName("Event Name")]
        public string Name { get; set; }
        [DisplayName("Location")]
        public string City { get; set; }

        [DataType(DataType.Date)]
        public DateTime Date { get; set; }

        public bool Approved { get; set; }
    }
}
```

The DataType attribute takes a value from the DataType enumeration as a parameter. I have selected the Date value, which displays only the date portion of a DateTime value, as shown in Figure 26-4.

Figure 26-4. *Formatting a DateTime value with the DataType attribute*

The DataType enumeration contains a wide range of formatting options, and I have described the most useful values in Table 26-5.

Table 26-5. *The Values of the DataType Enumeration*

Value	Description
DateTime	Displays a date and time (this is the default behavior for System.DateTime values).
Date	Displays the date portion of a DateTime.
Time	Displays the time portion of a DateTime.
Text	Displays a single line of text.
MultilineText	Displays the value in a **textarea** element.
Password	Displays the data so that individual characters are masked from view.

Value	Description
Url	The DisplayFor helper displays the data as a URL (using an HTML a element). The EditorFor helper displays the string value in a text box.
EmailAddress	The DisplayFor helper displays the data as an e-mail address (using an a element with a mailto href). The EditorFor helper displays the string value in a text box.

Note that applying the DataType attribute only formats the data. No checks are made to ensure that the value is of an appropriate type.

Using Metadata to Select a Template

As the name implies, the templated helpers use a set of templates to render values. So far, the only evidence of this we have seen is the way that the bool property in the view model object was rendered as a checkbox, rather than just the string value true or false.

The templated helpers have a number of built-in templates available, and we can specify which of them should be used to display a property using the UIHint attribute, as shown in Listing 26-16.

Listing 26-16. Using the UIHint attribute to specify a template

```
using System;
using System.ComponentModel;
using System.ComponentModel.DataAnnotations;

namespace EventRegistration.Models.View {

    public class CompetitionSummary {

        [DisplayName("Event Name")]
        public string Name { get; set; }

        [DisplayName("Location")]
        [UIHint("MultilineText")]
        public string City { get; set; }

        [DataType(DataType.Date)]
        public DateTime Date { get; set; }

        public bool Approved { get; set; }
    }
}
```

We specify the template to use by passing the template name as a string to the UIHint attribute. I have selected the MultilineText template for the City property in the listing. This causes the EditorFor helper to display the property in a multiline text box, as you can see in Figure 26-5.

Label	Display	Editor
Event Name	Mass Mangler	Mass Mangler
Location	Boston	Boston
Date	1/20/2013	1/20/2013
Approved	☑	☑

Figure 26-5. *Applying the MultilineText template*

Table 26-6 describes the built-in templates to which the `UIHint` attribute provides access. We must be careful when using the `UIHint` attribute that the data type of the property is suitable for the selected template. If it isn't, then an exception will be thrown when the MVC framework tries to convert the property type to the template type.

Table 26-6. *The Built-in Helper Templates*

Template	Description (EditorFor)	Description (DisplayFor)
Boolean	Renders a checkbox for `bool` values. For nullable `bool?` values, a `select` element is created with options for `True`, `False`, and `Not Set`.	As for the editor helpers, but with the addition of the `disabled` attribute that renders read-only HTML controls.
Collection	Renders the appropriate template for each of the elements in an `IEnumerable` sequence. The items in the sequence do not have to be of the same type.	As for the editor helpers.
Decimal	Renders a single-line text box `input` element and formats the data value to display two decimal places.	Renders the data value formatted to two decimal places.
EmailAddress	Renders the value in a single-line text box `input` element.	Renders a link using an HTML `a` element and an `href` attribute that is formatted as a `mailto` URL.
Html	Renders the value in a single-line text box `input` element.	Renders a link using an HTML `a` element.
MultilineText	Renders an HTML `textarea` element that contains the data value.	Renders the data value.

Template	Description (EditorFor)	Description (DisplayFor)
Password	Renders the value in a single-line text box input element so that the characters are not displayed but can be edited.	Renders the data value. The characters are not obscured.
String	Renders the value in a single-line text box input element.	Renders the data value.
Text	Identical to the String template.	Identical to the String template
Url	Renders the value in a single-line text box input element.	Renders a link using an HTML a element. The inner HTML and the href attribute are both set to the data value.

Using Metadata to Control Visibility and Editing

In Chapter 24, we added ID properties to the domain model classes so that we could more easily work with the Entity Framework. It was a small price to pay to get persistence for our model, but those properties don't have any bearing on our application, and we don't want our users to see or be able to edit the ID property values. They are plumbing that we don't want to expose. We can hide properties using the HiddenInput attribute, as shown in Listing 26-17.

Listing 26-17. Using the HiddenInput attribute to hide a model property

```
using System;
using System.ComponentModel;
using System.ComponentModel.DataAnnotations;
using System.Web.Mvc;

namespace EventRegistration.Models.View {

    public class CompetitionSummary {

        [DisplayName("Event Name")]
        public string Name { get; set; }

        [DisplayName("Location")]
        public string City { get; set; }

        [DataType(DataType.Date)]
        public DateTime Date { get; set; }

        [HiddenInput(DisplayValue=false)]
        public bool Approved { get; set; }
    }
}
```

657

The `DisplayFor` helper doesn't render any output at all for a property that has been annotated in this way. The `EditorFor` helper renders a hidden `input` element, which means we don't have to worry about providing values for hidden properties when forms are submitted. Here is the HTML that the `EditorFor` helper rendered for the `Approved` property in the listing:

```
<input id="Approved" name="Approved" type="hidden" value="True" />
```

If we want to display the value but not allow the user to edit it, we can change the value of the `DisplayValue` property to `true`, like this:

```
...
[HiddenInput(DisplayValue=true)]
public bool Approved { get; set; }
...
```

In this configuration, the `DisplayFor` helper renders the value, and the `EditorFor` helper renders the value and the hidden `input` element, like this:

```
True<input id="Approved" name="Approved" type="hidden" value="True" />
```

Figure 26-6 shows the effect on the content displayed by the browser.

Label	Display	Editor
Event Name	Mass Mangler	Mass Mangler
Location	Boston	Boston
Date	1/20/2013	1/20/2013
Approved	True	True

Figure 26-6. *Using the HiddenInput value to control editing*

Creating Custom Templates

We can go beyond the built-in templates and create our own. The process is reasonably simple, and by defining our own templates, we can gain complete control over how data types are displayed. We can create custom editor and display templates, but the MVC framework doesn't support custom label templates.

Creating a Custom Editor Template

We create custom editor and display templates separately, although the process is much the same. We will start with an editor template, which we create using a partial view (I introduced partial views in the previous chapter).

First, though, we need to create a folder called `EditorTemplates` in the `Views/Shared` folder. This is where the `EditorFor` helper looks for templates. Once you have created the new folder, right-click it and select Add ➤ View from the pop-up menus. We are going to create a partial view called City whose view model is a `string`. Figure 26-7 shows the required settings for the Add View dialog.

Figure 26-7. Adding a partial template that will be used as a custom template

It is important that the view model type for the partial view matches the property type that we are going to render. In this case, this partial view is going to be used to render the `City` property of the `CompetitionSummary` class, which is a `string`. (The name of the template view and the property don't need to match, although I usually name templates so that they do.) Listing 26-18 shows a very simple custom template.

Listing 26-18. *The City template/view*

```
@model string
```

```
@Html.DropDownListFor(x => x, new SelectList(new[] {"Boston", "New York", "London"}, Model))
```

We create templates as we would any other partial view. In this case, I have created a drop-down menu using the `Html.DropDownListFor` helper. We have access to the full range of Razor tags and helpers, and we can define static HTML if preferred. Once we have created the template, we can use the `UIHint` attribute to associate it with a property, as shown in Listing 26-19.

Listing 26-19. Using the UIHint property to select a custom template

```
using System;
using System.ComponentModel;
using System.ComponentModel.DataAnnotations;
using System.Web.Mvc;

namespace EventRegistration.Models.View {

    public class CompetitionSummary {

        [DisplayName("Event Name")]
        public string Name { get; set; }

        [DisplayName("Location")]
        [UIHint("City")]
        public string City { get; set; }

        [DataType(DataType.Date)]
        public DateTime Date { get; set; }

        [HiddenInput(DisplayValue=true)]
        public bool Approved { get; set; }
    }
}
```

I used the strongly typed `Html.DropDownListFor` helper because it will generate the correct values for the `ID` and `name` attributes of the `select` element when the view is rendered:

```
<select id="City" name="City"><option selected="selected">Boston</option>
    <option>New York</option>
    <option>London</option>
</select>
```

We can also specify the template to be used by passing its name to the HTML helper method, like this:

```
@Html.DisplayFor(x => x.City, "City")
```

▦ **Tip**   It is important that we reflect the name of the property in the rendered HTML elements so that the MVC framework can properly deal with form posts. The strongly typed HTML helper methods will take care of this automatically.

We can see the effect of the template in Figure 26-8.

Figure 26-8. *The effect of a custom editor template*

▦ **Tip**   If you don't want to use the HTML helpers, you can get details of the property that the template is being applied to through the ViewData.TemplateInfo property. This property returns a System.Web.Mvc.TemplateInfo containing the information you require. For example, the GetFullHtmlFieldName method returns the value that should be used for the name attribute of the HTML element you generate.

Creating a Custom Display Template

The process for creating a display template is similar to that for creating an editor template. We use partial views once again, but they are placed in the **Views/Shared/DisplayTemplates** folder. Listing 26-20 shows the contents of a custom display view I created called **City.cshtml**. Notice that I can use the same name for a display and an editor template in order to take advantage of the UIHint attribute shown in Listing 26-19.

Listing 26-20. *A custom display template*

```
@model string
```

```
<span style="font-weight:bold">@Model</span>
```

This template renders the model value in a bold font. You can see the effect of this template in Figure 26-9.

Label	Display	Editor
Event Name	Mass Mangler	Mass Mangler
Location	**Boston**	Boston ▾
Date	1/20/2013	1/20/2013
Approved	True	True

Figure 26-9. *The effect of a custom display template*

Creating a Type-Specific Template

If we create a custom template that has the name of a .NET type, then the templated helpers will use that template to render any property of that type they encounter. To demonstrate this, I have extended our view model object so that it has a new property, as shown in Listing 26-21.

Listing 26-21. Extending the view model object

```
using System;
using System.ComponentModel;
using System.ComponentModel.DataAnnotations;
using System.Web.Mvc;

namespace EventRegistration.Models.View {

    public enum StartTime {
        Morning,
        Midday,
        Evening
    }

    public class CompetitionSummary {

        [DisplayName("Event Name")]
        public string Name { get; set; }

        [DisplayName("Location")]
        [UIHint("City")]
        public string City { get; set; }

        [DataType(DataType.Date)]
        public DateTime Date { get; set; }

        [HiddenInput(DisplayValue=true)]
        public bool Approved { get; set; }

        public StartTime Start { get; set; }
    }
}
```

The `Start` property has a value from the `StartTime` enumeration. I have changed the `Summary` action method in the `CompetitionController` class to define a value for this property when the sample object is created, as shown in Listing 26-22.

Listing 26-22. Defining a value for the Start property of the view model object in the action method

```
using System.Web.Mvc;
using EventRegistration.Models.View;
```

```
namespace EventRegistration.Controllers {
    public class CompetitionController : Controller {

        public ActionResult Summary() {

            CompetitionSummary summary = new CompetitionSummary {
                Name = "Mass Mangler",
                City = "Boston",
                Date = new System.DateTime(2013, 1, 20),
                Approved = true,
                Start = StartTime.Evening
            };

            return View(summary);
        }
    }
}
```

I also need to update the view to render HTML for this new property. Listing 26-23 shows the Summary.cshtml view with these changes.

Listing 26-23. *Updating the Summary view to reflect an additional view model property*

```
@model EventRegistration.Models.View.CompetitionSummary

<style type="text/css">
    td {padding: 5px}
    th {text-align:left}
</style>

<table >
    <tr><th>Label</th><th>Display</th><th>Editor</th></tr>
    <tr>
        <td>@Html.LabelFor(x => x.Name)</td>
        <td>@Html.DisplayFor(x => x.Name)</td>
        <td>@Html.EditorFor(x => x.Name)</td>
    </tr>
    <tr>
        <td>@Html.LabelFor(x => x.City)</td>
        <td>@Html.DisplayFor(x => x.City)</td>
        <td>@Html.EditorFor(x => x.City)</td>
    </tr>
    <tr>
        <td>@Html.LabelFor(x => x.Date)</td>
        <td>@Html.DisplayFor(x => x.Date)</td>
        <td>@Html.EditorFor(x => x.Date)</td>
    </tr>
    <tr>
        <td>@Html.LabelFor(x => x.Approved)</td>
        <td>@Html.DisplayFor(x => x.Approved)</td>
        <td>@Html.EditorFor(x => x.Approved)</td>
    </tr>
```

```
    <tr>
        <td>@Html.LabelFor(x => x.Start)</td>
        <td>@Html.DisplayFor(x => x.Start)</td>
        <td>@Html.EditorFor(x => x.Start)</td>
    </tr>
</table>
```

We can see how the new property is rendered by the view in Figure 26-10.

Label	Display	Editor
Event Name	Mass Mangler	Mass Mangler
Location	**Boston**	Boston
Date	1/20/2013	1/20/2013
Approved	True	True
Start	Evening	Evening

Figure 26-10. *The default rendering of the newly added view model property*

Now we can add a type-specific template. Right-click the `Views/Shared/EditorTemplates` folder and select Add ➤ View from the pop-up menu.

■ **Tip** We can replace one of the built-in templates by creating a custom template of the same name. This is a big step and should not be taken lightly. It will change the way that every property of that type is rendered in your application. You can see the list of built-in templates and the names you must use to replace them in Table 26-6.

Create a view called `StartTime`, check the option to create a partial view, and set the view model type to `StartTime`, as shown in Figure 26-11.

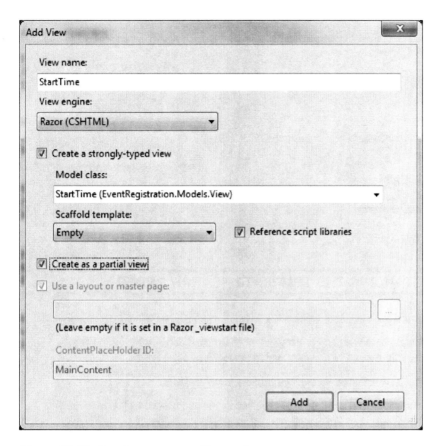

Figure 26-11. *Creating a type-specific template*

Click OK to create the new view and add the contents shown in Listing 26-24, which acts as an editor template for the StartTime type.

Listing 26-24. *A type-specific editor template*

```
@model EventRegistration.Models.View.StartTime

@Html.DropDownListFor(x => x, new SelectList(Enum.GetValues(Model.GetType()), Model))
```

Once again, you can see that the template is very simple. This is the nature of custom templates. In this example, I use the Html.DropDownListFor helper to render a select control that contains all the values of the StartTime enumeration.

We don't have to annotate our model class with attributes to use this template. The templated helper will use it automatically whenever it encounters a property of the StartTime type. You can see the effect of this custom template in Figure 26-12.

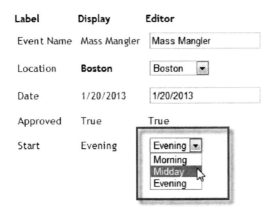

Figure 26-12. *The effect of a type-specific custom editor template*

UNDERSTANDING THE TEMPLATE SEARCH ORDER

There is a specific sequence that the templated helpers follow to find a suitable template for a property:

1. The template passed to the helper. For example, `Html.EditorFor(m => m.SomeProperty, "MyTemplate")` would lead to `MyTemplate` being used.

2. Any template that is specified by metadata attributes, such as `UIHint`.

3. The template associated with any data type specified by metadata, such as the `DataType` attribute.

4. Any template that corresponds to the.NET class name of the data type being processed.

5. If the data type being processed is a simple type, then the built-in `String` template.

6. Any template that corresponds to the base classes of the data type.

7. If the data type implements `IEnumerable`, then the built-in `Collection` template.

8. If all else fails, the `Object` template.

At each stage in the template search process, the MVC framework looks for a template called `EditorTemplates/<name>` or `DisplayTemplates/<name>` before using the built-in template. For our `StartTime` template, we satisfied step 4 in the search process. We created a template called `StartTime.cshtml` and placed it in the `~/Views/Shared/EditorTemplates` folder.

Using the Whole-Model Templated Helper Methods

There are three helper methods that we have yet to encounter. They operate on the whole of the view model as a single entity. Table 26-7 describes the helpers.

Table 26-7. *The Whole-Model Templated Helper Methods*

Helper	Example	Description
DisplayForModel	Html.DisplayForModel()	Renders a read-only view of the entire model object
EditorForModel	Html.EditorForModel()	Renders editor elements for the entire model object
LabelForModel	Html.LabelForModel()	Renders an HTML <label> element referring to the entire model object

The whole-model templated helpers are just a convenience. Rather than having to invoke helpers on each individual member, we can just work on the entire model. As an example, Listing 26-25 shows the `Summary.cshtml` view updated to use a whole-model helper.

Listing 26-25. *Using a whole-model helper*

```
@model EventRegistration.Models.View.CompetitionSummary

@Html.EditorForModel()
```

These helpers become useful only when we define custom templates for the view model types. The built-in templates are largely useless, as we can see in Figure 26-13. However, you should know that the metadata and custom templates we defined for individual properties have been correctly applied.

Figure 26-13. *The default output from the Html.EditorForModel helper*

If we create a type-specific model for CompetitionSummary, we can see the value of these helpers. Listing 26-26 shows a template I created in the Views/Shared/EditorTemplates folder called CompetitionSummary.cshtml.

Listing 26-26. *A type-specific template*

```
@model EventRegistration.Models.View.CompetitionSummary

<style type="text/css">
    td {padding: 5px}
    th {text-align:left}
</style>

<table >
    <tr><th>Label</th><th>Editor</th></tr>
    <tr>
        <td>@Html.LabelFor(x => x.Name)</td>
        <td>@Html.EditorFor(x => x.Name)</td>
    </tr>
    <tr>
        <td>@Html.LabelFor(x => x.City)</td>
        <td>@Html.EditorFor(x => x.City)</td>
    </tr>
    <tr>
        <td>@Html.LabelFor(x => x.Date)</td>
        <td>@Html.EditorFor(x => x.Date)</td>
    </tr>
    <tr>
        <td>@Html.LabelFor(x => x.Approved)</td>
        <td>@Html.EditorFor(x => x.Approved)</td>
    </tr>
    <tr>
        <td>@Html.LabelFor(x => x.Start)</td>
        <td>@Html.EditorFor(x => x.Start)</td>
    </tr>
</table>
```

I have used the property-level templated helpers to ensure that the metadata and custom templates are used. Figure 26-14 shows the effect of this template.

Figure 26-14. *A template used by the EditorForModel helper*

Summary

This chapter covered the helper methods that we can use in views to generate HTML flexibly and concisely. We saw how the basic helpers differ from the strongly typed helpers, how to create custom helper methods, and how to use and customize the templated helpers. There are a lot of different types of helper, but they are easy to master, and most programmers tend to settle on one type for most situations. I like to use the strongly typed helpers, but you may end up with a different style.

CHAPTER 27

Using Routing and Areas

Chapter 12 showed you how to use the ASP.NET routing system to create URLs that are independent from the pages that contained our markup. In that situation, routing was optional. We could just let the user request individual ASPX pages from the server, and our application would still function.

Routing is not optional in MVC framework applications. It is the means by which we map URLs requested by the user to action methods in controller classes. There is no page system for the MVC framework to fall back on. The only way we can process user requests is through the routing system. In this chapter, I'll show you how routing is employed by the MVC framework and explore a related feature called *areas*, which allow us to break up a large application into manageable chunks.

Note If you skipped over the early chapters to get started with the MVC framework, you'll need to go back and read at least Chapter 12 to make sense of this chapter.

Understanding Routing in the MVC Framework

In an MVC framework application, routes provide the mapping between requested URLs and action methods in a controller. In the examples I have given so far in this part of the book, I have told you to navigate to URLs in the format /<Controller>/<Action>. In doing this, I relied on the default routing configuration for an MVC framework application.

MVC framework routes are defined in the Global.asax file, but they use a slightly different format from the ones in Chapter 12. We are going to build on the example that we used in the previous chapter, and Listing 27-1 shows the Global.asax file from the EventRegistration project.

Listing 27-1. The Web.config file

```
using System;
using System.Collections.Generic;
using System.Linq;
using System.Web;
using System.Web.Mvc;
```

```
using System.Web.Routing;
using EventRegistration.Infrastructure;

namespace EventRegistration {

    public class MvcApplication : System.Web.HttpApplication {

        public static void RegisterGlobalFilters(GlobalFilterCollection filters) {
            filters.Add(new HandleErrorAttribute());
        }

        public static void RegisterRoutes(RouteCollection routes) {
            routes.IgnoreRoute("{resource}.axd/{*pathInfo}");

            routes.MapRoute(
                "Default",
                "{controller}/{action}/{id}",
                new { controller = "Home", action = "Index", id = UrlParameter.Optional }
            );
        }

        protected void Application_Start() {
            AreaRegistration.RegisterAllAreas();

            DependencyResolver.SetResolver(new CustomDependencyResolver());

            RegisterGlobalFilters(GlobalFilters.Filters);
            RegisterRoutes(RouteTable.Routes);
        }
    }
}
```

The `Application_Start` method (described in Chapter 5) contains a call to the `RegisterRoutes` method, which is where we define our routes. Visual Studio adds two routes to the `RegisterRoutes` method in a new project. The first is an instruction to the routing system to ignore requests for files with the `.axd` suffix. These are known as *web resource files* and include the trace viewer described in Chapter 7; they are not part of the MVC framework.

Using the MapRoute Method

Our goal in any MVC framework route is to obtain or provide values for two special route variables: `controller` and `action`. The values of these variables are used to identify the controller class and action method to which the request will be passed.

We register MVC framework routes using the `MapRoute` method, which is slightly different from the `MapPageRoute` method in Chapter 12, reflecting the different nature of the MVC framework. We provide at least two arguments: the name for the route and the URL that the route matches. Listing 27-2 shows a simple example.

Listing 27-2. *Creating a basic MVC route*

```
public static void RegisterRoutes(RouteCollection routes) {
    routes.IgnoreRoute("{resource}.axd/{*pathInfo}");

    routes.MapRoute(null, "{controller}/{action}");
}
```

This route will match any two-part URL. The first part of the URL will represent the controller, and the second part will represent the name of the action method. If we request the URL /Registration/Index, then we will invoke the Index method in the RegistrationController class. (We don't have to add Controller to map the requested controller to the class name. The MVC framework does this for us.)

The default route that Visual Studio adds to new projects goes further and defines additional URL segments and some default values:

```
public static void RegisterRoutes(RouteCollection routes) {
    routes.IgnoreRoute("{resource}.axd/{*pathInfo}");

    routes.MapRoute(
        "Default",
        "{controller}/{action}/{id}",
        new { controller = "Home", action = "Index", id = UrlParameter.Optional }
    );
}
```

In Chapter 12 we defined default values for routing variables using a RouteValueDictionary object, but when using the MapRoute method to define MVC framework routes, we use an anonymously typed object where the properties correspond to the names of the URL segments and property values correspond to the default values.

In the Default route, the default value for the controller variable is Home and Index for action. The id variable is an *optional variable*, which we denote by assigning the id parameter the UrlParameter.Optional value. An optional variable allows a route to match a broader range of URLs. If there is a third URL segment, it will be assigned to the id variable. If there are only two segments, the route will still match the URL, but the id variable won't be assigned a variable.

We don't have a HomeController class, so let's change the default value for the controller to match a controller that we *do* have, as shown in Listing 27-3.

Listing 27-3. *Routing requests to a default controller*

```
public static void RegisterRoutes(RouteCollection routes) {
    routes.IgnoreRoute("{resource}.axd/{*pathInfo}");

    routes.MapRoute(
        "Default",
        "{controller}/{action}/{id}",
        new { controller = "Registration", action = "Index", id = UrlParameter.Optional }
    );
}
```

The result of the three default values is that our route will match zero-, one-, two-, and three-part URLs, as shown in Table 27-1.

Table 27-1. *The URLs Supported by the Default Route*

URL	Controller	Action	ID
/Competition/Summary/1	Competition	Summary	1
/Competition/Summary	Competition	Summary	null
/Competition	Competition	Index	null
/	Registration	Index	null

By providing default values for the `controller` and `action` variables, we create a mapping between the default URL for our application (/) and an action method. This means we have the equivalent of a landing page for our application. Users who request the default URL cause the `Index` method of the `RegistrationController` class to be invoked, as shown in Figure 27-1.

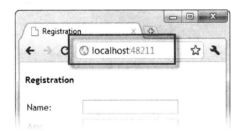

Figure 27-1. *Navigating to the default URL for an MVC framework application*

The importance of the `controller` and `action` variables is a convention applied by the MVC framework. The routing system itself has no knowledge of the special significant we accord these variables. This means it is possible to create routes that don't define the required variables without receiving a compiler warning. When such a route matches a URL, an HTTP `404 - Not Found` error will be reported to the user, whatever the details of the URL are.

Equally, the routing system doesn't check to ensure that the default values we supply correspond to controllers and action methods that exist, so it is important to test routes to ensure that the default values resolve to useful values.

Handling Routing Parameters in Action Methods

We can receive the values from optional routing parameters in our action methods by defining parameters of the same name. Listing 27-4 shows the `List` method of the `RegistrationController` class updated to deal with the optional `id` parameter defined in the default route.

▦ **Note** Routing variables can be incorporated into the model binding process. See Chapter 29 for details of model binding.

Listing 27-4. Handling a routing parameter in an action method

```
public ActionResult List(int? id) {
    ViewBag.Time = DateTime.Now;

    if (id.HasValue) {
        return View(repository.Registrations.OrderBy(x => x.ID)
            .Skip(id.Value - 1).Take(1));
    } else {
        return View(repository.Registrations);
    }
}
```

As you can see from the listing, I have defined a nullable int parameter called id. This is how the MVC framework will pass the value of the routing variable to the action method. I have used a nullable int because we have to deal with the possibility that the user has not requested a URL that includes a value for the routing variable. In this simple example, if there is a value available, I use it as an index to select a specific Registration record as the view model, and if not, the view model is the complete set of records.

▦ **Note** I have used the relative position of the records and not the value of the ID property. This is because the database generates unique values for the ID column, and they can become nonsequential when we delete records.

If the user requests /Registration/List/2, then the second record in the sequence is displayed, as shown in Figure 27-2.

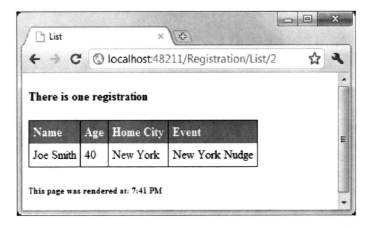

Figure 27-2. *Using a routing variable in an action method*

Notice that I set the type of the action method parameter to suit my purpose. When the request is processed, the MVC framework will try to convert the value extracted from the URL to the type of the action method parameter. If the conversion is successful, the value is passed via the parameter; if not, the parameter value will be **null**.

■ **Note** We can choose to ignore routing variables in an action method. The MVC framework will quietly discard the value if there is no parameter that matches the variable name.

Constraining MVC Framework Routes

We can restrict the way that routes match in MVC framework applications by providing *constraints*. These are similar to the constraints we used in Chapter 12, but they're expressed using an anonymously typed object passed to the **MapRoute** method. Listing 27-5 shows an example.

Listing 27-5. *Constraining a route for the MVC framework*

```
public static void RegisterRoutes(RouteCollection routes) {
    routes.IgnoreRoute("{resource}.axd/{*pathInfo}");

    routes.MapRoute(
        "Default",
        "{controller}/{action}/{id}",
        new { controller = "Registration", action = "Index", id = UrlParameter.Optional },
        new { controller = "Registration|Administration" }
    );
}
```

This additional parameter ensures that the route will only match URLs where the controller variable has the value `Registration` or `Administration`. In all other respects, the constraints for MVC framework routes are the same as the ones I showed you in Chapter 12.

Generating Outgoing URLs

Routes are more important in an MVC framework application than in a Web Forms application because we are intimately engaged in the HTML that our application generates. To that end, there are a set of helper methods that we can use in views to generate URLs from the routing system. The simplest way to generate an outgoing URL in a view is to call the `Html.ActionLink` helper. Listing 27-6 shows this helper used in the `List.cshtml` view of the `Registration` controller.

Listing 27-6. *Calling the ActionLink helper*

```
@model IEnumerable<EventRegistration.Models.Domain.Registration>
@using EventRegistration.Infrastructure
@{
    ViewBag.Title = "List";
    Layout = "~/Views/Shared/CustomLayout.cshtml";
}

@Html.RegistrationCount(@Model.Count())

<table rules="cols">
    <tr><th>Name</th><th>Age</th><th>Home City</th><th>Event</th></tr>

    @foreach (Registration reg in Model) {
        @Html.Partial("RegistrationTableRow", reg)
    }
</table>

<p />
@Html.ActionLink("Create New Registration", "Index")

<h6>This page was rendered at: @string.Format("{0:t}", ViewBag.Time) </h6>
```

The parameters to the `ActionLink` helper are the text for the link and the name of the action method that the link should target. The HTML that the `ActionLink` method generates is based on the routes defined in `Global.asax`. If we render this view with the route shown in Listing 27-5, we get the following HTML:

```
<a href="/">Create New Registration</a>
```

The URL that the helper has generated takes advantage of the default values that we defined in the route. When we specify just the action method, the helper assumes we want to target the current controller, which means that the value of our controller and action route variables must be `Registration` and `Index`, respectively. Since these are the default values that will be applied, we can use the default URL (/). If we target another action method, like this:

```
@Html.ActionLink("Create New Registration", "MyOtherAction")
```

then the helper can't rely on the default values, and we end up with a long URL. Here is the HTML that is rendered:

```
<a href="/Registration/MyOtherAction">Create New Registration</a>
```

■ **Caution** The helpers described in this chapter do not verify that the targets of the URLs they create exist. There is no MyOtherAction method in the RegistrationController class, but the Html.ActionLink helper happily generated the URL anyway. It is important to test the URLs that you create in views to ensure that they target valid action methods.

Targeting Other Controllers

The default version of the ActionLink method assumes you want to target an action method in the same controller that has caused the view to be rendered. To create an outgoing URL that targets a different controller, we can use a different overload that allows us to specify the controller name, as shown in Listing 27-7.

Listing 27-7. *Targeting a different controller using the ActionLink helper*

```
@Html.ActionLink("About this application", "About", "MyController")
```

When the view is rendered, we see the following HTML:

```
<a href="/MyController/About">About this application</a>
```

Passing Values for Routing Variables

We can provide values for routing segment variables using an anonymously typed object, where the property names correspond to the routing variables. Listing 27-8 shows an example.

Listing 27-8. *Passing a value for a routing variable to the ActionLink helper*

```
@Html.ActionLink("Show First Registration", "List", new { id = "1" })
```

In this example, I have provided a value for the optional id variable, resulting in the following HTML when the view is rendered:

```
<a href="/Registration/List/1">Show First Registration</a>
```

Avoiding the Routing Variable Reuse Trap

There is a pernicious oddity in the way that the MVC framework generates URLs. It causes a lot of confusion and unexpected behavior in applications. Our List action method in the RegistrationController class takes note of the id variable in our route. If the user provides a value for this variable in the requested URL, then we display just the specified records. In other words, requesting /Registration/List/2 shows just the second item.

To help the user, we might want to add a link that appears when a single record is being displayed that will display *all* the records, as shown in Listing 27-9.

Listing 27-9. *Creating a link to display all the registration records*

```
@model IEnumerable<EventRegistration.Models.Domain.Registration>
@using EventRegistration.Infrastructure
@{
    ViewBag.Title = "List";
    Layout = "~/Views/Shared/CustomLayout.cshtml";
}

@Html.RegistrationCount(@Model.Count())

<table rules="cols">
    <tr><th>Name</th><th>Age</th><th>Home City</th><th>Event</th></tr>

    @foreach (Registration reg in Model) {
        @Html.Partial("RegistrationTableRow", reg)
    }
</table>

<p />
@if (Model.Count() == 1) {
    @Html.ActionLink("Show All Registrations", "List")
}

<h6>This page was rendered at: @string.Format("{0:t}", ViewBag.Time) </h6>
```

We might expect that the URL generated by the helper would be this:

```
<a href="/Registration/List">Show All Registrations</a>
```

Clicking the link would call the List action method without a value for the id variable, and we'd see all of the records. However, that's not the URL that's generated. We get this instead:

```
<a href="/Registration/List/2">Show All Registrations</a>
```

This URL just puts the user into a loop. They click the link but see the same record again. What's happening here is called *routing variable reuse.*

In essence, the MVC framework will take values for routing variables from the *incoming* URL in order to generate an *outgoing* URL, even if the routing variable is optional and even if a perfectly valid URL could be created without reusing variables.

To prevent this from happening, we have to take care to provide values for all the variables in the route that is likely to be used in generating our outgoing URL, like this:

```
@Html.ActionLink("Show All Registrations", "List", new { id = string.Empty })
```

By providing the empty string as the value for the id variable, we get the URL we wanted in the first place:

```
<a href="/Registration/List">Show All Registrations</a>
```

If you are getting unexpected URLs from the helpers, then this is most likely the cause. This is an odd and frustrating behavior, and I have yet to meet anyone who finds it useful.

Specifying HTML Attributes

We've focused on the URL that the ActionLink helper generates, but remember that the method generates a complete HTML anchor (a) element. We can set attributes for this element by providing an anonymous type whose properties correspond to the attributes we require. Listing 27-10 demonstrates creating an id attribute and assigning a CSS class to the HTML element that the ActionLink helper creates.

Listing 27-10. Specifying HTML attributes when creating an outgoing URL

```
@Html.ActionLink("Show All Registrations", "List",
    new { id = string.Empty },
    new { id = "MyIDValue", @class = "MyCSSClass" })
```

The HTML that this generates is as follows:

```
<a class="MyCSSClass" href="/Registration/List" id="MyIDValue">Show All Registrations</a>
```

■ **Note**   Notice that I prepended the class property with an @ character. This is a C# language feature that lets us use reserved keywords as the names for class members.

Generating Fully Qualified URLs in Links

All the links that we have generated so far have contained relative URLs, but we can also use the ActionLink helper method to generate fully qualified URLs, as shown in Listing 27-11.

Listing 27-11. Generating a fully qualified URL

```
@Html.ActionLink("Show All Registrations", "List", "Registration", "https",
    "myserver.mydomain.com", "myFragmentName",
    new { id = string.Empty },
    new { id = "MyIDValue", @class = "MyCSSClass" })
```

This is the ActionLink overload with the most parameters, and it allows us to set values for the protocol, hostname, and the URL fragment in addition to the other values we have seen previously. Here is the HTML that the listing generates:

```
<a class="MyCSSClass" href="https://myserver.mydomain.com/Registration/List#myFragmentName"
    id="MyIDValue">Show All Registrations</a>
```

■ **Caution** I recommend sticking with relative URLs whenever possible. Fully qualified URLs create dependencies on the way your infrastructure is presented to users, and changes in hostnames or network infrastructure can break absolute URLs.

Generating URLs (and Not Links)

The `Html.ActionLink` helper method generates complete HTML a elements, which is exactly what we want most of the time. However, sometimes we just need a URL, which may be because we want to display the URL, build the HTML for a link manually, display the value of the URL, or include the URL as a data element in the HTML page being rendered. In such circumstances, we can use the `Url.Action` helper to generate just the URL and not the surrounding HTML, as Listing 27-12 shows.

Listing 27-12. Generating a URL (without any surrounding HTML)

```
My URL is @Url.Action("List", new { id = string.Empty })
```

The `Url.Action` method is prone to routing variable reuse, so I have taken the precaution of specifying a value for the `id` variable. The HTML that this helper renders is as follows:

```
My URL is /Registration/List
```

The `Url.Action` helper works in the same way as `Html.ActionLink`, except that it generates just the URL. The overloaded versions of the method and the parameters they accept are the same for both methods, and you can do all of the things with `Url.Action` that I demonstrated with `Html.ActionLink` in the previous sections.

■ **Note** The `Url.Content` helper generates a URL that targets a static file, usually a script library, an image, or a CSS style sheet. This helper is usually to be found in layouts, to ensure that the browser can reach the supporting files in an application.

Using Areas

The MVC framework supports organizing a web application into *areas*, where each area represents a functional segment of the application, such as administration, billing, customer support, and so on. This is useful in a large project, where having a single set of folders for all the controllers, views, and models can become difficult to manage.

Each MVC area has its own folder structure, allowing you to keep everything separate. This makes it more obvious which project elements relate to each functional area of the application and helps multiple developers work on the project without colliding with one another. As you'll see, areas are supported largely through the routing system. In this section, I'll show you how to set up and use areas in your MVC projects.

Creating an Area

To add an area to an MVC application, right-click the project item in the Solution Explorer window and select Add ➤ Area. Visual Studio will prompt you for the name of the area, as shown in Figure 27-3. We are going to create an area called Admin. This is a pretty common area to create, because many web applications need to separate the customer-facing and administration functions. Enter the name of the area to create and click the Add button.

Figure 27-3. *Adding an area to an MVC application*

After you click Add, you'll see some changes applied to the project. First, the project contains a new top-level folder called `Areas`. This contains a folder called `Admin`, which represents the area we just created. If we were to create additional areas, other folders would be created here. Inside the `Areas/Admin` folder, you will see that we have a mini-MVC project. There are folders called `Controllers`, `Models`, and `Views`. The first two are empty, but the `Views` folder contains a `Shared` folder and a `Web.config` file.

The other change is that there is a file called `AdminAreaRegistration.cs`, which contains the `AdminAreaRegistration` class, as shown in Listing 27-13.

Listing 27-13. *The AdminAreaRegistration class*

```
using System.Web.Mvc;

namespace EventRegistration.Areas.Admin {
    public class AdminAreaRegistration : AreaRegistration {
        public override string AreaName {
            get {
                return "Admin";
            }
        }
}
```

```
    public override void RegisterArea(AreaRegistrationContext context) {
        context.MapRoute(
            "Admin_default",
            "Admin/{controller}/{action}/{id}",
            new { action = "Index", id = UrlParameter.Optional }
        );
    }
}
}
```

The key part of this class is the **RegisterArea** method. As you can see from the listing, this method registers a route with the URL pattern **Admin/{controller}/{action}/{id}**. We can define additional routes in this method, which will be unique to this area.

▓ **Caution** If you assign names to your routes, you must ensure that they are unique across the entire application and not just the area for which they are intended.

We don't need to take any action to make sure that this registration method is called. It is handled for us automatically by the **Application_Start** method of **Global.asax**, which you can see in Listing 27-14.

Listing 27-14. Area registration called from Global.asax

```
protected void Application_Start() {
    AreaRegistration.RegisterAllAreas();

    DependencyResolver.SetResolver(new CustomDependencyResolver());

    RegisterGlobalFilters(GlobalFilters.Filters);
    RegisterRoutes(RouteTable.Routes);
}
```

The call to the static **AreaRegistration.RegisterAllAreas** method causes the MVC framework to go through all the classes in our application, find those that are derived from the **AreaRegistration** class, and call the **RegisterArea** method on each of them. The **AreaRegistrationContext** class that is passed to each area's **RegisterArea** method exposes a set of **MapRoute** methods that the area can use to register routes in the same way as the main application does in the **RegisterRoutes** method of **Global.asax**.

Populating an Area

Once we have created an area, we can populate it with controllers, views, and models as we have done for the main part of the application. To start, we are going to create a new controller. Right-click the **Areas/Admin/Controllers** folder, and select Add ➤ Controller from the pop-up menus. You'll see the standard Add Controller dialog. Set the controller name to RegistrationController, as shown in Figure 27-4.

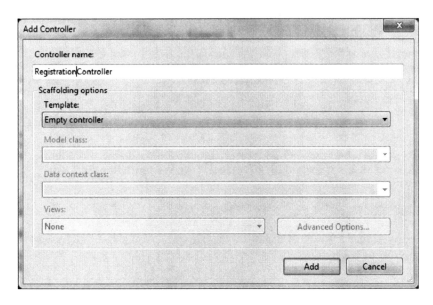

Figure 27-4. *Creating a controller in an area*

To emphasize the independence of each area, we are going to create a controller that has the same name as a controller in the main part of the application. When you have set the controller name in the dialog, click the Add button to create the controller class. We'll just create a very simple action method, as shown in Listing 27-15.

Listing 27-15. *A simple action method in the area controller*

```
using System.Linq;
using System.Web.Mvc;
using EventRegistration.Models.Domain.Repository;

namespace EventRegistration.Areas.Admin.Controllers {

    public class RegistrationController : Controller {
        private IRepository repository;

        public RegistrationController(IRepository repo) {
            repository = repo;
        }

        public ActionResult Index() {
            return View(repository.Registrations.Count());
        }
    }
}
```

Notice that we can still take advantage of the dependency injection we set up in Chapter 23 and that we can access the models and repository in the main part of the application. In the Index action method, I call the View method to render the default view associated with the action method and pass the number of Registration objects available as the view model object.

Right-click the Index method in the controller and select Add View from the pop-up menu. Check the option to create a strongly typed view and set the model class to int, as shown in Figure 27-5.

Figure 27-5. *Creating a view for an area controller*

Click the Add button to create the view. Notice that Visual Studio has maintained the separation of the area and created the view in the **Areas/Views/Registration** folder. Set the contents of the view to match those shown in Listing 27-16.

Listing 27-16. The area Index.cshtml view

```
@model int

@{
    ViewBag.Title = "Index";
}
```

```
<h4>Admin Registration Controller</h4>
```

```
There are @Model registrations in the database
```

This is a very simple view, but we just need something that will show that we have invoked the action methods of a controller within the area we created. To do this, start the application and navigate to /Admin/Registration/Index. You will see the result shown in Figure 27-6.

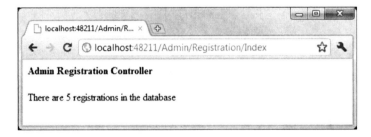

Figure 27-6. The output from the area view

The format for the URL to access the area is /Admin/<controller>/<action>, as defined in the AdminAreaRegistration class. We can, of course, change the format by changing the route definition, just as we would for regular routes.

Resolving the Ambiguous Controller Error

There is one issue to deal with. Although requests for the Registration controller in the area work properly, we can no longer access the original Registration controller in the main part of the application. If you navigate to /Registration/Index, you will see the error shown in Figure 27-7.

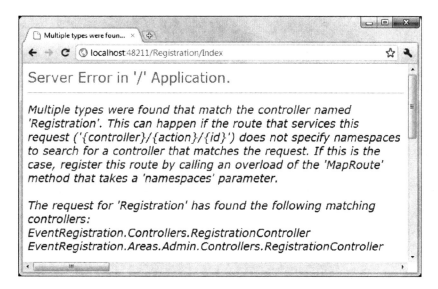

Figure 27-7. *The ambiguous controller error*

When a URL matches a route for an area, the MVC framework will only consider controller classes defined in that area. It does this by restricting the namespaces in which it will look for classes.

The same isn't true when a URL matches a route for the main part of the application. The MVC framework considers *all* controller classes to be possible candidates and can't differentiate between the `RegistrationController` class we created in the `Controllers` folder and the one we created in the `Areas/Admin/Controller` folder.

To fix this, we need to tell the MVC framework which namespace it should look in first when trying to deal with a URL that matches a route in the main application. We do this in the `RegisterRoutes` method in the `Global.asax` file, as shown in Listing 27-17.

Listing 27-17. *Specifying namespace priority*

```
public static void RegisterRoutes(RouteCollection routes) {
    routes.IgnoreRoute("{resource}.axd/{*pathInfo}");

    routes.MapRoute(
        "Default",
        "{controller}/{action}/{id}",
        new { controller = "Registration", action = "Index", id = UrlParameter.Optional },
        new { controller = "Registration|Administration" },
        new string[] {"EventRegistration.Controllers"}
    );
}
```

We add a new string array argument that contains the namespaces that we want to be treated as the priorities. In this case, I have specified that the `EventRegistration.Controllers` namespace takes priority, giving the MVC framework the information it needs to correctly select the controller.

Generating Links to Actions in Areas

We don't need to take any special steps to create links that refer to actions in the same MVC area that the user is already on. The MVC framework detects that the current request relates to an area, and outbound URL generation will find a match only among routes defined for that area. For example, if we add the following to the **/Areas/Admin/Views/Registration/Index.cshtml** view:

```
@Html.ActionLink("Click me!", "Index")
```

then we get the following HTML when we render the view:

```
<a href="/Admin/Registration">Click me!</a>
```

The default value for the `action` variable in the area route is `Index`, which is why we have a shortened URL in this case, but we also have the initial URL segment of `Admin`, which will direct the MVC framework to handle the request using the area controller.

To create a link to an action in a different area, or no area at all, we must create a variable called `area` and use it to specify the name of the area we want, like this:

```
@Html.ActionLink("Click me to go to another area", "Index", new { area = "Support" })
```

It is for this reason that **area** is reserved from use as a routing variable name. The HTML generated by this call is as follows (assuming that we created an area called `Support` that has the standard route defined):

```
<a href="/Support/Home">Click me to go to another area</a>
```

If we want to link to an action on one of the top-level controllers (a controller in the **/Controllers** folder), then you should specify the area as an empty string, like this:

```
@Html.ActionLink("Click me to go to another area", "Index", new { area = string.Empty })
```

Summary

This chapter showed how important the routing system is to the MVC framework. In lieu of a page-based model, the MVC framework relies on routes to be able to associate requests with controller classes and action methods. I showed you how to create and configure routes for MVC applications, building on the core routing information from Chapter 12. I also showed you how to generate URLs that are derived from routes in your views. Finally, we looked at areas, which allow us to break a large application into smaller, self-contained pieces.

CHAPTER 28

Working with Action Methods

In this chapter, you'll turn your attention to action methods—the critical part of a controller that allows us to respond to a request. I'll show you how to get the most from action methods, starting with the different kinds of object an action method can return and the effect they have on the MVC framework. I'll also show you how to pass data from an action method to a view, how to disambiguate action methods with the same name, and how to deal with unhandled exceptions that arise in action methods.

Preparing the Project

We are going to build on the example project from the previous chapter, focusing on the Competition controller and its actions. So that we have a clean slate to work with, reset the contents of the CompetitionController.cs file so that they match Listing 28-1.

Listing 28-1. *The contents of the CompetitionController.cs file*

```
using System.Web.Mvc;
using EventRegistration.Models.Domain;
using EventRegistration.Models.Domain.Repository;

namespace EventRegistration.Controllers {

    public class CompetitionController : Controller {
        private IRepository repository;

        public CompetitionController(IRepository repo) {
            repository = repo;
        }

        public ActionResult Index() {
            return View(repository.Competitions);
        }
    }
}
```

I have created a view for the Index action method, which is shown in Listing 28-2. This view simply enumerates the view model objects to create a table, using the Razor tags and techniques you have seen in previous chapters.

Listing 28-2. *The Views/Competition/Index.cshtml view*

```
@model IEnumerable<EventRegistration.Models.Domain.Competition>
@{
    ViewBag.Title = "Index";
}

<h3>Competitions</h3>

<table>
    <tr>
        <th>Name</th><th>Location</th><th>Date</th><th>Type</th><th>Registrations</th>
    </tr>

    @foreach (Competition comp in Model) {
        <tr>
            <td>@comp.Name</td>
            <td>@comp.Location</td>
            <td>@comp.Date.ToShortDateString()</td>
            <td>@comp.EventType</td>
            <td>@comp.Registrations.Count()</td>
        </tr>
    }
</table>
```

In the previous chapter, we added a restriction to the routes for the application that will stop us from using the Competition controller. Reset the contents of the RegisterRoutes method in Global.asax so that it matches Listing 28-3.

Listing 28-3. *Resetting the routes for the application*

```
public static void RegisterRoutes(RouteCollection routes) {
    routes.IgnoreRoute("{resource}.axd/{*pathInfo}");

    routes.MapRoute(
        "Default",
        "{controller}/{action}/{id}",
        new { controller = "Registration", action = "Index", id = UrlParameter.Optional }
    );
}
```

If we start the application and navigate to /Competition (since Index is the default value for the action variable for the application route), we see the details of the competitions show, as in Figure 28-1.

Figure 28-1. The rendered output from calling the Index action method

As you can see from the figure, I defined some basic CSS in the default layout, which is shown in Listing 28-4.

Listing 28-4. The CSS added to the _Layout.cshtml file

```
...
<head>
    <title>@ViewBag.Title</title>
    <link href="@Url.Content("~/Content/Site.css")" rel="stylesheet" type="text/css" />
    <script src="@Url.Content("~/Scripts/jquery-1.5.1.min.js")"
        type="text/javascript"></script>

    <style type="text/css">
        table {border:thin solid black}
        th {background-color:Gray; color:White; padding: 5px; text-align:left}
        td {padding: 5px}
    </style>
</head>
...
```

With these changes in place, we are ready to look at controllers and action methods in more depth.

Understanding Results from Action Methods

One of the most important aspects of an action method is its *result*. This instructs the MVC framework as to the next step to take in processing the request. The simplest kind of instruction is to do nothing, which we can express by defining an action method that has no return value, using the C# **void** keyword, as shown in Listing 28-5.

Listing 28-5. Defining an action method that defines no next step

```
using System.Linq;
using System.Web.Mvc;
using EventRegistration.Models.Domain;
using EventRegistration.Models.Domain.Repository;

namespace EventRegistration.Controllers {

    public class CompetitionController : Controller {
        private IRepository repository;

        public CompetitionController(IRepository repo) {
            repository = repo;
        }

        public ActionResult Index() {
            return View(repository.Competitions);
        }

        public void NoFurtherAction() {
            foreach (Competition comp in repository.Competitions.ToArray()) {
                comp.Date = comp.Date.AddMonths(1);
                repository.SaveCompetition(comp);
            }
        }
    }
}
```

This action method, which I have called NoFurtherAction, doesn't define a next step. It does, however, perform an action. So that we can see that it has been invoked, I have set the action method up so that it adds one month to the Date property of each Competition record in the database.

■ **Note** Notice that I force the evaluation of the LINQ to Entities query by calling ToArray on the Competitions property of the repository. This is a variation of the iteration problem I described in Chapter 25. Since I call the SaveCompetition method within the foreach loop, I am trying to modify data before it has been read from the server, which causes an exception. To avoid this problem, I call the ToArray method, which forces the data to be read into memory and allows me to make changes as I wish. An alternative approach would be to push the call to SaveCompetition outside of the foreach loop. A call to this method causes the Entity Framework to save all changes. This is the kind of compromise I described earlier with regard to separation of concerns. I would rather that the implementation detail of the repository didn't leak into the controller (however vaguely and indirectly it might be), but that is very hard to achieve.

If we start the application and navigate to the **/Competition/NoFurtherAction** URL, then we will see…well, nothing. The ASP.NET server sends an HTTP 200 (OK) code to the browser and closes the connection. We see an empty browser window. If we then navigate to **/Competition/Index**, we can see the effect on the data, as shown in Figure 28-2.

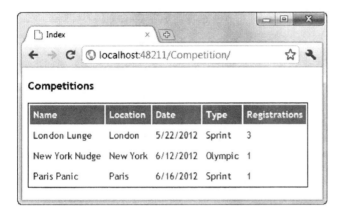

Figure 28-2. *The effect of the NoFurtherAction method*

■ **Caution** The NoFurtherAction method breaks one of the common patterns of web applications, which is that HTTP GET requests should be *safe*, such that they can be repeated over and over again without causing problems with the application state. Typically, this means that GET request should only read data. This is an important convention because a search engine or acceleration cache can index your site by following all of the GET links in your HTML and cause a lot of problems (if this seems unlikely to you, then look up the history of the Google Accelerator product; this is exactly what happened). Instead, changes should happen only as the result of a POST request. I have broken this convention for the sake of a simple example—a case of do what I say, not what I do.

Returning a String from an Action Method

The next step up from no instruction is a very simple one, which we can do by creating an action method that returns a string, as shown in Listing 28-6.

Listing 28-6. *Returning a string from an action method*

```
using System;
using System.Linq;
using System.Web.Mvc;
using EventRegistration.Models.Domain;
using EventRegistration.Models.Domain.Repository;
```

```
namespace EventRegistration.Controllers {

    public class CompetitionController : Controller {
        private IRepository repository;

        public CompetitionController(IRepository repo) {
            repository = repo;
        }

        public ActionResult Index() {
            return View(repository.Competitions);
        }

        public void NoFurtherAction() {
            foreach (Competition comp in repository.Competitions.ToArray()) {
                comp.Date = comp.Date.AddMonths(1);
                repository.SaveCompetition(comp);
            }
        }

        public string Time() {
            return string.Format("The time is: {0}", DateTime.Now.ToShortTimeString());
        }
    }
}
```

Returning a `string` from an action method tells the MVC framework that its next step is to send that string to the browser. It does this without wrapping the string in any HTML. It just adds the string to the response. Most browsers will just display the string, as shown in Figure 28-3.

Figure 28-3. *Returning a string from an action method*

Understanding Action Results

Actions that lead to no further steps or to returning simple strings are fine but not very useful. To get to the real power and flexibility of action methods, we need to return `ActionResult` objects, which is exactly what the `Index` method I added to the controller at the start of the chapter does:

```
public ActionResult Index() {
    return View(repository.Competitions);
}
```

There are a range of ActionResult subclasses, and returning each kind gives the MVC framework a different instruction. The View method that I used in the Index method tells the MVC framework to render a view. In this case, the default view is associated with the action method, using the value of the repository.Competitions property as the view model data.

The View method returns a ViewResult object, which is derived from ActionResult. We could rewrite the Index method like this if we wanted:

```
public ViewResult Index() {
    return View(repository.Competitions);
}
```

and get the same effect.

■ **Note** Notice that we are not responsible for performing the next step ourselves. We don't need to find the view, render it, and send the result as the response to the client. We just tell the MVC framework what do to. This is another example of the distinction between the components in the MVC framework.

In the following sections, I'll show you the most commonly used ActionResult subclasses and the methods that create them and explain their function.

■ **Note** We can also return JSON data from an action method to create a web service. I explain how to do this in Chapter 30.

Rendering a View

The majority of action methods cause a view to be rendered. This is how we generate HTML. As already explained, we use the View method to cause a view to be rendered, but this method has several overloads that allow us to specify view model objects and select which view is rendered. The simplest overload of the View method defined no parameters, like this:

```
public ViewResult Index() {
    return View();
}
```

This tells the MVC framework to render the view with the same name as the action method (Index in our case) and does not specify any view model object. We can specify a particular view by passing the view name as a string, like this:

```
public ViewResult Index() {
    return View("MyView");
}
```

There are overloads that allow us to specify view model objects, with and without specifying the view. Here is how we provide view data and use the default view:

```
public ViewResult Index() {
    return View(MyDataObject);
}
```

and here is how we provide view data and select a specific template:

```
public ViewResult Index() {
    return View("MyView", MyDataObject);
}
```

■ **Tip**   Confusion often arises when you want to use the default view and your view model is a `string`. You call `View(MyModelString)`, and the MVC framework throws an exception reporting that it can't find the view. This happens because we are unwittingly using the wrong overload and the value of the view model `string` is being taken as the required view name. The simplest way to address this is to cast your view model to an `object`, `View((object)MyModelString)`.

Finally, we can specify the layout that should be used with the view, overriding the value of the `Layout` property assigned in the view or the `_ViewStart.cshtml` file (see Chapter 25 for details of layouts). Here are the method calls, with and without view data:

```
return View("MyView", "MyLayout", MyDataObject);    // with view data
return View("MyView", "MyLayout");    // without view data
```

■ **Note**   You can also render partial views, which I described in Chapter 25. Rendering partial views is typically done as part of *child actions*, which I describe later in this chapter.

Performing a Redirection

Redirections are commonly performed to follow a pattern called *post/redirect/get*. When we return data from a POST request, we run the risk that the user will reload the page and resubmit the form. This is probably not what the user wanted to do and can cause an unexpected duplication of the last operation they performed. To get around this, we can redirect the user's browser so that it makes a GET request. The user can then reload the page without submitting data to the application.

We can choose between two kinds of redirection. The first is a *temporary redirection* and sends the HTTP code 302 to the browser. This is what we use when following the post/redirect/get pattern and in most other situations. The alternative is a *permanent redirection*, which should be used with caution. It tells the recipient of the redirection not to request the original URL every again by sending the HTTP code 301. For almost all situations, a temporary redirection is safer and more suitable. We can redirect in two different ways.

Redirecting to Another Action Method

The RedirectToAction method lets us perform a redirection to another action in the same controller and returns a RedirectToRoute result. Listing 28-7 shows an action method that performs a redirection using this method.

Listing 28-7. *Performing a redirection to another action in the same controller*

```
using System.Web.Mvc;
using EventRegistration.Models.Domain.Repository;

namespace EventRegistration.Controllers {
    public class CompetitionController : Controller {
        private IRepository repository;

        public CompetitionController(IRepository repo) {
            repository = repo;
        }

        ... other action methods omitted...

        public RedirectToRouteResult Redirect() {
            return RedirectToAction("Index");
        }
    }
}
```

We are assumed to be redirecting the user to an action in the current controller if we provide just one string argument, so if we navigate to **/CompetitionController/Redirect**, our browser will be redirected to Index method in the CompetitionController class. If we want to redirect the user to an action method in a different controller, then we can use the method overload that takes two string arguments, like this:

```
return RedirectToAction("MyAction", "MyOtherController");
```

The RedirectToActionPermanent method has the same two overloaded versions and makes permanent redirections.

Redirecting to a Literal URL

We can redirect the user to a specific URL by using the Redirect method and passing in the target URL as a string. Listing 28-8 contains a demonstration.

Listing 28-8. *Redirecting to a literal URL*

```
using System.Web.Mvc;
using EventRegistration.Models.Domain.Repository;

namespace EventRegistration.Controllers {
    public class CompetitionController : Controller {
        private IRepository repository;

        public CompetitionController(IRepository repo) {
            repository = repo;
        }

        ... other action methods omitted...

        public RedirectToRouteResult Redirect() {
            return RedirectToAction("Index");
        }

        public RedirectResult RedirectLiteral() {
            return Redirect("http://www.asp.net");
        }
    }
}
```

If we navigate to /Competition/RedirectLiteral, our browser will be redirected to www.asp.net. I recommend you only use literal redirections to redirect outside your MVC application. Otherwise, use the RedirectToAction method.

■ **Note**   Notice that the Redirect method returns a RedirectResult object, while the RedirectToAction method returns a RedirectToRouteResult object. If you switch from one type of redirection to the other, you'll have to change the result type for your action method as well.

Returning Errors and HTTP Codes

We can send a specific HTTP status code to the browser using the HttpStatusCodeResult class. There is no controller helper method for this, so we must instantiate the class directly, as shown in Listing 28-9.

Listing 28-9. *Sending a specific status code*

```
public HttpStatusCodeResult StatusCode() {
    return new HttpStatusCodeResult(404, "URL cannot be processed");
}
```

The constructor parameters for HttpStatusCodeResult are the numeric status code and an optional descriptive message. In the listing, we have returned code 404, which signifies that the requested resource doesn't exist.

Sending a 404 Result

We can achieve the same effect as Listing 28-4 using the more convenient `HttpNotFoundResult` class, which is derived from `HttpStatusCodeResult` and can be created using the controller `HttpNotFound` convenience method, as shown in Listing 28-10.

Listing 28-10. *Generating 404 results*

```
public HttpStatusCodeResult StatusCode() {
    return HttpNotFound();
}
```

Sending a 401 Result

Another wrapper class for a specific HTTP status code is `HttpUnauthorizedResult`, which returns the `401` code, used to indicate that a request is unauthorized. Listing 28-11 provides a demonstration.

Listing 28-11. *Generating a 401 result*

```
public HttpStatusCodeResult StatusCode() {
    return new HttpUnauthorizedResult();
}
```

There is no helper method available to create instances of `HttpUnauthorizedResult`, so we must do so directly. The effect of returning an instance of this class is usually to redirect the user to the authentication page, which I will explain in detail in Chapter 34.

Passing Data from the Action Method to the View

The most common result from a method is a `ViewResult`, causing a view to be rendered. All but the simplest of views require some form of data to operate on, and the MVC framework provides a range of different ways to pass data from the action method to a view. We have already encountered some of these techniques in previous chapters, but I'll recap them here for completeness.

■ **Note**　The three techniques that I describe next all pass data from an action method to a view for a single request. When the view has been rendered, the data is lost. The MVC framework supports session data if you want to pass data is a more long-lived way. See Chapter 6 for details of using session data.

Using a View Model Object

The view model object is the principle mechanism for passing data from the action method to the view, irrespective of whether the view is strongly typed. We set the view model object through the `View` method, described earlier in this chapter.

We can pass any object as the view object. This includes instances of classes from our domain model or classes that have been specifically created to convey information from the action to the view, known as *view model classes*.

View model classes are usually created to pass property values that span multiple objects. Listing 28-12 contains an example of a view model object that combines properties contained in both the Registration and Competition domain model classes. I like to keep my view models separate from my domain models, so I have created this class, called CompetitionNames, in the Models/View folder.

Listing 28-12. The CompetitionNames class

```
using System.Collections.Generic;

namespace EventRegistration.Models.View {
    public class CompetitionNames {
        public string EventName { get; set; }
        public IEnumerable<string> RegistrantNames { get; set; }
    }
}
```

To demonstrate this view model class, I have added a new action method to the CompetitionController class, as shown in Listing 28-13.

Listing 28-13. Adding an action method that uses a view model class

```
using System;
using System.Collections.Generic;
using System.Linq;
using System.Web.Mvc;
using EventRegistration.Models.Domain;
using EventRegistration.Models.Domain.Repository;
using EventRegistration.Models.View;

namespace EventRegistration.Controllers {

    public class CompetitionController : Controller {
        private IRepository repository;

        public CompetitionController(IRepository repo) {
            repository = repo;
        }

        public ActionResult Index() {
            return View(repository.Competitions);
        }
```

```
public ViewResult Registrants() {
    IList<CompetitionNames> names = new List<CompetitionNames>();
    foreach (Competition comp in repository.Competitions) {
        names.Add(new CompetitionNames {
            EventName = comp.Name,
            RegistrantNames = comp.Registrations.Select(e => e.Name).Distinct()
        });
    }
    return View(names);
}
    }
}
```

The Registrants action method creates a list of CompetitionNames objects from the set of Competition and associated Registration objects available through the repository. This list is then passed to the View method.

▧ **Note** I could have used Razor to extract the event name and the name of the registrants from the repository objects in the view, but I prefer to do as much processing as possible in the controller to maintain the spirit of the MVC pattern. I like the view to do only small amounts of work, but not everyone agrees about how much processing is acceptable in a view, and you will find a wide spectrum of opinion exists on this topic. As per my previous advice, I suggest you find the balance that works for you and your projects.

To complete this example, we need a view. Listing 28-14 shows the Views/Competition/ Registrants.cshtml view I created for this purpose.

Listing 28-14. *The Registrant view*

```
@model IEnumerable<EventRegistration.Models.View.CompetitionNames>
@{
    ViewBag.Title = "Registrants";
}

<h3>Registrants</h3>

<table>
    <tr>
        <th>Event Name</th>
        <th>Registrant Names</th>
        <th>Count</th>
    </tr>
```

```
@foreach (var comp in Model) {
    <tr>
        <td>@comp.EventName</td>
        <td>@string.Join(", ", comp.RegistrantNames)</td>
        <td>@comp.RegistrantNames.Count()</td>
    </tr>
}
</table>
```

If we start the application and navigate to /Competition/Registrants with a browser, we can see the rendered view, as shown in Figure 28-4.

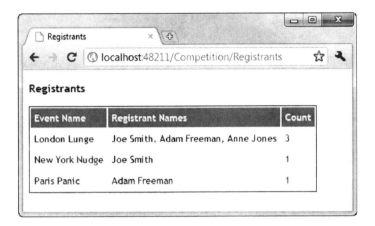

Figure 28-4. *Rendering a view that uses a view model class*

The decision about when to use a view model class is largely subjective. I find myself defining them when I'd have to use a Tuple to pass the data I need or when I'd need to add a lot of items to the ViewBag (described later in this chapter). There is no absolute right or wrong in these situations, but you should choose the approach that you think will make the most sense to other programmers and that will be the easiest to maintain over time.

Using the ViewBag

I introduced the ViewBag in Chapter 23. There is a ViewBag property in the base classes for both the controller and the view, and we can use the dynamic object that these properties return to pass data from the controller to the view.

Because the ViewBag is dynamic, we can define arbitrary properties just by assigning values to them. This is a neat and convenient trick. The drawback of using the ViewBag (as opposed to a view model object) is that we are responsible for ensuring that the property names we define are the same in the controller and the view and that the data types we send and expect are the same. Listing 28-15 shows a simple addition to the Registrants action method that uses the ViewBag to pass additional data to the view.

Listing 28-15. *Using the ViewBag in an action method*

```
public ViewResult Registrants() {
    IList<CompetitionNames> names = new List<CompetitionNames>();
    foreach (Competition comp in repository.Competitions) {
        names.Add(new CompetitionNames {
            EventName = comp.Name,
            RegistrantNames = comp.Registrations.Select(e => e.Name).Distinct()
        });
    }

    ViewBag.Time = DateTime.Now.ToShortTimeString();
    return View(names);
}
```

I find it preferable to use the ViewBag with data that is already prepared to be rendered as a string in the HTML. In the listing, you can see that I have called the ToShortTimeString method on the DateTime object so that the value assigned to the Time property in the ViewBag is just a simple string. This means I don't have to worry about data types in the view. I can just use a Razor @ tag to refer to the ViewBag property and have it inserted into the response, as shown in Listing 28-16.

Listing 28-16. *Using the ViewBag in a view*

```
@model IEnumerable<EventRegistration.Models.View.CompetitionNames>
@{
    ViewBag.Title = "Registrants";
}

<h3>Registrants</h3>

<table>
    <tr>
        <th>Event Name</th>
        <th>Registrant Names</th>
        <th>Count</th>
    </tr>
    @foreach (var comp in Model) {
        <tr>
            <td>@comp.EventName</td>
            <td>@string.Join(", ", comp.RegistrantNames)</td>
            <td>@comp.RegistrantNames.Count()</td>
        </tr>
    }
</table>

<p />
Page rendered at: @ViewBag.Time
```

Had I not prepared the DateTime object in the action method, I could have done so in the view, like this:

```
Page rendered at: @ViewBag.Time.ToShortTimeString()
```

We don't have to explicitly cast the value of the ViewBag.Time property to DateTime, but we do have to make sure that whatever object we set as the value of the Time property has a ToShortTimeString method to call. This means we must take care to keep the action method and the view in sync.

I tend to use the ViewBag incrementally. I will use it to supplement a view model object, but there comes a point where if I have more than a couple of properties defined, I start to think about using a view model class instead.

Using ViewData

ViewData is the precursor to the ViewBag and uses a key/value approach to passing data from the action method to the view. Listing 28-17 shows the Registrants action method updated to use ViewData.

Listing 28-17. Using ViewData to pass data from the action to the view

```
public ViewResult Registrants() {
    IList<CompetitionNames> names = new List<CompetitionNames>();
    foreach (Competition comp in repository.Competitions) {
        names.Add(new CompetitionNames {
            EventName = comp.Name,
            RegistrantNames = comp.Registrations.Select(e => e.Name).Distinct()
        });
    }

    ViewData["Time"] = DateTime.Now;
    return View(names);
}
```

The ViewData feature is implemented as a dictionary, so we define keys as strings and assign values to them, as shown in the listing. The main drawback of ViewData is that we have to perform casts to be able to operate on data objects, as shown in Listing 28-18.

Listing 28-18. Using ViewData in a view

```
@model IEnumerable<EventRegistration.Models.View.CompetitionNames>
@{
    ViewBag.Title = "Registrants";
}

<h3>Registrants</h3>
```

```
<table>
    <tr><th>Event Name</th><th>Registrant Names</th><th>Count</th></tr>
    @foreach (var comp in Model) {
        <tr>
            <td>@comp.EventName</td>
            <td>@string.Join(", ", comp.RegistrantNames)</td>
            <td>@comp.RegistrantNames.Count()</td>
        </tr>
    }
</table>

<p />
Page rendered at: @(((DateTime)ViewData["Time"]).ToShortTimeString())
```

This is pretty ugly when compared to using the ViewBag. The ViewBag was introduced in MVC version 3, and the only reason to use ViewData is when working with applications that were written against earlier versions of the MVC framework.

Using Child Actions

Child actions are action methods that we invoke from within a view. This lets us avoid repeating logic in our controller that we want to use in several places in the application.

■ **Note**   Child actions are to actions as partial views are to views. See Chapter 25 for details of partial views.

We might use a child action whenever we want to display some data-driven "widget" that appears on multiple pages and contains data unrelated to the main action that is running. This is commonly the case when we want part of the overall page to contain navigation links, where the data required to create navigation links is unrelated to the data being displayed by the main part of the view.

Creating a Child Action

Any action can be used as a child action. To demonstrate this feature, I have defined the action method shown in Listing 28-19.

Listing 28-19. Defining a child action

```
using System;
using System.Collections.Generic;
using System.Linq;
using System.Web.Mvc;
using EventRegistration.Models.Domain;
using EventRegistration.Models.Domain.Repository;
using EventRegistration.Models.View;
```

```
namespace EventRegistration.Controllers {

    public class CompetitionController : Controller {
        private IRepository repository;

        public CompetitionController(IRepository repo) {
            repository = repo;
        }

        public ActionResult Index() {
            return View(repository.Competitions);
        }

        public ViewResult Registrants() {
            IList<CompetitionNames> names = new List<CompetitionNames>();
            foreach (Competition comp in repository.Competitions) {
                names.Add(new CompetitionNames {
                    EventName = comp.Name,
                    RegistrantNames = comp.Registrations.Select(e => e.Name).Distinct()
                });
            }
            return View(names);
        }

        [ChildActionOnly]
        public PartialViewResult Footer() {
            ViewBag.CompCount = repository.Competitions.Count();
            ViewBag.RegCount = repository.Registrations.Count();
            return PartialView(DateTime.Now);
        }

        public void NoFurtherAction() {
            foreach (Competition comp in repository.Competitions.ToArray()) {
                comp.Date = comp.Date.AddMonths(1);
                repository.SaveCompetition(comp);
            }
        }

        public string Time() {
            return string.Format("The time is: {0}", DateTime.Now.ToShortTimeString());
        }
    }
}
```

The ChildActionOnly attribute ensures that an action method can be called only as a child method from within a view. An action method doesn't need to have this attribute to be used as a child action, but I tend to use this attribute to prevent the action methods from being invoked as a result of a user request.

Having defined an action method, we need to create the view that will be rendered when the action is invoked. Notice that my new action method returns the PartialViewResult type, which I generate using the PartialView method in the action method. Child actions are typically associated with partial views, although this is not compulsory. Listing 28-20 shows the partial `Footer.cshtml` view I created for this demonstration.

Listing 28-20. *A partial view for use with a child action*

```
@model DateTime

<table>
<tr>
    <td>Page rendered at @Model.ToShortTimeString()</td>
    <td>@Html.ActionLink((int)ViewBag.CompCount + " competitions", "Index")</td>
    <td>
        @Html.ActionLink((int)ViewBag.RegCount + " registrations", "List", "Registration")
    </td>
</tr>
</table>
```

This is a simple view that displays the time that the view was rendered and generates links that invoke the action methods that display the lists of registration and competition objects available in the repository. I pass the number of available objects of each type to the view using the `ViewBag`, just as we would for any regular action and view.

Rendering a Child Action

We invoke a child action using the `Html.Action` helper. The action method is executed, the `ViewResult` or `PartialViewResult` is processed, and the output is injected into the response to the client. Listing 28-21 shows how I have added a call to the child action to the `Registrants.cshtml` view.

Listing 28-21. *Calling a child action from a view*

```
@model IEnumerable<EventRegistration.Models.View.CompetitionNames>
@{
    ViewBag.Title = "Registrants";
}

<h3>Registrants</h3>

<table>
    <tr><th>Event Name</th><th>Registrant Names</th><th>Count</th></tr>
    @foreach (var comp in Model) {
        <tr>
            <td>@comp.EventName</td>
            <td>@string.Join(", ", comp.RegistrantNames)</td>
            <td>@comp.RegistrantNames.Count()</td>
        </tr>
    }
</table>

<p />
```

```
@Html.Action("Footer")
```

You can see the effect of rendering this view in Figure 28-5.

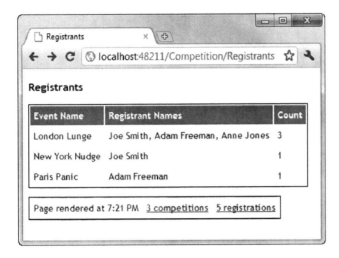

Figure 28-5. *Using a child action*

When I called the `Action` helper in the listing, I provided a single argument that specified the name of the action method to invoke. This causes the MVC framework to look for an action method in the controller that is handling the current request. We can call action methods in other controllers by providing the controller name, like this:

```
@Html.Action("Footer", "MyController")
```

We also can pass parameters to action methods by providing an anonymously typed object whose properties correspond to the names of the child action method parameters. So, for example, if we have a child action method like this:

```
[ChildActionOnly]
public ActionResult Time(DateTime time) {
    return PartialView(time);
}
```

then we can invoke it from a view as follows:

```
@Html.Action("Time", new { time = DateTime.Now })
```

Using the HTTP Method Selector Attributes

The routing system provides the MVC framework with details of which controller and action are targeted by a requested URL. These are the values assigned to the `controller` and `action` routing variables.

The MVC framework can figure out which class corresponds to the requested controller pretty easily (although it does sometimes need some help when areas are used, as I explained in Chapter 27). Working out which method the action corresponds to is more complicated, because C# allows us to create multiple methods of the same name but with different parameter signatures. Listing 28-22 shows a new controller class, called Reports, that I have added to the example project and that contains two methods called Index.

Listing 28-22. The Reports controller

```
using System.Web.Mvc;
using EventRegistration.Models.Domain.Repository;

namespace EventRegistration.Controllers {

    public class ReportsController : Controller {
        private IRepository repository;

        public ReportsController(IRepository repo) {
            repository = repo;
        }

        public ActionResult Index() {
            return View();
        }

        public ActionResult Index(string report) {
            switch (report) {
                case "Competitions":
                    return View("CompetitionReport", repository.Competitions);
                case "Registrations":
                    return View("RegistrationReport", repository.Registrations);
                default:
                    return View();
            }
        }
    }
}
```

If we request the URL /Reports/Index, the MVC framework won't be able to determine which of the Index methods should be used to process the request, and we'll see an error like the one shown in Figure 28-6.

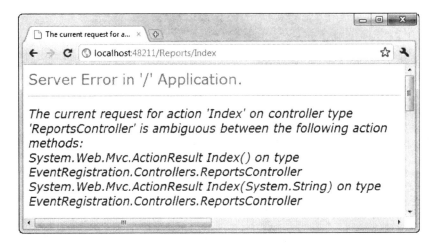

Figure 28-6. *The MVC framework cannot determine which method to invoke.*

We have to provide the MVC framework with some direction, which we do using the HTTP method selector attributes. There are four such attributes, corresponding to four HTTP methods: HttpGet, HttpPost, HttpPut, and HttpDelete.

■ **Note** There is an unfortunate conflict of terms here. HTTP has a number of verbs (GET, POST, DELETE, and so on) that are called *methods*. So, a GET request is a request that contains the GET verb and thus the GET method. This is distinct from the *action methods* that we define in our controller classes.

When we apply one of these attributes to an action method, we tell the MVC framework that the action method can be used for requests made with the associated HTTP method. Listing 28-23 shows the application of one of these attributes to disambiguate the Index methods in the controller.

Listing 28-23. *Applying an HTTP method selector attribute to an action method*

```
using System.Web.Mvc;
using EventRegistration.Models.Domain.Repository;

namespace EventRegistration.Controllers {

    public class ReportsController : Controller {
        private IRepository repository;
```

```
public ReportsController(IRepository repo) {
    repository = repo;
}

public ActionResult Index() {
    return View();
}

[HttpPost]
public ActionResult Index(string report) {
    switch (report) {
        case "Competitions":
            return View("CompetitionReport", repository.Competitions);
        case "Registrations":
            return View("RegistrationReport", repository.Registrations);
        default:
            return View();
    }
}
}
}
```

When the MVC framework checks for the presence of these attributes, it tries to determine which Index method should handle a request. It gives preference to the action method with the attribute that corresponds to the requested HTTP method. If there is no matching attribute, then the MVC framework looks for an action method with no attributes at all. This is the fallback position, and specifying no attributes tells the MVC framework that an action method is prepared to process requests for all HTTP methods.

In practical terms, if we make a POST request to the Index action in the Reports controller, the MVC framework will detect the HttpPost attribute and invoke the second of our Index methods. If we make a GET request, the MVC framework will look for the HttpGet attribute, fail to find it, and so invoke the first Index method (because it has no attributes).

We can apply multiple attributes to an action method to indicate that it is able to process different kinds of HTTP method, but we must take care to ensure that each attribute is used at most once. If we don't use all the attributes, then we must also ensure that there is at most one action method that doesn't have any attributes at all. If we don't follow these rules, then the MVC framework can't work out which action method should be used for each HTTP method.

The pattern I have shown in the listing is commonly used to handle forms. The first Index method responds to GET requests and is responsible for generating the HTML that contains the form element. The second Index method will receive the POST request when the form is submitted and is responsible for processing the form and generating the response for the user. We'll see this pattern in more detail in Chapter 29 when we look at model binding.

Dealing with Exceptions

We can deal with exceptions by using the HandleError attribute. This is an example of a filter, which allows us to deal with *cross-cutting concerns*. As I explained in Chapter 22, cross-cutting concerns are features or functions that are used through an application but that don't fit neatly into our MVC pattern. We'll see another example of filters when we look at authorization in Chapter 34.

Before we can use the `HandleError` attribute, we have to make an addition to the `Web.config` file, as shown in Listing 28-24.

Listing 28-24. *Enabling custom errors in Web.config*

```
<configuration>
  ...
  <system.web>

    <customErrors mode="On"/>

  </system.web>
  ...
</configuration>
```

We have to define the `customErrors` element with a value of `On` for the `mode` attribute. Without this element, the MVC framework will ignore our use of the `HandleError` attribute and use the standard error handling approach.

By changing the `Web.config` file, we change the way that errors are handled. We no longer get the Yellow Screen of Death generated by the core ASP.NET platform that I described in Chapter 7. Instead, we get a response generated by the MVC framework itself. To see the difference, start the application and navigate to `/Reports/Index`. We have yet to define a view for this action method, and so an exception will be thrown. You can see the message that is displayed in Figure 28-7.

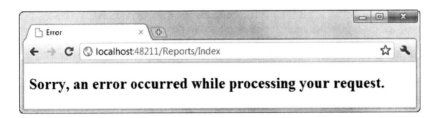

Figure 28-7. *The default custom error message*

Setting Global Error Handlers

We will start by improving the default error handling, which is set up in the `Global.asax` file, as shown in Listing 28-25.

Listing 28-25. *The global error filter in the Global.asax file*

```
using System;
using System.Collections.Generic;
using System.Linq;
using System.Web;
using System.Web.Mvc;
```

```
using System.Web.Routing;
using EventRegistration.Infrastructure;

namespace EventRegistration {

    public class MvcApplication : System.Web.HttpApplication {

        public static void RegisterGlobalFilters(GlobalFilterCollection filters) {
            filters.Add(new HandleErrorAttribute());
        }

        public static void RegisterRoutes(RouteCollection routes) {
            routes.IgnoreRoute("{resource}.axd/{*pathInfo}");

            routes.MapRoute(
                "Default",
                "{controller}/{action}/{id}",
                new { controller = "Registration", action = "Index",
                    id = UrlParameter.Optional }
            );
        }

        protected void Application_Start() {
            AreaRegistration.RegisterAllAreas();

            DependencyResolver.SetResolver(new CustomDependencyResolver());

            RegisterGlobalFilters(GlobalFilters.Filters);
            RegisterRoutes(RouteTable.Routes);
        }
    }
}
```

The `Application_Start` method called the `RegisterGlobalFilters` method, which in turn creates a new instance of `HandleErrorAttribute`. To change the way that errors are handled, we can set values for the properties that `HandleErrorAttribute` defines. The most important of these properties is `View`, as shown in Listing 28-26.

Listing 28-26. *Specifying a view for HandleErrorAttribute to use*

```
public static void RegisterGlobalFilters(GlobalFilterCollection filters) {
    filters.Add(new HandleErrorAttribute() { View = "CustomError"});
}
```

If we don't define a value for the `View` property, then the `Views/Shared/Error.cshtml` view will be used. This is the view that renders the content shown in Figure 28-7. In the listing, I have specified that a different view be used, one called `CustomError`. I have created a view called `CustomError.cshtml` in the `Views/Shared` folder; the contents are shown in Listing 28-27.

Listing 28-27. The CustomError.cshtml view

```
@model HandleErrorInfo

@{
    ViewBag.Title = "Unhandled Error";
}

<h2>Unhandled Error</h2>

<table>
    <tr><th>Controller</th><td>@Model.ControllerName</td></tr>
    <tr><th>Action</th><td>@Model.ActionName</td></tr>
    <tr><th>Type</th><td>@Model.Exception.GetType()</td></tr>
    <tr><th>Message</th><td>@Model.Exception.Message</td></tr>
</table>
```

The error view is like any other view, except that the view model is a `HandleErrorInfo` object. The `HandleErrorInfo` class defines three useful properties, which are described in Table 28-1.

Table 28-1. Properties of the HandleErrorInfo Class

Property	Description
ControllerName	The name of the controller (this will be Reports rather than ReportsController)
ActionName	The name of the action
Exception	The exception object that has been thrown

In the listing, I use these properties to display some simple information about the exception. You can see how the view renders in Figure 28-8.

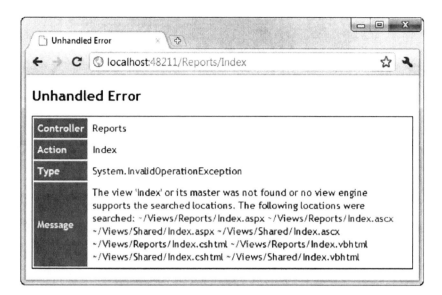

Figure 28-8. *Rendering a custom error view*

■ **Tip**   It is important to ensure that no exceptions are thrown when your custom error view is rendered. One way of doing this is to keep the view as simple as possible, but even so, you should test thoroughly to make sure that the view will always render. If an exception is thrown, then the default ASP.NET platform exception handling will be used, and you'll see the Yellow Screen of Death, defeating the point of defining and using custom error handlers.

Setting a Global Exception-Specific Error Handler

We can register additional instances of the `HandleErrorAttribute` to deal with specific types of exceptions. To demonstrate this, I have created a view for the `Index` action method (`Views/Reports/Index.cshtml`), which will throw an exception. Listing 28-28 shows the contents of this view.

Listing 28-28. *A view that throws an exception*

```
@{
    ViewBag.Title = "Index";
}

<h4>Index</h4>
```

```
@{
    throw new FormatException("This is my exception");
}
```

In this view, I create and throw a FormatException. We can create a handler for this type of exception, defining a new HandleErrorAttribute object in Global.asax and setting a value for the ExceptionType property, as shown in Listing 28-29.

Listing 28-29. *Defining a global type-specific handler*

```
public static void RegisterGlobalFilters(GlobalFilterCollection filters) {
    filters.Add(new HandleErrorAttribute() { View = "CustomError"});
    filters.Add(new HandleErrorAttribute() { ExceptionType=typeof(FormatException),
        View = "FormatError" });
}
```

This addition tells the MVC framework that if a FormatException is thrown, it should be handled by displaying the FormatError view. Listing 28-30 shows the contents of this view, created in the Views/Shared project folder.

Listing 28-30. *The FormatError.cshtml view*

```
@model HandleErrorInfo

@{
    ViewBag.Title = "Unhandled Format Error";
}

<h2>Format Error</h2>

<table>
    <tr><th>Controller</th><td>@Model.ControllerName</td></tr>
    <tr><th>Action</th><td>@Model.ActionName</td></tr>
    <tr><th>Message</th><td>@Model.Exception.Message</td></tr>
</table>
```

This is a simple variation on the previous error view but is distinct enough so that we can tell when the MVC framework uses it. If you start the application and navigate to /Reports/Index, you'll see the new template in use, as shown in Figure 28-9.

Figure 28-9. *A view rendered by a global type-specific error handler*

Defining a Local Error Handler

The previous examples have demonstrated how to handle exceptions that occur anywhere in the application. We can also be more specific and define a handler that applies to a single action method, as demonstrated by Listing 28-31.

Listing 28-31. *Defining a local error handler*

```
using System.Web.Mvc;
using EventRegistration.Models.Domain.Repository;
using System;

namespace EventRegistration.Controllers {

    public class ReportsController : Controller {
        private IRepository repository;

        public ReportsController(IRepository repo) {
            repository = repo;
        }

        [HandleError(ExceptionType=typeof(FormatException), View="CustomError")]
        public ActionResult Index() {
            return View();
        }

        [HttpPost]
        public ActionResult Index(string report) {
            switch (report) {
                case "Competitions":
                    return View("CompetitionReport", repository.Competitions);
```

```
                case "Registrations":
                    return View("RegistrationReport", repository.Registrations);
                default:
                    return View();
            }
        }
    }
}
```

This attribute will be applied to handle any exception that arises in one of the Index action methods in the controller, and this includes any exception that is thrown while rendering the view. The ExceptionType and View properties have the same meaning as when we used the HandleErrorAttribute class in Global.asax, so this attribute tells the MVC framework to display the CustomError view when a FormatException goes unhandled by the action method.

Attributes to an action method take precedence over those defined globally, as we can see if we navigate to /Reports/Index. Even though the global policy is to handle FormatException instances with the FormatError view, we see the CustomError view displayed in accordance with the attribute in the listing, as shown in Figure 28-10.

Figure 28-10. An error view rendered from an action method attribute

Summary

In this chapter, we looked at some of the important aspects of action methods and their role in the controller and the wider MVC framework application. I showed you how we can issue next-step instructions by returning ActionResult objects, how to pass data from an action method to a view, how to enrich views using child actions, and how to deal with exceptions that arise in an action method. I also showed you how to use HTTP method selector attributes. These are most often used to separate action methods to deal with GET and POST requests to simplify form processing, a topic we will examine in more depth in the following chapter.

CHAPTER 29

Working with Model Binding and Validation

In this chapter, we will look at model binding and validation. Model binding is one of the MVC framework features that I find most appealing. It removes the tedious work of constructing model objects from request data. Validation allows us to ensure that the data we receive can be used to create valid model objects, something that goes hand in hand with the model binding process.

Understanding Model Binding

Model binding is the process of creating .NET objects using the data sent by the browser in an HTP request. I touched on model binding in Chapter 23, but let's recap that example to set a foundation for this chapter, going back and resetting the code for our `RegistrationController` class. Listing 29-1 shows the contents of the controller.

Listing 29-1. The basic RegistrationController class

```
using System.Web.Mvc;
using EventRegistration.Models.Domain;
using EventRegistration.Models.Domain.Repository;

namespace EventRegistration.Controllers {

    public class RegistrationController : Controller {
        private IRepository repository;

        public RegistrationController(IRepository repo) {
            repository = repo;
        }
```

```
        public ActionResult Index() {
            ViewBag.Competitions = repository.Competitions;
            return View();
        }
    }
}
```

This controller contains a single action method, called **Index**. The action renders the default view and passes the set of **Competition** objects from the repository via the **ViewBag**. Listing 29-2 shows the **Views/Registration/Index.cshtml** view, rendered by the **Index** action method.

Listing 29-2. *The Index.cshtml view*

```
@{
    ViewBag.Title = "Registration";
}

<h4>Registration</h4>

@using (Html.BeginForm("HandleIndexPost", "Registration")) {
    <table>
        <tr><td>Name:</td><td>@Html.Editor("Name")</td></tr>
        <tr><td>Age:</td><td>@Html.Editor("Age")</td></tr>
        <tr><td>City:</td><td>@Html.Editor("HomeCity")</td></tr>
        <tr>
            <td>Competition:</td>
            <td>
                @Html.DropDownList("CompetitionID", new SelectList(ViewBag.Competitions,
                    "ID", "Name"))
            </td>
        </tr>
        <tr><td colspan="2"><input type="submit" value="Register" /></td></tr>
    </table>
}
```

Notice that I have used an overload of the **Html.BeginForm** helper, which lets me specify the action and controller to which the form posts back. I'll come back to this shortly. When we target the action method (by requesting **/Registration/Index**, for example), we see the form in Figure 29-1.

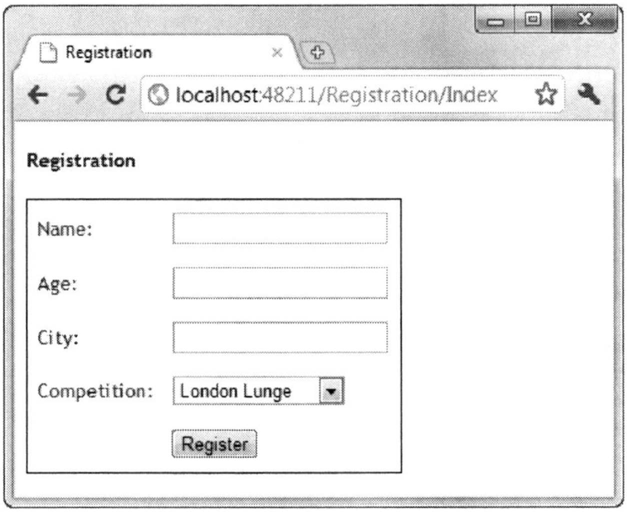

Figure 29-1. *Rendering a simple form*

The `input` elements in the HTML form gather values that correspond to the properties in the `Registration` object. By using the `Html.Editor` helpers, I ensure that the `ID` and `name` attribute values of the input elements are given values that match the properties to which they correspond. For example, here is the input element rendered by the call to `@Html.Editor("Name")`:

```
<input class="text-box single-line" id="Name" name="Name" type="text" value="" />
```

Handling the Form Post Without Model Binding

We need to handle the `POST` request when the user clicks the Register button and submits to the form, and this is where our model binding starts. Listing 29-3 shows how we would process a form post without any model binding at all.

Listing 29-3. *Handling the form post*

```
using System.Linq;
using System.Web.Mvc;
using EventRegistration.Models.Domain;
using EventRegistration.Models.Domain.Repository;

namespace EventRegistration.Controllers {

    public class RegistrationController : Controller {
        private IRepository repository;
```

```
    public RegistrationController(IRepository repo) {
        repository = repo;
    }

    public ActionResult Index() {
        ViewBag.Competitions = repository.Competitions;
        return View();
    }

    [HttpPost]
    public ActionResult HandleIndexPost() {

        Registration registration = new Registration();
        registration.Name = Request.Form["Name"];
        registration.Age = int.Parse(Request.Form["Age"]);
        registration.HomeCity = Request.Form["HomeCity"];
        registration.CompetitionID = int.Parse(Request.Form["CompetitionID"]);

        registration.Competition = repository.Competitions
            .Where(x => x.ID == registration.CompetitionID).FirstOrDefault();

        repository.SaveRegistration(registration);
        return View("RegistrationComplete", registration);
    }
  }
}
```

I have added a new action method called HandleIndexPost, which corresponds to the way I used the Html.BeginForm helper earlier. It is unusual to have two different action method names in this situation, but I want to demonstrate a method without parameters, and since I already have a parameterless Index method, I need to use a different name.

Without model binding, we have to take responsibility for obtaining the values from the form via the Request parameter, parsing the values to the correct types and assigning the results to the properties of a Registration object we created. This is a basic but serviceable approach and will be familiar to you if you have done web development with other frameworks (or Web Forms).

Handling the Form Post with Basic Binding

The most basic way of using model binding is to declare parameters with the same names as the input elements in the HTML form. Listing 29-4 shows how we can do this.

Listing 29-4. Using model-bound parameters

```
using System.Linq;
using System.Web.Mvc;
using EventRegistration.Models.Domain;
using EventRegistration.Models.Domain.Repository;

namespace EventRegistration.Controllers {
```

```
public class RegistrationController : Controller {
    private IRepository repository;

    public RegistrationController(IRepository repo) {
        repository = repo;
    }

    public ActionResult Index() {
        ViewBag.Competitions = repository.Competitions;
        return View();
    }

    [HttpPost]
    public ActionResult HandleIndexPost(string name, int age,
        string homecity, int competitionid) {

        Registration registration = new Registration();
        registration.Name = name;
        registration.Age = age;
        registration.HomeCity = homecity;
        registration.CompetitionID = competitionid;

        registration.Competition = repository.Competitions
            .Where(x => x.ID == registration.CompetitionID).FirstOrDefault();

        repository.SaveRegistration(registration);
        return View("RegistrationComplete", registration);
    }
}
```

We are still responsible for creating the **Registration** object, but the MVC framework will take the form values, convert them to the type specified by the parameter value, and pass them to our action method. During this process, the MVC framework looks for values in a range of places. In the case of the name parameter, it will check for the following:

- `Request.Form["name"]`

- `RouteData.Values["name"]`

- `Request.QueryString["name"]`

- `Request.Files["name"]`

The search stops as soon as a value is found. Notice that case doesn't matter. An action method parameter of name will match to an input element with Name for an attribute value.

Handling the Form Post with a Complex Type

The previous example showed how we can use model binding with simple types. This is useful, but we are still responsible for creating the **Registration** object we need and setting the values for the properties. Fortunately, the MVC framework also supports binding to complex types, which means we can tidy up our action method even further. Listing 29-5 shows how we do this.

Listing 29-5. Using complex-type model binding

```
using System.Linq;
using System.Web.Mvc;
using EventRegistration.Models.Domain;
using EventRegistration.Models.Domain.Repository;

namespace EventRegistration.Controllers {

    public class RegistrationController : Controller {
        private IRepository repository;

        public RegistrationController(IRepository repo) {
            repository = repo;
        }

        public ActionResult Index() {
            ViewBag.Competitions = repository.Competitions;
            return View();
        }

        [HttpPost]
        public ActionResult HandleIndexPost(Registration registration) {

            registration.Competition = repository.Competitions
                .Where(x => x.ID == registration.CompetitionID).FirstOrDefault();

            repository.SaveRegistration(registration);
            return View("RegistrationComplete", registration);
        }
    }
}
```

When we specify a complex type as the parameter for an action method, the MVC framework tries to find values for all of the properties and fields that the type defines. It then creates a new instance of the complex type, populates it with the values it finds, and passes it to the action method, performing any required type conversions along the way.

This is an incredibly neat and convenient feature. We get to focus on what we are doing with our model objects and ignore how they are being constructed from the form that the user has submitted.

Handling the Form Post with a Custom Model Binder

There is still a problem with the previous example. We have to set the Competition property of the Registration object ourselves. This is because Competition is a navigation property that is managed by the Entity Framework when we request objects from the repository, and the Registration object in the listing is created during the model binding process. We can address this by creating a custom model binding, which will be used any time that an action method demands a Registration parameter.

This simplest way to create a custom model binder is to derive a class from `DefaultModelBinder` and override the `BindModel` method. As long as we are careful to call the base class implementation of `BindModel`, we can benefit from the default binder's functionality and just add the logic we require to finish the binding process.

Listing 29-6 shows a model binder that creates `Registration` objects. I called this class `RegistrationModelBinder`, and I created it in the `Infrastructure` project folder.

Listing 29-6. *A custom model binder*

```
using System.Linq;
using System.Web.Mvc;
using EventRegistration.Models.Domain;
using EventRegistration.Models.Domain.Repository;

namespace EventRegistration.Infrastructure {
    public class RegistrationModelBinder : DefaultModelBinder {

        public override object BindModel(ControllerContext controllerContext,
            ModelBindingContext bindingContext) {

            Registration reg = (Registration)base.BindModel(controllerContext,
                bindingContext);

            reg.ID = int.Parse(GetValue(bindingContext, "ID", "0"));

            IRepository repo = DependencyResolver.Current.GetService<IRepository>();

            reg.Competition = repo.Competitions
                .Where(x => x.ID == reg.CompetitionID).FirstOrDefault();

            return reg;
        }

        private string GetValue(ModelBindingContext context, string key,
            string defaultValue = null) {

            ValueProviderResult vpr = context.ValueProvider.GetValue(key);
            return vpr == null ? defaultValue : vpr.AttemptedValue;
        }
    }
}
```

The MVC framework calls the `BindModel` method when it needs to create a `Registration` object as part of the model binding process. In this method, I call the base class `BindModel` implementation, which will return a `Registration` object that is populated with values from the request. To complete the binding process, I use the repository to find the appropriate `Competition` object and assign it to the `Registration` object's `Competition` property.

We don't have to rely on the default model binder to generate property values. We can do that ourselves as well. I have defined a convenience method in a custom model binder called `GetValue` that retrieves values from the request and simplifies dealing with the slightly awkward `ValueProvider` syntax. It also allows me to supply an optional parameter to deal with default values. In the listing, I use the

GetValue method to set a value for the ID property, with a default value of 0 if there is no value available for this property in the request.

Notice that I don't use dependency injection in the custom model binder class. This is because new instances are created through the System.Activator class, which requires a parameterless constructor. This can be changed through some of the advanced customization options that the MVC framework supports, but it is as easy to use the dependency resolver facility, like this:

```
IRepository repo = DependencyResolver.Current.GetService<IRepository>();
```

The static DependencyResolver.Current property returns our Ninject dependency resolver implementation, allowing me to request an implementation of the IRepository interface. We tell the MVC framework to use our custom model binder by applying the ModelBinder attribute to the model class, as shown in Listing 29-7.

Listing 29-7. Using the ModelBinder attribute to associate a custom model binder with a model type

```
using System.Web.Mvc;
using EventRegistration.Infrastructure;
namespace EventRegistration.Models.Domain {

    [ModelBinder(typeof(RegistrationModelBinder))]
    public class Registration {

        public int ID { get; set; }

        public string Name { get; set; }
        public string HomeCity { get; set; }
        public int Age { get; set; }

        public int CompetitionID { get; set; }

        public virtual Competition Competition {get; set;}
    }
}
```

The sole argument to the ModelBinder class is the type of the custom binder that should be used to bind instances from requests. As you might imagine, in this case the type is RegistrationModelBinder.

SOLVING THE TWO CONTEXT PROBLEM WITH NINJECT

In Chapter 24, I told you to apply the InRequestScope method to the Ninject registration statement for the IRepository interface. If we had not done this, we would see an exception thrown by the application, telling us that "An entity object cannot be referenced by multiple instances of IEntityChangeTracker."

If we let Ninject create a new EFRepository instance each time an implementation of IRepository is requested, then we create one instance in the model binder and one instance in the controller. The model binder loads a Competition object through one repository and assigns it to an object that is then saved to the database through the *other* repository. The Entity Framework can't cope with tracking objects across multiple repositories (which is fair enough, because it is fraught with difficulty) and so throws an exception.

There are several ways to handle this problem, but the simplest is to have Ninject create only one repository implementation per request. This ensures that all of the objects are loaded and saved through a single repository instance.

We can now simplify our action method even further, as shown by Listing 29-8.

Listing 29-8. *Further simplifying the action method*

```
using System.Linq;
using System.Web.Mvc;
using EventRegistration.Models.Domain;
using EventRegistration.Models.Domain.Repository;

namespace EventRegistration.Controllers {

    public class RegistrationController : Controller {
        private IRepository repository;

        public RegistrationController(IRepository repo) {
            repository = repo;
        }

        public ActionResult Index() {
            ViewBag.Competitions = repository.Competitions;
            return View();
        }

        [HttpPost]
        public ActionResult HandleIndexPost(Registration registration) {
            repository.SaveRegistration(registration);
            return View("RegistrationComplete", registration);
        }
    }
}
```

We have reached the point where our action method doesn't have to worry about creating any aspect of the Registration object from the form data. Everything is taken care of during the model binding process. All we have to do is save the object and tell the MVC framework to render the RegistrationComplete view.

Validating Models

The MVC framework automatically performs some basic validation when it performs model binding. In this section, I'll show you what we get built in and how we can add to that to perform more sophisticated validation.

Setting Up Basic Model Validation

The Age property in the Registration class is defined as an int, and during the model binding process, the MVC framework has to convert the string value that has been provided in the request. If the request value cannot be converted to an int, then the model is classified as *invalid*.

To detect and handle invalid models, we need to make some enhancements to our controller and view. Listing 29-9 shows the changes to the RegistrationController class.

Listing 29-9. *Enhancing the controller to support model validation*

```
using System.Linq;
using System.Web.Mvc;
using EventRegistration.Models.Domain;
using EventRegistration.Models.Domain.Repository;

namespace EventRegistration.Controllers {

    public class RegistrationController : Controller {
        private IRepository repository;

        public RegistrationController(IRepository repo) {
            repository = repo;
        }

        public ActionResult Index() {
            ViewBag.Competitions = repository.Competitions;
            return View(new Registration());
        }

        [HttpPost]
        public ActionResult HandleIndexPost(Registration registration) {
            if (ModelState.IsValid) {
                repository.SaveRegistration(registration);
                return View("RegistrationComplete", registration);
            } else {
                ViewBag.Competitions = repository.Competitions;
                return View("Index", registration);
            }
        }
    }
}
```

We can detect whether there has been a problem with the model binding validation by reading the ModelDate.IsValid property. If IsValid returns true, then we can proceed as normal and save the Registration object. If IsValid returns false, then we do something different. We render the Index view again, passing in the Registration object that the model binding process tried (and failed) to create.

■ **Note** Notice that I have also changed the `Index` method so that it creates a new `Registration` object and uses it as the view model object. This is to simplify making the view strongly typed.

This may seem counterintuitive, but the MVC framework has a clever trick when dealing with model objects that are invalid. To take advantage of this, we need to make a further change and make the `Index.cshtml` view strongly typed, as shown in Listing 29-10.

Listing 29-10. Making the Index view strongly typed

```
@model EventRegistration.Models.Domain.Registration
@{
    ViewBag.Title = "Registration";
}

<h4>Registration</h4>

@using (Html.BeginForm("HandleIndexPost", "Registration")) {
    @Html.HiddenFor(x => x.ID)
    <table>
        <tr><td>Name:</td><td>@Html.EditorFor(x => x.Name)</td></tr>
        <tr><td>Age:</td><td>@Html.EditorFor(x => x.Age)</td></tr>
        <tr><td>City:</td><td>@Html.EditorFor(x => x.HomeCity)</td></tr>
        <tr>
            <td>Competition:</td>
            <td>
                @Html.DropDownListFor(x => x.CompetitionID,
                    new SelectList(ViewBag.Competitions, "ID", "Name"))
            </td>
        </tr>
        <tr><td colspan="2"><input type="submit" value="Register" /></td></tr>
    </table>
}
```

I have added an `@model` directive and used the strongly typed templated helpers to generate editors for the properties in the `Registration` class. If we start the application and navigate to `/Registration/Index`, we see the view rendered as shown in Figure 29-1. The changes we have made are not visible yet.

■ **Note** I have also added a `hidden` element for the `ID` property. This is to make life easier later when we come to apply modelwide validation rules.

Here is the HTML generated by the `Html.EditorFor` helper for the `Age` property:

```
<input class="text-box single-line" data-val="true"
    data-val-number="The field Age must be a number."
    data-val-required="The Age field is required." id="Age" name="Age"
    type="text" value="" />
```

Ignore the `data-val-number` and `data-val-required` attributes for the moment. The purpose of these will become clear as we work through the examples in this chapter.

Now we can test the model validation. Enter the word twenty into the Age text box and click the Register button. Although twenty might be a valid age, we have expressed it in a way that the MVC framework cannot convert into an `int` value. This means that the model is invalid. We detect the validation issue in the action method and pass the malformed `Registration` object as the view model object to render the `Index` view again, but this time, the MVC framework highlights that there is a problem, as shown in Figure 29-2.

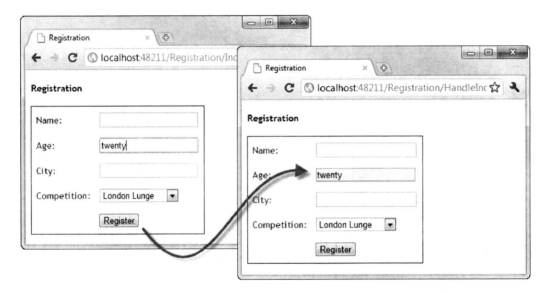

Figure 29-2. *The built-in model validation*

During the view rendering process, the templated helper has realized that there is a problem with the `Age` property and rendered different HTML.

```
<input class="input-validation-error text-box single-line" data-val="true"
    data-val-number="The field Age must be a number."
    data-val-required="The Age field is required." id="Age" name="Age"
    type="text" value="twenty" />
```

To reflect the validation error, the helper has added a new CSS class to the input element called `input-validation-error`. This class is defined in `Content/Site.css` (which is referenced by the default view, `_Layout.cshtml`) as follows:

```
.input-validation-error {
    border: 1px solid #ff0000;
    background-color: #ffeeee;
}
```

Model validation is performed each time the user clicks the Register button, and the model won't be valid until the user corrects the problem.

Using the Validation Helpers

We are now able to indicate to the user that there is a problem. To give them an idea about how they might correct the problem, we need to use some validation-specific helper methods in the Index.cshtml view. Listing 29-11 shows how we do this.

Listing 29-11. Adding validation details to the Index view

```
@model EventRegistration.Models.Domain.Registration
@{
    ViewBag.Title = "Registration";
}

<h4>Registration</h4>

@Html.ValidationSummary("Please fix the following errors:")

@using (Html.BeginForm("HandleIndexPost", "Registration")) {
    @Html.HiddenFor(x => x.ID)
    <table>
        <tr>
            <td>Name:</td>
            <td>@Html.EditorFor(x => x.Name)</td>
            <td>@Html.ValidationMessageFor(x => x.Name)</td>
        </tr>
        <tr>
            <td>Age:</td>
            <td>@Html.EditorFor(x => x.Age)</td>
            <td>@Html.ValidationMessageFor(x => x.Age)</td>
        </tr>
        <tr>
            <td>City:</td>
            <td>@Html.EditorFor(x => x.HomeCity)</td>
            <td>@Html.ValidationMessageFor(x => x.HomeCity)</td>
        </tr>
        <tr>
            <td>Competition:</td>
            <td>
                @Html.DropDownListFor(x => x.CompetitionID,
                    new SelectList(ViewBag.Competitions, "ID", "Name"))
            </td>
```

```
            <td>@Html.ValidationMessageFor(x => x.CompetitionID)</td>
        </tr>
        <tr><td colspan="2"><input type="submit" value="Register" /></td></tr>
    </table>
}
```

Two kinds of validation helper are available, and I have used them both in the view. The first is `Html.ValidationSummary`, and it generates a summary of all the validation errors that were detected. The second kind is `Html.ValidationMessageFor`, which reports on the validation errors for a single property.

■ **Note** The `Html.ValidationMessage` helper is the weakly typed equivalent to the `Html.ValidationMessageFor` helper. I like to use the strongly typed helpers, but either works.

When we submit the form now, we get some more useful information, as shown in Figure 29-3.

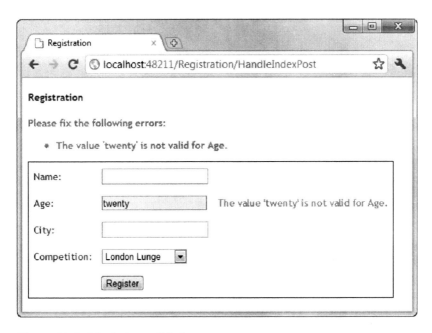

Figure 29-3. *Displaying validation messages*

It is overkill to duplicate the same message in the summary and alongside the property, but we'll tweak this later. Now the user knows that the value they have entered isn't valid and they can take steps to correct it.

Defining Validation Rules Using Metadata

Now that we have set up model validation, we can define our own validation rules using metadata applied to the model class. Listing 29-12 shows how we can do this.

Listing 29-12. *Applying validation attributes to a model class*

```
using System.Web.Mvc;
using EventRegistration.Infrastructure;
using System.ComponentModel.DataAnnotations;

namespace EventRegistration.Models.Domain {

    [ModelBinder(typeof(RegistrationModelBinder))]
    public class Registration {

        [Required]
        public int ID { get; set; }

        [Required]
        public string Name { get; set; }

        [Required]
        public string HomeCity { get; set; }

        [Required(ErrorMessage="Please enter an age")]
        [Range(18, 100, ErrorMessage = "Please enter an age between 18 and 100")]
        public int Age { get; set; }

        [Required]
        public int CompetitionID { get; set; }

        public virtual Competition Competition { get; set; }
    }
}
```

I have demonstrated a couple of different validation attributes in the listing. The Required attribute states that the user must provide a value for the property, and the Range attribute specifies that the value supplied must be within a given range (in this case between 18 and 100, inclusive).

■ **Note** Notice that I have added the Required attribute to the ID and CompetitionID properties. I have done this even though we don't use the ID property when gathering data for a new registration and that the CompetitionID value is set from a drop-down menu. This is because the validation attributes are applied to the model, not the controller or action method. If we created actions that let us edit existing records or select events by entering a name, we would want to ensure that values were supplied for these properties, too.

Table 29-1 shows the set of built-in validation attributes that the model binder recognizes.

Table 29-1. *The Built-in Validation Attributes*

Attribute	Example	Description
Compare	`[Compare ("MyOtherProperty")]`	Two properties must have the same value. This is useful when you ask the user to provide the same information twice, such as an e-mail address or a password.
Range	`[Range(10, 20)]`	A numeric value (or any property type that implements `IComparable`) must not lie beyond the specified minimum and maximum values. To specify a boundary on only one side, use a `MinValue` or `MaxValue` constant—for example, `[Range(int.MinValue, 50)]`.
RegularExpression	`[RegularExpression ("pattern")]`	A string value must match the specified regular expression pattern. Note that the pattern has to match the *entire* user-supplied value, not just a substring within it. By default, it matches case sensitively, but you can make it case insensitive by applying the `(?i)` modifier—that is, `[RegularExpression("(?i)mypattern")]`.
Required	`[Required]`	The value must not be empty or be a string consisting only of spaces. If you want to treat whitespace as valid, use `[Required(AllowEmptyStrings = true)]`.
StringLength	`[StringLength(10)]`	A string value must not be longer than the specified maximum length. We can also specify a minimum length: `[StringLength(10, MinimumLength=2)]`.

Each of the validation attributes will display a default error message to the user, but we can specify a custom message by setting a value for the `ErrorMessage` property, like this:

```
[Required(ErrorMessage="Please enter an age")]
```

We can see the effect of the validation attributes if we start the application; navigate to `/Registration/Index` and click the Register button without entering any values. The attributes that I applied to each property will cause the model validation process to fail, leading to the error messages shown in Figure 29-4.

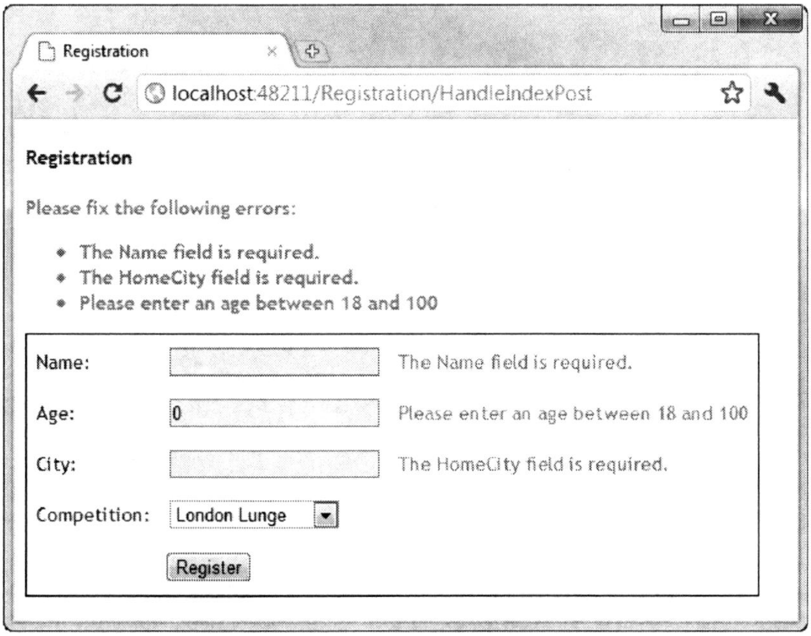

Figure 29-4. *Error messages resulting from validation metadata*

Each time we click the Register button, the data that we have entered into the fields is validated using the attributes we applied to the model.

The `Age` property has a default value of zero because we pass a newly created `Registration` object as the view model in the `Index` action method. We can fix this by changing the helper and checking for the zero value, like this:

```
<td>@Html.TextBox("Age", Model.Age == 0 ? "" : Model.Age.ToString())</td>
```

Performing Additional Property-Level Validation

The validation attributes are applied whenever our model type is bound. Sometimes, we need to perform more specialized validation, which can be unique to a given action method. Let's imagine that we need to make sure that the value of the `Name` property is unique only when a new registration is created. Listing 29-13 shows how we can perform validation on properties in the action method.

Listing 29-13. *Performing validation an action method*

```
[HttpPost]
public ActionResult HandleIndexPost(Registration registration) {

    if (ModelState.IsValidField("Name") &&
        repository.Registrations.Where(x => x.Name == registration.Name).Count() > 0) {
```

```
        ModelState.AddModelError("Name",
            "A registration has already been made in this name");
    }

    if (ModelState.IsValid) {
        repository.SaveRegistration(registration);
        return View("RegistrationComplete", registration);
    } else {
        ViewBag.Competitions = repository.Competitions;
        return View("Index", registration);
    }
}
```

By the time that the action method is invoked, our model has already been through validation. This means we can use the results of the validation to see whether it is worth performing our additional checks. We do this by calling the ModelState.IsValidField method, passing in the name of the property we want to check as an argument.

If the IsValidField method returns false, we know that the property value has not passed validation, and there is no point in us muddying the water by reporting additional errors. If the method returns true, then we know the property value has passed through validation and we can safely apply additional tests.

In the listing, I use LINQ to see whether there are any Registration objects that have the same Name value as the model object. If there are, then this fails my validation check, and I call the ModelState.AddModelError method to register the problem. The arguments to the AddModelError method are the name of the property and the error message to display.

If we submit the form using a Name value that we know exists in the database, we see the error message, as illustrated by Figure 29-5.

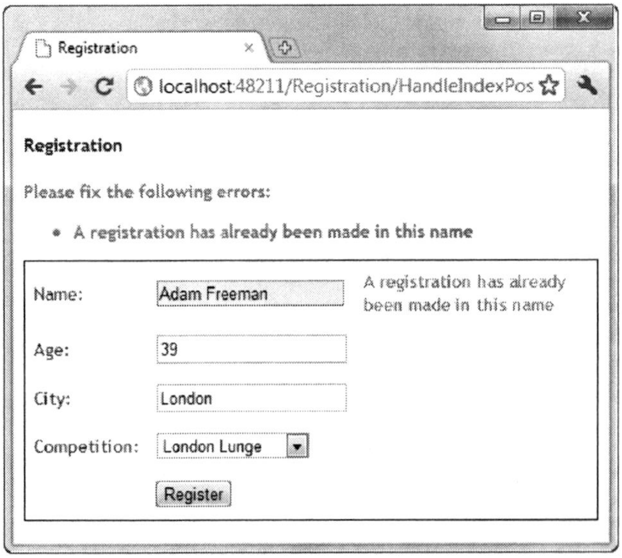

Figure 29-5. *An additional validation message*

In this way, we can add situation-specific validation to our model and go beyond what we have defined using metadata.

Performing Model-Level Validation

All of the validation we have done so far has been at the level of the individual property. Sometimes, however, we need to validate the overall model, ensuring that the combination of property values is valid. As an example, let's imagine that the Paris Panic event only allows competitors who are older than 40. Validating this rule requires checking the combination of the Age and CompetitionID properties. Listing 29-14 shows how we can perform this kind of validation.

Listing 29-14. Performing model-level validation

```
[HttpPost]
public ActionResult HandleIndexPost(Registration registration) {

    if (ModelState.IsValidField("Name") &&
        repository.Registrations.Where(x => x.Name == registration.Name).Count() > 0) {

        ModelState.AddModelError("Name",
            "A registration has already been made in this name");
    }

    if (ModelState.IsValidField("Age") && ModelState.IsValidField("CompetitionID")) {
        if (registration.Competition.Name == "Paris Panic" && registration.Age < 40) {
            ModelState.AddModelError(string.Empty,
                "You must be at least 40 to do the Paris Panic");
        }
    }

    if (ModelState.IsValid) {
        repository.SaveRegistration(registration);
        return View("RegistrationComplete", registration);
    } else {
        ViewBag.Competitions = repository.Competitions;
        return View("Index", registration);
    }
}
```

Once again I use the IsValidField method to check that the fields I need to work with have passed validation. I then perform my validation check. If there is a problem, I use the AddModelError method to register the problem. The difference is that I use the empty string as the property name. This tells the MVC framework that the problem is with the overall model, rather than an individual property. Figure 29-6 shows what happens when this validation message is displayed.

Figure 29-6. *A model-level validation error message*

The message is displayed only in the summary. There is no particular property to which the error can be attributed, of course. The final tweak we can make is to have the summary display *only* model-level errors. This prevents the duplication of error messages that can be attributed to individual properties, leaving only the model-level errors displayed. Listing 29-15 shows the required change to the Index.cshtml view.

Listing 29-15. *Showing only model-level errors in the validation summary*

```
@model EventRegistration.Models.Domain.Registration
@{
    ViewBag.Title = "Registration";
}

<h4>Registration</h4>

@Html.ValidationSummary(true, "Please fix the following errors:")

@using (Html.BeginForm("HandleIndexPost", "Registration")) {

    @Html.HiddenFor(x => x.ID)
```

```
<table>
    <tr>
        <td>Name:</td>
        <td>@Html.EditorFor(x => x.Name)</td>
        <td>@Html.ValidationMessageFor(x => x.Name)</td>
    </tr>
...
```

The additional argument I have added to call to the `Html.ValidationSummary` helper specifies that only model-level messages should be displayed, as shown in Figure 29-7.

Figure 29-7. *Limiting the validation summary to model-level validation errors*

Using Client-Side Validation

The validation in the previous examples has been performed at the server, in response to the form being submitted. The MVC framework supports *unobtrusive client-side validation.* The term *unobtrusive* means that validation rules are expressed using attributes added to the HTML elements that we generate. These are interpreted by a JavaScript library that is included as part of the MVC Framework, which uses the attribute values to configure the jQuery Validation library, which does the actual validation work. (We saw the jQuery Validation library in Chapter 10, but we will only work with it indirectly in this chapter.)

■ **Note** MVC version 3 introduced support for jQuery validation, whereas earlier versions relied on JavaScript libraries that Microsoft produced. These were not highly regarded, and although they are still included in the MVC framework, there is no reason to use them.

You will encounter the word *unobtrusive* used more broadly in the context of JavaScript. This is a loose term that has three key characteristics. The first is that the JavaScript that performs the validation is kept separate from the HTML elements, which means we don't have to include client-side validation logic in our views and that the HTML we generate is easier to read.

The second characteristic is that the validation is performed using *progressive enhancement*. This means that if a user's browser doesn't support all the JavaScript features we require for client-side validation, the validation will be performed using simpler techniques. For example, if the user has disabled JavaScript, then server-side validation will be seamlessly performed without the user being otherwise penalized (no unpleasant error messages or special steps to take). The third characteristic is a set of best practices to mitigate the effect of browser inconsistencies and behaviors. This is one of the main goals of the jQuery library.

The MVC framework support for client-side validation is controlled by two settings in the Web.config file, as shown in Listing 29-16.

Listing 29-16. Controlling client-side validation

```
<configuration>
  <appSettings>
    <add key="ClientValidationEnabled" value="true"/>
    <add key="UnobtrusiveJavaScriptEnabled" value="true"/>
  </appSettings>
...
```

Both of these settings must be true for client-side validation to work. When Visual Studio created your MVC 3 project, these entries were set to true by default. In addition to the configuration settings, we must ensure that there are references to three specific JavaScript libraries, as shown in Listing 29-17.

Listing 29-17. Referencing the JavaScript libraries required for client-side validation

```
<!DOCTYPE html>
<html>
<head>
    <title>@ViewBag.Title</title>
    <link href="@Url.Content("~/Content/Site.css")" rel="stylesheet" type="text/css" />

    <script src="@Url.Content("~/Scripts/jquery-1.5.1.min.js")"
        type="text/javascript"></script>

    <script src="@Url.Content("~/Scripts/jquery.validate.min.js")"
        type="text/javascript"></script>

    <script src="@Url.Content("~/Scripts/jquery.validate.unobtrusive.min.js")"
        type="text/javascript"></script>
```

```
</head>
<body>
    @RenderBody()
</body>
</html>
```

We can add these files to each and every view in which we want to use client-side validation, but it is usually simpler and easier to reference the files from a layout file, as shown in the listing.

■ **Caution** The order in which the jQuery files are referenced is significant. If you change the order, you will find that the client validation is not performed.

The scripts folder contains two versions of each JavaScript library. The versions whose name ends with min.js are the *minimized* versions, meaning that all the whitespace, comments, and other nonessential content have been removed to reduce the size of the library file. The minimized files can be much smaller and are typically used in production to reduce the amount of data that the client downloads. During development, the unminimized versions are typically used so that the JavaScript can be debugged (or just read) if problems arise.

The nice thing about the unobtrusive validation support is that it works on the HTML that is emitted as a consequence of applying our validation attributes. These are the data- attributes that we saw earlier in the chapter. We don't have to make any additional changes to get the client-side validation support.

■ **Note** There is one more client validation technique. It relies on Ajax, and I describe it in Chapter 30.

Summary

In this chapter, we have seen how the MVC framework supports model binding to help us simplify our action methods. Model binding is an elegant feature that allows us to focus our efforts on working with model objects, without having to pay attention to how they are created from the request data.

I showed you how to customize the model binding process and how you can validate that the data received as part of the request will lead to a valid model object. Finally, I showed you the support for unobtrusive client-side validation, which allows you to perform simple validation on property values before the form is submitted for processing.

Using Unobtrusive Ajax

The MVC framework contains support for *unobtrusive Ajax*. This is similar to the unobtrusive client-side validation in Chapter 18, in that it doesn't involve inserting extra blocks of JavaScript code at arbitrary points in your HTML document. Like the client-side validation support, MVC unobtrusive Ajax is based on the jQuery JavaScript library, which was introduced in Chapters 10 and 11.

Preparing the Project

We are going to build on the example we used in the previous chapter. In particular, we will focus on the `Report` controller, which we last saw in Chapter 28 when we looked at how to handle exceptions in controllers. Listing 30-1 shows the contents of the `ReportController` class, including some additions to prepare for this chapter.

Listing 30-1. The ReportController class

```
using System.Linq;
using System.Web.Mvc;
using EventRegistration.Models.Domain.Repository;

namespace EventRegistration.Controllers {

    public class ReportsController : Controller {
        private IRepository repository;

        public ReportsController(IRepository repo) {
            repository = repo;
        }

        public ActionResult Index(string competition) {
            ViewBag.CompetitionNames = repository.Competitions.Select(x => x.Name);
            if (string.IsNullOrEmpty(competition)) {
                return View((object)repository.Competitions.First().Name);
            } else {
                return View((object)competition);
            }
        }
    }
```

```
        [ChildActionOnly]
        public PartialViewResult RegistrationTable(string competition) {
            return PartialView(repository.Registrations
                .Where(x => x.Competition.Name == competition));
        }
    }
}
```

To keep things simple, I have defined only one action method, which we will use for both GET and POST requests. The sole parameter to the Index method is a string that specifies the name of the competition for which we are going to generate a report. I select the first competition from the repository if no value for the competition parameter is provided (which will be the case when the user performs the initial GET request).

The Index method uses the ViewBag to pass the set of competition names to the view and uses the name of the competition to be reported on as the view model object.

The controller also defines a child action called RegistrationTable, which renders a partial view. We'll return this method shortly. Listing 30-2 shows the main view for this controller, Index.chstml.

Listing 30-2. *The Views/Reports/Index.cshtml view*

```
@model string
@{
    ViewBag.Title = Model + " Report";
}

<h2>@Model</h2>

@using (Html.BeginForm()) {

    @Html.DropDownList("competition", new SelectList(ViewBag.CompetitionNames, Model))
    <input type="submit" value="Show Report" />
}

<p />

@Html.Action("RegistrationTable", new { competition = Model })
```

This view renders a drop-down list containing the names of the competitions, with the selected value being taken from the view model object. It also contains a call to the child action RegistrationTable, passing the name of the selected competition using an anonymously typed object. This value is bound to the parameter of the action method, which generates a list of the Registration objects associated with the selected competition, and uses them as the view model object for rendering the default partial view, shown in Listing 30-3.

Listing 30-3. *The RegistrationTable partial view*

```
@model IEnumerable<EventRegistration.Models.Domain.Registration>

<table id="datatable">
    <tr><th>Name</th><th>Home City</th><th>Age</th><th>Competition</th></tr>
```

```
@foreach (var reg in Model) {
    <tr>
        <td>@reg.Name</td>
        <td>@reg.HomeCity</td>
        <td>@reg.Age</td>
        <td>@reg.Competition.Name</td>
    </tr>
}
</table>
```

This partial view renders an HTML table and uses a Razor **@foreach** loop to generate a table row for each of the **Registration** objects in the view model. When we run the application and navigate to **/Reports/Index**, we have a simple report generator that allows us to select from the available competitions and see the set of registrations for each of them, as shown in Figure 30-1.

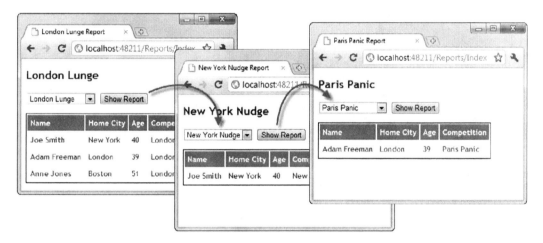

Figure 30-1. *A simple reporting web application*

We select an event from the drop-down list and click the Show Report button, and the form is submitted to the server. The response shows the set of registrations for the selected competition.

Enabling Unobtrusive Ajax

The process for enabling unobtrusive Ajax is similar to the one for unobtrusive client validation that I showed you in the previous chapter. To enable the feature, we set the value for **UnobtrusiveJavaScriptEnabled** to **true** in **Web.config**, as shown in Listing 30-4.

Listing 30-4. Enabling the unobtrusive JavaScript support in Web.config

```
<configuration>
  <appSettings>
    <add key="ClientValidationEnabled" value="true"/>
    <add key="UnobtrusiveJavaScriptEnabled" value="true"/>
  </appSettings>
...
```

In addition to setting the configuration option, we must also make sure that the required JavaScript libraries are referenced from the views in which we want to use Ajax. The simplest way to do this is to place the `script` elements in a layout, as shown in Listing 30-5.

Listing 30-5. Adding script elements to reference the required JavaScript libraries

```
<!DOCTYPE html>
<html>
<head>
    <title>@ViewBag.Title</title>
    <link href="@Url.Content("~/Content/Site.css")" rel="stylesheet" type="text/css" />
    <script src="@Url.Content("~/Scripts/jquery-1.5.1.min.js")"
        type="text/javascript"></script>
    <script src="@Url.Content("~/Scripts/jquery.unobtrusive-ajax.js")"
        type="text/javascript"></script>
</head>

<body>
    @RenderBody()
</body>
</html>
```

The two JavaScript library files are `jquery-1.5.1.min.js` (which is the core jQuery library) and `jquery.unobtrusive-ajax.js` (which is the MVC-specific wrapper around jQuery that provides the unobtrusive Ajax support).

Using Unobtrusive Ajax Forms

Let's use the MVC support for Ajax to add support for posting forms for updates. Listing 30-6 shows the changes to the `Index.cshtml` view to enable this feature.

Listing 30-6. Using Ajax forms

```
@model string
@{
    ViewBag.Title = Model + " Report";
    AjaxOptions ajaxOpts = new AjaxOptions {
        UpdateTargetId = "datatable"
    };
}
```

```
<h2>@Model</h2>

@using (Ajax.BeginForm("RegistrationTable", ajaxOpts)) {

    @Html.DropDownList("competition", new SelectList(ViewBag.CompetitionNames, Model))
    <input type="submit" value="Show Report" />
}

<p />

@Html.Action("RegistrationTable", new { competition = Model })
```

We have to make two changes to enable Ajax forms. The first is to define an `AjaxOptions` object, which is the mechanism by which we specify the settings for Ajax requests. Table 30-1 shows the available properties in the `AjaxOptions` class.

Table 30-1. *AjaxOptions Properties*

Property	Description
Confirm	Sets a message to be displayed to the user in a confirmation window before making the Ajax request.
HttpMethod	Sets the HTTP method that will be used to make the request. Must be either `Get` or `Post`.
InsertionMode	Specifies the way in which the content retrieved from the server is inserted into the HTML. The three choices are expressed as values from the `InsertionMode` enum: `InsertAfter`, `InsertBefore`, and `Replace` (which is the default).
LoadingElementId	Specifies the ID of an HTML element that will be displayed while the Ajax request is being performed.
LoadingElementDuration	Specifies the number of milliseconds over which the gradual appearance of the element specified by `LoadingElementId` will appear.
UpdateTargetId	Sets the ID of the HTML element into which the content retrieved from the server will be inserted.
Url	Sets the URL that will be requested from the server.

I have set up a very simple configuration in the listing, specifying a value for only the `UpdateTargetId` property. The MVC framework Ajax forms feature expects to retrieve HTML from the server, and the `UpdateTargetId` property specifies the ID of the element that this HTML will replace. In this example, I set the ID on the `table` element in the `RegistrationTable` partial view, like this:

```
...
<table id="datatable">
...
```

The second change we have to make to the listing is to use the `Ajax.BeginForm` helper to create the appropriate `form` element when the view is rendered, like this:

```
...
@using (Ajax.BeginForm("RegistrationTable", ajaxOpts)) {.
...
```

The parameters for this helper are the name of the action method to invoke using Ajax and the `AjaxOptions` object we created earlier. In this example, I have specified the child method in the same controller. We have one further change to make. We need to remove the `ChildActionOnly` attribute from the `RegistrationTable` method in the controller, as shown in Listing 30-7.

Listing 30-7. *Removing the ChildActionOnly attribute*

```
using System.Linq;
using System.Web.Mvc;
using EventRegistration.Models.Domain.Repository;

namespace EventRegistration.Controllers {

    public class ReportsController : Controller {
        private IRepository repository;

        public ReportsController(IRepository repo) {
            repository = repo;
        }

        public ActionResult Index(string competition) {
            ViewBag.CompetitionNames = repository.Competitions.Select(x => x.Name);
            if (string.IsNullOrEmpty(competition)) {
                return View((object)repository.Competitions.First().Name);
            } else {
                return View((object)competition);
            }
        }

        public PartialViewResult RegistrationTable(string competition) {
            return PartialView(repository.Registrations
                .Where(x => x.Competition.Name == competition));
        }
    }
}
```

This may seem like a trivial change, but it can have some serious consequences depending on your application. When the `ChildActionOnly` attribute is present, the MVC framework ignores URLs that target that action method, including Ajax requests. But when we remove the attribute, those requests will be serviced, and this allows users to access the content directly. So, for example, requesting this URL:

```
/Reports/RegistrationTable?competition=London%20Lunge
```

will return the HTML fragment containing all the registrations for the London Lunge event, as shown in Figure 30-2.

Figure 30-2. *Exposing fragments of data through previously child-only action methods*

Exposing fragments of HTML this way isn't a problem in my example. This is data that the user would have had access to anyway. But when promoting from a child action to a regular action method, it pays to make sure you are not publishing more data than you think, and you must take care to apply appropriate authentication and authorization measures. You can learn more about how to apply authentication and authorization in Chapter 34.

Performing Graceful Degradation

The `Ajax.BeginForm` helper doesn't generate the JavaScript directly. It just creates a form element with data attributes that are detected by the unobtrusive Ajax script, as follows:

```
<form action="/Reports/RegistrationTable" data-ajax="true"
    data-ajax-mode="replace" data-ajax-update="#datatable" id="form0" method="post">
```

The helper generates a valid `form` element, which means that the user can still post the form synchronously if JavaScript is disabled in the browser. That sounds like a great idea, but the URL that the form is posted to is the one that returns the fragment of HTML. You can see the effect of submitting the form without JavaScript in Figure 30-3.

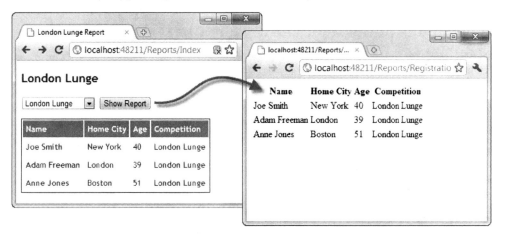

Figure 30-3. *Posting an unobtrusive Ajax form when JavaScript is disabled*

To solve this problem, we have to configure the Ajax request and the HTML form element slightly differently in the view. Listing 30-8 shows the changes that are required in the `Index.cshtml` view.

Listing 30-8. *Adding support for gracefully degrading Ajax forms*

```
@model string
@{
    ViewBag.Title = Model + " Report";
    AjaxOptions ajaxOpts = new AjaxOptions {
        UpdateTargetId = "datatable",
        Url = Url.Action("RegistrationTable")
    };
}

<h2>@Model</h2>

@using (Ajax.BeginForm("Index", ajaxOpts)) {

    @Html.DropDownList("competition", new SelectList(ViewBag.CompetitionNames, Model))
    <input type="submit" value="Show Report" />
}

<p />

@Html.Action("RegistrationTable", new { competition = Model })
```

We set a value for the `AjaxOptions.Url` property. This is the URL that the Ajax request will target. I set a value for this property using the `Url.Action` helper, which I described in Chapter 29. We then change the action name that we pass to the `Ajax.BeginForm` helper to be the one we want targeted when JavaScript isn't available, in this case, the `Index` action method, which will generate the selected report synchronously. With these changes, JavaScript users will get the Ajax experience, and non-JavaScript users will benefit from graceful degradation and still be able to use the application.

Providing Feedback to the User During a Request

One drawback of using Ajax is that it isn't obvious to the user that something is happening. We can remedy this problem using the `AjaxOptions.LoadingElementId` property, as shown in Listing 30-9.

Listing 30-9. *Giving feedback to the user with the LoadingElementId property*

```
@model string
@{
    ViewBag.Title = Model + " Report";
    AjaxOptions ajaxOpts = new AjaxOptions {
        UpdateTargetId = "datatable",
        Url = Url.Action("RegistrationTable"),
        LoadingElementId = "loading",
        LoadingElementDuration = 2000
    };
}
```

```
<h2>@Model</h2>

@using (Ajax.BeginForm("Index", ajaxOpts)) {

    @Html.DropDownList("competition", new SelectList(ViewBag.CompetitionNames, Model))
    <input type="submit" value="Show Report" />
}

<p />

@Html.Action("RegistrationTable", new { competition = Model })

<div id="loading" style="display:none; color:Red; font-weight: bold">
    <p>Loading Data...</p>
</div>
```

The `AjaxOptions.LoadingElementId` property specifies the `id` attribute value of a hidden HTML element that will be shown to the user while an asynchronous request is being performed. I have added a `div` element to the view, which is hidden using the `display:none` CSS value. Figure 30-4 shows the effect of this feedback.

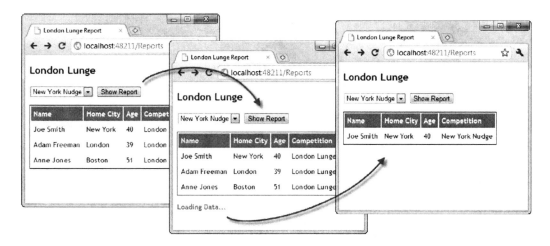

Figure 30-4. *Providing the user with feedback during an Ajax request*

The associated setting `AjaxOptions.LoadingElementDuration` allows us to specify the number of milliseconds during which the hidden panel will be revealed, using a simple animation. Once the Ajax request has completed, the element specified by the `LoadingElementId` property will be hidden once again.

Working with Ajax Callbacks

The `AjaxOptions` class defines a set of properties that allow us to specify JavaScript functions that will be called at various points in the Ajax request life cycle. These properties are described in Table 30-2.

Table 30-2. *AjaxOptions Callback Properties*

Property	jQuery Event	Description
OnBegin	beforeSend	Called immediately prior to the request being sent
OnComplete	complete	Called if the request is successful
OnFailure	error	Called if the request fails
OnSuccess	success	Called when the request has completed successfully

Each of the AjaxOptions callback properties correlates to an Ajax event supported by the jQuery library. I have listed the jQuery events in Table 30-2. You can see how they relate to regular jQuery Ajax in Chapter 11 and get the complete documentation at http://api.jquery.com/jQuery.ajax.

Listing 30-10 shows the callback I have added to Index.cshtml, which uses jQuery to remove the existing rows from the HTML table.

Listing 30-10. *Adding a callback to the view*

```
@model string
<script src="../../Scripts/jquery-1.5.1.js" type="text/javascript"></script>
<script src="../../Scripts/jquery-1.5.1-vsdoc.js" type="text/javascript"></script>
@{
    ViewBag.Title = Model + " Report";
    AjaxOptions ajaxOpts = new AjaxOptions {
        UpdateTargetId = "datatable",
        Url = Url.Action("RegistrationTable"),
        LoadingElementId = "loading",
        LoadingElementDuration = 2000,
        OnBegin = "ClearTableData"
    };
}

<script type="text/javascript">
    function ClearTableData() {
        $('#datatable td').remove();
    }
</script>

<h2>@Model</h2>

@using (Ajax.BeginForm("Index", ajaxOpts)) {

    @Html.DropDownList("competition", new SelectList(ViewBag.CompetitionNames, Model))
    <input type="submit" value="Show Report" />
}

<p />
```

```
@Html.Action("RegistrationTable", new { competition = Model })

<div id="loading" style="display:none; color:Red; font-weight: bold">
    <p>Loading Data...</p>
</div>
```

I registered the callback by setting the `AjaxOptions.OnBegin` property to the name of the function. Now the existing data is cleared from the table when the new data is requested.

Using Unobtrusive Ajax Links

The `Ajax` HTML helper will also produce links that are followed asynchronously using Ajax. I have used this feature in Listing 30-11 to create a set of links that load the data for each of the available events.

Listing 30-11. Generating Ajax links

```
@model string
@{
    ViewBag.Title = Model + " Report";
    AjaxOptions ajaxOpts = new AjaxOptions {
        UpdateTargetId = "datatable",
        Url = Url.Action("RegistrationTable"),
        LoadingElementId = "loading",
        LoadingElementDuration = 2000,
        OnBegin = "ClearTableData"
    };
}

<script type="text/javascript">

    function ClearTableData() {
        $('#datatable td').remove();
    }

</script>

<h2>@Model</h2>

@using (Ajax.BeginForm("Index", ajaxOpts)) {

    @Html.DropDownList("competition", new SelectList(ViewBag.CompetitionNames, Model))
    <input type="submit" value="Show Report" />
}

<p />
<table>
    <tr>
        @foreach (string comp in ViewBag.CompetitionNames) {
```

```
        <td>
            @Ajax.ActionLink(comp, "RegistrationTable", new {competition = comp},
                new AjaxOptions {UpdateTargetId = "datatable"})
        </td>
    }
    </tr>
</table>

<p />

@Html.Action("RegistrationTable", new { competition = Model })

<div id="loading" style="display:none; color:Red; font-weight: bold">
    <p>Loading Data...</p>
</div>
```

I use a Razor @foreach loop to call the Ajax.ActionLink helper on each of the competition names that the action method has passed through the ViewBag. The four parameters for this helper method are the text to be displayed in the link, the name of the action method to invoke when a link is clicked, additional values to be passed to the routing system, and an AjaxOptions object. I have created an AjaxOptions object for each iteration of the loop to demonstrate they can be created inline, but usually I prefer to define them in a code block as I did for the Ajax form example.

These links are laid out in a table, which you can see in Figure 30-5.

Figure 30-5. *Using Ajax-enabled links*

When we click one of the links, an Ajax request is made to the RegistrationTable action method, and the data is used to replace the table element in the page, just as for the Ajax form example earlier in the chapter.

Performing Graceful Degradation

One of the advantages of creating a separate `AjaxOptions` object for each of the links in the view is that we can more easily support graceful degradation for Ajax links. Listing 30-12 shows the changes that are required to make the links work without JavaScript.

Listing 30-12. Graceful degradation for Ajax links

```
...
<table>
    <tr>
        @foreach (string comp in ViewBag.CompetitionNames) {
            <td>
                @Ajax.ActionLink(comp, "Index", new {competition = comp},
                    new AjaxOptions {
                        UpdateTargetId = "datatable",
                        Url = Url.Action("RegistrationTable", new {competition = comp})
                    })
            </td>
        }
    </tr>
</table>
...
```

This is the same technique we used to support graceful degradation for the form, but creating a new `AjaxOptions` object for each link allows us to specify a different URL for each of them to follow, both synchronously and asynchronously.

Working with JSON

The examples so far in this chapter have worked on fragments of HTML, but the MVC framework makes it very easy to work with JSON data as well. Listing 30-13 shows how we create an action method that produces JSON data.

Listing 30-13. Creating an action method that produces JSON

```
using System.Linq;
using System.Web.Mvc;
using EventRegistration.Models.Domain.Repository;

namespace EventRegistration.Controllers {

    public class ReportsController : Controller {
        private IRepository repository;

        public ReportsController(IRepository repo) {
            repository = repo;
        }
```

```
public ActionResult Index(string competition) {
    ViewBag.CompetitionNames = repository.Competitions.Select(x => x.Name);
    if (string.IsNullOrEmpty(competition)) {
        return View((object)repository.Competitions.First().Name);
    } else {
        return View((object)competition);
    }
}

public PartialViewResult RegistrationTable(string competition) {
    return PartialView(repository.Registrations
        .Where(x => x.Competition.Name == competition));
}

public JsonResult RegistrationData(string competition) {

    var data = repository.Registrations
        .Where(x => x.Competition.Name == competition)
        .Select(x => new {
            x.Name,
            x.HomeCity,
            x.Age,
            Competition = x.Competition.Name
        });

    return Json(data, JsonRequestBehavior.AllowGet);
    }
  }
}
```

To create an action method that generates JSON, we just have to return a JsonResult. We can create the result object and produce the data by using the Json method. The arguments I passed to this method are the data that I want formatted as JSON and a value from the JsonRequestBehavior enumeration. By default, JSON action methods will respond only to POST requests, but I have specified the AllowGet enumeration value to permit the method to respond to GET requests as well.

Notice that I use LINQ to generate a sequence of anonymously typed objects to be converted to JSON data. I have done this because the MVC JSON serialization process has no special knowledge about the Entity Framework navigation properties that exist in the domain model classes. The serialization process starts with a Competition object, follows the Registrations property to include the Registration objects, follows the Registration.Competition object, and so on. If we pass our domain model objects to the Json method, we get an exception because the serializer detects the loop that the navigation properties introduce.

The simplest way to get around this problem is to use anonymously typed objects to select just the fields we want included in the JSON data. You can see how this data is serialized as JSON by requesting the URL that invokes the action in the browser. Figure 30-6 shows the data in Google Chrome. Other browsers download the data to a file.

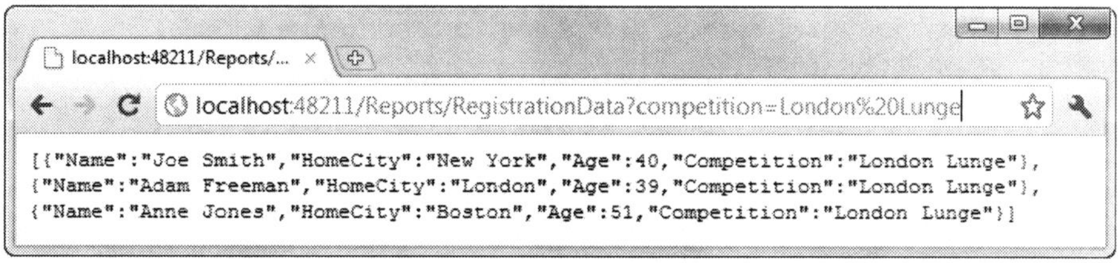

Figure 30-6. Requesting JSON data using the browser

Processing JSON at the Client

We can process JSON data using the unobtrusive Ajax feature by registering a function with the
OnSuccess property of the AjaxOptions object, as shown in Listing 30-14.

Listing 30-14. Handling JSON data using the unobtrusive Ajax feature

```
@model string
@{
    ViewBag.Title = Model + " Report";
    AjaxOptions ajaxOpts = new AjaxOptions {
        Url = Url.Action("RegistrationData"),
        OnBegin = "ClearTableData",
        OnSuccess = "ProcessData"
    };
}

<script type="text/javascript">

    function ClearTableData() {
        $('#datatable td').remove();
    }

    function ProcessData(data) {
        var target = $('#datatable');
        for (var i = 0; i < data.length; i++) {
            target.append('<tr><td>' + data[i].Name+ '</td>'
            + '<td>' + data[i].HomeCity + '</td>'
            + '<td>' + data[i].Age + '</td>'
            + '<td>' + data[i].Competition + '</td></tr>');
        }
    }

</script>

<h2>@Model</h2>

@using (Ajax.BeginForm("Index", ajaxOpts)) {
```

```
    @Html.DropDownList("competition", new SelectList(ViewBag.CompetitionNames, Model))
    <input type="submit" value="Show Report" />
}

<p />

@Html.Action("RegistrationTable", new { competition = Model })
```

Notice that I have removed the value for the `UpdateTargetId` property in the `AjaxOptions` object. If this property has a value, then the unobtrusive Ajax library will replace the targeted HTML with the JSON data. This makes a mess of the page.

I have created a function called `ProcessData` and assigned it as the function to call when a request is successful. The function iterates through the items in the JSON data array and generates a table row for each of them, much as the partial view did in the child action when we were retrieving HTML from the server.

Performing Remote Validation

The last Ajax feature we will look at in this chapter is *remote validation*. This is a hybrid of the model validation techniques I showed you in Chapter 29. The validity of a property is evaluated by an action method invoked using an Ajax call at the client. The first step in setting up remote validation is to add an action method to the controller to perform the evaluation. Listing 30-15 shows such a method, which I have added to the `RegistrationController` class since this is the controller that contains the validation logic from Chapter 29.

Listing 30-15. *Adding a remote validation action method to a controller*

```
using System;
using System.Linq;
using System.Web.Mvc;
using EventRegistration.Models.Domain;
using EventRegistration.Models.Domain.Repository;

namespace EventRegistration.Controllers {

    public class RegistrationController : Controller {
        private IRepository repository;

        public RegistrationController(IRepository repo) {
            repository = repo;
        }

        public ActionResult Index() {
            ViewBag.Competitions = repository.Competitions;
            return View(new Registration());
        }
```

```
public JsonResult ValidateCity(string HomeCity) {
    string[] cities = { "London", "New York", "Boston", "San Francisco", "Paris" };
    if (Array.Exists(cities, x => x == HomeCity)) {
        return Json(true, JsonRequestBehavior.AllowGet);
    } else {
        return Json(string.Format("Residents of {0} cannot register", HomeCity),
            JsonRequestBehavior.AllowGet);
    }
}

[HttpPost]
public ActionResult HandleIndexPost(Registration registration) {

    if (ModelState.IsValidField("Name") &&
        repository.Registrations
        .Where(x => x.Name == registration.Name).Count() > 0) {

        ModelState.AddModelError("Name",
            "A registration has already been made in this name");
    }

    if (ModelState.IsValidField("Age")
        && ModelState.IsValidField("CompetitionID")) {

        if (registration.Competition.Name == "Paris Panic"
            && registration.Age < 40) {

            ModelState.AddModelError(string.Empty,
                "You must be at least 40 to do the Paris Panic");
        }
    }

    if (ModelState.IsValid) {
        repository.SaveRegistration(registration);
        return View("RegistrationComplete", registration);
    } else {
        ViewBag.Competitions = repository.Competitions;
        return View("Index", registration);
    }
}
}
}
```

An action method that supports remote validation must return a JsonResult and have a single parameter that has the same name as the model property it is responsible for validating. In this case, my action method validates the HomeCity property.

We tell the client that the value is acceptable by passing true as the parameter to the Json method. Otherwise, pass a string to the same method with the error message that should be displayed to the user. In the listing, my validation method checks to see whether the value that the user has entered is on a set of approved cities, but this technique is usually used to validate values against a database, where it would be impracticable to ship all the possible permitted values to the browser.

Once we have defined the method, we must annotate the model class with the Remote attribute, as shown in Listing 30-16.

Listing 30-16. Applying the remote validation attribute to the domain model class

```
using System.ComponentModel.DataAnnotations;
using System.Web.Mvc;
using EventRegistration.Infrastructure;

namespace EventRegistration.Models.Domain {

    [ModelBinder(typeof(RegistrationModelBinder))]
    public class Registration {

        [Required]
        public int ID { get; set; }

        [Required]
        public string Name { get; set; }

        [Required]
        [Remote("ValidateCity", "Registration")]
        public string HomeCity { get; set; }

        [Required(ErrorMessage="Please enter an age")]
        [Range(18, 100, ErrorMessage = "Please enter an age between 18 and 100")]
        public int Age { get; set; }

        [Required]
        public int CompetitionID { get; set; }

        public virtual Competition Competition { get; set; }
    }
}
```

There are various overloads for this attribute, and I have chosen the one that lets me specify an action method and controller. Bear in mind that this action method will be used wherever validation is performed in your application. I usually put my validation methods in a separate controller. You can see the effect of this attribute (and the associated action method) in Figure 30-7.

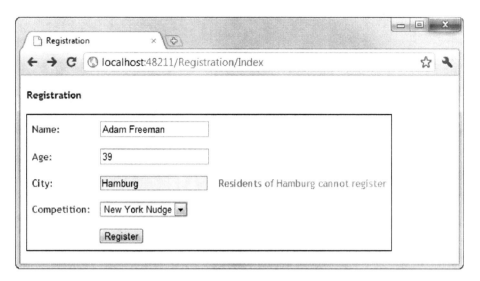

Figure 30-7. *Performing remote validation*

■ **Caution** Unlike the other validation attributes, the Remote attribute is not applied at the server. It is used only by the unobtrusive client validation library. This means you should enforce an explicit check on the value using the techniques I showed in Chapter 29.

Summary

In this chapter, I showed you the MVC framework's unobtrusive Ajax feature, which allows you to perform Ajax requests in a neat and elegant way. You could use jQuery directly for all of the features shown in this chapter, but the integration of the Ajax helper methods and the routing system make life easier in most MVC framework projects.

The MVC Framework Triathlon App

We are going to finish our tour of the MVC framework by re-creating the triathlon application that I started the book with. Doing so demonstrates some of the compromises and constraints that a project faces and gives you a more realistic demonstration of applying the MVC features that you learned about in earlier chapters, even if the example is still relatively simple.

Creating the Project

To get started, I have created a new project using the Visual Studio ASP.NET MVC 3 Web Application template and called the project TriathlonApp. I selected the Empty template, because I prefer to create an application from an empty project.

Creating the Model

Most projects start with the model. For this application, I am working with a preexisting database, so my model objects will simply represent the database tables. I created a new folder called Models/Domain and created the model classes. Listing 31-1 shows the Event class, which will represent rows of data in the Events database table.

Listing 31-1. The Event domain model class

```
using System;

namespace TriathlonApp.Models.Domain {
    public class Event {

        public int ID { get; set; }
        public DateTime Date { get; set; }
        public string Athlete { get; set; }
        public string Type { get; set; }
        public TimeSpan SwimTime { get; set; }
```

```
        public TimeSpan CycleTime { get; set; }
        public TimeSpan RunTime { get; set; }
        public TimeSpan OverallTime { get; set; }
    }
}
```

Listing 31-2 shows the `Athlete` class, which represents rows in the `Athletes` database table.

Listing 31-2. *The Athlete class*

```
using System.ComponentModel.DataAnnotations;

namespace TriathlonApp.Models.Domain {
    public class Athlete {

        [Key]
        public string Name { get; set; }
    }
}
```

The Entity Framework is pretty good at inferring the information it needs to know from the database or from our model classes, but sometimes it needs a helping hand. In this class, I have applied the `Key` attribute to the `Name` property because the Entity Framework is unable to infer the primary key for this class. It may seem obvious to you and I when we look at this class because there is only one property, but the Entity Framework makes certain assumptions when trying to figure out which property corresponds to the key column in the table. These assumptions work well when there in an `int` property that corresponds to a key column of the same name, but not so well otherwise.

KNOWING WHEN TO APPLY THE KEY ATTRIBUTE

You might be wondering how to tell when you need the `Key` attribute on your model classes. I always forget that the Entity Framework will infer only that certain types of properties are keys, and it isn't until I come to unit test the repository (or use the repository in a controller). At that point, I see the error message shown in Figure 31-1.

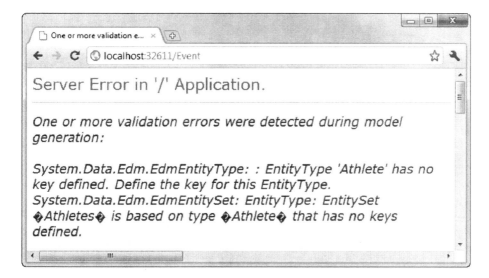

Figure 31-1. The error message shown when the Entity Framework can't infer the key

This is the moment when I slap my forehead and go back and add the Key attribute.

Listing 31-3 shows the EventType class, which represents rows in the EventTypes database table.

Listing 31-3. The EventType class

```
using System.ComponentModel.DataAnnotations;

namespace TriathlonApp.Models.Domain {
    public class EventType {

        [Key]
        public string Name { get; set; }
        public float SwimMiles { get; set; }
        public float CycleMiles { get; set; }
        public float RunMiles { get; set; }
    }
}
```

Once again, the Entity Framework won't be able to infer the key property in this model type, so I have applied the Key attribute. Listing 31-4 shows the ReferenceTime class, which represents rows from the ReferenceTimes database table.

Listing 31-4. The ReferenceTime class

```
using System;

namespace TriathlonApp.Models.Domain {
    public class ReferenceTime {
```

```
        public int ID { get; set; }
        public int OverallPos { get; set; }
        public TimeSpan OverallTime { get; set; }
        public int SwimPos { get; set; }
        public TimeSpan SwimTime { get; set; }
        public int CyclePos { get; set; }
        public TimeSpan CycleTime { get; set; }
        public int RunPos { get; set; }
        public TimeSpan RunTime { get; set; }
        public string Type { get; set; }
    }
}
```

The TrainingData database that we will be using has a couple of stored procedures that calculate rankings. I showed you how to import these procedures when creating a data model using the Entity Framework in Chapter 8. The code-first approach that I will be using for this application (which is the same one I showed you in Chapter 24) doesn't support stored procedures as easily. I'll come back to this when we create the repository later in the chapter. For the moment, though, I need to define a class that will represent rankings. Listing 31-5 shows the RankingSet class.

Listing 31-5. The RankingSet class

```
namespace TriathlonApp.Models.Domain {
    public class RankingSet {
        public int SwimRank { get; set; }
        public int CycleRank { get; set; }
        public int RunRank { get; set; }
        public int OverallRank { get; set; }
        public int RankCount { get; set; }
    }
}
```

As you can see from these classes, our model is pretty simple. I have not defined any navigation properties, meaning that each class is self-contained. The only new concept is the application of the Key property, which is a relatively common issue when using the Entity Framework.

Creating and Implementing the Repository

Now that we have defined the domain model classes, we can move on to the repository. I have added the folder Models/Domain/Repository in which I created a new interface, IRepository, shown in Listing 31-6.

Listing 31-6. The IRepository interface

```
using System.Collections.Generic;

namespace TriathlonApp.Models.Domain.Repository {

    public interface IRepository {
```

```
        IEnumerable<Event> Events { get; }
        void SaveEvent(Event ev);

        IEnumerable<EventType> EventTypes { get; }
        IEnumerable<ReferenceTime> ReferenceTimes { get; }
        IEnumerable<Athlete> Athletes { get; }

        RankingSet GetPersonalRank(Event ev);
        RankingSet GetReferenceRank(Event ev);
    }
}
```

I have defined properties that return enumerations of the different domain model classes. In this application, I only need to create new records in the Events table, which is why the SaveEvent method is the only one of its kind in this interface. I have marked the GetPersonalRank and GetReferenceRank methods in bold. These methods correspond to the stored procedures defined in the database.

Implementing the Repository

I am going to implement the repository following the same pattern that I showed you in Chapter 24. Listing 31-7 shows the EFAdpater class (which is derived from DbContext and is the entry point in to the Entity Framework) and EFRepository (which is the implementation of the IRepository interface).

Listing 31-7. The EFAdapter and EfRepository classes

```
using System.Collections.Generic;
using System.Data.Entity;
using System.Linq;

namespace TriathlonApp.Models.Domain.Repository {

    public class EFAdapter : DbContext {

        public EFAdapter(string connectionName)
            : base(connectionName) {
            // do nothing
        }

        public DbSet<Athlete> Athletes { get; set; }
        public DbSet<Event> Events { get; set; }
        public DbSet<EventType> EventTypes { get; set; }
        public DbSet<ReferenceTime> ReferenceTimes { get; set; }
    }

    public class EFRepository : IRepository {
        private EFAdapter adapter = new EFAdapter("EFRepository");
```

```
public IEnumerable<Event> Events {
    get { return adapter.Events; }
}

public void SaveEvent(Event ev) {
    if (ev.ID == 0) {
        adapter.Events.Add(ev);
    }
    adapter.SaveChanges();
}

public IEnumerable<EventType> EventTypes {
    get { return adapter.EventTypes; }
}

public IEnumerable<ReferenceTime> ReferenceTimes {
    get { return adapter.ReferenceTimes; }
}

public IEnumerable<Athlete> Athletes {
    get { return adapter.Athletes; }
}

public RankingSet GetPersonalRank(Event ev) {

    IEnumerable<Event> interimResults = adapter.Events
        .Where(x => x.Athlete == ev.Athlete && x.Type == ev.Type);

    return new RankingSet {
        SwimRank = interimResults.Count(x => x.SwimTime <= ev.SwimTime),
        CycleRank = interimResults.Count(x => x.CycleTime <= ev.CycleTime),
        RunRank = interimResults.Count(x => x.RunTime <= ev.RunTime),
        OverallRank = interimResults.Count(x => x.OverallTime <= ev.OverallTime),
        RankCount = interimResults.Count()
    };
}

public RankingSet GetReferenceRank(Event ev) {

    IEnumerable<ReferenceTime> interimResults = adapter.ReferenceTimes
        .Where(x => x.Type == ev.Type);

    return new RankingSet {
        SwimRank = interimResults
                    .Where(x => x.SwimTime >= ev.SwimTime).Min(x => x.SwimPos),
        CycleRank = interimResults
                    .Where(x => x.CycleTime >= ev.CycleTime).Min(x => x.CyclePos),
        RunRank = interimResults
                    .Where(x => x.RunTime >= ev.RunTime).Min(x => x.RunPos),
```

```
            OverallRank = interimResults
                        .Where(x => x.OverallTime >= ev.OverallTime)
                        .Min(x => x.OverallPos),
            RankCount = interimResults.Count()
        };
    }
  }
}
```

This approach to using the Entity Framework doesn't provide convenient access to the stored procedures in the database. There are several ways of addressing this. First, we could generate an Entity Framework data model and import the stored procedures into the model, as we did in Chapter 8. This provides us with a nice way of accessing the stored procedures but means that our domain model classes are generated by the Entity Framework. This is a compromise because switching away from the Entity Framework would involve changing the domain model classes.

Another approach would be to execute the stored procedures using SQL. The DbContext class has a Database property, through which we can execute SQL queries. I don't like this approach. One of the reasons I like using the Entity Framework is that I can avoid putting SQL into my applications and use LINQ instead.

The third approach is the least appealing in real projects but the most suited to my example application. I have ignored the stored procedures entirely and replicated them as a set of LINQ queries. I have chosen this approach because it is the simplest, and I want to focus on the MVC framework, but it generates a lot of additional work for the database, which is undesirable in a real project.

Defining the Connection String

We need to tell the Entity Framework how to connect to the database. Listing 31-8 shows the addition to the Web.config file, which is the same connection string I used in Chapter 24.

Listing 31-8. The database connection string

```
<configuration>
...
<connectionStrings>
    <add name="EFRepository" connectionString="Data Source=TITAN\SQLEXPRESS;Initial
        Catalog=TrainingData;Persist Security Info=True;User ID=adam;Password=adam;
        MultipleActiveResultSets=true" providerName="System.Data.SqlClient"/>
  </connectionStrings>
...
</configuration>
```

This connection string operates on the SQL Server Express installation on my database server, Titan. See Chapter 24 for details of how to figure out the connection string that you need for your environment.

Setting Up Dependency Injection

We want to be able to use the IRepository interface without needing to know any details of the implementation class. I am going to do this by using dependency injection, much as I did in Chapters 23 and 24.

To begin, I have added a reference to the Ninject assembly. This is the same assembly that I used previously, and I included in the source code download for this book. Next I have created a class called CustomDependencyResolver in a folder called Infrastructure. Listing 31-9 shows this class.

Listing 31-9. *The CustomDependencyResolver class*

```
using System;
using System.Collections.Generic;
using System.Web.Mvc;
using Ninject;
using Ninject.Syntax;
using TriathlonApp.Models.Domain.Repository;

namespace TriathlonApp.Infrastructure {
    public class CustomDependencyResolver : IDependencyResolver {
        private IKernel ninjectKernel;

        public CustomDependencyResolver() {
            ninjectKernel = new StandardKernel();
            AddDefaultBindings();
        }

        public object GetService(Type serviceType) {
            return ninjectKernel.TryGet(serviceType);
        }

        public IEnumerable<object> GetServices(Type serviceType) {
            return ninjectKernel.GetAll(serviceType);
        }

        public IBindingToSyntax<T> Bind<T>() {
            return ninjectKernel.Bind<T>();
        }

        private void AddDefaultBindings() {
            Bind<IRepository>().To<EFRepository>();
        }
    }
}
```

This is the same dependency resolver that I used in Chapter 23, updated with the namespaces for this project. I have added one binding, shown in bold, that makes the EFRepository class the implementation that will be used to service requests for the IRepository interface.

The last set in setting up dependency injection is to register the CustomDependencyResolver class with the MVC framework in Global.asax, as shown in Listing 31-10.

Listing 31-10. Registering the dependency resolver class with the MVC framework

```
using System.Web.Mvc;
using System.Web.Routing;
using TriathlonApp.Infrastructure;

namespace TriathlonApp {

    public class MvcApplication : System.Web.HttpApplication {
        public static void RegisterGlobalFilters(GlobalFilterCollection filters) {
            filters.Add(new HandleErrorAttribute());
        }

        public static void RegisterRoutes(RouteCollection routes) {
            routes.IgnoreRoute("{resource}.axd/{*pathInfo}");

            routes.MapRoute(
                "Default",
                "{controller}/{action}/{id}",
                new { controller = "Home", action = "Index", id = UrlParameter.Optional }
            );
        }

        protected void Application_Start() {
            AreaRegistration.RegisterAllAreas();

            DependencyResolver.SetResolver(new CustomDependencyResolver());

            RegisterGlobalFilters(GlobalFilters.Filters);
            RegisterRoutes(RouteTable.Routes);
        }
    }
}
```

Configure the Routing

The entry point into the application will be a controller called **Event**. This will generate the initial page for the user, showing the events data from the database. Before I start creating the controller, I like to get the routes set up so that the intended entry point maps to the default URL for the application. This means changing the value that will be used when no controller name is specified, as shown in Listing 31-11.

Listing 31-11. Changing the default controller in the route

```
using System.Web.Mvc;
using System.Web.Routing;
using TriathlonApp.Infrastructure;

namespace TriathlonApp {
```

```
public class MvcApplication : System.Web.HttpApplication {
    public static void RegisterGlobalFilters(GlobalFilterCollection filters) {
        filters.Add(new HandleErrorAttribute());
    }

    public static void RegisterRoutes(RouteCollection routes) {
        routes.IgnoreRoute("{resource}.axd/{*pathInfo}");

        routes.MapRoute(
            "Default",
            "{controller}/{action}/{id}",
            new { controller = "Event", action = "Index", id = UrlParameter.Optional }
        );
    }

    protected void Application_Start() {
        AreaRegistration.RegisterAllAreas();

        DependencyResolver.SetResolver(new CustomDependencyResolver());

        RegisterGlobalFilters(GlobalFilters.Filters);
        RegisterRoutes(RouteTable.Routes);
    }
}
}
```

Creating the Event Controller

As I mentioned, the Event controller will be the entry point into the application, so I have created a new controller class called EventController in the Controllers project folder (see Listing 31-12).

Listing 31-12. The initial version of the EventController class

```
using System.Linq;
using System.Web.Mvc;
using TriathlonApp.Models.Domain;
using TriathlonApp.Models.Domain.Repository;

namespace TriathlonApp.Controllers {
    public class EventController : Controller {
        private IRepository repository;

        public EventController(IRepository repo) {
            repository = repo;
        }
```

```
        public ActionResult Index() {
            return View();
        }
    }
}
```

In applications that have a common appearance, I like to get the layout as complete as possible as early as possible, so I tend to create a very simple action method and a correspondingly simple view. I use these as placeholders so I can edit and render the layout before returning and adding functionality to the controller. You can see the contents of the Index.cshtml view in Listing 31-13, which I created in the Views/Event folder.

Listing 31-13. *The initial version of the Index.cshtml view for the Event controller*

```
<h4>Content will go here</h4>
```

This is a trivially simple view, but we have now reached the point where we can start the application, request the default URL (/), and see the result, as shown in Figure 31-2.

Figure 31-2. *Rendering the skeletal view from the skeletal controller*

At the moment, this controller and view are just props so that I can see the effect of the layout, but we'll return to them soon enough and add some useful functionality.

Building the Layout

The layout for this application is simple enough; we are going to have to create a child action to generate the footer, since it relies on data aggregated from the repository. To being with, though, we can define the styles and static content.

Creating the CSS styles

I have created a new style sheet called Triathlon.css in the Content folder. These are the same styles that I used in the previous builds of this application. I am not going to list them here because CSS is verbose, and you can get the styles from the source code download that accompanies this book. I have referenced the new style sheet in the _Layout.cshtml file, as shown in Listing 31-14. This file is in the Views/Shared project folder and is the view I will be using by default.

Listing 31-14. *Adding a reference to a style sheet*

```
<!DOCTYPE html>
<html>
<head>
    <title>Triathlon Training Data</title>
    <link href="@Url.Content("~/Content/Site.css")" rel="stylesheet" type="text/css" />
    <link href="@Url.Content("~/Content/Triathlon.css")" rel="stylesheet" type="text/css" />
    <link href="@Url.Content("~/Content/jquery-ui-1.8.6.custom.css")" rel="stylesheet"
        type="text/css" />
    <script src="@Url.Content("~/Scripts/jquery-1.5.1.min.js")"
        type="text/javascript"></script>
    <script src="@Url.Content("~/Scripts/jquery-ui-1.8.6.custom.min.js")"
        type="text/javascript"></script>
    <script src="@Url.Content("~/Scripts/jquery.unobtrusive-ajax.min.js")"
        type="text/javascript"></script>
    <script src="@Url.Content("~/Scripts/jquery.validate.min.js")"
        type="text/javascript"></script>
    <script src="@Url.Content("~/Scripts/jquery.validate.unobtrusive.min.js")"
        type="text/javascript"></script>
</head>
<body>

<div id="bodydiv">
    @RenderBody()
</div>

</body>
</html>
```

I have used the `Url.Content` helper to generate URLs that will pass through the routing configuration. I have also taken the opportunity to add references to the script libraries that I'll need later, and this includes the custom jQuery library that I demonstrated in Chapter 10. I have also added the custom jQuery library, the CSS style sheet, and the set of jQuery images to the project.

I would usually be more selective and only add, for example, the validation libraries to those views where I know they are required, but for simplicity, I have included everything here. Finally, notice that I have defined a static value for the `title` element. This means that all of the views will generate pages with the same title, rather than supplying a title through the `ViewBag`.

Adding the Header and Footer

Listing 31-15 shows the additions I have made to the layout to define the header and footer, which provide the consistent visual theme through the application.

Listing 31-15. *Adding the header and footer to the layout*

```
<!DOCTYPE html>
<html>
<head>
    <title>Triathlon Training Data</title>
    <link href="@Url.Content("~/Content/Site.css")" rel="stylesheet" type="text/css" />
```

```
<link href="@Url.Content("~/Content/Triathlon.css")" rel="stylesheet" type="text/css" />
<link href="@Url.Content("~/Content/jquery-ui-1.8.6.custom.css")" rel="stylesheet"
    type="text/css" />
<script src="@Url.Content("~/Scripts/jquery-1.5.1.min.js")"
    type="text/javascript"></script>
<script src="@Url.Content("~/Scripts/jquery-ui-1.8.6.custom.min.js")"
    type="text/javascript"></script>
<script src="@Url.Content("~/Scripts/jquery.unobtrusive-ajax.min.js")"
    type="text/javascript"></script>
<script src="@Url.Content("~/Scripts/jquery.validate.min.js")"
    type="text/javascript"></script>
<script src="@Url.Content("~/Scripts/jquery.validate.unobtrusive.min.js")"
    type="text/javascript"></script>
</head>
<body>

<div class="header">
    <div class="title" id="titleDiv">
        <img src="@Url.Content("~/Content/triathlon.png")" />
        <h1>Triathlon Training Data</h1>
    </div>

<div>

<div id="bodydiv">
    @RenderBody()
</div>

<div class="footer">
    <h2>@Html.Action("FooterMessage", "ChildActions")</h2>
</div>

</body>
</html>
```

The footer for this application contains a summary of the data in the database, so I have used the
`Html.Action` helper method to call a child action to generate the summary. I like to put child actions that
are used throughout the application in a separate controller. In this case, I have called the controller
`ChildActions`, and the action method that generates the summary data is called `FooterMessage`. Listing
31-16 shows the `ChildActionsController` class.

Listing 31-16. *The ChildActionsController class*

```
using System;
using System.Linq;
using System.Web.Mvc;
using TriathlonApp.Models.Domain;
using TriathlonApp.Models.Domain.Repository;
```

```
namespace TriathlonApp.Controllers {
    public class ChildActionsController : Controller {
        private IRepository repository;

        public ChildActionsController(IRepository repo) {
            repository = repo;
        }

        [ChildActionOnly]
        public string FooterMessage() {

            float distance = repository.Events
                .GroupBy(x => x.Type)
                .Aggregate(0f, (sum, egroup) => {
                    EventType etype = repository.EventTypes.First(x => x.Name == egroup.Key);
                    return sum += egroup.Count() *
                        (etype.SwimMiles + etype.CycleMiles + etype.RunMiles);
                });

            TimeSpan time = repository.Events.Select(x => x.OverallTime)
                .Aggregate(TimeSpan.Zero, (total, newtime) => total.Add(newtime));

            return string.Format("{0} Events, {1:F1} Miles, {2} Hours and {3} Minutes",
                repository.Events.Count(), distance, time.Hours, time.Minutes);
        }
    }
}
```

The FooterMessage action method is marked with the ChildActionOnly attribute to prevent users from targeting the method with a URL request. I only need to generate a simple summary in this child action, so I have chosen to return a string, rather than a partial view. I generate the summary data with a pair of LINQ queries and use the composite string formatting feature to create the result. You can see the effect of these additions in Figure 31-3.

Figure 31-3. *Adding the header and footer to the layout*

Adding the Tabs

To complete the layout, we need to add the tabs that allow the user to select different areas of the application. To do this, I am going to use the jQuery UI tabs feature, but I am going to add some additional JavaScript to modify the default behavior. I don't think I have *ever* used the default jQuery tabs behavior. It never quite fits what I want, but one of the things that I like about jQuery is how easy it is to make adjustments. Listing 31-17 shows the default layout with the tabs.

Listing 31-17. Adding tabs to the default layout

```
<!DOCTYPE html>
<html>
<head>
    <title>Triathlon Training Data</title>
    <link href="@Url.Content("~/Content/Site.css")" rel="stylesheet" type="text/css" />
    <link href="@Url.Content("~/Content/Triathlon.css")" rel="stylesheet" type="text/css" />
    <link href="@Url.Content("~/Content/jquery-ui-1.8.6.custom.css")" rel="stylesheet"
        type="text/css" />
    <script src="@Url.Content("~/Scripts/jquery-1.5.1.min.js")"
        type="text/javascript"></script>
    <script src="@Url.Content("~/Scripts/jquery-ui-1.8.6.custom.min.js")"
        type="text/javascript"></script>
    <script src="@Url.Content("~/Scripts/jquery.unobtrusive-ajax.min.js")"
        type="text/javascript"></script>
    <script src="@Url.Content("~/Scripts/jquery.validate.min.js")"
        type="text/javascript"></script>
    <script src="@Url.Content("~/Scripts/jquery.validate.unobtrusive.min.js")"
        type="text/javascript"></script>

    <script type="text/javascript">
        $(document).ready(function () {

            $('#@ViewBag.TabName').attr('href', '#bodydiv');

            $('#tabs').tabs({
                selected: $('#tabs ul li a').index($('#@ViewBag.TabName')),
                select: function (event, ui) {
                    var url = $.data(ui.tab, 'load.tabs');
                    if (url) {
                        location.href = url;
                        return false;
                    }
                    return true;
                }
            });
        });
    </script>
</head>
<body>
```

```
<div class="header">
    <div class="title" id="titleDiv">
        <img src="@Url.Content("~/Content/triathlon.png")" />
        <h1>Triathlon Training Data</h1>
    </div>

<div>

<div id="tabs">
    <ul>
    <li><a id="Events" href="@Url.Action("Index", "Event")">Events</a> </li>
    <li><a id="Performance" href="@Url.Action("Index", "Performance")">Performance</a></li>
    <li><a id="Calculator" href="@Url.Action("Index", "Calculator")">Calculator</a></li>
    </ul>
    <div id="bodydiv">
        @RenderBody()
    </div>
</div>

<div class="footer">
    <h2>@Html.Action("FooterMessage", "ChildActions")</h2>
</div>

</body>
</html>
```

There are two areas of change; let's look at them in reverse order. The `div` element with the `id` of `tabs` defines the set of tabs that will be displayed by the layout. For each tab, I have used the `Url.Action` helper to generate a URL that will target the `Index` method of a controller. We've created only one of these controllers so far, but we'll get to the others later in the chapter. Notice that there is a nested `div` element with an `id` of `bodydiv`. This contains a call to the `RenderBody` method, which will insert the contents of the current view into the page.

The `script` element I added sets up and configures the tabs. The first statement finds the `a` element for the current tab (which the view provides via the `ViewBag`) and sets the `href` attribute so that the tab will display the `bodydiv` element, like this:

```
$('#@ViewBag.TabName').attr('href', '#bodydiv');
```

This means the tab will display content that is already in the page. When configuring the tabs, I set the selected tab by finding the index of the `a` element with the `id` value passed in from the view via the `ViewBag`, like this:

```
selected: $('#tabs ul li a').index($('#@ViewBag.TabName')),
```

I override the default selection behavior so that the browser follows the specified link, rather than displaying the contents returned by the URL in the current page. I wanted to do this so that I can create a more regular MVC framework application. Otherwise, all of the action methods in the other controllers would have been requested via Ajax and would have had to generate partial views.

There is nothing wrong with the Ajax approach, but I didn't want the design of the jQuery UI tabs to drive the shape of the entire application. (And I do the manipulation using JavaScript so that non-JavaScript browsers are still supported.) Before we can test the tabs, we have to make a tweak to the `Views/Event/Index.cshtml` view, as shown in Listing 31-18.

Listing 31-18. Passing the name of the desired tab to the layout via the ViewBag

```
@{
    ViewBag.TabName = "Events";
}
```

```
<h4>Content will go here</h4>
```

This approach will be useful when I come to create the pages that allow the user to create, edit, or delete events. These should appear on the Events tab if we are to faithfully re-create the earlier incarnations of this application. Figure 31-4 shows the effect of the tabs. However, clicking the Performance and Calculator tabs shows an error since we have yet to create the controllers and action methods that these tabs target.

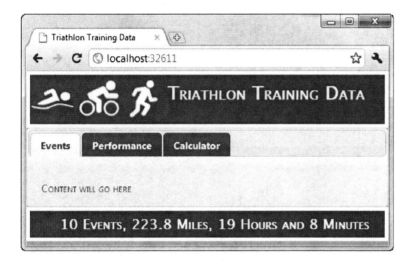

Figure 31-4. Adding the tabs to the layout

Building the Events Tab

We can now return to the `EventController` class and flesh out the `Index` action method and the associated view. Our goal is to display a table of event and ranking information, with links so that the user can edit or delete existing records or add new ones. We also need to allow the user to filter the set of events that are displayed based on the event type.

To begin, we need a view model object. I want to pass all the information needed for each row in the table in a single object, which means we need something to convey an `Event` domain model object and two values representing the personal rank and the reference rank. I created a new folder, `Models/View`, and added a new class called `EventAndRankSummary`. Listing 31-19 shows this class.

Listing 31-19. The EventAndRankSummary view model class

```
using TriathlonApp.Models.Domain;

namespace TriathlonApp.Models.View {
    public class EventAndRankSummary {
        public Event Event { get; set; }
        public int PersonalRank {get; set;}
        public int ReferenceRank {get; set;}
    }
}
```

We can begin to use this class in the controller. Listing 31-20 shows some additions to the
EventController class to support rendering the table.

Listing 31-20. Enhancing the EventController class

```
using System.Linq;
using System.Web.Mvc;
using TriathlonApp.Models.Domain.Repository;
using TriathlonApp.Models.View;

namespace TriathlonApp.Controllers {
    public class EventController : Controller {
        private IRepository repository;

        public EventController(IRepository repo) {
            repository = repo;
        }

        public ActionResult Index(string eventFilter = "All") {

            var selectedEvents = (eventFilter == "All" ? repository.Events
                : repository.Events.Where(x => x.Type == eventFilter))
                .Select(x =>
                    new EventAndRankSummary {
                        Event = x,
                        PersonalRank = repository.GetPersonalRank(x).OverallRank,
                        ReferenceRank = repository.GetReferenceRank(x).OverallRank
                });

            if (Request.IsAjaxRequest()) {
                return PartialView("EventsTable", selectedEvents);
            } else {
                ViewBag.EventTypes
                    = new string[] {"All"}.Concat(repository.EventTypes.Select(x => x.Name));
                return View(selectedEvents);
            }
        }
    }
}
```

The Index action method defines an optional parameter that defaults to All if no value is supplied in the request. I use the parameter value to filter the Event objects available in the repository and project a series of EventAndRankSummary objects into the selectedEvents variable. (I get the ranking information by calling the replacements for the stored procedures in the select clause of the LINQ query. Once again, I am going to gloss over the inefficiency of this approach.)

I am going to use unobtrusive Ajax to update the contents of the table when the user changes the filter. Rather than create an action method that returns just a partial view, I have used the Request.IsAjaxRequest method to determine the result of the action method. For regular requests, I return the Index view, and for Ajax requests I return the EventsTable partial view. Both of these views use the sequence of EventAndRankSummary objects as the view model. In addition to this, I pass the set of event types to be used as filters via the ViewBag when rendering the full view.

Defining the Views

The first view I created is Views/Event/EventsTable.cshtml, the contents of which are shown in Listing 31-21. This is the partial view, and it renders the table element that contains data values taken from the EventAndRankSummary objects.

Listing 31-21. The EventsTable partial view

```
@model IEnumerable<TriathlonApp.Models.View.EventAndRankSummary>

<table id="datatable" class="dataview" rules="cols">
    <tr>
        <th>Date</th>
        <th>Athlete</th>
        <th>Event Type</th>
        <th>Swim</th>
        <th>Cycle</th>
        <th>Run</th>
        <th>Overall</th>
        <th>Rank</th>
        <th>Ref Rank</th>
        <th>Edit</th>
        <th>Delete</th>
    </tr>

    @foreach (var item in Model) {
        <tr class="dataitem">
            <td>@item.Event.Date.ToString("MM/dd")</td>
            <td>@item.Event.Athlete</td>
            <td>@item.Event.Type</td>
            <td>@item.Event.SwimTime</td>
            <td>@item.Event.CycleTime</td>
            <td>@item.Event.RunTime</td>
            <td>@item.Event.OverallTime</td>
            <td>@item.PersonalRank</td>
            <td>@item.ReferenceRank</td>
```

```
            <td>@Html.ActionLink("Edit", "Edit", new { id = item.Event.ID})</td>
            <td>@Html.ActionLink("Delete", "Delete", new { id = item.Event.ID})</td>
        </tr>
    }
</table>
```

The last two columns of the table contain links that allow the user to edit or delete the record shown in the row. They point to two action methods (`Edit` and `Delete`) and use the optional `id` routing variable (shown in Listing 31-11) to pass the `ID` value of the selected event, such that the requested URLs will be of the following form, for example:

`/Event/Edit/9`

We'll implement these actions later. The `Views/Event/Index.cshtml` view is used for non-Ajax requests and includes the partial view, as you can see in Listing 31-22.

Listing 31-22. *The Index view*

```
@model IEnumerable<TriathlonApp.Models.View.EventAndRankSummary>
@{
    ViewBag.TabName = "Events";
    AjaxOptions ajaxOpts = new AjaxOptions {
        UpdateTargetId = "datatable"
    };
}

@Html.Partial("EventsTable", Model)

@using (Ajax.BeginForm(ajaxOpts)) {

    <table>
        <tr>
            <td>Event Type:</td>
            <td>@Html.DropDownList("EventFilter", new SelectList(ViewBag.EventTypes))</td>
            <td><input type="submit" value="Filter"/></td>
            <td>@Html.ActionLink("Add Event", "Add")</td>
        </tr>
    </table>
}
```

This is effectively a superset of the partial view. I render the `table` containing the data and use another `table` to create a simple grid effect for the event type filter, a submit button, and a link to the (as yet undefined) `Add` action, which the user will click when they want to add a new event. I have used the `Ajax.BeginForm` helper to create the form element, but I don't have to define a target URL in the `AjaxOptions` object since the same action method is used for Ajax and regular requests.

We can see the effect of these changes by starting the application and navigating to the default URL, as shown in Figure 31-5.

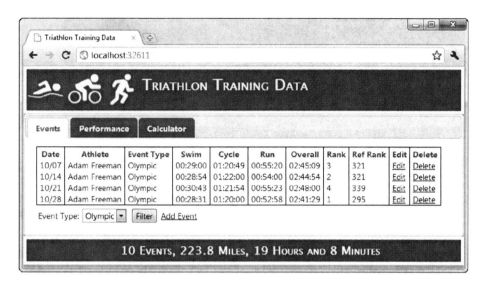

Figure 31-5. *Displaying the event data*

Ajax is used to update the table when the user selects an event type from the drop-down list and clicks the Filter button. The appearance is slightly less appealing for non-JavaScript browser, as shown in Figure 31-6, but everything still works. However, clicking the Filter button causes the browser to load a new HTML page, rather than just replace the `table` element.

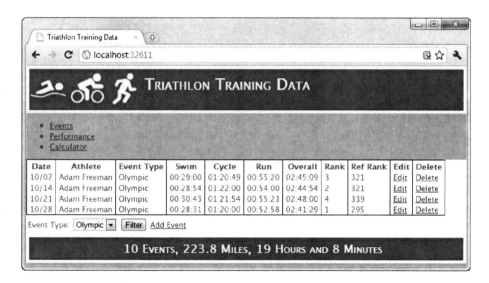

Figure 31-6. *Displaying the event data when JavaScript is disabled*

Adding Some jQuery Polish

We can improve the appearance of the page for JavaScript-enabled browsers using some of the jQuery techniques I showed you in Chapter 10. Listing 31-23 shows the additions to the Views/Event/Index.cshtml view.

Listing 31-23. Adding jQuery to the view

```
@model IEnumerable<TriathlonApp.Models.View.EventAndRankSummary>
@{
    ViewBag.TabName = "Events";
    AjaxOptions ajaxOpts = new AjaxOptions {
        UpdateTargetId = "datatable",
        OnSuccess = "PolishTable"
    };
}
<script type="text/javascript">

    function PolishTable() {
        $('#datatable a').button().addClass("linkbutton");
    }

    $(document).ready(function () {
        PolishTable();
        $('#filterSubmit').hide();
        $('#EventFilter').change(function () {
            $('form').submit();
        });
        $('#AddLink').button();
    });

</script>

@Html.Partial("EventsTable", Model)

@using (Ajax.BeginForm(ajaxOpts)) {

    <table>
        <tr>
            <td>Event Type:</td>
            <td>@Html.DropDownList("EventFilter", new SelectList(ViewBag.EventTypes))</td>
            <td><input id="filterSubmit" type="submit" value="Filter"/></td>
            <td>@Html.ActionLink("Add Event", "Add", null, new { id = "AddLink" })</td>
        </tr>
    </table>
}
```

The PolishTable function uses the jQuery UI button feature to transform the links for editing and deleting events into buttons. This function is called by the unobtrusive Ajax OnSuccess callback and in the other function I added, which is called when the document loads. In addition to calling PolishTable, this function also changes the Add Event link into a button, hides the submit element, and registers an event callback that posts the form to the server when a new value is selected from the drop-down menu. You can see the effect of this script in Figure 31-7.

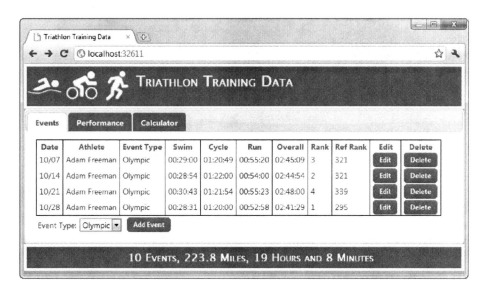

Figure 31-7. *Adding some jQuery to polish the appearance of the page*

Building the Add Event Feature

The user can add a new event to the database by clicking the Add Event button. Before we implement the action method that this button targets, I am going to add some validation and display attributes to the **Event** model class, as shown in Listing 31-24.

Listing 31-24. *Adding display and validation attributes to the Event domain model class*

```
using System;
using System.ComponentModel.DataAnnotations;
using System.Web.Mvc;

namespace TriathlonApp.Models.Domain {
    public class Event {

        [HiddenInput(DisplayValue=false)]
        public int ID { get; set; }
        [DataType(DataType.Date)]
        public DateTime Date { get; set; }
        [Required]
        public string Athlete { get; set; }
        public string Type { get; set; }
```

```
    [Required]
    public TimeSpan SwimTime { get; set; }
    [Required]
    public TimeSpan CycleTime { get; set; }
    [Required]
    public TimeSpan RunTime { get; set; }
    [HiddenInput(DisplayValue=true)]
    public TimeSpan OverallTime { get; set; }
  }
}
```

I explained the meaning of these attributes in Chapters 26 and 29. The next step is to add the action methods to the controller, which you can see in Listing 31-25.

Listing 31-25. Implementing the Add action

```
using System;
using System.Linq;
using System.Web.Mvc;
using TriathlonApp.Models.Domain;
using TriathlonApp.Models.Domain.Repository;
using TriathlonApp.Models.View;

namespace TriathlonApp.Controllers {
    public class EventController : Controller {
        private IRepository repository;

        ...constructor and Index action omitted for brevity...

        public ActionResult Add() {
            ViewBag.EventTypes = repository.EventTypes.Select(x => x.Name);
            ViewBag.Athletes = repository.Athletes.Select(x => x.Name);
            return View(new Event { Date = DateTime.Now });
        }

        [HttpPost]
        public ActionResult Add(Event ev) {

            ValidateEvent(ev);

            if (ModelState.IsValid) {
                ev.OverallTime = ev.SwimTime + ev.CycleTime + ev.RunTime;
                repository.SaveEvent(ev);
                return RedirectToAction("Index");
            } else {
                ViewBag.EventTypes = repository.EventTypes.Select(x => x.Name);
                ViewBag.Athletes = repository.Athletes.Select(x => x.Name);
                return View(ev);
            }
        }
    }
```

```
        private void ValidateEvent(Event ev) {
            if (ModelState.IsValidField("SwimTime") && ev.SwimTime == TimeSpan.Zero) {
                ModelState.AddModelError("SwimTime", "Enter a time");
            }
            if (ModelState.IsValidField("CycleTime") && ev.CycleTime == TimeSpan.Zero) {
                ModelState.AddModelError("CycleTime", "Enter a time");
            }
            if (ModelState.IsValidField("RunTime") && ev.RunTime == TimeSpan.Zero) {
                ModelState.AddModelError("RunTime", "Enter a time");
            }
        }
    }
}
```

The first **Add** method takes no parameters and is used to service **GET** requests. Details of the registered athletes and event types are passed to the view using the **ViewBag**, and a new **Event** object is created and used as the view model object. This allows me to pass the current date to the view.

The second **Add** method is used to process **POST** requests and relies on model binding to receive an **Event** parameter. I use model validation to report an error to the user if any of the individual activity times are zero. If there are no model errors, I save the new **Event** object to the repository and redirect the user to the **Index** action. If there are model errors, then I redisplay the **Event** object so that the validation messages are shown to the user. Listing 31-26 shows the **Views/Event/Add.cshtml** view, used by both overloads of the action method.

Listing 31-26. *The Add view*

```
@model TriathlonApp.Models.Domain.Event

@{
    ViewBag.TabName = "Events";
}

<script type="text/javascript">
    $(document).ready(function () {
        $(':submit').attr('value', 'Add');
    });
</script>

<h2>Add New Event</h2>
<p />

@using (Html.BeginForm()) {

    @Html.Partial("EventEditor", Model);
}
```

This is very simple. Most of the hard work is done in the **EventEditor** partial view. I created **EventEditor.cshtml** in the **Views/Shared** folder. We'll use it later when we come to implement the edit feature. The only point of note is the small script in this view that changes the value attribute of **submit** elements to **Add**. This tailors the generic Submit button that is in the partial view to the current task but still lets me use the view for non-JavaScript browsers. Listing 31-27 shows the contents of the **EventEditor** partial method.

Listing 31-27. *The EventEditor partial view*

```
@model TriathlonApp.Models.Domain.Event

<script type="text/javascript">
    $(document).ready(function () {
        $(':submit, #cancellink').button();
        $('#eventtable select, #eventtable td input').width("150");
        $('#Date').datepicker();
    });
</script>

@Html.HiddenFor(x => x.ID)

<table id="eventtable">
    <tr><th>Date:</th>
        <td>@Html.EditorFor(x => x.Date)</td>
        <td>@Html.ValidationMessageFor(x => x.Date)</td></tr>
    <tr><th>Athlete:</th>
        <td>@Html.DropDownList("Athlete", new SelectList(ViewBag.Athletes))</td>
        <td> @Html.ValidationMessageFor(x => x.Athlete)</td></tr>
    <tr><th>Event Type:</th>
        <td>@Html.DropDownList("Type", new SelectList(ViewBag.EventTypes))</td>
        <td> @Html.ValidationMessageFor(x => x.Type)</td></tr>
    <tr><th>Swim Time:</th>
        <td>@Html.EditorFor(x => x.SwimTime)</td>
        <td> @Html.ValidationMessageFor(x => x.SwimTime)</td></tr>
    <tr><th>CycleTime:</th>
        <td>@Html.EditorFor(x => x.CycleTime)</td>
        <td>@Html.ValidationMessageFor(x => x.CycleTime)</td></tr>
    <tr><th>Run Time:</th>
        <td>@Html.EditorFor(x => x.RunTime)</td>
        <td>@Html.ValidationMessageFor(x => x.RunTime)</td></tr>
    <tr style="text-align:center">
        <th colspan="2">
            <input type="submit" value="Submit" />
            @Html.ActionLink("Cancel", "Index", null, new {id = "cancellink"})
        </th>
    </tr>
</table>
```

The main part of this partial view creates a table to provide a grid structure around a set of labels, editors, and validation messages for the properties of the Event view model object. The Athlete and Type parameters are represented by drop-down lists. I have added a small script to this view. Here is the first statement:

```
$(':submit, #cancellink').button();
```

This statement selects the input element and the link element that I added at the bottom of the table and turns them into buttons. These allow the user to submit the form or return to the Index action. The second statement is as follows:

```
$('#eventtable select, #eventtable td input').width("150");
```

This statement sets the **select** and **input** elements in the table to be similar sizes. The final statement enables the jQuery UI date picker on the **Date** attribute editor:

```
$('#Date').datepicker();
```

I showed you the date picker in Chapter 10. However, I am using all of the default settings in this view, since the layout we are working with is simpler. You can see the rendered view in Figure 31-8.

Figure 31-8. *Adding a new event to the database*

I added the unobtrusive validation library to the layout earlier in the chapter, which means that the validation I defined using attributes will be enforced at the client as well as at the server. The checks for zero times, which you can see in the figure, are performed in the action method and so won't be applied until the user clicks the Add button and posts the form.

Building the Edit Feature

Now that we have the main structure of the application in place, adding the ability to edit events is straightforward. Listing 31-28 shows the Edit action methods, defined in the EventController class.

Listing 31-28. Implementings the Edit action

```
using System;
using System.Linq;
using System.Web.Mvc;
using TriathlonApp.Models.Domain;
using TriathlonApp.Models.Domain.Repository;
using TriathlonApp.Models.View;

namespace TriathlonApp.Controllers {
    public class EventController : Controller {
        private IRepository repository;

        ...constructor, Index and Add actions omitted for brevity...

        public ActionResult Edit(int id) {
            ViewBag.EventTypes = repository.EventTypes.Select(x => x.Name);
            ViewBag.Athletes = repository.Athletes.Select(x => x.Name);
            Event ev = repository.Events.Where(x => x.ID == id).FirstOrDefault();
            if (ev.ID > 0) {
                return View(ev);
            } else {
                return RedirectToAction("Index");
            }
        }

        [HttpPost]
        public ActionResult Edit(Event ev) {
            ValidateEvent(ev);
            if (ModelState.IsValid) {
                ev.OverallTime = ev.SwimTime + ev.CycleTime + ev.RunTime;
                repository.SaveEvent(ev);
                return RedirectToAction("Index");
            } else {
                return View(ev);
            }
        }

        private void ValidateEvent(Event ev) {
            if (ModelState.IsValidField("SwimTime") && ev.SwimTime == TimeSpan.Zero) {
                ModelState.AddModelError("SwimTime", "Enter a time");
            }
            if (ModelState.IsValidField("CycleTime") && ev.CycleTime == TimeSpan.Zero) {
                ModelState.AddModelError("CycleTime", "Enter a time");
            }
```

```
            if (ModelState.IsValidField("RunTime") && ev.RunTime == TimeSpan.Zero) {
                ModelState.AddModelError("RunTime", "Enter a time");
            }
        }
    }
}
```

The first overload of the `Edit` method takes an `int` parameter that corresponds to the optional `id` routing variable. I use this to retrieve the `Event` object that the user wants and pass it as the view model object to the default view. If there is no `Event` object with the specified ID, I redirect the user back to the `Index` action.

The second overload of the `Edit` method is used for `POST` requests. It performs validation in the same way that the `Add` action did, generates the value for the `OverallTime` property, and stores the modified event using the repository before redirecting the user to the `Index` action. Listing 31-29 shows the `Edit.cshtml` view, created in the `Views/Event` folder.

Listing 31-29. *The Edit view*

```
@model TriathlonApp.Models.Domain.Event

@{
    ViewBag.TabName = "Events";
}

<script type="text/javascript">
    $(document).ready(function () {
        $(':submit').attr('value', 'Save');
    });
</script>

<h2>Edt an Event</h2>
<p />

@using (Html.BeginForm()) {

    @Html.Partial("EventEditor", Model);
}
```

This is a minor variation on the `Add` view, with some minor changes to reflect the current task. The bulk of the HTML that this view generates comes from the `EventEditor` partial view.

Fixing the Repository

We have to fix a wrinkle in the repository before the edit functionality will work. This is the same problem we faced when we looked at model binding in Chapter 29. The MVC framework creates an `Event` object and uses model binding to assign values to the object's properties. Unfortunately, the Entity Framework doesn't know anything about the object that the MVC framework created and doesn't detect the changes that the user has made. To fix this, I have made the changes to the `SaveEvent` method in the repository implementation shown in Listing 31-30.

Listing 31-30. Forcing change detection in the repository implementation

```
...
public void SaveEvent(Event ev) {
    if (ev.ID == 0) {
        adapter.Events.Add(ev);
    } else {
        Event rev = Events.Where(x => x.ID == ev.ID).FirstOrDefault();
        if (rev.ID > 0) {
            rev.Date = ev.Date;
            rev.Athlete = ev.Athlete;
            rev.Type = ev.Type;
            rev.SwimTime = ev.SwimTime;
            rev.CycleTime = ev.CycleTime;
            rev.RunTime = ev.RunTime;
            rev.OverallTime = ev.OverallTime;
        }
    }
    adapter.SaveChanges();
}
...
```

These changes locate the Event object that the Entity Framework *does* know about and copies the property values from the doppelganger that the MVC framework created. This makes the Entity Framework detect the changes that the user has made, such that the subsequent call to SaveChanges will update the database correctly.

Building the Delete Feature

Before we can implement a delete action, we will have to update the repository so that it supports deleting event objects. Listing 31-31 shows the modifications required for the IRepository interface.

Listing 31-31. Adding a delete method to the IRepository interface

```
using System.Collections.Generic;

namespace TriathlonApp.Models.Domain.Repository {

    public interface IRepository {

        IEnumerable<Event> Events { get; }
        void SaveEvent(Event ev);
        void DeleteEvent(Event ev);

        IEnumerable<EventType> EventTypes { get; }
        IEnumerable<ReferenceTime> ReferenceTimes { get; }
        IEnumerable<Athlete> Athletes { get; }
```

```
        RankingSet GetPersonalRank(Event ev);
        RankingSet GetReferenceRank(Event ev);
    }
}
```

I have added a `DeleteEvent` that defines a parameter, which is the `Event` to delete. Listing 31-32 shows the corresponding method in the implementation.

Listing 31-32. Implementing the delete method in the repository implementation

```
using System.Collections.Generic;
using System.Data.Entity;
using System.Linq;

namespace TriathlonApp.Models.Domain.Repository {

    public class EFRepository : IRepository {
        private EFAdapter adapter = new EFAdapter("EFRepository");

        public IEnumerable<Event> Events {
            get { return adapter.Events; }
        }

        public void SaveEvent(Event ev) {
            if (ev.ID == 0) {
                adapter.Events.Add(ev);
            } else {
                Event rev = Events.Where(x => x.ID == ev.ID).FirstOrDefault();
                if (rev.ID > 0) {
                    rev.Date = ev.Date;
                    rev.Athlete = ev.Athlete;
                    rev.Type = ev.Type;
                    rev.SwimTime = ev.SwimTime;
                    rev.CycleTime = ev.CycleTime;
                    rev.RunTime = ev.RunTime;
                    rev.OverallTime = ev.OverallTime;
                }
            }
            adapter.SaveChanges();
        }

        public void DeleteEvent(Event ev) {
            Event rev = Events.Where(x => x.ID == ev.ID).FirstOrDefault();
            if (rev.ID > 0) {
                adapter.Events.Remove(rev);
                adapter.SaveChanges();
            }
        }
    }
```

```
            ...methods omitted for brevity...

    }
}
```

We have to take the same precautions in the `DeleteEvent` method as we did in `SaveEvent`. The `Event` object that the MVC framework model binding process creates is unknown to the Entity Framework and so we must retrieve a matching `Event` object from the database and then pass this to the `Remove` method of the `Events` property of the adapter. Now that we have added support for deleting events from the repository, we can implement the `Delete` action, as shown in Listing 31-33.

Listing 31-33. Implementing the Delete action methods

```
using System;
using System.Linq;
using System.Web.Mvc;
using TriathlonApp.Models.Domain;
using TriathlonApp.Models.Domain.Repository;
using TriathlonApp.Models.View;

namespace TriathlonApp.Controllers {
    public class EventController : Controller {
        private IRepository repository;

        ...constructor and other methods omitted for brevity...

        public ActionResult Delete(int id) {
            Event ev = repository.Events.Where(x => x.ID == id).FirstOrDefault();
            if (ev.ID > 0) {
                return View(ev);
            } else {
                return RedirectToAction("Index");
            }
        }

        [HttpPost]
        public ActionResult Delete(Event ev) {
            repository.DeleteEvent(ev);
            return RedirectToAction("Index");
        }
    }
}
```

The first of the `Delete` methods deals with GET requests and retrieves an `Event` object from the repository using the `id` parameter, which corresponds to the id routing variable. This object is passed to the default view for rendering. The second of the `Delete` methods deals with POST requests and calls the `DeleteEvent` method in the repository and then redirects the user to the `Index` action. I created the `Delete.cshtml` view in the `Views/Event` folder, and Listing 31-34 shows the contents.

Listing 31-34. The Delete view

```
@model TriathlonApp.Models.Domain.Event

@{
    ViewBag.TabName = "Events";
}

<script type="text/javascript">
    $(document).ready(function () {
        $(':submit, #cancellink').button();
    });
</script>

<h2>Delete Event</h2>
<p />

@using (Html.BeginForm()) {
    @Html.HiddenFor(x => x.ID)
    <table id="eventtable">
        <tr><th>Date:</th><td>@Html.DisplayFor(x => x.Date)</td></tr>
        <tr><th>Athlete:</th><td>@Html.DisplayFor(x => x.Athlete)</td></tr>
        <tr><th>Event Type:</th><td>@Html.DisplayFor(x => x.Type)</td></tr>
        <tr><th>Swim Time:</th><td>@Html.DisplayFor(x => x.SwimTime)</td></tr>
        <tr><th>CycleTime:</th><td>@Html.DisplayFor(x => x.CycleTime)</td></tr>
        <tr><th>Run Time:</th><td>@Html.DisplayFor(x => x.RunTime)</td></tr>
          <tr><th>Overall Time:</th><td>@Html.DisplayFor(x => x.OverallTime)</td></tr>
        <tr style="text-align:center">
            <th colspan="2">
                <input type="submit" value="Delete" />
                @Html.ActionLink("Cancel", "Index", null, new { id = "cancellink" })
            </th>
        </tr>
    </table>
}
```

This view presents the user with a read-only view of the Event and the option to delete it or cancel and return to the event list. This view is broadly similar to the ones we have used for adding and editing events.

Building the Performance Tab

The Performance tab displays the best performance for each event type for a selected athlete. To make it easier to pass this information from the controller to the view, I have defined a couple of view model classes, as shown in Listing 31-35. I created these classes in the Models/View folder.

Listing 31-35. View model classes for use in the Performance tab

```
using System;
using TriathlonApp.Models.Domain;

namespace TriathlonApp.Models.View {

    public class PerformanceSummary {
        public string Athlete { get; set; }
        public RankingSet SprintRanks { get; set; }
        public TimeSet SprintTimes { get; set; }
        public RankingSet OlympicRanks { get; set; }
        public TimeSet OlympicTimes { get; set; }
    }

    public class TimeSet {
        public TimeSpan SwimTime { get; set; }
        public TimeSpan CycleTime { get; set; }
        public TimeSpan RunTime { get; set; }
        public TimeSpan OverallTime { get; set; }
    }
}
```

These classes are collections of properties that express the data required in the tab. Notice that I use the RankingSet domain model class to avoid creating two classes with equivalent data values. The next step is to create and implement the PerformanceController class, as shown in Listing 31-36.

Listing 31-36. The PerformanceController class

```
using System;
using System.Collections.Generic;
using System.Linq;
using System.Web.Mvc;
using TriathlonApp.Models.Domain;
using TriathlonApp.Models.Domain.Repository;
using TriathlonApp.Models.View;

namespace TriathlonApp.Controllers {
    public class PerformanceController : Controller {
        private IRepository repository;

        public PerformanceController(IRepository repo) {
            repository = repo;
        }

        public ActionResult Index(string athlete) {

            if (string.IsNullOrEmpty(athlete)) {
                athlete = repository.Athletes.First().Name;
            }
```

```
        PerformanceSummary data = new PerformanceSummary {
            Athlete = athlete,
            SprintTimes = GetTimeData(athlete, "Sprint"),
            OlympicTimes = GetTimeData(athlete, "Olympic")
        };

        data.OlympicRanks = GetRankData("Olympic", data.OlympicTimes);
        data.SprintRanks = GetRankData("Sprint", data.SprintTimes);

        ViewBag.Athletes = repository.Athletes.Select(x => x.Name);

        if (Request.IsAjaxRequest()) {
            return PartialView("PerformanceTable", data);
        } else {
            return View(data);
        }
    }

    private TimeSet GetTimeData(string athlete, string eventType) {

        TimeSet result = new TimeSet();

        IEnumerable<Event> events = repository.Events
            .Where(x => x.Athlete == athlete && x.Type == eventType);

        if (events.Count() > 0) {
            result.SwimTime = events.Min(x => x.SwimTime);
            result.CycleTime = events.Min(x => x.CycleTime);
            result.RunTime = events.Min(x => x.RunTime);
            result.OverallTime = events.Min(x => x.OverallTime);
        }

        return result;
    }

    private RankingSet GetRankData(string eventType, TimeSet times) {

        if (times.SwimTime == TimeSpan.Zero || times.CycleTime == TimeSpan.Zero
            || times.RunTime == TimeSpan.Zero || times.OverallTime == TimeSpan.Zero) {
            return new RankingSet();
        } else {
            return repository.GetReferenceRank(new Event {
                Type = eventType,
                SwimTime = times.SwimTime,
                CycleTime = times.CycleTime,
                RunTime = times.RunTime,
                OverallTime = times.OverallTime
            });
        }
    }
}
}
```

I have defined only one action method in the controller. It will handle GET and POST requests. It will render a partial view called PerformanceTable when it receives an Ajax request and a view called Index otherwise. The GetTimeData and GetRankData methods get the time and rank data required for the display and are used by the Index method to populate the PerformanceSummary object, which is used as the view model object in both the partial and full views. Listing 31-37 shows the PerformanceTable partial view. I created this view in the Views/Performance folder.

Listing 31-37. *The PerformanceTable partial view*

```
@model TriathlonApp.Models.View.PerformanceSummary

@helper FormatTime(TimeSpan time) {
    if (time == TimeSpan.Zero) {
        @:---
    } else {
        @time
    }
}

@helper FormatRank(int rank) {
    if (rank == 0) {
        @:---
    } else {
        @rank
    }
}

<table class="centerTable">
    <colgroup><col /><col width="100px" /><col /><col width="40px" /></colgroup>
    <tr><th colspan="4">Sprint Results</th></tr>
    <tr>
        <td>Best Swim Time:</td><td>@FormatTime(Model.SprintTimes.SwimTime)</td>
        <td>Best Swim Rank:</td><td>@FormatRank(Model.SprintRanks.SwimRank)</td>
    </tr>
    <tr>
        <td>Best Cycle Time:</td><td>@FormatTime(Model.SprintTimes.CycleTime)</td>
        <td>Best Cycle Rank:</td><td>@FormatRank(Model.SprintRanks.CycleRank)</td>
    </tr>
    <tr>
        <td>Best Run Time:</td><td>@FormatTime(Model.SprintTimes.RunTime)</td>
        <td>Best Run Rank:</td><td>@FormatRank(Model.SprintRanks.RunRank)</td>
    </tr>
    <tr>
        <td>Best Overall Time:</td><td>@FormatTime(Model.SprintTimes.OverallTime)</td>
        <td>Best Overall Rank:</td><td>@FormatRank(Model.SprintRanks.OverallRank)</td>
    </tr>
</table>
```

```
<table class="centerTable">
    <colgroup><col /><col width="100px" /><col /><col width="40px" /></colgroup>
    <tr><th colspan="4">Olympic Results</th></tr>
    <tr>
        <td>Best Swim Time:</td><td>@FormatTime(Model.OlympicTimes.SwimTime)</td>
        <td>Best Swim Rank:</td><td>@FormatRank(Model.OlympicRanks.SwimRank)</td>
    </tr>
    <tr>
        <td>Best Cycle Time:</td><td>@FormatTime(Model.OlympicTimes.CycleTime)</td>
        <td>Best Cycle Rank:</td><td>@FormatRank(Model.OlympicRanks.CycleRank)</td>
    </tr>
    <tr>
        <td>Best Run Time:</td><td>@FormatTime(Model.OlympicTimes.RunTime)</td>
        <td>Best Run Rank:</td><td>@FormatRank(Model.OlympicRanks.RunRank)</td>
    </tr>
    <tr>
        <td>Best Overall Time:</td><td>@FormatTime(Model.OlympicTimes.OverallTime)</td>
        <td>Best Overall Rank:</td><td>@FormatRank(Model.OlympicRanks.OverallRank)</td>
    </tr>
</table>
```

This view creates a pair of table elements and populates them with the time and ranking information for each type of event. I have defined a couple of inline helpers (as described in Chapter 25) so that I can create a meaningful display when the selected athlete hasn't recorded any events for a specific event type. Listing 31-38 shows the Views/Performance/Index.cshtml view.

Listing 31-38. The Index.cshtml view for the Performance controller

```
@model TriathlonApp.Models.View.PerformanceSummary

@{
    ViewBag.TabName = "Performance";
    AjaxOptions ajaxOpts = new AjaxOptions {
        UpdateTargetId = "dataElement"
    };
}

<script type="text/javascript">
    $(document).ready(function () {
        $(':submit').hide();
        $('#athlete').change(function () {
            $('form').submit();
        });
    });

</script>
```

```
@using (Ajax.BeginForm(ajaxOpts)) {
<div id="selectDiv">
    Athlete: @Html.DropDownList("athlete", new SelectList(ViewBag.Athletes, Model.Athlete))
    <input type="submit" value="Select" />
</div>
}

<div id="dataElement">
    @Html.Partial("PerformanceTable", Model)
</div>
```

This view starts by specifying that it should be displayed on the Performance tab and by defining an **AjaxOptions** object that I used to create an Ajax form. I don't have to worry about configuring a fallback URL for non-JavaScript clients because the action method will respond correctly depending on the kind of request it receives.

The user is able to select the athlete whose performance data should be displayed using a drop-down list, and the data itself is rendered using the **PerformanceTable** partial view. I have added a small script to this view to add some polish for JavaScript-enabled browsers. I simply hide the submit element and add a handler that posts the form when the user selects a value using the drop-down list. You can see the Performance tab in Figure 31-9.

Figure 31-9. *The completed Performance tab*

Building the Calculator Tab

The last area of functionality we have to build is the Calculator tab. I have started by creating a couple of view model classes in the Models/View folder. The classes are called CalcData and CalcResult and are shown in Listing 31-39.

Listing 31-39. *View model classes to support the Calculator tab*

```
using System.ComponentModel.DataAnnotations;
namespace TriathlonApp.Models.View {

    public class CalcData {

        public CalcData() {
            Laps = 80;
            PoolLength = 20;
            Minutes = 60;
            CalsPerHour = 1070;
        }

        [Required]
        [Range(1, 500)]
        public int Laps { get; set; }
        [Required]
        [Range(10, 500)]
        public int PoolLength { get; set; }
        [Required]
        [Range(1, 500)]
        public int Minutes { get; set; }
        [Required]
        [Range(1, 5000)]
        public int CalsPerHour {get; set;}

        public CalcResult Result { get; set; }
    }

    public class CalcResult {
        public float Distance { get; set; }
        public int CaloriesBurned { get; set; }
        public int Pace { get; set; }
    }
}
```

The CalcData class contains a property of the CalcResult type. I am going to use this relationship to do something different with the view, just for some variety. CalcData objects will be created during the model binding process, so I have added some validation attributes to ensure that I receive data values for the user that I can work with. Listing 31-40 shows the CalculatorController class.

Listing 31-40. The CalculatorController class

```
using System.Web.Mvc;
using TriathlonApp.Models.Domain.Repository;
using TriathlonApp.Models.View;

namespace TriathlonApp.Controllers {
    public class CalculatorController : Controller {
        private const float metersToMiles = 0.00062137119223733f;
        private const float minsPerHour = 60f;
        private IRepository repository;

        public CalculatorController(IRepository repo) {
            repository = repo;
        }

        public ActionResult Index() {
            return View(new CalcData());
        }

        [HttpPost]
        public ActionResult Index(CalcData calcData) {
            if (ModelState.IsValid) {
                calcData.Result = new CalcResult {
                    Distance = (calcData.Laps * calcData.PoolLength) * metersToMiles,
                    CaloriesBurned = (int)((calcData.Minutes / minsPerHour)
                        * calcData.CalsPerHour),
                    Pace = (int)((calcData.Minutes * minsPerHour) / calcData.Laps),
                };
            }
            return View(calcData);
        }
    }
}
```

This controller is very simple. The first Index method deals with GET requests and renders the default view, passing a new CalcData object as the view model so that the user sees the default values defined in the CalcData constructor.

The second Index method checks the model state and, if there are no errors, sets the Result property of the CalcData object created by the model binder to a new CalcResult object that contains the calculation results. Both of the action methods use the default view, which is Views/Calculator/Index.cshtml, as shown in Listing 31-41.

Listing 31-41. The Index view for the Calculator controller

```
@model TriathlonApp.Models.View.CalcData
@{
    ViewBag.TabName= "Calculator";
}
```

```
<script type="text/javascript">
    $(document).ready(function () {
        $(':submit').button();
    });
</script>

@using (Html.BeginForm()) {

<table id="calcDataTable">
    <colgroup><col /><col width="80px" /><col /><col width="20px"/><col/></colgroup>
    <tr>
        <th>Laps:</th>
        <td>@Html.EditorFor(x => x.Laps)</td>
        <td>@Html.ValidationMessageFor(x => x.Laps)</td>
        @if (Model.Result != null) {
            <th colspan="2" style="text-align:center">Results</th>
        }
    </tr>
    <tr>
        <th>Pool Length:</th>
        <td>@Html.EditorFor(x => x.PoolLength)</td>
        <td>@Html.ValidationMessageFor(x => x.PoolLength)</td>
        @if (Model.Result != null) {
            <th>Distance:</th>
            <td>@string.Format("{0:F2} miles", Model.Result.Distance)</td>
        }
    </tr>
    <tr>
        <th>Minutes:</th>
        <td>@Html.EditorFor(x => x.Minutes)</td>
        <td>@Html.ValidationMessageFor(x => x.Minutes)</td>
        @if (Model.Result != null) {
            <th>Calories:</th>
            <td>@string.Format("{0:F0} calories", Model.Result.CaloriesBurned)</td>
        }
    </tr>
    <tr>
        <th>Calories/Hour:</th>
        <td>@Html.EditorFor(x => x.CalsPerHour)</td>
        <td>@Html.ValidationMessageFor(x => x.CalsPerHour)</td>
        @if (Model.Result != null) {
            <th>Pace:</th>
            <td>@string.Format("{0:F0} seconds/lap", Model.Result.Pace)</td>
        }
    </tr>
    <tr>
        <td colspan="2" style="text-align:center">
            <input type="submit" value="Calculate" />
        </td>
    </tr>
</table>
}
```

What I've done here is put a modicum of logic into the view, such that if the `Result` property `CalcData` view model object isn't `null`, then the view displays extra columns in the table to show the results of the calculation. You can see how this works in Figure 31-10.

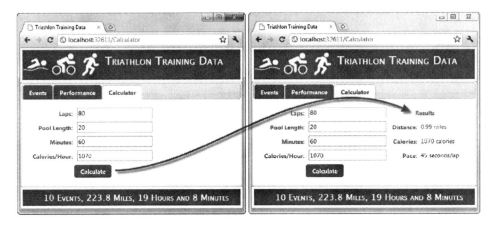

Figure 31-10. *Conditionally displaying data in a view*

I have also included validation messages in the view, which you can see in Figure 31-11.

Figure 31-11. *Displaying validation messages in the Calculator tab*

I am relying on the default validation messages that the validation attributes produce, but you get the idea. To be honest, rendering view content conditionally like this is something that I rarely do in a real project, but I wanted to show you that it is possible (and that it is easy to do). I like to keep my views as simple as possible, which means that I would most likely have created multiple views to handle the different outcomes of posting the form, and to reduce duplication, I would have used a partial view.

Summary

In this chapter, I showed you how we can use the features of the MVC framework to build the triathlon application. You've seen how to create this application using the core ASP.NET features, using the Web Forms controls, and, now, using the MVC framework. Each has a very different nature and presents the developer with a different experience. My feeling when using the MVC framework is that there is a slow start that has to be endured (creating the model, the repository, the layout, and so on), and then functionality starts to come together with increasing speed and ease.

P A R T V

Wrapping Up

The last three chapters of this book apply to all of the different types of ASP.NET applications that we have created. In Chapters 32 and 33, I'll show you how to prepare and deploy an ASP.NET application to Internet Information Services (IIS). In Chapter 34, I'll show you how to perform authentication and authorization in ASP.NET.

CHAPTER 32

Preparing a Server
for Deployment

Developing an ASP.NET application is only part of the story. We also have to deploy it so that our application can be used. This chapter will show you how to deploy an ASP.NET application to Internet Information Services (IIS), which is the Microsoft application and web server product.

Tip   You don't have to deploy to your own server. A common alternative is to deploy to a third-party hosting company. There is a huge choice of ASP.NET hosting providers with differing levels of service and price points. When you sign up for a hosting service, you will be sent instructions for how to deploy your application. Many, but not all, hosting services will send you instructions that are similar to the examples in Chapter 34.

IIS is included with most versions of Windows, including the client versions such as Windows Vista and Windows 7. I don't recommend deploying an MVC application to a client operating system. There are some fundamental restrictions in these versions of Windows that make them unsuitable for all but the smallest and simplest web applications. Instead, I recommend you use Windows Server. The current version as I write this is Windows Server 2008 R2, which comes with IIS version 7.5, and this is the combination for which this chapter provides instructions.

Note   It is possible to deploy MVC 3 applications to IIS version 6, which is the version that was included with Windows Server 2003 and 2003 R2. I am not going to cover IIS 6 in this book, but a deployment walk-through is available at http://haacked.com/archive/2008/11/26/asp.net-mvc-on-iis-6-walkthrough.aspx.

In the sections that follow, I describe only the minimum steps required to configure a server so that you can deploy and run an ASP.NET application: enable the Web Server role, install .NET Framework version 4 and the Web Deployment Tool, and set up web deployment. I am going to assume you are working with a freshly installed copy of Windows Server. For best-practice information about deploying Windows Server and IIS in production environments, visit the IIS Learning Center at www.iis.net, where you'll find extensive reference information.

Enabling the Web Server Role

The first step is to enable the Web Server (IIS) role on Windows Server. Open the Server Manager tool, and select Add Roles from the Rules Summary section, as shown in Figure 32-1.

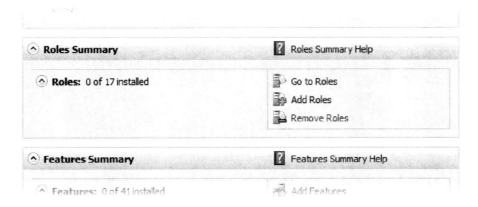

Figure 32-1. *Adding a role to Windows Server*

The Add Roles Wizard will start. You will see a list of available roles (the set of roles depends on which edition of Windows Server 2008 R2 you are using). Check the box for the Web Server (IIS) role and click the Next button. Continue through the wizard until you reach the list of role services that are available for the Web Server (IIS) role. Ensure that the following services are checked:

- ASP.NET (in the Application Development category)

- Management Service (in the Management Tools category)

The ASP.NET role service is essential. You can't run install and run ASP.NET applications without it. The Management Service role service is required for use with the Web Deployment tool, which we will install next.

Continue through the wizard until you reach the summary of the roles and role services that will be enabled. From that page, click the Install button.

After the installation process has completed, you should be able to test the basic functionality of IIS using a browser. Navigate to the default URL for your server, either from the server itself (http://localhost) or from another machine (http://mywindowsserver). If everything has installed properly, you will see the IIS 7.5 Welcome page, as shown in Figure 32-2.

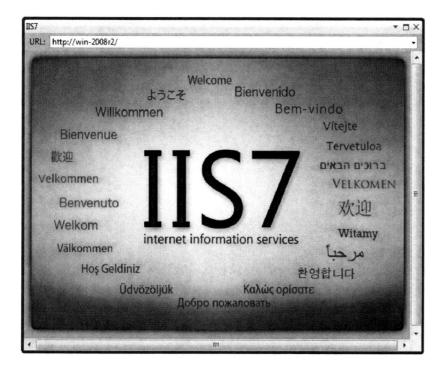

Figure 32-2. The IIS Welcome page

Installing Additional Components

The next step is to use the WebPI on the server to obtain and install additional software components. You need only two components:

- .NET Framework version 4

- Web Deployment Tool 2.0

Using the Web Deployment Tool is only one of the ways for deploying an MVC application, but you'll need this component if you want to follow the deployment demonstrations in Chapter 33.

■ **Note** If you have not yet installed a database on your server, you can select the option to include SQL Server Express 2008 R2 here. If you install SQL Server Express, you'll be prompted to select an authentication mode. Choose Mixed Mode Authentication, and create a password for the sa account. Make a careful note of this.

You can, optionally, select the MVC framework for installation as well. The MVC framework is obviously optional for servers that will run applications built using the core ASP.NET platform or using the Web Forms controls, but it is also optional for a server that will run MVC framework applications. It may seem odd that the MVC framework is optional, but you can choose to include the framework libraries with the application when you deploy it. This is especially useful when deploying an application to a server that you don't control. I'll show you this technique in Chapter 33.

If you don't have a dedicated database server available, you can install SQL Server on the same server that runs IIS. This step is optional, but in Chapter 33, I'll show you how to deploy databases as part of the application deployment process, and you'll need an instance of SQL Server for this.

Setting Up Web Deployment

In Chapter 33, I'll show you how to use the Web Deployment feature to deploy an MVC framework application to a server. However, before you can do that, you need to configure IIS to accept such requests.

■ **Note** We are configuring web deployment so that any administrator account on the server can be used to deploy our MVC framework applications. Delegating this process to nonadministrative accounts is a lengthy process. For a comprehensive tutorial, see http://learn.iis.net/page.aspx/984/configure-web-deploy.

Open the Internet Information Service (IIS) Manager tool, which can be found in the Start menu. In the Connections panel on the left side of the window, select the server. It will be identified by name. Our server is called WIN-2008R2, as you can see in Figure 32-3.

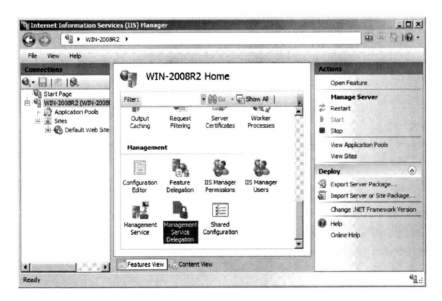

Figure 32-3. *Using the IIS Manager tool*

Double-click the Management Service Delegation icon, which you will find by scrolling down to the Management section in the main part of the window (see Figure 32-3). Click the Edit Feature Settings link, and ensure that the "Allow administrators to bypass rules" option is checked, as shown in Figure 32-4. Click OK to dismiss the dialog box.

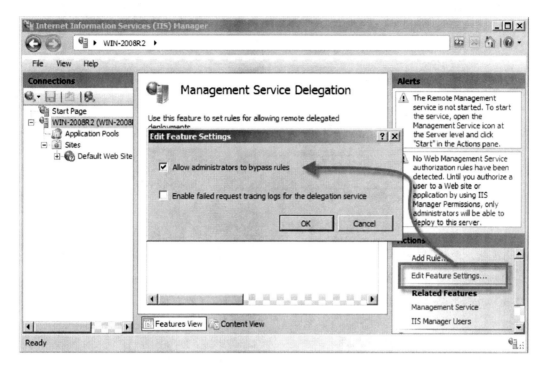

Figure 32-4. *Editing the Management Service Delegation feature settings*

Click the Back button to return to the Management home page for your server. Double-click the Management Service icon, check the "Enable remote connections" option, and then click the Start link, as shown in Figure 32-5.

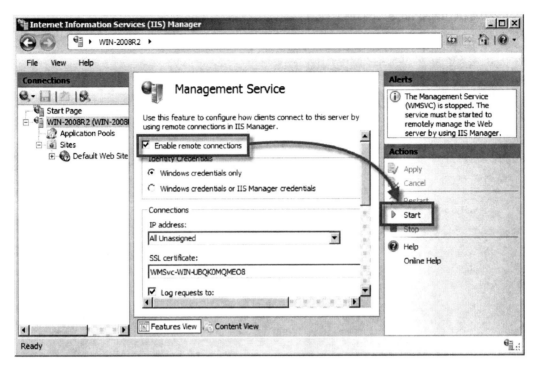

Figure 32-5. *Enabling the Management Service*

■ **Note** The Management Service won't start automatically when you restart the server. To fix this, go to the Services control panel and change the Startup Type option for the Web Management Service to Automatic or Automatic (Delayed).

To test whether the Web Deployment feature is working properly, open a browser and navigate to the following URL:

`https://<server-name>:8172/MsDeploy.axd`

The Web Deployment service requires a secure connection (which is why we request `https` and not regular `http`) and operates on port 8172. If everything is working, you will be see a certificate warning and then be prompted for a username and password. (If you don't see the username and password prompt, then the most likely cause is that a firewall is blocking port 8172.)

Understanding the IIS Fundamentals

As I mentioned, IIS is the application server built into the Windows operating system. In this section, I'll provide some background on how IIS operates so that you have some context for deployment.

Understanding Web Sites

IIS can host multiple independent web sites simultaneously. For each web site, you must specify a *root path* (a folder either on the server's file system or on a network share), and then IIS will serve whatever static or dynamic content it finds in that folder.

To direct a particular incoming HTTP request to a particular web site, IIS allows you to configure *bindings.* Each binding maps all requests for a particular combination of IP address, TCP port number, and HTTP hostname to a particular web site (see Figure 32-6). I'll explain bindings shortly.

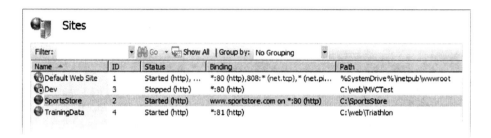

Figure 32-6. *IIS 7 Manager showing a set of simultaneously hosted web sites and their bindings*

Understanding Virtual Directories

As an extra level of configuration, we can add *virtual directories* at any location in a web site's folder hierarchy. Each virtual directory causes IIS to take content from some other file or network location and serve it as if it were actually present at the virtual directory's location under the web site's root folder (see Figure 32-7).

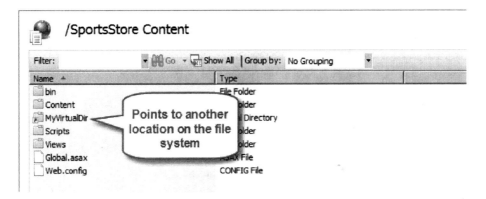

Figure 32-7. *A virtual directory displayed in the IIS Manager content view*

Each virtual directory can be marked as an independent application, in which case it gets its own separate application configuration and state. It can even run a different version of ASP.NET than its parent web site.

Understanding Application Pools

IIS supports *application pools* (usually called *app pools*) as a mechanism to increase isolation between different web applications running in the same server. Each app pool runs a separate worker process, which can run under a different identity (affecting its level of permission to access the underlying OS) and defines rules for maximum memory usage, maximum CPU usage, process-recycling schedules, and so on. Each web site (or virtual directory marked as an independent application) is assigned to one of these app pools. If one application crashes, then the web server itself and applications in other app pools won't be affected.

Binding Web Sites to Hostnames, IP Addresses, and Ports

Since the same server might host multiple web sites, it needs a system to dispatch incoming requests to the right one. As mentioned previously, we can bind each web site to one or more combinations of the following:

- Port number (in production, of course, most web sites are served on port 80)

- Hostname

- IP address (relevant only if the server has multiple IP addresses—for example, if it has multiple physical or virtual network adapters)

When creating a binding, we can choose not to specify a value. This gives the effect of a wildcard—matching anything not specifically matched by a different web site. If multiple web sites have the same binding, then only one of them can run at any particular time. Virtual directories inherit the same bindings as their parent web site.

Preparing the Server for the Application

We have to configure IIS to create a new ASP.NET web site before we can deploy our application. In the following chapter, I'll show you how to deploy the MVC framework version of the triathlon application we created in Chapter 31. In this section, I'll show you how to get the server ready to receive this application. Follow these steps to create a new web site if you are using IIS 7:

1. Open IIS Manager (from Start ➤ Administrative Tools).

2. In the left column, expand the node representing your server, and expand its Sites node. For any unwanted sites already present in the list (such as Default Web Site), either right-click and choose to remove them or select them and use the column on the right to stop them.

3. Add a new web site by right-clicking Sites and choosing Add Web Site. Enter a descriptive value for the site name; I have entered Triathlon.

4. Enter the physical path where you want your application files to reside. I have specified C:\Triathlon.

5. If you want to bind to a particular hostname, IP address, or port, then provide values in the Binding part of the window. For this chapter, we are going to use the default settings.

Figure 32-8 shows the Add Web Site dialog populated for the triathlon application.

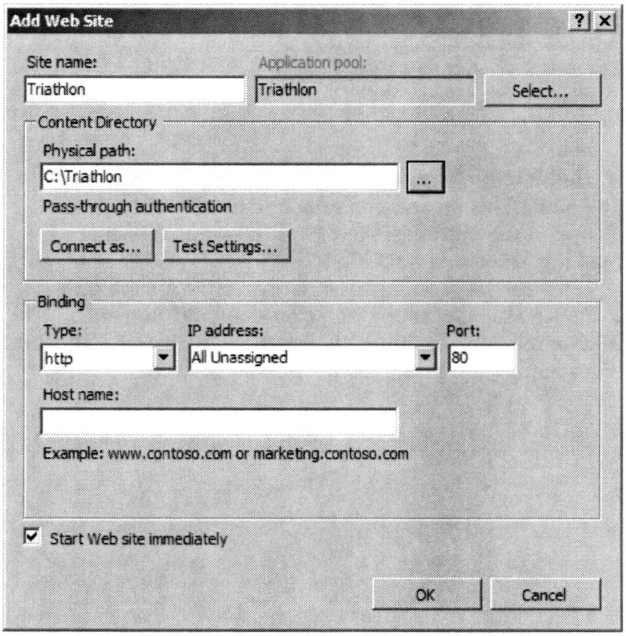

Figure 32-8. *Creating a new web site for the triathalon application*

When you are happy with the configuration for the new site, click the OK button.

WHERE SHOULD I PUT MY APPLICATION?

You can deploy your application to any folder on the server. When IIS first installs, it automatically creates a folder for a web site called Default Web Site at c:\Inetpub\wwwroot\, but you shouldn't feel any obligation to put your application files there. It's common to host applications on a different physical drive from the operating system (for example, in e:\websites\example.com\). It's entirely up to you and may be influenced by concerns such as how you plan to back up the server.

If the binding configuration you have selected conflicts with another web site that IIS is hosting, then you will see a warning like the one in Figure 32-9.

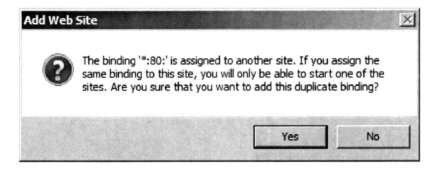

Figure 32-9. *A warning shown when there is a binding conflict*

The configuration that we specified for our triathlon application conflicts with the binding used for the default web site that is created when IIS is installed. This means that only one of our web sites can operate at any given moment, unless we modify one of the bindings. We care only about a single application in this chapter, so click the Yes button if you see this warning.

IIS creates a new application pool for our application but configures it to use .NET version 2. To correct this, click the Application Pools node in the IIS Manager tool, right-click the Triathlon entry, and select Basic Settings from the pop-up menu. Change the .NET Framework version value to .NET version 4, as shown in Figure 32-10. Click the OK button to apply the change to the application pool.

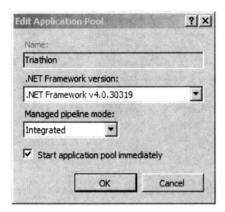

Figure 32-10. Configuring the application pool to use .NET version 4

The final step is to start the application. Click the Sites node in the IIS Manager tool to see a list of the applications available. Select Default Web Site in the list and click Stop in the Manage Web Site panel on the right. Now select Triathlon and click Start in the Manage Web Site panel.

We've started the application, but we haven't deployed any content. This means you will be shown an error if you go to the default URL for the server (`http://win-2008r2/` in my case). We'll fix this in the next chapter when we deploy the application.

Summary

In this chapter, you learned how to prepare Windows Server 2008 R2 and IIS 7.5 so that you can deploy an ASP.NET application. In the next chapter, I'll show you how to prepare and deploy the application.

CHAPTER 33

Deploying an ASP
.NET Application

In the previous chapter, I showed you how to prepare Windows Server and IIS for deployment. This chapter will show you how to prepare the application itself and, of course, do the deployment itself.

I have also included some basic information about using IIS, just enough to understand and perform an ASP.NET application deployment. If you want to learn more about IIS, then I recommend looking at the extensive documentation available at www.iis.net.

I recommend you practice deployment using a test application and server before attempting to deploy a real application into a production environment. Like every other aspect of the software development life cycle, the deployment process benefits from testing. It is not that the ASP.NET deployment features are especially dangerous—they are not—but rather, any interaction that involves a running application with real user data deserves careful thought and planning.

Preparing for Deployment

In this chapter, I am going to deploy the MVC framework version of the triathlon application we created in Chapter 31. Deployment is the same for all types of ASP.NET application, with a couple of exceptions. I'll explain those issues when we get to them.

Enabling Dynamic Page Compilation

One of the most important Web.config settings to pay attention to when deploying an application is compilation, as shown in Listing 33-1.

Listing 33-1. *The compilation setting in Web.config*

```
<configuration>
    <!-- other settings removed for clarity -->
    <system.web>
```

```
<compilation debug="true" targetFramework="4.0">
<assemblies>
    <add assembly="System.Web.Abstractions, Version=4.0 ...
    ...
```

As I explained earlier in the book, ASPX pages and Razor views are compiled into .NET classes at runtime. The compilation setting in Web.config determines whether the compilation will be performed in debug or release mode. The debug mode is intended for use in the development process, and it causes the compiler to do the following:

- Omit some code optimizations so that the compiler can step through the code line-by-line

- Compile each view as it is requested, rather than compiling all the views in a single batch

- Disable request timeouts so that we can spend a long time in the debugger

- Limit the way that browsers will cache content

These are all useful features when we are developing the application, but they hinder performance in deployment. As you might imagine, the solution is to change the value of the debug setting to false, like this:

```
<compilation debug="false" targetFramework="4.0">
```

If we are deploying our application to IIS 7.*x*, we can use the IIS Manager's .NET Compilation tool, which overrides the Web.config settings automatically. To do this, open the IIS Manager, navigate to the home page for the server, and double-click the .NET Compilation item, which is in the ASP.NET section. Ensure that the Debug setting is False and click Apply, as shown in Figure 33-1.

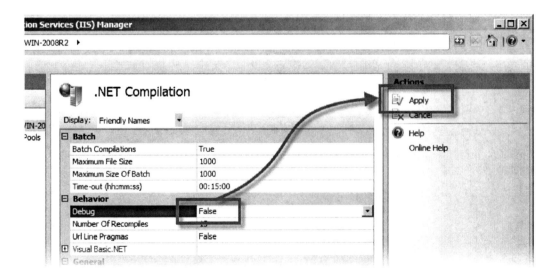

Figure 33-1. *Using the .NET Compilation tool*

Preparing the Web.config File for Transformation

We usually need to change some of the configuration settings in Web.config when we deploy an application. At the very least, we have to change the connection strings that we use for any databases so that we connect to our production servers and not those used for development and testing. Visual Studio provides a useful feature that lets us generate different versions of Web.config for different stages in the development life cycle.

■ **Note**   The Web.config transformations are applied only when deploying the application using one of the techniques described later in this chapter. The transformations are not applied when doing a regular build in Visual Studio.

If you look at the Web.config file in the Solution Explorer window, you will see that there are two additional files, Web.Debug.config and Web.Release.config, as shown in Figure 33-2.

Figure 33-2. The Web.config transformation files

These files correspond to the Debug and Release build configurations that we can select in Visual Studio, as shown in Figure 33-3.

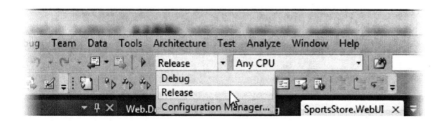

Figure 33-3. Selecting the build configuration

When we select one of these build configurations and then deploy our application, the instructions in the corresponding Web.xxx.config file are used to transform the contents of Web.config. Listing 33-2 demonstrates a sample transformation file.

Listing 33-2. A Web.config transformation file

```
<?xml version="1.0"?>

<configuration xmlns:xdt="http://schemas.microsoft.com/XML-Document-Transform">

  <connectionStrings>
    <add name="EFRepository" connectionString="Data Source=.\SQLEXPRESS;Initial
        Catalog=TrainingData;Persist Security Info=True;User
        ID=adam;Password=adam;MultipleActiveResultSets=true"
        xdt:Transform="SetAttributes" xdt:Locator="Match(name)"/>
  </connectionStrings>

  <system.web>
    <compilation xdt:Transform="RemoveAttributes(debug)" />
  </system.web>
</configuration>
```

I have created a simplified release environment for this chapter. In development, I have my workstation plus a database server called Titan. In production, both the application and the database will run on the same machine, called Win-2008R2. I require two transformations in our Web.config file: the first is that we want to change the connection string used by the Entity Framework so that connections are made to the local machine, not Titan.

■ **Note** Please don't write in and tell me how foolish I am for using a database connection secured with a user name and password of adam. I know this is not secure, but the Apress testing lab is isolated from the public Internet, and I want to keep the examples as simple as possible.

The second transformation is that we want to remove the debug attribute from the compilation configuration element (I explained why this is important in the previous section). When the transformation file in the listing is applied to the application, we'll end up with a new database connection string and with dynamic page compilation enabled.

In the following sections, I'll show you some of the different transformations that we can apply to the Web.config file, and along the way, you'll see how the transformations in the listing actually work.

Understanding the Transformation Structure

The basic structure of a transformation file echoes that of Web.config. We define the configuration element and then replicate the hierarchy of each node that we want to transform. So, connection strings are contained in the connectionStrings element, which is a child of configuration, and the compilation element is contained within system.web, which is also a child of configuration. This means that for our target transformations, we start by creating the skeletal structure shown in Listing 33-3.

Listing 33-3. *A skeletal transformation file structure*

```
<?xml version="1.0"?>
<configuration xmlns:xdt="http://schemas.microsoft.com/XML-Document-Transform">

  <connectionStrings>
    ...transformation for connection string goes here...
  </connectionStrings>

  <system.web>
    ...tranformation for compilation goes here...
  </system.web>

</configuration>
```

For each transformation we want to perform, we define the target element, the type of transformation we require, and any additional values that the transformation demands. So, for example, if we want to transform the compiler attribute, then we define a transformation like this:

```
<compilation xdt:Transform="RemoveAttributes(debug)" />
```

The Transform attribute specifies which of the available transformation attributes we want to apply to the compilation element in the Web.config file. In this example, I have selected the RemoveAttributes transformation and passed in an argument of debug. As you might expect, this has the effect of removing the debug attribute from the compilation element. If we start with an element like this in Web.config:

```
<compilation debug="true" targetFramework="4.0">
```

and then deploy using the Release configuration, then we end up with an element like this:

```
<compilation targetFramework="4.0">
```

Table 33-1 shows the set of transformations that are supported.

Table 33-1. Web.config Transformations

Transformation	Description
Insert	Inserts the containing element into Web.config
InsertBefore InsertAfter	Inserts the containing element before or after the specified element
Remove	Removes a single element
RemoveAll	Removes all the elements that are the same as the containing element
RemoveAttributes	Removes a set of attributes from the containing element
SetAttributes	Sets the value of one or more attributes
Replace	Replaces a set of elements

The following sections provide demonstrations of each of the transformations. I have applied the examples to the configuration file shown in Listing 33-4. To make the examples easier to read, I have omitted all but a couple of configuration options and simplified the assembly references and connection strings. They can't be used in a real Web.config file, but they will help illustrate the transformations that are available.

Listing 33-4. A sample Web.config file

```
<?xml version="1.0"?>

<configuration>

  <connectionStrings>
    <add name="EFRepository" connectionString="Data Source=TITAN\SQLEXPRESS;Initial
        Catalog=TrainingData;Persist Security Info=True;UserID=adam;
        Password=adam;MultipleActiveResultSets=true"
      providerName="System.Data.SqlClient"/>
  </connectionStrings>

  <system.web>
    <compilation debug="true" targetFramework="4.0">
      <assemblies>
        <add assembly="System.Web.Abstractions, Version=4.0.0.0, Culture=neutral" />
        <add assembly="System.Web.Helpers, Version=1.0.0.0, Culture=neutral" />
      </assemblies>
    </compilation>
  </system.web>
</configuration>
```

Inserting Configuration Elements

We can add new elements to existing collections of elements in Web.config using the Insert transformation. Listing 33-5 contains an example transformation.

Listing 33-5. *Adding a new element*

```
<?xml version="1.0"?>
<configuration xmlns:xdt="http://schemas.microsoft.com/XML-Document-Transform">

  <connectionStrings>
    <add name="NewConnection" connectionString="MyConnectionString" xdt:Transform="Insert"/>
  </connectionStrings>

</configuration>
```

Listing 33-6 shows the result of this transformation.

Listing 33-6. *The effect of adding a new configuration element*

```
<?xml version="1.0"?>

<configuration>

  <connectionStrings>
    <add name="EFRepository" connectionString="Data Source=TITAN\SQLEXPRESS;Initial
        Catalog=TrainingData;Persist Security Info=True;User ID=adam;
        Password=adam;MultipleActiveResultSets=true" providerName="System.Data.SqlClient" />
    <add name="NewConnection" connectionString="MyConnectionString" />
  </connectionStrings>

  <system.web>
    <compilation debug="true" targetFramework="4.0">
      <assemblies>
        <add assembly="System.Web.Abstractions, Version=4.0.0.0, Culture=neutral" />
        <add assembly="System.Web.Helpers, Version=1.0.0.0, Culture=neutral" />
      </assemblies>
    </compilation>
  </system.web>
</configuration>
```

The transformation attribute is appended to the corresponding region of the Web.config file, as the listing shows. All of the attributes, except the one that specifies the transformation, are preserved.

To exert more control over where a new attribute is inserted, we can use the InsertBefore and InsertAfter transformations, as shown in Listing 33-7.

827

Listing 33-7. *Using the InsertBefore and InsertAfter transformations*

```
<?xml version="1.0"?>
<configuration xmlns:xdt="http://schemas.microsoft.com/XML-Document-Transform">
  <connectionStrings>

    <add name="NewConnection" connectionString="MyConnectionString"
      xdt:Transform
      ="InsertBefore(/configuration/connectionStrings/add[@name='EFRepository'])"/>

    <add name="OtherConnection" connectionString="MyOtherConnectionString"
      xdt:Transform
      ="InsertAfter(/configuration/connectionStrings/add[@name='NewConnection'])"/>

  </connectionStrings>
</configuration>
```

The InsertBefore and InsertAfter transformations require a parameter that identifies the element in the Web.config file relative to where our new element will be inserted. The parameters are expressed using the XPath notation, such that elements are identified by their location in the Web.config document, like this:

```
/configuration/connectionStrings/add
```

This example selects all the add elements contained within the connectionStrings element, which in turn is contained within the top-level configuration element. We can select individual elements by specifying the names and values for attributes, like this:

```
/configuration/connectionStrings/add[@name='NewConnection']
```

This selects the single add element that has a name attribute with a value of NewConnection. Listing 33-8 shows the effect of applying these transformations to the sample Web.config.

Listing 33-8. *The result of applying the InsertBefore and InsertAfter transformations*

```
<?xml version="1.0"?>

<configuration>

  <connectionStrings>
    <add name="NewConnection" connectionString="MyConnectionString" />
    <add name="OtherConnection" connectionString="MyOtherConnectionString" />
    <add name="EFRepository" connectionString="Data Source=TITAN\SQLEXPRESS;Initial
        Catalog=TrainingData;Persist Security Info=True;User ID=adam;
        Password=adam;MultipleActiveResultSets=true" providerName="System.Data.SqlClient" />
  </connectionStrings>
```

```
<system.web>
  <compilation debug="true" targetFramework="4.0">
    <assemblies>
      <add assembly="System.Web.Abstractions, Version=4.0.0.0, Culture=neutral" />
      <add assembly="System.Web.Helpers, Version=1.0.0.0, Culture=neutral" />
    </assemblies>
  </compilation>
</system.web>
</configuration>
```

Removing Configuration Elements

We can remove elements using the Remove transformation, as shown in Listing 33-9.

Listing 33-9. Using the Remove transformation

```
<?xml version="1.0"?>
<configuration xmlns:xdt="http://schemas.microsoft.com/XML-Document-Transform">
  <system.web>
    <compilation>
      <assemblies>
        <add xdt:Transform="Remove"/>
      </assemblies>
    </compilation>
  </system.web>
</configuration>
```

The Remove transformation in this example matches all the add elements in the assembly region. When more than one element matches, only the first is removed. Listing 33-10 shows the result of this transformation.

Listing 33-10. The effect of the Remove transformation

```
<?xml version="1.0"?>

<configuration>

  <connectionStrings>
    <add name="EFRepository" connectionString="Data Source=TITAN\SQLEXPRESS;Initial
        Catalog=TrainingData;Persist Security Info=True;User ID=adam;
        Password=adam;MultipleActiveResultSets=true" providerName="System.Data.SqlClient" />
  </connectionStrings>

  <system.web>
    <compilation debug="true" targetFramework="4.0">
      <assemblies>
        <add assembly="System.Web.Helpers, Version=1.0.0.0, Culture=neutral" />
      </assemblies>
    </compilation>
  </system.web>
</configuration>
```

To remove multiple elements, we can use the RemoveAll transformation, which will remove all matching elements.

Setting and Removing Attributes

We can use the SetAttributes and RemoveAttributes transformations to manipulate attributes in the Web.config file, as shown in Listing 33-11.

Listing 33-11. *Manipulating configuration element attributes*

```
<?xml version="1.0"?>
<configuration xmlns:xdt="http://schemas.microsoft.com/XML-Document-Transform">

  <connectionStrings>
    <add name="EFRepository" xdt:Transform="SetAttributes(connectionString)"
      connectionString="MyNewConnection"/>
  </connectionStrings>

  <system.web>
    <compilation xdt:Transform="RemoveAttributes(targetFramework)"  />
  </system.web>
</configuration>
```

The first transformation in this example changes the value of a connection string, and the second removes the targetFramework attribute from the compilation element. Listing 33-12 shows the effect of these transformations.

Listing 33-12. *Applying transformations to attributes*

```
<?xml version="1.0"?>

<configuration>

  <connectionStrings>
    <add name="EFRepository" connectionString="MyNewConnection"
      providerName="System.Data.SqlClient" />
  </connectionStrings>

  <system.web>
    <compilation debug="true">
      <assemblies>
        <add assembly="System.Web.Abstractions, Version=4.0.0.0, Culture=neutral" />
        <add assembly="System.Web.Helpers, Version=1.0.0.0, Culture=neutral" />
      </assemblies>
    </compilation>
  </system.web>
</configuration>
```

Replacing Elements

We can replace entire sections of Web.config with the Replace transformation, as shown by Listing 33-13.

Listing 33-13. Replacing configuration elements

```
<?xml version="1.0"?>
<configuration xmlns:xdt="http://schemas.microsoft.com/XML-Document-Transform">

  <connectionStrings xdt:Transform="Replace">
    <add name="MyFirstConnection" connectionString="MyConnection1"/>
    <add name="MySecondConnection" connectionString="MyConnection2"/>
    <add name="MyThirdConnection" connectionString="MyConnection2"/>
  </connectionStrings>

</configuration>
```

In this example, we remove all the Web.config elements items contained within the connectionStrings element with the new set of elements defined in the transformation file. Listing 33-14 shows the effect of this transformation on the sample Web.config file.

Listing 33-14. The effect of replacing configuration elements

```
<?xml version="1.0"?>

<configuration>
  <connectionStrings>
    <add name="MyFirstConnection" connectionString="MyConnection1"/>
    <add name="MySecondConnection" connectionString="MyConnection2"/>
    <add name="MyThirdConnection" connectionString="MyConnection2"/>
  </connectionStrings>

  <system.web>
    <compilation debug="true" targetFramework="4.0">
      <assemblies>
        <add assembly="System.Web.Abstractions, Version=4.0.0.0, Culture=neutral" />
        <add assembly="System.Web.Helpers, Version=1.0.0.0, Culture=neutral" />
      </assemblies>
    </compilation>
  </system.web>

</configuration>
```

Using the Locator Attribute

The Locator attribute allows us to be more specific about which element or elements we are interested in. Consider the example in Listing 33-15, which doesn't use the Locator attribute.

Listing 33-15. *A transformation with specificity issues*

```
<?xml version="1.0"?>
<configuration xmlns:xdt="http://schemas.microsoft.com/XML-Document-Transform">

  <system.web>
    <compilation debug="true" targetFramework="4.0">
      <assemblies>
        <add xdt:Transform="Remove"/>
      </assemblies>
    </compilation>
  </system.web>

</configuration>
```

I have created a transformation that will remove an add entry from the assemblies section of the configuration file. As I mentioned previously, if there are multiple matches in Web.config, the Remove transformation will remove the first element it finds. Alternatively, we can use the RemoveAll transformation to remove *all* the elements.

If there are (or might be) multiple matches and we want to transform only one of them, then we can use the Locator attribute. Listing 33-16 shows how we can apply Locator to the previous example.

Listing 33-16. *Using the Locator attribute*

```
<?xml version="1.0"?>
<configuration xmlns:xdt="http://schemas.microsoft.com/XML-Document-Transform">

 <system.web>
   <compilation debug="true" targetFramework="4.0">
     <assemblies>
       <add xdt:Transform="Remove" xdt:Locator="Condition(contains(@assembly,'Helpers'))" />
     </assemblies>
   </compilation>
 </system.web>

</configuration>
```

The value we assigned to the Locator attribute restricts our transformation to those elements that have an assembly attribute value that contains Helpers. The expression that we have specified is combined with the path of the transformation element. We are transforming elements that have the path /configuration/compilation/assemblies/add and that have a matching assembly attribute. There are three different modes that we can use for the Locator attribute, as described in Table 33-2.

Table 33-2. *Locator Attribute Modes*

Mode	Usage	Description
Condition	xdt:Locator="Condition(*Expression*)"	Combines the relative XPath expression with the implied path of the transformation element to limit the element selection
XPath	xdt:Locator="XPath(Expression)"	Applies the absolute XPath expression to limit the element selection
Match	xdt:Locator="Match(*attribute name*)"	Limits the selection to those elements that have attributes whose values match those of the transformation element

When using the Condition mode, we can use XPath operators such as contains and starts-with to create complex search patterns. We can also use the or and and operators to create compound expressions, as shown in Listing 33-17.

Listing 33-17. *Creating compound XPath expressions with the Locator attribute and condition model*

```
<?xml version="1.0"?>
<configuration xmlns:xdt="http://schemas.microsoft.com/XML-Document-Transform">

  <connectionStrings>

    <add xdt:Transform="SetAttributes(connectionString)" connectionString="MyConnection"
        xdt:Locator=
          "Condition(starts-with(@name, 'EF') and contains(@providerName, SqlClient))"/>

  </connectionStrings>
</configuration>
```

■ **Tip**   I am not going to go into the details of XPath in this chapter, but you can get full details, including the list of available operators, at www.w3.org/TR/xpath.

The XPath mode allows us to specify an absolute XPath expression, which is *not* combined with the implicit path of the transformation element. Listing 33-18 contains an example, which is functionally equivalent to Listing 33-17.

Listing 33-18. *Using an absolute XPath expression*

```
<?xml version="1.0"?>
<configuration xmlns:xdt="http://schemas.microsoft.com/XML-Document-Transform">

  <connectionStrings>

    <add xdt:Transform="SetAttributes(connectionString)" connectionString="MyConnection"
        xdt:Locator=
        "XPath(/configuration/connectionStrings/add[starts-with(@name, 'EF') and
            contains(@providerName, 'SqlClient')])"/>
  </connectionStrings>
</configuration>
```

If our goal is to match specific attribute values, then we can use the Match mode, as shown in Listing 33-19.

Listing 33-19. *Using the Match locator mode*

```
<?xml version="1.0"?>
<configuration xmlns:xdt="http://schemas.microsoft.com/XML-Document-Transform">

  <connectionStrings>

    <add xdt:Transform="SetAttributes(connectionString)" connectionString="MyConnection"
        xdt:Locator="Match(name, providerName)"
        name="EFRepository"
        providerName="System.Data.SqlClient"/>

  </connectionStrings>
</configuration>
```

The Match mode takes one or more attribute names and will match against Web.config elements that have the same values for the named attributes as the transformation element *and* that have the same path.

In this example, I specified the name and providerName attributes, which means our transformation will applied to those elements that have the path /configuration/connectionStrings/add, have a name attribute value of EFRepository, and have a providerName attribute value of System.Data.EntityClient.

Preparing the Project for Database Deployment

Another excellent deployment feature that we can use is the ability to deploy a database as part of our project. We can elect to copy the schema and/or data from our development database to our production server as part of the deployment process.

■ **Caution**   This feature can be very useful but should be used with care. In particular, we must ensure that we don't overwrite real user data with any test data that we may be using in development.

To start, set the build configuration for the project to be deployed to Release, either using the drop-down menu shown in Figure 33-3 or using the Configuration Manager, which can be accessed through the Build menu.

Next, right-click the project that will be deployed in the Solution Explorer window, and select Properties from the pop-up menu. The settings for the project will be displayed. Switch to the Package/Publish Web tab, and check the "Include all databases configured in Package/Publish SQL tab" option, as shown in Figure 33-4.

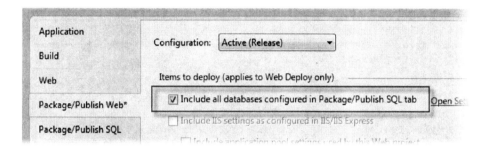

Figure 33-4. *Enabling database deployment*

Next, switch to the Package/Publish SQL properties tab. This is where we configure which databases will be deployed alongside our application. Click the Import from Web.config button to import the database connection string, as shown in Figure 33-5.

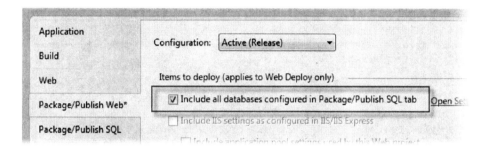

Figure 33-5. *Importing connection strings from Web.config*

This connection string is used to read the schema and data from the development database. The read operation will be performed from our development workstation, which means that the Web.config connection string is usually the one we want. If we need to use a different connection string, then we can enter it manually after clicking the Add button.

■ **Tip**   The deployment process can deploy multiple databases, but we will deploy only the single database that the triathlon application uses in this chapter.

The next step is to enter the connection string for the destination database. For the examples in this chapter, we are going to run the production database and the application server on the same machine, named Win-2008r2. To create the destination connection string, I copied the source string that Visual Studio imported from Web.config and edited the server name, as shown in Figure 33-6.

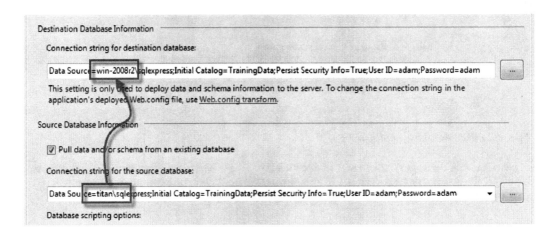

Figure 33-6. Entering the source and destination connection strings

My source and destination connection strings are very similar, which makes copying and editing the most convenient approach. If the connection strings are more disparate, then we can click the ellipsis button (the one marked "..."), which opens a connection builder dialog.

■ **Tip**   The destination connection string is used only to set up the database during the deployment process. See the "Preparing the Web.config File for Transformation" section for details of creating production-environment connection strings for applications.

Next, we must select what is deployed. We can choose to deploy the schema, the schema and any data, or just the data, as shown in Figure 33-7.

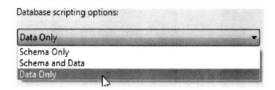

Figure 33-7. *Selecting the deployment type*

Some care should be taken when deciding which option is required. The SQL script that is generated to deploy databases doesn't delete the existing schema and data. This means that if we try to deploy a schema when one already exists or try to deploy data that conflicts with existing data (violating a key constraint, for example), our deployment will fail. Further, we must make sure that the destination connection string we specified earlier will allow the deployment option to function. This means we have to create any required accounts and assign appropriate permissions to allow for the creation of new databases, new tables, and so on. Finally, save the deployment configuration by pressing Ctrl+S or by selecting File ➤ Save Selected Items.

Preparing for a Bin Deployment (MVC Framework Only)

As I mentioned in the part of the book that deals with the MVC framework, the core ASP.NET platform is tied to the main .NET Framework release cycle, but the MVC framework is not. This means we face the prospect of deploying to servers that have the latest version of the .NET Framework and ASP.NET, but not of the MVC framework. (This is especially prevalent in the hosting services world, where providers are reluctant to invest in the cost and disruption of upgrading their servers until there is sufficient demands for the new features.)

To get around this, we can choose to include the MVC libraries as part of our application deployment. We do this by performing what is called a *bin deployment*, so-called because the libraries are included in the bin directory of the project.

Using Visual Studio 2010 SP1 or newer, we can prepare our application for bin deployment in just a few clicks. Right-click the project name in the Solution Explorer window and select Add Deployable Dependencies. In the pop-up menu, select ASP.NET MVC, as shown in Figure 33-8. Finally, click OK.

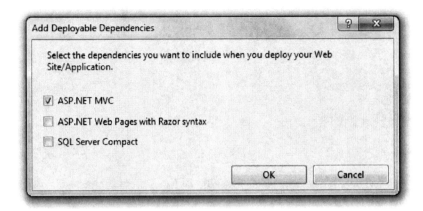

Figure 33-8. *Adding ASP.NET MVC as a deployable dependency*

Visual Studio will then automatically add a new folder to the project, _bin_deployableAssemblies, containing various assemblies required for ASP.NET MVC 3 and the Razor view engine. When we compile our application, those assemblies will be copied to the bin directory of our project folder structure, and these assemblies will be copied to the server when we deploy the project. This means our application can run successfully whether or not the ASP.NET MVC 3 assemblies have been installed by the server's administrators.

Deploying an Application

In the sections that follow, I'll show you different techniques to deploy an ASP.NET application to IIS. All of these techniques create the same result, but the degree of automation varies significantly.

▪ **Note** Before starting any of these deployment techniques, make sure you have selected the desired build configuration, either using the drop-down menu shown in Figure 33-3 or using the Configuration Manager, which can be opened from the Build menu.

Deploying an Application by Copying Files

The most basic way to deploy an application is to copy the required files from our development machine to the target directory on our server. We need to copy the following files from the project on our development machine:

- The compiled .NET assemblies (which are in the /bin folder)
- Configuration files (Web.config and Global.asax)

- The uncompiled views and web pages (*.cshtml, *.aspx, *.ascx, and so on)

- Static files (including images, CSS files, and JavaScript files)

We need to maintain the structure of the project. This means we copy the bin directory and its contents, for example, rather than just the files in the directory. For security reasons, it is better not to copy the files that are required only for development. Don't copy the following:

- C# code files (*.cs, including Global.asax.cs and other code-behind files)

- Project and solution files (*.sln, *.suo, *.csproj, or *.csproj.user)

- The \obj folder

- Anything specific to your source control system (for example, .svn folders if you use Subversion, or the .hg or .git folders if you use Mercurial or Git)

We must copy the files to the directory that we specified when we configured IIS. For this example, this is C:\Triathlon. Figure 33-9 shows the content view for the application. To select the content view, click the triathlon web site in the IIS Manager tool and then click the Content button at the bottom of the window.

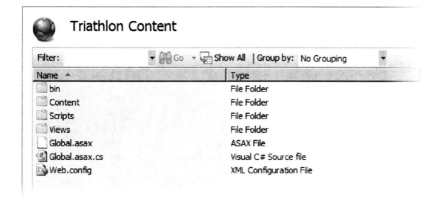

Figure 33-9. *The content view for the triathlon site*

Not only is this the most basic deployment technique, but it is also the most manual. This deployment process will not transform the Web.config file or deploy the databases associated with our application, which means we must take responsibility for deploying the database and changing the application configuration for the production environment.

For the triathlon application, this means we have to set up the schema for the database on the server and load the data that the application requires. We also have to edit the Web.config file to update the connection string so that the application connects to the production database, not our development database server. I recommend caution. It is easy to make a mistake and end up with a production system that is using development or test systems. It is equally important to change the settings back after deployment. Otherwise, future development or testing will be done using databases and other servers that contain real user data. Once we have copied the files into the target directory on the server, we can test the application by requesting the server's default URL, as shown in Figure 33-10.

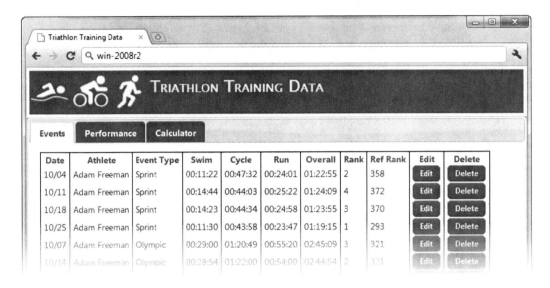

Figure 33-10. *The (manually) deployed application*

The first request to the server can take a while to complete. This is because all the views are compiled as a batch. Subsequent requests will be much quicker.

Using a Deployment Package

A *deployment package* is a zip file containing the application files. Visual Studio generates the package for us, and we deploy the application by copying the package to the server and using the IIS Manager tool. Deployment packages support Web.config transformation and database deployment, which makes the deployment process much more streamlined and consistent than manually copying the files.

■ **Note** Deployment packages rely on the Web Deployment feature, which must be installed on the server. See Chapter 33 for details.

Creating the Deployment Package

To create a deployment package, select the project to deploy in the Solution Explorer window and then select Project ➤ Build Deployment Package. Visual Studio will build the project and generate a zip file that contains the files required to deploy the application and any database schemas and data that we specified when preparing the project. By default the zip file is created in the project folder as obj\Release\Package\<project name>.zip, which means that for our example Visual Studio creates the package as obj\Release\Package\TriathlonApp.WebUI.zip.

■ **Tip**   We can change the location where the deployment package is created on the Package/Publish Web tab
of the project properties.

Deploying the Package

We must begin by copying the deployment package that Visual Studio creates to the server on which we
want to deploy the application. Once that is done, start the IIS Manager tool, and navigate to the
triathlon web site we created earlier. Click the Import Application link on the right of the window, as
shown in Figure 33-11.

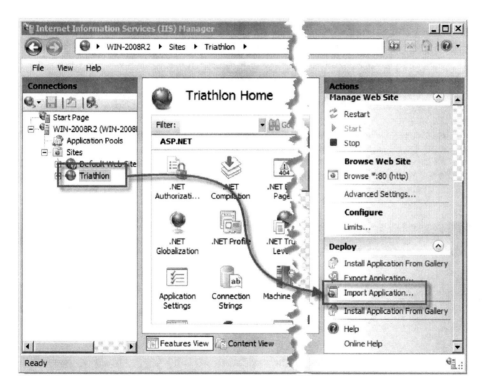

Figure 33-11. Loading a deployment package

The Import Application Package wizard will start. Select the deployment package zip file, and click
the Next button. The contents of the package will be read, and the deployment steps will be displayed, as
shown in Figure 33-12.

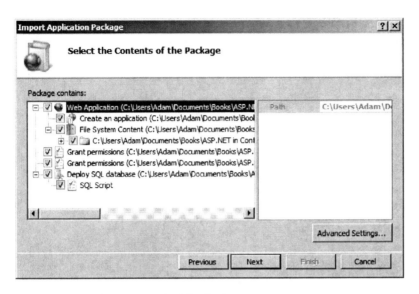

Figure 33-12. *The steps required for deployment*

At this stage, we can uncheck individual items in the package to prevent them from being deployed. This is most useful if the package contains a database that already exists in production. For this example, we are going to deploy all the items in the package, including the data and schema. (Prior to deploying this package, I set up the database on the application server.) Click the Next button. The wizard will display some additional configuration options, as shown in Figure 33-13.

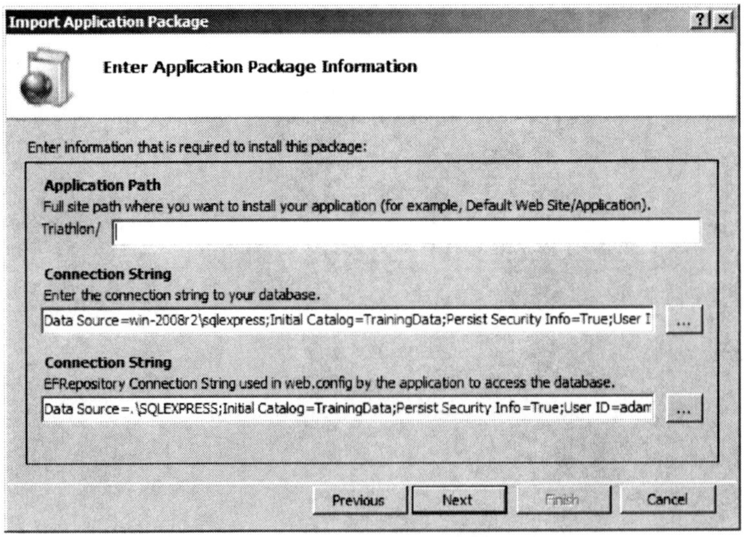

Figure 33-13. *Configuring the application path and connection strings*

The application path determines where in the web site the application will be deployed. We are going to deploy only a single application, so I have cleared the path text box so that the application will be installed in the root directory. A web site can have multiple applications, in which case we can differentiate between them using different paths.

We can also edit the connection strings for the database. The first string will be used to connect to the database to perform the deployment tasks, and the second is the one that will be used in the Web.config file by the application (this will be the transformed value if we have used Web.config transformations). Click the Next button to continue, and click the OK button to dismiss the warning about installing an application to the root directory of a web site.

The application will be deployed, and the database will be installed. When the deployment process has completed, a summary similar to the one shown in Figure 33-14 will be displayed.

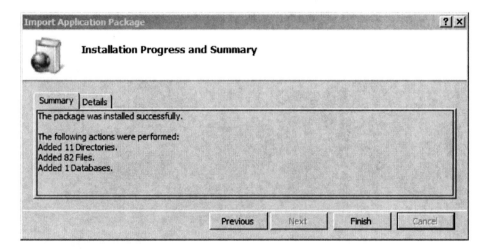

Figure 33-14. The deployment summary

Click the Finish button to close the wizard. The application (and the database) are now installed and are ready to be used.

Using One-Click Publishing

If our development workstation is able to connect to the application server, then we can deploy our application directly, without having to copy files around. We do this using the one-click publishing support built into Visual Studio.

░ **Note** One-click publishing replies on the Web Deployment feature, which must be installed on the server. See Chapter 32 for details.

To use one-click publishing, right-click the project to be deployed in the Solution Explorer window, and select Publish from the pop-up menu (or select Publish <project name> from the Build menu). The Publish Web dialog will be shown, as illustrated by Figure 33-15.

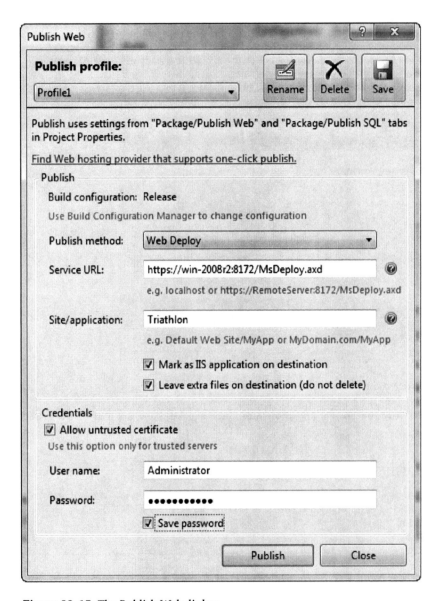

Figure 33-15. *The Publish Web dialog*

Visual Studio supports a range of different publication methods, but the one we want is Web Deploy, which can be selected from the "Publish method" drop-down menu.

The service URL is very specific, as follows:

```
https://<server-name>:8172/MsDeploy.axd
```

The only part of this URL that we edit is the name of the server. In particular, note that the connection uses HTTPS and not regular HTTP. The "Site/application" option determines where the application is deployed to. For our example, this is simply Triathlon since we want to deploy our application to the root directory of the web site we created in the previous chapter.

Ensure that the "Mark as IIS application on destination" and "Allow untrusted certificate" options are checked. Enter the account name and password of an account on the server that has administration rights. As I mentioned in the previous chapter, we have configured the Web Deploy feature to allow administrative users to deploy applications, since delegating this function to other accounts is an involved process.

When all the options are configured, click the Publish button. The deployment package is created and pushed to the server automatically, where it is processed and the application (and any associated databases) is deployed.

Summary

In this chapter, you learned how to prepare an application for deployment and some different ways in which the deployment can be done. I recommend particular care when deploying an application. It is an error-prone task, and it is easy to make a mistake that disrupts service. I suggest you practice deployment in a safe environment, validate that the deployment went as planned, and only then deploy into production.

CHAPTER 34

Authentication and Authorization

In this final chapter, I explain how to perform authentication and authorization in ASP.NET applications. The functionality for these features is built into the core of ASP.NET and is consumed slightly differently depending on what kind of application you are building. There are a wide range of authentication models supported, but the one that I'll demonstrate fully is *Forms Authentication*. This is the most flexible and the most suitable for Internet-facing applications.

Setting Up Authentication

In software terms, *authentication* means determining who somebody is. This is completely separate from *authorization*, which means determining whether a certain person is allowed to do a certain thing. Authorization usually happens after authentication. Appropriately, ASP.NET's authentication facility is concerned only with securely identifying visitors to your site and setting up a security context in which you can decide what that particular visitor is allowed to do.

Using Windows Authentication

The first kind of authentication we can use is *Windows Authentication*. This is where the details of users and their security credentials are stored and managed by the operating system. We essentially inherit whatever authentication system our Windows server is configured to use, including complex Active Directory deployments. We enable Windows Authentication in our application's Web.config file, as shown in Listing 34-1.

Listing 34-1. *Enabling Windows Authentication*

```
<configuration>
    <system.web>
        <authentication mode="Windows" />
    </system.web>
</configuration>
```

When we use Windows Authentication, ASP.NET relies on IIS to authenticate requests from users. IIS in turn uses one of the modes described in Table 34-1.

Table 34-1. *IIS Authentication Modes*

Authentication Mode	Description
Anonymous Authentication	Allows any user to access content without providing a user name and password; the mode is enabled by default on IIS 7.
Basic Authentication	Requires that a user provide a valid user name and password for an account on the server; the credentials provided by the user are sent from the browser to the server as plain text, so this mode should be used only over an SSL connection.
Digest Authentication	Requires that a user provides a valid user name and password, which are transmitted from the browser to the server using a cryptographically secure hash code. This is more secure than the Basic Authentication mode but works only when the server is a domain controller.
Windows Authentication	The identity of the user is established transparently through the Windows domain, without requiring the user to provide any credentials. Transparency requires the client and server to be in the same domain or in domains that have a trust relationship. If domain trust cannot be established, then the user is prompted for a user name and password. This mode is widely used in corporate LANs but is not well-suited to Internet-facing applications.

We can choose which modes are enabled using the Authentication feature in IIS Manager. Select the web site to be configured, and double-click the Authentication icon, which appears in the IIS feature group. Authentication modes can be enabled and disabled, as shown in Figure 34-1.

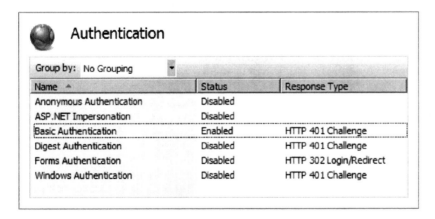

Figure 34-1. *The IIS Authentication feature*

If we want to restrict access such that requests for all content require authentication, then we must disable the Anonymous Authentication feature. If we want to restrict access to certain parts of the application, then we can leave the Anonymous Authentication option enabled and apply authentication selectively, using the techniques I describe later in the chapter. The specific technique differs based on which kind of ASP.NET application is being configured.

If some of the authentication options are not displayed, then we must run the Server Manager tool and use the Add Role Services option for the Web Server (IIS) Role setting. The roles we require can be found in the Security section, as shown in Figure 34-2.

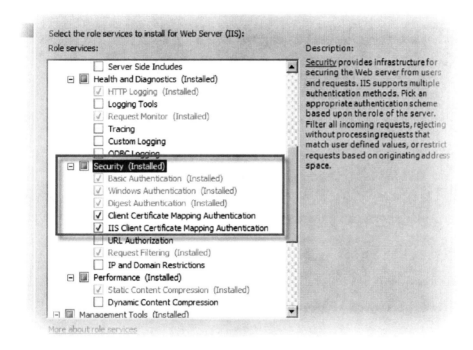

Figure 34-2. *Adding Web Server role features*

Windows Authentication (the broader feature, not the specific IIS mode) can be extremely useful if you are deploying an application in a corporate intranet and there is an established domain infrastructure. Users don't have to manage duplicate sets of credentials, and we don't have to manage account creation and deletion.

This form of authentication doesn't work so well for Internet-facing applications. We *could* create accounts for Internet users in a Windows domain, but it's unlikely that you'd want to give Windows domain accounts to every visitor from the public Internet, so most ASP.NET applications tend to rely on Forms Authentication instead.

Using Forms Authentication

Forms Authentication is ideally suited for use in Internet-facing applications. It takes a little more effort to set up than Windows Authentication, but it is a lot more flexible once everything is in place.

The security of Forms Authentication relies on an encrypted browser cookie called .ASPXAUTH. If you look at the contents of an .ASPXAUTH cookie (either by using a tool like Fiddler or by looking at your browser's cookie cache), you will see something similar to Listing 34-2.

Listing 34-2. *An example of an .ASPXAUTH cookie*

9CC50274C662470986ADD690704BF652F4DFFC3035FC19013726A22F794B3558778B12F799852B2E84
D34D79C0A09DA258000762779AF9FCA3AD4B78661800B4119DD72A8A7000935AAF7E309CD81F28

If we pass this value to the FormsAuthentication.Decrypt method, we can get a FormsAuthenticationTicket object that has the properties shown in Table 34-2.

Table 34-2. *Properties and Values of an Authentication Cookie Object*

Property	Type	Value
Name	string	admin
CookiePath	string	/
Expiration	DateTime	3/20/2011 12:38:54 PM
Expired	bool	false
IsPersistent	bool	false
IssueDate	DateTime	3/18/2011 12:38:54 PM
UserData	string	(Empty String)
Version	int	2

The key property encoded in the cookie is Name. This is the identity that will be associated with the requests that the user makes. The security of this system comes from the fact that the cookie data is encrypted and signed using our server's *machine keys*. These are generated automatically by IIS, and without these keys, the authentication information contained in the cookie cannot be read or modified.

■ **Note** When deploying an application that uses Forms Authentication to a farm of servers, we must either ensure that requests always go back to the server that generated the cookie (known as *affinity*) or ensure that all of the servers have the same machine keys. Keys can be generated and configured using the Machine Keys option in IIS Manager (the icon is in the ASP.NET section).

Setting Up Forms Authentication

We enable Forms Authentication in `Web.config`, as shown in Listing 34-3.

Listing 34-3. Enabling Forms Authentication in Web.config

```
<configuration>
  <system.web>
    <authentication mode="Forms">
      <forms loginUrl="~/Account/LogOn" timeout="2880" />
    </authentication>
  </system.web>
</configuration>
```

■ **Note** When we create a new MVC framework application using the Internet Application project template, the Visual Studio template enables Forms Authentication by default.

This simple configuration is suitable for most applications, but for more control, we can define additional attributes to the forms node in the `Web.config` file. Table 34-3 describes the most useful of them.

Table 34-3. Properties and Values of an Authentication Cookie Object

Attribute	Default Value	Description
name	.ASPXAUTH	The name of the cookie used to store the authentication ticket.
timeout	30	The duration (in minutes) after which authentication cookies expire. Note that this is enforced on the server, not on the client; authentication cookies' encrypted data packets contain expiration information.
slidingExpiration	true	If true, ASP.NET will renew the authentication ticket on every request. That means it won't expire until timeout minutes after the most recent request.

Continued

Attribute	Default Value	Description
domain	None	If set, this assigns the authentication cookie to the given domain. This makes it possible to share authentication cookies across subdomains (for example, if your application is hosted at www.example.com, then set the domain to .example.com to share the cookie across all subdomains of example.com).
path	/	This sets the authentication cookie to be sent only to URLs below the specified path. This lets you host multiple applications on the same domain without exposing one's authentication cookies to another.
loginUrl	/login.aspx	When Forms Authentication requires a user login, it redirects the visitor to this URL.
cookieless	UseDeviceProfile	Enables cookieless authentication; we return to this topic later in the chapter.
requireSSL	false	If set to true, then Forms Authentication sets the "secure" flag on its authentication cookie, which advises browsers to transmit the cookie only during requests encrypted with SSL.

As an alternative to editing the Web.config file, we can configure Forms Authentication using the Authentication option in the IIS Manager tool. This is the same tool that we used to configure Windows Authentication earlier. Ensure that Forms Authentication is enabled and then click Edit to configure the settings, as shown in Figure 34-3.

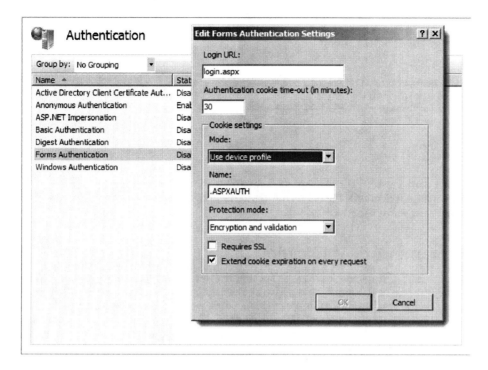

Figure 34-3. *Using the IIS Manager Authentication feature to configure Forms Authentication*

With Forms Authentication enabled in the Web.config file, when an unauthenticated visitor tries to access any part of the application that requires authentication, they'll be redirected to the login URL we specified.

Performing Authentication and Authorization

Setting up authentication is only part of the job. We also have to implement authorization so that ASP.NET knows what a user can do once they have been authenticated. The technique required for this differs between the MVC framework and other ASP.NET applications. I describe both in the sections that follow.

To make demonstrating authorization simpler, I have created some credentials in the Web.config file of the MVC framework and Web Forms triathlon applications (both follow the same format for this because both rely on the same core ASP.NET authentication feature). Listing 34-4 shows the additions I have made.

Listing 34-4. Defining credentials in Web.config

```
<authentication mode="Forms">
    <forms loginUrl="~/Account/LogOn" timeout="2880">
        <credentials passwordFormat="Clear">
          <user name="adam" password="adam" />
          <user name="joe" password="joe" />
        </credentials>
    </forms>
</authentication>
```

This is the MVC framework version. The value of the loginUrl attribute will be slightly different when we come to Web Forms applications. I don't recommend defining credentials like this for real applications, but it is useful for simple demonstrations.

Using an MVC Framework Application

We apply authorization in an MVC framework using the Authorize filter. As I explained previously, filters are a way in which we can express functionality that pervades the application but does not fit neatly into one of our defined concerns. We saw another example of filters when we looked at MVC framework exceptions in Chapter 28. Listing 34-5 shows how I have applied this filter to the EventController class.

Listing 34-5. Applying authentication to the Event controller

```
using System;
using System.Linq;
using System.Web.Mvc;
using TriathlonApp.Models.Domain;
using TriathlonApp.Models.Domain.Repository;
using TriathlonApp.Models.View;

namespace TriathlonApp.Controllers {

    [Authorize]
    public class EventController : Controller {
        private IRepository repository;

        public EventController(IRepository repo) {
            repository = repo;
        }

        ...action methods omitted for brevity...

    }
}
```

When applied without parameters, the Authorize filter will only allow requests to target the action methods in the controller if the user has been authenticated. This means that the request contains a valid authentication cookie. We can be more specific by providing values for the Users and Roles parameters of the Authorize attribute. These properties are described in Table 34-4.

Table 34-4. *AuthorizeAttribute Properties*

Name	Type	Description
Users	string	Comma-separated list of usernames that are allowed to access the action method.
Roles	string	Comma-separated list of role names. To access the action method, users must be in at least one of these roles.

So, for example, we can limit access to a specific set of users by listing their names in the Users property, like this:

```
...
[Authorize(Users="adam, bob")]
public class EventController : Controller {
private IRepository repository;
...
```

I'll come back to roles, and how they can make authorization simpler, later in the chapter. If we start the application, we can see the effect that the filter has, as shown in Figure 34-4.

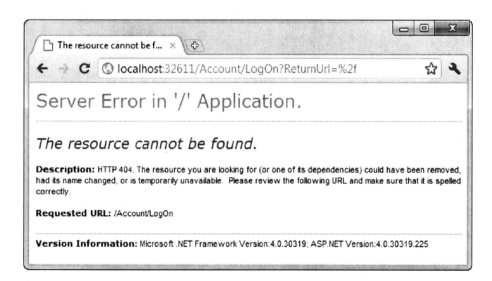

Figure 34-4. *Trying to access an action that requires authentication*

When an unauthenticated request is received for an action method that requires authentication, ASP.NET redirects the user's browser to the URL we specified when we set up Forms Authentication, as follows:

```
<forms loginUrl="~/Account/LogOn" timeout="2880">
```

Under the default routing configuration, this URL will target an action method called LogOn in a controller called Account. We are responsible for implementing this controller and action method so that the user can provide the credentials for authentication. The first step is to create a view model class so that we can rely on the model validation and templated helper features. Listing 34-6 shows this class, called LogOnViewModel, which I created in the Models/View folder.

Listing 34-6. *The LogOnViewModel class*

```
using System.ComponentModel.DataAnnotations;

namespace TriathlonApp.Models.View {
    public class LogOnViewModel {

        [Required]
        public string UserName { get; set; }

        [Required]
        [DataType(DataType.Password)]
        public string Password { get; set; }
    }
}
```

This class defines a property for the user name and another for the password. Both are annotated with the Required attribute so that the user is forced to provide a value. The Password property is annotated with the DataType attribute, specifying that this is a password and that the contents should be masked. We can now create the controller. I have created a class called AccountController in the Controllers project folder, which is shown in Listing 34-7.

Listing 34-7. *The AccountController class*

```
using System.Web.Mvc;
using System.Web.Security;
using TriathlonApp.Models.View;

namespace TriathlonApp.Controllers {
    public class AccountController : Controller {

        public ActionResult LogOn() {
            return View();
        }

        [HttpPost]
        public ActionResult LogOn(LogOnViewModel creds, string returnURL) {
            if (ModelState.IsValid) {
                if (FormsAuthentication.Authenticate(creds.UserName, creds.Password)) {
                    FormsAuthentication.SetAuthCookie(creds.UserName, false);
                    return Redirect(returnURL ?? Url.Action("Index", "Event"));
                } else {
                    ModelState.AddModelError("", "Incorrect username or password");
                }
            }
```

```
            return View(creds);
        }
    }
}
```

The action method that handles the post requests performs the authentication. The parameters are the LogOnViewModel object (created by the model binding process) and the URL that the user should be redirected to if they are successfully authenticated.

The FormsAuthentication class contains the methods we need to perform the work. The Authenticate method takes user name and password arguments and returns true if the user has provided valid credentials (and false otherwise). The SetAuthCookie method sets a cookie in the response to the browser. The arguments are the user name that has been authenticated and whether or not the cookie should persist between sessions (I have selected false for this option).

If the user is authenticated, I redirect the browser to the specified URL. Or, if no URL has been provided, I redirect them to the Index action in the Event controller. We won't be passed a URL if the user has gone straight to the logon page.

If the user isn't authenticated, I add an error to the model state, which will be displayed in the view. You can see the view in Listing 34-8. It is called Logon.cshtml, and it resides in the Views/Account folder.

Listing 34-8. *The Logon.cshtml view*

```
@model TriathlonApp.Models.View.LogOnViewModel

@{
    ViewBag.TabName= "Events";
}

<h2>Please log in</h2>

@using (Html.BeginForm()) {
    @Html.ValidationSummary(true)
    @Html.EditorForModel()

    <p>
        <input type="submit" value="Log In" />
    </p>
}
```

This view uses the templated helpers we looked at in Chapter 26 to render elements from the model object. I have also added a validation summary, configured not to display property-level messages. This is where the message will be displayed if the user doesn't provide valid credentials. If we start the application and go to the default URL, we are redirected to the logon page, as shown in Figure 34-5.

Figure 34-5. *Logging on to the application*

That's all there is to it. Once we enter some valid credentials, we will be redirected to the event controller, and we will see the normal events listing.

Using a Web Forms Application

We configure authorization Web Forms (and core ASP.NET) applications using the Web.config file. Listing 34-9 provides an example.

Listing 34-9. *Configuring authorization in the Web.config file*

```
<configuration>

  <location path="Events.aspx">
    <system.web>
      <authorization>
        <deny users="?"/>
            <allow users="adam" roles="SiteAdmin"/>
        <deny users="*"/>
      </authorization>
    </system.web>
  </location>
```

```
<system.web>
  <authentication mode="Forms">
    <forms loginUrl="~/Login.aspx" timeout="2880">
      <credentials passwordFormat="Clear">
        <user name="adam" password="adam" />
        <user name="joe" password="joe" />
      </credentials>
    </forms>
  </authentication>
</configuration>
```

The `location` element is a child of `configuration` and contains its own `system.web` element. The `path` attribute of the `location` element defines the URL to which the policy applies:

```
<location path="Events.aspx">
```

In this example, the authorization policy will apply to the `Events.apsx` page. The next line denies access to the page for all anonymous users:

```
<deny users="?"/>
```

We then enable access for the user `adam` and any user in the `SiteAdmin` role:

```
<allow users="adam" roles="SiteAdmin"/>
```

Finally, we deny access for any other authenticated users:

```
<deny users="*"/>
```

When users do not have access, the URL authorization feature generates an HTTP 401 response (which means "not authorized"), and this triggers the Forms Authentication system and directs users to our application's login URL. Notice that I have set this to be `~/Login.aspx`.

We need to create the `Login.aspx` page to handle the authentication requests. Listing 34-10 shows this page.

Listing 34-10. *The Login.aspx page*

```
<%@ Page Language="C#" AutoEventWireup="true" CodeBehind="Login.aspx.cs"↵
  Inherits="TriathlonApp.Login" %>

<!DOCTYPE html PUBLIC "-//W3C//DTD XHTML 1.0 Transitional//EN"↵
  "http://www.w3.org/TR/xhtml1/DTD/xhtml1-transitional.dtd">

<html xmlns="http://www.w3.org/1999/xhtml">
<head runat="server">
    <title></title>
</head>
<body>
    <form id="form1" runat="server">
        <h2>Log In</h2>
    <p>
        Please enter your username and password.
    </p>
```

```
        <table>
            <tr>
                <td>Username:</td>
                <td><input type="text" id="username" runat="server" /></td>
            </tr>
            <tr>
                <td>Password:</td>
                <td><input type="password" id="password" runat="server" /></td>
            </tr>
            <tr>
                <td colspan="2" style="text-align:center">
                    <input type="submit" value="Log In" />
                </td>
            </tr>
        </table>
        </form>
</body>
</html>
```

I have gone for a very simple approach here—just the required elements in an HTML form. Web Forms includes some controls to aid with authenticating users, including creating new accounts. The easiest way to see these controls is to create a project using the Visual Studio ASP.NET Web Application template and take a look at the Accounts/Login.aspx page.

I have chosen this approach because it allows me to use similar code in the code-behind class as I did in the controller for the MVC framework application. Listing 34-11 shows the Login.aspx.cs file.

Listing 34-11. *The login code-behind class*

```
using System;
using System.Web.Security;

namespace TriathlonApp {
    public partial class Login : System.Web.UI.Page {

        protected void Page_Load(object sender, EventArgs e) {

            if (IsPostBack) {
                string user = Request["username"];
                string pass = Request["password"];

                if (FormsAuthentication.Authenticate(user, pass)) {
                    FormsAuthentication.SetAuthCookie(user, false);
                    Response.Redirect(Request["ReturnUrl"] ?? "~/Events.aspx");
                }
            }
        }
    }
}
```

I extract the username and password values from the request and use them to attempt authentication through the FormsAuthentication class.

Using Membership, Roles, and Profiles

To demonstrate authentication and authorization, I stored the user credentials in the Web.config file. This is acceptable for small and simple applications where the list of users is unlikely to change over time, but there are two significant limitations to this approach. The first problem is that anyone who can read the Web.config file might be able to figure out the passwords, even when they are stored using cryptographic hashes rather than plain text (if you don't believe this, create some hash codes for typical passwords and then search Google for each hash code; it won't take much effort to figure out at least one of the passwords).

The second problem is administration. Putting the credentials in the Web.config file is workable when you have a small number of users, but it is impossible to manage when there are hundreds or thousands of users. Aside from the difficulty of correctly editing a file with innumerable entries, remember that IIS will restart the application as soon as we change Web.config. This will reset all the active sessions, and users will lose their progress in the application.

As you might expect, ASP.NET has a solution to these problems—a standardized user accounts system that supports all the common user account tasks, including registering, managing passwords, and setting personal preferences. There are three key functional areas:

- *Membership*, which is about registering user accounts and accessing a repository of account details and credentials

- *Roles*, which are about putting users into a set of (possibly overlapping) groups, typically used for authorization

- *Profiles*, which let you store arbitrary data on a per-user basis (for example, personal preferences)

ASP.NET provides some standard implementations for each of these three areas, but we can mix and match with our own custom implementations if we need to, through a system of *providers*. There are built-in providers that can store data in different ways, including SQL Server and Active Directory. There are some solid advantages in using the built-in providers for membership, roles, and profiles:

- Microsoft has already gone through a lengthy research and design process to come up with a system that works well in many cases. Even if you just use the APIs (providing your own storage and UI), you are working to a sound design.

- For simple applications, the built-in storage providers eliminate the work of managing your own data access. Given the clear abstraction provided by the API, you could in the future upgrade to using a custom storage provider without needing to change any UI code.

- The API is shared across all ASP.NET applications, so you can reuse any custom providers or UI components across projects.

- It integrates well with the rest of ASP.NET. For example, User.IsInRole() is the basis of many authorization systems, and it obtains role data from your selected roles provider.

And, of course, there are disadvantages:

- The built-in SQL storage providers need direct access to your database, which feels a bit dirty if you have a strong concept of a domain model or use a particular ORM technology elsewhere.

- The built-in SQL storage providers demand a specific data schema that isn't easy to share with the rest of your application's data schema.

- The Web Forms controls that ASP.NET includes alongside the authentication providers don't work in MVC applications, so we need to create our own UI.

I think it is worth following the API, because it provides a nice separation of concerns and is nicely integrated into the rest of the ASP.NET framework.

Setting Up and Using Membership

The framework comes with membership providers for SQL Server (SqlMembershipProvider) and Active Directory (ActiveDirectoryMembershipProvider). In this section, we'll show you how to set up the most commonly used, which is SqlMembershipProvider. There are also providers available from third parties, including ones based around Oracle, NHibernate, and XML files, although we won't demonstrate them here.

■ **Tip** Roles are applied to MVC framework applications using authorization filters. See Chapter 13 for more details and examples of using roles for authorization.

Setting Up SqlMembershipProvider

When we create a new MVC project using the Internet Application template, Visual Studio configures the application to use the SqlMembershipProvider class by default. The easiest way to get started in other project types is to copy this configuration. You can see this in Listing 34-12, which shows the relevant sections from the Web.config file created for a new project.

Listing 34-12. The default membership provider configuration in a new project

```
<configuration>
  <connectionStrings>
    <add name="ApplicationServices"
        connectionString="data source=TITAN\SQLEXPRESS;Integrated Security=SSPI;
                        AttachDBFilename=|DataDirectory|aspnetdb.mdf;User Instance=true"
                        providerName="System.Data.SqlClient" />
  </connectionStrings>
  ...
  <system.web>
  <membership>
    <providers>
      <clear/>
```

```
        <add name="AspNetSqlMembershipProvider"
             type="System.Web.Security.SqlMembershipProvider"
             connectionStringName="ApplicationServices"
             enablePasswordRetrieval="false"
             enablePasswordReset="true"
             requiresQuestionAndAnswer="false"
             requiresUniqueEmail="false"
             maxInvalidPasswordAttempts="5"
             minRequiredPasswordLength="6"
             minRequiredNonalphanumericCharacters="0"
             passwordAttemptWindow="10"
             applicationName="/" />
      </providers>
    </membership>
</system.web>
</configuration>
```

Web Forms and MVC applications created using the Empty template don't include these configuration elements, so we have to add them manually.

Using SqlMembershipProvider with SQL Server Express

SQL Server Express supports a feature called *user instance* databases. These are databases that don't have to be configured before they are used. We simply open a connection to SQL Server Express, and the .mdf file that we specify is created automatically (or loaded if it already exists). This can be a convenient way of working with databases because we won't have to worry about creating user accounts in SQL Server Management Studio, assigning database access rights, and doing all the other database setup tasks usually required.

You can see how user instance databases are configured in the listing. The connection string that Visual Studio puts in Web.config specifies User Instance is true and that SQL Server Express should use a file called aspnetdb.mdf. The |DataDirectory| portion of the connection string specifies that the file will be created in the project App_Data directory. ASP.NET will take care of creating the tables and stored procedures for the database to support the membership, roles, and profiles features.

▪ **Tip**　The default settings that Visual Studio creates assume you are running SQL Server Express on the same machine on which you are doing development. If you prefer to run your database on a separate machine, as I do, then you should change the data source part of the connection string. For example, my database server is called TITAN, so I changed the data source from data source=.\SQLEXPRESS to data source=TITAN\SQLEXPRESS.

Manually Preparing SQL Server

The paid-for (non-Express) editions of SQL Server do not support user instance databases, which means we must prepare the database ahead of time so that support for membership, roles, and profiles is ready for the application.

We can use the ASP.NET SQL Server Setup Wizard to configure the database. Run aspnet_regsql.exe, which can be found in the .NET Framework directory (this will be \Users*yourName*\Windows\Microsoft.NET\Framework\v4.0.30319 for 32-bit systems and \Users*yourName*\Windows\Microsoft.NET\Framework64\v4.0.30319 for 64-bit systems).

Click Next to move past the welcome screen. Select "Configure SQL Server for application services" on the next screen. Keep clicking Next until you see the screen shown in Figure 34-6.

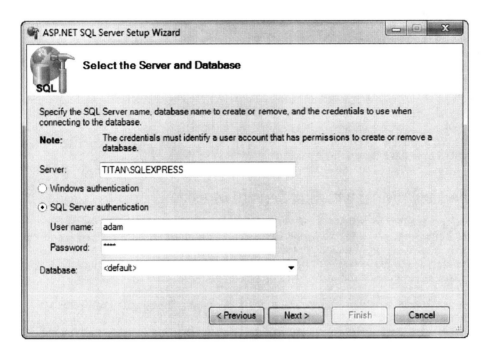

Figure 34-6. Selecting the database

Enter the name of the SQL Server (in this case I am working with the instance of SQL Express running on my development server) and the credentials required to connect to the database. Leave Database as <default>. This will create a database called aspnetdb.

Continue through the wizard by clicking the Next button, and the database will be created and populated. Remember to change the connection string in Web.config to reflect the new database. Listing 34-13 shows the connection string for the database created the figure.

Listing 34-13. A connection string for the authentication database

```
<connectionStrings>
  <add name="ApplicationServices"
       connectionString="data Source=TITAN\SQLEXPRESS;
                         Initial Catalog=aspnetdb;
                         Persist Security Info=True;
                         User ID=adam;Password=adam"
```

```
        providerName="System.Data.SqlClient" />
</connectionStrings>
```

If you are unsure of the connection string, the easiest way to find out what it should be is to open the Server Explorer view in Visual Studio, right-click Data Connections, and select Add Connection. You can get the connection string from the properties of the newly created connection. You can also see the tables that have been created, as shown in Figure 34-7.

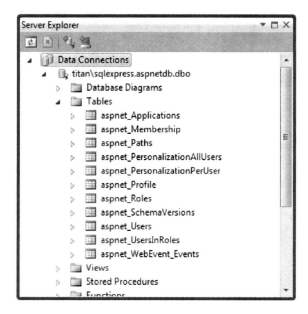

Figure 34-7. *The tables created for the authentication database*

Managing Membership

The Membership API contains methods for administering your set of registered users: methods for adding and removing user accounts, resetting passwords, and so on. It's likely that you'll want to implement your own web-based administrative UI (which internally calls these methods) to let site administrators manage the user account database.

However, in some simple cases, you might be able to get away without implementing any custom user administration UI and instead use one of the platform's two built-in administration UIs: the *Web Site Administration Tool* (WAT) or the IIS *.NET Users* tool.

Using the Web Site Administration Tool (WAT)

During development, we can manage membership using the WAT, which is included with Visual Studio. The WAT is a web-based UI and can be started by selecting Project ➤ ASP.NET Configuration in Visual Studio. One of the options on the home page is Security, which takes you to the features available for managing users and roles, as shown in Figure 34-8.

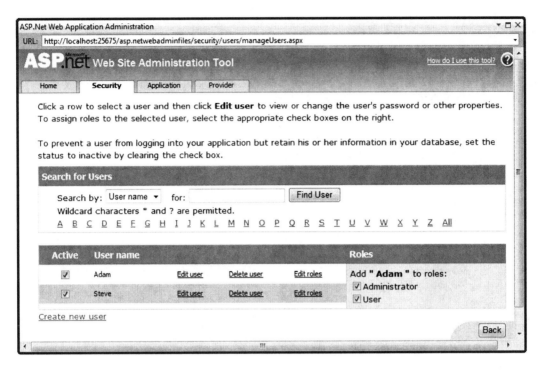

Figure 34-8. *The Web Site Administration Tool*

Using the IIS .NET Users Tool

Once we deploy our application, we can manage our application's users through the IIS .NET Users option, but doing so requires us to work around a deficiency of the IIS Manager tool.

When we use the .NET Users option, the IIS Manager tool reads our `Web.config` file and tries to ensure that the membership provider we are using is trustworthy. Unfortunately, IIS Manager was written using .NET 2 and has yet to be updated to support the provider classes that are used in ASP.NET 4. In current IIS versions, Microsoft has elected to simply disable the .NET Users option for web applications that use .NET 4, not the most useful solution.

We can work around this by creating a very simple application on IIS that uses .NET 2.0 and that connects to our membership database. We will use the same connection string as for our real application so that changes we make through our workaround take effect in both applications.

The first step is to create an empty directory on the server that will hold the workaround application. On our server, we create a directory called `C:\AuthManager`. Next, create a file called `Web.config` in the directory and set the contents to match Listing 34-14.

Listing 34-14. *A Web.config file for managing membership*

```
<?xml version="1.0" encoding="UTF-8"?>

<configuration>
  <connectionStrings>
```

```
        <add name="ApplicationServices" connectionString="data Source=TITAN\SQLEXPRESS;
            Initial Catalog=aspnetdb;
            Persist Security Info=True;
            User ID=adam;Password=adam"
                providerName="System.Data.SqlClient" />
    </connectionStrings>

    <system.web>

        <authentication mode="Forms">
            <forms loginUrl="~/Account/LogOn" timeout="2880" />
        </authentication>

        <membership>
            <providers>
                <remove name="AspNetSqlMembershipProvider"/>
                <add name="AspNetSqlMembershipProvider"
                    type="System.Web.Security.SqlMembershipProvider,
                    System.Web, Version=2.0.0.0, Culture=neutral,
                    PublicKeyToken=b03f5f7f11d50a3a"
                    connectionStringName="ApplicationServices"
                    applicationName="/"
                />
            </providers>
        </membership>
    </system.web>
</configuration>
```

This is a cut-down Web.config file that has two configuration sections. The first is the connection string for the membership database. You should edit this to match your environment. The second region specifies the .NET 2.0 version of the membership provider class. You must take care to copy this exactly as I have shown it. The second attribute shown in bold is the name of the connection string. This must match the name given to the connection string earlier in the file.

Open IIS Manager, right-click a web site, and select Add Application. Set the name of the application to be something memorable (I used AuthManager), and set the physical path to be the directory you created earlier, as shown in Figure 34-9.

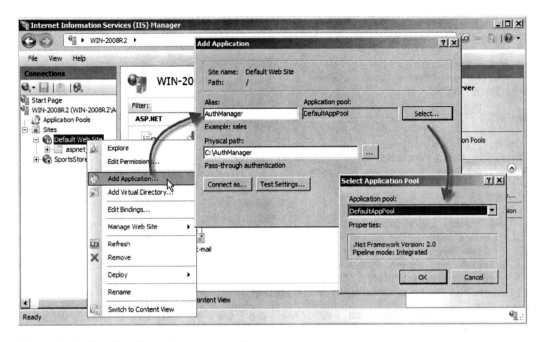

Figure 34-9. *Creating the workaround application*

When you create the application, make sure you assign it to an application pool that uses version 2.0 of the .NET Framework. As you can see in the figure, I have assigned the application to DefaultAppPool.

Once you have created the application, select it in the left panel of the IIS Manager window. If you have followed the instructions, you should see a feature called .NET Users, which is shown in Figure 34-10.

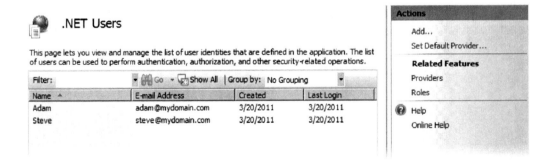

Figure 34-10. *The IIS .NET Users feature*

Using this feature, we can manage the users for our application, just as we did using the WAT during development.

Setting Up and Using Roles

So far, we've seen how the framework manages your application's set of credentials and validates login attempts (via a membership provider) and how it keeps track of a visitor's logged-in status across multiple requests (via Forms Authentication). Both of these are facets of authentication, which means securely identifying who a certain person is.

Another common security requirement is *authorization*, which is the process of determining what a user is allowed to do once they have been authenticated. ASP.NET uses a *role-based authorization* approach, which means that actions are restricted to a set of roles, and users are allowed to perform the action if they have been assigned to one of these roles.

A role is represented using a unique string value. For example, we might choose to define three roles, as follows:

- ApprovedMember

- CommentsModerator

- SiteAdministrator

These are just arbitrary strings, but they gain meaning when, for example, our application grants administrator access only to members in the SiteAdministrator role. Each role is totally independent of the others—there's no hierarchy—so being a SiteAdministrator doesn't automatically grant the CommentsModerator role or even the ApprovedMember role. Each one must be assigned independently; a given member can hold any combination of roles. Just as with membership, the ASP.NET platform expects us to work with roles through its provider model, offering a common API (the RoleProvider base class) and a set of built-in providers you can choose from. And of course, we can implement our own custom provider.

Setting Up SqlRoleProvider

The SqlRoleProvider class is the complement to SqlMembershipProvider and uses the same database schema to provide support for roles. When we create an MVC Framework project using the Internet Application template, Visual Studio automatically adds elements to the Web.config file to set up SqlRoleProvider, as shown in Listing 34-15.

Listing 34-15. The SqlRoleProvider configuration created by Visual Studio

```
<configuration>
  <system.web>
    <roleManager enabled="false">
      <providers>
        <clear/>
        <add name="AspNetSqlRoleProvider"
             type="System.Web.Security.SqlRoleProvider"
             connectionStringName="ApplicationServices"
             applicationName="/" />
```

```
        <add name="AspNetWindowsTokenRoleProvider"
             type="System.Web.Security.WindowsTokenRoleProvider"
             applicationName="/" />
      </providers>
    </roleManager>
</configuration>
```

Two role providers are registered, but by default, neither is enabled. To set up SqlRoleProvider, we must change the roleManager element like this:

```
<roleManager enabled="true" defaultProvider="AspNetSqlRoleProvider">
```

▓ **Tip** AspNetSqlRoleProvider uses the same database schema as SqlMembershipProvider, which means that the database has to be prepared using one of the techniques I showed you earlier in the chapter. If you have already prepared the database for SqlMembershipProvider, then you don't have to repeat the process.

Alternatively, we can select AspNetWindowsTokenRoleProvider as the role provider if we are using Windows Authentication and would like users' roles to be determined by their Windows Active Directory roles.

Managing Roles

We can manage roles using the same techniques as for managing members—either by implementing our own web-based management UI or by using the WAT during development and using the IIS Manager .NET Users feature once the application has been deployed. In the latter case, we still have to implement the workaround to use the IIS Manager feature, which is shown in Figure 34-11.

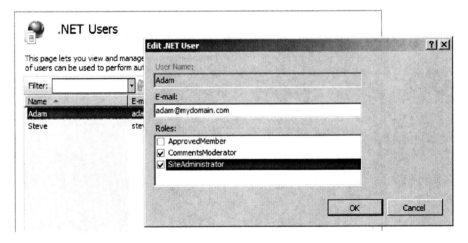

Figure 34-11. Managing roles using the IIS Manager .NET Users tool

We have to add some configuration elements to the `Web.config` file of the workaround application to enable support for the role provider, as follows:

```
<roleManager enabled="true" defaultProvider="AspNetSqlRoleProvider">
    <providers>
        <clear/>
        <add name="AspNetSqlRoleProvider"
            type="System.Web.Security.SqlRoleProvider,
             System.Web, Version=2.0.0.0, Culture=neutral,
             PublicKeyToken=b03f5f7f11d50a3a"
            connectionStringName="ApplicationServices"
            applicationName="/" />
    </providers>
</roleManager>
```

Setting Up and Using Profiles

Membership keeps track of our users, and *roles* keep track of what they're allowed to do. If we want to keep track of other per-user data like "member points" or "site preferences" or "favorite foods," then we can use *profiles*—a general purpose, user-specific data store that follows the same provider pattern as membership and roles.

This is an appealing feature for smaller applications that are using `SqlMembershipProvider` and `SqlRoleProvider`, because the profiles are maintained using the same database schema. In larger applications, though, where there is a custom database schema and a stronger notion of a domain model, you will probably have a different, better infrastructure for storing per-user data specific to your application.

Setting Up SqlProfileProvider

We add the element to configure `SqlProfileProvider` in the `Web.config` file, as shown in Listing 34-16. You can see from the listing that the approach for setting up `SqlProfileProvider` follows the same pattern as the other two providers.

Listing 34-16. Setting Up SqlProfileProvider

```
<configuration>
  <system.web>
    <profile>
      <providers>
        <clear/>
        <add name="AspNetSqlProfileProvider"
            type="System.Web.Profile.SqlProfileProvider"
            connectionStringName="ApplicationServices"
            applicationName="/" />
      </providers>
    </profile>
  </system.web>
</configuration>
```

Configuring, Reading, and Writing Profile Data

Before we can use the profile feature, we must define the structure of the profile data that we want to work with. We do this by adding properties elements inside the Web.config profile element, as shown in Listing 34-17.

Listing 34-17. Defining the structure of profile data

```
<profile>
  <providers>
    <clear/>
    <add name="AspNetSqlProfileProvider"
         type="System.Web.Profile.SqlProfileProvider"
         connectionStringName="ApplicationServices"
         applicationName="/" />
  </providers>
  <properties>
    <add name="Name" type="String"/>
    <group name="Address">
      <add name="Street" type="String"/>
      <add name="City" type="String"/>
      <add name="ZipCode" type="String"/>
      <add name="State" type="String"/>
    </group>
  </properties>
</profile>
```

As you can see from the listing, we can define individual profile properties or group-related properties together. All the properties we have defined in the listing are strings, but the profile system supports any .NET type that can be serialized. However, we pay a performance penalty if we use custom types, because the SqlProfileProvider class can't determine whether an object created from a custom type has been modified and will write the object to the database every time the profile is modified.

When using ASP.NET Web Forms, the profile data is accessed through a proxy object whose properties correspond to the profile properties. This feature isn't available for MVC framework applications, but we can access the profile properties using the HttpContent.Profile property, which is available through the Controller class, as shown in Listing 34-18.

Listing 34-18. Reading and writing profile properties

```
public ActionResult Index() {

    ViewBag.Name = HttpContext.Profile["Name"];
    ViewBag.City = HttpContext.Profile.GetProfileGroup("Address")["City"];

    return View();
}

[HttpPost]
public ViewResult Index(string name, string city) {
```

```
HttpContext.Profile["Name"] = name;
HttpContext.Profile.GetProfileGroup("Address")["City"] = city;

    return View();
}
```

The ASP.NET framework uses the profile provider to load the profile properties for a user the first time we access the profile data and writes any modifications back through the provider at the end of the request. We don't have to explicitly save changes; it happens automatically.

Enabling Anonymous Profiles

By default, profile data is available only for authenticated users, and an exception will be thrown if we attempt to write profile properties when the current user hasn't logged in. We can change this by enabling support for *anonymous profiles*, as shown in Listing 34-19.

Listing 34-19. *Enabling support for anonymous profiles*

```
<configuration>
  <system.web>
    <anonymousIdentification enabled="true"/>
    <profile>
      <providers>
        <clear/>
        <add name="AspNetSqlProfileProvider"
             type="System.Web.Profile.SqlProfileProvider"
             connectionStringName="ApplicationServices"
             applicationName="/" />
      </providers>
      <properties>
        <add name="Name" type="String" allowAnonymous="true"/>
        <group name="Address">
          <add name="Street" type="String"/>
          <add name="City" type="String" allowAnonymous="true"/>
          <add name="ZipCode" type="String"/>
          <add name="State" type="String"/>
        </group>
      </properties>
    </profile>
  </system.web>
</configuration>
```

When anonymous identification is enabled, the ASP.NET framework will track anonymous users by giving them a cookie called .ASPXANONYMOUS that expires after 10,000 minutes (that's around 70 days). We can enable anonymous support for profile properties by setting the allowAnonymous attribute to true; in the listing, we have enabled anonymous support for the Name and City properties.

Enabling anonymous profiles makes it possible to read and write profile data for unauthenticated users, but beware, every unauthenticated visitor will automatically create a user account in the profile database.

Summary

In this chapter, you learned how to configure and apply authentication and authorization to ASP.NET applications. The functionality is built into the core ASP.NET platform and is consumed slightly differently depending on the type of application in use. Setting up the underlying database can be a frustrating process, but once it is done, the task of performing authentication and applying authorization is simple and straightforward.

Index

■ G

■**T**

W

CPSIA information can be obtained at www.ICGtesting.com
Printed in the USA
LVOW130004041011

248966LV00003B/1/P